After Monte Albán

Mesoamerican Worlds: From the Olmecs to the Danzantes

After Monte Albán: Transformation and Negotiation in Oaxaca, Mexico, JEFFREY P. BLOMSTER, EDITOR

The Apotheosis of Janaab' Pakal: Science, History, and Religion at Classic Maya Palenque, GERARDO ALDANA

Commoner Ritual and Ideology in Ancient Mesoamerica, NANCY GONLIN AND JON C. LOHSE, EDITORS

Eating Landscape: Aztec and European Occupation of Tlalocan, PHILIP P. ARNOLD

Empires of Time: Calendars, Clocks, and Cultures, Revised Edition, ANTHONY AVENI

Encounter with the Plumed Serpent: Drama and Power in the Heart of Mesoamerica, MAARTEN JANSEN AND GABINA AURORA PÉREZ JIMÉNEZ

In the Realm of Nachan Kan: Postclassic Maya Archaeology at Laguna de On, Belize, MARILYN A. MASSON

Invasion and Transformation: Interdisciplinary Perspectives on the Conquest of Mexico, REBECCA P. BRIENEN AND MARGARET A. JACKSON, EDITORS

Life and Death in the Templo Mayor, EDUARDO MATOS MOCTEZUMA

The Madrid Codex: New Approaches to Understanding an Ancient Maya Manuscript, GABRIELLE VAIL AND ANTHONY AVENI, EDITORS

Mesoamerican Ritual Economy: Archaeological and Ethnological Perspectives, E. CHRISTIAN WELLS AND KARLA L. DAVIS-SALAZAR, EDITORS

Mesoamerica's Classic Heritage: Teotihuacan to the Aztecs, DAVÍD CARRASCO, LINDSAY JONES, AND SCOTT SESSIONS, EDITORS

Mockeries and Metamorphoses of an Aztec God: Tezcatlipoca, "Lord of the Smoking Mirror," GUILHEM OLIVIER, TRANSLATED BY MICHEL BESSON

Rabinal Achi: A Fifteenth-Century Maya Dynastic Drama, ALAIN BRETON, EDITOR; TRANSLATED BY TERESA LAVENDER FAGAN AND ROBERT SCHNEIDER

Representing Aztec Ritual: Performance, Text, and Image in the Work of Sahagún, ELOISE QUIÑONES KEBER, EDITOR

Ruins of the Past: The Use and Perception of Abandoned Structures in the Maya Lowlands, TRAVIS W. STANTON AND ALINE MAGNONI, EDITORS

Skywatching in the Ancient World: New Perspectives in Cultural Astronomy—Studies in Honor of Anthony F. Aveni, CLIVE RUGGLES AND GARY URTON, EDITORS

The Social Experience of Childhood in Mesoamerica, TRACI ARDREN AND SCOTT R. HUTSON, EDITORS

Stone Houses and Earth Lords: Maya Religion in the Cave Context, KEITH M. PRUFER AND JAMES E. BRADY, EDITORS

Tamoanchan, Tlalocan: Places of Mist, ALFREDO LÓPEZ AUSTIN

Thunder Doesn't Live Here Anymore: Self-Deprecation and the Theory of Otherness Among the Teenek Indians of Mexico, ANATH ARIEL DE VIDAS; TRANSLATED BY TERESA LAVENDER FAGAN

Topiltzin Quetzalcoatl: The Once and Future Lord of the Toltecs, H. B. NICHOLSON

The World Below: Body and Cosmos in Otomi Indian Ritual, JACQUES GALINIER

After Monte Albán

Transformation and Negotiation in Oaxaca, Mexico

EDITED BY JEFFREY P. BLOMSTER

UNIVERSITY PRESS OF COLORADO

Published by the University Press of Colorado
5589 Arapahoe Avenue, Suite 206C
Boulder, Colorado 80303

First paperback edition 2017

The University Press of Colorado is a proud member of
the Association of American University Presses.

The University Press of Colorado is a cooperative publishing enterprise supported, in part, by Adams State College, Colorado State University, Fort Lewis College, Mesa State College, Metropolitan State College of Denver, University of Colorado, University of Northern Colorado, and Western State College of Colorado.

Library of Congress Cataloging-in-Publication Data

After Monte Alban : transformation and negotiation in Oaxaca, Mexico / edited by Jeffrey P. Blomster.
p. cm. — (Mesoamerican worlds)
Includes bibliographical references and index.
ISBN 978-0-87081-896-7 (hardcover) — ISBN 978-1-60732-597-0 (pbk)
1. Indians of Mexico—Mexico—Oaxaca Valley—Antiquities. 2. Indians of Mexico—Mexico—Oaxaca Valley—Historiography. 3. Ethnohistory—Mexico—Oaxaca Valley. 4. Ethnoarchaeology—Mexico—Oaxaca Valley. 5. Monte Alban Site (Mexico) 6. Oaxaca Valley (Mexico—Antiquities. I. Blomster, Jeffrey P. (Jeffrey Paul)
F1219.1.O11A46 2008
972'.74—dc22

2007043718

Design by Daniel Pratt

Dedicated to Bruce Byland

Tee dakuá'á ña'a, tee nakanú-íchí ña'a, tee xito-tá'án

teacher, mentor, friend

Contents

Part III. Continuity and Abandonment of Houses in the Valley of Oaxaca: Lambityeco and Macuilxóchitl

Part IV. Changing Power Relations and Interaction in the Lower Río Verde Valley

Part V. Sacred History and Legitimization in the Mixteca Alta

Part VI. New Research Frontiers in Oaxaca and Eastern Guerrero

Lindsay Jones

Foreword

After Monte Albán: Transformation and Negotiation in Oaxaca, Mexico provides a welcome addition to the series Mesoamerican Worlds: From the Olmecs to the Danzantes. Indeed, *After Monte Albán* is a fresh contribution that extends somewhat the boundaries implied by the series' subtitle. The so-called Danzantes, famed carvings of human figures in an array of contorted poses, belong to the earliest era of the great Zapotec capital Monte Albán, which emerged sometime around 500 BCE. Objects of endless debate, these highly distinctive carvings—dozens of which were found either in their original positions on the façade of Building L, one of the oldest structures at the site, or scattered elsewhere around the ruined city—were at one point thought to depict individuals engaged in ritual dances. Following a raft of alternate interpretations, the prevailing, though by no means unanimous, opinion at present is, however, that the weirdly twisted Danzante figures represent slain and mutilated captives of those that ruled Monte Albán during the city's initial surge toward greatness.

The intensity and longevity of debate surrounding these Danzante figures, which were unearthed and sketched by Guillermo Dupaix in 1806 and so-named by Leopold Batres during his work at the site from 1901 to 1902, instantiate the disproportionate attention that has been paid to the early stages in the development of the Zapotec capital. The Aztec and Maya regions have attracted more scrutiny, but this early period of Oaxacan history, along with the circumstances that led to the emergence and ascent of Monte Albán as the dominant capital city in the region, have received an abundance of serious and sustained academic attention since the pathbreaking work of Alfonso Caso in the 1930s. The circumstances connected with Monte Albán's decline and the Oaxaca region in the wake of the great capital's demise—that is to say, the era and circumstances on which this book focuses—have, by contrast, been object of far less scholarly investigation and interpretation.

After Monte Albán, by focusing attention on the "critical junction" between the Late Classic and Postclassic eras in Oaxaca, goes a long way in rectifying that imbalance. Of interest to Oaxacan specialists and more general readers, this volume contains both abundant attention to detail concerning recent excavations and revised chronologies as well as more broadly sweeping arguments concerning the distinctive, if more decentralized, pattern of authority that characterized Oaxaca following Monte Albán's decline. Solidly grounded in state-of-the-art archaeology, several chapters capitalize also on the greater abundance of extant codices and ethnohistorical resources for this later period. Attentive to new research on the much-studied central valley and Mixteca regions, the collection addresses as well Postclassic developments in several other regions of Oaxaca and even neighboring eastern Guerrero that are highly relevant but seldom discussed. Moreover, these essays engage both the local dynamics and responses to the collapse of Monte Albán as well as investigating Oaxaca's participation in pan-Mesoamerican Postclassic political, economic, and social changes, a strategy that helps to explain important linkages between the respective demises of Monte Albán, Teotihuacan, and several of the great Classic Maya cities. And, as a consequence of the interplay between those tight and wide-angled views of the aftermath of Monte Albán, the volume brings to the fore not only ways in which Postclassic Oaxacan society was more similar to its contemporaneous counterparts in Central Mexico and the Maya zone than we would have imagined but also ways in which Oaxaca's approach to polity and trade was unique and decidedly different from that which was obtained in those more fully studied regions.

Additionally, by appreciating this late period in Oaxaca not simply as a degenerate version of the preceding era but instead as a time of distinctive creativity—in fact, a kind of florescence in its own right—this collection brings new subtlety to the old question of continuities and changes between the Classic and Postclassic eras. We are apprised, on the one hand, that even in the wake of the collapse of Monte Albán, the quotidian lives of ancient Oaxaca's lower classes proceeded much as they had before. To a remarkable extent, Postclassic means of subsistence and food production, house construction and domestic technologies, "core beliefs" and ritual practices, particularly those associated with burial and the treatment of the non-elite dead, were virtually indistinguishable from their Classic era precedents. On the other hand, the collapse of Monte Albán's centralized authority precipitated an unprecedentedly complex and factional political landscape. Instead of one dominant center, Postclassic influence in the Valley of Oaxaca was distributed among more than a dozen largely autonomous city-states, or *cacicazgos*, each with its own sacred ruling dynasty. Instead of stability, populations and territorial control constantly fluctuated, a fluidity that stimulated very different strategies for the legitimation of authority, which were likewise reflected in very different distributions of public, religious, and private architecture as well as very different media of expression wherein elite, ritual, and astronomical activities that had previously been recorded on carved stone monuments were now expressed in codices or painted books. The decentralization of authority, moreover, spurred fundamental economic changes wherein new products, new forms of wealth, along with new and more vigorously trafficked networks of exchange among the major city-states all represented significant disjunctions with the past. We learn, in fact, that in these last centuries prior to the arrival of the Spaniards, Oaxaca was a prime participant in the most intense period of trade and interaction in Mesoamerica's history.

In sum, *After Monte Albán* demonstrates an emerging and overdue consensus that there are benefits to appreciating the Postclassic in Oaxaca not simply as a shadowy remnant of the brilliant Classic past but as a time of great opportunity and inventiveness. Yet, besides scholarly agreement, the volume is also forthright in demonstrating a healthy divergence of opinions on several of the large issues, for instance, whether the vigorously interconnected economies and interdependencies that developed during this era actually qualify as a "world system." Via that combination of abundant collaboration and occasional contention, this collection takes a large step toward rectifying the neglect of Postclassic Oaxaca and, even more, serves as an incitement for additional work focused on this fascinating, still underrepresented component of the ancient Mesoamerican past.

Preface

IN THE SHADOW OF THE CLASSIC: POSTCLASSIC OAXACA IN A MESOAMERICAN WORLD

Upon their sixteenth-century arrival in the region now referred to as Oaxaca State, in southern Mexico, the Spanish invaders witnessed the results of an amazing cultural florescence. Throughout Oaxaca, small city-states, or *cacicazgos*, each with its own sacred ruling dynasty, competed with each other. Alliances proved ephemeral, with marriages serving as a political strategy more frequently than military domination. Although the Central Mexican Aztecs had impacted parts of Oaxaca, they had also met stiff resistance, often in the form of multi-ethnic alliances. An extraordinary visual and performative culture flourished. From the Aztecs, the Spanish knew of the great skills of Oaxacan artisans, especially those who crafted gold.

What the Spanish did not know was that 700 or more years before their arrival, major sociopolitical transformations occurred during the Late Classic/Postclassic transition throughout Oaxaca. Large nucleated states had collapsed, roughly contemporaneous to the decline of other Classic (ca. 200–800 CE) states throughout Mesoamerica. The decline of the great Zapotec state centered in the Valley of Oaxaca, Monte Albán, especially resonated throughout parts of Oaxaca. The end of the Late Classic and the beginning of the Postclassic is a critical junction, with processes of great interest to anthropologists underway. Sociopolitical organization, and many aspects of elite culture, fundamentally changed after the Late Classic/Postclassic transition, with new strategies of legitimization necessary on the part of the many ruling dynasties that proliferated in this new political landscape. While elites devised new leadership strategies, the vast majority of the population's lifestyle endured, with continuities marking aspects of quotidian and religious life and cosmology. Commoners also played a role in the negotiations of social practice that precluded any other large centralized states comparable to Monte Albán from developing and continued a way of life still in place upon the arrival of the Spanish and beyond.

For many years, archaeology has contributed little to understanding the Postclassic and the transition from the Late Classic throughout Oaxaca. Archaeologists often focus on the rise of major Classic states rather than on their decline and the emergence of new forms of political organization. In Oaxaca, part of the problem also lies in the nature of the evidence. Because of the rich ethnohistoric documents preserved in Oaxaca, which provide a wealth of data on life before, during, and after the arrival of the Spanish, archaeology for this era may seem less pressing. Perhaps the problem that has most plagued Late Classic/Postclassic studies is the poorly understood ceramic chronology, with its decided lack of temporal sensitivity. Further, Oaxaca is often ignored by archaeologists working elsewhere in Mesoamerica as irrelevant to larger phenomena. Despite its central position in many trade routes between the highland of Mexico and the Pacific Coast and Guatemala, Oaxaca is often written off as simply a series of competing states, somehow insulated or uninterested in macro-regional trends (except for its role in the nebulous "Mixteca-Puebla style"). Archaeologists, confronted with the rich material culture of the Classic and Postclassic, often neglect larger trends and influences that may have impacted Oaxaca.

In the summer of 2002, it appeared that critical mass was being achieved in exploring these issues. Large-scale excavations at Macuilxóchitl, and other sites in the Tlacolula branch of the Valley of Oaxaca impacted by a highway project, began to provide new data, while materials from other recently excavated sites in the Mixteca Alta and along the western Oaxaca Coast, in the lower Río Verde region, were being analyzed. Codex scholars were increasingly seeing multi-ethnic alliances and appropriation of foreign symbols in Postclassic politics in Oaxaca. It seemed fitting that after an era—the Classic period—so associated with Monte Albán, some of the most intriguing data on the Postclassic come from outside the Valley of Oaxaca. Geoffrey McCafferty and I, sensing the time was ripe, organized a symposium for the Society for American Archaeology meetings in Milwaukee in 2003, with scholars from Mexico, the United States, Canada, and Europe. Although other commitments—and Nicaragua—occupied McCafferty, additional scholars joined with those from the symposium for the current collection of contributions that both synthesizes and challenges the way we see Oaxaca after the collapse of Monte Albán.

This book presents data and interpretations from three well-studied regions of Oaxaca—the lower Río Verde Valley of the western coast, the Valley of Oaxaca, and the Mixteca Alta—to examine changes (and continuities) and to better contextualize these processes within a larger Mesoamerican perspective. The goal is not only to put Oaxaca "back on the map" for this period but also to show its potential to examine larger anthropological issues within Oaxaca. The chapters in this book explore broad issues, such as interregional interaction and sociopolitical organization, but more specifically consider the following areas:

- the reconfiguration of political power in Oaxaca after the collapse of Monte Albán and other Classic states in the Mixteca and lower Río Verde
- strategies—both new and old—by which leaders were able to maintain social differentiation and power after the collapse of Classic states
- how architecture and imagery, as material symbols, promote social distinctions and how material culture can inform us about power relations and the ways they are contested
- the impact of political transformations on regional settlement systems
- the relationship between polities, boundaries, and ethnic identities
- what aspects of culture are less impacted by dramatic political changes; in other words, continuities in quotidian life and belief
- differences and interactions between regions of Oaxaca
- how Oaxaca participated in larger interactions across Mesoamerica involving both exchange and ideology
- the indigenous perspective of this dramatic transition and responses to it

The chapters in this volume are grouped into six parts. Chapter 1 deals with overarching themes and problems in Oaxacan archaeology; it both synthesizes the major transformations and continuities that result from the Late Classic/Postclassic transition and contextualizes events in Oaxaca with those in larger Mesoamerica. Chapter 1 argues against seeing the Classic and Postclassic as two separate, static phases but instead encourages viewing the changes that characterize the Postclassic as transformations and continuities with earlier practices.

The three chapters in the second part, Chronology, Continuity, and Disjunction, also deal with larger themes. Chapters 2 and 3 both examine chronology. In Chapter 2, Robert Markens presents the results of a major seriation analysis of ceramic vessels from a series of burials throughout the Valley of Oaxaca. He provides solid evidence—and a revised chronology—for refining the ceramic sequence from the Late Classic through the end of the Postclassic. In contrast to Markens's etic approach,

Michel Oudijk uses ethnohistoric documents to construct an emic chronology based on events that ancient Oaxacans may have found significant. As he notes, Oudijk is limited by how far back dates from ethnohistoric documents can be extended, but he presents an excellent non-archaeological complement to Markens's research. Chapter 4, by Byron Hamann, pushes further toward an emic understanding of how ancient Oaxacans viewed the Classic/Postclassic transition. He presents compelling evidence, drawn from ethnohistoric sources, that Postclassic people considered the Late Classic/Postclassic transition to be a substantial rupture with the past.

Part III consists of two chapters, both of which focus on house abandonment and later reutilization of Zapotec sites in the Tlacolula sub-valley of the Valley of Oaxaca. Chapter 5 details house construction and abandonment at Lambityeco, an important Late Classic secondary center to Monte Albán. Michael Lind exposes dramatic patterns of abandonment by the Early Postclassic, probably due to suppression from Monte Albán, but with continued use of the area for salt production after it ceased to be a living community. Moving east along the highway in the Tlacolula Valley, the recent excavations at Macuilxóchitl, on which Markens, Marcus Winter, and Cira Martínez López focus in Chapter 6, provide crucial architectural and temporal data for understanding transformations and continuities from the Late Classic through the Postclassic. They see much of elite culture—what they term the "Zapotec great tradition"—ending by the end of the Late Classic, with the Early Postclassic being a time of dramatic political crisis. They establish continuities by looking at house construction and location, seeing reuse of house lots even after a period of decline if not actual abandonment.

Although recent ceramic analysis from the lower Río Verde Valley shows the potential of refining the Postclassic chronology, data from this region have proven crucial in overturning some of the Valley of Oaxaca–centric perspectives often promulgated in Oaxaca studies—as shown by both chapters in Part IV. In Chapter 7, Arthur Joyce presents a history of the waxing and waning of centralized authority on the Oaxaca Coast; rather than seeing the Early Postclassic as a dramatic break with the past, he interprets it as the inevitable outcome of tenuous power relationships that could not overcome inherent social contradictions. The collapse of Monte Albán probably had little impact on the western coast around the lower Río Verde Valley. Stacie King focuses on the Early Postclassic in Chapter 8, exploring the diversity of agricultural products, exotic tropical goods, and marine resources with which coastal people supplied the highlands. Rather than a coastal trade route, she explores the socioeconomic organization and the niche markets they filled. She sees interaction as particularly important with the Mixteca Alta rather than with the Valley of Oaxaca.

In Part V, the geographic focus switches to the Mixteca Alta. Due to their brilliant painted picture books, or codices, the Mixtec people are well-known through ethnohistoric documents for the Postclassic and Colonial periods. In Chapter 9, I identify biases in the way in which political histories have been generated from surviving codices and present a material correlate to new legitimization strategies devised by Postclassic leaders. At Etlatongo, from which no codices survive (nor is Etlatongo treated extensively in any of the extant codices), a possible carved bench exhibits a format generally associated with Central Mexican states and empires—the Toltecs and Aztecs. But rather than representing conquest or integration of Etlatongo by outside groups, the bench materializes local appropriation of outside alliances and authority, a perspective supported by codical histories. In Chapter 10, Bruce Byland focuses on what the codices can reveal about sociopolitical transformations during and after the Classic/Postclassic transition. He views the transition in the context of local political action through the intersection of sacred and secular history at the important shrine center of Achiutla and emphasizes the importance of sacred history and belief systems in political transformation.

The final segment—Part VI—presents two especially useful chapters, as they synthesize data for regions culturally related to those on which this book focuses but from which very little is known. Acknowledging that modern political boundaries are artificial, Gerardo Gutiérrez explores eastern Guerrero, along the western border of Oaxaca, in Chapter 11. He sees both contrasts and influences with adjacent cultures in Oaxaca and other regions of Mesoamerica and finds greater continuity between the Classic and Postclassic than throughout Oaxaca. Indeed, as suggested by his title, the archaeological evidence in eastern Guerrero indicative of drastic changes is limited. In Chapter 12, Winter synthesizes data from four poorly known regions of Oaxaca: the Mazateca, Chinantla, Mixe, and southern Isthmus. The richness of material culture that emerges from the fragmentary data that have been documented, as well as the lack of participation in some regions (such as the Mixe) in external styles, serves to caution those who would characterize Oaxaca as a cultural unit with data from only the three best known regions. Winter's chapter points to the need for more research in these areas and cautions against applying a world systems model to Postclassic Oaxaca until basic data from its many diverse regions are available, refusing to cast them as peripheries without the benefit of investigation. I sincerely hope that the compelling data presented in these final two chapters inspire additional and more extensive investigations in these regions.

I anticipate that the chapters in this volume will allow investigators both inside and outside of Oaxaca to see the richness and diversity of sociopolitical organization and interaction within this region and encourage greater consideration of Oaxaca in larger pan-Mesoamerican linkages. Additional data are clearly needed; perhaps the greatest result of this volume would be to stimulate additional projects throughout all regions of Oaxaca.

All that remains is to thank the many people who helped bring this volume to fruition. In addition to the initial inspirational role played by Geoffrey McCafferty, I appreciate the support and encouragement of many colleagues, some of whom are authors in this volume. Constructive criticisms by Marilyn Masson and Heather Orr have greatly benefited this volume, as has the editorial skill of Darrin Pratt, Laura Furney, and Daniel Pratt at the University Press of Colorado. Mickey Lind, Carlos Rincón Mautner, and Nancy Troike contributed greatly to both the underlying ideas and the completion of Chapter 10 but declined Bruce Byland's offer to be included as coauthors; I gratefully acknowledge their efforts. Stacey Thompson assisted in the preparation of this book. Much of the initial editing of this volume was made possible by a fellowship at the Sainsbury Research Unit, University of East Anglia.

The minor revisions and corrections to this book in 2016 are due to the continued encouragement of Darrin Pratt and his team at Colorado, while the Mixtec dedication to our much missed colleague Bruce Byland was translated by Sue Hugghins.

Jeffrey P. Blomster, Washington, DC

After Monte Albán

PART I

The Late Classic/Postclassic in Oaxaca

AN INTRODUCTION

1

Jeffrey P. Blomster

Changing Cloud Formations

THE SOCIOPOLITICS OF OAXACA IN LATE CLASSIC/POSTCLASSIC MESOAMERICA

The origin and collapse of sociopolitical organizations remain topics of fundamental importance to anthropological archaeology. Sometime after 700 CE, both processes unfolded in various parts of modern Oaxaca State, a region in the southern highlands of Mexico (Figure 1.1) encompassing a mosaic of cultures and landscapes (Figure 1.2). One of the first states in the New World emerged after 200 BCE in the Valley of Oaxaca, centered at the Zapotec city of Monte Albán, founded ca. 500 BCE on a hill in the center of the valley. While Monte Albán and other states in disparate regions of Oaxaca began downward spirals of political control and hegemony after 700 CE, territorially small city-states emerged and became the political organization in place when the Spanish first arrived in 1519 in what we now call Mexico. The disjunction in politics contrasts with the persistence of many aspects of daily life and non-elite culture.

Except for studies of Postclassic style and imagery, external relationships and how Oaxacan cultures were situated in a post–Monte Albán world has received less attention than the rise and study of the Monte Albán state. The impact of events outside of Oaxaca that bookend the period of time on which this chapter and volume focuses—the collapse of Teotihuacan in Central Mexico after 600 CE and the

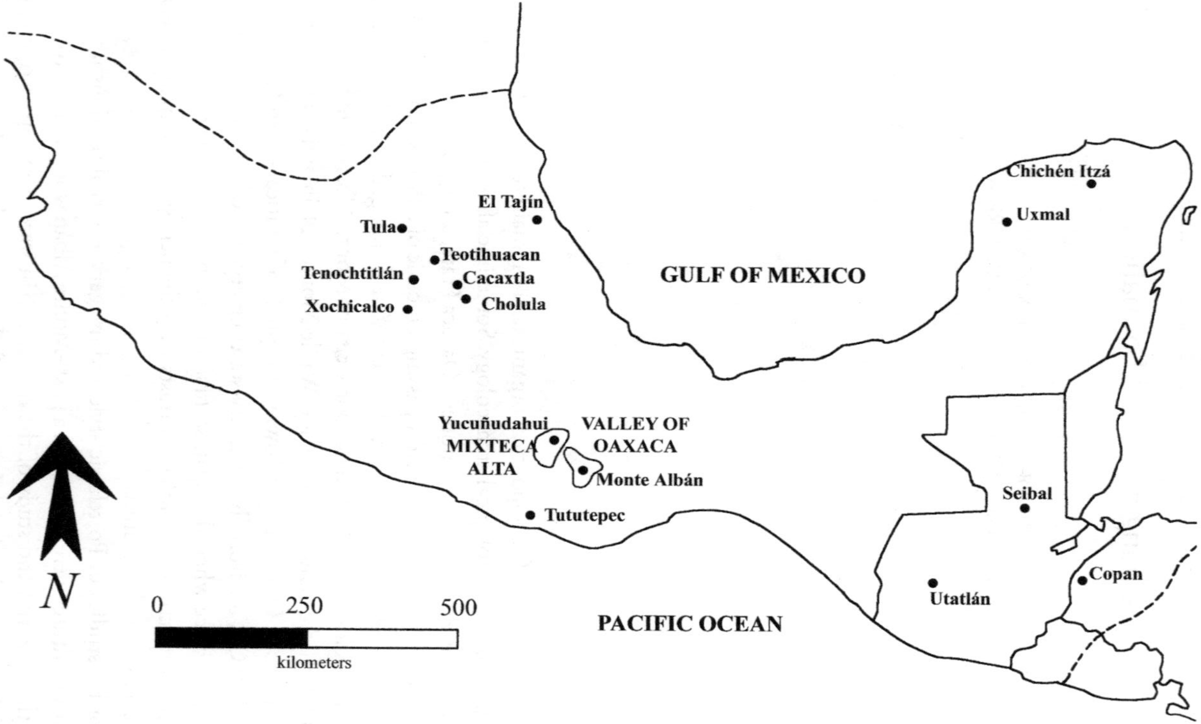

1.1 Map of Late Classic and Postclassic Mesoamerica, showing major sites mentioned in the text. Dashed lines delimit the boundaries of Mesoamerica, and solid lines mark both cultural regions and modern national boundaries. Geographic/cultural regions are indicated in uppercase letters, and sites are in lowercase letters.

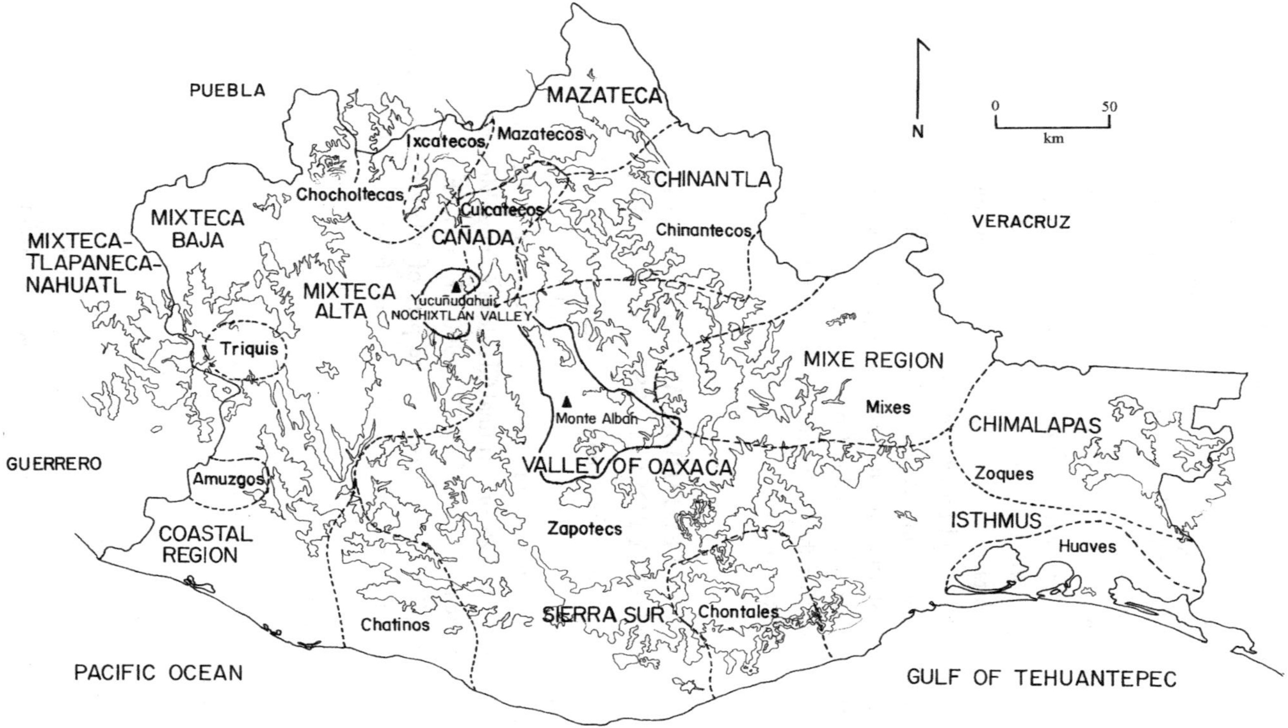

1.2 Map of Oaxaca State and adjacent regions, showing cultural regions (in capital letters) and language groups (in lowercase letters). The important Late Classic urban centers of Yucuñudahui and Monte Albán are represented by triangles. Map by Juan Cruz Pascual, based on Barabas et al. 2003:map 1.

dual incursions of the so-called Aztec Empire into various parts of Oaxaca in the fifteenth century and the Spanish Invasion of the sixteenth century—remain poorly understood and conceptualized. The nature of interregional interaction of Oaxacan societies within the context of larger Mesoamerica, and between the many cultural regions of Oaxaca, remains poorly defined. To many Mesoamerican scholars, Oaxaca remains "off the map" during this time—too focused on balkanized internal politics to have been particularly impacted by or relevant to the transformations occurring throughout ancient Mexico.

After establishing the larger Mesoamerican context in which Oaxaca is situated, this chapter explores what is known about the Late Classic and Postclassic throughout Oaxaca, especially from the three best studied regions: the Valley of Oaxaca, the Mixteca Alta, and the coast/lower Verde Valley (Figure 1.2). Instead of categorizing Late Classic and Postclassic Oaxaca as static and decadent compared to the glories of Classic Monte Albán, this chapter synthesizes the sociopolitical continuities and transformations after the collapse of Classic Oaxacan states. The focus is on themes and analysis of data from recent excavations, surveys, documents, art, and iconography that show Oaxaca's contribution to Postclassic Mesoamerica and larger issues in anthropology.

AFTER TEOTIHUACAN: LATE CLASSIC AND EARLY POSTCLASSIC MESOAMERICA

The demise of the massive urban center at Teotihuacan, situated in the Basin of Mexico (Figure 1.1), impacted other Classic states throughout Mesoamerica, leading to new patterns of interaction, political institutions, and ruling ideologies. Some authors refer to the Late or Terminal Classic in Central Mexico from the fall of Teotihuacan to the rise of Tula (600/700–900 CE) as the Epiclassic (Jiménez Moreno 1966). Teotihuacan's demise may be part of a larger phenomenon of Classic states disintegrating throughout Mesoamerica, from Maya centers (such as Palenque, Tikal, and Copan) to Monte Albán. Although the nature of the demise of Classic states remains uncertain, the usual suspects include warfare, environmental degradation, climate change, internal revolt, and/or commoner agency in rejecting waning Late Classic elite domination (Culbert 1973; Diehl and Berlo 1989; Joyce et al. 2001).

Following Teotihuacan's demise, new cities, or formerly subordinate ones, flourished throughout Mesoamerica, such as El Tajín, Xochicalco, Uxmal, and Cacaxtla (Figure 1.1). The new powers that arose in Central Mexico had roots extending prior to the fall of Teotihuacan. Arising in areas that had been politically marginal zones, none of these new centers approached Teotihuacan's size and influence (Diehl and Berlo 1989:4). Whereas the Classic settlement pattern of the Basin of Mexico had been dominated by only one center, after the demise of Teotihuacan six population clusters emerged, each centered on a major urban center (Sanders et al. 1979).

New connections developed between regions, with trade becoming more decentralized as it flourished in both central and formerly "peripheral" zones. Groups moved throughout Mesoamerica, as often depicted in public art. In the Maya region, the Classic city of Seibal erected stelae in the Late/Terminal Classic featuring individuals with foreign physiognomies—probably the intrusive Putún Maya. Alternatively, these figures on Seibal stelae have been interpreted as representing a greater range of statuses or stylistic temporal variation rather than different cultural identities (Tourtellot and González 2004:64). The highland Mexico sites of Cacaxtla and Xochicalco epitomize the eclectic network of influences and people of the Late/Terminal Classic. The murals of Cacaxtla, primarily painted in Maya style and using the distinctive "Maya-blue" paint, exhibit Central Mexican and Mayan warriors locked in mortal combat. The Temple of Quetzalcoatl at Xochicalco displays lords with Mayan characteristics enveloped by undulating feathered serpents. At both Cacaxtla and Xochicalco, there is a cosmopolitan mixing of influences from throughout Mesoamerica, including Oaxaca as evinced by hieroglyphic elements. Both sites also document the development of state-sponsored militarism, prior to the emergence of the Toltecs at Tula, with the presence of warrior orders (Hirth 1989).

Toltecs: Tula, Chichén Itzá, and Cholula

The impact of the Toltecs, centered at Tula, Hidalgo, on early Postclassic Mesoamerica (900–1200 CE) remains contested. Indeed, although the word "Toltec" is used throughout this volume and usually refers to the people of Tula, it is not assumed that all Toltec elements originated or were even fully expressed at Tula. The Nahuatl term for Tula, "Tollan," actually is much more generic, less geographically specific (see below); many "Toltec" lords noted throughout Postclassic Mesoamerica had little or no connection to Tula. The use of "Tula" refers specifically to the large center in Hidalgo, whereas "Tollan" may refer to several different places. At its height, Tula covered sixteen square kilometers, with an organized city plan and militaristic public art and architecture (Mastache et al. 2002). Ethnohistoric and archaeological data are equivocal on the relationship between Tula and Chichén Itzá, an important late Maya site on the Yucatan peninsula. Beginning with Désiré Charney (1887), some scholars postulate an invasive Toltec presence at Chichén Itzá based on ethnohistoric data, architectural features (such as the "Temple of the Warriors" at each site), sculpture (the recumbent chacmools, receptacles for sacrifices), and iconographic imagery (such as the similar depictions of jaguars and eagles devouring hearts). The work of George Kubler (1961) represents a more recent break from this interpretation, which has long had detractors, focusing instead on local Maya development at Chichén Itzá (see Cobos 2006 for a recent summary). The iconography at Chichén Itzá clearly shows some kind of ethnic opposition or differentiation, as does the art of Late Classic Cacaxtla and Seibal. Some scholars stress, however, that the theme at Chichén Itzá is really elite interaction rather than the conquest or domination of one region by another; what appears to be different ethnic groups may be allies or clients, and they may be relatively local. William Ringle (2004) suggests that elites at centers across Mesoamerica (such as Tula, Chichén Itzá, and El Tajín) were all linked through a shared cult and investiture rituals focused on Quetzalcoatl, a deity whose origins can be traced to the time prior to the Classic period in several regions of Mesoamerica. The importance of shared investiture rituals and symbols reappears elsewhere in this volume (Chapters 3, 9, and 10).

In addition to monuments, Toltec contact is often associated with certain types of pottery, such as Silho Fine Orange and Tohil Plumbate, a distinctive ware with a lustrous gray surface actually produced in the area around Takalik Abaj in the western coastal plain of Guatemala (Neff 2002; Shepard 1948). The production of plumbate extends back to the later portion of the ninth century—almost a half century prior to the Tollan phase (the time of the Toltecs) at Tula (Cobos 2006:181). Thus, its association with Toltec "influence" remains problematic, although the Toltecs may have controlled later distribution of this prized ware. Similarly, the distribution of Silho Fine Orange also lay outside of Tula; Cobos (ibid.) notes that its distribution in the Maya Lowlands was controlled by Chichén Itzá, and that this ware (which also existed prior to the Toltecs) did not actually reach Tula. The movement of ceramics, such as Tohil Plumbate and Fine Orange from the Gulf Coast, epitomize the flourishing trade during the Early Postclassic. Rather than focusing on their Toltec associations, these ceramics served as a canvas for a set of common symbols that spread along trade routes and may be linked with the diffusion of the new international religion and series of rituals (discussed previously) focused on Quetzalcoatl. This symbol set may be a precursor to the Mixteca-Puebla style that characterizes interaction in the Late Postclassic.

A final complicating factor in the supposed Toltec domination of Chichén Itzá is the recent reconsideration of the site's chronology. Rather than being an Early Postclassic center, Chichén Itzá increasingly is referred to by some scholars as a Terminal Classic center in terms of monument construction and elite activity (Andrews et al. 2003). This multi-ethnic center became an important capital as early as the ninth century; its influence was greatly diminished by the first half of the eleventh century. In this view, Chichén Itzá does not represent a break with the Classic Maya past but would have overlapped with important Terminal Classic Maya cities such as Uxmal (ibid.). Both the chronology, however, of Chichén Itzá and the timing of "Toltec" sculptural and architectural elements at this center remain debated, as recent research at Chichén Itzá supports substantial overlap between such features at both sites and the continuation of Chichén Itzá as an important political and economic center through the eleventh century (Schmidt 2007:194). Additionally, there is a growing awareness that although much of the scholarly focus has centered on Tula and Chichén Itzá, they operated in a larger context of competing centers (including Alta Vista and La Quemada to the northwest of Tula in Zacatecas) that also contributed elements shared by both centers (Kristan-Graham and Kowalski 2007:26). Similarities at Tula and Chichén Itzá may represent participation in a larger pan-Mesoamerican cult, some elements of which have antecedents. Indeed, some of the Toltec or Central Mexican imagery at Chichén Itzá may derive from Late Classic Mayan utilization of Teotihuacan imagery (Kowalski 2007:295).

Ethnohistoric documents from the Quiché region of highland Guatemala have also been interpreted as showing the importance of Toltec connections, with clear "Mexican" influence (such as I-shaped ballcourts) first apparent archaeologically in the Epiclassic period and increasing during the Early Postclassic (Fox 1980) and Late Postclassic (Carmack 1981). John Fox (1980:51), among others, interprets ethnohistoric accounts (such as the Sacapulas document) as evidence that actual Toltec lineages came into the Río Negro Valley, conquered the inhabitants, and built much of the public sectors at Chutinamit. The later Quiché Maya adopted Toltec symbols of authority as part of the justification and legitimation of the Quiché state (Carmack 1981:369). Some scholars, however, dispute the notion of Quiché migrations and importance of Toltec connections, preferring a local development, or "ethnogenesis," model, based on contact with Aztec neighbors in Soconusco, to account for the Late Postclassic transformation of elite culture (Braswell 2003).

"Tollan" (Place of the Reeds) may have been a concept linked with several important centers in the Early Postclassic. Throughout the Postclassic, "Tollan" referred to both sacred space and actual places; in addition to towns named with variants of "reed place" throughout the Mexican states of Hidalgo, Veracruz, and Oaxaca, the Aztec capital was sometimes referred to as Tollan Tenochtitlán (Kristan-Graham and Kowalski 2007:22). Although the Toltecs were celebrated, and appropriated by the Aztecs as great warriors and artisans, Tula was simply one Tollan, as were Chichén Itzá and El Tajín, or in highland Guatemala, Nacxit has been suggested as a local Tollan (Fox 1980). Ringle (2004) suggests this pattern extends back to Teotihuacan and sees these cities as legitimating centers for large hinterlands. The recent discovery (Stuart 2000:501–506) of a Classic Mayan glyph of a cattail reed at Tikal and Copan, in texts that refer to the arrival of foreigners with Teotihuacan-style features, supports the idea that Teotihuacan may have been a Tollan, or reed place.

Early Postclassic Cholula, Puebla, may also have been a Tollan (Byland and Pohl 1994). As part of the movement of peoples during the Early Postclassic, the Olmeca-Xicallanca, a mercantile group from the Gulf Coast, occupied Cholula (McCafferty 1996). Much of the massive pyramid at Cholula was constructed at this time. Cholula evinces significant changes during the end of the Late Classic/ Early Postclassic (including a shift to seated flexed burials), and Cholula's identity as a sacred place—the site of a Late Postclassic cult center—may have been established at this time. The ritual authority of Cholula would have far exceeded in distance its limited direct political control (Ringle 2004). Cholula's proximity to Oaxaca may have made it the most referenced Tollan among Oaxacans vying for political power (see below). Despite the various local understanding of "Tollan," Toltecs remain frequently cited in the origins of dynastic lineages, from the Quiché Maya (Carmack 1981) to the Late Postclassic Aztecs, or Mexica. For Postclassic elites, Tollan served as a place for investiture of titles and insignia, with nose-piercing at various Tollans explicitly depicted in Mixtec codices.

LATE POSTCLASSIC MESOAMERICA: MIXTECA-PUEBLA STYLE AND THE AZTECS

The small size, limited political power, and shared ideology of competitive city-states throughout Mesoamerica was conducive to the expansion of commercial exchange and stylistic communication, the hallmark of the Late Postclassic (Smith and Berdan 2003a). In Central Mexico, city-states varied greatly in size and power, with some developing specialties, from markets to centers of law (Texcoco). Michael Smith (2003a:37) suggests that it was the Postclassic development of strong and autonomous commercial institutions that precluded the development of powerful centralized states prior to the Aztecs. Two significant Late Postclassic phenomena impact Oaxaca: the Mixteca-Puebla style and the Aztec Empire.

During the Late Postclassic, a style and iconography emerged that are often referred to as the Postclassic International Style (Robertson 1970), which includes the Mixteca-Puebla style, Aztec painting, coastal Maya mural style, and southwest Maya style. Oaxaca remains inextricably linked to the Mixteca-Puebla style (Brown and Andrews 1982; Nicholson and Quiñones Keber 1994). Starting in the late 1930s, George Vaillant (1938) introduced the concept as part of his effort to describe post-Teotihuacan Central Mexico; he named it Mixteca-Puebla in reference to its supposed place of origin. The concept was more fully elaborated by H. B. Nicholson (1960, 1982), who argued for it as primarily stylistic and iconographic. Noting that it appears in various media, including codices, polychrome murals, ceramics, and turquoise mosaics, Nicholson characterized the Mixteca-Puebla style by its "almost geometric precision in the delineation of its images, both figural and symbolic. The former often represented deities important in the pantheon, usually identifiable by their relatively standardized insignia" (Nicholson and Quiñones Keber 1994:vii).

Detailed stylistic and compositional analysis of polychrome ceramics in the Mixteca-Puebla style have determined the existence of multiple production loci (Lind 1987; Neff et al. 1994). The application of Mixteca-Puebla is confined to Middle and Late Postclassic codices, ceramics, and murals from the Mixteca-Puebla region (Nicholson and Quiñones Keber 1994; Smith 2003b:182); however, material in related local variants are found throughout Mesoamerica, where it is often cited as evidence of "Mexican" contact or participation in pan-Mesoamerican phenomenon. In the Quiché region, materials visually related to the Mixteca-Puebla style (most notably the mural paintings at Iximché and Utatlán) are seen as the most substantial Mexican influence in the highlands, although Robert Carmack (1969) notes that its expression is a local variant, from general presentation to specific features.

Sharing of the Mixteca-Puebla style and iconography followed alliance corridors. Rather than the outcome of a purely economic exchange, the use of certain iconographic symbols and stylistic features of the Mixteca-Puebla style represented a comprehendible form of communication for leaders speaking a plethora of different languages and formed parts of their strategies for social and political interaction (Byland and Pohl 1994; Smith 2003b:181). Its dissemination may also reflect the emergence of an important pilgrimage center at Cholula (see previous discussion). During the Late Postclassic, Cholula became the site of an important oracular shrine for Quetzalcoatl that attracted pilgrims from as far away as Guatemala (McCafferty 2001; Ringle et al. 1998). Reflecting the more commercialized nature of the Late Postclassic, Cholula was also a major mercantile center. The sacred and the profane were closely intertwined at Cholula. The link between the spread of religious ideology and trade networks is symbolized at Cholula by the depiction of Quetzalcoatl as Yacatecuhtli, the Nahua merchant deity (Pohl 2003a:174).

In addition to movement of styles, objects, and iconography, one group—the Aztecs—also intruded into many regions of Late Postclassic Mesoamerica. The Aztecs, based at their capital of Tenochtitlán, formed one of the most expansive empires in the New World. With their allies, the Aztec Triple Alliance incorporated vast regions of Mesoamerica into their empire, whereas other regions—such as the Tarascan Empire—remained largely free from Aztec tribute demands. The impact of the Aztecs varied across Mesoamerica; they often did little to disturb the underlying foundations of the city-states that they incorporated into their empire, with ruling elites allowed to maintain their position as long as tribute flowed to the Triple Alliance. Some towns became well integrated into the Aztec Empire, but others paid tribute only under threat of an Aztec attack.

1.3 The public core of Monte Albán; view of the Main Plaza, looking south.

OAXACA AS A REGION

The Spanish arrived in what is now Oaxaca State to find one to three million people with rich, diverse regional cultures (Figure 1.2). At least sixteen distinct ethnic and linguistic groups are generally acknowledged in Oaxaca State (Flannery and Marcus 1983; Winter 1989), the vast majority of which remain poorly known and studied (Chapter 12). Some Oaxaca-related cultures, of course, are not limited by modern state boundaries, making recent investigations in eastern Guerrero—adjacent to Oaxaca—of great interest (Chapter 11). The best-studied cultures, the Mixtec and the Zapotec, occupy the largest valleys in Oaxaca; in addition to their own knowledge traditions, aspects of their cultures are documented by early colonial Spanish records and subsequent anthropological projects. Information available on the Zapotec and Mixtec should caution scholars in how carefully to treat intra-group diversity. Neither group ever dominated all of Oaxaca State or formed a unified ethnic group—there was never a unified "Zapotec" nation; rather, there were always factional divisions that cut across and within cultural and linguistic boundaries (Byland and Pohl 1994). Indeed, the Nahuatl names assigned by the Aztecs to these groups remain useful because they are generic names. Variations of indigenous names used by Oaxacan groups (such as the Bènizàa for some Zapotec groups or the Ñuu Dzavui/Ñudzahui for some Mixtec groups)—often glossed as meaning

"people of the rain or clouds"—epitomize the regional, linguistic, and cultural diversity among what are often stereotyped as well-defined "ethnic" groups (Jansen and Pérez Jiménez 2000).

The Valley of Oaxaca

Systematic archaeological investigations in the Valley of Oaxaca date back to 1931 and the pioneering efforts of Alfonso Caso and his associates. Covering 2500 square kilometers and at approximately 1,500 meters in elevation, the Valley of Oaxaca is well studied archaeologically through surface surveys and extensive excavations (see Kowalewski et al. 1989, Winter 1989). Much research in Oaxaca focuses on the emergence of the first urban center at Monte Albán (Figure 1.3), on a series of hills in the center of where the three sub-valleys of the Oaxaca Valley converge. After 200 BCE, Monte Albán became the head of a Zapotec state, with a complex four-tier settlement hierarchy in the Valley of Oaxaca and incursions—the nature of which remains debated—into surrounding regions (Joyce 1991; Marcus and Flannery 1996; Winter 1989). At its Classic period height the city probably covered 6.5 square kilometers (Blanton 1978). Although substantially modified (see Figure 2.1), the ceramic chronology for much of Oaxaca is based on the initial efforts of Caso, Ignacio Bernal, and Jorge Acosta (1967) at Monte Albán.

Mixteca Alta and Baja

The various Mixtec regions cover approximately 50,000 square kilometers of rugged terrain. The largest of these regions, the Mixteca Alta, features mountains that surround small, irregular valleys, which account for only 20 percent of the land mass (Smith 1976:24). Much of the archaeological research in the Mixteca Alta centers on the largest valley, the Nochixtlán, which was systematically surveyed by Ronald Spores in the 1960s (Spores 1972) and was the setting for the large Classic/Late Classic urban center of Yucuñudahui. Other areas of the Mixteca Alta, such as the valleys at Teposcolula (Stiver 2001), Huamelulpan (Gaxiola González 1984), and Tamazulapan (Byland 1980), have been increasingly explored. A recent literature review by Spores (2001) summarizes both historic and recent work throughout the Mixteca Alta. The Mixteca Baja, the lower, "hot" Mixtec region of the Ñuiñe culture (the term also refers to a style, people, and phase name; see Winter 1989, 1994) centered at Cerro de las Minas, exhibits shared and contrasting cultural traits with the Alta (Paddock 1966; Rivera Guzmán 2002). The relationships between Classic Mixtec centers in adjacent valleys remain unclear. The impact of Monte Albán's demise on Mixtec states varied, as ongoing archaeological research demonstrates their multiplicity of external relations that went beyond the Zapotec state.

The Lower Río Verde Valley

Beginning with research in the late 1980s (Joyce 1991), a long-term project in the lower Río Verde Valley, a low, hot, coastal plain along the western Pacific Oaxaca Coast, has provided data critical for challenging many Valley of Oaxaca–centric interpretations. A combined program of survey and excavation have shown that trends in political centralization culminated during the Terminal Formative (150 BCE–250 CE) in the emergence of a state centered at Río Viejo. Rather than interpretations that focus on Zapotec conquest (Marcus and Flannery 1996), the ongoing research suggests a complex indigenous development, marked by periods of political collapse and centralization, with political and economic ties that distinguish it from the Valley of Oaxaca.

Other Regions of Oaxaca

Other parts of Oaxaca State remain underexplored. The best documented is the Cuicatlán Cañada, a deep canyon between the Mixtec, Zapotec, and Mazatec regions that served as an important trade corridor and was heavily impacted by the Monte Albán state (Spencer 1982). One contribution of the present volume is providing data on other poorly known Oaxacan regions during the Late Classic through Postclassic (Chapter 12). In addition to the culturally related eastern part of Guerrero (Chapter 11), other parts of Oaxaca included in this volume are the Mixe region (the mountains east/northeast of the Valley of Oaxaca), the Chinantla (the mountainous area on the northern extreme of the Zapotec Sierra and the river valleys/piedmont that slope down to the Gulf Coast), the Mazateca (an area of highland and river valleys northwest of the Chinantla), and the southern Isthmus (the coastal plain of the Isthmus of Tehuantepec and adjacent low hills) (Figure 1.2).

CHALLENGES: CHRONOLOGY, METHOD, AND THEORY

At the foundation of many of the unresolved issues facing the Oaxacan Late Classic/Postclassic is a highly problematic chronology; failure to devise more temporally sensitive ceramic phases has led to basic problems in estimating population and settlement during this period. Methods and prevailing theories have also influenced interpretations.

Chronology, Methods, and Hiatus

Archaeologists construct ceramic chronologies, supported by absolute dates, for the regions in which they work. The problems in Oaxaca chronology are especially pronounced at the end of the Late Classic and Postclassic. As traditionally outlined, the Postclassic alone encompasses six centuries—an untenable situation. The ceramic chronology defined by Caso and his collaborators (Caso, Bernal, and Acosta 1967) featured periods I through V, beginning with the founding of Monte Albán around 500 BCE and ending with the arrival of the Spanish. They correlated Period IIIB with the Late Classic, whereas Period IV represented Oaxaca after the collapse of Monte Albán—the Early Postclassic (Chapter 2; Figure 2.1). As the surveyors were unable to distinguish between diagnostic ceramics from these periods, they combined them into Phase IIIB-IV. Some sites once considered the type sites of the Early Postclassic, such as Lambityeco (Chapter 5), have been radiocarbon dated to the 650–750 interval before the Monte Albán collapse and are similar to dates from Cacaxtla and Xochicalco. The confusion with this part of the chronology masks important stylistic changes and political disjunction.

The problem has recently been tackled by Robert Markens (Chapter 2). Using Valley of Oaxaca burial lots, he distinguishes early and late sub-phases in the Xoo (600–800), Liobaa (800–1200), and Chila (1200–1521) phases (see Figure 2.1). The proposed ceramic sequence has received confirmation through radiocarbon dates from recent excavations at sites in the Tlacolula branch of the Valley of Oaxaca, such as Macuilxóchitl (Chapter 6) and Xaagá. Additionally, Michel Oudijk analyzes ethnohistoric documents to provide an alternative chronology starting at 963 CE, with three well-defined phases starting at 1100 (Chapter 3). Oudijk's chronology was developed independently of ceramics and archaeological sources and is based on the foundation of lineages, suggesting there are three critical moments in which it may be possible to divide the Postclassic period. Both chronologies may be useful and inform each other; they represent emic (Oudijk) and etic (Markens) approaches. Finally, recent work in the lower Río Verde opens new possibilities for understanding differences between Early Postclassic ceramics and those from the Late Classic and Late Postclassic (Chapters 7 and 8).

The long-standing confusion with the chronology render problematic basic data on Postclassic population, as much of the data come from surface survey. As William Sanders (1989:216) asked, "How can we accept settlement and population histories from an area when the basic chronology is so confused?" Many regions of Oaxaca have been surveyed, and the surface surveys are extremely valuable tools for identifying sites. The Valley of Oaxaca was the location of a full-coverage survey, directed by Richard Blanton and Stephen Kowalewski and completed in 1980; 2,700 archaeological sites were recorded (Kowalewski et al. 1989). In addition to site formation processes, which lead to the underrepresentation of earlier deposits that lie buried in multi-component sites (Brown 1975), the poor ceramic chronology led to what appears to be drastic population decreases and movements in some areas. For example, recent research at Macuilxóchitl (Chapter 6) underscores problems with reliance on surface survey. Excavations at Mound 1, categorized as Late Formative and Early Classic by the Prehistoric Settlement Patterns of the Valley of Oaxaca Project (Kowalewski et al. 1989), revealed only Late Classic and Postclassic materials (Markens, personal communication, 2004).

Due partially to a problematic chronology, archaeologists disagree on the issue of regional abandonment. Marcus Winter (Chapter 12) proposes an abandonment of parts of the Valley of Oaxaca at the end of the Late Classic. In addition to drastic population decline at the end of the Xoo phase (800 CE) at Monte Albán, excavations at Lambityeco, a major salt-producing center in the Valley of Oaxaca, document the abandonment of houses between 700 and 800, although some salt making continued at the site into the Postclassic (Chapter 5). Indeed, it appears that the depopulation of Lambityeco represents repression and political domination of a competing center by the Monte Albán state prior to its collapse (see below). In addition to hiatuses in the Mazatec, Chinantla, and Mixe regions, Winter (1994:217) has proposed a "dark age" in the Mixtec urban centers as well, including Cerro de las Minas. In the lower Río Verde Valley, where the ceramic chronology is more refined for the Late Classic/Early Postclassic, the data do not support a hiatus. Although Río Viejo declined in size, at 140 hectares it remained a significant center in the Early Postclassic (Chapter 7).

New Theoretical Approaches

In terms of theoretical approaches, much of the research and syntheses that have been published for Oaxaca are based on an explicitly cultural evolutionary perspective (Flannery and Marcus 1983; Marcus and Flannery 1996). Although an effort has been made to lose the ethnocentric baggage and more extreme biological analogies of cultural evolution by referring to it as "social evolution," the promise of an "evolution without stages" has not been fulfilled (see Flannery 2002:240). New theoretical approaches further illuminate our understanding of the Late Classic and Postclassic.

The majority of chapters in this volume approach political and social phenomena through a practice/praxis or agency perspective (Ortner 1984). A practice perspective explores the relationships of human agents within larger systems (structures). Neither random nor unrestrained, actions occur within a structural context, constrained by both the biophysical and sociocultural environment. Individuals pursue self-interested goals and strategies; they make decisions in relation to multiple factors, structures, and other agents (Bourdieu 1977; Giddens 1984). The archaeologists' emphasis is on social identities and behavioral strategies rather than on details of individual lives, although the details provided by the codices of individual lives (albeit invariably those of the elite) flesh out the roles and structure of Postclassic society. Rather than perspectives that solely focus on the negotiations of elites, efforts have been made to explore commoner agency as well (Chapters 5 and 8; Joyce et al. 2001). Such approaches are also more sympathetic to emic perspectives, such as how people living in Early and Late Postclassic Oaxaca viewed the Late Classic/Postclassic transition (Chapters 3 and 4).

MONTE ALBÁN'S COLLAPSE AND ITS IMPACT IN OAXACA: DISJUNCTION?

Although a series of internal factors were probably most responsible for the post–700 CE collapse of the Zapotec state at Monte Albán, ripples from events occurring elsewhere in Mesoamerica—such as the demise of Teotihuacan—may have disrupted exchange networks that the ruling elite depended on for exotic goods, prestige, trade, and power. In the case of Monte Albán, the demise of a potential threat like Teotihuacan may have undermined the necessity for such a large, nucleated population to resist it. The collapse of Monte Albán and other Classic period states in Oaxaca initiated political changes but represents a transformation rather than a sudden event. With a 600 CE population of at least 30,000 people living at and on the sides of this hilltop center (Blanton 1978), the process of overexploitation of the region had been well under way for generations. Competing centers, such as Lambityeco, Mitla, Jalieza, and Zaachila, had already appeared in the Valley of Oaxaca. During this transition, leaders of nascent city-states would have negotiated a challenging political climate in order to assert independence from Monte Albán while still referencing that ancient city as a source of legitimacy, especially those that served its secondary administrative centers. The demise of effective power at Monte Albán allowed the ideological adjustments and political realignments to flourish.

Monte Albán was not the only large Classic center in the various cultural regions of Oaxaca; other large states were centered, for example, at Yucuñudahui in the Nochixtlán Valley and Río Viejo in the lower Río Verde Valley. Such states engaged in diplomatic, economic, and martial relationships with other large states beyond Monte Albán. Although elements of elite culture at Yucuñudahui, for example, show Zapotec influence, artisans drew from an array of inspirations, such as the local distinctive square main chamber and Ñuiñe-style carvings from Tomb 1 (Caso 1938; Winter 1989). Relationships beyond those with the Zapotec state in the Mixteca and lower Verde encouraged different dynamics in the wake of the collapse of Monte Albán. In the Mixteca Alta, the Classic hilltop centers may have survived the collapse of Monte Albán (Spores 1984); however, due to the problematic nature of the Late Classic Mixtec ceramic chronology, this observation is tentative.

In the lower Río Verde Valley, collapse began around 800 CE after a marked Classic period of population nucleation and political centralization focused at Río Viejo. Although the dominant ruling regime ended, the site remained occupied but without construction of additional public architecture—a pattern seen during this time at other sites in Oaxaca. The end of what Arthur Joyce (Chapter 7) refers to as a period of unstable rulership represents the failure to establish long-term legitimacy.

Although archaeological evidence of a true hiatus (depending on how "hiatus" is defined) in any region of Oaxaca remains problematic, some important sites throughout Oaxaca were largely abandoned. The ideological impact may have been substantial; the Late Classic to Postclassic transition may have been perceived as a significant disjunction from the Classic. Byron Hamann (Chapter 4; 2002) interprets Postclassic pictorial histories as emphasizing a rupture with the Classic, which is treated as a different age, or "Sun," from which the Postclassic present emerged. Interpretation of this rupture presented both challenges and opportunities to individuals from the full spectrum of economic and political status. In the Mixteca Alta, much of the rupture may correspond with an event from the tenth century first identified by Alfonso Caso (1960) and now referred to as the "War of Heaven." Sites that appeared in pictorial histories prior to this event vanish as living communities; Bruce Byland and John Pohl (1994) have been able to link several of them with Classic period ruins around Tilantongo. The dramatic political changes in the lower Verde Valley lend some support to this perspective, with images of elites from the previous order treated with a decided lack of respect in the Early Postclassic (Chapter 8). Similarly, the abandoned Late Classic palaces at the Valley of Oaxaca administrative center of Lambityeco were reused by commoners in the Early Postclassic for salt production (Chapter 5).

LATE CLASSIC/POSTCLASSIC BALKANIZATION IN OAXACA: TRANSFORMATIONS

After 700 CE, a wave of major sociopolitical transformations surged across much of Oaxaca. The diversity of responses to the collapse of major states throughout Oaxaca evinces the great variety of contact and integration between regions.

Political Transformation

With the demise of large centers, small, competing cacicazgos flourished in Oaxaca. As with other parts of Mesoamerica (Diehl and Berlo 1989), the emergence of city-states was tied with new alliance formations, many of which predated the final decline of Monte Albán. Many of the ruling lineages of newly ascendant city-states in the Valley of Oaxaca may have administered secondary centers for the Zapotec capital or may have been factions within the ruling elite at Monte Albán and desired more independence or pragmatically viewed the irreversible demise of Monte Albán as an opportunity to establish themselves elsewhere. The post–Monte Albán elites would have emphasized their genealogy and marriage alliances—a trend begun in Xoo phase Monte Albán, with the importance of "genealogical registers" (Marcus 1989) manifested in stone sculpture. That fact that other Xoo centers in the Valley of Oaxaca illustrate comparable scenes shows that Monte Albán was no longer able to suppress such statements at competing centers.

The failure of some emerging centers to flourish after the Xoo phase testifies to the potential repressive force exercised by Monte Albán. Some lineages of competing centers may have simply been premature in pursuing economic or political independence, or expressed it in a way that the Monte Albán leaders could not ignore. Lambityeco, a secondary administrative center or district capital for the Tlacolula arm of the Valley of Oaxaca, became a major salt-producing center in the early Xoo phase, with numerous households in charge of production. Michael Lind (Chapter 5) documents the increasing wealth and power of the Lambityeco rulers, appointed by the Monte Albán king; elite houses at Lambityeco, such as Structure 4, were larger than corresponding ones at Monte Albán. The increasing wealth and independence of Lambityeco may have been viewed as a challenge to Monte Albán, which after 700 CE reacted by deposing the local ruling lineage and drastically reorganizing salt production in a government workshop. Rather than becoming an important Early Postclassic center, Lambityeco was largely abandoned as a living community, serving primarily as a locus for salt production throughout the Postclassic (Chapter 5). Similar dynamics played out in the Mixteca Alta as well, although in the absence of a central state as hegemonic as Monte Albán, the processes began earlier and may not have been met with successful repression as in the case of Lambityeco and Monte Albán.

Demographics and Settlement Patterns

Upheavals in the Late Classic/Postclassic transition are reflected in demography. Throughout regions of Oaxaca, settlement patterns changed. For example, the major Classic center of Río Viejo lost half of its Late Classic population by the Early Postclassic (Chapter 7). Although some formerly large states experienced depopulation as part of political decentralization, population was redistributed in emerging first-order sites. Beginning in the Early Postclassic, a trend develops whereby people moved into the piedmont from the west to the east side of the Río Verde; by the Late Postclassic, piedmont occupation accounts for 93.2 percent of settlement in this region, as opposed to comprising only 34.2 percent in the Late Classic (Joyce et al. 2004).

In the Valley of Oaxaca, some Late Classic sites were abandoned or reduced substantially in population (such as Monte Albán); many Xoo phase houses fell into ruin. As noted above with the Lambityeco example, the failure of some Xoo centers to thrive in the Early Postclassic was not necessarily a demographic collapse but rather a response by the remaining occupants to the successful political repression by Monte Albán.

In contrast to the conflicting evidence from the Early Postclassic, the Late Postclassic appears to be a time of incredible growth throughout all regions of Oaxaca. While earlier sites remain occupied, people tended to select higher elevations for new sites in the Late Postclassic (Kowalewski et al. 1989:307). The foundation of a new noble house and a population expansion reenergized Macuilxóchitl, and it became one of many important players in Late Postclassic politics in the Valley of Oaxaca (Chapter 6).

The Late Postclassic represents the time of maximum population in the Mixteca. In the Tamazulapan Valley, the number of occupied sites doubles (Byland 1980). Spores (1972) notes a substantial change in the location of major centers in the Nochixtlán Valley—on the valley floors rather than hills, where the old hilltop localities continued to serve as ritual centers and places of legitimacy and power.

Mixtec Invasions and Ethnicity

A long-standing problem in Oaxaca archaeology is the presence of Mixtecs in the Valley of Oaxaca documented by the sixteenth-century Spanish; to some, this signals a Mixtec invasion of the Zapotec Oaxaca Valley (Paddock 1983:274). Although ethnohistoric documents clearly mention Mixtec incursions (Chapter 3), archaeological evidence of a forced Mixtec entry in the Valley of Oaxaca has proven elusive. Mixtecs occupied the western Valley of Oaxaca in the sixteenth century (Burgoa 1989), but how they entered remains problematic. Many of the claims of a Mixtec conquest of the Valley of Oaxaca come from the Mixtecs themselves and were motivated by both pride and a desire to negotiate a specific identity and place for themselves in colonial society. Rather than envisioning hoards of Mixtecs (who were never a unified "ethnic" group) swarming into the Valley of Oaxaca, we should view Mixtec entry into the Valley of Oaxaca as following the same patterns of negotiations as between Mixtec cacicazgos. The sixteenth-century Relaciones Geográficas indicate Zapotec cities interacted with specific Mixtec cacicazgos and elite lines, facilitating Mixtec entry into the Valley of Oaxaca, at least initially as partners, affinal kin, and allies.

The specter of a Mixtec invasion reflects the problematic associations between different geographic areas, material culture, and ethnicity. Archaeologists often essentialize the concept of ethnicity, when in fact there may be many underlying features to unpack. As a situational phenomenon, ethnicity can be both claimed by the agent and also assigned by others and includes tangible and intangible features (Barth 1969; Cohen 1978). This is not to deny that ethnic distinctions may have been extremely important to ancient Mesoamericans. The use of ethnic markers to distinguish groups from each other can be seen at Late and Terminal Classic sites such as Cacaxtla, Seibal, and Chichén Itzá, where artists juxtaposed different physiognomies, styles of clothing, ornamentation, and weaponry. At Classic Monte Albán, supposed Teotihuacan visitors were differentiated from Zapotecs appearing on the same stone monuments, such as the Lápida de Bazán (see Figure 4.12) and various stelae from the South Platform. Esther Pasztory (1989:18) notes that ethnic styles often serve as badges of group identity—differentiating members of one group from "the other." Although she notes that style juxtapositions in Mesoamerican art are rare, they generally occur in public areas—a politically sanctioned attitude that speaks to the official perception of these cultures.

Archaeologists can only approach ethnicity through multiple lines of evidence (Stein 2002), recognizing the different agendas and points of view in each type of source. Archaeologists attempting to characterize Mixtec and Zapotec ethnic groups in Late Classic to Postclassic Oaxaca face numerous challenges. For example, ethnographies demonstrate that individual identity remains contingent and variable. Modern Zapotec villagers associate themselves with their specific village or community, which they differentiate from others, rather than a vague concept of "Zapotec" (Dennis 1987). In other circumstances, a larger group identity may have been advantageous—even a form of resistance. The frequent use of the term for Mixtec, Ñudzahui, in indigenous sixteenth- to eighteenth-century documents may reflect an attempt at maintaining group boundaries and identity in the face of colonialism (Terraciano 2001:318). Furthermore, the material culture that archaeologists excavate provides only tenuous links with ethnicity. Pottery is especially difficult to link with ethnic groups in the Postclassic; some pottery types may have been produced at specialized pottery-making centers and were widely available across ethnic lines (Marcus and Flannery 1983:225).

A Shifting Mosaic: Cacicazgos in Postclassic Oaxaca

Although the basic city-state (cacicazgo or señorío) format existed prior to the demise of large states like Monte Albán, its Postclassic florescence introduced new features and transformed others. Throughout the world, city-states often, but not inevitably, emerge after the collapse of larger central states, such as in Greece after the collapse of centralized Mycenaean palace societies (Snodgrass 1977). As autonomous polities, city-states exert less economic control over populations—especially those living in towns and villages outside of the center.

The extent and identity of a Mesoamerican city-state is defined by affiliation with a ruler rather than a territory (Smith 2003a:36). A royal family rules a cacicazgo, with close kinsmen as noble administrators; each has a capital center (*cabecera*) and surrounding subject communities that provide labor and support (Spores 1967). Social stratification is well developed, often with beliefs in separate origins for nobles and commoners. The well-documented city-states (*altepetl*) of Central Mexico had additional classes, including slaves and different divisions of commoners based on access to land.

Reflecting local practice, Oaxaca exhibits much variety in the constitution of its city-states. In the Mixteca Alta, the word for a populous settlement is *yuhuitayu* and combines the Mixtec words for "reed mat" and "pair/couple," referring literally to the city-state as the seat of rulership for a married couple (Terraciano 2001:103). In the Nochixtlán Valley, an average cacicazgo, or kingdom, contained a population of 2,000 to 10,000 people (Winter 1994:217), with larger ones, such as Yanhuitlán, having populations of 25,000 or more. The basic patterns documented by Spores (1972) for the Nochixtlán Valley are typical. The center of the cacicazgo lay near the valley bottomland, often with a fortified palace on a nearby ridge—a place that could be defended in times of conflict (Pohl 2003b).

Postclassic cabeceras also differ from Classic centers in their internal organization. There is a dramatic reduction in the amount of monumental and civic-ceremonial architecture; what ceremonial structures exist are less imposing than in the Classic (Spores 1972). In the lower Río Verde, Early Postclassic centers lack public architecture (Chapter 7). This represents the reduced territorial and ideological integration of the Postclassic, as smaller, adjacent kingdoms competed against each other. Larger structures are generally palaces, celebrating elite lineages, rather than large public monuments that glorify the state and its ideology. Palaces feature rooms organized around one or more open patios and vary greatly in size, depending on the power of the lineage and the position of the city. Throughout Mesoamerica, private residences of the elite overshadowed public architecture; the Quiché palaces at Utatlán became so massive and elaborate that the Spanish approvingly referred to them as castles (Carmack 1981:193). Large Postclassic structures, of course, exist—the massive Temple of Heaven at Tilantongo rivals the size of Classic Mixtec mounds, although it does not appear to be part of a formal layout of public architecture as at the nearby, and earlier Late Formative center, Monte Negro. And in the Late Postclassic, the double-temple of the Aztec Templo Mayor was a massive and imposing structure that represented the heart of their cosmological and political empire.

Zapotec kingdoms (*gueche*) in the Valley of Oaxaca were similar to those in the Mixteca, with connections based on trade and marriage. Oudijk (2002:80) suggests that the Valley of Oaxaca can be provisionally divided into eleven to thirteen major cacicazgos, whose size, population, and territory constantly changed over time. None of the large cabeceras approached the size of Monte Albán, and populations were less nucleated. Although many of the best-known Postclassic centers and dynasties in the Valley of Oaxaca had Classic antecedents, others, such as Macuilxóchitl, appear to have had a new noble house established in the Postclassic. Fortifications at some Zapotec sites (such as Mitla, Yagul, Huitzo, and Zaachila) are usually placed on a hill and indicate some degree of warfare or raiding during the Postclassic. The boundaries of a cacicazgo were circumscribed, but influence—and even control—extended irregularly beyond them.

Cacicazgos differed greatly in size and importance. Along the western coast of Oaxaca, Tututepec became a massive center in the Late Postclassic, sitting atop a five-tier site hierarchy and perhaps covering as much as 2,185 hectares (Joyce et al. 2004). The ca. 1100 foundation of Tututepec, as depicted in the codices, involves the famed Lord 8 Deer Jaguar Claw and a possible strategic alliance with the Toltec-Chichimeca after a period of political instability in the Early Postclassic. The polity centered at Tututepec may have controlled an empire of 25,000 square kilometers. To the west, the Tlapa-Tlachinollan formed a major Postclassic state—controlling some 150,000 people—along modern Oaxaca's border with eastern Guerrero and extending south to the Costa Chica (Chapter 11). In the Mixteca Alta, Achiutla was famed both for sacred tree birth and the seat of a solar oracular shrine controlled by a powerful priest; due to the supernatural power centered in this place, the Achiutla oracle was often consulted by Mixtec rulers (Chapter 10). Another important Mixtec oracular shrine—for Lady 9 Grass—was located in Chalcatongo. To the north, the multi-ethnic city of Coixtlahuaca became a major mercantile center; its market attracted merchants from Tenochtitlán and other large cities (Durán 1994). In the Valley of Oaxaca, places such as Cuilapan and Mitla had important religious and market functions. The elegant palaces at Mitla served to celebrate the administrative powers of the royal line as well as entomb great Zapotec rulers. Mitla also served as the residence of one of the most important Zapotec priests, who served to mediate political disputes—leading to Spanish comparisons with the Vatican (Canseco 1905; Pohl 1999); the Achiutla oracle also arbitrated conflicts between competing royal families (Chapter 10).

City-states also varied greatly in their level of political independence. Some city-states successfully dominated others. Zaachila served as a political center for at least part of the Valley of Oaxaca, with places as far as Macuilxóchitl apparently subject to it. The control exercised by important city-states such as Zaachila or Tilantongo waxed and waned. This pattern is common in Postclassic Mesoamerica, where competing kingdoms were sometimes centralized or controlled for a period of time under multiple regional centers, such as Utatlán and Iximché in the Quiché region of highland Guatemala or the series of city-states around Lake Texcoco that tried to exercise control over the Valley of Mexico prior to the successful domination of that region by the Aztecs.

Other institutions played important political functions. Relatives of the ruling elite often filled administrative roles, whereas members of the priesthood filled positions of secular authority in both the Postclassic and early Colonial eras; a council of four priests has been suggested as particularly significant in the Mixteca (Pohl 1994). Judith Zeitlin (1994) has explored the role of the barrio, or residential ward, in the functioning and integration of city-state organization. She sees the plaza-centered public architecture at Panteón Antiguo, Tehuantepec, as identifying it as a corporate community, the focus of religious and administrative features (such as overseeing public works projects) and physically separate from other communities (1994:291).

Power and Legitimization: Alliances, Marriages, Factions, and Conquest

From Late Classic to Postclassic, the legitimization strategies employed by the ruling elite changed. With the collapse of Monte Albán and other large states, alliances between city-states became increasingly important in reinforcing both the power and legitimacy of lineages and the position of the cacicazgo in regional politics. New forms of legitimization focused on the complex ways in which dynasties were founded—reflective of the complex, factional politics of the Postclassic. Yuhuitayu, the Mixtec term used for large settlements (see previous discussion), specifically associates place with a ruling couple's union.

Marriages linked dynasties and connected them to larger political networks. Places that had venerated supernatural connections, such as Achiutla, and/or ancient and well-established genealogies, such as Tilantongo, Jaltepec, Tlaxiaco, and Coixtlahuaca (Chapter 10; Pohl 2003b), produced royals who made especially desirable marriage partners, and ambitious elites (often from less important lineages) vied for these marriage partners to enhance their own legitimacy and reputation of their dynasty. Beyond the initial marital merger, the stability of the union also remained a paramount concern. Based on early colonial documents, Kevin Terraciano (2001:103–104) notes that rulership as inscribed in yuhuitayu refers to a married pair representing different ruling lineages; this union joined the resources and authority of two places without compromising their separateness. The continued viability of these relationships could be reaffirmed through multiple marriages between important figures from both places, such as between Achiutla and Hill of the Wasp (Chapter 10).

Alliances could prove crucial in the origin of a ruling dynasty. Throughout Oaxaca, challenges—both internal and external—to a ruling dynasty were often met by enhanced alliances and, in times of crisis, linked with the foundation of a new dynasty. Zaachila rulers routinely made alliances, generally through marriage, with Mixtec ruling dynasties, and as Oudijk shows (Chapter 3), in one case (Cosijoeza), the alliance was actually used to initiate a campaign of colonization. Sometimes alliance involved external parties. The founding and promotion of the Coixtlahuaca dynasty, for example, extended back to eleventh-century alliances made with a "Toltec" lord, 4 Jaguar, who materialized alliances and promoted his supporters through a nose-piercing ceremony (Doesburg and van Buren 1997). The same Lord 4 Jaguar proved crucial to the ambitions of Lord 8 Deer Jaguar Claw; the Toltec connection is further discussed below. Such alliances transmitted powerful messages to competing dynasties within and outside of a particular city-state.

In the face of factional opposition, the position of ruler was continually reconstituted, along with the associated practices, as part of a recursive ordering of social conditions (Giddens 1984). Within cacicazgos, rulers created heroic histories for their lineage that blended historical actions with a larger ideology that celebrated the "nationality" or origin of that cacicazgo, attempting to rise above factional disputes (Pohl 2003c). Military conflict and conquest was an additional tool of rulership and incorporation. Lord 8 Deer Jaguar Claw, of Tilantongo, deployed the whole gamut of strategies as he incorporated a series of city-states under his rule.

New Ideology, Paraphernalia, Media, and Modes of Visual Expression

After the Late Classic, some cultural elements associated with elites, such as ceramic effigy vessels depicting elites impersonating deities, vanish from the archaeological record. New badges of office and power—such as turquoise nose ornaments presented at nose-piercing ceremonies at a Tollan, symbolic of promotion to the rank of Toltec lord—represent the mosaic of relationships and alliances in which rulers engaged, both with neighbors and distant city-states and their kings.

Zapotec hieroglyphic writing ceases at the end of the Late Classic, as does one format on which it appeared—the stone genealogical registers portraying elites in rites of passage at sites such as Monte Albán. Throughout Oaxaca, there is a clear shift away from Classic monuments that show individual aggrandizement and dominance. Although still showing important personages, three Early Postclassic carved stones recovered at Río Viejo do not show them adorned in elaborate headdresses and other regal paraphernalia, as had Late Classic carved stones. Also, the Early

Postclassic stones were positioned on a natural hill (Chapter 7), not in the Late Classic acropolis. The appearance of women on these stones has been suggested as evidence of a change in gender ideology, with more equality in the Early Postclassic than in the Late Classic (Joyce et al. 2001:373). Oval monumental stones, with pecked depressions, were found associated with Río Viejo house patios, suggestive of an Early Postclassic change in venue for at least some ceremonies to more private space as commoners appropriated the sacrificial rituals of elite specialists (Chapter 7; Joyce et al. 2001).

The themes previously expressed in Late Classic carved stone monuments are expressed in a distinct new form—the codex or painted book—that records elite, ritual, and astronomical activities. Codices, screenfold documents generally painted on animal hides, provide both secular and sacred stories, foundation narratives, and royal genealogies that illustrate how the ruling class obtained their position (see Chapter 10). Although images on Maya pottery document the presence of codices among the Classic Maya, no such evidence exists for pre-Postclassic codex use in Oaxaca. Codices served to legitimate and celebrate the accomplishments of the ruling dynasty and the sacred history of their cacicazgo. Specialists interpreted codices for a variety of audiences (Byland and Pohl 1994; Smith 1983). In lieu of carved stones, some codices may have hung from palace walls, and fragments of codex-like scenes painted directly on doorway lintels still remain at Mitla. Applying concepts developed by Marshall Sahlins (1985), codices can be considered "heroic histories" in which the central heroic agent's actions influence and reflect the larger society, which the agent embodies (Joyce et al. 2004; Zeitlin 1994). The codices document a significant representational break with the Xoo phase in that Zapotec hieroglyphic writing is absent; only symbols for dates, places, and names are present.

Political themes in some codices relating to the legitimization of ruling dynasties may have been expressed in other media and venues. Procession scenes and images of past ancestors may have been expressed in stone benches or "banquettes," similar to those from Tula, and later copied in an archaizing fashion by the Aztecs at Tenochtitlán (Chapter 9). In addition, John Pohl (1999) has suggested that the codices themselves were meant be performed, providing public spectacle and constant renegotiation and legitimization of the painted images.

Other paraphernalia associated with legitimacy and power, such as sacred bundles, emerged in the Postclassic. Made of paper, cloth, or vegetable materials that enveloped sacred objects (such as the greenstone *penates* found at Postclassic sites), these bundles represented deified founding ancestors (Oudijk 2002). The sacred bundles may also have contained the bones of royal ancestors and served as the focus of offerings and shrines. In the Mixtec codices, four priests carry the bundles (Pohl 1994), which represent the sacred charter of rulership. The sharing of bundles among four priests also reflects the less hegemonic rule of Postclassic kings.

In the Late Classic and Postclassic, dead rulers were transformed into religious objects and badges of authority in the form of mummies or through curation of specific body parts. Displays of ancestral bones appear throughout Late Classic and Postclassic Mesoamerica, with femora held by warriors on the Cacaxtla murals. Elites were depicted holding femora—probably from their ancestors—on tomb friezes at Lambityeco, where the removal of long bones from corpses has been documented (Lind and Urcid 1983). In the Postclassic, Mixtec mummy bundles served as physical proof of the royal line of succession upon which social order was defined—with the physical remains of the royal ancestors providing the current leader's "bona fides." The legitimating power of ancestors remained important during this time of change; as Byland (Chapter 10) notes, the dramatic political changes involving Tilantongo, and the establishment of a new dynasty, would not have been considered legitimate without the approval of the Achiutla oracle.

Economic Transformations, Exchange, and World Systems

The period from the Late Classic/Early Postclassic transition through the Late Postclassic represents a time of fundamental economic transformation in much of Mesoamerica, marked by a high level of commercialization. Although rulers continued to control land, labor, and tribute, commercial exchange systems developed that were only loosely connected with state institutions (Smith and Berdan 2003a:12). Compared to the Classic period, the Postclassic is marked by an enhanced role for merchants, markets, and money throughout Mesoamerica. Markets provided additional integration within cacicazgos.

Without the strictures of a large centralized state, elites in emerging city-states engaged in fierce economic competition both with internal factions and with other city-states. One manifestation of changing political economy in Oaxaca is the proliferation of important markets, some of which occurred between major city-states (Pohl et al. 1997). In the Classic period, household-level specialization is evidenced for a variety of craft industries, such as ornamental shell production at Ejutla (Feinman 1999) and the fiber industries proposed for El Palmillo, in the eastern edge of the Valley of Oaxaca (Feinman et al. 2002). In some cases, such as in late Xoo phase salt production at Lambityeco, the state attempted to impose workshop labor organization after generations of household production; as noted previously, this change was met with resistance (Chapter 5). In the Postclassic, some villages may have turned to more specialized production, such as the thicker cotton produced at Río Viejo, which may have had its own market niche (Chapter 8). There is also evidence that Postclassic organization of production went beyond the household level generally proposed for Classic Oaxaca (Feinman 1999). The small Late Postclassic Valley of Oaxaca village of Llily Gueeubin may have specialized in coarseware ceramic production at the community-based workshop level (Fargher

2003). These contrasting patterns of production evince the transformations that occurred in the increasingly commercialized economy of the Postclassic.

Throughout Postclassic Mesoamerica, trade goods diversified and new forms of wealth increased in circulation (Smith and Berdan 2003a:7). Items that formerly were restricted prestige goods became available for sale in markets as commercial luxury goods. The new inventory of rich material culture that appeared by the Early Postclassic includes bichrome pottery, flutes, earspools, and spindle whorls. After 1200 CE, metalworkers in Oaxaca—as well as Guerrero—produced relatively standardized types of copper objects: the famous "axe-monies," often cited as a form of currency or medium of exchange. Turquoise from the American Southwest became more widely available, and in Oaxaca the coastal region became particularly important as a source of raw materials, such as feathers, marine shells, *pupura* dye, and cacao (Chapter 8). Sites such as Río Viejo engaged in multiple exchange networks, with connections to the Mixteca Alta, Cholula, and Tula. Early Postclassic pottery from the lower Verde Valley documents the increase in stylistic cross-ties between that region and highland Mexico (Joyce et al. 2001:377). The new products, different regional partners, and the mechanisms of exchange and distribution represented significant disjunctions with the past.

As trade and interaction reached new heights of intensity throughout Mesoamerica in the centuries before the arrival of the Spanish, the agents of this exchange varied between regions. Rather than a specialized long-distance trader class, such as the Aztec *pochteca*, it appears that among the Mixtecs it was the junior nobility who organized expeditions for rulers (Pohl 2003a). Commoners also appear to have been heavily involved in exchange and markets. Due to the antagonistic relationships between Mixtec city-states, exchange often took place at annual religious events in the boundary areas between major cacicazgos. Thus, political conflicts did not disrupt economic relationships (Pohl et al. 1997).

To some, the interconnected economies and interdependencies that developed during the Postclassic in Mesoamerica formed a world system (Smith and Berdan 2003a). One recent effort at defining a Postclassic world system conceives it as a "large-scale zone of economic and social interactions that tied together independent polities, and these interactions had significant impacts on the participating societies" (Smith and Berdan 2003a:4). Rather than using terms such as "core," "periphery," and "underlying hierarchy," Smith and Berdan (2003b:24) usefully conceive of a series of zones: core zones, affluent production zones, resource extraction zones, unspecialized peripheral zones, and contact peripheries. Areas included in each zone change through time, with generally four to five core zones at any given time in the Postclassic. In the Late Postclassic, the "Mixteca/Valley of Oaxaca" region is considered a core zone (Berdan et al. 2003:314), although elsewhere Smith and Berdan (2003b:26) note that the small size of Oaxacan urban centers precludes core status. It is premature to apply world systems concepts to Oaxaca as a region until more data are available from throughout Oaxaca, especially from areas that are considered "peripheral" primarily due to a lack of research (Chapter 12).

POST-TRANSITION CONTINUITIES IN OAXACA

Although the settlement and demographic changes outlined above certainly impacted the population, it was elite culture and political structure that experienced the most disjuncture. Continuities characterize several realms of life for most Oaxacans from the Late Classic throughout the Postclassic, especially in the realm of subsistence, houses, burials, beliefs, and rituals. Similarly, despite the massive impact that the decline of Teotihuacan had on Mesoamerican prehistory in general, continuities have been noted in ceremonies, subsistence, social organization, urban patterns, and religion in Central Mexico (Diehl and Berlo 1989). Much of what marks Mesoamerica as a unified cultural region is the consistency of core beliefs; common people are the major stakeholders and reproducers of what continues—often referred to as central social propositions (Sahlins 1985). It is daily practice that represents the constitution of society (Bourdieu 1977).

Quotidian Life

Although the material culture of the elite experienced drastic changes, objects used in commoners' daily lives demonstrate great continuity, as with the ceramics in the lower Verde Valley from Late Classic to Early Postclassic. In some parts of Oaxaca, such as the Mixteca Alta, subsistence practices may have become more intensive to accommodate an increased Postclassic population, but there are no drastic changes in technology and food produced. The daily life of a farming family would have been virtually indistinguishable before and after the Late Classic/Postclassic transition.

One of the most striking continuities is expressed in houses. During the Xoo phase, the typical house layout becomes a patio surrounded by rooms at Monte Albán and Lambityeco (Chapter 5); this template serves at the floor plan for Postclassic palaces at Mitla, Yagul, and Zaachila (Winter 1989). The recent excavations at Macuilxóchitl exposed primarily a Xoo occupation with a very limited Early Postclassic (Liobaa) component. When the community underwent extensive reoccupation during the Late Postclassic (Chila), a Chila phase residence at Mound 1 was constructed over the remains of an earlier Xoo phase structure and exhibits surprising continuity with the earlier residence in terms of architectural layout and household activities (Chapter 6). In the Mixteca Alta and Baja, there is also continuity in house layout and construction, with block-and-slab construction continuing in use from Late Classic Ñuiñe (Winter 1994:218).

Although many aspects of commoner life demonstrate great continuity between the Late Classic and Early Postclassic, recent research in the lower Río Verde Valley suggests commoners thrived during this transition; they engaged in a more diverse domestic economy and had more access to imported prestige goods (see previous discussion). They also may have played a more expansive role in this period of sociopolitical transformations. At Río Viejo, commoners may have seen the waning power of elites as an opportunity for them to change the nature of what had become an increasingly exploitative relationship (Joyce et al. 2001). Freed of the coercive power of Late Classic elites, commoners played an active role in the denigration of what had come before, reusing both space and objects associated with elites; a similar important role by commoners may have been crucial in the post-Xoo depopulation of Lambityeco (see previous discussion). Commoners constructed their own meanings for the ruins of Late Classic monumental architecture among which they lived in the Early Postclassic; as Hamann (Chapter 4) suggests, they may have viewed these ruins as evidence of the failed, decadent, and hierarchical society that had come before. Arthur Joyce and colleagues (2001) see the Early Postclassic as making visible a previously hidden transcript of more subtle resistance and negotiation between commoners and elites.

Imagery, Rituals, and Ideology

Although the new suite of paraphernalia has been emphasized as showing drastic transformations in elite culture and imagery, elements of it have Xoo phase, and earlier, roots. Motifs associated with Postclassic imagery, such as grecas, have clear Late Classic antecedents (Winter 1989). In some places, such as the lower Verde Valley, carved stones continue into the Early Postclassic, albeit with very different imagery and messages (see above). The carving of animal bones, which reached an extraordinary height in the Postclassic at Monte Albán's Tomb 7, also has Classic manifestations across Oaxaca, although with the hieroglyphic writing that is lacking in the Postclassic. Mural painting, exemplified in Classic and Late Classic Monte Albán tombs, also continues into the Postclassic. Indeed, codices may represent a transformation of this venerable tradition onto a more portable medium. Perhaps the appearance of codices reflects the Late Classic trend of smaller sites throughout the Valley of Oaxaca erecting genealogical registers that celebrate activities of their ruling elite.

Many of the prehispanic beliefs that continue to manifest themselves in modern Oaxaca villages have roots that extend prior to the Late Classic/Postclassic transition. For example, the manner of internment has remained stable. In the Mixteca Alta, internment took the form of seated burials and continued unchanged during this period of transition. In the Valley of Oaxaca, the continuity in burials involved household heads buried in family tombs with junior family members placed in simple graves beneath house floors (Chapter 6). Also, tombs, especially at Monte Albán, were reused from generation to generation, cutting across the transition from the Late Classic to Early Postclassic (Winter 1989). By the Late Postclassic, possible Xoo phase tomb reuse occurred at Zaachila, but elsewhere, such as at Mitla, the form and placement of new tombs differed from those of the Xoo phase. Throughout these burial rituals, the importance of the ancestors, and their legitimating force, remained constant.

Deeper beliefs evocative of cosmology also continue from the Late Classic throughout the Postclassic and beyond. Continuities in the calendar system exemplify the resilience of such deep-seated beliefs (see Chapter 11). The importance of sacred mountains to cultures throughout Mesoamerica probably extends back to the Olmec; among the Classic Maya, pyramidal platforms represented these mountains and glyphs refer to them, as well as to the temple atop, as a particular sacred mountain. The Mixtec codices document the names of sacred mountains and places across an animate landscape. In the Valley of Oaxaca, modern residents of Macuilxóchitl continue a Classic—or earlier—tradition of seeing the adjacent Cerro Danush as a sacred mountain. Earlier beliefs, style, and iconography were also reimagined through archaizing, a common trend throughout Postclassic Mesoamerica (Umberger 1987).

OAXACA IN LATE CLASSIC AND EARLY POSTCLASSIC MESOAMERICA: "TOLTECS"

Oaxaca is often not considered a participant in the new patterns of interaction that emerged during and after the Late Classic/Postclassic transition, as the region is too often characterized as a series of insular city-states. Given its strategic geographic setting, Oaxaca clearly lay at the crossroads of many of these reconstituted interactions, exchange routes, and movements of people—and contributed to them. For example, the art programs at sites such as Cacaxtla and Xochicalco depict non-Mexican individuals and exhibit glyphs that show Zapotec and Ñuiñe influences from Oaxaca mixed with possible Teotihuacan precursors (Berlo 1989; Moser 1977; Nagao 1989).

Material evidence of outsiders impacting Oaxaca is limited. In terms of sculpture, John Pohl (1999:184) suggests that Tututepec Monument 6 resembles the colossal atlantid warriors from Tula, but the sculpture itself is probably Late Postclassic and is related to Toltec imagery in only the general, non-Tula-specific sense (see Chapter 9). The stone bench fragment from Etlatongo may appropriate a form of Toltec imagery but is also probably significantly later than the era of Tula. Winter (Chapter 12) documents the presence of Maya Jaina-style figurines in the Isthmus and suggests a Late Classic/Early Postclassic complex, multi-ethnic panorama for that area, perhaps reflecting on a smaller scale the larger Mesoamerican population movements seen at Cacaxtla and Xochicalco. Tohil Plumbate, problematically associated with the movement of "Toltecs," is rare in the Valley of Oaxaca and Mixteca Alta but appears on the Isthmus (at Paso Aguascalientes), which was part of an important trading network including the source of plumbate pottery. The recent excavation of several intact plumbate vessels at Paso Aguascalientes (Chapter 12) substantially expands the surprisingly small sample of such pots from throughout Oaxaca. Although acknowledging the occupants may have been Zapotec, Winter also suggests the site may have been occupied by an outside group—perhaps a merchant colony or enclave from the Soconusco. Along the western coast of Oaxaca, no plumbate has been found at Río Viejo (Chapter 7). In the Mixteca Alta, a Toltec-related bowl, in terms of style, has been found at Yucuita in the Nochixtlán Valley (Winter, personal communication, 2003). Another purported ware that evinces interregional interaction, Silho Fine Orange, has been found in the Valley of Oaxaca, at Lambityeco (Chapter 5). Numerous problems abound in associating scattered plumbate and Silho ceramic sherds with "Toltecs," especially if by "Toltec," a presence from Tula is suggested; as noted above, neither plumbate nor Silho Fine Orange were made at Tula.

Although material evidence of Toltec contact is limited, evidence occurs in codical documents, as well as the painted murals at Mitla (Pohl 1999), and ethnohistoric manuscripts. These sources emphasize the ideological importance of the Toltecs, or "Tollan," in Oaxaca rather than any large-scale presence of a foreign group. As noted above, it is crucial to make the distinction between the site of Tula in Hidalgo state and what these sources refer to as "Tollan," a generic term for a sacred or important place or center of culture—a place of legitimization. The "Toltec" Lord 4 Jaguar, mentioned in several documents (such as the *Lienzo de Tlapiltepec*) as involved in the founding of the Coixtlahuaca dynasty, as well as abetting the ambitions of Lord 8 Deer Jaguar Claw of Tilantongo, probably came from the relatively nearby Tollan of Cholula (also known as Tollan-Cholula; see Chapter 3). Coixtlahuaca itself may ultimately have been viewed as a Tollan (Chapter 10). Given the similarity in nose-piercing as investiture ceremonies from Oaxaca to the Maya Highlands, a chain of Tollans, linked spatially and temporally, became associated with political investiture of Postclassic lords (Kristan-Graham and Kowalski 2007:22).

Beginning in the Early Postclassic, association with Toltec elites—wherever they were from—apparently formed an important legitimizing narrative in Oaxaca. Toltec connections also assisted in accessing exchange routes and the common elite leadership imagery and rituals discussed above, which some scholars link with a pan-Mesoamerican cult of Quetzalcoatl (Ringle 2004). As with other groups in Mesoamerica, such as the Quiché (Carmack 1981:374), competitive lineages in Oaxaca acquired Toltec imagery, icons, and ancestors as one of many strategies in negotiating power. In Oaxaca, association with "Toltec" appears to be more invoked after the demise of Tula (Chapter 9), and similar to the appropriation and creation of Toltec by the Aztec, the "civilizing" aspect of the Toltec was desired. If Oudijk (Chapter 3) is correct in his linking of the concept he interprets as "Lagoon of Blood" with Tollan, many ruling houses throughout Oaxaca invoked "Toltecs" in their founding narratives.

OAXACA IN LATE POSTCLASSIC MESOAMERICA: MIXTECA-PUEBLA AND AZTECS

Oaxaca, particularly the Mixteca, has been proposed as a possible origin for the Mixteca-Puebla style, especially due to the presence of codices in the Mixteca Alta. For some scholars (Jiménez Moreno 1966; McCafferty 1994; Nicholson 1982), the early importance of polychromes at Cholula (by at least 900 CE) and architectural antecedents for images on the later codex-style vessels implicate Cholula in the origins of the Mixteca-Puebla style. Some imagery encompassed under Mixteca-Puebla style appears in Toltec and earlier Central Mexican art. Although its origins remain unclear, the sharing of this style and associated iconography reflected Late Postclassic interaction and materialized the alliance corridors and elite leadership rituals that connected groups within Oaxaca and beyond; such sustained contact among elites developed from the Tollan phenomenon discussed above, which probably predates the city of Tula.

In Oaxaca, the Mixteca-Puebla style usually appears on small objects, especially ceramics and codices, reflecting the reduced nature of public spectacle from the Classic. Examples in larger media, such as the stucco figures from the Zaachila tombs or on stone benches (Chapter 9), are consistently at a smaller than life-size scale. The distribution of Mixteca-Puebla-style (especially "codex"-style) pottery remains uneven throughout Oaxaca. Generally rare at houses in both the Teposcolula Valley (Pérez Rodríguez 2004) and Nochixtlán Valley (Blomster 1998, 2004; Lind 1987; Spores 1972), 10,000 Mixtec polychrome sherds were recovered by Alfonso Caso (1938) in his excavations of a Chachoapan midden; it is not clear how many of these truly represent the Mixteca-Puebla codex style rather than simple geometric polychromes. Concentrations of Mixteca-Puebla pottery are scattered in the Valley of Oaxaca, often appearing in spectacular tombs (Caso 1969); only at the Casa Mixteca, on the lower terraces of Monte Albán, have extremely high quantities of this material been documented (Salinas Contreras 2004). Although not frequent throughout the lower Verde Valley, polychromes with Mixteca-Puebla-style designs are found in relatively high quantities at the massive kingdom of Tututepec (Joyce et al. 2004; Levine 2006). Spectacular Mixteca-Puebla objects, both in textile fragments and turquoise mosaics, have come from caves in the Cuicatlán Cañada and Mazatec regions (Chapter 12; González Licón and Márquez Morfín 1994). Only in the Mixe (see Figure 1.2) region have no Mixtec polychrome or codex-style designs been reported, which may represent the resilience of indigenous representational conventions and iconography or even actual resistance to the dominant Postclassic ideology. Until substantial archaeological data are reported from the Mixe region, such interpretations remain speculative at best.

Aztec impact throughout Mesoamerica varied, and regions of Oaxaca reflect the differing strategies, successes, and failures of the Aztec imperial machine (see also Chapter 11). Although there is little archaeological evidence of Aztec domination of Oaxaca, ethnohistoric documents reveal that the Aztec incursions into Oaxaca began as early as during the reign of Aztec ruler Moctecuhzoma I, who ventured into northern Oaxaca, supposedly conquering Coixtlahuaca around 1458 (Marcus 1983:314; Pohl 2003c:61). Conflict with the Aztecs in Oaxaca intensified during the reign of Ahuitzotl, who attacked at least sixteen localities throughout Oaxaca, while his successor, Moctecuhzoma II (the Aztec emperor in power upon the arrival of the Spanish in 1519), subdued forty-four places. Some episodes involved substantial violence, such as the conquest of Coixtlahuaca, whose leader, Atonal, unsuccessfully attempted to forge an alliance capable of resisting the armies of the Aztec Triple Alliance. The *Codex Mendoza* (66) documents the Aztec garroting of the defeated Atonal (Berdan and Anawalt 1997; Townsend 2000:98), and, according to some accounts, the Aztec supposedly established a garrison at Coixtlahuaca. Thus, Coixtlahuaca can serve as an example of the impact of direct Aztec hostile contact. Although the documents record their assassination of the ruler, their impact on the majority of the population is not directly detailed in the indigenous and colonial documents. At both Coixtlahuaca (particularly from Ignacio Bernal's excavations at Ingüiteria, on a small hill near the current center of Coixtlahuaca) and Zaachila, Aztec burnished red occurs primarily with elite burials and tombs (Bernal 1949; Gallegos Ruiz 1978). In 1998, Ronald Spores directed a brief surface survey of the residential areas on the hills surrounding the modern town of Coixtlahuaca, where much of the Postclassic population lived; few Aztec-related ceramics were observed on these eroded residential slopes. Utilization of Aztec material goods may have been confined to only a small sector of society, with minimal impact on daily lives for the majority.

The Aztecs resonated in Oaxacan alliance structures. Although alliances were between individual cacicazgos rather than ethnic groups, larger scale, strategic alliances were attempted in order to resist the Aztecs. One such alliance between Zapotecs and Mixtecs culminated in the late-fifteenth-century battle at the Zapotec fortress site of Guiengola, on the southern Isthmus of Tehuantepec (Peterson and MacDougall 1974). Alliance strategies used within Oaxaca also could be applied to the Nahua intruders, with marriages between Zapotecs and Aztecs documented in the final years before the arrival of the Spanish, such as the famous marriage between the last prehispanic king of Zaachila, Cocijoeza, and Coyolicatzin ("Cotton Puff"), daughter of the Aztec king Ahuitzotl (Burgoa 1989). This alliance ended the Aztec siege at Guiengola and produced offspring who continued to form alliances with other kingdoms into the Colonial era.

IN THE SHADOW OF THE CLASSIC: A REAPPRAISAL OF THE POSTCLASSIC IN OAXACA

Reappraising the Postclassic, and Oaxaca's role in prehispanic Mesoamerica, is linked with changing views of the Classic period in Mesoamerica. Previous models viewed Classic Teotihuacan as a peaceful theocracy, where high priests dispatched artists to other parts of Mesoamerica to spread the Tlaloc cult; the Postclassic was portrayed in a negative light, formed by barbarians who lacked the culture of Teotihuacan (Jiménez Moreno 1966:50). The Postclassic too often has been defined by what it lacks compared to the Classic, with the Late Classic/Postclassic transition considered a time of decadence. Recent research reveals the Postclassic as a vital, dynamic time during which Oaxacan cultures flourished.

Because domination systems are negotiated and unstable, civilizations are not static; they experience continual change as their fortunes wax and wane (Bourdieu 1977; Diehl and Berlo 1989; Giddens 1984). In many regions of Oaxaca, the unstable nature of Classic states such as Monte Albán, Yucuñudahui, and Río Viejo, as well as the disruption of important networks of interregional relations with the demise of Teotihuacan, resulted in the radical political and social transformations of the Postclassic. The collapse of interregional communication networks may have signaled to both competing centers and commoners within each center the weakness of rulership and its associated ideology and institutions, leading to further erosion of legitimacy and power at these places (Joyce et al. 2001:375). Although the formation of city-states often follows the collapse of a major polity throughout the world (Marcus 1989), in some regions of Oaxaca city-states existed prior to the collapse of centralized states, both within and outside of the territory of places such as Monte Albán. Elite culture fundamentally changed following the major political realignment, but great continuity characterizes commoner household organization throughout Oaxaca.

Although regions of Oaxaca interacted with other parts of Mesoamerica prior to the Late Classic, relations shifted during this time of sociopolitical upheaval. Populations adjusted to new political challenges and opportunities; new alliances developed, within and outside of Oaxaca. Both elites and commoners displayed new items of material wealth, some of which originated in areas largely ignored in previous eras, such as metal from West Mexico. The internal and external relations of city-states appear driven by factional competition, with new strategies employed to show the legitimacy and stability of ruling lineages.

As opposed to large centralized Classic states, Postclassic city-states allowed many Oaxacan communities to withstand two subsequent invasions—both the Aztec and the Spanish—with at least initially only limited disruptions in socio-political institutions and quotidian life; the elites simply channeled tribute to the intruders, whether Aztec or Spanish. Postclassic institutions and agents, such as the residential ward with hereditary barrio leaders, facilitated community survival during the ultimate demise of native elite rule under Spanish colonialism (Zeitlin 1994:276). Despite Spanish efforts to eradicate indigenous religion and its practitioners, deeply held religious beliefs persisted, drawing from the Postclassic, Classic, and earlier. Rather than a mere shadow of the Classic "golden age" of Oaxaca, the Postclassic actually provides continuities and links with earlier eras and elements of political, economic, and religious organization, even as the Spanish imposed new institutions. The Postclassic was a time of innovation, as original solutions emerged for problems stemming from the collapse of Classic states and institutions. In at least some parts of Oaxaca, the Postclassic represents an unprecedented rise in the power and autonomy of commoners. The continued resilience of indigenous people throughout Oaxaca in the face of a vast array of hegemonic forces remains as testimony to the enduring institutions and traditions that continued and/or were developed during the Postclassic.

ACKNOWLEDGMENTS

I would like to thank all of the volume participants for offering ideas and suggestions, which I have incorporated into this chapter, although I alone remain responsible for how they have been represented. Several colleagues, particularly Arthur Joyce and Marcus Winter, struggled through various drafts of this chapter, while others—Robert Markens and Carlos Rincón Mautner—shared their expertise on certain portions. I also acknowledge the helpful comments of Marilyn Masson, Heather Orr, and Darrin Pratt.

REFERENCES

Andrews, Anthony P., E. Wyllys Andrews, and Fernando Robles Castellanos
2003 The Northern Maya Collapse and Its Aftermath. *Ancient Mesoamerica* 14(1): 151–156.

Barabas, Alicia Mabel, Miguel Alberto Bartolomé, and Benjamín Maldonado
2003 *Los pueblos indígenas de Oaxaca: Atlas Etnográfico*. Fondo de Cultura Económica, Mexico City.

Barth, Fredrik
1969 Introduction. In *Ethnic Groups and Boundaries: The Social Organization of Cultural Difference*, edited by F. Barth, pp. 1–38. Little, Brown and Company, Boston.

Berdan, Frances F., and Patricia R. Anawalt
1997 *The Essential Codex Mendoza*. University of California Press, Berkeley.

Berdan, Frances F., Susan Kepecs, and Michael E. Smith
2003 A Perspective on Late Postclassic Mesoamerica. In *The Postclassic Mesoamerican World*, edited by M. Smith and F. Berdan, pp. 313–317. University of Utah Press, Salt Lake City.

Berlo, Janet C.
1989 Early Writing in Central Mexico: *In Tlilli, In Tlapalli* before A.D. 1000. In *Mesoamerica after the Decline of Teotihuacan, A.D. 700–900*, edited by R. Diehl and J. Berlo, pp. 19–47. Dumbarton Oaks Research Library and Collection, Washington, DC.

Bernal, Ignacio
1949 Exploraciones en Coixtlahuaca, Oaxaca. *Revista Mexicana de Estudios Antropológicos* 10:5–76.

Blanton, Richard E.
1978 *Monte Alban: Settlement Patterns at the Ancient Zapotec Capital*. Academic Press, New York.

Blomster, Jeffrey P.
1998 At the Bean Hill in the Land of the Mixtec: Early Formative Social Complexity and Interregional Interaction at Etlatongo, Oaxaca, Mexico. Unpublished Ph.D. Dissertation, Department of Anthropology, Yale University, New Haven, Connecticut.
2004 *Etlatongo: Social Complexity, Interaction, and Village Life in the Mixteca Alta of Oaxaca, Mexico*. Wadsworth, Belmont, California.

Bourdieu, Pierre
1977 *Outline of a Theory of Practice*. Cambridge University Press, New York.

Braswell, Geoffrey E.
2003 K'iche'an Origins, Symbolic Emulation, and Ethnogenesis in the Maya Highlands. In *The Postclassic Mesoamerican World*, edited by M. Smith and F. Berdan, pp. 297–303. University of Utah Press, Salt Lake City.

Brown, James A.
1975 Deep-site Excavation Strategy as a Sampling Problem. In *Sampling in Archaeology*, edited by J. W. Mueller, pp. 155–169. University of Arizona Press, Tucson.

Brown, Jennifer S.H., and E. Wyllys Andrews V (editors)
1982 *Aspects of the Mixteca-Puebla Style and Mixtec and Central Mexican Culture in Southern Mesoamerica*. Middle American Research Institute, Occasional Paper 4. Tulane University, New Orleans.

Burgoa, Francisco de
1989 *Geográfica Descripción* [1674]. Editorial Porrua, Mexico City.

Byland, Bruce E.
1980 Political and Economic Evolution in the Tamazulapan Valley, Mixteca Alta, Oaxaca. Unpublished Ph.D. Dissertation, Department of Anthropology, Pennsylvania State University, State College.

Byland, Bruce E., and John M.D. Pohl
1994 *In the Realm of 8 Deer: The Archaeology of the Mixtec Codices.* University of Oklahoma Press, Norman.

Canseco, Alonso de
1905 Relación de Tlacolula y Mitla hecha en los dias 12 y 23 de agosto respectivamente [1580]. In *Papels de Nueva España: Segunda serie, Geografía y Estadística,* Vol. 4, edited by F. del Paso y Troncoso, pp. 144–154. Madrid.

Carmack, Robert M.
1969 Quichean Art: A Mixteca-Puebla Variant. *Katunob* 7(3):12–35.
1981 *The Quiché Mayas of Utatlán.* University of Oklahoma Press, Norman.

Caso, Alfonso
1938 *Exploraciones en Oaxaca: Quinta y sexta temporadas 1936–1937.* Publicación No. 34. Instituto Panamericano de Geografía e Historia, Mexico City.
1960 *Interpretation of the Codex Bodley 2858.* Translated by Ruth Morales and John Paddock. Sociedad Mexicana de Antropología, Mexico City.
1969 *El tesoro de Monte Albán.* Memorias del Instituto Nacional de Antropología e Historia, No. 3. INAH, Mexico City.

Caso, Alfonso, Ignacio Bernal, and Jorge R. Acosta
1967 *La cerámica de Monte Albán.* Memorias del Instituto Nacional de Antropología e Historia, No. 13. INAH, Mexico City.

Charnay, Désiré
1887 *The Ancient Cities of the New World: Being Voyages and Explorations in Mexico and Central America from 1857–1882.* Translated by J. Gonine and H. Conant. Harper Brothers, New York.

Cobos, Rafael
2006 The Relationship between Tula and Chichén Itzá: Influences or Interactions? In *Lifeways in the Northern Maya Lowlands: New Approaches to Archaeology in the Yucatán Peninsula,* edited by J. Matthews and B. Morrison, pp. 173–183. University of Arizona Press, Tucson.

Cohen, Ronald
1978 Ethnicity: Problems and Focus in Anthropology. *Annual Review of Anthropology* 7:379–403.

Culbert, T. Patrick (editor)
1973 *The Classic Maya Collapse.* University of New Mexico Press, Albuquerque.

Dennis, Philip A.
1987 *Intervillage Conflict in Oaxaca.* Rutgers University Press, New Brunswick, New Jersey.

Diehl, Richard A., and Janet C. Berlo
1989 Introduction. In *Mesoamerica after the Decline of Teotihuacan, A.D. 700–900,* edited by R. Diehl and J. Berlo, pp. 1–8. Dumbarton Oaks Research Library and Collection, Washington, DC.

Doesburg, Sebastian van, and Olivier van Buren
1997 The Prehispanic History of the Valley of Coixtlahuaca, Oaxaca. In *Códices, Caciques y Comunidades,* edited by M. Jansen and L. Reyes García, pp. 103–160. Cuadernos de Historia Latinoamericana, No. 5. AHILA, Ridderkerk.

Durán, Fray Diego
1994 *The History of the Indies of New Spain* [1581], translated by Doris Heyden. University of Oklahoma Press, Norman.

Fargher, Lane F.
2003 Specialized coarse-ware ceramic production in Postclassic Oaxaca. Paper presented at the 68th Annual Meeting of the Society for American Archaeology, Milwaukee, Wisconsin.

Feinman, Gary M.
1999 Rethinking our Assumptions: Economic Specialization at the Household Scale in Ancient Ejutla. In *Pottery and People: Dynamic Interactions,* edited by J. Skibo and G. Feinman, pp. 81–98. University of Utah Press, Salt Lake City.

Feinman, Gary M., Linda M. Nicholas, and Helen R. Haines
2002 Houses on a Hill: Classic Period Life at El Palmillo, Oaxaca, Mexico. *Latin American Antiquity* 13(3):251–277.

Flannery, Kent V.
2002 Prehistoric Social Evolution. In *Archaeology: Original Readings in Method and Practice,* edited by P. Peregrine, C. Ember, and M. Ember, pp. 225–244. Prentice Hall, Saddle River, New Jersey.

Flannery, Kent V., and Joyce Marcus
1983 The Changing Politics of A.D. 600–900. In *The Cloud People: Divergent Evolution of the Zapotec and Mixtec Civilizations,* edited by K. Flannery and J. Marcus, pp. 183–185. Academic Press, New York.

Fox, John W.
1980 Lowland and Highland Mexicanization Processes in Southern Mesoamerica. *American Antiquity* 45(1):43–54.

Gallegos Ruiz, Roberto
1978 *El Señor 9 Flor en Zaachila.* Universidad Nacional Autónoma de México, Mexico City.

Gaxiola González, Margarita
1984 *Huamelulpan: Un centro urbano de la Mixteca Alta*. Colección Científica, No. 114. Instituto Nacional de Antropología e Historia, Mexico City.

Giddens, Anthony
1984 *The Constitution of Society: Outline of the Theory of Structuration*. University of California Press, Berkeley.

González Licón, Ernesto, and Lourdes Márquez Morfín
1994 Rito y Ceremonial Prehispánico en la Cuevas de La Cañada, Oaxaca. In *Mixteca-Puebla: Discoveries and Research in Mesoamerican Art and Archaeology*, edited by H. B. Nicholson and E. Quiñones Keber, pp. 223–234. Labyrinthos, Culver City, California.

Hamann, Byron
2002 The Social Life of Pre-Sunrise Things. *Current Anthropology* 43(3):351–382.

Hirth, Kenneth G.
1989 Militarism and Social Organization at Xochicalco, Morelos. In *Mesoamerica after the Decline of Teotihuacan, A.D. 700–900*, edited by R. Diehl and J. Berlo, pp. 69–81. Dumbarton Oaks Research Library and Collection, Washington, DC.

Jansen, Maarten, and Gabina Aurora Pérez Jiménez
2000 *La Dinastía de Añute; Historia, literatura e ideología de un reino mixteco*. CNWS Publications, Vol. 87. Research School of Asian, African, and Amerindian Studies, University of Leiden, Leiden.

Jiménez Moreno, Wigberto
1966 Mesoamerica before the Toltecs. In *Ancient Oaxaca: Discoveries in Mexican Archeology and History*, edited by J. Paddock, pp. 3–82. Stanford University Press, Stanford, California.

Joyce, Arthur A.
1991 Formative Period Occupation in the Lower Río Verde Valley, Oaxaca, Mexico: Interregional Interaction and Social Change. Unpublished Ph.D. Dissertation, Department of Anthropology, Rutgers University, New Brunswick, New Jersey.

Joyce, Arthur A., Laura Arnaud Bustamante, and Marc N. Levine
2001 Commoner Power: A Case Study from the Classic Period Collapse on the Coast of Oaxaca. *Journal of Archaeological Method and Theory* 8(4):343–385.

Joyce, Arthur A., Andrew G. Workinger, Byron Hamann, Peter Kröfges, Maxine Oland, and Stacie M. King
2004 Lord 8 Deer "Jaguar Claw" and the Land of the Sky: The Archaeology and History of Tututepec. *Latin American Antiquity* 15(3):273–297.

Kowalewski, Stephen A., Gary M. Feinman, Laura M. Finsten, Richard E. Blanton, and Linda M. Nicholas
1989 *Monte Albán's Hinterland, Part II: Prehispanic Settlement Patterns in Tlacolula, Etla and Ocotlán, the Valley of Oaxaca, Mexico*. Memoirs of the Museum of

Anthropology, University of Michigan, No. 23. University of Michigan, Ann Arbor.

Kowalski, Jeff Karl
2007 What's "Toltec" at Uxmal and Chichén Itzá? Merging Maya and Mesoamerican Worldviews and World Systems in Terminal Classic to Early Postclassic Yucatan. In *Twin Tollans: Chichén Itzá, Tula, and the Epiclassic to Early Postclassic Mesoamerican World,* edited by J. Kowalski and C. Kristan-Graham, pp. 251–313. Dumbarton Oaks Research Library and Collection, Washington, DC.

Kristan-Graham, Cynthia, and Jeff Karl Kowalski
2007 Chichén Itzá, Tula, and Tollan: Changing Perspectives on a Recurring Problem in Mesoamerican Archaeology and Art History. In *Twin Tollans: Chichén Itzá, Tula, and the Epiclassic to Early Postclassic Mesoamerican World,* edited by J. Kowalski and C. Kristan-Graham, pp. 13–83. Dumbarton Oaks Research Library and Collection, Washington, DC.

Kubler, George
1961 Chichén Itzá y Tula. *Estudios de Cultura Maya* 1:47–79.

Levine, Marc N.
2006 Residential Excavations at Yucu Dzaa (Tututepec, Oaxaca). Paper presented at the 13th Mixtec Gateway, Las Vegas.

Lind, Michael
1987 *The Sociocultural Dimensions of Mixtec Ceramics.* Vanderbilt University Publications in Anthropology, No. 33. Nashville, Tennessee.

Lind, Michael, and Javier Urcid
1983 The Lords of Lambityeco and Their Nearest Neighbors. *Notas Mesoamericanas* 9:76–111.

Marcus, Joyce
1983 Aztec Military Campaigns against the Zapotecs: The Documentary Evidence. In *The Cloud People: Divergent Evolution of the Zapotec and Mixtec Civilizations,* edited by K. Flannery and J. Marcus, pp. 314–318. Academic Press, New York.
1989 From Centralized Systems to City-States: Possible Models for the Epiclassic. In *Mesoamerica after the Fall of Teotihuacan, A.D. 700–900,* edited by R. Diehl and J. Berlo, pp. 201–208. Dumbarton Oaks Research Library and Collection, Washington, DC.

Marcus, Joyce, and Kent V. Flannery
1983 The Postclassic Balkanization of Oaxaca: An Introduction to the Late Postclassic. In *The Cloud People: Divergent Evolution of the Zapotec and Mixtec Civilizations,* edited by K. Flannery and J. Marcus, pp. 217–226. Academic Press, New York.
1996 *Zapotec Civilization: How Urban Society Evolved in Mexico's Oaxaca Valley.* Thames and Hudson, New York.

Mastache, Alba Guadalupe, Robert Cobean, and Dan Healan
2002 *Ancient Tollan: Tula and the Toltec Heartland.* University Press of Colorado, Boulder.

McCafferty, Geoffrey G.
1994 The Mixteca-Puebla Stylistic Tradition at Early Postclassic Cholula. In *Mixteca-Puebla: Discoveries and Research in Mesoamerican Art and Archaeology*, edited by H. B. Nicholson and E. Quiñones Keber, pp. 53–77. Labyrinthos, Culver City, California.
1996 Reinterpreting the Great Pyramid of Cholula. *Ancient Mesoamerica* 7(1):1–18.
2001 Mountain of Heaven, Mountain of Earth: The Great Pyramid of Cholula as Sacred Landscape. In *Landscape and Power in Ancient Mesoamerica*, edited by R. Koontz, K. Reese-Taylor, and A. Headrick, pp. 279–315. Westview Press, Boulder, Colorado.

Moser, Christopher L.
1977 *Ñuiñe Writing and Iconography of the Mixteca Baja.* Vanderbilt University Publications in Anthropology, No. 19. Nashville, Tennessee.

Nagao, Debra
1989 Public Proclamation in the Art of Cacaxtla and Xochicalco. In *Mesoamerica after the Decline of Teotihuacan, A.D. 700–900*, edited by R. Diehl and J. Berlo, pp. 83–104. Dumbarton Oaks Research Library and Collection, Washington, DC.

Neff, Hector
2002 Nuevos hallazgos relacionados con la producción de la Vajilla Plomiza. In *XV Simposio de Investigaciones Arqueológicas en Guatemala, 2001*, edited by J. Laporte, H. Escobedo, and B. Arroyo, pp. 529–542. Museo Nacional de Arqueología y Etnología, Guatemala City.

Neff, Hector, Ronald L. Bishop, Edward B. Sisson, Michael D. Glascock, and Penny R. Sisson
1994 Neutron Activation Analysis of Late Postclassic Polychrome Pottery from Central Mexico. In *Mixteca-Puebla: Discoveries and Research in Mesoamerican Art and Archaeology*, edited by H. B. Nicholson and E. Quiñones Keber, pp. 117–141. Labyrinthos, Culver City, California.

Nicholson, H. B.
1960 The Mixteca-Puebla Concept in Mesoamerican Archaeology: A Reexamination. In *Men and Cultures: Selected Papers from the Fifth International Congress of Anthropological and Ethnological Sciences*, Philadelphia, September 1–9, 1956, edited by A. Wallace, pp. 612–617. University of Pennsylvania, Philadelphia.
1982 The Mixteca-Puebla Concept Revisited. In *The Art and Iconography of Late Post-Classic Central Mexico*, edited by E. Boone, pp. 227–254. Dumbarton Oaks Research Library and Collection, Washington, DC.

Nicholson, H. B., and Eloise Quiñones Keber
1994 Introduction. In *Mixteca-Puebla: Discoveries and Research in Mesoamerican Art and Archaeology*, edited by H. B. Nicholson and E. Quiñones Keber, pp. vii–xv. Labyrinthos, Culver City, California.

Ortner, Sherry B.
1984 Theory in Anthropology since the Sixties. *Comparative Studies in Society and History* 26:126–166.

Oudijk, Michel R.
2002 The Zapotec City-State. In *A Comparative Study of Six City-State Cultures: An Investigation Conducted by the Copenhagen Polis Centre*, edited by M. Hansen, pp. 73–90. Royal Danish Academy of Sciences and Letters, Copenhagen.

Paddock, John
1966 Oaxaca in Ancient Mesoamerica. In *Ancient Oaxaca: Discoveries in Mexican Archeology and History*, edited by J. Paddock, pp. 82–242. Stanford University Press, Stanford, California.
1983 Mixtec Impact on the Postclassic Valley of Oaxaca. In *The Cloud People: Divergent Evolution of the Zapotec and Mixtec Civilizations*, edited by K. Flannery and J. Marcus, pp. 272–277. Academic Press, New York.

Pasztory, Esther
1989 Identity and Difference: The Uses and Meanings of Ethnic Styles. In *Cultural Differentiation and Cultural Identity in the Visual Arts*, edited by S. J. Barnes and W. S. Melion, pp. 15–38. Studies in the History of Art, No. 27. National Gallery of Art, Washington, DC.

Pérez Rodríguez, Verónica
2004 La Casa Mixteca Posclásica y su Cerámica. Paper presented at the Cuarta Mesa Redonda de Monte Albán: Taller de Cerámica. Oaxaca.

Peterson, David A., and Thomas B. MacDougall
1974 *Guiengola: A Fortified Site in the Isthmus of Tehuantepec*. Vanderbilt University Publications in Anthropology, No. 10. Nashville, Tennessee.

Pohl, John M.D.
1994 *The Politics of Symbolism in the Mixtec Codices*. Vanderbilt University Publications in Anthropology, No. 46. Nashville, Tennessee.
1999 The Lintel Paintings of Mitla and the Function of the Mitla Palaces. In *Mesoamerican Architecture as a Cultural Symbol*, edited by J. Kowalski, pp. 176–197. Oxford University Press, New York.
2003a Ritual Ideology and Commerce in the Southern Mexican Highlands. In *The Postclassic Mesoamerican World*, edited by M. Smith and F. Berdan, pp. 172–177. University of Utah Press, Salt Lake City.
2003b Royal Marriage and Confederacy Building among the Eastern Nahuas, Mixtecs, and Zapotecs. In *The Postclassic Mesoamerican World*, edited by M. Smith and F. Berdan, pp. 243–248. University of Utah Press, Salt Lake City.

2003c Creation Stories, Hero Cults, and Alliance Building: Confederacies of Central and Southern Mexico. In *The Postclassic Mesoamerican World*, edited by M. Smith and F. Berdan, pp. 61–66. University of Utah Press, Salt Lake City.

Pohl, John M.D., John Monaghan, and Laura Stiver
1997 Religion, Economy, and Factionalism in Mixtec Boundary Zones. In *Códices y Documentos sobre México. Segundo Simposio. Volumen I*, edited by S. Rueda Smithers, C. Vega Sosa, and R. Martínez Baracs, pp. 205–232. Instituto Nacional de Antropología e Historia and Consejo Nacional para la Cultura y las Artes, Mexico City.

Ringle, William M.
2004 On the Political Organization of Chichen Itza. *Ancient Mesoamerica* 15(2): 167–218.

Ringle, William M., Tomás Gallareta Negrón, and George J. Bey III
1998 The Return of Quetzalcoatl: Evidence for the Spread of a World Religion during the Epiclassic Period. *Ancient Mesoamerica* 9(2):193–232.

Rivera Guzmán, Iván
2002 Cerámica de Tequixtepec. Paper presented at the Tercera Mesa Redonda de Monte Albán: Taller de Cerámica. Oaxaca.

Robertson, Donald
1970 The Tulum Murals: The International Style of the Late Post-Classic. In *Verhandlungen del XXXVIII Internationalen Amerikanisten-Kongres, Stuttgar-München, 1968*, Vol. 2, pp. 77–88. Kommissionsverlag Klaus Renner, Munich.

Sahlins, Marshall
1985 Other Times, Other Customs: The Anthropology of History. In *Islands of History*, pp. 32–72. University of Chicago Press, Chicago.

Salinas Contreras, Adrián
2004 Cerámica Posclásica de Monte Albán de la Casa Mixteca. Paper presented at the Cuarta Mesa Redonda de Monte Albán: Taller de Cerámica. Oaxaca.

Sanders, William T.
1989 The Epiclassic as a Stage in Mesoamerican Prehistory: An Evaluation. In *Mesoamerica after the Decline of Teotihuacan, A.D. 700–900*, edited by R. Diehl and J. Berlo, pp. 211–218. Dumbarton Oaks Research Library and Collection, Washington, DC.

Sanders, William T., Jeffrey R. Parsons, and Robert S. Santley
1979 *The Basin of Mexico: Ecological Processes in the Evolution of a Civilization*. Academic Press, New York.

Schmidt, Peter J.
2007 Birds, Ceramics, and Cacao: New Excavations at Chichén Itzá, Yucatan. In *Twin Tollans: Chichén Itzá, Tula, and the Epiclassic to Early Postclassic Mesoamerican World*, edited by J. Kowalski and C. Kristan-Graham, pp. 151–203. Dumbarton Oaks Research Library and Collection, Washington, DC.

Shepard, Anna O.
1948 *Plumbate, a Mesoamerican Trade Ware*. Publication No. 573. Carnegie Institution of Washington, Washington, DC.

Smith, C. Earle, Jr.
1976 *Modern Vegetation and Ancient Plant Remains of the Nochixtlán Valley, Oaxaca*. Vanderbilt University Publications in Anthropology, No. 16. Nashville, Tennessee.

Smith, Mary Elizabeth
1983 Regional Points of View in the Mixtec Codices. In *The Cloud People: Divergent Evolution of the Zapotec and Mixtec Civilizations*, edited by K. Flannery and J. Marcus, pp. 260–266. Academic Press, New York.

Smith, Michael E.
2003a Small Polities in Postclassic Mesoamerica. In *The Postclassic Mesoamerican World*, edited by M. Smith and F. Berdan, pp. 35–39. University of Utah Press, Salt Lake City.
2003b Information Networks in Postclassic Mesoamerica. In *The Postclassic Mesoamerican World*, edited by M. Smith and F. Berdan, pp. 181–185. University of Utah Press, Salt Lake City.

Smith, Michael E., and Francis F. Berdan
2003a Postclassic Mesoamerica. In *The Postclassic Mesoamerican World*, edited by M. Smith and F. Berdan, pp. 3–13. University of Utah Press, Salt Lake City.
2003b Spatial Structure of the Mesoamerican World System. In *The Postclassic Mesoamerican World*, edited by M. Smith and F. Berdan, pp. 21–31. University of Utah Press, Salt Lake City.

Snodgrass, Anthony M.
1977 *Archaeology and the Rise of the Greek State*. Cambridge University Press, New York.

Spencer, Charles S.
1982 *The Cuicatlán Cañada and Monte Albán: A Study of Primary State Formation.* Academic Press, New York.

Spores, Ronald A.
1967 *The Mixtec Kings and Their People*. University of Oklahoma Press, Norman.
1972 *An Archaeological Settlement Survey of the Nochixtlán Valley, Oaxaca*. Vanderbilt University Publications in Anthropology, No. 1. Nashville, Tennessee.
1984 *The Mixtecs in Ancient and Colonial Times*. University of Oklahoma Press, Norman.
2001 Estudios mixtecos, ayer, hoy y mañana: Dónde estábamos, dónde estamos, hacia dónde vamos? In *Memoria de la Primera Mesa Redonda de Monte Albán: Procesos de cambio y conceptualización del Tiempo,* edited by N. Robles, pp. 167–181. CONACULTA-INAH, Mexico City.

Stein, Gil J.

2002 From Passive Periphery to Active Agents: Emerging Perspectives in the Archaeology of Interregional Interaction. *American Anthropologist* 104(3):903–916.

Stiver, Laura

2001 Prehispanic Mixtec Settlement and State in the Teposcolula Valley of Oaxaca, Mexico. Unpublished Ph.D. Dissertation, Department of Anthropology, Vanderbilt University, Nashville, Tennessee.

Stuart, David

2000 "The Arrival of Strangers": Teotihuacan and Tollan in Classic Maya History. In *Mesoamerica's Classic Heritage: From Teotihuacan to the Aztecs,* edited by D. Carrasco, L. Jones, and S. Sessions, pp. 465–513. University Press of Colorado, Boulder.

Terraciano, Kevin

2001 *The Mixtecs of Colonial Oaxaca: Ñudzahui History, Sixteenth through Eighteenth Centuries*. Stanford University Press, Stanford, California.

Tourtellot, Gair and Jason J. González

2004 The Last Hurrah: Continuity and Transformation at Seibal. In *The Terminal Classic in the Maya Lowlands: Collapse, Transition, and Transformation,* edited by A. Demarest, P. Rice, and D. Rice, pp. 60–82. University Press of Colorado, Boulder.

Townsend, Richard F.

2000 *The Aztecs*, Revised edition. Thames and Hudson, New York.

Umberger, Emily

1987 Antiquities, Revivals, and References to the Past in Aztec Art. *Res: Anthropology and Aesthetics* 13:62–105.

Vaillant, George C.

1938 A Correlation of Archaeological and Historical Sequences in the Valley of Mexico. *American Anthropologist* 40:535–573.

Winter, Marcus

1989 *Oaxaca: The Archaeological Record*. Minutiae Mexicana, Mexico City.

1994 The Mixteca Prior to the Late Postclassic. In *Mixteca-Puebla: Discoveries and Research in Mesoamerican Art and Archaeology*, edited by H. B. Nicholson and E. Quiñones Keber, pp. 201–221. Labyrinthos, Culver City, California.

Zeitlin, Judith F.

1994 Precolumbian Barrio Organization in Tehuantepec, Mexico. In *Caciques and their People: A Volume in Honor of Ronald Spores,* edited by J. Marcus and J. Zeitlin, pp. 275–300. Anthropological Papers, No. 89. Museum of Anthropology, University of Michigan, Ann Arbor.

PART II

Chronology, Continuity, and Disjunction

ETIC AND EMIC PERSPECTIVES

2

Robert Markens

Advances in Defining the Classic-Postclassic Portion of the Valley of Oaxaca Ceramic Chronology

OCCURRENCE AND PHYLETIC SERIATION

Few archaeologists would argue against the need for a well-defined chronology; without it, observations and inferences regarding the material record cannot be anchored in time. Yet, as Americanist archaeology broke free from an overwhelming concern with culture history in the 1960s to address what were seen as more stimulating issues, interest in chronology in Oaxaca generally lapsed. This is made most apparent by reviewing the existing regional ceramic chronologies for the State of Oaxaca (Figure 2.1). Although many of the state's regional chronologies were formulated decades ago, phases lasting 500 years or even longer are immediately apparent in a number of regions. The Valley of Oaxaca is a case in point, where one long-standing chronological concern has been left in a state of limbo: the definition of ceramic phases spanning the Classic-Postclassic period transition (see Smith and Berdan 2003:4; Winter 1989b).

Here I report on a facet of recent research designed to illuminate the Classic-Postclassic period transition in the Valley of Oaxaca's ceramic chronology. Applying techniques of occurrence and phyletic seriation to a sample of seventy-three Valley of Oaxaca tomb and grave lots consisting of pottery vessels, I establish a chronological sequence for the materials permitting the definition of three ceramic phases for the

Postclassic period: the Early Liobaa phase (800–1000 CE), the Late Liobaa phase (1000–1200 CE), and the Chila phase (1200–1521 CE). I also divide the Late Classic period into two phases: the Peche (500–600 CE) and Xoo (600–800 CE) phases, following Martínez López and her colleagues (2000). The major ceramic forms and variable states for each phase are described and illustrated in an effort to make this information available (Chapter 3; Oudijk 2000, 2002). The seriation is supported in its major contours by existing Valley of Oaxaca radiocarbon dates as well as by a new series of dates from the sites of Macuilxóchitl, Lambityeco, and Xaagá acquired during recent salvage excavations carried out in 2002 and 2003 in connection with the widening of the Pan-American Highway (Mexico 190).[1]

A Select Overview of the Problem of Defining a Ceramic Chronology for the Classic-Postclassic Transition in the Valley of Oaxaca

For those Mesoamericanists specializing in the study of the prehispanic societies in the Valley of Oaxaca, the monograph titled *La cerámica de Monte Albán* remains an indispensable reference work more than forty years after its publication in 1967. Compiled by the eminent Mexican archaeologists Alfonso Caso, Ignacio Bernal, and Jorge Acosta, this volume is the product of their pioneering excavations conducted primarily during the 1930s and 1940s at the ancient Zapotec metropolis of Monte Albán, a mountaintop site overlooking Oaxaca City, the capital of the State of Oaxaca.

It is in this 1967 volume, which supersedes several of their earlier preliminary reports and syntheses, that Caso and his colleagues classified the pottery from the ancient center in detail and developed the site's ceramic chronology most completely. As Monte Albán is the valley's largest archaeological site and was presumed to possess a long history of occupation, its pottery sequence was formulated with the purpose of establishing a master ceramic chronology applicable to the region as a whole. Spanning the millennia from the city's founding at about 500 BCE to the Spanish Conquest, when the center's Main Plaza lay in ruins and its environs had come to be used in part as a necropolis, or burial ground, the ceramic chronology that Caso and his associates devised for Monte Albán has served as the cornerstone upon which all subsequent research in the valley concerned with this interval has been based.

Although the regional ceramic chronology is confirmed in its essential contours, it is on closer examination punctuated by some phases that are still undesirably long and by those that are more difficult than others to identify in the context of survey and excavation (Figure 2.1). For the Valley of Oaxaca, the phase believed to coincide with the decline and abandonment of Monte Albán as the region's

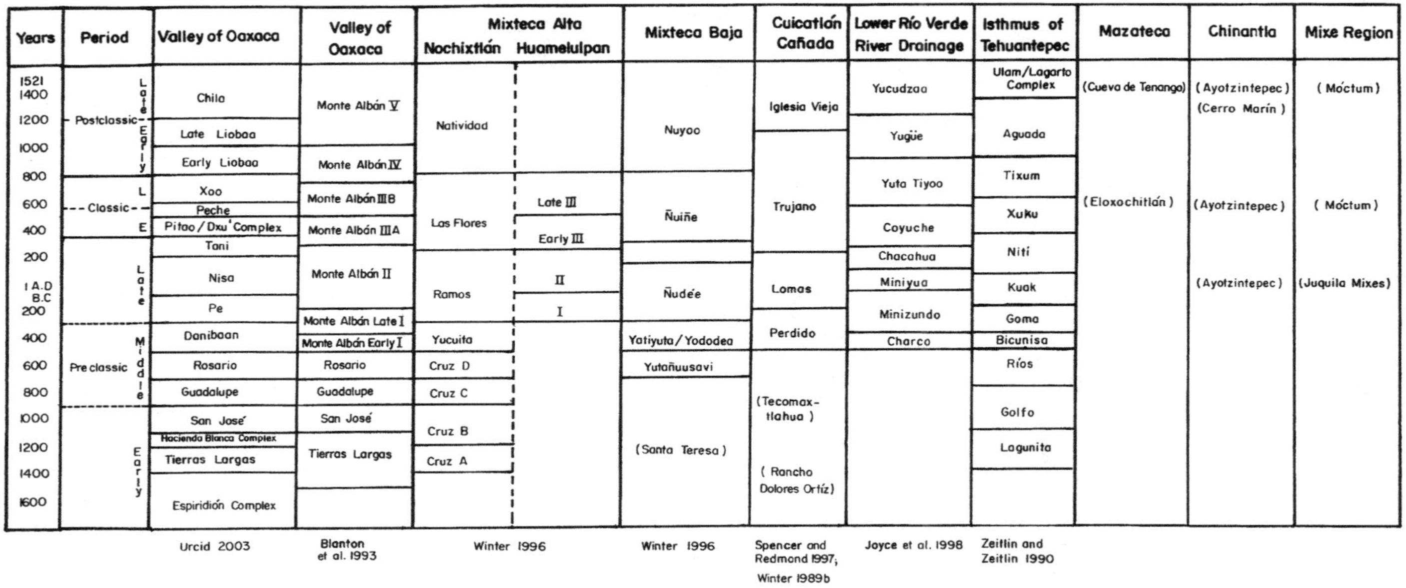
Years
Period
Valley of Oaxaca
Valley of Oaxaca
Mixteca Alta
Nochixtlán
Huamelulpan
Mixteca Baja
Cuicatlán Cañada
Lower Río Verde River Drainage
Isthmus of Tehuantepec
Mazateca
Chinantla
Mixe Region
1521
1400
1200
1000
800
600
400
200
1 A.D
B.C
200
400
600
800
1000
1200
1400
1600
Postclassic
Late
Early
Classic
L
E
Late
Preclassic
Middle
Early
Chila
Late Liobaa
Early Liobaa
Xoo
Peche
Pitao / Dxu' Complex
Tani
Nisa
Pe
Danibaan
Rosario
Guadalupe
San José
Hacienda Blanca Complex
Tierras Largas
Espiridión Complex
Monte Albán V
Monte Albán IV
Monte Albán IIIB
Monte Albán IIIA
Monte Albán II
Monte Albán Late I
Monte Albán Early I
Rosario
Guadalupe
San José
Tierras Largas
Natividad
Las Flores
Ramos
Yucuita
Cruz D
Cruz C
Cruz B
Cruz A
Late III
Early III
II
I
Nuyoo
Ñuiñe
Ñudée
Yatiyuta / Yododea
Yutañuusavi
(Santa Teresa)
Iglesia Vieja
Trujano
Lomas
Perdido
(Tecomaxtlahua)
(Rancho Dolores Ortíz)
Yucudzaa
Yugüe
Yuta Tiyoo
Coyuche
Chacahua
Miniyua
Minizundo
Charco
Ulam/Lagarto Complex
Aguada
Tixum
Xuku
Nití
Kuak
Goma
Bicunisa
Ríos
Golfo
Lagunita
(Cueva de Tenango)
(Eloxochitlán)
(Ayotzintepec)
(Cerro Marín)
(Ayotzintepec)
(Ayotzintepec)
(Móctum)
(Móctum)
(Juquila Mixes)
Urcid 2003
Blanton et al. 1993
Winter 1996
Winter 1996
Spencer and Redmond 1997;
Winter 1989b
Joyce et al. 1998
Zeitlin and Zeitlin 1990

2.1 Chronological chart of ceramic phases for archaeological regions of the state of Oaxaca, Mexico. Some of the regional ceramic chronologies have been modified based on recent research. Two ceramic sequences for the Valley of Oaxaca are presented; the one on the left is based on recent research. Names in parentheses represent archaeological sites; blank spaces indicate phases yet to be defined.

preeminent political and urban center during the Early Postclassic period is widely acknowledged as the weakest link in the sequence (Chapter 1; Drennan 1983:370; Kowalewski et al. 1989:251; Lind 1991–1992:178; Oudijk 2002:75; Winter 1989a:123). The identification of reliable, commonly occurring ceramic markers necessary to define this interval in a viable way posed a problem that Caso, Bernal, and Acosta (1967:84–86, 381–385) never adequately solved and it is one that continues to vex Oaxaca specialists today.

In the late 1960s, John Paddock (Paddock et al. 1968; see also Paddock 1978, 1983b) defined the ceramic phase he called Phase IV based on his excavations at the site of Lambityeco in the Tlacolula arm of the Valley of Oaxaca (Chapter 5) to partially fill the vacuum in the chronology for the Early Postclassic period. While most Oaxaca specialists accept Paddock's solution (see Finsten 1995; Kowalewski et al. 1989; Spencer and Redmond 1997:fig. 4.1), there is also consensus that more attention to this issue is essential, since subsequent research has produced findings inconsistent with the phase's placement in the Early Postclassic period (Kowalewski et al. 1989:252–253; Lind 1991–1992:180; Miller 1995:137–141; Winter 1989a).

Recently I concluded, as have others, that Paddock's Phase IV corresponds to the Late Classic period and not the Early Postclassic (Markens 2004; see also Lind 1991–1992; Martínez López et al. 2000; Smith and Lind 2005; Winter 1989a). I base this conclusion on the striking similarity of the pottery from Lambityeco with that of other Late Classic period valley sites (Markens and Martínez López 2001; Martínez López et al. 2000) as well as on a consideration of radiocarbon dates from Lambityeco and other valley sites where pottery is associated and described.

It should be a straightforward matter deciding to which period Phase IV corresponds, especially since the suite of highly consistent radiocarbon dates that Paddock obtained from Lambityeco fall in the Late Classic and not the Early Postclassic period (see Table 2.2 and Chapter 5).[2] Nonetheless, the issue has been clouded by the practice common among Oaxaca specialists, considered both individually and collectively, of using a number of terms to refer to the divisions of the regional ceramic sequence; these terms include "phase," "period," "stage," and the Spanish word "*época*" ("epoch" in English) (see Blanton 1978; Blanton et al. 1981, 1982; Blanton et al. 1993; Kowalewski et al. 1989; Markens and Martínez López 2001; Martínez López et al. 2000; Paddock 1978; Winter 1989a). In some instances the terms are used in ways that are not conceptually equivalent, confounding criteria of ceramic chronology with those of cultural development. This practice has facilitated reasoning that is at times incomprehensible and led to conclusions that are erroneous. Such is the case with Paddock, whose seminal writings on the matter illustrate the situation. Three examples are cited.

Paddock (1978) was well aware of the fact that his proposed Early Postclassic period Phase IV overlapped temporally with the Late Classic period phase known as IIIB. Further, upon examination of a large collection of Phase IIIB Late Classic pottery from Monte Albán, he observed that it is "virtually indistinguishable from Period IV materials found at Lambityeco" (Paddock 1978:55–56n4). Yet he nonetheless reconciled the impossibility of two contemporaneous ceramic phases:

> What has been clarified through recent work is that while IIIB norms were continuing at Monte Albán and in its surroundings, the stage called Monte Albán IV was already beginning in parts of the Valley of Oaxaca farthest from Monte Albán (Lambityeco, Mitla, Miahuatlán, and probably Huitzo and Macuilxóchitl as well).[3] (Paddock 1986:6)

> That IV and V are at least partially contemporary has long been believed by Caso and his collaborators; that IIIB overlaps both of them in some degree is no great new complication. (Paddock 1978:50)

I believe that the terminological ambiguity that characterizes Paddock's writings concerning chronology as well as those of many Oaxacan specialists has obscured the very real problems generated by research treating Phase IV as an Early Postclassic period interval (Kowalewski et al. 1989:252–253; Lind 1991–1992:180; Miller 1995:137–141; Winter 1989a). If my analysis is correct in placing Phase IV in the latter part of the Late Classic based on radiocarbon dates from Lambityeco and the conspicuous similarity of its pottery with that of other Late Classic period valley sites, then the ceramic chronology for the interval 800–1200 CE remains to be defined. It is to this task that I now turn.

THE SAMPLE

The number of tombs and burials excavated in the Valley of Oaxaca dating to the Classic and Postclassic periods is probably well in excess of 250. A large number of the tomb and grave offerings are published either whole or in part in monographs, book chapters, and journals, and some are known through theses, technical reports, and manuscripts with a more limited circulation. There are uncounted others, tucked away in laboratory storage spaces that remain unanalyzed to this day.

Among the collections that constitute the corpus of Classic and Postclassic period funerary offerings, the largest and most important is the one Caso, Bernal, and Acosta assembled during the era of their explorations at Monte Albán. Consisting of nearly 150 tomb and burial caches (Caso et al. 1967:tables 16 and 18), this invaluable resource is inaccessible, having been dispersed among a number of museums and storage facilities in Mexico City and Oaxaca City.

What is readily available of the Monte Albán collection to students of Oaxaca archaeology is the monograph Caso and his associates (Caso et al. 1967) painstakingly assembled: *La cerámica de Monte Albán*. Although the authors' principal objective was to classify the pottery from the ancient Zapotec metropolis and formulate on that basis a regional ceramic chronology applicable to the Valley of Oaxaca, the volume is furnished with a number of tables that make it possible to reconstitute, albeit with limitations, the ceramic offerings that accompanied the deceased in tombs and graves.

For the ceramic seriations to follow, I make use of those tomb and burial grave lots recovered during the explorations of Caso and his associates at Monte Albán (Proyecto Monte Albán, hereafter abbreviated as PMA) that are problem-free, or nearly so. The ceramic offerings of Tombs 34, 40, 47, and 52 are several among a good number of proveniences that are particularly well described and/or illustrated; the pottery offering found in Tomb 2 is not only inventoried in Table 16 but also appears in a photograph in Caso's companion monograph, *El tesoro de Monte Albán* (Caso 1969:fig. 11). Similarly, the contents of a number of burials are for the most part straightforward, and these proveniences are included in the study as well. Other important tomb and burial collections from Monte Albán integrated into this study come from the Proyecto Salvamento Carretera Monte Albán 1991 (hereafter abbreviated as PSCMA), directed by Ernesto González Licón, and from the more recent Proyecto Especial Monte Albán 1992–1994 (hereafter abbreviated as PEMA), directed by Marcus Winter. Finally, there are the numerous contexts from other Valley of Oaxaca sites that round out this study. All tomb and grave lots that I use appear in Table 2.1, where I provide information as available on the number, relative age, and sex of the individuals found within each tomb or burial. This information is essential for demonstrating the suitability of Zapotec tomb lots for purposes of seriation—an issue addressed in a section to follow.

PRINCIPLES OF OCCURRENCE AND PHYLETIC SERIATION AND THE PRESENT STUDY

There are a number of excellent essays and helpful primers that examine the principles on which seriation techniques are based (e.g., Cowgill 1972; Lyman et al. 1998; Marquardt 1978; O'Brien and Lyman 1999; Rouse 1967). It is beyond my purpose to duplicate those efforts here. Rather, I explain the essentials of the method as they relate to the present case study.

The term "seriation" designates a group of related formal logical analytic techniques that place archaeological entities or units—such as site components, middens, and tomb or grave lots, for example—in sequence, based on their varying degree of formal similarity with one another (Cowgill 1972:381; see also Marquardt 1978:258). Any two adjacent contexts in a seriation share with each other the greatest number of criteria judged to be chronologically sensitive relative to the rest of the sample units; neighboring contexts are therefore closest in time as well as in

Table 2.1 List of tomb and grave lots used in this study

#	*Provenience*	*Individuals*	*Source*
1	Cuilapan T.8	1 adult	Bernal 1958
2	Cuilapan, COBAO T.1	3 adult males, 2 adult females	analyzed for this study
3	Dainzú T.1	no information available	antechamber contents analyzed for this study; Bernal and Oliveros 1988
4	Dainzú T.6	no information available	Bernal and Oliveros 1988
5	Dainzú Bur.5	1 adult female	Bernal and Oliveros 1988
6	Fábrica San José Bur.41	3 adults, 2 males, 1 sex indeterminate	Drennan 1976
7	Hacienda El Alemán T.1980-1	17 adults, 7 males, 8 females, 2 sex indeterminate	analyzed for this study
8	Hacienda El Alemán T.1980-3	at least 3 adults	analyzed for this study
9	Huitzo T.1981	no information available	analyzed for this study
10	Huitzo, Barrio del Rosario T.1	7 adults, 1 male, 1 female, 5 sex indeterminate	analyzed for this study
11	Huitzo Barrio del Rosario Bur.1967-7	no data available	analyzed for this study
12	Huitzo T.1994-1	5 adults, 1 female, 4 sex indeterminate, 1 neonate	Martínez López et al. n.d.
13	Lambityeco T.11	no information available	analyzed for this study
14	Lambityeco T.12	3 individuals	Zárate Morán 1993
15	Lambityeco Bur.1977-1	1 adult	analyzed for this study
16	Lomas de la Cascada Bur. 1980-1	no information available	analyzed for this study
17	Macuilxóchitl Bur.1996-1	1 adult	analyzed for this study
18	Macuilxóchitl Bur.1996-2	no information available	analyzed for this study
19	Monte Albán, PMA T.2	no information available	Caso 1969; Caso et al. 1967
20	Monte Albán, PMA T.15	no information available	Caso et al. 1967
21	Monte Albán, PMA T.34	no information available	Caso et al. 1967
22	Monte Albán, PMA T.40	no information available	Caso et al. 1967
23	Monte Albán, PMA T.46	no information available	Caso et al. 1967
24	Monte Albán, PMA T.47	no information available	Caso et al. 1967
25	Monte Albán, PMA T.52	no information available	Caso et al. 1967
26	Monte Albán, PMA T.59	no information available	Caso et al. 1967
27	Monte Albán, PMA T.63	no information available	Caso et al. 1967
28	Monte Albán, PMA T.75	no information available	Caso et al. 1967
29	Monte Albán, PMA T.80	no information available	Caso et al. 1967
30	Monte Albán, PMA T.93	no information available	Caso et al. 1967
31	Monte Albán, T.172	3 adult males, 1 adult female, 1 adult sex indeterminate	Winter et al. 1998
32	Monte Albán, PMA Bur.V-20	no information available	Caso et al. 1967
33	Monte Albán, PMA Bur.V-21	no information available	Caso et al. 1967
34	Monte Albán, PMA Bur.V-50	no information available	Caso et al. 1967
35	Monte Albán, PSCMA 1991 T.181	1 adult male, 1 adult female, at least 1 neonate	Martínez López 1998
36	Monte Albán, PSCMA 1991 T.183	no information available	Martínez López 1998

continued on next page

Table 2.1—*continued*

#	*Provenience*	*Individuals*	*Source*
37	Monte Albán, PSCMA 1991 T.184	at least 1 adult	Martínez López 1998
38	Monte Albán, PSCMA 1991 T.188	2 adults	Martínez López 1998
39	Monte Albán, PEMA T.195	1 adult male, 1 adult female	Martínez López et al. 2001
40	Monte Albán, PEMA T.196	5 adults, 2 males, 3 sex indeterminate	Martínez López et al. 2001
41	Monte Albán, PEMA T.197	1 adult	Martínez López et al. 2001
42	Monte Albán, PEMA T.198	at least 4 adults	Martínez López et al. 2001
43	Monte Albán, PEMA T.200	at least 3 adults	Martínez López et al. 2001
44	Monte Albán, PEMA T.205	1 adult	Martínez López et al. 2001
45	Monte Albán, PEMA T.206	1 adult	Martínez López et al. 2001
46	Monte Albán, PEMA T.207A	4 adults, 2 female, 2 sex indeterminate	Martínez López et al. 2001
47	Monte Albán, PEMA T.207B		Martínez López et al. 2001
48	Monte Albán, PEMA T.208	9 adults, 4 males, 2 females, 3 sex indeterminate	Martínez López et al. 2001
49	Monte Albán, PEMA T.209	at least 1 adult female	Martínez López et al. 2001
50	Monte Albán, PEMA T.211	at least 2 adult males	Martínez López et al. 2001
51	Monte Albán, PEMA Bur.1 1993-2	adult male	Martínez López et al. 2001
52	Monte Albán, PEMA Bur. 1993-13	1 infant	Martínez López et al. 2001
53	Monte Albán, PEMA Bur. 1993-15	1 infant	Martínez López et al. 2001
54	Monte Albán, PEMA Bur. 1993-35	1 infant	Martínez López et al. 2001
55	Monte Albán, PEMA Bur. 1993-37	1 infant	Martínez López et al. 2001
56	Monte Albán, PEMA Bur. 1994-68	1 adult female	Martínez López et al. 2001
57	Monte Albán, PEMA Bur. 1994-69	1 adult female	Martínez López et al. 2001
58	Monte Albán, PEMA Bur. 1994-70	1 adult male, 1 sex indeterminate	Martínez López et al. 2001
59	San José Mogote T.3-96	3 adults	analyzed for this study with C. Martínez López
60	San Pablo Etla T.76-1	1 adult	Winter et al. 1977
61	Santa Ana del Valle T. no number	no information available	Winter 2000
62	Santa Cruz Mixtepec T.2	at least 2 adult males	Winter 1978
63	Suchilquitongo T.1/81	13 adult males, 1 adult female	Arriola Rivera 1987
64	Suchilquitongo, Yutendahue T. 1986-1	11 adults, 4 males, 5 females, 2 sex indeterminate	Winter and Guevara Hernández 2000
65	Xoxocotlán T.1987-1	6 adult males, 6 adult females	analyzed for this study
66	Yagul T.23	at least 6 individuals	Bernal and Gamio 1974

continued on next page

Table 2.1—*continued*

#	*Provenience*	*Individuals*	*Source*
67	Yagul T.24A	16 individuals	Bernal and Gamio 1974
68	Yagul T.24B	8 individuals	Bernal and Gamio 1974
69	Yagul Bur.6	1 adult male	Bernal and Gamio 1974
70	Zaachila T.3	2 adults	analyzed for this study
71	Zimatlán 1997 T.1	4 individuals	Herrera Muzgo and Winter 2003
72	Zimatlán 1997 T.2	1 individual	Herrera Muzgo and Winter 2003
73	Zimatlán 1997 T.3	1 adult, 1 child	Herrera Muzgo and Winter 2003

formal resemblance to one another. Those applications that seriate contexts in terms of the presence/absence of temporally diagnostic criteria are known as "occurrence seriations," and this is the first of two techniques that I apply to the Valley of Oaxaca study sample.

I apply a second technique known as "phyletic seriation" (O'Brien and Lyman 1999) to the ordering of grave and tomb lots achieved through occurrence seriation. Phyletic seriation traces what might be called "lineages of descent" within one or more domains of artifact form or decoration based on principles of similarity; those entities closest in formal resemblance to one another in terms of a given characteristic are placed in sequence. Such an analysis may reveal developmental trends through time within a particular class of form or decorative tradition and thus facilitate a more subtle ordering of the seriated contexts. This is precisely the seriation technique that Sir Flinders Petrie developed and popularized over one hundred years ago in his study of Egyptian predynastic grave lots (see Deetz 1967: fig. 6).

Constraints on Sample Units to Be Seriated

There are a number of constraints to which the sample contexts selected for seriation should ideally conform (Cowgill 1972; Rouse 1967). The entities to be seriated ought to be of equal and preferably of short duration. The units should come from a geographically circumscribed or local area, and the units must pertain to the same cultural tradition. If these conditions are satisfied and the position of some of the seriated contexts is consistent with other sources of information regarding their relative or absolute temporal placement (e.g., radiocarbon or archaeomagnetic dates), then the ordering is inferred to be a chronological one. I detail issues relevant to only the first condition, although I note that this last requirement is of particular interest, as it bears directly on the issue of Mixtec immigration and the displacement of Zapotecs in the Valley of Oaxaca—a topic of long-standing debate among Oaxaca scholars (see Bernal and Gamio 1974; Caso 1969; Caso et al. 1967; Oudijk 2000; Paddock 1983a).

Tomb and grave lots are considered excellent candidates for seriations as they are ideally the product of an event occurring at a moment in time when a number of vessels constituting part of a ceramic assemblage then in use was brought together as an offering to be deposited with a deceased individual (Rouse 1967:158). Zapotec mortuary practices in prehispanic Oaxaca, however, may constitute an important exception to this rule that invalidates the use of tomb offerings for purposes of seriation. Researchers (Lind 2004; Lind and Urcid 1983; Middleton et al. 1998; Urcid 1996) have illuminated the ancient Zapotec burial practices relevant to this exception.

During the Late Classic period, Zapotecs of middle and upper status in the Valley of Oaxaca buried male and female household heads in well-built tombs installed beneath the floors of their residences. Junior family members, such as adolescents, children, and perhaps other unrelated individuals who may have been attached to the household, were sometimes placed in stone-lined graves or more often in simple pits also excavated beneath the house floor, as was the practice among families of lower standing in Zapotec society (Winter 1974:984, figs. 3–5; 1986:353, figs. 9–11). Subsequently, the tombs were periodically reopened for a variety of reasons.

When the head of a household died, he or she was laid to rest most often in an extended supine position, occupying the tomb's center, together with ceramic and other kinds of offerings. As a spouse or a household head of the next generation passed away, the tomb was reopened and the deceased was often placed alongside the earlier burial; it is not uncommon to find two, three, or four skeletons in extended position at the tomb's center. With the passing of time and the death of subsequent family members, it often became necessary to clear a space for the newly deceased. Accordingly, the skeletal remains of preceding generations were frequently removed and piled up in the rear of the tomb (Urcid 1996:7–8), and the accompanying ceramic offerings were placed in a corner or niche of the tomb or left outside its entrance.

Urcid (1996:7–8) has also observed that the skeletons found in household tombs were often covered with a fine dust of red ochre that was probably applied after the soft body tissues had disintegrated and therefore after interment. Whether tombs were periodically reopened specifically to commune with the spirits of ancestors, during which time they sprinkled red pigment over the deceased relative, or whether the pigment was deposited while laying to rest a newly departed relative is unknown. It has also been demonstrated that some high-status tombs at Lambityeco were reopened at some point in order to retrieve the femora of deceased ancestors

(Chapter 1). Friezes found within one of the palaces (Structure 195) suggest that these bones were used to validate exalted inherited rank from an important ancestor (Lind and Urcid 1990:289). Finally, when house lots were abandoned, the mortal remains of family members and the accompanying offerings may have been retrieved from the family tomb and carried off to wherever the household members had decided to move (Caso 1938:86; Miller 1995).

The phenomenon of tomb reuse and alteration in the Valley of Oaxaca during the Classic period and earlier is a well-documented fact, and thus the tomb contents in most cases do not represent a single episode of deposition but rather a sequence of events taking place intermittently throughout some interval of time. Nonetheless, I do not believe this practice to be an obstacle invalidating the use of tomb offerings for the purposes of ceramic seriation. By referring to Figure 2.2, it is apparent that most of the tombs within the sample contain on the average two to three pairs of adults. If Lind and Urcid (1990) and others are correct that the individuals laid to rest in the tombs are married household heads buried generationally, then it appears that the tombs and the houses under which they were constructed were occupied on the average for forty to sixty years. As ceramic chronologies seldom achieve a resolution finer than one hundred years, the pattern of tomb reuse in the Valley of Oaxaca may be regarded as if the sequential burials took place at a moment in time, probably before most changes in pottery styles would become manifest. As I am interested in refining what is a 1,000-year interval (Late Classic period 500–800 CE and Postclassic period 800–1521 CE), this pattern of tomb reuse should cause little trouble. I observe, however, that some tombs contain the remains of many more individuals. Even so, if these represent married generational household heads, the tomb's duration would amount to approximately 175 years.

Given the assumptions of the seriation technique and the nature of the sample contexts, it is probable that there are a number of factors responsible for the ceramic variation in the pottery sample in addition to that of time. These most probably include geography (i.e., contemporary subregional ceramic variation within the Valley of Oaxaca), status, and gender. I would argue, however, that tombs and burials do not correspond entirely to elite versus non-elite statuses (Urcid 1996:9), as some researchers have argued (Sejourné 1960; Wilkinson and Norelli 1981). After all, both burials and tombs are found in the same high-status residences. My expectation, however, is that time is a more significant factor than others (Cowgill 1972:384). It is for this reason I have chosen to use an explicitly multi-variate technique, non-metric multidimensional scaling, for this seriation, as it tests precisely this premise: that the overall pattern of change within the ceramic sample can be related primarily to the passage of time (Cowgill 1972:383–384; Steponaitis 1983:86–87).

NON-METRIC MULTIDIMENSIONAL SCALING AND SERIATION

Non-metric multidimensional scaling (NMDS) is a computer technique originally conceived and developed for application to problems in psychology, but it is also a procedure well-suited to the requirements of archaeological seriation. NMDS is especially useful for seriation when there are indications that there may be sources of variation within a dataset due to factors other than the passage of time. NMDS programs first assess the formal similarity among the units to be seriated in terms of the temporally sensitive diagnostic criteria they share. This is accomplished by calculating for every unit a measure of similarity vis-à-vis each of the remaining ones through the application of a suitable coefficient of similarity. It is the resulting similarity values that the NMDS program then scales or places in rank order in two or more dimensions of variation. If the sequencing can be accomplished in two or more dimensions as determined by a goodness-of-fit measure that NMDS programs calculate, and if there is external evidence that the resulting order is indeed a temporal series (e.g., radiocarbon or archaeomagnetic dates), then most of the variation in the dataset is explained by the first dimension, which is inferred to represent time.

For this study I apply the NMDS program available in the *UCINET 5.0 Version 1.00* statistics package (Borgatti et al. 1999). The *UCINET* version of NMDS makes use of an algorithm based on the MDS(X) MINISSA program developed by Guttman and Lingoes (Lingoes 1972). Goodness-of-fit is assessed in terms of Kruskal's measure of stress, which calculates the extent to which the resulting order departs from the ideal pattern. In an archaeological occurrence seriation that conforms to the ideal, each chronologically sensitive variable appears in an unbroken sequence or string of contexts. Stress values below 0.1 are excellent; those between 0.1 and 0.2 are acceptable and those above 0.2 are not (Borgatti et al. 1999).

OCCURRENCE SERIATION BASED ON VALLEY OF OAXACA CERAMIC TOMB AND GRAVE LOTS FROM THE LATE CLASSIC AND POSTCLASSIC PERIODS

Based on the descriptive classification of Late Classic and Postclassic pottery from the sample tomb and grave lots (Markens 2004), I selected what I believe are thirty-eight chronologically sensitive variables distributed among the seventy-three funerary contexts. A preliminary inspection and sequencing of the ceramic tomb and grave lots by hand revealed that a number of ceramic categories were rare, occurring in only one or two of the tomb or grave lots. Others, such as certain varieties of *comales* (tortilla griddles) and *patojos* (boot-shaped jars), are temporally sensitive, but since they find their way into tomb and grave lots only sporadically, they are poor candidates for a seriation exercise. Further, a number of graves and tombs contained but one or two of the selected ceramic variables. As these variables and contexts appeared to contribute little information to the overall seriation, they were removed where possible from the dataset in order to facilitate calculation of the clearest possible scaling solution. Exceptions to this rule were made in instances where a rare variable is known to be a particularly good temporal marker. Plumbate glaze and orange-paste vessels are two cases in point. The removal of infrequently occurring and inappropriate ceramic variables and tombs or burials with few diagnostic traits produced a final dataset of twenty-one diagnostic ceramic traits and forty-one mortuary contexts to be seriated.

The first step in executing a seriation using an NMDS computer program is to select a suitable coefficient of similarity from the many available to assess the formal resemblance among the contexts to be seriated. Here I use Jaccard's coefficient of similarity. Use of this algorithm is recommended when the dataset contains some rarely occurring variables, as is the case here. This coefficient of similarity places greater weight on those variables shared by two units by omitting from its calculation of similarity the number of absent-absent matches they possess in common. Accordingly, an index of similarity was calculated for the tomb and grave lots using the UCINET statistics package. The results were then scaled in two dimensions using the UCINET NMDS program, which reads the similarity values for the units to be scaled as just that—similarities.

I ran the NMDS program several times and from these trials the most compelling seriation sequence was selected on the basis of what is known about the dating of the units constituting the sample. Kruskal's stress value for the seriation is 0.084, a value appearing in the range that is considered excellent. The earliest contexts in Figure 2.2 appear in the upper left portion of the table; moving to the right the contexts are progressively more recent. The order of the seriated contexts presented in Figure 2.2 was determined by first drawing a diagonal line by eye passing through the long axis of the scaled similarity values—that is, from lower left to upper right. Next, a line perpendicular to the diagonal was drawn from the diagonal to each point. The scaling or sequence of contexts corresponds to the order in which the points are connected to the diagonal (see Cowgill 1972:407).

The results of this occurrence seriation are significant and constitute what I consider an important first step toward clarifying the ceramic chronology for the Valley of Oaxaca during the Classic and Postclassic periods. What the seriation shows is that the tomb and grave lots in this sample can be seriated based on the selected ceramic variables. Although other factors, such as geography, differences in status, and gender, may contribute to some of the variation seen in the tomb and burial sample, the overall pattern of ceramic change, nonetheless, can be explained by the passage of time. Conical G.35 bowls,[4] so common during the Peche and Xoo phases, are compressed into the first part of the graph representing the pottery in use during the Late Classic period. The painted polychromes and vessels with

CERAMIC CATEGORIES	Santa Cruz Mixtepec T.2	Monte Albán, PEMA T. 206	Monte Albán, PEMA T.196	Monte Albán, PMA T.34	Monte Albán, PEMA T. 207	Monte Albán, PEMA T.195	Monte Albán, PSCMA 1991 T.188	Monte Albán, PSCMA 1991 T.183	Monte Albán, PMA T.40	Monte Albán, PEMA T. 205	Lambityeco T.11
Grayware conical bowl with hollow hemispherical support attached to the base	1	1	1	1							
Gray or brownware sahumador with hemispherical bowl and large perforations	1	1	1	1	1	1	1				
Small grayware olla with subspherical body, neck-rim straight-divergent with bridge handles		1	1	1							
Large and medium gray and creamware conical bowl without supports (G.35)			1	1	1		1	1	1	1	1
Large and medium grayware conical bowl with solid conical supports				1	1	1	1	1	1		
Brownware conical bowl						1	1		1	1	
Brownware hemispherical bowl									1		
Grayware hemispherical bowl or plate (G.3M)								1			
Gray, brown or creamware handled censer with or without small perforations with or without decoration							1	1	1	1	
Gray, brown or creamware miniatures						1	1		1	1	1
Orangeware vessels											
Cream or orangeware ollas with basket type handle											
Composite silhouette olla,Tohil Plumbate type											
Gray, brown or orangeware conjoint vessels											
Huitzo Polished Cream type											
Large brown or creamware handled sahumador with long handle and without perforations in bowl											
Grayware composite silhouette bowl (G.3M)											
Gray, brown or creamware vessels with long hollow supports											
Polychrome vessels											
Small or medium gray, brown or polychrome olla with handles on the body											
Gray, brown and creamware medium or small pitchers with loop handle											

2.2 Occurrence seriation of forty-two tomb and grave lots. The number 1 signifies the presence of a ceramic category.

					1	1			1		1	1	1				1				San José Mogote T.3-96
					1				1		1						1				Hacienda El Alemán T.1980-1
									1		1	1					1				Hacienda El Alemán T.1980-3
								1		1	1	1					1				Monte Albán, PMA T. 52
								1	1	1	1	1					1	1			Monte Albán, PMA T. 47
											1	1	1								Monte Albán, PEMA T. 208
											1	1	1								Monte Albán, PEMA T. 209
							1				1		1								Cuilapan T. 8
				1			1				1	1	1	1	1						Cuilapan, COBAO T.1
				1			1			1	1	1	1								Zaachila T.3
				1			1				1	1	1								Zimatlán 1997 T. 2
				1							1	1	1								Zimatlán 1997 T. 1
				1							1	1	1	1							Zimatlán 1997 T.3
				1							1	1	1	1	1						Monte Albán, PMA T.75
				1	1						1		1	1							Monte Albán, PMA T.46
											1	1	1	1							Dainzú T. 1
				1							1		1	1							Monte Albán, PMA T.63
1				1									1	1							Monte Albán, PMA T.59
	1			1									1								Huitzo T. 1981
1	1	1	1	1									1								Huitzo, Barrio del Rosario T.1
	1		1	1																	Huitzo Barrio del Rosario Bur. 1967-7
	1	1	1	1									1								Huitzo T.1994-1
				1		1							1								Suchilquitongo, Yutendahue T. 1986-1
1	1		1	1								1	1								Suchilquitongo T.1/81
		1	1	1																	Monte Albán, PMA Bur.V-20
				1	1	1															Infonavit T.1/1978
1	1	1	1	1									1								Xoxocotlán T. 1987-1
			1	1									1								Yagul Bur. 6

elongated hollow supports terminating with serpent or eagle heads or deer hooves, for example, are concentrated into the opposite extreme of the table, which represents the Late Postclassic period Chila phase.

Similarly, there are a number of pottery categories occupying the middle range of the table and pertaining to the Early Postclassic. These are Huitzo Polished Cream bowls, thin-walled pottery fired a bright orange color, multiple conjoint vessels, vessels with basket-type handles, Tohil Plumbate, brownware hemispherical bowls, and commonly occurring miniature toylike vessels. It is also in the middle portion of Figure 2.2 that one sees the Postclassic period hemispherical and composite silhouette bowls made of the fine, hard paste, known as G3M, replacing the ubiquitous conical serving bowls of the Late Classic period. This is perhaps one of the most striking changes in the Zapotec ceramic tradition in the Valley of Oaxaca.

On a more concrete level, the series of contexts produced by the NMDS program can be shown to be a temporal one, for it is consistent in broad strokes with existing radiocarbon dates and with ceramic cross-ties with other regions of Mesoamerica (Table 2.2). The conical bowls with hemispherical supports attached to the base have been found in a trash pit at Monte Albán (*Elemento* 9) that yielded a carbon sample dating to 500±60 CE, corresponding to the Peche phase (Winter 1994:120). Similarly, PEMA Tomb 209, containing Early Postclassic pottery, was found deep beneath a defensive wall covering part of the southern portion of the Main Plaza. The carbon extracted from the soil below the defensive wall's foundation was dated to 1320±50 CE (ibid.). Tomb 209 therefore was constructed and used some time before that date and is probably several hundred years older. The presence of Tohil Plumbate *floreros* in PMA Tombs 47 and 52 date those contexts by ceramic cross-ties to the Early Postclassic period, about 900–1000 CE. Tomb 3 from Zaachila contains an orangeware chimney-shaped florero similar to X Fine Orange specimens made in the Maya area during the Early Postclassic (Acosta 1972: fig. 2, second from right; R. Smith 1958:figs. 3a and 3f). Tomb 3 from Zimatlán is radiocarbon dated to 1250±40 CE (Herrera Muzgo T. and Winter 2003:43). Finally, there is the Postclassic period polychrome pottery.

Lind (1994) has observed that the polychrome pottery in the Valley of Oaxaca is virtually identical to that found in the adjacent Mixteca Alta, where it is designated Pilitas Polychrome. The reason for this similarity is explained by the fact that the Valley of Oaxaca together with the Mixteca Alta formed part of an elite interaction sphere during the Late Postclassic period. Sharing or making use of a common set of principles, individuals of the highest standing sought to enhance their power by forging political alliances with leaders of adjacent *señoríos* or those further removed through the exchange of marriage partners (Chapters 1 and 10; Oudijk 2000:181–183; Pohl 2003) and sumptuary goods. The common values of this elite culture appear to find expression in a range of material culture items decorated in the same style. These are found throughout the area of this interaction sphere and include polychrome pottery. Pilitas Polychrome is radiocarbon dated in the Mixteca Alta to about 1340±90 CE (Lind 1994)—a date that is probably applicable to the Valley of Oaxaca.

Building on the foundation of existing radiocarbon determinations for the Valley of Oaxaca presented in Table 2.2, I present the results of a new set of twelve radiocarbon dates obtained from three valley sites key to understanding the Classic-Postclassic period transition: Lambityeco, Macuilxóchitl, and Xaagá (Table 2.3). The third site, Xaagá, is a dispersed village community located in the Mitla hinterland. The carbon samples were recovered during the Proyecto Salvamento Arqueológico Carretera Oaxaca-Mitla carried out in 2002 and 2003 in conjunction with improvements made to the Pan-American Highway (Mexico 190) between Oaxaca City and the Isthmus of Tehuantepec. The dates offer robust support for the division of the valley's prehispanic pottery into the Late Classic, Early Postclassic, and Late Postclassic periods obtained by means of the seriation exercise. The new dates from Lambityeco are of special interest since Lambityeco is the type site for Early Postclassic period pottery defined by Paddock and his colleagues in 1968.

There are in total five new radiocarbon assays from Lambityeco. The first three dates (Beta-205982, 205983, and 205985) are derived from organic materials recovered from three tombs found in two of the center's residences. All three tombs and/or residences contained Late Classic period Xoo phase pottery identical to the assemblage Paddock (Paddock et al. 1968) described in his Lambityeco excavations (see also Chapter 5). The three radiocarbon determinations range from 450±60 to 560±40 CE, and like the dates Paddock obtained, these correspond to the Late Classic and not the Early Postclassic period, taking into consideration their margins of error.

Subtler distinctions within the Late Classic period valley ceramic complex are less clear-cut. If the earliest date is correct (Beta-205982, 450±60 CE), the corresponding carbon sample should be associated with Peche phase ceramic material (only a handful of Pitao phase sherds were recovered during our excavations at Lambityeco).Yet Peche phase pottery diagnostic attributes appear to be absent from this context.

The Peche phase, dating to 500–600 CE (see Figure 2.1), was first identified in the pottery at Monte Albán by Caso and his colleagues (Caso et al. 1967:365–378)[5] and later expanded and refined by dividing the Xoo phase pottery at Monte Albán into earlier and later moments (Martínez López et al. 2000). Since then, Urcid (2003) has defined a Peche phase for Zapotec funerary urns at Monte Albán and ceramic attributes diagnostic of the Peche phase have been identified in the Late Classic pottery samples recovered from residences excavated during the 2002 salvage project at Macuilxóchitl. The absence of identifiable Peche phase pottery

Table 2.2 Radiocarbon dates for the Valley of Oaxaca, after Drennan 1983. All dates are uncalibrated and uncorrected. Those assays that are clear outliers are omitted here.

Laboratory Number	*Uncalibrated and Uncorrected Radiocarbon Date*	*Corresponding Period and Phase*	*Site*	*Provenience*
Beta-63236	500+60 CE	Late Classic period Peche phase	Monte Albán	North Platform, Vértice Geodésico, Pit 7P. Associated with Peche phase pottery.
I-15921	710+80 CE	Late Classic period Xoo phase	Monte Albán	Mound III South Platform. Associated with Xoo phase pottery.
TX-1815	740+100 CE	Late Classic period Xoo phase	Monte Albán	Terrace 634-6, Feature 72-19. Associated with Xoo phase pottery.
I-15920	750+80 CE	Late Classic period Xoo phase	Monte Albán	Mound III South Platform. Associated with Danibaan/Pe and Peche phase pottery.
GX-1480	640+100 CE	Late Classic period Xoo phase	Lambityeco	Mound 190, Floor 2. Associated with Xoo phase pottery.
GX-1482	690+100 CE	Late Classic period Xoo phase	Lambityeco	Mound 195, Tomb 6. Associated with Xoo phase pottery.
I-3258	700+95 CE	Late Classic period Xoo phase	Lambityeco	Mound 195, offering. Associated with Xoo phase pottery.
I-2679	720+100 CE	Late Classic period Xoo phase	Lambityeco	Mound 195, offering. Associated with Xoo phase pottery.
I-3257	730+100 CE	Late Classic period Xoo phase	Lambityeco	Mound 195. Associated with Xoo phase pottery.
GX-1573	755+90 CE	Late Classic period Xoo phase	Lambityeco	Building 195-sub. Associated with Xoo phase pottery.
M-2096	620+130 CE	Late Classic period Xoo phase	Guilá Naquitz	Zone A. Associated with Xoo phase pottery.
SI- 514	740+40 CE	Late Classic period Xoo phase	Guilá Naquitz	Zone A. Associated with Xoo phase pottery.
M-1251	840+110 CE	Early Postclassic period Liobaa phase	Mitla	South group Tomb 3. Associated with Liobaa phase pottery.
Beta-138612	1250+40 CE	Early Postclasic period Late Liobaa phase	El Sabino, Zimatlán	Tomb 3. Associated with Late Liobaa phase pottery.
M-1248	1200+100 CE	Late Postclassic period Chila phase	Yagul	Room 13, North sub-floor hearth. Associated with Chila phase pottery.
M-1250	1250+100 CE	Late Postclassic period Chila phase	Yagul	Patio A, North Room, sub-floor hearth. Associated with Chila phase pottery.
SI-513	1270+80 CE	Late Postclassic period Chila phase	Guilá Naquitz	Feature 7. Associated with Chila phase.
Beta-66503	1320+50 CE	Late Postclassic period	Monte Albán	Soil layer above Tomb 209. Associated with Late Liobaa phase pot- tery.
SI-510	1430+50 CE	Late Postclassic period Chila phase	Cueva Blanca	Zone A. Associated with Chila phase pottery.

Table 2.3 Radiocarbon dates from the Proyecto Salvamento Arqueológico Carretera Oaxaca-Mitla 2002–2003. All samples are uncalibrated and uncorrected to facilitate comparison with the radiocarbon dates presented in Table 2.2.

Laboratory Number	*Uncalibrated and Uncorrected Radiocarbon Date*	*Corresponding Period and Phase*	*Site*	*Provenience*
Beta-205982	450+60 CE	Early Classic period Tani phase / Late Classic Peche phase	Lambityeco	Area B. Tomb 19 of Residence B1. Associated with Xoo phase pottery.
Beta-205983	520+70 CE	Late Classic period Peche/Xoo phase	Lambityeco	Area B. Tomb 25 of Residence B4. Associated with Xoo phase pottery.
Beta-205985	560+40 CE	Late Classic period Peche/Xoo phase	Lambityeco	Area B. Tomb 22 of Residence B1. Residence. Associated with Xoo phase pottery.
Beta-205986	920+30 CE	Early Postclassic period Early Liobaa phase	Lambityeco	Area B. Feature 55. Oven intrusive into Xoo phase house. No pottery recovered.
Beta-205984	940+60 CE	Early Postclassic period Early Liobaa phase	Lambityeco	Area A. Feature 10. Outdoor oven associated with Liobaa phase pottery.
Beta-205989	880+40 CE	Early Postclassic period Early Liobaa phase	Xaagá	Area E. Tomb 2003-2. Associated with Liobaa phase pottery.
Beta-205987	920+70 CE	Early Postclassic period Early Liobaa phase	Xaagá	Area H. Tomb 2003-6. Associated with Liobaa phase pottery.
Beta-205990	1160+60 CE	Early Postclassic period Late Liobaa phase	Xaagá	Area E. Tomb 2003-1. Associated with Liobaa phase pottery.
Beta-205988	1200+50 CE	Late Postclassic period Chila phase	Xaagá	Area B, sub-floor offering associated with kiln containing Chila phase pottery.
Beta-205980	1390+40 CE	Late Postclassic period Chila phase	Macuilxóchitl	Mound 1. Residence, Feature 39, sub-floor offering in south patio. Associated with Chila phase pottery.
Beta-205991	1580+50 CE	Early Colonial period	Xaagá	Area C. Residence C2, Feature 19, sub-floor hearth. Residence associated with Chila phase pottery and T-shaped copper axes.
Beta-205992	1760+40 CE	Late Colonial period	Xaagá	Area C. Residence C1, Feature 17, sub-floor hearth. Residence associated with Chila phase pottery.

in the residence at Lambityeco yielding the earliest radiocarbon date (see above) remains unexplained for the present.

The final two dates from Lambityeco correspond to the Early Postclassic period. One of the radiocarbon samples (Beta-205986) dating to 920±30 CE comes from an oven dug through the floor in one room of an abandoned Xoo phase house. No pottery was found in the feature. The second date, Beta-205984, corresponds to an outdoor oven or hearth dating to 940±60 CE and is associated with Liobaa phase pottery. Liobaa phase pottery is wholly unlike the ceramic material Paddock described in defining his Phase IV (Paddock et al. 1968) at Lambityeco. Made from coarse brown paste, the Liobaa assemblage at Lambityeco consists of *ollas*, patojos, miniature vessels, and poorly made *sahumadores*. The pottery occurs as a widespread but light scatter in the plow zone of the site. In no case was a single sherd of it found in any of the nine tombs, thirty-four burials, or sealed features of the seventeen residences explored during the recent salvage project at the site.

Three tombs explored at the dispersed village site of Xaagá contained pottery identical to the Liobaa phase pottery found on the surface of Lambityeco. Radiocarbon samples from each of the three tombs provide dates entirely consistent with the Early Postclassic period (Table 2.3). These are Beta-205989, yielding a date of 880±40 CE; Beta-205987, which provided a date of 920±70 CE; and Beta-205990, which yielded a date of 1160±60 CE. Xoo phase materials are entirely absent from the Xaagá site.

Finally, two radiocarbon samples from Xaagá (Beta-205988 and Beta-205991) provide dates for the Late Postclassic Chila phase pottery of 1200±50 and 1580±50 CE, respectively. A third radiocarbon sample (Beta-205980) yielded a date of 1390±40 CE and was found in association with a Chila phase pottery cache in a residence at Macuilxóchitl.

PHYLETIC SERIATION

It should be possible to improve upon the ceramic seriation for the Late Classic and Postclassic periods presented in Figure 2.3 by following two steps. (1) Making use of the principle of phyletic seriation, I look more closely within diagnostic ceramic categories that are broadly conceived. "Gray- and creamware conical bowls" and "miniatures" are two examples. Such an analysis may reveal developmental trends through time within a given class of form or decoration and thus facilitate a more subtle ordering of the seriated contexts. (2) I then reinsert the purged ceramic variables, tomb, and grave contexts back into the seriation in a way that does little or no violence to the general order already achieved. This will allow me to expand the list of pottery categories possibly in use during the Late Classic and Postclassic periods and to better propose where this ceramic continuum may be divided into phases.

I begin this discussion by drawing attention to the fact that although the ordering of contexts achieved through NMDS generally conforms to what is known about the absolute or relative temporal position of several of the contexts, there are also a number of apparent reversals in the order of some of the sample tombs and graves. For example, Tombs 47 and 52 from Monte Albán are key contexts as they each contain a Tohil Plumbate composite silhouette olla—a ceramic type widely recognized as a reliable horizon marker for the Early Postclassic period in Mesoamerica (Chapter 1). Yet, Tomb 11 from Lambityeco—a reliable Late Classic period context—is sequenced *after* the tombs containing Tohil Plumbate vessels. There are three likely reasons for the inversions. First, NMDS scaling solutions are not unique. This means that more than one ordering of the contexts may produce the same level of stress. Second, as the NMDS program sorts and resorts the contexts, it may reach a point of diminishing returns and shut down before arriving at the best scaling solution. It is for these reasons that the placement of contexts within a seriation generated by NMDS cannot be taken too literally. What NMDS programs accomplish is a very good general ordering of the sample contexts, so that temporally recent units will all be placed together, chronologically intermediate contexts will be grouped together, and so on. The exact position of a context within its group may be less precise (Cowgill 1972:385–386, 417; Steponaitis 1983:88–90). The final reason explaining the temporal reversal of some contexts is the generality with which some of the key diagnostic ceramic variables were defined. The categories of conical bowls; G3M paste hemispherical bowls; and gray-, brown-, and creamware handled censers are all broadly conceived. Developmental trends within each category were identified by examining some of the temporally secure contexts. This permitted a refining of the tomb and grave contexts. These refined contexts appear in Figure 2.3.

The continuum of ceramic change appearing in Figure 2.3 was divided into five blocks based on the simultaneous appearance or disappearance of a number of ceramic variables. Each block corresponds to a phase. Accordingly, I identify a Peche phase (500–600 CE), represented by the first block of contexts that occupy the upper left-hand corner of Figure 2.3. The second block of tomb and grave lots represents the Xoo phase (600–800 CE). The following two blocks represent the Early (800–1000 CE) and Late (1000–1200 CE) Liobaa phases, respectively, corresponding to the Early Postclassic period. Finally, the last block represents the Chila phase, dating to the Late Postclassic period (1200–1521 CE).

MAJOR CERAMIC VARIABLES DURING THE LATE CLASSIC AND POSTCLASSIC PERIODS

In this section, I describe the major ceramic variables that characterize the phases defined above. For purposes of illustration, a series of companion figures accompany

CERAMIC CATEGORIES	Santa Cruz Mixtepec T.2	Monte Albán, PMA T.80	Monte Albán, PSCMA 1991 T.181
Large conical bowl with low walls and black slip, without supports			
Grayware conical bowl with hollow semispherical supports attached to the base	1	1	
Grayware florero with high narrow neck, spherical body without supports			1
Gray or brownware sahumador with semispherical bowl and large perforations	1		
Large semispherical wide mouthed gray bowl with hollow semispherical supports			
Medium grayware cilindrical cup with excurvate rim			
Grayware olla with spherical body, neck-rim straight-divergent with coarse sand on exterior base			
Small grayware olla with subspherical body, straight-divergent neck-rim with bridge handles			
Large and medium gray and creamware conical bowl without supports		1	1
Large grayware conical bowl with hollow semispherical supports attached to the basal angle			
Small grayware semispherical bowl with restricted mouth and incurvate rim, no supports			
Grayware florero with wide neck and body without supports			
Large and medium grayware conical bowl with solid conical supports			
Small gray or brownware conical or semispherical bowl with or without solid conical supports			
Grayware florero with wide neck and body and mask of Cociyo			
Gray or brownware cup with claw			
Brownware conical bowl			
Brownware semispherical bowl			
Grayware semispherical bowl without supports, wide mouthed and with burnished waxy-like surface			
G3M semispherical bowl or plate			
Gray or brownware sahumador with conical bowl and small perforations			
Gray, brown or creamware handled sahumador with or without small perforations, with or without incised decoration			
Gray, brown and creamware miniatures			
Orangeware vessels			
Cream and orangeware olla with basket type handle			
Composite silhouette olla, Tohil Plumbate type			
Gray, brown or orangeware conjoint vessels			
Semispherical bowl, Huitzo Polished Cream type			
Large brown or creamware handled sahumador without perforations and a long handle			
Gray, brown or creamware patojo with handles			
Grayware vessels with short hollow supports			
G3M composite silhouette bowl			
Gray, brown or creamware vessels with elongated hollow supports			
Polychrome vessels			
Small or medium gray, brownware or polychrome olla with handles on the body			
Gray, brown and creamware medium or small pitcher with loop handle			
Brown paste excised censer with phallic supports with or without graphite paint			

2.3 Refined seriation of seventy-four tomb and burial contexts and division of sequence of contexts into phases. The number 1 signifies the presence of a ceramic category.

Monte Albán, PEMA T.207A	Monte Albán, PEMA T.198	Monte Albán, PEMA T.206	Monte Albán, PEMA Bur. 1993-2	Monte Albán, PEMA Bur. 1993-15	Monte Albán, PMA T.34	Monte Albán, PMA, T.2	Macuilxóchitl Bur. 1996-1	Monte Albán, PSCMA 1991 T.183	Monte Albán, PSCMA 1991 T.184	Monte Albán, PEMA T.200	Monte Albán, PEMA T.207B	Monte Albán, PEMA T.211	Monte Albán, PEMA Bur. 1994-68	Monte Albán, PEMA Bur. 1994-69	Monte Albán, PEMA Bur. 1994-70	Lambityeco Bur. 1977-1	Monte Albán, PEMA Bur. 1993-13	Monte Albán, PEMA Bur. 1993-35	Monte Albán, PEMA Bur. 1993-37	Lambityeco T.12	Lambityeco T.11	Monte Albán, PMA T.40	Monte Albán, T.172	Monte Albán, PSCMA 1991 T.188	Monte Albán, PEMA T.195	Monte Albán, PEMA T.205	Fábrica San José Bur. 41	San José Mogote T.3-96	Hacienda El Alemán T.1980-1	Hacienda El Alemán T.1980-3	Monte Albán, PMA T.47	Monte Albán, PMA T.52
			1		1																											
		1		1	1																											
1					1																											
1	1	1	1		1	1											1						1	1	1							
		1					1																									
			1																													
		1		1													1	1	1													
		1			1																										1	
1					1		1	1		1				1	1	1		1	1	1	1	1	1	1		1		1	1	1	1	1
					1	1																										
				1									1																			
1																									1							
					1			1	1								1					1	1	1	1							
								1		1	1			1							1						1					
									1											1												
																1				1												
										1		1										1		1	1	1	1					
																						1					1					
		1													1									1								
								1						1														1	1			
												1												1	1							
								1					1							1		1	1	1		1		1		1	1	1
																					1	1	1	1	1	1	1	1	1	1	1	1
																															1	1
																												1	1	1	1	
																															1	1
																												1				
																											1	1	1			
																												1				
																													1			

CERAMIC CATEGORIES	Monte Albán, PMA T.15	Cuilapan T. 8	Cuilapan, COBAO T.1
Large conical bowl with low walls and black slip, without supports			
Grayware conical bowl with hollow semispherical supports attached to the base			
Grayware florero with high narrow neck, spherical body without supports			
Gray or brownware sahumador with semispherical bowl and large perforations			
Large semispherical wide mouthed gray bowl with hollow semispherical supports			
Medium grayware cilindrical cup with excurvate rim			
Grayware olla with spherical body, neck-rim straight-divergent with coarse sand on exterior base			
Small grayware olla with subspherical body, straight-divergent neck-rim with bridge handles			
Large and medium gray and creamware conical bowl without supports	1		
Large grayware conical bowl with hollow semispherical supports attached to the basal angle			
Small grayware semispherical bowl with restricted mouth and incurvate rim, no supports			
Grayware florero with wide neck and body without supports			
Large and medium grayware conical bowl with solid conical supports			
Small gray or brownware conical or semispherical bowl with or without solid conical supports			
Grayware florero with wide neck and body and mask of Cociyo			
Gray or brownware cup with claw	1		
Brownware conical bowl			1
Brownware semispherical bowl	1		1
Grayware semispherical bowl without supports, wide mouthed and with burnished waxy-like surface			
G3M semispherical bowl or plate	1	1	1
Gray or brownware sahumador with conical bowl and small perforations			
Gray, brown or creamware handled sahumador with or without small perforations, with or without incised decoration	1		1
Gray, brown and creamware miniatures	1	1	1
Orangeware vessels			
Cream and orangeware olla with basket type handle			
Composite silhouette olla, Tohil Plumbate type			
Gray, brown or orangeware conjoint vessels		1	1
Semispherical bowl, Huitzo Polished Cream type			
Large brown or creamware handled sahumador without perforations and a long handle			
Gray, brown or creamware patojo with handles	1		
Grayware vessels with short hollow supports			
G3M composite silhouette bowl			1
Gray, brown or creamware vessels with elongated hollow supports			
Polychrome vessels			
Small or medium gray, brownware or polychrome olla with handles on the body			
Gray, brown and creamware medium or small pitcher with loop handle			
Brown paste excised censer with phallic supports with or without graphite paint			

2.3—continued

					1	1				1				1	1		1																				Zimatlán 1997 T. 2
							1							1	1		1																				Monte Albán, PEMA T.208
														1	1		1																				Monte Albán, PEMA T.209
					1				1								1																				Suchilquitongo, Yutendahue T. 1986-1
					1		1	1						1			1		1				1														Monte Albán, PMA T.46
					1		1							1			1		1																		Monte Albán, PMA T.63
					1									1	1		1		1	1	1																Monte Albán, PMA T.75
					1	1								1	1		1																				Zimatlán 1997 T. 1
							1							1	1		1		1																		Dainzú T. 1
							1							1			1																				Dainzú T. 6
							1							1			1																				Dainzú Bur. 5
					1									1	1		1		1																		Zimatlán 1997 T.3
					1												1																				San Pablo Etla T.76-1
						1											1																				Santa Ana del Valle T.without number
																	1		1	1																	Yagul T.24A
															1		1		1																		Yagul T.24B
		1			1												1																				Huitzo T. 1981
	1				1												1		1																		Monte Albán, PMA T.59
	1	1	1	1	1												1																				Huitzo, Barrio del Rosario T.1
		1		1	1																																Huitzo Barrio del Rosario Bur. 1967-7
1		1	1	1	1												1																				Huitzo T.1994-1
	1	1		1	1										1		1																				Suchilquitongo T.1/81
1				1	1		1																1														Monte Albán, PMA T.93
			1	1	1		1																														Monte Albán, PMA Bur.V-20
				1			1																														Monte Albán, PMA Bur. V-21
				1															1																		Monte Albán, PMA Bur.V-50
					1	1											1																				Macuilxóchitl Bur. 1996-2
				1	1	1													1																		Lomas de la Cascada Bur. 1980-1
	1	1	1	1	1												1																				Xoxocotlán T. 1987-1
1						1									1		1		1																		Yagul T.23
				1	1												1																				Yagul Bur. 6

this discussion. Following a phyletic approach, I discuss the pottery in terms of major form classes and show how these change from the Late Classic through the Postclassic period phases defined above.

Conical Bowls

The large and medium conical bowls made from G.35 paste are the ceramic hallmark of the Late Classic period. They often exhibit a flat base but also may display three basal supports. During the Peche phase (500–600 CE) the most salient characteristic is the presence of three hollow hemispherical supports attached to the base of large bowls (Figure 2.4). This mode of attachment of supports to the vessel's base is a continuation of the practice that began in the Pitao phase, when the G.35 conical bowl (variant II in Caso's terms [Caso et al. 1967]) first appears. A variation on this theme is the use of molded supports in the likeness of simians. These, too, are attached to the vessel base. Conical bowls during the Late Classic were frequently decorated with a burnished geometric design hastily executed on the vessel's interior base.

More common in the Peche phase is the innovation of placing the hemispherical supports on the basal angle of the vessel. This placement of the vessel support continues in the Xoo phase but attaching supports to the vessel base does not. Simple G.35 conical bowls without supports were produced in vast quantities throughout the Peche and Xoo phases. During the Xoo phase, the medium size G.35 conical bowl becomes common. It is also during this time that conical bowls appear in small quantities in brown paste.

Conical bowls diagnostic of the Xoo phase (600–800 CE) are recognized by the presence of solid conical supports that appear on large- and medium-size grayware conical bowls. They also appear on small conical bowls that appear for the first time during the Xoo phase and continue into the Postclassic Early Liobaa phase. These are made of gray or brown paste.

During the Early Liobaa phase (800–1000 CE), the conical bowl appears to continue in gray and brown paste, but it is also made for the first time in a cream paste. The Early Liobaa form of the conical bowl is distinguished by a noticeably thickened base. It has in some instances the appearance of having been squashed down when the clay was still wet, for the clay extrudes unevenly around the vessel base. The interior contour of the conical bowl is more hemispherical than conical, unlike the conical bowls of the Late Classic period. Finally, the conical bowls from the Hacienda El Alemán, Cobao, and San José Mogote tombs are smoothed with an instrument, perhaps a corncob, leaving swaths of short rough parallel lines. There are no examples of conical bowls for the Late Liobaa phase (1000–1200 CE) in the sample universe. The fact that conical bowls are present in the Chila phase (1200–1521 CE) suggests that its absence from Late Liobaa phase is the result of sampling error in this study.

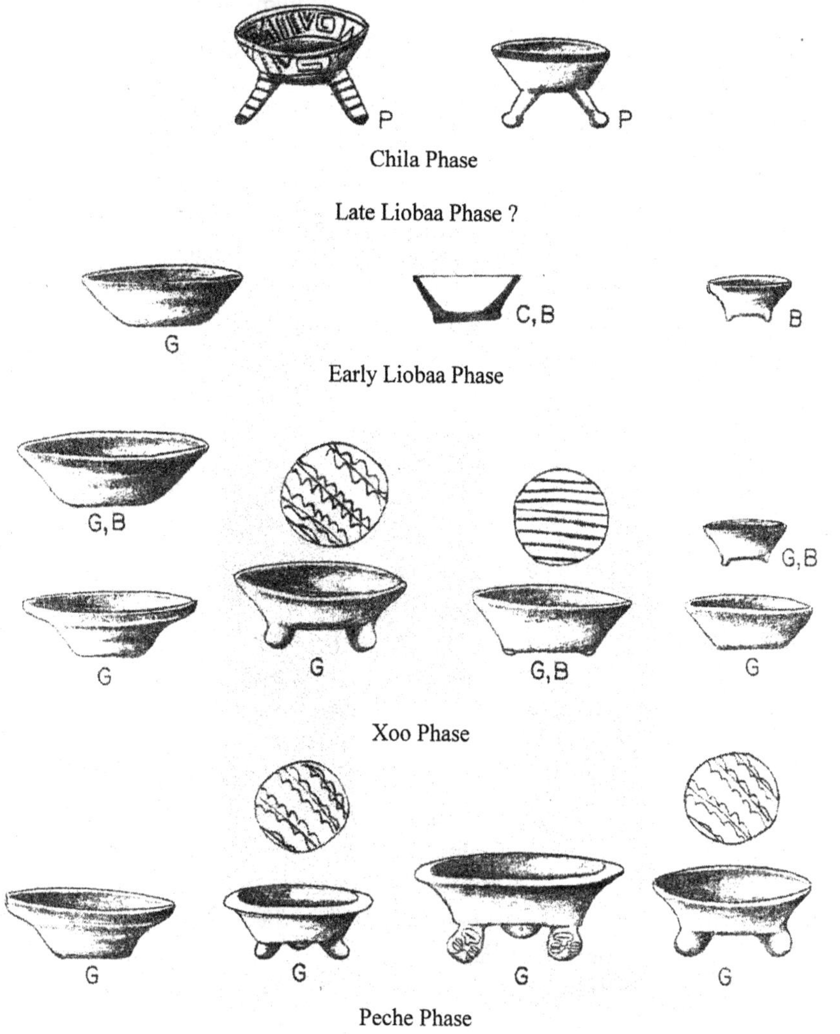

2.4 Development of conical bowls from Peche (bottom) through Chila phases (top); B=brownware, C=creamware, G=grayware, P=polychrome.

During the Chila phase (1200–1521 CE), conical bowls appear with hollow elongated or slab legs and are polychrome painted.

Hemispherical Bowls

During the Peche and Xoo phases, large hemispherical bowls with wide, open mouths and three hemispherical supports are present (Figure 2.5). Like the conical bowls they too were frequently decorated with a burnished design in the interior base. There are also attractive well-burnished, medium-size black-slipped bowls whose walls and lips are slightly curvo-convergent. These disappear by the onset of Xoo phase times.

During the Xoo phase there are a number of varieties of hemispherical bowls in use. The wide-mouth bowl with three hollow hemispherical supports continues. A medium-size hemispherical bowl with a slightly restricted mouth becomes common. This vessel is somewhat coarse in appearance as it is scraped on the outside and hastily burnished. At times, it is furnished with two handles attached horizontally below the lip. Finally, small hemispherical bowls made from brown paste and furnished with three conical supports appear during this time.

The Early Liobaa phase is distinguished by medium- and large-size hemispherical bowls with low walls made from G3M and brown paste. These are scraped on the outside and sometimes left unburnished on the exterior surface. Also present in the sample are medium and large hemispherical bowls that appear in some ways as transitional to the well-made G3M bowls of the Late Liobaa and Chila phases. In some instances, the paste is coarse and resembles that of the G.35 bowl. The two-tone differential firing effect is also often poorly executed at this time and may be accidental rather than intentional.

As mentioned above, the Early Postclassic period was the time of a notable change in the history of the Valley of Oaxaca Zapotec pottery tradition. The hemispherical bowl largely superseded the conical bowl, which had functioned as the primary serving vessel and all-purpose bowl for hundreds of years prior to the Early Liobaa phase. Instructive in this regard are the Early Liobaa hemispherical bowls from Zaachila Tomb 3, the Cobao tomb, and PEMA Tombs 208 and 209. Many of the G3M hemispherical bowls appearing in these Early Postclassic tombs were finished and decorated in the way that is typical of the conical serving bowls they were replacing; the hemispherical G3M bowls from these tombs are scraped and left unburnished on the outside, and a simple geometric pattern is burnished or incised on the interior base. Thus, it appears that potters conceived the hemispherical bowl as the functional equivalent of the conical bowl it was displacing.

It is during the Early Liobaa phase that Huitzo Polished Cream bowls appear—a ceramic category that Paddock long ago believed was a hallmark of the Early Postclassic period (Paddock 1966:figs 260–261). They also appear in the form of conjoint vessels.

The G3M and brownware hemispherical bowls continue into the Late Liobaa phase. The brownware bowls sometimes are provided with a thickened base.

Composite Silhouette Bowls

G3M composite silhouette bowls first appear in the Early Liobaa phase but they are often difficult to reliably distinguish. In many cases the contour break

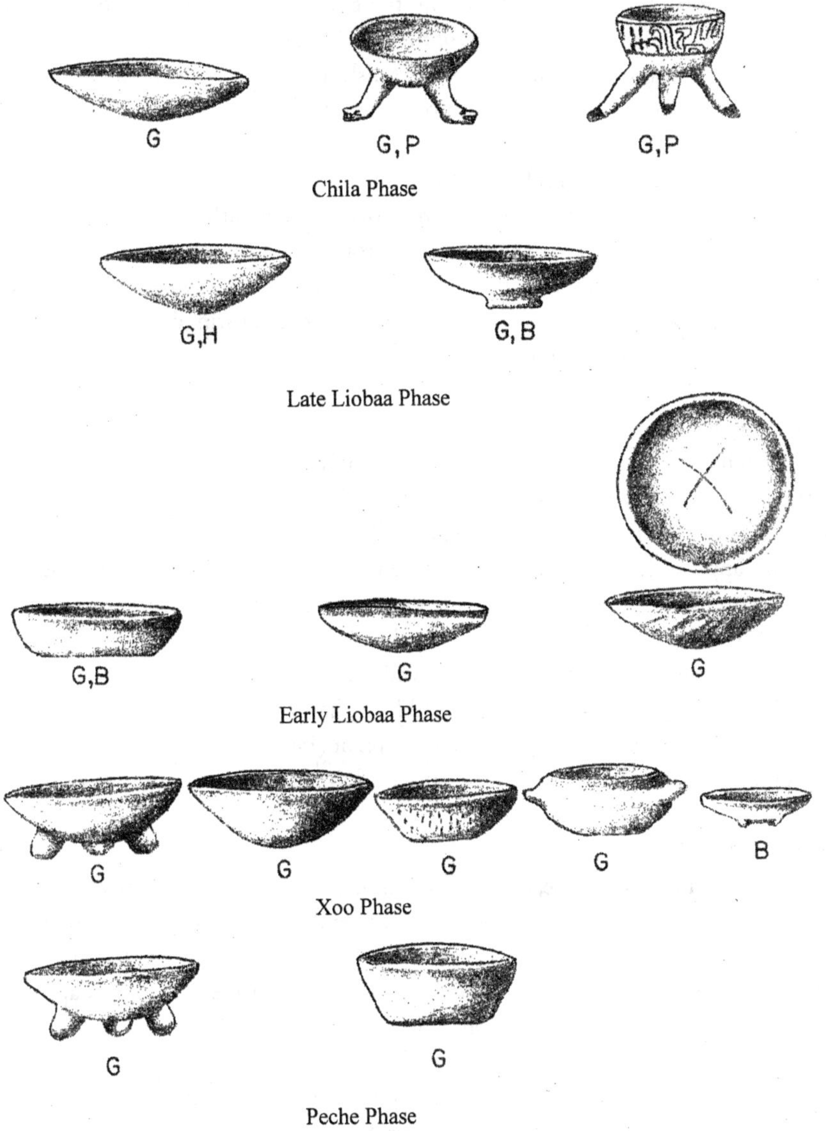

2.5 Development of hemispherical bowls from Peche (bottom) through Chila phases (top); B=brownware, C=creamware, G=grayware, H=Huitzo Polished Cream, P=polychrome.

appears to be a by-product of the forming and finishing techniques applied to G3M hemispherical bowls. The hemispherical bowl is scraped on the exterior surface, beginning at the lip and continuing to the bowl's base. It is this scraping process that sometimes produces an angle in the bowl's contour, high up on the wall beneath the lip (Figure 2.6). In many examples from the Early Liobaa phase, the break is not uniform around significant portions of the vessel circumference, suggesting that the contour break was more a function of the finishing process than an intended shape modification. There are examples, however, where the contour break appears uniform and well defined.

It is during the Late Liobaa and Chila phases when the composite silhouette bowls are unmistakably defined. The break occurs frequently on both the interior and exterior surfaces. The vessel wall, rising from the contour break to the lip, may be vertical or recto-divergent. Two-tone differential firing is present on many vessels. Chila phase composite silhouette bowls are further distinguished by the addition of elongated hollow supports.

Botellones

Botellones, sometimes called floreros, appear in the Peche phase where they are distinguished by high narrow necks and spherical bodies—characteristics that carry on from the Early Classic Pitao phase (Figure 2.7). A somewhat squatter variant also appears during the Xoo phase, and it is this form that prevails throughout the remainder of the phase. Particularly distinctive of the Xoo phase is the addition of a Cociyo (Zapotec rain deity) mask to the vessel's neck. During the Early Liobaa phase, botellones may be recognized by a wide neck and a composite silhouette body. The flattened everted rim of the Peche and Xoo phases also disappears. It is this shape that appears decorated with Red-on-Cream paint (Huitzo Polished Cream) or with a plumbate glaze. One zoomorphic example is known from the Chila phase.

Cups

During the Peche phase, cups are present in a variety of forms. Made from grayware paste, they may be quite simple in form, resembling a drinking cup, or they may be decorated with appliqué bat or tiger claws (Figure 2.8). The bat claw cups continue in the Xoo phase when the modeled claws are sometimes replaced by appliqué cones. The tiger claw vessels apparently do not extend into the Xoo phase.

Larger cylindrical cups displaying vertical or composite silhouette walls were also produced during the Peche and Xoo phases. Balancán Fine Orange, the Late Classic period ceramic marker, appears during the Xoo phase in two forms: composite silhouette and barrel-shaped cups.

Chimney-shaped cups, made of orangeware, occur in the Early Liobaa phase, and bat claw cups also continue into the Late Liobaa phase. This is also the time when bat claw vessels made from the distinctive A.7 paste appear—a category Caso (Caso et al. 1967:86) identified as belonging to the Early Postclassic. Finally, the distinctive vibrantly polychrome painted and fine G3M-paste tripod cups appear during the Chila phase.

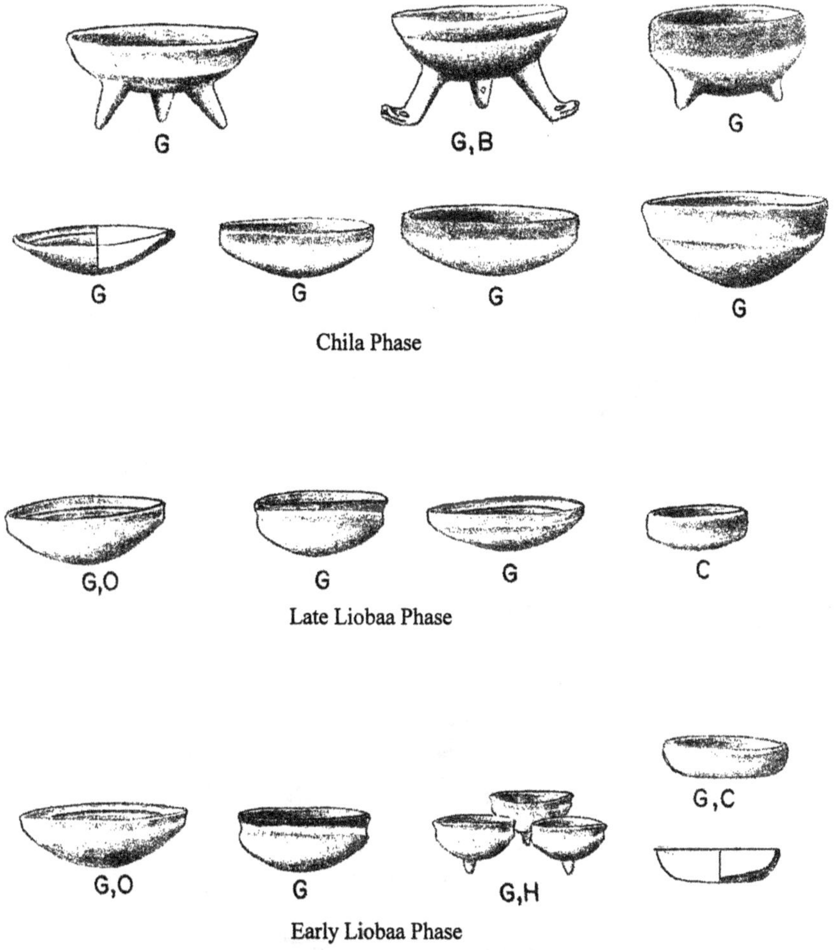

2.6 Development of composite silhouette bowls from Early Liobaa (bottom) through Chila phases (top); B=brownware, C=creamware, G=grayware, H=Huitzo Polished Cream, O=orangeware, P=polychrome.

Ollas

Ollas during the Xoo phase are made predominantly from grayware paste. They were made in a number of sizes ranging from small to large; the smaller vessels were used for storage or serving, and the larger ones served storage and cooking purposes. Distinctive of the Peche phase is the small biconical olla furnished with a vertical spout (Figure 2.9a). This form is also known from the preceding Pitao phase. Small ollas with vertical bridge handles joining the neck and rim are found throughout the Xoo phase and continue in use into the Early Liobaa phase.

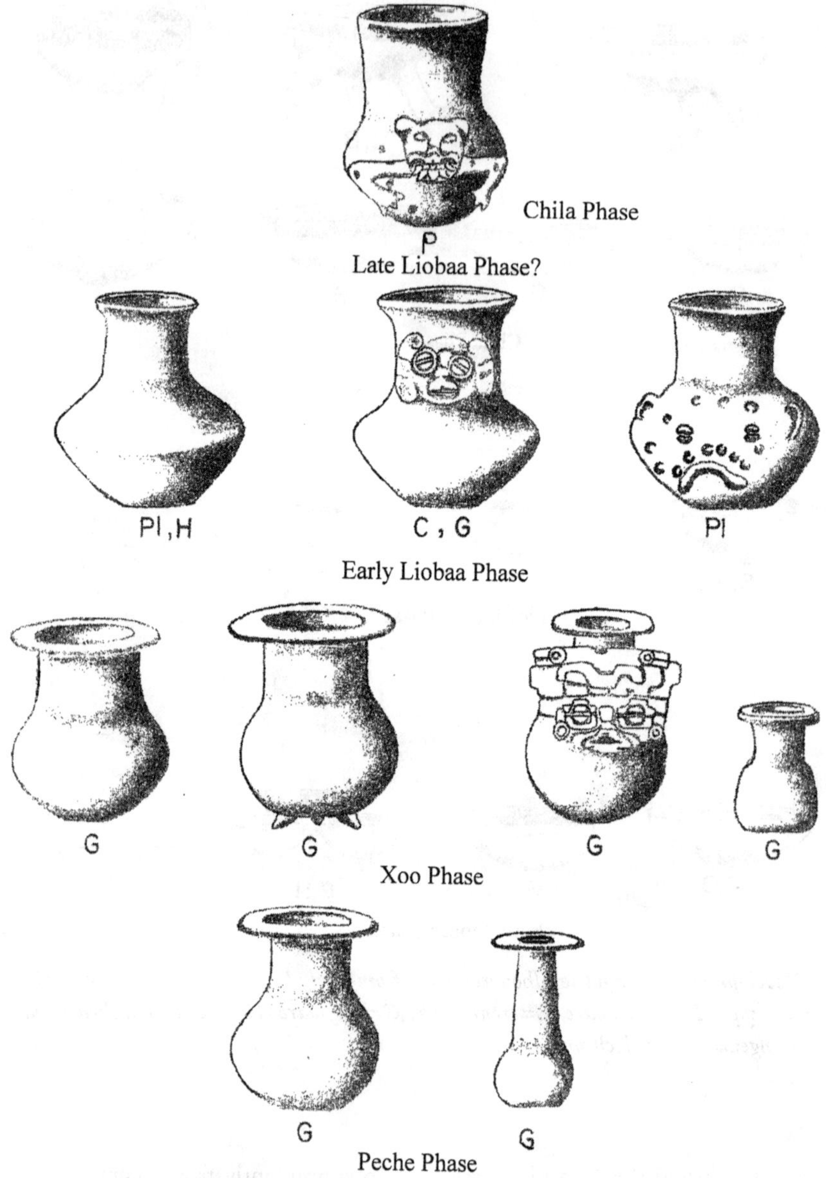

2.7 Development of florero from Peche (bottom) through Chila phases (top); C=creamware, H=Huitzo Polished Cream, P=polychrome, Pl=Plumbate.

Double-spouted ollas appearing in the Xoo phase bear a Cociyo mask, and in this way they are similar to some botellones for this time, for they too are adorned with Cociyo masks. Distinctive of the Xoo phase are large barrel-shaped ollas fitted with

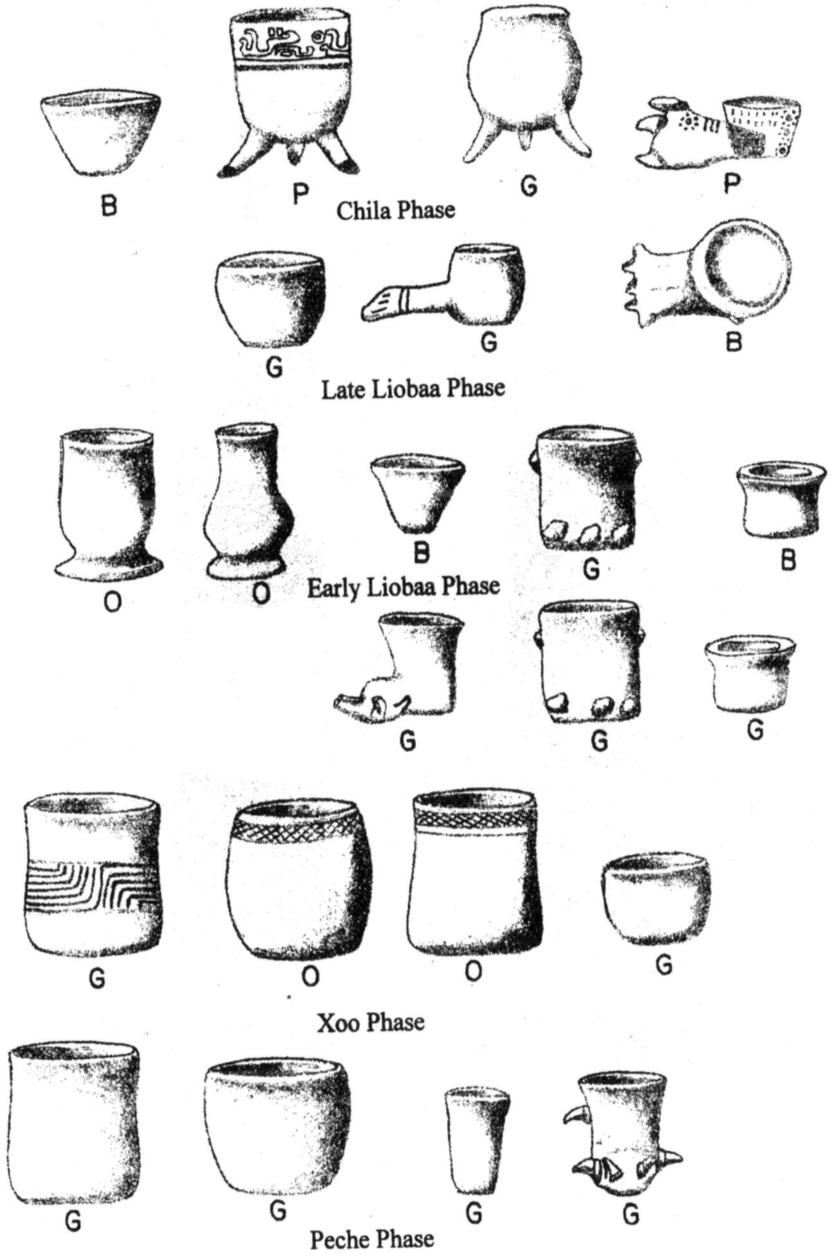

2.8 Development of cups from Peche (bottom) through Chila phases (top); B=brownware, G=grayware, O=orangeware, P=polychrome.

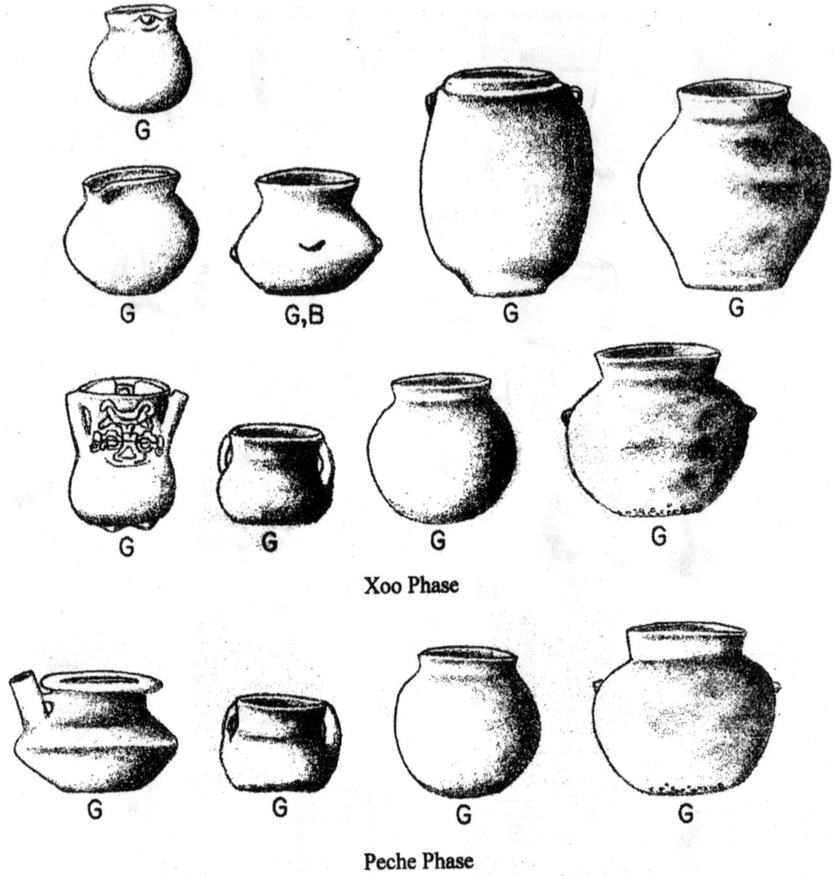

2.9a Development of ollas: from Peche (bottom) through Xoo phases (top); B=brownware, G=grayware.

a rim to which a lid appears to have been attached. Made from gray pastes, they are also furnished with loop handles.

A number of smaller ollas may have been made for special purposes. Fashioned principally in grayware pottery, some are furnished with a simple spout whereas others bear a spout capped horizontally with a strip of clay. Another small form made from gray or brown paste is distinguished by appliqué cones attached to the vessel body.

During the Early Liobaa phase, a host of novel and perhaps rare forms appear. These include the small spouted olla made from A.7 paste. A larger form, provided with a spout that is lenticular in vertical cross section, appears in grayware and orangeware. There are also small ollas with basket-type handles made from cream

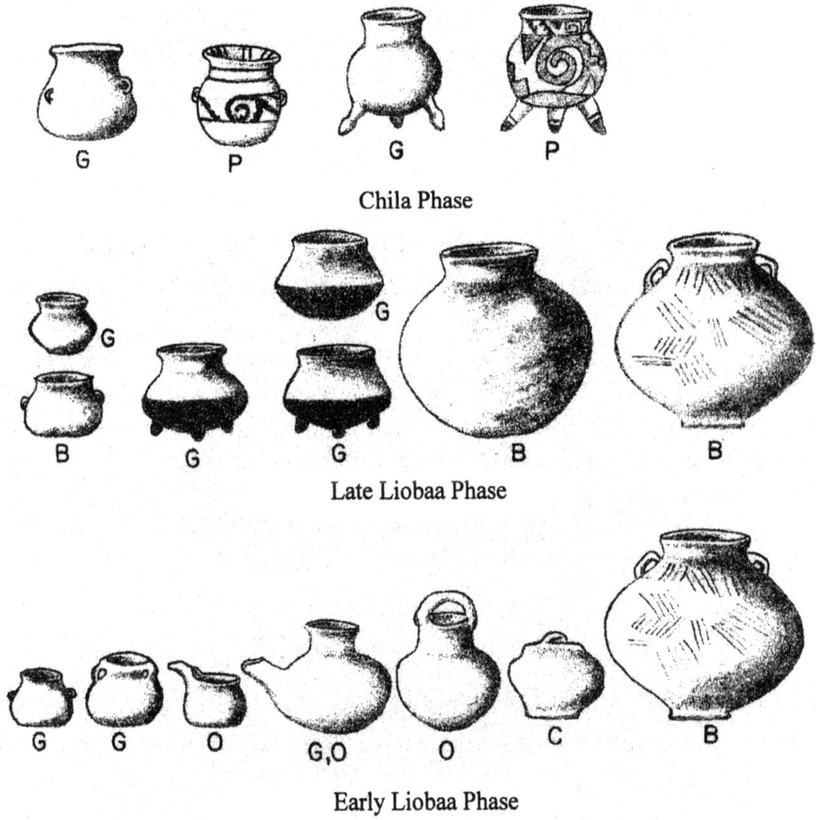

2.9b Development of ollas from Early Liobaa through Chila phases; B=brownware, G=grayware.

and orange pastes. Storage jars, made in brownware pottery, typify the Early and Late Liobaa phases. Particularly distinctive is the finishing technique, which left swaths of short, rough parallel lines over the vessel surface.

During the Late Liobaa phase, composite silhouette ollas appear in G3M pastes. They are sometimes provided with short hollow supports. Ollas with restricted mouths and hollow elongated supports appear in the Chila phase; they are often polychrome painted. A final form, the small olla with vertical handles on the body, is an excellent Chila phase marker.

Cántaros

Cántaros, or water-carrying vessels, are not often found in tombs or graves. The sample in this study is therefore small. Cántaros during the Xoo phase are made from a fine gray paste. Many bear a wide burnished band on the shoulder (Figure 2.10). During the Early and Late Liobaa phases, small grayware cántaros sometimes bear a burnished geometric decoration on the vessel shoulder. Finally, Chila phase grayware cántaros may be adorned with a starburst burnished pattern radiating downward from the neck.

Sahumadores

Sahumadores, or handled censers, characterize both the Late Classic and Postclassic ceramic assemblages in the Valley of Oaxaca. During the Peche phase, grayware hollow-handled sahumadores are fitted with a hemispherical receptacle and sport large holes in the vessel wall (Figure 2.11). These continue into the Xoo phase when they are joined by hollow-handled sahumadores fitted with a conical receptacle. During the Xoo phase, perforations in the vessel wall of sahumadores with hemispherical receptacles may be large or small, whereas the holes in conical receptacles are small or absent.

During the Early Liobaa phase, sahumadores undergo two striking changes. First, the handle in some instances is greatly elongated. The more dominant change is a decline in the quality of manufacture. Sahumadores corresponding to this second trend are made of coarse gray- or brownware pottery. The handles are solid or longitudinally traversed by a small perforation. The receptacle is hemispherical and is sometime adorned with a hastily incised circle and/or X design, and it may also be provided with holes that many times do not penetrate the vessel wall. The solid-handled variety continues into the Late Liobaa phase but may disappear by the onset of the Chila phase. The *sahumerio*, or excised censer, appears in the Early Liobaa phase and becomes prevalent during the Chila phase.

Miniatures

Although miniatures appear at the end of the Xoo phase, they are diagnostic of both the Early and Late Liobaa phases. Made of gray- and brownware pastes, miniatures during the Xoo phase are rendered in *olla* and *tecomate* forms and are sometimes fitted with lids (Figure 2.12). These forms are perhaps short-lived as they do not appear in the Chila phase sample contexts. During the Early and Late Liobaa phases, miniatures were made in gray-, brown-, and creamware. The forms include hemispherical bowls, trays (*charolas*), wide-mouthed ollas, sahumadores, and bat-claw vessels.

A FINAL WORD ON THE CERAMIC SERIATION

If the ceramic seriation I propose is correct—at least in bold strokes—then it should now be straightforward to identify contexts and components belonging to the Late

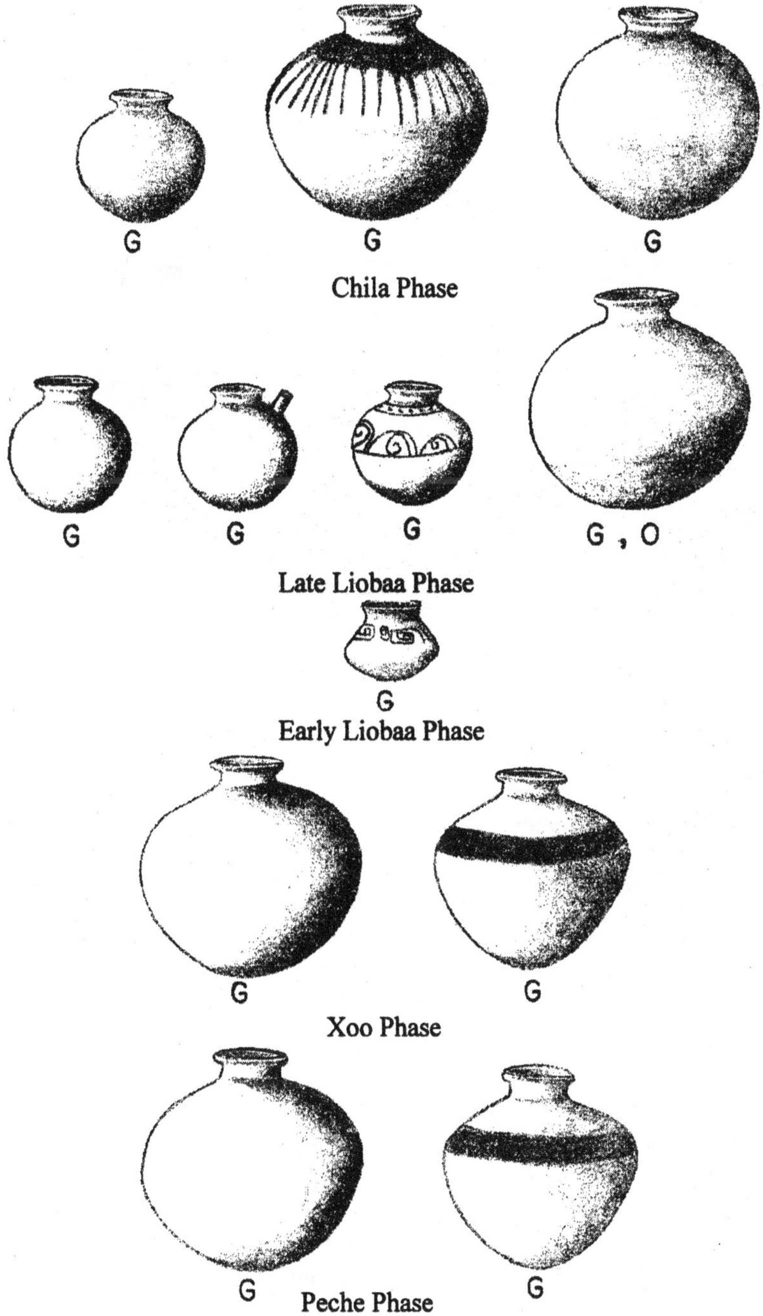

2.10 Development of cántaros from Peche (bottom) through Chila phases (top); G=grayware, O=orangeware.

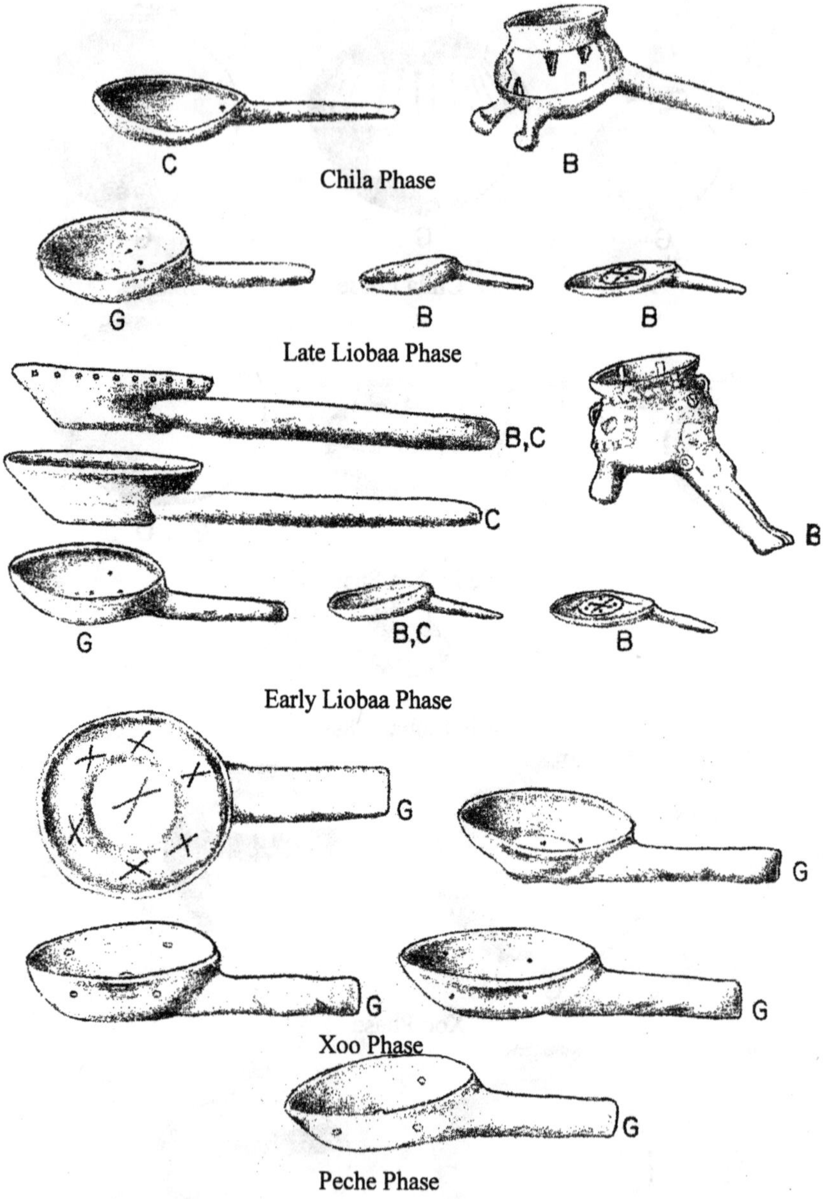

2.11 Development of sahumador and excised censers from Peche (bottom) through Chila phases (top); B=brownware, C=creamware, G=grayware.

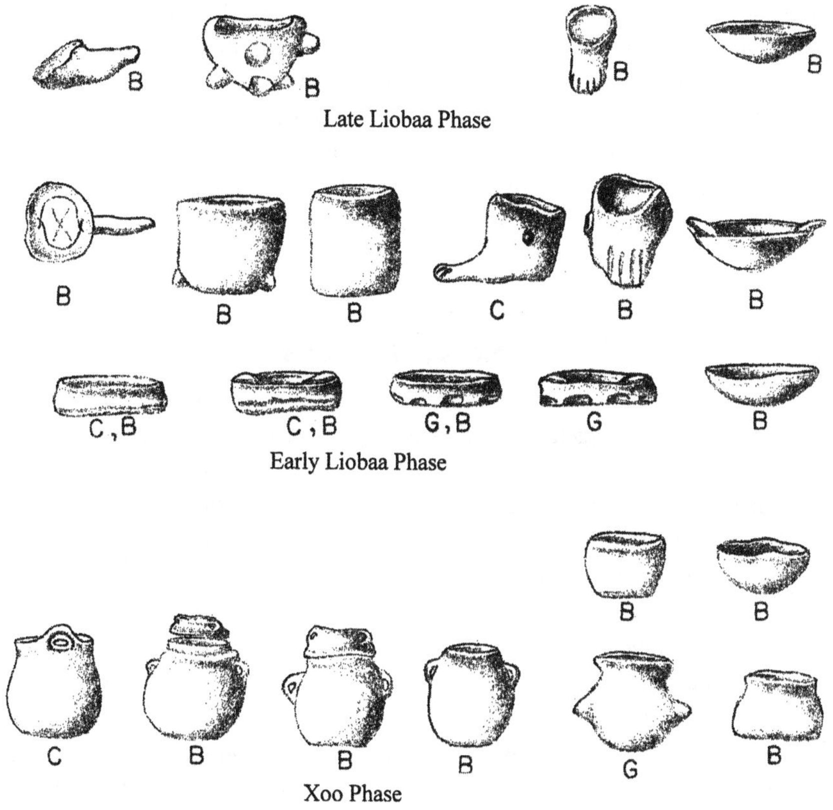

2.12 Development of miniatures from Xoo (bottom) through Late Liobaa phases (top); B=brownware, C=creamware, G=grayware.

Classic and Early and Late Postclassic periods in the context of fieldwork. There are a good number of diagnostic ceramic categories that appear to have been in vogue during each of these periods. Repositioning Paddock's Phase IV to the Late Classic period is key to identifying a viable Early Postclassic pottery complex in the Valley of Oaxaca.

On the other hand, I consider this study a work in progress as I am keenly aware of its limitations. Although the existing valley radiocarbon dates as well as the new series of dates presented here offer strong support for the division of the valley's prehispanic pottery into the Late Classic, Early Postclassic, and Late Postclassic periods obtained by means of the seriation exercise, finer discriminations require more work. Peche phase pottery could not be identified at Lambityeco although one radiocarbon assay indicates the site was occupied at this time. Whether the Peche phase was a valley-wide phenomenon remains to be determined. Similarly, only a single

Early Postclassic Liobaa phase is at present recognizable at Lambityeco and Xaagá although I was able to define Early and Late Liobaa phases in the seriation. Some of the pottery types enabling the subdivision of the Liobaa phase in the seriation may be rarely occurring pottery categories. As the Late Classic, Early Postclassic, and Late Postclassic periods are still on the order of three to four hundred years long, I am optimistic that the work presented here can be greatly improved upon through diligent effort and a renewed recognition of the importance of ceramic chronology among students of the archaeology of Oaxaca.

ACKNOWLEDGMENTS

I am most grateful to Dr. Marcus Winter, Director of the Proyecto Especial Monte Albán 1992–1994, for generously making available to me the ceramic tomb and grave offerings recovered during that project. Dr. Winter and Lic. Cira Martínez López have been a constant source of guidance throughout the course of this study. Dr. Robert Drennan, University of Pittsburgh, most kindly offered advice on coefficients of similarity. I also give thanks to Lic. Jesús M. Arvizu, Director of El Museo de las Culturas in Oaxaca City, who graciously and most expeditiously facilitated access to the ceramic offerings from Tomb 3, Zaachila. I give earnest thanks to Dr. Jeffrey P. Blomster for his editorial skill in helping pare down an excessively long chapter. The figures were selected and assembled by Cira Martínez López and skillfully executed by Juan Cruz Pascual. This study is based on my doctoral dissertation, which was made possible by a number of grants from the Sachar International Fellowship Program and the Department of Anthropology of Brandeis University as well as a Collection Study Grant from the American Museum of Natural History in New York City. I acknowledge this support with gratitude.

NOTES

1. This is the Proyecto Salvamento Arqueológico Carretera Oaxaca-Mitla, directed by Marcus Winter.

2. Paddock (Paddock et al. 1968:23) dismissed an anomalous sixth radiocarbon date, GX-1481 1055±95 CE, because it is inconsistent with the other five highly consistent dates from various layers within Mounds 190 and 195 at Lambityeco.

3. This is my translation from Spanish into English. Paddock alludes to his proposal that Monte Albán was shrinking as an urban center and diminished in power while Lambityeco and other distant centers (Mitla, Miahuatlán, Huitzo, and Macuilxóchitl) flourished politically independent of Monte Albán. Here Paddock is in fact describing the regional political landscape of autonomous city-states, a criterion essential to his definition of the stage/period he calls variously Late Urbanism or the Late Postclassic (Paddock 1966:200–231; 1983c:2).

4. The system that Caso and his colleagues used to classify the pottery from Monte Albán is a hierarchical one. They classify their pottery by applying the three nominal variables in the following order: (1) *barro* or clay, which takes into account clay color, texture, and slip; (2) vessel form; and (3) decoration (Caso et al. 1967:17). In the case of the category G.35, the "G" refers to the gray color of the paste whereas the number 35 is a finer designation within the category of gray-paste pottery based on aspects of form and decoration.

5. Caso, Bernal, and Acosta refer to this phase as Epoca de Transición IIIA-IIIB. The phase was based on two tomb lots of pottery: PMA Tombs 103 and 104.

REFERENCES

Acosta, Jorge R.

1972 Nuevos descubrimientos en Zaachila (1971). *Boletín del Instituto Nacional de Antropología e Historia*, Epoca II, 3:27–34.

Arriola Rivera, María Victoria

1987 Exploración de una tumba Postclásica en Santiago Suchilquitongo, Etla, Oaxaca. Unpublished Licenciatura Thesis, Department of Anthropology, Universidad Veracruzana, Xalapa, Veracruz.

Bernal, Ignacio

1958 Exploraciones en Cuilapan de Guerrero, 1902–1954. Informe 7. Dirección de Monumentos Prehispánicos, Instituto Nacional de Antropología e Historia, Mexico City.

Bernal, Ignacio, and Lorenzo Gamio

1974 *Yagul: El palacio de los seis patios*. Instituto de Investigaciones Antropológicas, Universidad Nacional Autónoma de México, Mexico City.

Bernal, Ignacio, and Arturo Oliveros

1988 Exploraciones arqueológicas en Dainzú, Oaxaca. Colección Científica, No. 167. Instituto Nacional de Antropología e Historia, Mexico City.

Blanton, Richard E.

1978 *Monte Albán: Settlement Patterns at the Ancient Zapotec Capital*. Academic Press, New York.

Blanton, Richard E., Stephen A. Kowalewski, Gary M. Feinman, and Jill Appel

1981 *Ancient Mesoamerica: A Comparison of Change in Three Regions*. Cambridge University Press, New York.

1982 *Monte Albán's Hinterland, Part I: Prehispanic Settlement Patterns of the Central and Southern Parts of the Valley of Oaxaca, Mexico*. Memoirs of the Museum of Anthropology, University of Michigan, No. 15. University of Michigan, Ann Arbor.

Blanton, Richard E., Stephen A. Kowalewski, Gary M. Feinman, and Laura M. Finsten

1993 *Ancient Mesoamerica: A Comparison of Change in Three Regions*. 2nd Edition. Cambridge University Press, New York.

Borgatti, Steve, Martin Everett, and Lin Freeman

1999 *UCINET 5.0 VERSION 1.00*. Analytic Technologies, Natick.

Caso, Alfonso

1938 *Exploraciones en Oaxaca: Quinta y Sexta Temporadas, 1936–1937*. Publicación No. 34. Instituto Panamericano de Geografía e Historia, Mexico City.

1969 *El tesoro de Monte Albán*. Memorias del Instituto Nacional de Antropología e Historia, No. 3. INAH, Mexico City.

Caso, Alfonso, Ignacio Bernal, and Jorge R. Acosta

1967 *La cerámica de Monte Albán*. Memorias del Instituto Nacional de Antropología e Historia, No. 13. INAH, Mexico City.

Cowgill, George L.

1972 Models, Methods and Techniques for Seriation. In *Models in Archaeology*, edited by D. Clarke, pp. 381–424. Methuen & Company, London.

Deetz, James

1967 *Invitation to Archaeology*. Natural History Press, Garden City.

Drennan, Robert D.

1976 *Fabrica San Jose and Middle Formative Society in the Valley of Oaxaca*. Memoirs of the Museum of Anthropology, University of Michigan, No. 8. University of Michigan, Ann Arbor.

1983 Appendix: Radiocarbon Dates from the Oaxaca Region. In *The Cloud People: Divergent Evolution of the Zapotec and Mixtec Civilizations*, edited by K. Flannery and J. Marcus, pp. 363–370. Academic Press, New York.

Finsten, Laura

1995 *Jalieza, Oaxaca: Activity Specialization at a Hilltop Center.* Vanderbilt University Publications in Anthropology, No. 48. Nashville, Tennessee.

Herrera Muzgo T., Alicia, and Marcus Winter

2003 *Tres Tumbas Postclásicas en el Sabino, Zimatlán, Oaxaca*. CONACULTA-INAH, Oaxaca.

Kowalewski, Stephen A., Gary M. Feinman, Laura M. Finsten, Richard E. Blanton, and Linda M. Nicholas

1989 *Monte Albán's Hinterland, Part II: Prehispanic Settlement Patterns in Tlacolula, Etla and Ocotlán, the Valley of Oaxaca, Mexico*. Memoirs of the Museum of Anthropology, University of Michigan, No. 23. University of Michigan, Ann Arbor.

Lind, Michael D.

1991–92 Unos problemas con la cronología de Monte Albán y una nueva serie de nombres para las fases. *Notas Mesoamericanas* 13:177–192.

1994 Cholula and Mixteca Polychromes: Two Mixteca-Puebla Regional Substyles. In *Mixteca- Puebla: Discoveries and Research in Mesoamerican Art and Archaeology*, edited by H. B. Nicholson and E. Quiñones Keber, pp. 79–100. Labyrinthos, Culver City, California.

2004 Lambityeco, Tomb 6. In *Homenaje a John Paddock*, edited by P. Plunket, pp. 45–66. Universidad de Las Américas, Cholula, Puebla.

Lind, Michael D., and Javier Urcid

1983 The Lords of Lambityeco and Their Nearest Neighbors, *Notas Mesoamericanas* 9:78–111.

1990 La zona arqueológica de Lambityeco. In *Lecturas históricas del Estado de Oaxaca*, Vol.1: *Epoca prehispánica*, edited by M. Winter, pp. 287–307. Instituto Nacional de Antropología e Historia, Mexico City.

Lingoes, James C.

1972 A General Survey of the Guttman-Lingoes Non-metric Program Series. In *Multidimensional Scaling: Theory and Applications in the Behavioral Sciences*, Vol. 1: *Theory*, edited by R. Shepard, A. Romney, and S. Nerlove. Seminar Press, New York.

Lyman, R. Lee, Steve Wolverton, and Michael J. O'Brien

1998 Seriation, Superposition, and Interdigitation: A History of Americanist Graphic Depictions of Culture Change. *American Antiquity* 63(2):239–261.

Markens, Robert

2004 Ceramic Chronology in the Valley of Oaxaca, Mexico during the Late Classic and Postclassic Periods and the Organization of Ceramic Production. Unpublished Ph.D. Dissertation, Department of Anthropology, Brandeis University. Waltham, Massachusetts.

Markens, Robert, and Cira Martínez López

2001 Resumen de cerámica de la fase Xoo (Monte Albán IIIB-IV). In *Memoria de la Primera Mesa Redonda de Monte Albán: Procesos de cambio y conceptualización del Tiempo,* edited by N. Robles, pp. 301–327. CONACULTA-INAH, Mexico City.

Marquardt, William H.

1978 Advances in Archaeological Seriation. In *Advances in Archaeological Method and Theory*, Vol. 1, edited by M. Schiffer, pp. 257–314. Academic Press, New York.

Martínez López, Cira

1998 Contextos mortuorios en unidades habitacionales de Monte Albán, Oaxaca, de la Epoca II Temprana a la Epoca V. Unpublished Licenciatura Thesis, Escuela Nacional de Antropología e Historia. Mexico City.

Martínez López, Cira, Lucina Cruz Hernández, Gustavo Gámez Goytia, and Luz María Borja Torres

n.d. Informe del rescate de la tumba Huitzo 1994-1 en San Pablo, Huitzo, Etla, Oaxaca. Report on file at the Centro INAH Oaxaca, Oaxaca.

Martínez López, Cira, Robert Markens, Marcus Winter, and Michael Lind

2000 *Cerámica de la Fase Xoo (Monte Albán IIIB–IV) del Valle de Oaxaca.* Proyecto Especial Monte Alban 1992–1994, Contribución No. 8. Centro INAH Oaxaca, Oaxaca.

Martínez López, Cira, Marcus Winter, and Pedro Antonio Juárez

1995 Entierros humanos del Proyecto Especial Monte Albán 1992–1994. In *Entierros humanos de Monte Albán: Dos estudios*, edited by M. Winter, pp. 79–244. Proyecto Especial Monte Alban 1992–1994, Contribución No. 7. Centro INAH Oaxaca, Oaxaca.

2001 Las tumbas exploradas durante el Proyecto Especial Monte Albán. Vol. 7. Proyecto Especial Monte Albán 1992–1994, Informe Final, edited by M. Winter. Centro INAH Oaxaca. Report submitted to the Instituto Nacional de Antropología e Historia, Mexico City.

Middleton, William D., Gary M. Feinman, and Guillermo Molina Villegas

1998 Tomb Use and Reuse in Oaxaca, Mexico. *Ancient Mesoamerica* 9(2):297–307.

Miller, Arthur G.

1995 *The Painted Tombs of Oaxaca, Mexico: Living with the Dead.* Cambridge University Press, New York.

O'Brien, Michael J., and R. Lee Lyman

1999 *Seriation, Stratigraphy and Index Fossils: The Backbone of Archaeological Dating.* Kluwer Academic / Plenum Publishers, New York.

Oudijk, Michel R.

2000 *Historiography of the Bènizàa: The Postclassic and Early Colonial Periods (1000–1600 A.D.).* CNWS Publications, Vol. 84. Research School of Asian, African, and Amerindian Studies, University of Leiden, Leiden.

2002 The Zapotec City-state. In *A Comparative Study of Thirty City-state Cultures*, Supplement, edited by M. Hansen, pp. 73–90. Royal Danish Academy of Sciences and Letters, Copenhagen.

Paddock, John

1966 Oaxaca in Ancient Mesoamerica. In *Ancient Oaxaca: Discoveries in Mexican Archeology and History*, edited by J. Paddock, pp. 83–242. Stanford University Press, Stanford, California.

1978 The Middle Classic Period in Oaxaca. In *Middle Classic Mesoamerica: A.D. 400–700*, edited by E. Pasztory, pp. 45–62. Columbia University Press, New York.

1983a *Lord 5 Flower's Family: Rulers of Zaachila and Cuilapan.* Vanderbilt University Publications in Anthropology, No. 29. Nashville, Tennessee.

1983b Lambityeco. In *The Cloud People: Divergent Evolution of the Zapotec and Mixtec Civilizations*, edited by K. Flannery and J. Marcus, pp.197–204. Academic Press, New York.

1983c Some Thoughts on the Decline of Monte Albán. In *The Cloud People: Divergent Evolution of the Zapotec and Mixtec Civilizations,* edited by K. Flannery and J. Marcus, pp. 186–188. Academic Press, New York.

1986 Reflexiones en torno a la tumba 7 de Monte Albán: Cincuenta años después de su descubrimiento. *Cuadernos de Arquitectura Mesoamericana* 7:3–8.

Paddock, John, Joseph R. Mogor, and Michael D. Lind
1968 Lambityeco tomb 2: A preliminary report. *Boletín de Estudios Oaxaqueños,* No. 25. Oaxaca.

Pohl, John M.D.
2003 Creation Stories, Hero Cults and Alliance Building: Confederacies of Central and Southern Mexico. In *The Postclassic Mesoamerican World,* edited by M. Smith and F. Berdan, pp. 61–66. University of Utah Press, Salt Lake City.

Rouse, Irving B.
1967 Seriation in Archaeology. In *American Historical Anthropology: Essays in Honor of Leslie Spier,* edited by C. Riley and W. Taylor, pp. 153–195. Southern Illinois University Press, Carbondale.

Sejourné, Laurette
1960 El simbolismo de los rituales funerarios en Monte Albán. *Revista Mexicana de Estudios Antropológicos,* No. 16.

Smith, Michael E., and Frances F. Berdan (editors)
2003 *The Postclassic Mesoamerican World.* University of Utah Press, Salt Lake City.

Smith, Michael E., and Michael D. Lind
2005 Xoo Phase Ceramics from Oaxaca Found at Calixtlahuaca in Central Mexico. *Ancient Mesoamerica* 16(1):169–177.

Smith, Robert E.
1958 The Place of Fine Orange Pottery in Mesoamerican Archaeology. *American Antiquity* 24(1):151–160.

Spencer, Charles S., and Elsa M. Redmond
1997 *Archaeology of the Cañada de Cuicatlán, Oaxaca.* Anthropological Papers of the American Museum of Natural History, No. 80. New York.

Steponaitis, Vincas P.
1983 *Ceramics, Chronology and Community Patterns: An Archaeological Study at Moundville.* Academic Press, New York.

Urcid, Javier
1996 Zapotec Mortuary Practices: Implications for the Oaxaca Barrio at Teotihuacan. Paper presented at the 61st Annual Meeting of the Society for American Archaeology, New Orleans.
2003 Las urnas del Barrio Zapoteca de Teotihuacan. *Arqueología Mexicana* 11(64): 54–57.

Wilkinson, Richard G., and Richard J. Norelli
1981 A Biocultural Analysis of Social Organization at Monte Albán. *American Antiquity* 48(1):17–43.

Winter, Marcus
1974 Residential Patterns at Monte Albán, Oaxaca, Mexico. *Science* 186:981–987.

1978 *Cerro de la Cruz: Una zona arqueológica del Clásico en Santa Cruz Mixtepec y San Bernardo Mixtepec, Distrito de Zimatlán, Oaxaca.* Estudios de Antropología e Historia, No. 12. Centro INAH Oaxaca, Oaxaca.

1986 Unidades habitacionales prehispánicas en Oaxaca. In *Unidades habitacionales mesoamericanas y sus areas de actividad,* edited by L. Manzanilla, pp. 325–374. Universidad Nacional Autónoma de México, Mexico City.

1989a From Classic to Post-Classic in Prehispanic Oaxaca. In *Mesoamerica after the Decline of Teotihuacan, A.D. 700–900,* edited by R. Diehl and J. Berlo, pp. 123–130. Dumbarton Oaks Research Library and Collection, Washington, DC.

1989b *Oaxaca: The Archaeological Record.* Minutiae Mexicana, Mexico City.

1994 Nuevas determinaciones de radiocarbono de Monte Albán. In *Monte Albán: Estudios Recientes,* edited by M. Winter, pp. 119–120. Proyecto Especial Monte Alban 1992–1994, Contribución 2. Centro INAH Oaxaca, Oaxaca.

2000 Apéndice D: Un lote de vasijas del Postclásico procedentes de Santa Ana del Valle, Distrito de Tlacolula, Oaxaca. In *Cerámica de la fase Xoo (epoca Monte Alban IIIB-IV) del Valle de Oaxaca,* by C. Martínez López, R. Markens, M. Winter, and M. D. Lind, pp. 285–286. Proyecto Especial Monte Alban 1992–1994, Contribución no. 8. Centro INAH Oaxaca, Oaxaca.

Winter, Marcus, Daria Deraga, and Rodolfo Fernández

1977 *Una tumba Postclásica en San Pablo Etla, Oaxaca.* Estudios de Antropología e Historia, No. 3. Centro INAH Oaxaca, Oaxaca.

Winter, Marcus, and Jorge Guevara Hernández

2000 Apéndice E: Una tumba Postclásica (Tumba 1986-1) de loma y untendahue, Santiago Suchilquitongo, Etla, Oaxaca. In *Cerámica de la fase Xoo (epoca Monte Alban IIIB-IV) del Valle de Oaxaca,* by C. Martínez López, R. Markens, M. Winter, and M. D. Lind, pp. 287–297. Proyecto Especial Monte Alban 1992–1994, Contribución no. 8. Centro INAH Oaxaca, Oaxaca.

Winter, Marcus, Alicia Herrera Muzgo T., and Peggy Wilner

1998 La tumba 172 de Monte Albán. In *Tiempo, población y sociedad: Homenaje al maestro Arturo Romano Pacheco,* edited by M. Jaén Esquivel et al., pp. 517–529. Colección Científica, No. 365. Instituto Nacional de Antropología e Historia, Mexico City.

Zárate Morán, Roberto

1993 La Tumba 12 de Lambityeco. *Cuadernos del Sur* 2:5–22.

3

Michel R. Oudijk

The Postclassic Period in the Valley of Oaxaca

THE ARCHAEOLOGICAL AND ETHNOHISTORICAL RECORDS

The correlation of archaeological and ethnohistorical information should be one of the key methods in the determination of historical processes and events in the Valley of Oaxaca during the Postclassic period. The mere existence of alphabetical and pictorial historical documentation in a region that has received extensive archaeological investigations over the last half a century creates possibilities that scholars in many other Mesoamerican regions envy. It is consequently disturbing and disappointing that historians and archaeologists alike have not taken full advantage of this opportunity. There are two principal reasons for this failure. On the one hand, ethnohistorical studies using pictorials and documents written in Tíchazàa, or the Zapotec language, have only recently begun and the results are still undergoing considerable changes when new material is found or studied. On the other hand, the chronology of the Postclassic period has largely been ignored by archaeologists, leaving an unacceptably long period without any significant subdivisions and making it almost useless for the correlation with short-period historical processes (Chapters 1 and 2). An additional problem is that the archaeological and ethnohistorical discourses are handicapped by the existence of opposing "camps" of scholars, making the exchange of ideas and a constructive discussion virtually impossible.

Within the discussion on the Postclassic period, ethnohistorical and archaeological evidence has been used without making any distinction between the two. Consequently, one of the major issues of discussion was caused by an adaptation of the archaeological evidence to the historical model—the fall of Monte Albán. That is, the distinction between two archaeological phases (MA IIIB and IV) was made based on the historical event of the fall of Monte Albán rather than the archaeological evidence. At no time have the two disciplines and the information generated by them been compared independently. The objective of this chapter is to propose a Postclassic chronology based on ethnohistorical information that can then be used for comparison and correlation with the archaeological chronology. With such a method I follow Michael Smith (1987:38), who suggests that "the archaeological and ethnohistorical records should be analyzed independently to yield their own separate conclusions before correlation is attempted. When the two records are compared, one should not confuse any resulting composite models with the independent primary data sets." This approach forms part of a broader discussion in historical archaeology, and between archaeologists and historians in general, concerning the nature and status of their respective sources: the thing and the word (Andrén 1998; Malina and Vasicek 1990; Moreland 2001; Small 1995; Trigger 1989). Although there is still much to be said about this issue, in practice it seems best to follow the method of keeping independent records.

THE ETHNOHISTORICAL DISCUSSION

For an ethnohistorian it is surprising that in the discussion about the Postclassic period, which is so intertwined with the historical event of the fall of Monte Albán, only one kind of source material has been used—archaeological artifacts. Of course, the discussion is one among archaeologists, some of whom may have a deeply ingrained distrust for historical sources; but it is unfortunate that in discussions about Oaxaca State, which is so well-known for its pictorial manuscripts, we generally do not see reference to these sources (see Chapters 1 and 4). In my opinion, it has become untenable for archaeologists and ethnohistorians not to share information or cooperate more closely; many of the authors in the current volume attempt to bridge this gap. The Early Postclassic period (after 800 CE) may be a bit early for any relationships between archaeology and ethnohistory, but the tenth and eleventh centuries are fully displayed in the pictorials and are investigated by a range of scholars. Each discipline needs the input of the other. Works like those of Maarten Jansen (1998) about the relationship between communities on the hills of Monte Albán and those from the Mixteca Alta may be controversial for some but can also be regarded as new challenges. John Pohl's (1999, 2003a, 2003b, 2003c) extensive work on the corridors of information linking the Central Highlands, Puebla, the Mixteca Alta, and the

Valley of Oaxaca into an intricate web of exchange is yet another source of inspiration. Bas van Doesburg and Olivier van Buren's (1997) work on the Coixtlahuaca region has shown the extensive ties between this region and that of Southern Puebla. Finally, my own work (Oudijk 2000) has shown continuous contacts between the Mixteca Alta and the Valley of Oaxaca throughout the Postclassic, and more recently evidence for direct contact with Cholula has emerged. All of these, as well as others, have shown that the Valley of Oaxaca was part of a complex web of exchange of people, materials, and ideas, which was in full swing since at least the tenth century. Such ethnohistorical evidence cannot and should not be ignored in the discussion on the Postclassic Valley of Oaxaca since it can give crucial information about the difficult period in which the transition from the Classic to the Postclassic took place.

The ethnohistorical discussion is not without its problems. It is a fairly young discipline if we consider constructive interrelated studies. Before Joseph Whitecotton (1990a) presented his results on the Bènizàa, or Zapotec, pictorial materials, only isolated, uncritical, and/or unsystematic studies of indigenous sources had been published. I have published a broad overarching history based on a study of Bènizàa pictorial and alphabetical documents (Oudijk 2000), but there are still many unanswered questions and uncertainties. Consequently, Francisco de Burgoa, Martínez Gracida, and Antonio Gay's mytho-historical version of the Bènizàa Postclassic Valley of Oaxaca is still pervasive but not seriously considered by "scientific" archaeologists.

Finally, a strong polemic exists between the main scholars working with the Postclassic and Colonial ethnohistory of the Valley of Oaxaca. Whitecotton (1990a) was the first to make an integrated study of various Bènizàa pictorial documents, reaching conclusions that confirmed political and military opposition between Ñuu Dzavui (Mixtec) and Bènizàa groups in the valley as was recorded in the above-mentioned mytho-historical version. My own work (2000) has questioned the historical value of the traditional sources, and through an analysis and comparison of indigenous sources I have come to the conclusion that ethnicity was not an important factor in Postclassic Oaxaca but rather factionalism and interfactional relationships were responsible for shaping Postclassic Oaxaca. This interpretation has led to a totally new Postclassic and Early Colonial history of the Bènizàa relating the Valley of Oaxaca with the Mixteca Alta, the Sierra Zapoteca, and the Isthmus of Tehuantepec into one large complex historical process.

In order to make useful comparisons of the archaeological and ethnohistorical information it is thus necessary to create two independent models for analysis (Table 3.1). Although we are still far from a solid ethnohistorical dataset that allows us to make any profound analysis in relation to the archaeological dataset, there certainly is enough to create a tentative chronology that can be used as a guideline for future ethnohistorical research and as a tool for archaeological comparison.

Table 3.1 Archaeological and ethnohistorical chronologies for the Valley of Oaxaca

<table>
<tr><th colspan="2">Blanton et al. 1982</th><th colspan="2">Martínez López et al. 2000</th><th colspan="2">Oudijk (ethnohistory)</th></tr>
<tr><td rowspan="5">1000–1521</td><td rowspan="5">Monte Albán V</td><td rowspan="3">1200–1521</td><td rowspan="3">Chila phase</td><td>1440–1521</td><td>Cuilapan</td></tr>
<tr><td>1280–1440</td><td>Zaachila</td></tr>
<tr><td rowspan="2">1100–1280</td><td rowspan="2">Quelatini</td></tr>
<tr><td rowspan="4">800–1200</td><td rowspan="4">Liobaa phase</td></tr>
<tr><td rowspan="2">963–1100</td><td rowspan="2">Tanipaa</td></tr>
<tr><td rowspan="2">800–1000</td><td rowspan="2">Monte Albán IV</td></tr>
<tr><td colspan="2" rowspan="2">no records</td></tr>
<tr><td>500–800</td><td>Monte Albán IIIB</td><td>500–800</td><td>Xoo phase</td></tr>
</table>

THE ETHNOHISTORICAL CHRONOLOGY

Until two decades ago the Bènizàa pictorial documents had received relatively little attention from ethnohistorians. Only the famous *Lienzo de Guevea* had been the object of study since Eduard Seler's analysis (1906) over a hundred years ago. Since then, only some partial studies of this same document have been done (Cruz 1983; Marcus 1980, 1983; Paddock 1983a, 1983b). This situation persisted until the 1980s when Whitecotton (1982, 1983a, 1983b, 1990a, 1990b) began to publish his studies of little or unknown pictorial manuscripts. Instead of discussing these as isolated documents, Whitecotton demonstrated that it was necessary to relate the information contained in each of these with each other in order to reach a better understanding of the history they were telling.[1] In my own studies (Oudijk 2000),

Table 3.2 Bènizàa documents with genealogical information

Valley of Oaxaca	*Sierra Zapoteca*	*Isthmus of Tehuantepec*
Genealogía de Quialoo	*Lienzo de Tabaá*	*Lienzo de Guevea*
Genealogía de Macuilxochitl	*Lienzo de Tiltepec*	*Lienzo de Huilotepec*
Genealogía de Quiaviní	*Lienzo de Yatao*	
Genealogías de Etla		
Genealogía de San Bernardo Mixtepec		
Genealogía de Juan Ramírez	*Zoogocho* (alphab.)	
Genealogía Oaxaqueña (San Antonino)	*Yatzachi el Bajo* (alphab.)	

I have contextualized the pictorial documents by using alphabetical Tíchazàa and Spanish manuscripts, through the analysis and comparison of oral history, and by working with indigenous people. In this way I have been able to relate the pictorials to the geographical and historical reality. With these studies, we can now look at the pictorials as a corpus and draw certain conclusions that we could never have drawn if we had been working with only one.

We know twelve pictorial and two alphabetical documents, all Bènizàa, which contain genealogical information that goes back into prehispanic times (Table 3.2).[2]

The document from San Antonino, called *Genealogía Oaxaqueña* (BNAH 35-104), is badly damaged in certain crucial parts, which makes it impossible to verify how many lords are represented and what kind of relationship exists between them. We thus will ignore this document in the following discussion.

So, as a start, if we count the generations or, more accurately, the consecutive lords that make up the genealogies in the different documents, we encounter quite an interesting pattern (Table 3.3). There are three groups of documents: those of one to four generations,[3] those of six to nine generations,[4] and those of twelve to seventeen generations. Assuming that the existence of these groups is not merely accidental, we thus could identify certain periods related with the foundations of the lineages or dynasties as represented in these documents; at certain times, specific historical processes were in progress that resulted in the foundation of lineages during particular periods. Only if we can date these periods, however, will we be able to identify the reasons that motivated these foundations.

The easiest method for dating foundations in genealogical pictorials is to count the generations and multiply them by a particular number of years, although how many years remains contested. Various scholars have proposed different estimations. For example, Alfonso Caso (1977–1979, 1:128) calculated 22.5 years per generation. Mary Elizabeth Smith, in agreement with Emily Rabin, used 23 years for every generation (Smith and Parmenter 1991:45), whereas Jansen and Pérez Jiménez (2000:147) count 18 to 20 years for each generation. It is not clear how

Table 3.3 Number of genealogies in the Bènizàa pictorials

Place	*Prehispanic Generations*	*Colonial Generations*
Tabaá 3	1	(4)
Tehuantepec (*L. de Huilotepec*)	2	2
Tehuantepec (*L. de Guevea*)	2	1
Quiaviní	3	3
Tiltepec 3	(4)	4
Etla	6	4
Zoogocho	7	—
Yatzachi el Bajo	7	—
Zaachila (*L. de Guevea / C. Nuttall*)	5 (+2)	—
Yatao	9	1
Macuilxochitl	12	2
Tetipac (*Tabaá 2*)	12 (+1)	
Juan Ramírez	13	2
San Bernardo Mixtepec	(14)	2
Quiachila (*S. Matheo Mixtepec*)	15	6
Quialoo	17	5

Table 3.4 Determining average years per generation

Village	*Period*	*Generations*	*Average*
Acatlan	1232–1550	15	21.2
Ñuñaha	1248–1521	11	24.8
Teozacoalco	1125–1450	13	25.0
Tilantongo	990–1450	19	24.2
Añute	968–1521	23	24.0
Coixtlahuaca	1096–1457	18	21.8
			141.0 / 6 = 23.5

these estimates were determined, but if we gather the information rendered by genealogies that can be dated, an average of 23.5 years per generation is reached.

What Are Lineages, Genealogies, and Generations?

Ethnohistorians are notorious for their loose use of terminology. For example, we use the term "genealogy" when anthropologically speaking it is not a genealogy to which we refer. Although anthropologists do not always distinguish between lineage and genealogy, here I use that distinction. I use the term "lineage" to refer to the maximum lineage, or "all the generations and all colateral descendants of the first ancestor" (Harris 2001:434). The most extensive documents that exist (*Codices Bodley, Nuttall, and Selden*) only give "the cognatic lineage which uses both filiations, masculine and feminine, to . . . deduce their obligations, rights and privileges in respect to other persons and in relation with many other aspects of social life" (ibid.:428). The use of the term "genealogy" will be restricted to the series of consecutive lords of a city-state; that is, to the succession itself and thus ignoring the affiliation between its members. Finally, "generation" will refer to a particular level within a genealogy; thus, each new lord will represent a new generation. Within the discipline of pictorial studies, the Aztec rulers Axayacatl and Tizoc are counted as two distinct generations in the well-known Mexica-Tenochca genealogy even though we know they were brothers.[5]

In the majority of the documents related with the nobility, the succession of rulers is represented as a genealogy—lords who ruled one after the other in their *señorío,* or kingdom. Such a representation suggests a direct line, or an ideal inheritance, from father to son during various generations. Although this situation is possible, in many cases the reality was probably different. The few examples that permit us to verify it show this reality: in the lienzos from Guevea and Santo Domingo Petapa the *coquis,* or rulers, of Zaachila are represented as if they succeeded in a direct line, but *Codex Nuttall* 33–35 makes it clear that this was not the case. The son of the founder never ruled, probably because he had died before he could rise to the throne. The grandson succeeded the founder, but this grandson was not the oldest son since he went to Teozacoalco to found the fourth dynasty of that town. The successor of the founder of Zaachila was therefore the youngest child and second son. There is another case within this same genealogy in which, after the penultimate ruler of the dynasty died without leaving any children, a half-uncle succeeded on the throne (a half brother of the father). Outside of the Valley of Oaxaca we find another case in the *Lienzo de Tabaá I* that shows a founder followed by three coquis. These, however, cannot be considered to represent three generations. Internal information about the lienzo and the Primordial Title of the town proves that the three sons of the founder ruled together in a form of government that is quite common in the Sierra Zapoteca (Chance 1989:128).

This information obviously has serious consequences for using generations as a method for dating historical events or processes. Furthermore, since there are very few cases for which we have historical information, we always have to consider a certain margin of error if we date an event based on a genealogy about which we do not have sufficient information. There are also methods to limit the margin of error. After all, pictorial documents with precise chronological information do exist, such as the Ñuu Dzavui codices and some Nguigua (Chochona) lienzos, which depict long lineages with their corresponding dates. These manuscripts also suffer from the same problems that I mentioned above, but if we can join a good number of them, with their well-dated lineages and genealogies, we can possibly determine an average for a generation. This average then can be used in documents like those of the Bènizàa. It is of the utmost importance to bring together as large a number as possible of datable genealogies since the more genealogies we have, the more trustworthy the average will be.

Another problem is how to count the generations. Many of the genealogical documents begin in prehispanic times and end in the Colonial period. The first colonial ruler is normally easy to recognize because he tends to be represented with some Spanish element, be it his name, clothes, or a beard. This is not always the case, however, as we can see in the *Codices Tulane* and *Selden*, which include colonial rulers depicted in a prehispanic style and simply ignore the arrival of the Spaniards and their culture. When counting generations, we have to decide whether to include the first colonial ruler. This point seems trivial, but if we consider the situation of the Zaachila-Tehuantepec genealogy, the problem will become clear

Around 1260 CE, the genealogy of Zaachila (Figure 3.1) was initiated by Coqui 9 Serpent when he married Xonaxi 11 Rabbit.[6] Their eldest son was the famous 5 Flower, who was buried in Tomb 1 in Zaachila and whose marriage is mentioned in the *Relaciones Geográficas* of Zaachila. This matrimony took place around 1280 CE, but we know that 5 Flower never ruled in Zaachila. His son, Coqui 3 Crocodile, did rule and he succeeded Coqui 9 Serpent. This means that with 3 Crocodile we jump one generation, although in the lienzos from Guevea and Santo Domingo Petapa this is simply represented as if this coqui was the next generation. From here on the problems multiply. Coqui 3 Crocodile married two women, apparently at two very distinct moments. From the first marriage he had a son called Cosijoeza 11 Water, who later received the throne. From the second marriage, much later when 11 Water was probably some twenty years old, he had another son, 1 Grass. We do not have any dates for this part of the genealogy, but the information of the next generation suggests that these two sons had long lives. Coqui Cosijoeza 11 Water also had two wives.[7] With the first he had a son, Quixicayo 6 Water, who later became coqui of Zaachila. He was born more or less at the same time as, or even before, his half-uncle 1 Grass. Quixicayo played an important role in the Valley of Oaxaca and was responsible for the deaths of two rulers in 1372.[8]

A second date of this period relates to a daughter of the second marriage of Coqui 11 Water, the so-called Xonaxi 3 Crocodile. She married a ruler of Tlaxiaco and had a son in 1402. Considering that the age to have children is between fifteen and thirty, this lady must have been born between 1372 and 1387 CE, making her much younger than her half brother Quixicayo. These dates are therefore another indication that the marriages of prehispanic rulers could take place at very distinct moments in time: while Quixicayo was conquering in 1372, his half-sister, 3 Crocodile, was not even born. Such information has serious consequences for our understanding of genealogies.

When Coqui 6 Water died, he did not have children to succeed him and so his half-uncle, Lord 1 Grass, became coqui. He was of the same age as, and possibly younger than, Coqui 6 Water. As he was not the son of 6 Water, his enthronement probably caused some controversy and political opposition. Consequently, when

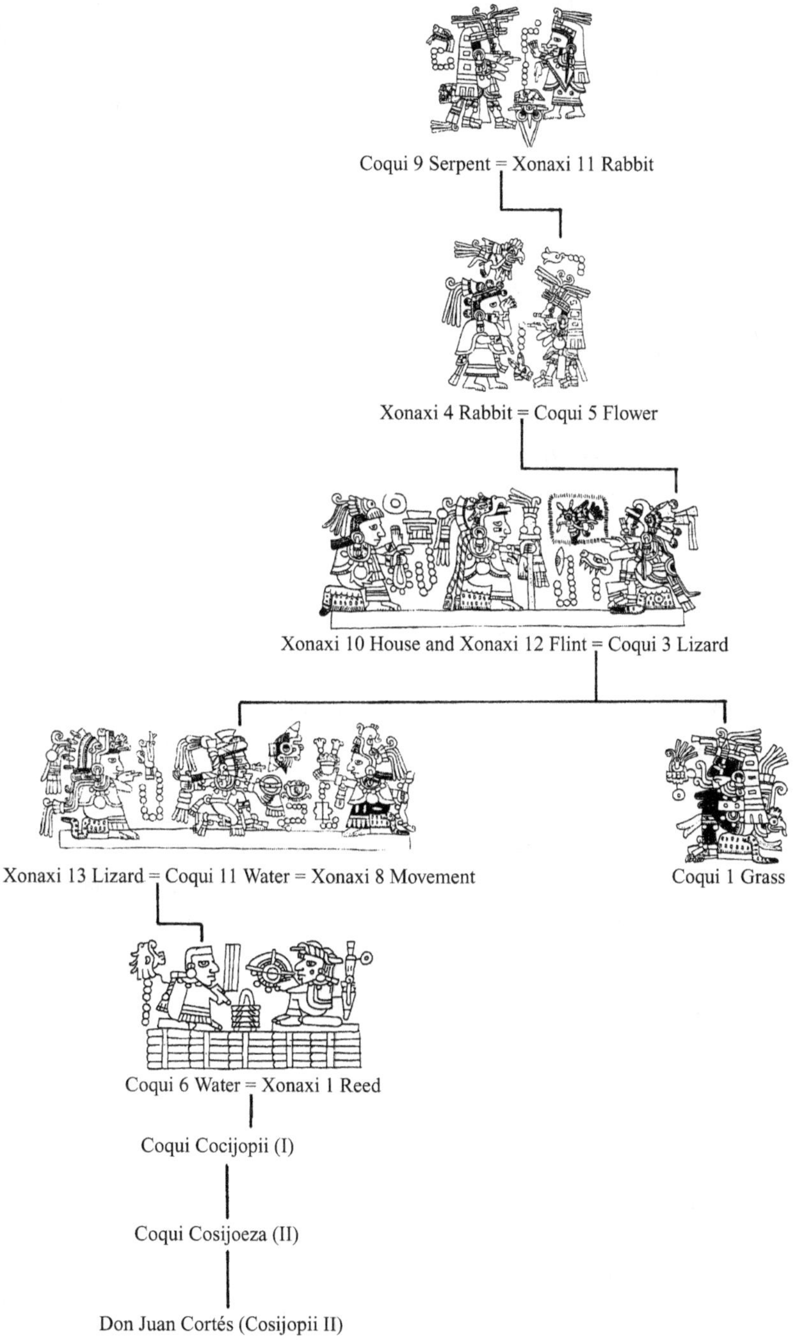

3.1 The genealogy of Zaachila according to the Codex Nuttall *and the* Lienzo de Guevea.

Coqui 1 Grass died, serious problems about the succession began within the ruling house of Zaachila. The result was a power struggle that ended with one part of this noble house going to Tehuantepec. We know that this move took place between 1440 and 1450 CE and that the founder of the new ruling house in the Isthmus of Tehuantepec was called Coqui Cosijopii (I). According to the sources that we have, around 1450 CE Cosijopii was succeeded by his son Cosijoeza (II), who in turn had a son, probably from a late marriage, in 1492. This son seems to have been called Cosijopii (II) like his grandfather. It was this Cosijopii who, as a child, succeeded his father on the throne of Tehuantepec in 1502 and who was still ruling at the time of the Spanish arrival. Later, Cosijopii II was baptized and received the name Don Juan Cortés, with which he is registered in the pictorial documents as first colonial ruler. He finally died in 1562 while being investigated for idolatry.

I have presented these detailed discussions of the ruling houses of Zaachila and Tehuantepec in order to demonstrate the existing difficulties in the genealogies and to make the problem of the first colonial ruler clear. We have seen that in 1260 CE, Coqui 9 Serpent founded the genealogy or dynasty of Zaachila and that the lienzos from Guevea and Santo Domingo Petapa show seven prehispanic generations (excluding 5 Flower and Don Juan but including 1 Grass). For seven generations, and to get to 1521, we have 261 years, or 37.3 years per generation, which is a very high average compared to that of the Mixteca. If we count until 1502, the year Cosijoeza died, instead of 1521, the average is only 34.6 years per generation. We could also include Lord 5 Flower, who did not rule but does represent a generation. This would bring us to an average of 30.3 years per generation. This average is still high but possible, especially considering the old age at which some of the rulers of this dynasty died.[9] Yet, the problem is clear. The exclusion of the first colonial ruler can have significant consequences when we date events through genealogies,[10] but in the case where there is not sufficient historical information about a genealogy it seems better not to include him in the count.

THE FOUR POSTCLASSIC ETHNOHISTORICAL PHASES IN THE VALLEY

Returning to the historical processes in the Valley of Oaxaca, we can recognize three moments of distinct foundations in the Bènizàa documents, from most recent to the earliest possible with the documents.

The Cuilapan phase (1440–1521 CE)

For the first (or most recent) group—that of one to four generations representing the Cuilapan phase—the additional information that exists makes it possible to identify the related historical events that occurred and caused these genealogies to be founded. As was explained previously, the genealogy of Tehuantepec was founded by Coqui Cosijopii when his faction opted to leave Zaachila. In 1554, various witnesses swore under oath that it was Cosijopii who had conquered the region and who had founded Tehuantepec (AGIE 160b), and they furthermore said that his son Cosijoeza had succeeded him to the throne in 1450. The related year with Cosijoeza in the *Lienzo de Guevea* seems to be 1446 CE, but it is not clear if this concerns his succession or his birth. What is clear is that Cosijopii founded the ruling house of Tehuantepec shortly before or after 1440 CE, the year in which Moctecuhzoma Ilhuicamina received the throne in Tenochtitlán and as *tlatoani* of the Mexicas conquered Oaxaca and various other places in the valley. At that time Cosijopii had already left Zaachila. His abandonment of Zaachila, together with many of his allies, left behind a chaotic situation in the valley (Oudijk 2000:102–112) in which the ruling houses and the members of the lineages that stayed behind had to reevaluate their alliances and look for new political relationships. In the meantime, the fights and wars between the different factions continued. The insecurity, which had made an important faction of the ruling house of Zaachila leave, now worked as an accelerator. This process was further stimulated when Cosijopii sent messengers to the Valley of Oaxaca to invite people to migrate to the Isthmus, the new land that had been conquered so recently (AGIE 160b:255v).

The crisis in the Valley of Oaxaca around 1440 CE seems reason enough to explain the foundations of new genealogies, which, according to the documents with one to four generations, took place outside of the valley. Two are in the Sierra Zapoteca[11] and two in the Isthmus (see Figure 1.1). The fifth genealogy is from Quiaviní, a village on the border of the Valley of Oaxaca and the Sierra Sur. Documentation related to this village informs us that it was (re)founded "so they have an entrance and exit in the town of Tehuantepec [which] is where the founders and conquerors stay" (*Mapa de San Lucas Quiaviní*; Oudijk 2000:155–159, 284).[12] The faction that founded Tehuantepec left Zaachila but did not forget the valley. In the great reorganization of the political relationships that took place in the valley, this faction continued to influence the señoríos with which it always had had ties and to found and recognize lineages, and it probably promoted the division between the different existing factions.

The Zaachila Phase (1280–1440 CE)

The group of documents with six to nine generations, representing the Zaachila phase, shows other dynamics. Whereas the foundations of the first group of genealogies took place as a consequence of times of crisis, the foundations of the second group were caused by the opposite: a policy of expansion and integration that resulted in a chain of señoríos related through matrimonies and, surely, ties of reciprocity or clientelism.

As noted above, the genealogy of Zaachila, which forms part of this group, was founded approximately in 1260 CE. It is anomalous, however, due to at least two very long generations that we should not expect to find in the other genealogies of this group. If we consider the average as calculated above, the genealogies of Zoogocho, Yatzachi, and Etla were probably founded in the period 1356–1380. This period is relatively well-known. The coqui of Zaachila at that time was Cosijoeza 11 Water, whom we know developed a policy based on the establishment of alliances through matrimonial ties. The foci of his alliances were the ruling houses of the Mixteca Alta. This practice was not unprecedented considering that his grandfather, 5 Flower, was married to a noble woman from Teozacoalco and his uncle was the founder of the fourth dynasty in that same town after his marriage to a noble woman from Tilantongo. Thus, it is not surprising that Cosijoeza's son, Quixicayo 6 Water, married a noble woman from Tlaxiaco and that one of his daughters went to rule in Teozacoalco after her marriage to the town's ruler. What is new is that Cosijoeza, probably together with his son Quixicayo, used his alliances to initiate a campaign of colonization.

The documents from the village of Santo Domingo Petapa on the Isthmus suggest that various villages were founded during this campaign (ABCP, Libro 2). These villages, situated within a region dominated by Huaves and Mixes, were converted into fortifications and colonies in order to control the commercial route to Soconusco and Coatzacoalco. We know that during this campaign the region of Nejapa was also conquered and that fortifications were built at Quiavicuzas, Quiegolani, Quiechapa, and Nejapa, creating a corridor between the Valley of Oaxaca and the Isthmus of Tehuantepec (Burgoa 1989, 2, ch. 65:236). Military campaigns and foundations of genealogies took place in the Sierra Zapoteca at the same time. At the least, Zoogocho and Yatzachi el Bajo were founded during Cosijoeza's rule (AVA, Exp. 196:2r–4v; AGNC 390, Exp. 4:277r–v). The situation of Yatao is distinct, as it has nine generations and it is not clear if it concerns an early foundation or that its generations are actually short. If the latter is the case, its foundation may also have taken place during Cosijoeza's rule. Unfortunately, there is very little information about this village, which no longer exists. It is interesting, however, to note that the three villages are located in the southern part of the Sierra Zapoteca—close to the Valley of Oaxaca. The genealogies of the first group (one to four generations) are located in the northern part. I would like to suggest, tentatively, that the villages of the second group were used as stepping-stones for the people of the first group on their way to conquering the northern part of the Sierra Zapoteca.

The last genealogy of the second group is that of Etla, a large and important village with powerful caciques during the Colonial period (Taylor 1972; Whitecotton 1990a). Etla's early colonial and prehispanic history is quite enigmatic. At the moment of its foundation, approximately in 1380 (1521– [6 x 23.5]), Coqui 6 Water was involved in wars in this part of the valley. In 1372, together with the ruler of Macuilxóchitl, he killed the rulers of Huitzo and Mazaltepec, which is probably an indication of the conquest of these towns. Both the alliance between Macuilxóchitl and Zaachila and the conquest of Huitzo and Mazaltepec appear to have incorporated the señoríos of the Valley of Oaxaca into a large confederation that extended at least from Tilantongo, Tlaxiaco, and Teozacoalco in the Mixteca Alta to Huitzo, Etla, Zaachila, and Macuilxóchitl in the valley.

The Quelatini Phase (1100–1280 CE)

The last group consists of the documents with genealogies of 12 to 17 generations which represent the Quelatini phase. Based on the established average, we get the period 1121–1239 CE. Three of the genealogies (from Teticpac, Juan Ramírez, and San Bernardo Mixtepec) simply begin without giving information about the place of origin of their founders, and we do not have other information that we can use to say anything about these foundations. The genealogy of Quiachila, or San Mateo Mixtepec, is derived from the genealogy of Quialoo, or Santa Cruz Mixtepec (Oudijk 2000:177–181), as the second son of the founding couple of Quialoo left to found his own genealogy in 1168 CE, according to my calculations. There is more information about the genealogy of Quialoo. Three "brothers" went to Zaachila to ask for a lord to rule their village. After reaching an agreement, the three returned to Quialoo carrying Pechetene, a new lord and ruler, on their backs. Pechetene married a Xonaxi, initiating a genealogy (ibid.:158–171). Obviously, the role of Zaachila is important here because it shows that the foundation of the Zaachila genealogy was actually that of a dynasty rather than a ruling house. Furthermore, the house of Zaachila clearly legitimated rulers and their genealogies. It is a function well-known from the Ñuu Dzavui documents in which Tilantongo has the same role.

Before continuing, it is important to point out that all the genealogies of this group are from the Valley of Oaxaca, the place of origin of the Bènizàa. The founding ancestors must also have come from somewhere. For example, the founder of the genealogy of Macuilxóchitl is associated with a gloss that explains that he came from *quilatinizoo,* or Lagoon of Primordial Blood. It concerns a typical place of origin, a sacred place, which can be compared to those represented in the Ñuu Dzavui codices, where the founders are born from trees, hills, and rivers, or the Nguigua lienzos, where they are also born from rivers. There is one Bènizàa pictorial example that refers to this Lagoon of Blood: the *Genealogy of Quiavini* (Figure 3.2). It shows a founding ancestor who not only originated the genealogy included in the first group discussed above but who seems to be a much older founder who came from the Lagoon of Blood. He also comes from *billegaa* (Cave Nine) and

3.2 Cave Seven, Cave Nine, and the Lagoon of Primordial Blood according to the Genealogy of Quiaviní.

billehegache (Cave Seven). Chicomoztoc, as it is known in Nahuatl, is mentioned and depicted numerous times as place of origin of various Nahua groups or as one of the places the Mexicas passed through during their migration to the Valley of Mexico. In the *Historia Tolteca-Chichimeca* (Kirchhoff et al. 1989), the barbarian Teochichimecs leave their place of origin (Chicomoztoc) to go to Cholula; during the migration they go through a process of transformation toward civilization, which is marked by the consumption of corn and, related to this, Nahuatl speech. So from the Oaxacan point of view, on the one hand, Chicomoztoc is related to Nahuatl speaking groups, civilization, farmers, and artists, and, on the other hand, is it related with Chichimecs, barbarians, hunters, and warriors. We also see this ambivalence reflected in the Mexica-Tenochcas who identified themselves as Culhua-Chichimecs, or descendants of the Toltecs and the Chichimecs, taking the best of both worlds.

In documents from the Mixteca we also encounter representations of Chicomoztoc. The *Lienzo de Tlapiltepec* shows that the descendants of Atonal, founder of the genealogy of Coixtlahuaca, came from Chicomoztoc. In this case, the place is related to Nahua groups because we know that Atonal came from Tamazolac in the Valley of Mexico. Another case is depicted in the *Codex Nuttall*; page 14 depicts a number of primordial places of the Ñuu Dzavui, one of which is Chicomoztoc, where we see the primordial couple, Lord 5 Flower and Lady 3 Flint, emerging from one of the caves (Anders et al. 1992:118). Here, however, Chicomoztoc seems to be related more with the concept of "place of origin" or "beginning" than with Nahuas of Chichimecs.

The importance and possible exchange of information with Nahua groups in the Mixteca has been demonstrated by a number of investigators. The *Lienzo de Tlapiltepec* is an extraordinary example showing that the arrival of the founder Atonal and the establishment of his ruling house in the Coixtlahuaca region are closely related with the presence of a warrior called 4 Jaguar (Doesburg and van Buren 1997:114–116; Jansen 1996). It was this Lord 4 Jaguar who helped the famous Lord 8 Deer Jaguar Claw take control of Tilantongo and began a large expansion with the objective of uniting the whole region under his rule. Jansen (ibid.) has made clear that Lord 4 Jaguar, identified by him as a Toltec, came from Cholula (also known as Tollan-Cholula). I refer to Tollan, with its connotations of important and sacred place, as a legitimator of power, whereas "Toltec" refers to a person from such a place (real or perceived). Famous "Tollans" were Teotihuacan, Tula (Hidalgo), and Tenochtitlán, as well as Cholula (Chapters 1 and 9).

Whereas the arrival of Atonal in the Coixtlahuaca region took place during the period 1086–1096 CE, the alliance with Lord 8 Deer began in 1097. In order to consolidate his alliance with this Toltec ruler, 8 Deer organized marriages between some of his family members with people from Cholula. Due to these kinds of relationships, corridors of contact were established between the two regions that were based on the exchange of people, ideas, beliefs, and goods (Pohl 1999, 2003a, 2003b, 2003c; Pohl and Hook 2001:12). Cultural expressions extended across large regions, ignoring ethnic boundaries.

Considering this exchange of people and ideas, we can try to relate this third group's period of foundations with a historical process. Various elements of the discussed documents suggest that the foundations of this group are related to migrations that began during the process of decay and fall of Tula, which continued over a long period. More specifically, they seem to be related to the arrival of Lord 4 Jaguar in what today is known as the state of Oaxaca. There is no information about Lord 4 Jaguar in the Valley of Oaxaca, but there are indications suggesting that the foundations under discussion here took place at the time the "Toltecs" arrived in the valley. In the *Genealogy of Quialoo*, the son and successor of the founder bothered the people of Zaquita. Zaaguijta is the Bènizàa name of Mexico City and can be translated as "Place of Reed"—Tollan. Obviously, at the time these events took place Tenochtitlán was not yet a place of any importance. Thus, the Tollan to which those of Quialoo are referring is probably Cholula, which was going through a process of expansion at that time.

Furthermore, there are indications that the Lagoon of Primordial Blood—place of origin of the founders of Quialoo and Quiaviní—is a reference to a conceptual place related with foundations, places of origin and beginning. In litigation between Santo Domingo Yojovi and Santa Catarina Yetzelalag, their authorities presented a *probanza*, which begins with the following text:

3.3 Tollan and the Lagoon of Primordial Blood according to the Relación Geográfica *of Cholula.*

> [T]itza diaa la Provanza resolao yelayeti yelayaa racagobechi ditza *niga yaggahua yelarene niga saguita* goca sichite gati bida benee gastila laa cortez bida xie guia yeche niga *saguita* goxie yogo benee goqui dipalachijhui yala quie gosalanie *yaggahua yelarenee* goca sichijte goca titza galag goti Rey quie bene yndio.
>
> [Word of the Generation, and Probanza: It begins in peace and conformity. The word was negotiated *there in the court of Mexico*, there was much affliction and sorrow when the Spaniards came; called Cortes, he came to take the mountain and the people of *Mexico*, he took all the brave caciques [and] with their soldiers he left, and followed *the Lagoon of Blood*, there was much affliction, it was the word until the King of Indians died.] (AVA, Civil, Leg. 15, Exp. 6, ff. 4r, 6v)[13]

I have presented the important and corresponding parts in italics. The Tíchazàa text literally reads "here in Yaggahua, the Lagoon of Blood, here in Tollan," which is translated as "there in the court of Mexico." That is, neither the word *yaggahua* nor *yelarene* are translated. Yaggahua is a bit difficult to translate but seems to mean "my tree" (= my throne?). I have not encountered this term in any colonial or modern vocabulary or in any other alphabetical text in Tíchazàa. The second time it is used in the text, *yelarene* is translated as "Lagoon of Blood." There is a totally regular change from *tini* in Valley Tíchazàa to *rene* in Sierra Tíchazàa. The context of the text suggests that this lagoon is situated close to Mexico City, but it seems more probable that it actually is a conceptual place like Chicomoztoc or Tollan and that it is related to such a place of origin.

The 1581 *Relación Geográfica* of Cholula is accompanied by a painting of the city in which one block is called "Tollan-Cholula" (Figure 3.3). This is where the pyramid is located; at its foot we see reeds growing out of water, that is, Tollan. A series of red scrolls is represented atop this water, which in Mesoamerican pictography means blood. Thus, Tollan is related to a place of water and blood. A similar yet much clearer representation is depicted on folios 16r–v of the *Historia Tolteca-Chichimeca*. Folio 16r shows the scene of Chicomoztoc, place of origin of the (Teo)Chichimecs. We also see a Colhuacan, or "Curved Hill," and a scene of New Fire, all elements of beginnings and origin. The painting on folio 16r continues on the verso (Figure 3.4), where we see more places of beginnings and origin. The central scene is Tollan, or Place of Reeds, plants growing in a lagoon of which the water is divided into two parts. One side is blue and the other side is red—again, an association of Tollan with water and blood. Trees are depicted on both sides of the lagoon. If we now read the Tíchazàa text again, it is clear to what the author was referring: "Here in My Tree, in the Lagoon of Blood, here in Tollan." So it seems that the Bènizàa of Macuilxóchitl, Quiaviní, Yatzachi el Bajo, and Yojovi are indicating that they have their origins in Tollan. That is, they are Toltecs, or civilized people. Such claims make sense if we consider them within the historical events of the eleventh and twelfth centuries when various Oaxacan ruling houses were established with help of the "Toltecs." Torquemada (1969, book 3:ch. 7) informs us:

> [Nacxitl Topiltzin Quetzalcoatl] came to Cholullan, where he lived many years with his people; whom he sent from there to the provinces of Huaxyacac [Oaxaca] to populate them and all of the Mixteca Baja and Alta, and Zapotecas. And these people say that they built large and sumptuous Roman buildings in Mictlan, which means "hell" in the Mexican language, which certainly is a building worth seeing, because it is claimed that those who made and built it were people of very great understanding and greatness and of very great strengths.[14]

If this indeed concerns the same phenomenon as that recorded in the Nguigua and Ñuu Dzavui pictorials, we could conclude that the Bènizàa foundations of the group of twelve to seventeen generations began at the end of the eleventh century or the beginning of the twelfth and were related with the arrival of "Toltec" lords.

The Tanipaa Phase (963–1100 CE)

Finally, the earliest phase of my proposed ethnohistorical chronology—the Tanipaa—is still shrouded in obscurity. Information from the ethnohistoric sources begins at 963 CE (3 Reed), which is based on the year the War of the Stone Men took place (*Codex Nuttall*, pp. 3–4, 20–21). Traditionally, this war is supposed to have taken place in the Mixteca Alta, but the latest investigations by Jansen (1998, 2001) and Jansen and Aurora Pérez Jiménez (2007) suggest it was actually related

3.4 Tollan and the Lagoon of Primordial Blood according to the Historia Tolteca-Chichimeca.

with the place of Monte Albán and what probably were the last remnants of the state. Some of the communities on the hills of Monte Albán seem to have obtained some of the legitimating aspects of this old powerful center. Of course, this does not mean that at this time Monte Albán was still a powerful polity controlling the Valley of Oaxaca. Rather, the opposite seems to have been true. At no time is Monte Albán represented as an all pervasive polity, but it is rather related with ritual and ceremonies, which could be an indication of its role in the Early Postclassic sociopolitical landscape. In fact, it seems that the War of the Stone Men represents the end of what was left of the power of Monte Albán (see also Chapter 4). For more than a century after these events, no ethnohistorical record exists for the Valley of Oaxaca, until the foundations of the Quelatini phase began and the suggested relation with Cholula became apparent.

CONCLUSION

The pictorial information from the Valley of Oaxaca shows four distinct phases, and during three of them certain circumstances made it possible or necessary to found new ruling houses. About the first phase hardly anything is known besides the War of the Stone Men, in which the last rulers of Monte Albán possibly played a determining role. The second phase, called Quelatini, concerns the eleventh century, when "Toltec" lords entered the Oaxacan region. There they established alliances with the local rulers and, as such, created a corridor of contacts that included the Nahua ruling houses of the Tlaxcala and Puebla regions, Nguigua rulers from the Coixtlahuaca Valley, and ruling houses from the Mixteca Alta and the Valley of Oaxaca. Although the nature of the relationships between the Bènizàa rulers in the Valley of Oaxaca and Nahua lords is not yet clear, the arrival of the latter clearly created a favorable situation for the foundation of houses in Quiaviní, Quialoo, San Bernardo Mixtepec, and Teticpac.

Almost 200 years later another period of foundations began—the Zaachila phase. In this phase, the rulers of Zaachila established a large confederation that extended well into the Mixteca Alta. The army of this alliance made a first entrance into the Isthmus of Tehuantepec under the leadership of Coqui Cosijoeza, lord of Zaachila. Furthermore, this confederation colonized the southern part of the Sierra Zapoteca and took over power in the Etla arm of the Valley of Oaxaca, which made necessary the foundation of new ruling houses in these regions whose rulers are registered in documents like the probanzas of Zoogocho and Yatzachi el Bajo, the *Genealogía de Yatao*, and the *Genealogía de Etla*.

Finally, the last phase—the Cuilapan—was of a very different character. Dynastic problems in the ruling house of Zaachila around the mid-fifteenth century caused chaos and continuous battle to take place in the Valley of Oaxaca, producing massive migrations from this region to the Isthmus of Tehuantepec and the northern part of the Sierra Zapoteca. Once these migrating groups arrived at their destiny, they founded new ruling houses, which are represented in documents like the *Lienzo de Guevea* and those of Santo Domingo Petapa, Tabaá, and Tiltepec.

NOTES

1. Although our interpretations, translations, and paradigms are totally different, the importance of Joseph Whitecotton's work for Bènizàa historiography is considerable. His 1977 book *The Zapotecs* is up to now the only volume that considers Bènizàa history from prehispanic times until the present. Furthermore, it was Whitecotton who initiated the systematic study of glosses in pictorial documents, clarifying the system of calendar and personal names. These are the foundations on which we are working today.

2. Another genealogical document called the *Lienzo de Santa Catarina Ixtepeji* exists, but it is not included here since it only contains colonial information (Doesburg 2000).

3. The number of generations of Tiltepec is in parentheses because I am not sure if it is correct. The lienzo shows four consecutive lords, but the *Lienzo de Tabaá*, which is identical in format and internal organization, also represents other lords. In the case of the Tabaá, we have additional information that demonstrates it does not concern consecutive generations but rather brothers who ruled together—a kind of governing organization that seems to have been common in the Sierra Zapoteca (Chance 1989:128). It is thus possible that the "generations" of the *Lienzo de Tiltepec* actually also represent brothers, but there is not sufficient information to verify this possibility.

4. The number in parentheses does not mean doubt here: the lineage of Zaachila is represented in the *Lienzo de Guevea*, the *Lienzo de Santo Domingo Petapa*, and the *Codex Nuttall*. The last seems to register six consecutive lords, but one did not rule and the last one is the uncle of the penultimate. That is, a new lord does not necessarily mean a new generation. Furthermore, the lineage, or maybe the dynasty, terminated two generations before the Spanish Conquest as is clearly represented in the lienzos from Guevea and Santo Domingo Petapa.

5. Obviously, because at the moment we are going to date historical events based on the Tenochca genealogy, we have to present the real relationship that existed between these two personages. In any analysis one has to use all existing information.

6. The date of 1260 CE is based on the marriage of the son of this couple, Lord 5 Flower; see Oudijk (2000).

7. It is possible that he had more wives, which was common for prehispanic rulers. The *Codex Nuttall*, however, only shows two of them.

8. These two lords are 3 Crocodile and 7 House from Mazaltepec and Huitzo, respectively. Their capture and deaths are registered in the *Codex Selden* 12.IV–13.I and in the *Genealogía de Macuilxóchitl*. The *Codex Selden* also gives the year in which this took place; see Oudijk (2000:132–135).

9. We have to take into account the possibility that two consecutive rulers died at an age of seventy. In that case the genealogy would jump four generations.

10. The effect is even more significant if the first colonial ruler was at an advanced age when he was baptized. For example, if Don Juan had been 55 years old at the time of the Conquest instead of 29, the average would have been 29.4 years per generation instead of 34.6.

11. The genealogy called *Tabaá 3* is that of the village of Tabaá itself whereas the so-called *Tabaá 2* is that of the town of origin, Teticpac. These denominations are based on an analysis of the *Lienzo de Tabaá* (Oudijk 2000:185–208). The Tabaá 3 only has one prehispanic generation and it does not seem likely that it was founded in the period 1440–1450. It is possible that the first colonial ruler was at an advanced age at the time of the Conquest, which would solve the problem. Furthermore, we can imagine a scenario in which the people of Tabaá did not leave the Valley of Oaxaca during 1440–1450 but endured the explosive situation for five or ten years more before leaving for the Sierra. It is easy to imagine that the people of Tabaá, through communication with others who had already migrated to the Sierra (Tiltepec?), knew what they could expect in the new region. Such a situation is quite common among migrants today as it probably was in the past.

12. "[P]ara que tengan entrada y salida en la villa de Teuantepeque [que] es a donde quedo los fundadores y conquistadores."

13. Palabra de la Generacion, y Probanza: Comienza en paz y conformidad. Se negocio la palabra *alla en la corte de Mexico*, fue mucho pezar y sentimiento quando vinieron los españoles, llamado Cortes, vino a ganar el cerro y Pueblo de Mexico, cogio a todos los Caziques valientes con sus soldados fue, y siguio *la Laguna de Sangre*, fue de mucho pezar, fue la palabra hasta que murio el Rey de los Yndios.

14. [Nacxitl Topiltzin Quetzalcoatl] vino a Cholullan, donde habitó muchos años con sus gentes; de las cuales envió desde allá a las provincias de Huaxyacac a poblarla y a toda esa Mixteca Baja y alta y tzapotecas. Y estas gentes dicen que hicieron aquellos grandes y sumptuosísimos edificios romanos de Mictlan, que quiere decir "infierno" en la lengua mexicana, que ciertamente es edificio muy de ver, porque se arguye de aquellos que lo obraron y edificaron ser hombres de muy gran entendimiento y para mucho y de muy grandes fuerzas.

REFERENCES

Abbreviations:

ABCP	Archivo de Bienes Comunales de Santo Domingo Petapa.
AGIE	Archivo General de Indias, Ramo Escribanía
AGNC	Archivo General de la Nación, Ramo Civil
AVA	Archivo de Villa Alta, Archivo del Poder Judicial del Estado de Oaxaca
BNAH	Biblioteca Nacional de Antropología e Historia

Anders, Ferdinand, Maarten Jansen, and Gabina Aurora Pérez Jiménez

1992 *Crónica Mixteca: El rey 8 Venado, Garra de Jaguar, y la dinastía de Teozacualco-Zaachila: Libro explicativo del llamado Códice Zouche-Nuttall.* ADEVA/Fondo de Cultura Económica, Mexico City.

Andrén, Anders

1998 *Between Artifacts and Texts: Historical Archaeology in Global Perspectives.* Plenum Publishers, New York.

Blanton, Richard E., Stephen Kowalewski, Gary Feinman, and Jill Appel

1982 *Monte Albán's Hinterland, Part 1: The Prehispanic Settlement Patterns of the Central and Southern Parts of the Valley of Oaxaca, Mexico.* Memoirs of the Museum of Anthropology, University of Michigan, No. 15. University of Michigan, Ann Arbor.

Burgoa, Fray Francisco de

1989 *Geográfica Descripción . . .* (I, II). Publicaciones del AGN 25, 26. Mexico City.

Caso, Alfonso

1977–79 *Reyes y reinos de la mixteca; diccionario biográfico de los señores mixtecos.* 2 Vols. Fondo de Cultura Económica, Mexico City.

Chance, John K.

1989 *Conquest of the Sierra: Spaniards and Indians in Colonial Oaxaca.* University of Oklahoma Press, Norman.

Cruz, Victor de la
1983 *Genealogía de los Gobernantes de Zaachila*. Oaxaca.

Doesburg, Sebastian van
2000 El lienzo de Santa Catarina Ixtepeji: Un documento pictográfico tardío de la Sierra Juárez. *Acervos* 4(17):28–34.

Doesburg, Sebastian van, and Olivier van Buren
1997 The Prehispanic History of the Valley of Coixtlahuaca, Oaxaca. In *Códices, Caciques y Comunidades,* edited by M. Jansen and L. Reyes García, pp. 103–160. Cuadernos de Historia Latinoamericana, No. 5. AHILA, Ridderkerk.

Harris, Marvin
2001 *Introducción a la antropología general* [Translation of *Culture, People, and Nature: An Introduction to General Anthropology*, 1981]. Alianza Editorial, Mexico City.

Jansen, Maarten
1996 Lord 8 Deer and Nacxitl Topiltzin. *Mexicon* 18(2):25–29.
1998 Monte Albán y Zaachila en los Códices Mixtecos. In *The Shadow of Monte Alban: Politics and Historiography in Postclassic Oaxaca, Mexico*, edited by M. Jansen, P. Kröfges, and M. Oudijk, pp. 67–122. CNWS Publications, Vol. 64. Research School of Asian, African, and Amerindian Studies, University of Leiden, Leiden.
2001 Monte Albán y el Origen de las Dinastías Mixtecas. In *Procesos de cambio y conceptualización del tiempo: Memoria de la Primera Mesa Redonda de Monte Albán*, edited by N. Robles García, pp. 149–164. CONACULTA-INAH, Mexico City.

Jansen, Maarten, and Gabina Aurora Pérez Jiménez
2000 *La Dinastía de Añute; Historia, literatura e ideología de un reino mixteco*. CNWS Publications, Vol. 87. Research School of Asian, African, and Amerindian Studies, University of Leiden, Leiden.
2007 *Encounter with the Plumed Serpent: History and Power in the City-States of Ñuu Dzavui, Mexico*. University Press of Colorado, Boulder.

Kirchhoff, Paul, Lina Odena Güemes, and Luis Reyes García
1989 *Historia Tolteca-Chichimeca*. Fondo de Cultura Económica, Mexico City.

Malina, Roslav J.A., and Zdenek Vasicek
1990 *Archaeology Yesterday and Today: The Development of Archaeology in the Sciences and Humanities.* Cambridge University Press, New York.

Marcus, Joyce
1980 Zapotec Writing. *Scientific American* 242:50–64.
1983 The Reconstructed Chronology of the Later Zapotec Rulers, A.D. 1415–1563. In *The Cloud People: Divergent Evolution of the Zapotec and Mixtec Civilizations,* edited by K. Flannery and J. Marcus, pp. 310–308. Academic Press, New York.

Martínez, Cira, Robert Markens, Marcus Winter, and Michael Lind

2000 *Cerámica de la Fase Xoo (Monte Albán IIIB–IV) del Valle de Oaxaca.* Proyecto Especial Monte Alban 1992–1994, Contribución No. 8. Centro INAH Oaxaca, Oaxaca.

Moreland, John

2001 *Archaeology and Text.* Duckworth, London.

Oudijk, Michel R.

2000 *Historiography of the Bènizàa: The Postclassic and Early Colonial Periods (1000–1600 A.D.).* CNWS Publications, Vol. 84. Research School of Asian, African, and Amerindian Studies, University of Leiden, Leiden.

Paddock, John

1983a Comments on the Lienzos of Huilotepec and Guevea. In *The Cloud People: Divergent Evolution of the Zapotec and Mixtec Civilizations,* edited by K. Flannery and J. Marcus, pp. 308–313. Academic Press, New York.

1983b *Lord 5 Flower's Family: Rulers of Zaachila and Cuilapan.* Vanderbilt University Publications in Anthropology, No. 29. Nashville, Tennessee.

Pohl, John M.D.

1999 The Lintel Paintings of Mitla and the Function of the Mitla Palaces. In *Mesoamerican Architecture as a Cultural Symbol,* edited by J. Kowalski, pp. 176–197. Oxford University Press, New York.

2003a Creation Stories, Hero Cults, and Alliance Building: Confederacies of Central and Southern Mexico. In *The Postclassic Mesoamerican World,* edited by M. Smith and F. Berdan, pp. 61–66. University of Utah Press, Salt Lake City.

2003b Ritual Ideology and Commerce in the Southern Mexican Highlands. In *The Postclassic Mesoamerican World,* edited by M. Smith and F. Berdan, pp. 172–177. University of Utah Press, Salt Lake City.

2003c Ritual and Iconographic Variability in Mixteca-Puebla Polychrome Pottery. In *The Postclassic Mesoamerican World,* edited by M. Smith and F. Berdan, pp. 201–206. University of Utah Press, Salt Lake City.

Pohl, John M.D., and Adam Hook

2001 *Aztec Warrior: A.D. 1325–1521. Weapons, Armor, Tactics.* Osprey Military Warrior Series, No. 32. Osprey Publishing, Oxford.

Seler, Eduard

1906 Das Dorfbuch von Santiago Guevea. *Zeitschrift für Ethnologie* 38:121–155.

Small, David B. (editor)

1995 *Methods in the Mediterranean: Historical and Archaeological Views on Texts and Archaeology.* E. J. Brill, Leiden.

Smith, Mary Elizabeth, and Ross Parmenter

1991 *The Codex Tulane.* Publication 61. ADEVA, Graz.

Smith, Michael E.

1987 The Expansion of the Aztec Empire: A Case Study in the Correlation of Diachronic Archaeological and Ethnohistorical Data. *American Antiquity* 51(1): 37–54.

Taylor, William B.

1972 *Landlord and Peasant in Colonial Oaxaca.* Stanford University Press, Stanford.

Torquemada, Fray Juan de

1969 *Monarquia Indiana*. 3 Volumes. Editorial Porrua, Mexico City.

Trigger, Bruce

1989 *A History of Archaeological Thought.* Cambridge University Press, New York.

Whitecotton, Joseph W.

1977 *The Zapotecs: Princes, Priests, and Peasants*. University of Oklahoma Press, Norman.

1982 Zapotec Pictorials and Zapotec Naming: Towards an Ethnohistory of Ancient Oaxaca. In *Native American Ethnohistory*, edited by J. W. Whitecotton and J. B. Whitecotton, pp. 285–344. University of Oklahoma Papers in Ethnohistory, Vol. 23(2). University of Oklahoma, Norman.

1983a The Genealogy of Macuilxochitl: A 16th-Century Pictorial from the Valley of Oaxaca. *Notas Mesoamericanas* 9:58–75

1983b The Yale Zapotec Genealogy: A Recently Identified 16th Century Pictorial from the Valley of Oaxaca. Paper presented at the Meeting of the Society for American Ethnohistory in Albuquerque, New Mexico.

1990a *Zapotec Elite Ethnohistory: Pictorial Genealogies from Eastern Oaxaca.* Vanderbilt University Publications in Anthropology, No. 39. Nashville, Tennessee.

1990b Zapotec Elite Pictorial Genealogies: New Evidence for Zapotec-Mixtec Interactions in Postclassic Oaxaca. *Mexicon* 12:66–73.

4

Byron Ellsworth Hamann

Heirlooms and Ruins

HIGH CULTURE, MESOAMERICAN CIVILIZATION, AND THE POSTCLASSIC OAXACAN TRADITION

On March 31, 2000, the name of Oaxacanist John Pohl was projected onto thousands of movie screens across the United States: he was listed as visual consultant in the credits to DreamWorks' animated *The Road to El Dorado*. This film chronicled the adventures of Miguel and Tulio, two European castaways who stumble across the fabled Amerindian City of Gold. Although the story was set in the sixteenth century, the architecture of the film's volcano-shadowed city merged 3,000 years of Mesoamerican visual history. From the Formative period (1200 BCE–250 CE) came colossal Olmec heads and "were-jaguar" architectural masks. From the Classic period (250–900 CE) came Tikal-style pyramids, Yaxchilan-referencing stelae, and Bonampak-inspired murals. And from the Postclassic period (900–1521 CE) came the dominant style of the city, the complex stone mosaics of Yucatec Maya architecture. The film even suggested that the sixteenth-century El Doradeños were creating new objects in these ancient styles: during the festivities of the song and dance "It's Tough to be a God," Miguel and Tulio drunkenly cavort on a Formative-inspired colossal stone head carved in Miguel's likeness.

Now it would be too easy (and oh so clichéd) to dismiss this hybrid architecture as the inevitable product of Hollywood fantasy, a postmodern pastiche in which the history of indigenous peoples is evaporated in order to create an exoticizing spectacle—or to further U.S. manifest destiny even as southern borders are increasingly militarized (cf. Lerner 2000). "What else could one expect," the whiny cultural critic would say, "from Southern California, that earthquake-prone land of ruins?" Indeed, an assertion of ahistorical fantasy is exactly how the creators of *El Dorado* describe their Mesoamerican city. Art director Paul Lasaine comments: "A great deal of research went into this film, but we had to keep in mind that it's set in a mythological place. A lot of the design was inspired by the Mayan civilization and other cultures, but it's not meant to be an exact reflection of any one culture." Producer Brooke Breton added: "This is a fantasy. We applied what we learned of the civilization and the surroundings and took it to a surreal realm, weaving in the fantasy elements to achieve a look that is really original" (http://www.roadtoeldorado.com/index_main.html, see "Production/Finding El Dorado"; file accessed May 1, 2006).

These comments aside, a much more interesting way to think about the seeming discord of time in El Dorado is to realize that the merger of stylistic millennia in Hollywood's sixteenth-century city is far more faithful to indigenous practices than one might expect. Formative and Classic period objects and buildings *were* incorporated into Postclassic social lives. Formative objects were worn as heirloom ornaments and were buried in the dedications of Postclassic buildings. The ruins of Classic period cities were visited for religious observances. New architecture and statuary were created in archaizing Classic styles (R. Joyce 2000a, 2000b; Masson 2000; Umberger 1987). Indeed, Postclassic indigenous histories tell of the literal emergence of the Postclassic present from the ruins of the Classic past (Byland and Pohl 1994; Hamann 2002; Sahagún 1950–1982, 3:1–3). And this is something that John Pohl is well aware of. In discussing the earliest historical events in the Postclassic Ñudzavui (Mixtec) screenfolds, Pohl notes that Ñudzavui rulers "are trying to refer to family origins, not as people who come directly from the Classic, but rather as people who are emerging from the ruins of old Classic sites" (Bakewell and Hamann 2001:Debates/History or Propaganda/Pohl). Revivals of the past were central features of Postclassic Mesoamerican societies, central not just to Postclassic ideas about history but to the genealogical origins of elite social life in the Postclassic present.

Scholars of Mesoamerica have long realized the importance of written records in indigenous understandings of time (Caso 1928; Goodman 1905; Jiménez Moreno and Mateos Higuera 1940:69–76). And archaeologists working in twentieth- and twenty-first-century Mesoamerica have repeatedly observed prehispanic reuses of material remains from the past (Caso 1932; Coe 1981:136–39; Gussinyer 1970; King 2003:188–90; López-Lujan 1989; López Lujan et al. 2000; Masson 2000; Matos Moctezuma 1979; Proskouriakoff 1968; Spinden 1913:199–204; Spores

1983; Umberger 1987). In this chapter, I draw on these two traditions of research to explore a less-studied issue: the many ways in which Postclassic Mesoamericans (like twenty-first-century archaeologists) shaped their understanding of time through the active use of material artifacts. This chapter, then, is about the varied techniques of Postclassic indigenous archaeologies, practices that gave meaning to ancient objects in Postclassic Mesoamerica (see Hamann 2002; Umberger 1987:63; Watkins 2000:xiii). When interpreted by indigenous archaeologies, ancient objects were used to shape Postclassic understandings of time on a number of scales, from intimate (as with the familial time bridged by the handing down of heirloom names from one generation to the next) to cosmic (as with the rifts in time between ages of creation evidenced by abandoned settlements and megafauna bones). By engaging with these indigenous archaeological traditions, this chapter hopes to contribute, from a material perspective, to anthropology's long-standing interest in the cultural construction of time reckoning (Durkheim and Mauss 1963[1903]; Evans-Pritchard 1940; Gell 1992; Levi-Strauss 1966; Munn 1986; Sahlins 1985), as well as to more recent interests in the study of archaeology as a social practice (Abu El-Haj 1998; Dietler 1994; Schmidt and Patterson 1995; Trigger 1980; Watkins 2000).

Specifically, this chapter focuses on the indigenous archaeologies of the Postclassic Oaxacan Tradition—that is, the ways in which Postclassic Oaxacans interacted with the physical heritage of what twenty-first-century archaeologists call the Classic and Formative past. Two questions will be central. First, how did Postclassic Oaxacans use and interpret ancient remains? Second, how did ancient remains both shape and constrain the Postclassic present? I will pursue these questions by drawing on material practices (the reuses of ancient objects and places that we can observe archaeologically) as well as on the discourses about ancient ruins and things recorded in Late Postclassic histories (primarily the Ñudzavui screenfolds, but also the wall paintings at Mitla and the imagery of a turquoise mosaic disk). Four themes will be explored in four main sections: Ruins, Heirlooms, High Culture? and Mesoamerican Civilization.

In Ruins, I argue that Postclassic Oaxacans had a visual convention for representing ruined settlements (i.e., Classic or Formative sites) in their written histories. By recognizing this visual convention for ruins, we can see how important ruined places were in indigenous representations of the Postclassic landscape. And by looking for patterns in how these ruins were represented, we can learn about how people thought about ruins—the remains of Classic and Formative buildings. In Heirlooms, I narrow the scale, focusing on the portable artifacts from the pre-Postclassic past that circulated in Postclassic Oaxacan communities. Again I draw on both textual and material evidence, arguing that the inheritance of an unusual personal name by a daughter from her mother in the *Codex Nuttall* may indicate the inheritance of an heirloomed Classic greenstone face. The third and fourth sections broaden in scope. Since both Ruins and Heirlooms are dependent on written records created by and concerned with the elite class, the third section—High Culture?—critiques recent claims that an interest in the physical remains of the past was necessarily limited to elites. Excavated evidence from two "post-collapse societies" in Early Postclassic Oaxaca and Honduras reveals how the members of minimally stratified societies reoccupied, reused, and meaningfully manipulated the detritus of ruined Classic period centers. Finally, in Mesoamerican Civilization I consider how indigenous interactions with the physical remains of the past may have shaped the dynamic creation of continuities in beliefs and practices that characterize the culture area of Mesoamerica across 3,000 years. In sum, Ruins and Heirlooms focus on how Postclassic peoples interpreted their past and the things they inherited from it. High Culture? and Mesoamerican Civilization ask how Postclassic indigenous archaeologies can illuminate the role of ancient things in the dynamics (and inertias) of social transformation.

RUINS

The Ñudzavui screenfolds (or codices) make up a corpus of seven indigenous books painted during the fifteenth and sixteenth centuries in what is now the Mexican state of Oaxaca. They recount eight centuries of elite Ñudzavui history, with their latest accounts ending around 1560 CE and their beginnings dated to around 950 CE (see Chapters 1 and 10). This tenth-century period of origin is extremely significant, because this is roughly the period in which twenty-first-century archaeologists date the emergence of Postclassic social orders after the pan-Mesoamerican collapse of Classic period societies in the ninth century (see Chapters 2 and 3; Joyce et al. 2001; Manahan 2003:339–342). The Ñudzavui screenfolds may therefore provide an indigenous historical account of the Late Classic to Early Postclassic transition (at least as this period was retrospectively viewed in the fifteenth and sixteenth centuries). Over the past two decades Oaxacanists have studied Ñudzavui histories alongside archaeological evidence in order to see what the combination of these two types of sources can tell us about this poorly understood period of social transformation.

The origin of this approach dawned in 1960, when Alfonso Caso, in his pioneering study of the *Codex Bodley*, noted that a number of sites that appear early in Ñudzavui codical histories (such as Hill that Opens-Wasp) vanish from codical narratives after an important early event that he called the War that Came From Heaven. In the 1970s, Emily Rabin's revised (but unpublished) correlations of Ñudzavui codical dates with the Christian calendar revealed that the earliest codical events were dated by Ñudzavui authors to the tenth century (Rabin 2004).

Bruce Byland and John Pohl took up these observations in the 1980s, as part of a research project that combined archaeological survey and excavation, ethnographic interviews, and a study of the screenfolds. They linked Caso's disappearing sites—such as Hill that Opens-Wasp—to sites on the ground in the Dzini Ñudzavui (the Mixteca Alta). These sites proved to be the locations of Classic period settlements (Chapter 10; Byland and Pohl 1994). More recently, Maarten Jansen (1998) has tried to correlate these vanishing codical sites to a different set of Classic period locations on the summit of Monte Albán. Although Jansen's interpretations have been critiqued (Pohl 1999a; Pohl and Aguilar 2003:16–23; Pohl 2004), Byland and Pohl and Jansen all agree that the early events in the Ñudzavui screenfolds, including the War that Came From Heaven, are indigenous accounts of the Late Classic to Early Postclassic transition. These accounts therefore should allow us to understand how fifteenth- and sixteenth-century Ñudzavui understood their history through reference to ruined places.

My own work on this topic has considered the cosmological implications of the War that Came From Heaven (Hamann 2002:358–363). I showed that screenfold accounts explicitly depict this foundational war as taking place in a previous age of creation. One account in the *Nuttall* even concluded the war by showing the First Sunrise—a cataclysmic event that ended the previous age of creation and brought about its successor (Figure 4.3). I also argued that the indigenous interpretation of ruined sites as evidence for the destruction of a prior age of creation by the dawning of the "present" is well documented in both sixteenth- and twentieth-century Mesoamerica (e.g., Parsons 1936:1, 216, 220–221; Redfield and Villa Rojas 1934:330–331; Sahagún 1950–1982, 10:191; Shaw 1971:124–126; Tozzer 1907:153). Postclassic Ñudzavui may therefore have interpreted the ruins of Formative and Classic settlements not simply as evidence of a vanished social order but also as evidence of an ancient apocalypse out from which their present, Postclassic age emerged. Rupture, not continuity, was demonstrated to be a repeated theme in indigenous Mesoamerican archaeologies of the sixteenth and twentieth centuries, archaeologies in which abandoned sites have been repeatedly mobilized as physical evidence supporting narratives of originary destruction (but cf. Chapter 11; R. Joyce 2000a:74 on contrastive views of time during the Classic period; Taube 1986 on originary floods).

I also argued that this originary destruction had important social implications, for elites claimed to play a key role in maintaining the new cosmic order under the current sun. Their intercessions with the divine prevented another apocalypse from overwhelming the present age (Hamann 2002:361–2; cf. R. Joyce 2000a:64, 67). As mentioned by Pohl above, in the Postclassic, Dzini Ñudzavui elites traced their genealogical origins back to the War that Came From Heaven. A key component of the truce that ended that war and made way for the present was an agreement between elites and the Earth and Rain. The Earth and Rain would allow humans to practice agriculture in the age of creation about to dawn—as long as elites provided Earth and Rain with sacrifices in repayment (cf. Monaghan 1990, 1995). According to these narratives, pre-Sunrise ruins (as tangible evidence for the destruction of an uncivilized preagricultural era) were reminders to all members of Postclassic society of the role of elites past and present in making agriculture, and thus the civilized existence of the present age, possible.

In the following pages I argue that indigenous elite histories may provide an additional means through which to study Postclassic Oaxacan understandings of the ruined settlements of the Classic and Formative past. I argue that Postclassic Oaxacan histories used a visual convention to explicitly depict ruined Classic and Formative sites (which seem to not have been differentiated, in contrast to the temporal typologies of twenty-first-century archaeologists; cf. Umberger 1987:97). This convention is an architectural platform drawn *without* a building on top. Figure 4.1, from *Codex Vienna* 7–8, comparatively illustrates architectural platforms with and without crowning buildings.

Evidence for identifying the plain architectural platform as the Ñudzavui convention for "ruin" is first provided by a 1593 Spanish–to–Dzaha dzavui (Mixtec-language) vocabulary, Fray Francisco de Alvarado's *Vocabulario en lengua Misteca*. There, the Dzaha dzavui translation for "antiguo lugar"—"ancient place"—is given as *chiyoyata*. *Yata* meant "ancient" or "old," as in *sanahasayata*, "anciently," or *tai yata*, "old man" (Alvarado 1593:22r, 202; Smith 1973a:47). *Chiyo* appears in a number of entries in Alvarado's *Vocabulario*, including in "to build a foundation" ("Fundar, poner fundamento"; which is distinguished from "Fundar, principar alguna cosa"), "foundation of a building" ("Cimiento"), and "site for a house or place" ("Sitio por asiento de casa o lugar") (Alvarado 1593:113v, 63v, 189v; Smith 1973a:45, 47).

An alphabetically glossed pictorial text, the *Codex Muro*, reveals that Colonial era Ñudzavui applied the term *chiyo* to images of architectural platforms. On pages 4, 6, and 8 of the *Muro*, a pair of rulers painted above an architectural platform with a flowering plant growing from it is labeled as *yya chyo yuhu*: Elites [yya] of the Platform [chiyo] of the White Flowering [Strawberry] Tree [*yuhndu*] (Smith 1973b:91, 93, 95; Jansen and Pérez Jiménez 2005:45). Considered together, the *Muro* and the *Vocabulario* attest that Colonial era Ñudzavui described drawings of architectural platforms as chiyo and described "ancient places" as *chiyoyata*, "ancient *platforms*" or "ancient *foundations*." In the following paragraphs, I argue that perhaps all of the platforms without buildings in the Ñudzavui screenfolds are representations of ruins: that every codical images of a chiyo, a platform, is an image of a chiyo yata, an "antiguo lugar" or ancient place. I also suggest that this convention for ruins was not limited to the Dzini Ñudzavui—the wall paintings at Mitla sug-

4.1 Architectural platforms on Codex Vienna *7–8: (a) with and (b) without crowning building. Line drawings by the author.*

gest that the inhabitants of the Valley of Oaxaca used a similar convention to represent ruined places.

Representing ruined sites by synecdochically reducing them to a single platform should make intuitive sense to any readers who are twenty-first-century archaeologists. Ancient architectural platforms are a common feature of the Mesoamerican landscape; it is very rare for the buildings once at their summits to have survived. This intuitive logic behind the depiction of ruins as platforms can be further supported by considering the contexts in which platform-places appear in the Ñudzavui screenfolds, and by linking these depicted chiyo-places to sites on the ground. Both approaches provide further support for thinking about chiyo-places as representations of ruins.

Contextual evidence for the interpretation of screenfold-depicted chiyo as chiyoyata is provided, first, by the frequency with which screenfold representations of

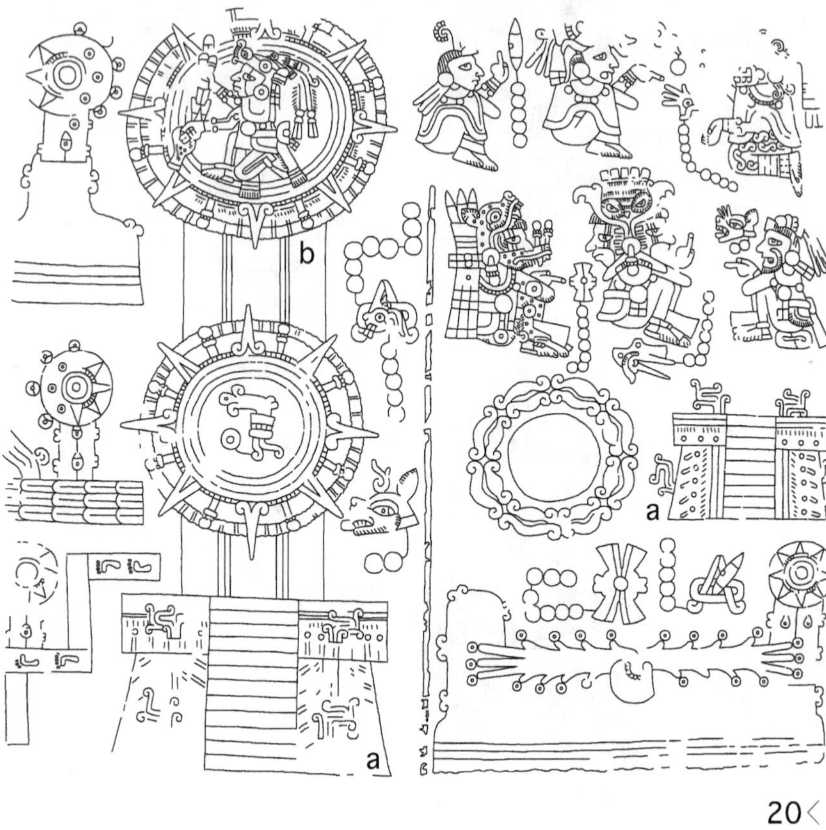

4.2 Ruins and the First Sunrise on Codex Vienna *23: (a) chiyo with song scrolls; (b) the First Sunrise. Line drawing by the author.*

the cataclysmic First Sunrise are associated with architectural platforms. As I mentioned previously, a number of sixteenth- and twentieth-century indigenous archaeologies interpret ruined buildings as physical evidence for the cosmic devastation wrought when a prior age of creation was destroyed by the First Sunrise of the present era. An iconographic connection of First Sunrises with ruined places is not a surprising association, given alphabetically recorded interpretations of ruins from throughout sixteenth- and twentieth-century Mesoamerica. Indeed, the sixteenth-century Central Mexican *Códice de Huamantla* depicts the sun rising above the ruined Classic pyramids of Teotihuacan (Aguilera 2005:8–12).

Similarly, at least five images of sunrises associated with architectural platforms can be found in Postclassic Oaxacan art. Consider the depiction of the First Sunrise on page 23 of the *Vienna*, a Ñudzavui screenfold that recounts the creation of the world (Figure 4.2). On the first (right) half of the page, six deities are shown gathered near a chiyo (from which song scrolls emerge; a twentieth-century Ñudzavui account of the First Sunrise describes a great noise accompanying that event; Dyk 1959:3–4). On the left, a blazing sun rises into the sky above another song-bursting chiyo. This page resonates with the sixteenth-century Central Mexican narratives about the origins of the present age, in which the gods gather at the ruins of Teotihuacan to bring about the First Sunrise (cf. Sahagún 1950–1982, 3:1–3).

A second association of First Sunrises and ruins is found on pages 21–22 of the *Nuttall* (Figure 4.3). These pages mark the conclusion to the War that Came From Heaven. On page 21, the "Skull Sun" of a new age of creation rises into the sky, replacing the "Motion Sun" that lit the sky of the previous age of creation (Hamann 2002:360–1). Immediately after this First Sunrise, page 22 is taken up by a large-scale portrayal of the landscape revealed by the Skull Sun's dawn. This landscape is dominated by the Black Mountain of Monte Negro, Yucu Tnoo in Dzaha dzavui. The black-and-white place sign of the Postclassic polity of Ñuu Tnoo ("Black Town," Tilantongo) is drawn in the shadow of the black summit, and standing upon that summit is a pair of chiyo. Presumably, these chiyo are meant to indicate the impressive ruins of the Formative period city constructed atop Monte Negro (Caso 1938). Again, a representation of the First Sunrise is directly linked to a representation of (ruined) chiyo.

A third iconographic connection between Sunrises and chiyo-platforms appears on a turquoise mosaic disk in the collections of the Art Institute of Chicago (Figure 4.4). Two round suns blaze at the top of the disk above a poorly understood scene of war and sacrifice (perhaps yet another version of the War that Came From Heaven). The sun on the right is shown resting on the top of an architectural platform. As with the aforementioned First Sunrise in the *Vienna* or in Central Mexican narratives about Teotihuacan, this may be a depiction of a First Sunrise dawning from ancient ruins (and thereby replacing the sun of the previous age of creation on the left).

A possible image of a First Sunrise from the Valley of Oaxaca suggests that the association of architectural platforms and ruins was not limited to the Dzini Ñudzavui. This example could once be seen on the wall paintings of the palaces of Mitla, preserved for us in early-twentieth-century drawings (Figure 4.5). There, two platforms without temples, one black and one white, are painted on the back of a jaguar-shaped hill. A starry skyband shines above. Emerging from its orifices are men who hold the white cord of the ecliptic, the path in which the sun travels across the sky every day, and in which the signs of the zodiac travel every night—indeed the murals depict a scorpion along this path (cf. Freidel et al. 1993:75–107). Using this cord, the men pull the sun into the sky from between the twin platforms without temples. The jaguar-shaped hill has been identified as that of Monte Albán.

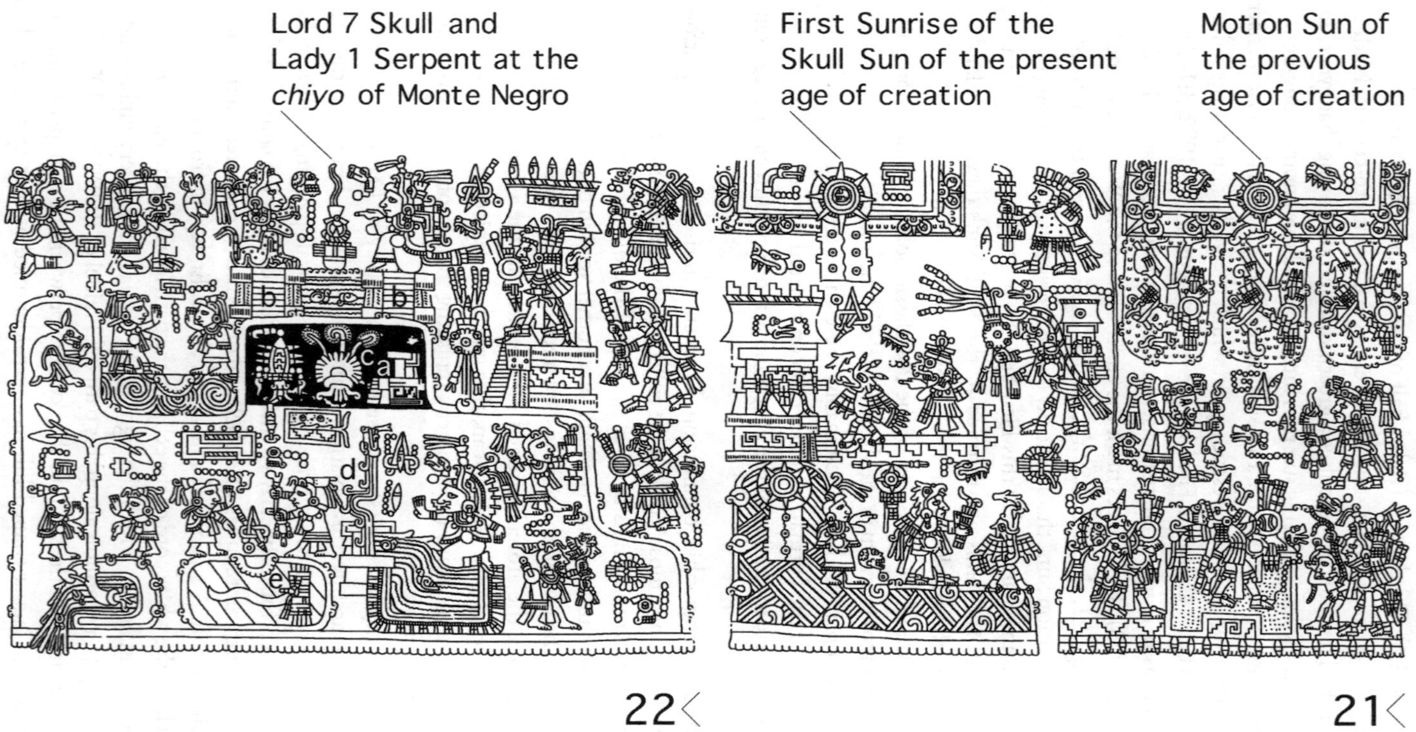

4.3 Ruins and the First Sunrise on Codex Nuttall *21–22. Parts a–e correspond to landscape features surrounding Yucu Tnoo (Monte Negro) also shown on* Codex Vienna *42 (see Figure 4.6). Line drawing by the author.*

4.4 Mixtec culture, mosaic disk, fifteenth century, turquoise, shell, gold leaf, ceramic, twelve-inch diameter (30.5 cm), The Art Institute of Chicago. Through prior gifts of Louise A. and Ruth G. Allen, and Mrs. Daniel Catton Rich, 1997.57. Pre-Treatment. Photograph by Bob Hashimoto, photography © The Art Institute of Chicago. Mosaic background digitally darkened by the author.

Colonial sources reveal that the mountain on which Monte Albán is located was once called Hill of the Jaguar. Documents studied by Wilfrido Cruz in Xoxocotlán named Monte Albán as "Hill of 20 Jaguars" in Dzaha dzavui and "Hill of the Tiger" in Spanish (Cruz 1946:159–60). The 1717 *Mapa de Xoxocotlán* depicts one of Monte Albán's peaks as a hill with a jaguar, and that peak is glossed in Dzaha dzavui as either "Hill of the Jaguar Lords" or "Peak of the Jaguar" (Jansen 1998:73; Pohl 1999b; Pohl and Aguilar 2003; Smith 1973a:205–206). If Mitla's Jaguar Hill is meant to represent Monte Albán, then the platforms without temples at its summit

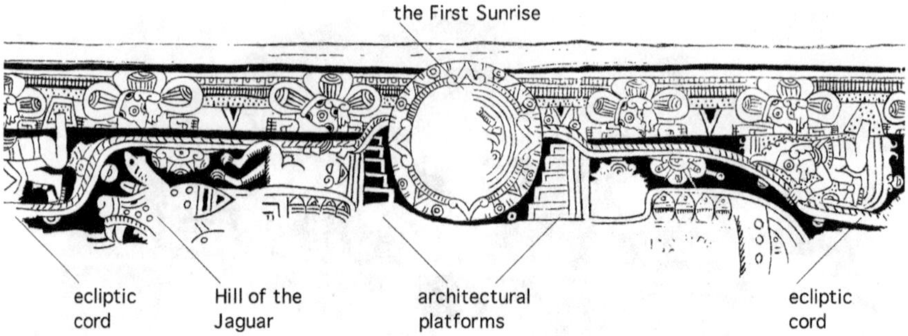

4.5 Ruins and the First Sunrise, Mitla wall painting. Drawing from León 1901.

provide a prehispanic representation of the ruined ceremonial center. Furthermore, Martínez Gracida recorded a Zapotec name for Monte Albán as Yoho Dipaa Copicha, which he translated as "Temple or Fortress of the Sun" (Martínez Gracida 1910). As in sixteenth-century Central Mexican beliefs about Teotihuacan, the Mitla murals show the sun rising from the ruins of a Classic period city. Indeed, although he does not mention the Mitla murals, Jansen has suggested that the sun shining above a colonial depiction of a walled Jaguar Hill in the "Coat of Arms of Cuilapan" may also represent the sun rising from Monte Albán (Jansen 1998:78).

Finally, a fifth chiyo-platform depiction can be linked to the First Sunrise indirectly. At the bottom of page 2 of the *Bodley* is painted a Chiyo of the Axe—Place of Heaven. A Ñudzavui creation narrative recorded in Cuilapan by Fray Gregorio Garcia in the early seventeenth century describes the building of a mountaintop palace near the Ñudzavui community of Yuta Tnoho (Apoala). That palace was marked by a copper axe with its blade turned upward to the sky. The narrative also says that this construction took place at a time when "the world was in shadows and darkness"—that is, before the dawn of the First Sunrise. Indeed, although Garcia's narrative tells of a creational flood, it also tells how the inhabitants of that palace "supplicated their ancestors to let the light appear" (quoted in Pohl 1995; cf. Taube 1986). The Yuta Tnoho palace, then, was a pre-Sunrise construction and would have been left in ruins when the light of the new age of creation appeared—which, if screenfold chiyo are always chiyoyata, is the state in which the *Bodley*'s Axe-Heaven location is depicted. Furthermore, a Ñudzavui cacique's testament from 1612 (written a few years after Garcia's 1607 account was published) mentions a barrio of Yuta Tnoho named "Chilloniñe." This may be translated as "platform" (or ruin-chiyo) of the palace (*aniñe*) (Archivo General de la Nación, Ramo Tierras, Volumen 3689, Expediente 7, folio 7v; Alvarado 1593:160v).

Five Postclassic Oaxacan images of architectural platforms can therefore be linked to First Sunrises. But evidence for the interpretation of chiyo-images as representations of ruined places is not limited to the painted and tessellated images of elite courtly art. Further support for the idea that Postclassic depictions of chiyo were meant to refer to chiyoyata is provided by correlating depictions of chiyo to archaeological sites on the ground. In two of the First Sunrise locations described above, Monte Negro and Monte Albán, images of platforms without crowning buildings can be linked to sites (the first Formative, the second Formative to Classic) that were in ruins by the Postclassic. In addition, the place signs for three Postclassic Ñudzavui communities (Ñuu Tnoo, Chiyoyuhu, Sachiyo) may make reference to nearby Formative and Classic ruins. An image on page 42 of the *Vienna* suggests that the ruins at Monte Negro (which we saw in Figure 4.3 on *Nuttall* 21–22) were called Chiyo Tnoo. *Vienna* 42 depicts the well-known black frieze place sign (Ñuu Tnoo, Black Town) for the community of Ñuu Tnoo (Tilantongo). Representations of Ñuu Tnoo often involve not only this black frieze but also a star-marked temple: in the 1580 *Relación Geográfica* of Ñuu Tnoo the town was named not simply as Ñuu Tnoo but Ñutnoo Huahindehui: Black Town, Temple of Heaven (Acuña 1984:234; Figure 4.6). However, on *Vienna* 42 the Ñuu Tnoo frieze is surmounted not by a Temple of Heaven but by a black chiyo-platform. This may be a representation of the Formative ruins of Monte Negro. This Chiyo Tnoo, Black Platform, would be linked by name to the Yucu Tnoo (Black Mountain) on which the Formative site was built, as well as to the community of Ñuu Tnoo (Black Town) constructed in its shadow (compare *Vienna* 42 and the aforementioned *Nuttall* 22; cf. Caso 1938:55 on Ñuu Tnoo taking its name from Yucu Tnoo).

More intimate linguistic ties between ruined sites and Postclassic communities may be found in the names of the Ñudzavui communities of Chiyoyuhu ("Platform of the White Flowering [Strawberry] Tree"—Suchixtlán in Nahuatl) and Sachiyo ("At the Foot of the Platform") (Figure 4.7). The twenty-first-century town of Chiyoyuhu (and its Postclassic predecessor) is located two kilometers east of the hilltop ruins of Cerro Jasmín ("Hill of the White Flowering Tree"), a site primarily occupied during the Classic (but that continued to be inhabited, if far less intensely, in the Postclassic; Byland and Pohl 1994:100–103; Pohl 2004:233–234; Spores 1972:86–88). Archaeological survey revealed that all of the other sites around Chiyoyuhu are either entirely or predominantly Postclassic. Cerro Jasmín would therefore have been the most important "ruined" site near Postclassic Chiyoyuhu. Perhaps, as Byland and Pohl have suggested, the Postclassic polity took its name (Platform of the White Flowering [Strawberry] Tree) in order to reference the nearby Cerro Jasmín, its ruins, and its vegetation—in the late twentieth century, at least, this hill was a microenvironment favoring a species of white-flowering tree (Byland and Pohl 1994:102–103; cf. Jansen and Pérez Jiménez 2005:45). Similarly, the twenty-first-century community of Sachiyo is located immediately to the east of a high hill called El Pedimento, which has the remains of stone buildings on its

4.6 Variations of the Ñuu Tnoo (Black Town, Tilantongo) place sign. Top left: Ñuu Tnoo Huahi Andehui (Black Town, Temple of Heaven) on the Mapa de Teozacoalco. *Top right: Ñuu Tnoo Huahi Andehui (Black Town, Temple of Heaven) on* Codex Nuttall *42. Bottom: Ñuu Tnoo Chiyo Tnoo (Black Town, Black Platform) on* Vienna *42. Parts a–e correspond to landscape features surrounding Yucu Tnoo (Monte Negro) also shown on* Codex Nuttall *22 (see Figure 4.3). Line drawings by the author.*

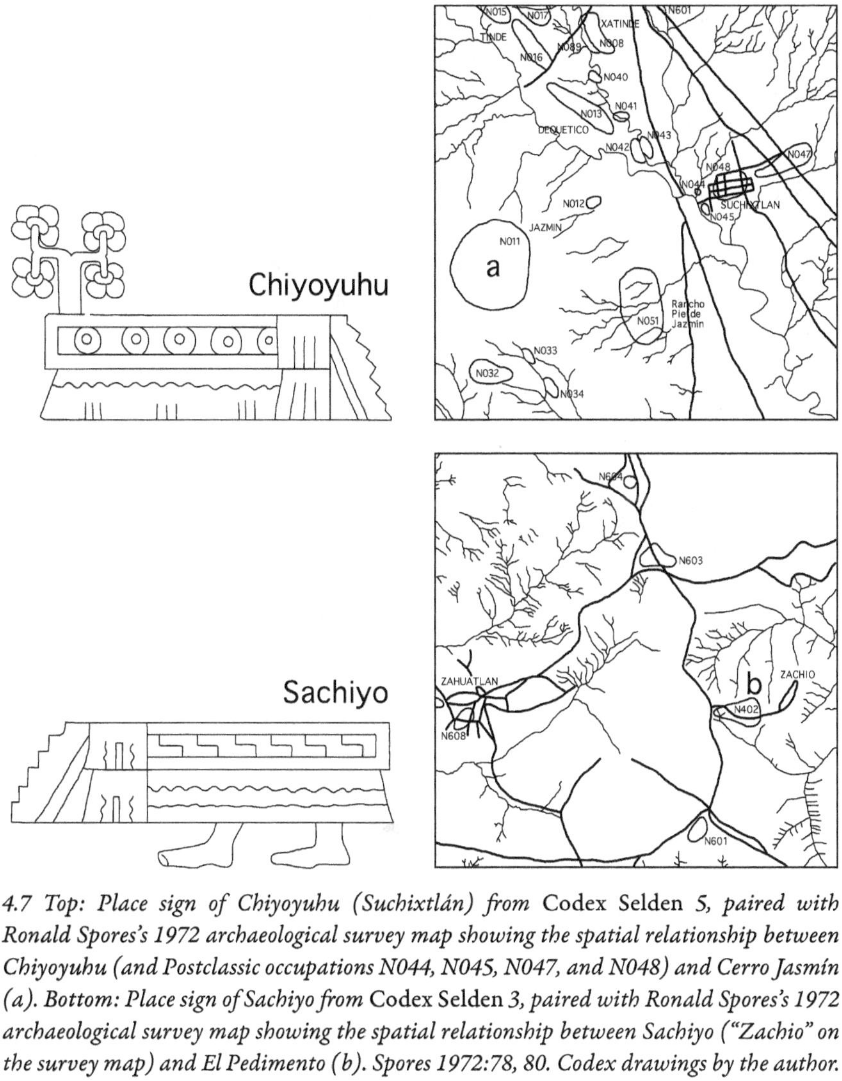

4.7 Top: Place sign of Chiyoyuhu (Suchixtlán) from Codex Selden 5, *paired with Ronald Spores's 1972 archaeological survey map showing the spatial relationship between Chiyoyuhu (and Postclassic occupations N044, N045, N047, and N048) and Cerro Jasmín (a). Bottom: Place sign of Sachiyo from* Codex Selden 3, *paired with Ronald Spores's 1972 archaeological survey map showing the spatial relationship between Sachiyo ("Zachio" on the survey map) and El Pedimento (b). Spores 1972:78, 80. Codex drawings by the author.*

summit. A lower hill adjoins El Pedimento; Spores groups the occupations on both hills as a single site and reports an equal mix of Classic and Postclassic sherds (Spores 1972:129). Additional archaeological work is needed to determine if the higher portion of the site (and its buildings) is Classic and the lower portion Postclassic (and thus literally "At the Foot of the Ruins"; cf. Spores 1983). In any case, regardless of whether Sachiyo's Postclassic occupants were the direct heirs of the Classic inhabitants or moved in after a period of abandonment (cf. Joyce et al. 2001; Manahan 2003, 2004), the place where they lived was a chiyoyata, an "antiguo lugar."

In the previous paragraphs I argued that Postclassic Oaxacan imagery frequently linked architectural platforms to First Sunrises, and I suggested that four sites represented with architectural platforms in Postclassic Oaxacan imagery can be archaeologically linked to what would have been "ancient places" (Formative or Classic sites) to Postclassic observers. Unfortunately, of the over sixty platform-represented places in the Ñudzavui screenfolds, only Monte Negro, Chiyoyuhu, and Sachiyo have been identified so far. It is therefore possible that not all of the chiyo in the Ñudzavui screenfolds are meant to represent ruined chiyoyata. Some depictions of chiyo may represent Postclassic buildings newly constructed for sacrifice or performance; another interpretation (which I critique in the next paragraphs) interprets these chiyo not as Classic and Formative ruins but as Postclassic "altars." Future research may demonstrate that not every chiyo was meant to represent a chiyoyata. At present, however, all of the chiyo places we can link to sites on the ground are linked to sites that would have been in ruins in the Postclassic (which would make the use of a chiyo image on the cover of Ron Spores's *The Mixtecs in Ancient and Colonial Times* (1984) unintentionally appropriate for a work on archaeology and ethnohistory; see Figure 4.8).

An alternative interpretation exists for translating chiyo images in the Ñudzavui screenfolds, which I would briefly like to address. One of the translations for chiyo offered in Alvarado's 1593 *Vocabulario* is "altar." This is the translation that Maarten Jansen and Gabina Aurora Pérez Jiménez have given to depictions of chiyo-places in their important commentaries on the Ñudzavui screenfolds (Jansen 1982:199; Jansen and Pérez Jiménez 2005:25, 45). In a narrow sense, I believe that this interpretation is incorrect: both linguistic and visual evidence suggests that "platform" or "foundation" (and by extension "ancient place") are better interpretations of these images than "altar." However, in a broader and perhaps more important sense, we *can* think of these ancient places as altars—as appropriate locations for making offerings and contacting the sacred.

Alvarado's 1593 *Vocabulario* offers two separate entries for "altar." Altars, of course, were key sites in both Ñudzavui and Christian ritual, and we know that the use of indigenous terms to describe Christian concepts was controversial in sixteenth-century Mesoamerica (Burkhart 1989). Indeed, in 1555 the first Mexican synod ordered that all sermons in native languages be confiscated, because some translations were thought to confuse Christian and indigenous ideas about the divine (Ricard 1966[1933]: 57). It is therefore no surprise that there are two entries for "altar" in Brother Alvarado's *Vocabulario*. One entry reads simply "Altar. chiyo"—but the other reads "Altar de demonios tayuquacu. tayudzana" (Alvarado 1593:17b). I believe that the first entry was meant to describe an altar to the Christian gods, and that the second entry was meant to describe an altar (*tayu*; literally, "throne" or "seat") to the Ñudzavui gods (disparagingly dismissed as "demonios"). The

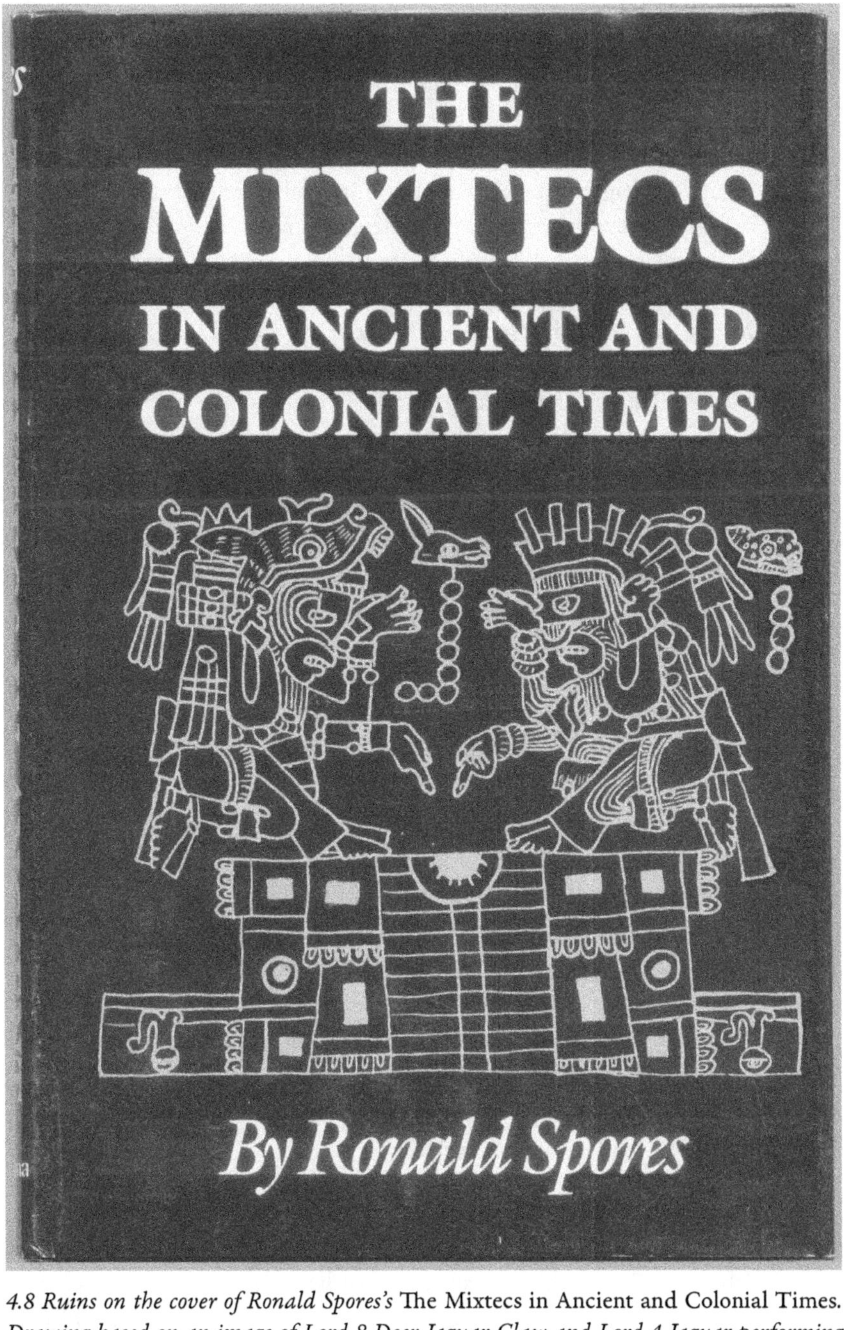

4.8 Ruins on the cover of Ronald Spores's The Mixtecs in Ancient and Colonial Times. *Drawing based on an image of Lord 8 Deer Jaguar Claw and Lord 4 Jaguar performing a ritual on page 79 of the* Codex Nuttall. *Image used by permission of the University of Oklahoma Press.*

translation of chiyo as "altar" would seem to be a Colonial period innovation meant to distinguish Christian altars from their indigenous counterparts, and therefore we should not use "altar" to translate representations of architectural platforms in Ñudzavui pictorials.

Visual evidence also suggests that translating these platforms as "altars" is problematic. Figure 4.1 demonstrated that empty chiyo platforms are formally identical to the platforms or foundations that buildings stand upon. In contrast, Ñudzavui representations of altars where sacrifices are held appear as tall, rounded stones (*Nuttall* 3; *Selden* 8, 12). Indeed, an image on pages 41–42 of the *Codex Borgia* (not a Ñudzavui document but stylistically related and created in the region immediately to the north of the Dzini Ñudzavui) depicts one of these rounded altars mounted on a chiyo-like architectural platform. There is only one occurrence in the Ñudzavui screenfolds where the chiyo platform functions as an altar, piled high with offerings: on *Nuttall* 17. But even here I would argue that what is being shown is the presentation of offerings at a ruined building. And here is where indigenous concepts of altars and ancient places may come together. We know that ruined buildings for centuries have been places where Ñudzavui have made offerings to the sacred. At least one architectural platform among the Classic ruins on the summit of Yucuñudahui, the mountain towering above the Postclassic community of Yuta Ñani (Chachoapan), was repaved during the Postclassic. Obsidian blades and incense burners make it clear that Postclassic Ñudzavui made offerings there (Spores 1983; see Chapter 6 on Postclassic offerings made at the Classic period ruins on the summit of Cerro Danush). Similarly, Classic and Postclassic portable objects were deposited amidst the Formative period ruins of the mountaintop site of Monte Negro (Spores 1967:42). And in *Huisi Tacu* Maarten Jansen tells how ruined architectural mounds were the focus for offerings by Ñudzavui in the late twentieth century, and includes a beautiful photo of such prestations (Jansen 1982:299). So although, strictly speaking, images of chiyo should not be translated as "altars" (since that translation bears the strong marks of colonial Christianity), we should be aware that ancient places were, and still are, places where offerings were made, and in this way served as "altars" in a broader sense. Indeed, as I will address shortly, the Ñudzavui screenfolds often depict ancestors and supernatural beings seated upon chiyo.

Although we can currently only link three of the sixty-plus chiyo-places in the Ñudzavui screenfolds to sites on the ground, a better understanding of Ñudzavui ideas about the material past can be revealed by considering how painted chiyo are visually elaborated. Briefly, chiyo are associated with origins and First Sunrises, with the dead, and with supernatural beings. The connection between chiyo and First Sunrises has been discussed above; further evidence for the association of chiyo with the beginnings of Postclassic time appears on the first two pages of the *Bodley*, which have one of the highest concentrations of chiyo representations of any pages of the Ñudzavui corpus. As John Pohl has observed (see previous discussion), these pages depict the ancestors of Postclassic elites literally being born from ruins: umbilical cords or footprint-pathways trace the emergence of elites from fissures in multiple chiyo.

Whereas *Bodley* pages 1–2 link chiyo to the birth of Postclassic ancestors, other images in the *Bodley*, *Nuttall*, and *Vienna* connect chiyo to the bundled bodies of the dead (Figure 4.9; Byland and Pohl 1994:193–202). This textual association is supported by archaeological evidence: Formative and Classic period tombs have been discovered by twentieth-century excavations at the mountaintop sites of Monte Negro and Yucuñudahui, and recent excavations of Classic period platforms at Huamelulpan and Río Viejo have revealed intrusive Postclassic burials (Chapters 5, 7, and 8; Acosta and Romero 1992; Caso 1938; Joyce et al. 2001; King 2003; Martínez López and Winter n.d.). The Huamelulpan and Río Viejo excavations suggest that one of the reasons we see screenfold images of the bundled dead associated with chiyo-platforms is because Postclassic Ñudzavui actually used chiyoyata as places for burial (cf. Caso 1932). Significantly, the dead were not separated from Postclassic Ñudzavui social life. Scenes in the *Nuttall* (page 44) and *Colombino-Becker* (pages III–IV) show the living consulting mortuary bundles for advice; images in the *Vienna* (pages 27, 24) even show "speaking" mortuary bundles wreathed in song scrolls. Ruins may therefore have been seen as places where one could go to ask advice from the buried elites of both past and present ages of creation (cf. Pohl 1994:69–82).

Closely related to their association with departed ancestors, chiyo are also depicted as the seats of supernatural beings in both the *Vienna* (52, 48, 24, 7) and *Nuttall* (18, 22) (Figure 4.10). The idea that divine beings inhabit ancient ruins is found throughout Mesoamerica (Durán 1994:497–501; Redfield and Villa Rojas 1934:120–121, 341, 349, 356). Indeed, in the late twentieth-century Dzini Ñudzavui, Byland and Pohl learned that ruin-occupying supernaturals protected their homes from being disassembled by killing would-be stone looters (Byland and Pohl 1994:75). Dangerous ruins are not found everywhere in the contemporary Dzini Ñudzavui, where ancient stonework is often recycled for contemporary construction (Chapter 9; Workinger 2002:69–70). However, the connection of ruins with the dead, and with dangerous supernatural forces, may help us better interpret the meaning (and power and danger) involved in prehispanic "looting." Simple convenience does not explain why worked stones were removed from the Classic period buildings at the not-so-accessible summit of Yucuñudahui in the Dzini Ñudzavui. Why was so much effort invested in dragging stones from this high peak? (See Caso 1938:44 and cf. Chapter 7 for the use of stones from Late Classic buildings at Río Viejo to build early Postclassic residences.) What were the risks involved in taking

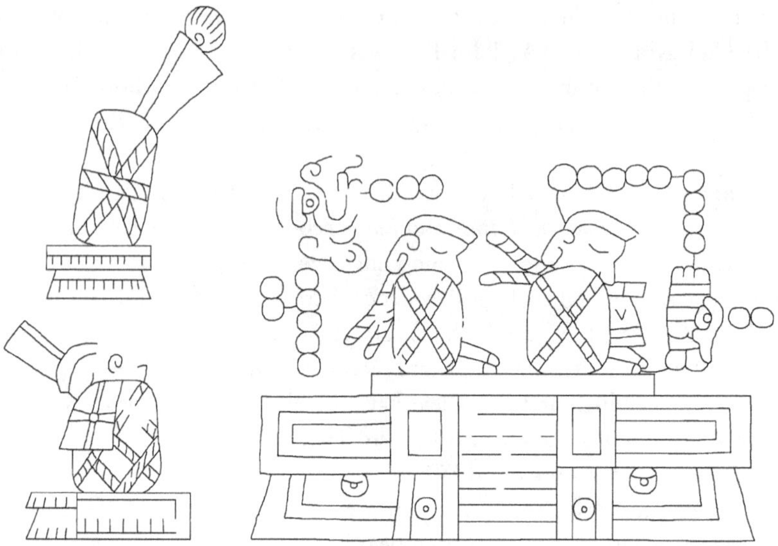

4.9 Mortuary bundles placed upon ruins: upper left: Codex Nuttall *1; lower left:* Codex Vienna *40; right:* Codex Bodley *35. Line drawings by the author.*

stones from such supernaturally inhabited locations? What were the benefits of incorporating such stones into new buildings? What were the moral implications of repairing ruins, as was done in the Postclassic to some of the Classic platforms of Yucuñudahui (Spores 1983)?

Given the rich conceptual associations of ruins for Postclassic Ñudzavui, the prehispanic "looting" of ancient sites and the reincorporation of ancient stonework into new Postclassic buildings may have been deeply meaningful practices in which the architectural spaces of present social life were literally constructed from the power-laden detritus of the past (cf. Hamann 2002; on place and the construction of identity in Mesoamerica, see Joyce and Hendon 2000; Monaghan 1995:9). In the next section I consider a more intimate scale at which Postclassic social life was constructed out of materials inherited from the past. Whereas this section has argued that Postclassic Oaxacan *communities* sometimes took their names from the ruins of ancient settlements, the following section argues that Postclassic Oaxacan *people* sometimes took their names from ancient artifacts.

HEIRLOOMS

The boundary between things and people is an unstable one; anthropologists and sociologists have long discussed the ways in which objects become intimately tied

4.10 Supernaturals seated upon ruins: left: unnamed progenitor couple on Codex Vienna *52; right: Lady 9 Reed on* Codex Vienna *8. See also Figure 4.3 for the* Codex Nuttall *22 depiction of supernaturals seated upon ruins at the summit of Monte Negro. Line drawings by the author.*

to human *being* (Appadurai 1986; Kopytoff 1986). Anthropomorphized things are often important in reproducing social relations between people across space and time (Mauss 1967[1925]; Munn 1986). W.H.R. Rivers's famed "genealogical method of anthropological inquiry," for example, proposed that social relations across generations could be productively studied by tracing how inherited lands and names were passed down from person to person over time (Rivers 1910:7–9). Similarly, E. E. Evans-Pritchard argued that the movement of cattle as part of Nuer marriage agreements was "equivalent to the lines on a genealogical chart"; and he more generally suggested that "material objects are the chains along which social relationships run" (Evans-Pritchard 1940:89). Although many of British social anthropology's genealogical claims have since been critiqued (Schneider 1984), this interest in the importance of things to the production of kinship is shared by a number of anthropological and sociological studies of house-based social relations. House-based social relations build networks of kinship not from ideas about blood and birth descent but from residence in a particular place, participation in the activities of that place, and the rotating possession of material and immaterial property of that place: from names, to dances, to heirloomed objects. Since the early twentieth century, a French tradition of scholarship has explored house-based social relations among the Kwakiutl (Levi-Strauss 1982; Mauss 1967[1925]:41–45), classical Romans (Halbwachs 1992:58–64; Mauss 1967[1925]:47–53), and medieval Europeans (Halbwachs 1992:120–138; Levi-Strauss 1982). More recent research has argued that the house provides a powerful model for thinking about social relations in the Dzini Ñudzavui specifically (Hamann 2004; Monaghan 1996) and in Mesoamerica generally (R. Joyce 2000b, 2001a; cf. Morgan 1881 and critiques by Watanabe 2004).

Names and portable objects are some of the most important possessions circulated among the members of such houses. In Melanesia and along the Northwest Coast of North America, heirloomed portable objects often have their own names, and the names given to humans are themselves often heirlooms, their circulation limited to household members and their possession limited to one holder at a time (Mauss 1967[1925]:22, 42; Munn 1986). Archaeological and textual evidence from Mesoamerica reveals similarly intimate connections between names and things. Names for people in Mesoamerica are often names of portable objects (the Maya Lady Stone Celt, Lord 8 Deer Jaguar Claw), and names are often graphically worn as costume elements (Houston and Stuart 1998:82–83). Among the Classic Maya, heirloomed costume elements (earspools, pendants), excavated in contexts generations or centuries after their creation, were often incised with the hieroglyphic names of their original owners (R. Joyce 2000b:202–210). Thus heirloomed things were vehicles through which the names of ancestors were remembered and preserved across time. Similarly, noble men and women depicted in the Ñudzavui screenfolds often take their personal names from costume elements (quechquemitls, necklaces, jaguar claws) that they wear or hold, and these representations provide some information on how these name-things may have been heirloomed. In the use of personal names—often taken from tangible objects—we may gain a small window onto intra-household relations within Ñudzavui communities.

People in the Ñudzavui screenfolds have two types of names. One is their calendar name, which consists of a number (indicated by a count of dots) and a glyph (Flint, Wind, Rain, Reed, and so forth), as in "Lord 8 Deer." The other is a "personal name," which in codical writing is indicated by the depiction of an object either worn by its possessor or drawn beside their calendar name, as in "Jaguar Claw." Calendar names were supposedly assigned according to the day on which a person was born, but the unequal distribution of these names in the screenfolds suggests that some names were more auspicious than others (and so in some cases naming may have been delayed a day or two in order for an inauspicious period to pass; cf. Sahagún 1950–1982, 4:113). It is less clear, however, how personal names were assigned. Page 8 of the *Selden* has one unusual image of a woman (Lady 6 Monkey Serpent Quechquemitl) undergoing a ceremony to receive a second personal name (Warband Quechquemitl) after her victories in combat. Other than this one image, however, we have little indication of how, when, or why personal names were assigned.

The distribution of personal names does little to illuminate our understanding. Only rarely do a parent and child share the same personal name, so the passing down of personal names from generation to generation is not something regularly recorded in the screenfolds. Jansen and Pérez Jiménez (n.d.) draw attention to the sixteenth-century Dzaha dzavui expression *dzeque iya nisanu ninaquaiya*, the "name taken from a forefather," and suggest this refers to Ñudzavui personal names. Along these lines, visual evidence suggests that, as with the names owned by Kwakiutl houses, certain personal names were associated with particular Ñudzavui royal dynasties. On page 5 of the *Selden*, the Second Dynasty of Añute (Jaltepec) is shown being founded by the actions of Lady 9 Wind Flint Quechquemitl. Generations later, on page 13, a daughter born to the then-ruling couple at Añute is again named Lady 9 Wind Flint Quechquemitl. Perhaps this was an heirloomed name (or the right to wear an heirloomed style of garment) that was specific to the royal house of Añute (but see Jansen and Pérez Jiménez 2005:15 for a linguistic interpretation of quechquemitl images). Another possible example of heirlooming from Añute is provided by the last noble to be born in the *Selden*, Lord 7 Crocodile, who wears his personal name of "Serpent Skull." Like "Flint Quechquemitl," this is an unusual attribute in the Ñudzavui screenfolds. The only other appearance of this costume element in the *Selden* is in a scene of creation at the very beginning of the narrative, where ancestor Lord 2 Grass Serpent Skull is born from a celestial tree on page 2. Thus, the final child shown born to Añute's lineage in the *Selden* is linked to the origins of Añute's dynasty through an heirloomed "Serpent Skull." Lord 7 Crocodile may have been alive when this copy of the *Selden* was painted, and so this materially signified claim of ancestry and continuity needs to be considered in light of the charged colonial legal situation in which the *Selden* was painted (Jansen and Pérez Jiménez 2000; Smith 1994). In other words, a simple depiction of the wearing of the heirloomed "Serpent Skull" title may indicate a potent form of political action (cf. Chapter 10 on the possible lineage-specificity of Lady 12 Vulture's sun disk–fan personal name).

In the *Selden*, then, Flint Quechquemitls and Serpent Skulls appear to be important names, important objects, linked to dynastic foundations and then later resurfacing in the royal history of Añute. An additional case of name inheritance is found in the *Nuttall*, in which a daughter inherits a personal name from her mother—and as with the personal names discussed for the *Selden*, this one is unusual (Figure 4.11). On page 23 of the *Nuttall*, the third king of the First Dynasty of Ñuu Tnoo (Lord 10 Lizard Arrow-Footed) is shown marrying two women (Lady 4 Crocodile Jeweled Face and Lady 4 Flint Eagle-Quetzal Feathers) within the outlines of a palace (or, more accurately, a house; Hamann 2004:108–115). Lady 4 Crocodile's personal name appears twice within this palace, both on her quechquemitl and drawn above her head. The name consists of a green face from which three green pendants hang, and which is marked with "hair," a "necklace," and earspools. The use of green is significant, indicating an object made of greenstone as opposed to blue turquoise mosaic. The face that Lady 4 Crocodile wears is further marked by an unusual upturned nose. On page 24, the children born to these marriages are shown. One daughter, Lady 1 Flint, both wears and is accompanied by a greenstone face hung with pendants (only this time the face is shown frontally, not in profile). As with Lady 4 Crocodile, these faces are made of greenstone; as with Lady 4 Crocodile, these faces are hung with greenstone pendants and are elaborated with "hair," a "necklace," and earspools. Lady 4 Crocodile is also depicted on page 5 of the *Bodley*, and again she is shown with a curved-nose "Jeweled Face" personal name (which has both hair and a collar but lacks pendants and, due to the discoloration of paint in the *Bodley*, the original color of the face is unclear).

That face is a curious object, especially in its long-nosed depictions. A similar object is depicted as part of a place sign on page 9 of the *Vienna*. This face is painted in blue and green (the once-brilliant vegetable dye has now faded to a dull olive), is frontally drawn, is hung with three pendants (one blue, two green), and wears earspools and "hair" and "neck" detailing. Similar faces with three pendants are worn on *Vienna* 25, 24, and 18 by the sun gods Lord 7 Flower and Lord 1 Skull (a perhaps predictable wearing of pre-Sunrise things by solar deities). Another such object may have once been shown on page XVI of the *Codex Colombino-Becker*. Alas, many of the faces in this codex have been scratched away, and this was also done to the surface of the object on page XVI—but it shares the same outline as the greenstone faces on page 9 of the *Vienna* and on page 24 of the *Nuttall*, and it has earspools and hair and neck treatment. Like the face in the *Bodley*, it lacks pendants, and it is not worn but is attached to a baton held in the hand of a protagonist.

Given the unusual visual form of this object, and its unusual appearance as a nickname passed from mother to daughter in the *Nuttall*, I suggest that this is an "heirloomed" object from the Classic past: one of the greenstone faces hung with celt pendants that are well attested from the Valley of Oaxaca. Achromatic representations of these objects appear on the Lápida de Bazán (Figure 4.12) and on ceramic urns. A green pectoral face is painted on the walls of Tomb 105 at Monte Albán (Caso 1938:19, 85, Lámina II-A). And at least one of these objects actually survives: the greenstone bat's head hung with three pendant celts now in the National Museum of Anthropology in Mexico City (Trueblood 1968:110). Given the important connections between the Valley of Oaxaca and the Dzini Ñudzavui during the Postclassic (Byland and Pohl 1994:176–181; Jansen 1998; Paddock 1983), it is quite possible that some of these Valley of Oaxaca–attested objects traveled to the Dzini Ñudzavui to become Postclassic heirlooms. This may be what we see on pages 23 and 24 of the *Nuttall*.

This greenstone face raises an important issue about the reuse of ancient things in prehispanic Mesoamerica: the question of how often we, in the twenty-first century, cannot see such reuses of the past. Round greenstone beads, for example, were found with the Postclassic offerings in Monte Albán's reused Classic period Tomb 7 (Caso 1932) and often appear in necklaces in the Ñudzavui screenfolds. But were these objects newly made in the Postclassic, or do they represent recycled heirlooms

4.11 The "Jeweled Face" personal name: upper left: Lady 4 Crocodile on Codex Bodley *5; lower left: Lady 1 Flint from* Codex Nuttall *24; right: Lord 10 Lizard, Lady 4 Crocodile, and Lady 4 Flint on* Codex Nuttall *23. (a) "Jeweled Face" personal names of Lady 4 Crocodile; (b) "Jeweled Face" personal names of Lady 1 Flint. Line drawings by the author*

inherited from family members, unearthed from tombs, or encountered in fields when planting crops? This is an issue that concerns the study of heirlooms throughout Mesoamerica. Joyce comments: "Undoubtedly many other examples of conservation of earlier valuables are not recognized because they do not differ as obviously in style from the later materials with which they were finally deposited" (R. Joyce 2000b:205; see Manahan 2003:259–160 on the Postclassic reuse of Classic jade at Copan). The heirlooming and circulation of ancient objects in Postclassic society may have been far more prevalent than we are currently able to detect.

HIGH CULTURE?

The previous two sections, on ruins and heirlooms, have provided initial forays into what we might be able to know about specific features of the indigenous archaeologies of Postclassic Oaxaca. The following two sections expand in focus to consider more general implications of such reuses of the past. First, how were objects from the past (and narratives that interpreted those objects) used to legitimize class inequalities in Mesoamerican societies? And second, what are the ways in which the reuse of objects from the past can illuminate the continuities and disjunctures spanning the 3,000 years of what Rosemary Joyce calls "Mesoamerican civilization"?

In Ruins, I argued that Postclassic Oaxacan elites mobilized physical remains of the past to create social memories of an ancient devastation that, in fact, no

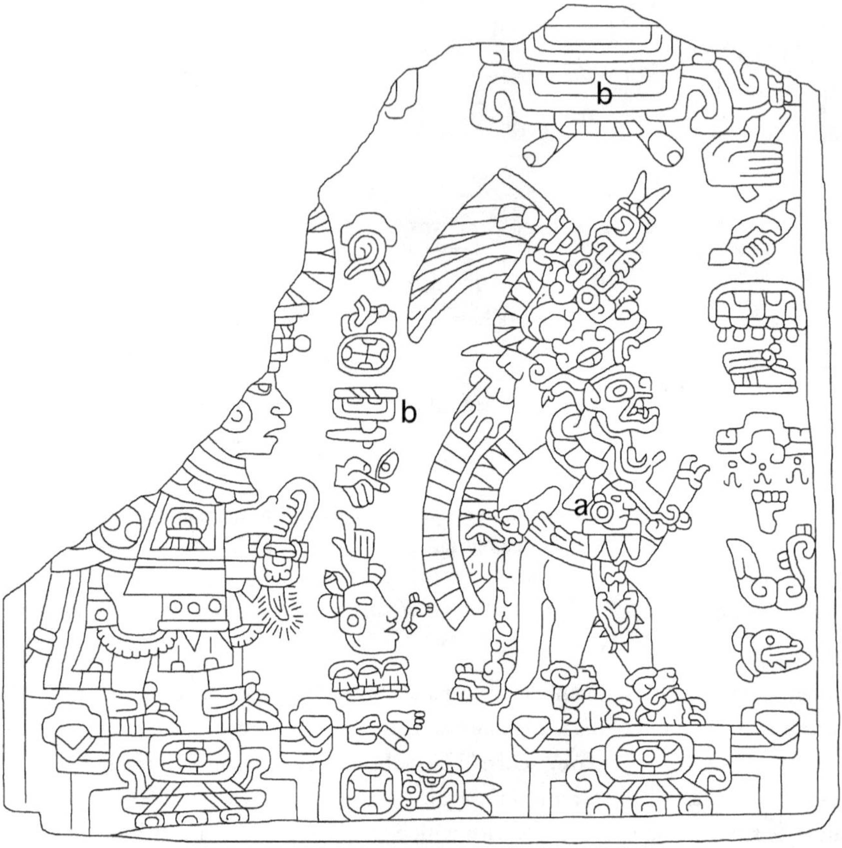

4.12 Lápida de Bazán: (a) pectoral with celt pendants; (b) celestial curved brackets. Redrawn by the author from Caso 1938:fig. 25.

living members of Postclassic society had ever experienced. Ruined sites reminded their viewers of the agriculture-creating covenants with Earth and Rain created by ancient elites, covenants still upheld in the Postclassic present by the descendants of those elites. The use of physical objects to provide tangible support for historical narratives is, of course, not uncommon (R. Joyce 2000b:193, 196, 201; cf. Levi-Strauss 1966:87–88, 237–234 and Gell 1992:26–28 on Australian *chirunga*). In the case of indigenous Oaxacan archaeology, these materially supported memories commemorated the origins of class inequality and the importance of elite religious practice in maintaining the fragility of an agricultural society annually indebted to the gifts of Earth and Rain (Hamann 2002; A. Joyce 2000).

But one of the difficulties of studying Postclassic Oaxacan discourses on ancient ruins is that our main sources—elite art and writing—offer only a limited perspective on the interpretation of these places. Since the meanings of places are always multiple, fragmented according to one's social perspective (Bender 1993; Joyce and Hendon 2000), our understanding of indigenous archaeological discourses will always be incomplete. However, two recent commentaries on elite uses of the past have argued that engagement with the material detritus of Mesoamerican "High Culture" *was* a phenomenon limited to the elite class. Rosemary Joyce, at the conclusion to her "High Culture, Mesoamerican Civilization, and the Classic Maya Tradition," writes:

> Elites become exemplary participants in that cosmic order. As Baines and Yoffee argue, there is little incentive for non-elites to question the order in which they now live. And perhaps even the strongest claim Baines and Yoffee make—that most high culture is essentially self-referential and unconcerned with non-elites—can be sustained, with Classic Maya art directed primarily at a narrow audience of elites, motivated primarily to satisfy their felt need for luxuries that were their unquestioned right within the Mesoamerican civilizational order. (R. Joyce 2000a:76; see also 69, 71)

Similarly, Michael E. Smith argues that it was unlikely that Central Mexican commoners would have had access to the pre-Sunrise things displayed in the ceremonial center of Tenochtitlán, and he sees an interest in past relics as an elite-focused practice:

> [A]ppreciation for ancient objects was a widespread phenomenon and an important cultural trait in Mesoamerica. It may be that in some settings commoners participated in this domain. . . . But Mesoamerican practices and beliefs that were culturally dominant and geographically widespread were not necessarily equally shared by commoners and elites. [Rosemary] Joyce (2000) points out that many of the traits used traditionally to define Mesoamerica as a cultural area—traits common to most ancient Mesoamerican cultures—were aspects of elite culture. The beliefs and practices associated with "pre-sunrise things" as discussed by Hamann provide another example of this pattern. (Smith 2003:271)

Both of these arguments for limiting an interest in the ancient things of "High Culture" to elites are problematic for several reasons. First, in a number of Mesoamerican societies discourses about the origins of this present age of creation made explicit reference to the emergence of agriculture—and elite participation in agriculture—as one of the consequences of the First Sunrise. These appeals to agriculture were appeals that would have resonated to all members of society, elite and commoner alike. This is a topic I addressed above in relation to Rosemary Joyce's ideas about civilizational fragility and the need for elites to maintain cosmic order. Ñudzavui elites made claims about their crucial role in maintaining the universe at a very basic level—making Earth and Rain bring forth agricultural crops that commoner men grew and that commoner women processed into edibles to feed all classes of society. Elite claims about their own agricultural importance (in societies where commoners in fact did the bulk of physical labor of agriculture) are found throughout Mesoamerica. Indeed, much of the symbolism of the sacred precinct in Tenochtitlán focuses on agricultural fertility—symbolism generally downplayed because of long-standing Western obsessions with Central Mexican religion as war, blood, and celestial cycling (Boone 1989; Hamann 2003; Smith 2003). By appealing to their role in agriculture (and to ruins as signs of the origins of the agricultural order), Mesoamerican elites were thus appealing to basic commoner concerns. Furthermore, just as twenty-first-century archaeologists rely on the upturned soil of agricultural fields to make potsherds visible, so too would prehispanic commoner agriculturalists be constantly encountering the ancient fragments of the past (even without bladed plows: digging sticks rupture the earth, and freezing and thawing churns up its surfaces).

Claims that only elites were interested in the use and meaning of ancient objects are problematic for a second reason: such claims justify studies of Mesoamerican iconography and materiality that ignore commoners. If elite art and elite heirloom practices concern only a narrow audience of elites, commoners do not need to be considered when dealing with these sources on prehispanic social life. Now, to their credit, the work of Rosemary Joyce and Michael Smith does not fall into this pitfall: both study the range of class inequalities observable in the archaeological record. But claims of elite exceptionalism can too easily lead to scholarship that isolates elites from commoners, as if these two classes were not living in the same communities and did not sustain each other through material and religious labor.

A recent essay by Linda A. Brown (2000) has argued for the importance of "commoner" archaeology (the engagement with ancient objects by non-elites) at the sixth-century site of Cerén and in a number of twentieth-century Maya communities. In the following paragraphs, I discuss similar examples of an interest in the physical remains of the past by members of minimally hierarchized communities. Two early Postclassic "post-collapse societies"—that is, "Early Postclassic groups living in or near ceremonial centers following the collapse" (Manahan 2004:109; see also Joyce et al. 2001; cf. Harrison 1999:192–198)—allow us to further consider whether uses of archaeological ruins, and discourses about those ruins, were truly an insular feature of Mesoamerican elite culture.

The first comes from the Oaxacan coast, with the Early Postclassic occupation of the site of Río Viejo (800–1100 CE; Chapters 7 and 8). A. Joyce and his colleagues (2001) have argued that the occupation of the site's ceremonial center by minimally hierarchized inhabitants immediately after the collapse of the Late Classic Río Viejo polity should be interpreted as an example of "commoner power," in which symbols of a failed hierarchical order were appropriated and symbolically denigrated (Chapter 7). Excavations on the acropolis, the elite sacred center of the Late Classic city, revealed a drastic shift in occupation in the Early Postclassic. Modest, densely packed houses were constructed on the acropolis; men and women were interred with simple burial offerings (Chapters 7 and 8; Joyce et al. 2001:360; King 2003:194–202). Crucially, excavations revealed stratigraphic continuity between Late Classic and Early Postclassic occupations. There are no indications of a hiatus in occupation, no indications that Río Viejo was abandoned and then resettled by foreign migrants (Joyce et al. 2001:345, 361). Joyce and his colleagues argue that this shift in occupation and hierarchization at Río Viejo's center should be interpreted not simply as an opportunistic reuse of space but as a meaningful symbolic statement by people who remembered—or whose parents or grandparents remembered—the hierarchical control of this space in the Late Classic. The very act of living in spaces once limited to elites provides one example of symbolic denigration (see also Chapter 5); an even more powerful example is Stacie King's discovery of a fragment of a carved stela broken and reused as a metate (King 2003:188–190, 352–353). Since representations of Mesoamerican elites were often interpreted as the living selves of those elites, using a stela as a grinding stone would have been a powerfully symbolic act (see Houston and Stuart 1998:95 on the vandalization of elite Maya images; and Thomas 1971:75 for an analogous case of the utilitarian desecration of sacred objects by commoners in Reformation England; but cf. King 2003:349–355).

Ironically, these Early Postclassic practices of "commoner power" share a number of features with the discourses on ruins recorded in texts from the hierarchical societies of the Late Postclassic Dzini Ñudzavui. As was argued above in Ruins, Late Postclassic Ñudzavui texts viewed Formative and Classic ruins as evidence of a failed civilizational order, a corrupt order without agriculture that was destroyed by a First Sunrise in order to bring about a new age of creation—an age in which humans could practice agriculture, thanks to originary covenants with Earth and Rain forged by elites. All of these interpretations of ruins can, perhaps, also be applied to the practices of "commoner power" at Río Viejo. For its Early Postclassic occupants, the ruined city of Río Viejo would have been powerful testimony of the failure of a hierarchical society, a society corrupt and decadent and thus destroyed to make way for a new, egalitarian order in the Early Postclassic (cf. Sullivan 1988:109–110 on cosmic catastrophe and social critique in indigenous South America). Even the agricultural symbolism we see in later highland narratives may be at play at Río Viejo: the useless stones of elite aggrandizement are reworked to make tools for processing agricultural products. The practices of the minimally hierarchized occupants of Río Viejo's post-collapse society (and their possible parallels to later elite-aggrandizing discourses) suggest that discourses about the past and uses of its material remains were not intrinsically dependant on an insular elite society.

At about the same time that the ruins of Río Viejo were being occupied by minimally hierarchized inhabitants, other minimally hierarchized settlers were moving into the abandoned Maya city of Copan (950–1100 CE; Manahan 2003, 2004). However, unlike the inhabitants of Río Viejo, these southern settlers were foreign immigrants, not descendants of the site's Classic period inhabitants. A comparison of material culture from the Late Classic and Early Postclassic occupations of Copan reveals a whole series of disjunctive contrasts, including changes in styles of houses, lithics, and ceramics; diet; and the treatment of the dead (Manahan 2003:268–330; Manahan 2004:111–115). Furthermore, although the material practices of the Early Postclassic occupants of Copan differ radically from those of the site's Classic occupants, they have much in common with traditions of material culture from Central Honduras and El Salvador, suggesting a westward migration of settlers into the abandoned city (Manahan 2003:299, 344; 2004:114–115). These immigrants chose not to dwell in Copan's ruined palaces and temples but instead quarried stone from its buildings in order to construct their own houses. They used abandoned temples as burial places for their dead and deposited offerings within temples (sometimes encountering, but apparently not disturbing, Classic period offerings). The new settlers did, however, harvest relics from the ruins (Manahan 2003:351–375). Jade beads and obsidian cores were reused, and carved stones were placed in burials and incorporated into the façades of new houses. Significantly, these carvings were often combined at random: Manahan (2003:372) notes that the placement of some carved stones upside down reveals that "the post-collapse society members were not fluent in the iconographic language of the dynastic period Copaneco elites." Yet even if these new users were illiterate in Classic Maya iconography, they clearly cared enough about these ancient carvings to visibly incorporate them into their new constructions and to systematically inter them with their dead (Longyear 1952:71; Manahan 2003:361–362). These stones were being manipulated in specific ways; their reuse cannot be interpreted as a mindless recycling of raw materials (see also R. Joyce 2000b:206; Ruins, above). So at Copan, as at Río Viejo, we have an example of a minimally hierarchized society (Manahan 2003:332, 392–393) making meaningful use of ancient ruins. A more detailed understanding of exactly what Copan's ruins meant to the new settlers is at present elusive (but see Manahan 2003:346–394); the important point here is that, as at Río Viejo, elites and a hierarchical society are not required for the practice of indigenous Mesoamerican archaeologies.

Copan's new inhabitants could not decipher Copan's Classic period iconography. In contrast, the Early Postclassic occupants of Río Viejo reused the stone portrait of a vanquished elite in a symbolically charged way. This points to a final question, a final issue for this chapter. Was iconographic incomprehension a standard reaction to the imagery of ancient objects? Or were reusers of ancient objects and buildings able to "read" their meanings in ways their original creators had intended? And if such decipherments were possible, how can the reuse of ancient objects help us to better understand the "three millennia of continuity covered by the term Mesoamerica" (R. Joyce 2000a:64)?

MESOAMERICAN CIVILIZATION

The mutual entanglement of the present and the past has troubled Western social thought for centuries. Writers since Machiavelli have focused on the ways in which the past and its material traces are actively manipulated and reshaped according to the needs of various presents (Chapters 9 and 10; Davis 1997:85; Halbwachs 1992:116, 125, 138; Hobsbawm and Ranger 1983; Machiavelli 1996[ca. 1519]:60–61; Marx 1972[1852]:437). Yet at the same time, such social constructivist interpretations have been faced with the "nightmare" of history: the ways in which the past constrains and shapes the present in ways the present may not even recognize (Chakrabarty 2000:238–253; Halbwachs 1992:224, 232; Marx 1972[1852]:437; Trouillot 1995). Most studies of archaeology as a social practice published in the past two decades have focused on the nineteenth- and twentieth-century West, and on the ways in which the present reinvents the past according to its changing needs (Abu El-Haj 1998; Dietler 1994; Trigger 1980). In contrast, this chapter concludes by considering the ways in which the constraining material traces of the past may have produced continuities in the ever-changing presents of Mesoamerica across 3,000 years.

Two famous images of these continuities have been published, one by Miguel Covarrubias in 1957 and another by Karl Taube in 1996 (Figure 4.13). Covarrubias illustrates the transformations of the faces of Mesoamerican rain deities: arrows sprout from a Formative visage at the bottom of the page and link later faces of the rain until, at the top, the arrows arrive at the Postclassic faces of a Yucatec Chac and a Central Mexican rain vessel (see Taube 1995:94–95 for a reaffirmation of this genealogy). Taube's illustration does the same thing, beginning with a Formative maize deity at the bottom and, with arrows, climbing up the page to end in a maize deity from a Postclassic Maya book. These charts, and the alphabetic arguments that accompany them, demonstrate that forms and meanings have endured for millennia in Mesoamerica. But what exactly is going on in all of the spaces these two charts mark with demure arrows? What processes to those arrows represent? How can we talk about *processes* of continuity?

Mesoamerican scholarship has often assumed the existence of long-term continuities over time and space, variously justified in terms of Selerian "geographical provinces," Boasian "culture areas," or the essentialist premises of the Direct Historic Approach (Freidel et al. 1993; Marcus and Flannery 1994). Unfortunately, all of

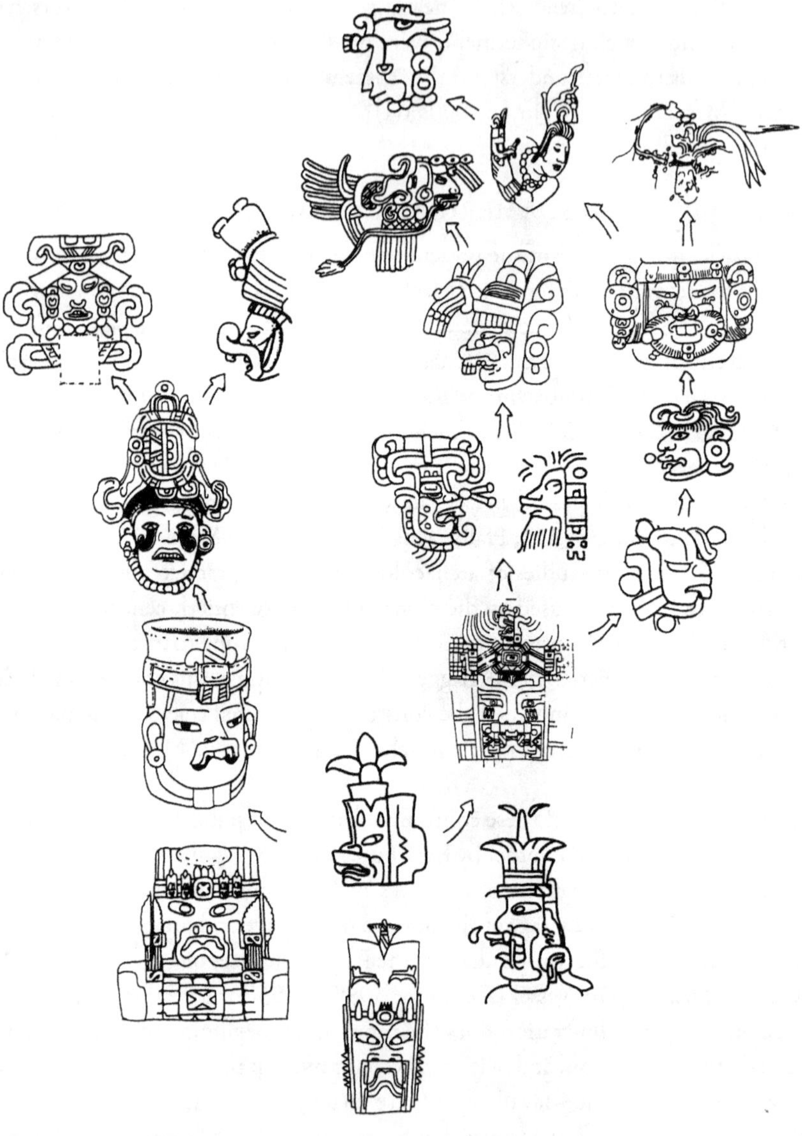

4.13 The Face of Maize in Mesoamerican art. From Taube 1996:70. Image used by permission from Karl A. Taube.

these approaches to regional integration and temporal continuity fail to specify the *processes* through which such spatial and temporal unities might be produced (but see Kubler 1962 and R. Joyce 2000a). I hope to outline some of these processes in the pages that follow.

First, we can think of how continuities are the result of implicit orientations to the world—those shaped by language and bodily practice. A striking illustration of how the orientations to the world encoded in language and bodily practice can shape "revivals" of continuity is provided by John Monaghan's work with twentieth-century Nuyooteco Ñudzavui drawings (Monaghan 1989). The composition of many of these drawings revealed strong similarities to the images in fifteenth- and sixteenth-century Ñudzavui screenfolds. Since "no folk tradition of visual representation exists in the Mixteca," these images suggest a number of ways in which representational continuities may endure even in the absence of a continuous tradition of graphic representation (Figure 4.14). Nuyootecos produced images of women in profile seated with bent knees—just like the basic representations of women in the screenfolds. Monaghan explains this parallel with reference to enduring assumptions about bodily composure: "The remarkable similarity between the drawings made by Mixtec Indians today and those by their ancestors centuries ago can be attributed, in part, to the fact that what is represented has not changed greatly. Thus women continue to sit in the same way today as they did in prehispanic times, on the floor with their legs folded under them and to one side" (Monaghan 1989:18; cf. Connerton 1989)

But why are human forms across 500 years depicted in a profile view? This continuity points to another factor in these visual parallels: language and the ways language categorizes the world.

> There are sound theoretical and empirical grounds for assuming that, given continuity between speakers of a language, continuity will also exist in the way the world is perceived and in the way these perceptions are represented. Since there is a close relationship between the Mixtec spoken at the time the codices were produced and that of today, there is reason to suspect that present-day Mixtec speakers will perceive, organize, and categorize objects in a way similar to their Post-Classic ancestors. (Monaghan 1989:13)

Thus, in speaking about the parallels of Postclassic and twentieth-century depictions of chains of mountains, Monaghan writes:

> There may, however, also be a much deeper, perceptual reason, a way of looking at the world that is fundamentally Mixtec. The similarities between the depictions of mountain chains by people in Nuyoo and the artists of the *Codex Nuttall* suggest that the Mixtec represent the physical world in a manner not necessarily inherent in the objects themselves, but instead based in the Mixtec experience of their environment, and perhaps in categories of relationships between objects which are rooted in Mixtec language and discourse. (Monaghan 1989:18)

There is no biological determinism involved in these arguments: Monaghan writes of learned, implicit modes of thinking about the world, acting in it, and

4.14 Comparison of drawing styles in Postclassic codical art and twentieth-century Nuyoo. Top: drawings of seated women by J. L. Nuñez and from the Codex Nuttall *13. Bottom: drawings of mountainous landscape by J. L. Nuñez and from the* Codex Vienna *21. From Monaghan 1989:13–14. Images used by permission from John Monaghan.*

dividing it for perception. Bourdieu argued that people interpret and interact with their world according to a few basic schema and approach new challenges in their worlds by using practices and assumptions that are familiar from other contexts

(Bourdieu 1977). This, no doubt, is what we can see in the Nuyooteco drawings: asked to draw for perhaps the first time, Nuyootecos draw on a whole host of background assumptions about the world and its ordering—and so produce drawings that are remarkably similar (but, crucially, not identical, and that encompass representations of objects—trucks and stereos—that no sixteenth-century Ñudzavui would have seen) to those created by people who spoke a similar language and lived in a similar environment 500 years ago.

Continuities may also be sustained by explicitly articulated assumptions about the nature of the world, such as those found in spoken and written narratives. When Marshall Sahlins was asked to answer the "how" of continuity in regards to his claims about the long-term importance of Original Sin in Western thought, he argued that continuities are explained by central social propositions in canonic theological writings:

> When confronted by a structure of the *longue durée* such as the tragic view of human imperfection, we are dealing with a kind of ideological dominance that no contingent functional value or political motivation will account for. Rather, it seems that the continuity of the ideology of human evil comes from its positional value in a cultural scheme of universal dimensions. Its historical dominance is the temporal expression of a pivotal structural role. The fall of man has been the condition of possibility of a great complex of interrelated theological dogmas. The whole redemptive Christology depends on the inherent wickedness of humanity. (Sahlins 1996:424; cf. Kubler 1962:22 on religious persistence)

Sahlins goes on to specify that canonic alphabetic texts, such as the Bible and the writings of St. Augustine, preserved and reproduced the idea of original sin and its implications across centuries. But even without canonic alphabetic enshrinement, narratives can show a surprising persistence and continuity over time. Consider the social life of the *Chanson de Roland*. First written down in late-eleventh-century France, later oral and alphabetic variations of this narrative are attested across the centuries that follow, even appearing in popular ballads in twentieth-century Brazil (Fentress and Wickham 1992:51–59, 103–106, 159–160). Non-sacred, popular narratives can thus endure in non-elite culture for centuries, without the benefit of an authoritative sacred text (Fentress and Wickham 1992:77–78). A similar process of transmission, in which oral and written relays were both important, probably shaped the life history of the narrative we now know as the *Popol Vuh*. We can glimpse the process of this narrative's transmission from its appearance on Formative Izapan stela, on Classic Maya ceramics, and, a millennium later, in the writing of an alphabetic Quiché version in 1565 (Coe 1973; Freidel et al. 1993; Tedlock 1996). Ñudzavui narratives of the Covenants with Earth and Rain also demonstrate how socially important narratives about the nature of the world can endure (if transformed) for centuries independently of written records (Hamann 2002; Monaghan 1990). Of course, neither the *Chanson de Roland* nor the *Popol Vuh* nor Ñudzavui Covenant narratives exhibit a fixed stability but rather involve a core narrative and core sets of characters that are preserved across thousands of years. Karl Taube, for example, has shown that Classic Maya ceramics depict episodes that are lost in the sixteenth-century version of the *Popol Vuh* (Taube 1992:55–58).

Finally, continuities may also be sustained by material things. Rosemary Joyce, in one of the articles that inspired the title to this chapter, has explored the possible material processes that link the Olmec images at the bottoms of Covarrubias's and Taube's charts to images further up the page. Joyce considers how a "Formative Revolution" created a basic corpus of elite practices whose material precedent forever constrained the options for aggrandizement available for later Mesoamerican elites. These material precedents included "certain forms of public architecture, notably monumental platforms; the employment of relief carving as a medium for public and semi-public political imagery; and the use of a restricted range of materials (especially jade) to produce costume ornaments and sumptuary goods" (R. Joyce 2000a:67). Joyce argues that these material precedents did not produce stasis for subsequent history but rather an inertia of practice: "[T]he iconographic motifs and selection of valuable materials that were transmitted to successor societies constrained reinterpretation. New meanings could, of course, become attached to these practices, but always with a residual weight derived from histories of their prior use" (R. Joyce 2000a:72). "Later polities worked within a history framed by these initial developments" (R. Joyce 2000a:67). The constraint exercised by Formative period precedents could take extremely literal forms. In Postclassic Veracruz, a new settlement was constructed over the remains of Formative period San Lorenzo Tenochtitlán. The new buildings followed the site's original layout and were thus physically constrained by foundations established thousands of years before (Coe 1981:136–139; cf. Halbwachs 1992:232 on similar cases in twelfth-century Jerusalem).

In addition to showing how basic forms and object types (like mirrors and earspools) created in the Formative endured for thousands of years, Joyce also demonstrates how Formative objects themselves, once created, continued to circulate in elite households thousands of years and hundreds of kilometers from the times and places where they were first made and used. One can therefore read the charts of Covarrubias and Taube not simply as genealogies of ancestral and descendant forms but as actual pathways along which heirloomed objects traveled through time—such as the Formative period jade mask that was discovered among the Postclassic deposits in the foundations of the Templo Mayor in Tenochtitlán (Matos Moctezuma 1979).

The charts of Covarrubias and Taube are productive tools for another reason. An important feature of the persistences attested by language and bodily practice, and by the transmission of oral and written narratives, is that whole networks of mutually implicated associations are involved. These examples thus stand in contrast to trait-transmission approaches of early-twentieth-century anthropology, and to Kubler's claims about "the extinction of *motifs* in pre-Columbian art" (Kubler 1961; emphasis mine). Boasian diffusionism saw "traits" as independent units that traveled across time and space and glibly changed their meanings as they went (transformations sometimes explained by the influence of the "pattern of culture" into which they were adopted; Boas 1940[1903]:555–562). When dealing with languages, systems of bodily comportment, and narratives, we are not dealing with isolated motifs: we are dealing with networks of associations, and these networks, I would argue, constrain reinterpretation in a way that is very different from the reinterpretation possible for isolated atomized "motifs." Indeed, Kubler himself noted that "symbolic clusters" of visual and formal motifs could inhibit changes in individual forms—and thus, I would argue, in the meanings of the cluster as a whole (Kubler 1962:viii)

The same holds true for Mesoamerican visual culture. Motifs, especially those of complex iconography, are never encountered floating in space, separated from objects or from contextual association with other motifs—broken pots and stela do not shatter jigsaw-puzzle-like into separate single-motif fragments. Just as people do not learn their first language from a grammar book but from examples of speech used in daily life (Bakhtin 1990), and just as people do not learn social norms from sets of rules but from the "tacit knowledge" acquired from the constant implicit and explicit pedagogy of social interaction (Bourdieu 1977; Kuhn 1962), so too were the viewers of ancient relics met by complete works of art, entire compositions in which "rules" of representation were encountered only as they were instantiated in complex images. Thus when Mesoamerican peoples encountered the "motifs" of ancient representational systems, they encountered a whole system of images linked to the material vehicle on which they were displayed (cf. Kubler 1962:viii). These contexts would have constrained the reading (and appropriation) of iconography. This returns us to all that is *not* shown in the Rain and Corn genealogy charts of Covarrubias and Taube. Both illustrate continuities by isolating faces from their bodies and objects of context. This isolation makes the kinship of forms clear: it is by focusing on motifs that we can trace particular continuities. But I would argue that those continuities were partially made possible by what these genealogical charts do not show: that is, the repeated material contexts in which Mesoamerican people looking at ruins would have encountered particular faces of Rain and Maize.

When the same practice appears over and over across time—as with the Formative to Postclassic traditions of wearing earspools or binding stone celts to the body (Joyce 2001b; Taube 1996)—it is hard to say whether such continuity is the result of the observation of specifically material archaeology or the result of a more diffuse continuity of bodily practice, language, and narrative (a survival or revival, using terms from Greenhalgh 1978; cf. Masson 2000 on revitalization). It is only with radical revivals—as with the parallels linking Formative statuary at Laguna de los Cerros to the similarly in-the-round statuary of Classic Tonina, discussed in Proskouriakoff's (1968) ground-breaking article on indigenous archaeology—that we can speak confidently of materially inspired revivals. However, Proskouriakoff's study was only able to observe the formal parallels linking statuary at Laguna de los Cerros and Tonina. It is difficult to say whether that Classic revival of form also involved a revival of symbolic meanings, other than a diffuse revival of ancient—and thus historically legitimizing—modes of presenting elite bodies. In contrast, Umberger's (1987) studies of Aztec revivals of Toltec, Teotihuacano, and Xochicalcan art revealed not only that the Aztecs recognized the formal variations of these styles but also had different sets of associations for each—so the Aztecs did not simply view ancient objects as formally homogenous things whose only meaning was derived from their legitimizing antiquity. However, as Umberger emphasizes, the Aztecs were most concerned with giving ancient forms meanings relevant to the Late Postclassic (Umberger 1987:98–99). In some cases, as when a Teotihuacan god of fire was used as formal model for an Aztec rain god, the ancient meanings of the form are ignored (Umberger 1987:88–89). But in other cases, as with the use of a skeletal Teotihuacan god as a model for an equally skeletal Aztec goddess, or with evocations of Xochicalco-style date glyphs, or with the use of a Teotihuacan vessel marked with funerary and militaristic symbols to house cremated Aztec remains, it does seem that Postclassic Central Mexicans were using ancient objects in a manner sensitive to the ancient meanings of those objects (López Lujan et al. 2000:242; Umberger 1987:86–87, 90–92). We do have some evidence, then, that Mesoamericans were subtle readers of the iconographic variation of ancient objects. I therefore want to end with an example of revival that not only bridges thousands of years but suggests that Postclassic people were able to read, and comprehend, Formative and Classic iconography.

This example comes from a place and a building we have already encountered: the Temple of Heaven of Ñuu Tnoo, as represented in the 1580 *Mapa de Teozacoalco* (one of sixty-nine surviving maps linked to the royal Relaciones Geográficas survey circulated in the late 1570s; Jansen and Pérez Jiménez 2005:25–28; Mundy 1996:112–117). As was discussed above in Ruins, representations of the site of Ñuu Tnoo in the Ñudzavui screenfolds usually depict a two-part place sign, combining a black frieze with a temple whose roof is marked with a blue skyband (Figure 4.6). Colonial documents—such as Ñuu Tnoo's *Relación Geográfica*—reveal these two place signs as visualizations of the full Dzaha dzavui name for the town, Ñutnoo Huahindehui: "Black Town, Temple of Heaven." Dozens of representations of this Temple of Heaven (and indeed skybands generally) are found in the Ñudzavui screenfolds. Almost all of them represent the heavens as a rectangular blue skyband marked with eyeball-shaped stars. Such starry eyes also appear on the *Mapa de Teozacoalco* temple. But instead of combining these with a standard blue rectangle, the roof is marked with a curving bracket. This curved bracket is, to my knowledge, a unique method of representing a skyband in the Ñudzavui corpus: again, we have dozens of representations of "heaven" in the screenfolds and none of them uses this convention. However, this is not the only example from the history of Mesoamerican iconography in which such brackets (opening upward or downward) were used to represent the sky. As Taube (1995:91) shows, they were quite common in Formative period iconography and represented the gum brackets of a sky serpent. These representations of the bracketed sky appeared on Formative period stela and also on portable celts and ceramics—objects that were still circulating in Postclassic Mesoamerica. Bracketed skybands also appear in the Classic period Lápida de Bazán (Figure 4.12), as well in the murals of the Classic period Tomb 105 at Monte Albán. Perhaps images from heirlooms or visitations to Classic tombs inspired the Colonial period painters of the *Mapa de Teozacoalco* to represent the sky using an ancient bracket. Indeed, the alphabetic texts of a number of other Relaciones Geográficas specifically mention the role of "ancient pictures" in the creation of their images and the drafting of their alphabetic commentaries (Mundy 1996:40, 87, 92). In sum, the representation of the sky in the *Mapa de Teozacoalco* suggests that Ñudzavui scribes looked at the iconography of objects from the ancient past, were able to read that iconography in a way its ancient makers intended, and could mobilize that iconography meaningfully for purposes in the sixteenth-century present.

The possibility of more or less accurate readings of ancient objects should not surprise us, for the reading of ancient texts and images has been a repeated feature of the West's various revivals of the Greco-Roman past (Greenhalgh 1978; Hamann 2002:367–368; Haskins 1927). Of course, these Western revivals have never involved the perfect re-creation of Greco-Roman iconography or a perfect reading of ancient Latin texts—to the consternation of Renaissance Latinists forced to deal with a millennium-long tradition of increasingly sloppy Latin and flawed translations (Alberti 1986[1432]:83). But thinking about the traditions of the reading of Latin in the West for over 2,000 years is a useful analogy to the traditions of reading ancient iconography that existed in Mesoamerica. Postclassic Ñudzavui were used to reading the images of their own writing system (indeed, used to reading the images of a pan-Mesoamerican "Mixteca-Puebla" style; cf. Chapter 1). We must assume they would have brought this skill in reading complexly composed images to their encounters with ancient artifacts. Similarly, Renaissance Europeans were used to applying their corrupted, medievalized style of Latin to texts created in the very different Latin of the ancient Romans. Both Mesoamerican and European processes of reading ancient texts were fraught with difficulties—indeed, fifteenth- and sixteenth-century European readers of Classical Latin became increasingly aware of the inertia of these texts: the way they enshrined traces of a pagan world radically different from the Renaissance present, a pagan world of gods and sacrifices whose traces were all but ignored by the medieval tradition of textual interpretation (Franklin 1963:7–35; Pocock 1967:1–29). But in both Renaissance Europe and Postclassic Mesoamerica, practices of reading inherited from precedents in the past were recursively deployed to reapproach and understand ancient artifacts. And the inherited influence of these ancient artifacts shaped the conditions of possibility of their anachronistic rereadings in both Renaissance and Postclassic presents.

ACKNOWLEDGMENTS

Many thanks go to Jeff Blomster and Geoff McCafferty for inviting me their Changing Cloud Formations session at the 2003 SAA meetings in Milwaukee, Wisconsin. Geoff was especially persistent in pestering me until I finally gave in and agreed to participate, so it is due to him that this essay exists at all. A later version of these arguments was presented at the 2004 Mixtec Gateway Meetings in Las Vegas, Nevada, organized by Nancy Troike and Mannetta Braunstein. Jeff Blomster, Mannetta Braunstein, Bruce Byland, Aurore Giguet, Gerardo Gutiérrez, Scott R. Hutson, Art Joyce, Stacie King, Michael Lind, Kam Manahan, Carlos Rincón Mautner, Geoff McCafferty, John Pohl, Nancy Troike, and Marc Winter provided comments on these earlier versions, and Michael E. Smith offered his always-appreciated skepticism. John Monaghan and Karl Taube kindly gave permission to reproduce images from their publications, and Scott R. Hutson overcame a number of difficulties to provide me with digital copies of Figures 4.5 and 4.13.

REFERENCES

Abu El-Haj, Nadia

1998 Translating Truths: Nationalism, Archaeological Practice, and the Remaking of Past and Present in Contemporary Jerusalem. *American Ethnologist* 25(2):1–23.

Acosta, Jorge R., and Javier Romero

1992 *Exploraciones en Monte Negro, Oaxaca: 1937–38, 1938–39, y 1939–40*. Instituto Nacional de Antropología e Historia, Mexico City.

Acuña, René (editor)

1984 *Relaciones Geográficas del siglo XVI: Antequera*, vol. 1. Universidad Autónoma de México, Mexico City.

Aguilera, Carmen

2005 *El códice de Huamantla*. CD-ROM and booklet. Serie Códices de México 1, Instituto Nacional de Antropología e Historia, Mexico City.

Alberti, Leon Battista
1986 On the Family [1432]. In *University of Chicago Readings in Western Civilization 5: The Renaissance*, edited by E. Cochrane and J. Kirshner, pp. 78–103. University of Chicago Press, Chicago.

Alvarado, Fray Francisco de
1593 *Vocabulario en lengua Misteca*. Pedro Balli, Mexico City.

Appadurai, Arjun
1986 Introduction: Commodities and the Politics of Value. In *The Social Life of Things: Commodities in Cultural Perspective*, edited by A. Appadurai, pp. 3–63. University of Cambridge Press, New York.

Bakewell, Liza, and Byron Hamann
2001 *Mesolore: Exploring Mesoamerican Culture*. CD-ROM. Brown University, Providence, Rhode Island.

Bakhtin, Mikhail
1990 The Problem of Speech Genres. In *The Problem of Speech Genres and Other Late Essays*, edited by M. Holquist and C. Holquist, pp. 60–103. University of Texas Press, Austin.

Bender, Barbara
1993 *Landscape: Politics and Perspectives*. Berg, Providence, Rhode Island.

Boas, Franz
1940 The Decorative Art of the North American Indians [1903]. Reprinted in Franz Boas, *Race, Language, and Culture*, pp. 546–563. Free Press, New York.

Boone, Elizabeth H.
1989 Incarnations of the Aztec Supernatural: The Image of Huitzilopochtli in Mexico and Europe. *Transactions of the American Philosophical Society* 79(2):1–107.

Bourdieu, Pierre
1977 *Outline of a Theory of Practice*. Cambridge University Press, New York.

Brown, Linda A.
2000 From Discard to Divination: Demarcating the Sacred through the Collection and Curation of Discarded Objects. *Latin American Antiquity* 11(4):319–333.

Burkhart, Louise
1989 *The Slippery Earth: Nahua-Christian Moral Dialogue in Sixteenth-Century Mexico*. University of Arizona Press, Tucson.

Byland, Bruce, and John M.D. Pohl
1994 *In the Realm of Eight Deer: The Archaeology of the Mixtec Codices*. University of Oklahoma Press, Norman.

Caso, Alfonso
1928 *Las estelas zapotecas*. Talleres Gráficos de la Nación, Mexico City.

1932 *La exploraciones en Monte Albán: Temporada 1931–1932*. Publicación No. 7. Instituto Panamericano de Geografía e Historia, Mexico City.

1938 *Exploraciones en Oaxaca: Quinta y sexta temporadas 1936–1937*. Publicación No. 34. Instituto Panamericano de Geografía e Historia, Mexico City.

1960 *Interpretation of the Codex Bodley 2858*. Translated by Ruth Morales and revised by John Paddock. Sociedad Mexicana de Antropología, Mexico City.

Chakrabarty, Dipesh

2000 *Provincializing Europe: Postcolonial Thought and Historical Difference*. Princeton University Press, Princeton, New Jersey.

Coe, Michael D.

1973 *The Maya Scribe and His World*. Grolier Club, New York.

1981 San Lorenzo Tenochtitlán. In *Supplement to the Handbook of Middle American Indians*, Vol. 1: *Archaeology*, edited by V. Bricker, J. Sabloff, and P. Andrews, pp. 117–146. University of Texas Press, Austin.

Connerton, Paul

1989 *How Societies Remember*. Cambridge University Press, New York.

Covarrubias, Miguel

1957 *Indian Art of Mexico and Central America*. Alfred A. Knopf, New York.

Cruz, Wilfrido

1946 *Oaxaca recóndita*. Mexico City.

Davis, Richard

1997 *Lives of Indian Images*. Princeton University Press, Princeton, New Jersey.

Dietler, Michael

1994 "Our Ancestors the Gauls": Archaeology, Ethnic Nationalism, and the Manipulation of Celtic Identity in Modern Europe. *American Anthropologist* 96:584–605.

Durán, Fray Diego

1994 *The History of the Indies of New Spain* [1581], translated by Doris Heyden. University of Oklahoma Press, Norman.

Durkheim, Emile, and Marcel Mauss

1963 *Primitive Classification* [1903]. University of Chicago Press, Chicago.

Dyk, Anne

1959 *Mixteco Texts*. Summer Institute of Linguistics, Norman, Oklahoma.

Evans-Pritchard, E. E.

1940 *The Nuer: A Description of the Modes of Livelihood and Political Institutions of a Nilotic People*. Oxford University Press, New York.

Fentress, James, and Chris Wickham

1992 *Social Memory*. Blackwell Publishing, Malden, Massachusetts.

Franklin, Julian H.

1963 *Jean Bodin and the Sixteenth-Century Revolution in the Methodology of Law and History*. Columbia University Press, New York.

Freidel, David, Linda Schele, and Joy Parker

1993 *Maya Cosmos: Three Thousand Years on the Shaman's Path*. William Morrow and Company, New York.

Gell, Alfred

1992 *The Anthropology of Time: Cultural Constructions of Temporal Maps and Images*. Berg, Oxford.

Goodman, Joseph Thompson

1905 Maya Dates. *American Anthropologist* 7:642–647.

Greenhalgh, Michael

1978 *The Classical Tradition in Art*. Duckworth, London.

Gussinyer, Jordi

1970 Un adoratorio dedicado a Tlaloc. *Boletín del INAH* 39:7–12.

Halbwachs, Maurice

1992 *On Collective Memory*, translated and edited by L. A. Coser. University of Chicago Press, Chicago.

Hamann, Byron

2002 The Social Life of Pre-sunrise Things. *Current Anthropology* 43(3):351–382.

2003 Reply: What Did Mesoamerican Commoners Think of "Pre-Sunrise Things"? *Current Anthropology* 44(2):272–273.

2004 Seeing and the Mixtec Screenfolds. *Visible Language* 38(1):66–124.

Harrison, Peter T.

1999 *The Lords of Tikal*. Thames and Hudson, New York.

Haskins, Charles Homer

1927 *The Renaissance of the Twelfth Century*. Harvard University Press, Cambridge, Massachusetts.

Hobsbawm, Eric, and Terence Ranger

1983 *The Invention of Tradition*. Cambridge University Press, New York.

Houston, Stephen, and David Stuart

1998 The Ancient Maya Self: Personhood and Portraiture in the Classic Period. *Res: Anthropology and Aesthetics* 33:73–101.

Jansen, Maarten

1982 *Huisi Tacu: Estudio interpretivo de un libro mixteco antiguo: Codice Vindobonensis Mexicanus 1*. Incidentale Publicaties 24, vols. 1 and 2. Centro de Estudios y Documentación Latinoamericanos, Amsterdam.

1998 Monte Albán y Zaachila en los Códices Mixtecos. In *The Shadow of Monte Alban: Politics and Historiography in Postclassic Oaxaca, Mexico*, edited by M. Jansen,

P. Kröfges, and M. Oudijk, pp. 67–122. CNWS Publications, Vol. 64. Research School of Asian, African, and Amerindian Studies, University of Leiden, Leiden.

Jansen, Maarten, and Gabina Aurora Pérez Jiménez

2000 *La Dinastía de Añute: Historia, literatura e ideología de un reino mixteco.* CNWS Publications, Vol. 87. Research School of Asian, African, and Amerindian Studies, University of Leiden, Leiden.

2005 *Codex Bodley.* Bodleian Library, Oxford.

n.d. *Deciphering the Mixtec Pictorial Manuscripts: Historiography of Ancient City-States.* Edwin Mellen Press, Ceredigion (in press).

Jiménez Moreno, Wigberto, and Salvador Mateos Higuera

1940 *Códice de Yanhuitlán.* Instituto Nacional de Antropología e Historia, Mexico City.

Joyce, Arthur A.

2000 The Founding of Monte Albán: Sacred Propositions and Social Practices. In *Agency in Archaeology,* edited by M. Dobres and J. Robb, pp. 71–91. Routledge, New York.

Joyce, Arthur A., Laura Arnaud Bustamante, and Marc N. Levine

2001 Commoner Power: A Case Study from the Classic Period Collapse on the Oaxaca Coast. *Journal of Archaeological Method and Theory* 8(4):343–385.

Joyce, Rosemary A.

2000a High Culture, Mesoamerican Civilization, and the Classic Maya Tradition. In *Order, Legitimacy, and Wealth in Ancient States,* edited by J. Richards and M. Van Buren, pp. 64–76. Cambridge University Press, New York.

2000b Heirlooms and Houses: Materiality and Social Memory. In *Beyond Kinship: Social and Material Reproduction in House Societies,* edited by R. Joyce and S. Gillespie, pp. 189–212. University of Pennsylvania Press, Philadelphia.

2001a Burying the Dead at Tlatilco: Social Memory and Social Identities. In *Social Memory, Identity, and Death: Anthropological Perspectives on Mortuary Rituals,* edited by M. Chesson, pp. 12–26. Archaeological Papers of the American Anthropological Association, No. 16. American Anthropological Association, Washington, DC.

2001b Negotiating Sex and Gender in Classic Maya Society. In *Gender in Pre-Hispanic America,* edited by C. Klein, pp. 109–142. Dumbarton Oaks Research Library and Collection, Washington, DC.

Joyce, Rosemary A., and Julia M. Hendon

2000 Heterarchy, History, and Material Reality: "Communities" in Late Classic Honduras. In *The Archaeology of Communities,* edited by M. Canuto and J. Yaeger, pp. 143–160. Routledge, New York.

King, Stacie M.

2003 Social Practices and Household Organization in Ancient Coastal Oaxacan Households. Unpublished Ph.D. Dissertation, Department of Anthropology, University of California, Berkeley.

Kopytoff, Igor

1986 The Cultural Biography of Things: Commoditization as Process. In *The Social Life of Things: Commodities in Cultural Perspective,* edited by A. Appadurai, pp. 64–91. Cambridge University Press, New York.

Kubler, George

1961 On the Colonial Extinction of the Motifs of Pre-Columbian Art. In *Essays on Pre-Columbian Art and Archaeology*, edited by S. Lothrop, pp. 14–34. Harvard University Press, Cambridge, Massachusetts.

1962 *The Shape of Time: Remarks on the History of Things*. Yale University Press, New Haven, Connecticut.

Kuhn, Thomas

1962 *The Structure of Scientific Revolutions*. University of Chicago Press, Chicago.

León, Nicolás

1901 *Lyobaa o Mictlan: Guía Histórico-Descriptiva*. La Europea, Mexico City.

Lerner, Jesse

2000 A Fevered Dream of Maya: Robert Stacy-Judd. www.tortugamarina.com/articulos/lerner/stacy-judd.html. Accessed June 2004.

Levi-Strauss, Claude

1966 *The Savage Mind*. Weidenfeld and Nicholson, London.

1982 The Social Organization of the Kwakiutl. In *The Way of the Masks*, pp. 167–187. University of Washington Press, Seattle.

Longyear, John M.

1952 *Copan Ceramics: A Study of Southeastern Maya Pottery*. Publication No. 597. Carnegie Institute of Washington, Washington, DC.

López Lujan, Leonardo

1989 *La recuperación mexica del pasado teotihuacano*. Instituto Nacional de Antropología e Historia, Mexico City.

López Lujan, Leonardo, Hector Neff, and Saburo Sugiyama

2000 The 9-Xi Vase: A Classic Thin Orange Vessel Found at Tenochtitlán. In *Mesoamerica's Classic Heritage: From Teotihuacan to the Aztecs*, edited by D. Carrasco, L. Jones, and S. Sessions, pp. 219–249. University Press of Colorado, Boulder.

Machiavelli, Niccolò

1996 *Discourses on Livy* [ca. 1519], translated by H. C. Mansfield and N. Tarcov. University of Chicago Press, Chicago.

Manahan, T. Kam

2003 The Collapse of Complex Society and Its Aftermath: A Case Study from the Classic Maya Site of Copan, Honduras. Unpublished Ph.D. Dissertation, Department of Anthropology, Vanderbilt University. Nashville, Tennessee.

2004 The Way Things Fall Apart: Social Organization and the Classic Maya Collapse of Copan. *Ancient Mesoamerica* 15(1):107–125.

Marcus, Joyce, and Kent V. Flannery

1994 Ancient Zapotec Ritual and Religion: An Application of the Direct Historic Approach. In *The Ancient Mind: Elements of Cognitive Archaeology*, edited by C. Renfrew and E. Zubrow, pp. 55–74. Cambridge University Press, New York.

Martínez Gracida, Manuel

1910 Los Indios Oaxaqueños y sus Monumentos Arqueológicos: Tomo IV Arquitectura. Unpublished and unpaginated. Microfilm copy in the collections of the Biblioteca Nacional de Antropología e Historia-Subdirección Técnica, Serie: Manuel Martínez Gracida, Rollo 13.

Martínez López, Cira, and Marcus Winter

n.d. *Excavaciones arqueológicas en San Martin Huamelulpan* (in press).

Marx, Karl

1972 The Eighteenth Brumaire of Louis Bonaparte [1852]. In *The Marx-Engels Reader*, edited by R. Tucker, pp. 436–525. W. W. Norton and Company, New York.

Masson, Marilyn

2000 *In the Realm of Nachan Kan*. University Press of Colorado, Boulder.

Matos Moctezuma, Eduardo

1979 Una máscara olmeca en el Templo Mayor de Teotihuacan. *Anales de Antropología* 16:11–19.

Mauss, Marcel

1967 *The Gift: Forms and Functions of Exchange in Archaic Societies* [1925]. W. W. Norton & Company, New York.

Monaghan, John.

1989 The Feathered Serpent in Oaxaca: An Approach to the Study of the Mixtec Codices. *Expedition* 31(1):12–18.

1990 Sacrifice, Death, and the Origins of Agriculture in the Codex Vienna. *American Antiquity* 55(3):559–569.

1995 *The Covenants with Earth and Rain: Exchange, Sacrifice, and Revelation in Mixtec Sociality*. University of Oklahoma Press, Norman.

1996 The Mesoamerican Community as a "Great House." *Ethnology* 35(3):181–194.

Morgan, Lewis H.

1881 *Houses and House-Life of the American Aborigines*. Government Printing Office, Washington, DC.

Mundy, Barbara E.

1996 *The Mapping of New Spain: Indigenous Cartography and the Maps of the Relaciones Geográficas*. University of Chicago Press, Chicago.

Munn, Nancy

1986 *The Fame of Gawa: A Symbolic Study of Value Transformation in a Massim (Papua New Guinea) Society*. Duke University Press, Durham, North Carolina.

Paddock, John

1983a *Lord 5 Flower's Family: Rulers of Zaachila and Cuilapan*. Vanderbilt University Publications in Anthropology, No. 29. Nashville, Tennessee.

Parsons, Elsie Clews

1936 *Mitla, Town of Souls*. University of Chicago Press, Chicago.

Pocock, J.G.A

1967 *The Ancient Constitution and Feudal Law: A Study of English Historical Thought in the Seventeenth Century*. W. W. Norton and Company, New York.

Pohl, John M.D.

1994 *The Politics of Symbolism in the Mixtec Codices*. Vanderbilt University Publications in Anthropology, No. 46. Nashville, Tennessee.

1995 Codex Vindobonensis Mexicanus I: Notebook for the Mixtec Pictographic Writing Workshop at Texas. Manuscript on file, Department of Art History, University of Texas, Austin.

1999a Review of *The Shadow of Monte Alban: Politics and Historiography in Postclassic Oaxaca* by M. Jansen, P. Kröfges, and M. R. Oudijk. *Latin American Antiquity* 10(3):317–318.

1999b The Lintel Paintings at Mitla and the Function of the Mitla Palaces. In *Mesoamerican Architecture as a Cultural Symbol*, edited by J. Kowalski, pp. 176–197. Oxford University Press, New York.

2004 The Archaeology of History in Postclassic Oaxaca. In *Mesoamerican Archaeology: Theory and Practice*, edited by J. Hendon and R. Joyce, pp. 215–238. Blackwell Publishing, Malden, Massachusetts.

Pohl, John M.D., and Manuel Aguilar

2003 Codex Nuttall: The Zapotec Dynasty of Zaachila. Notebook for the Mixtec Pictographic Workshop at Texas. Manuscript on file, Department of Art History, University of Texas, Austin.

Proskouriakoff, Tatiana

1968 Olmec and Maya Art: Problems of Their Stylistic Relation. In *Dumbarton Oaks Conference on the Olmec*, edited by E. Benson, pp.119–134. Dumbarton Oaks Research Library and Collection, Washington, DC.

Rabin, Emily

2004 Toward a Unified Chronology of the Historical Codices and Pictorial Manuscripts of the Mixteca Alta, Costa, and Baja: An Overview. In *Homenaje a John Paddock*, edited by P. Plunket, pp. 101–136. Universidad de las Américas, Cholula, Puebla.

Redfield, Robert, and Alfonso Villa Rojas

1934 *Chan Kom: A Maya Village*. Carnegie Institution of Washington, Washington, DC.

Ricard, Robert

1966 *The Spiritual Conquest of Mexico: An Essay on the Apostolate and the Evangelizing Methods of the Mendicant Orders in New Spain 1523–1572.* University of California Press, Berkeley.

Rivers, W.H.R.

1910 The Genealogical Method of Anthropological Inquiry. *Sociological Review* 3:1–12.

Sahagún, Bernardino de

1950–82 *Florentine Codex: General History of the Things of New Spain,* vols. 1–13 [1547–1579]. Edited and translated by A. Anderson and C. Dibble. University of Utah Press, Salt Lake City.

Sahlins, Marshall

1985 Other Times, Other Customs: The Anthropology of History. In *Islands of History,* pp. 32–72. University of Chicago Press, Chicago.

1996 The Sadness of Sweetness. *Current Anthropology* 37(3):395–427.

Schmidt, Peter, and Thomas Patterson

1995 *Making Alternative Histories: The Practice of Archaeology and History in Non-Western Settings.* School of American Research Press, Santa Fe, New Mexico.

Schneider, David

1984 *A Critique of the Study of Kinship.* University of Chicago Press, Chicago.

Shaw, Mary

1971 *According to Our Ancestors: Folk Texts from Guatemala and Honduras.* Summer Institute of Linguistics and University of Oklahoma Press, Norman.

Smith, Mary Elizabeth

1973a *Picture Writing from Ancient Southern Mexico: Mixtec Place Signs and Maps.* University of Oklahoma Press, Norman.

1973b The Relationship between Mixtec Manuscript Painting and the Mixtec Language. In *Mesoamerican Writing Systems,* edited by E. Benson, pp. 47–98. Dumbarton Oaks Research Library and Collection, Washington, DC.

1994 Why the Second Codex Selden Was Painted. In *Caciques and Their People: A Volume in Honor of Ron Spores,* edited by J. Marcus and J. Zeitlin, pp. 111–141. Anthropological Papers, No. 89. Museum of Anthropology, University of Michigan, Ann Arbor.

Smith, Michael E.

2003 What Did Mesoamerican Commoners Think of "Pre-Sunrise Things"? *Current Anthropology* 44(2):271.

Spinden, Herbert J.

1913 *A Study of Maya Art.* Memoirs of the Peabody Museum of American Archaeology and Ethnology, Harvard University, Vol. 6. Peabody Museum, Cambridge, Massachusetts.

Spores, Ronald
1967 *The Mixtec Kings and Their People*. University of Oklahoma Press, Norman.
1972 *An Archaeological Settlement Survey of the Nochixtlán Valley, Oaxaca*. Vanderbilt University Publications in Anthropology, No. 1. Nashville, Tennessee.
1983 Yucuñudahui. In *The Cloud People: Divergent Evolution of Mixtec and Zapotec Civilizations,* edited by K. Flannery and J. Marcus, pp. 155–158. Academic Press, New York.
1984 *The Mixtecs in Ancient and Colonial Times*. University of Oklahoma Press, Norman.

Sullivan, Lawrence Eugene
1988 *Icanchu's Drum: An Orientation to Meaning in South American Religions*. Macmillan, New York.

Taube, Karl
1986 The Teotihuacan Cave of Origin. *Res: Anthropology and Aesthetics* 12:51–82.
1992 The Temple of Quetzalcoatl and the Cult of Sacred War at Teotihuacan. *Res: Anthropology and Aesthetics* 21:54–87.
1995 The Rainmakers: The Olmec and Their Contribution to Mesoamerican Belief and Ritual. In *The Olmec World: Ritual and Rulership*, edited by J. Guthrie, pp. 83–117. The Art Museum, Princeton University, Princeton, New Jersey.
1996 The Olmec Maize God: The Face of Corn in Formative Mesoamerica. *Res: Anthropology and Aesthetics* 29/30:39–81.

Tedlock, Dennis
1996 *Popol Vuh: The Maya Book of the Dawn of Life and the Glories of Gods and Kings,* 2nd ed. Simon and Schuster, New York.

Thomas, Keith
1971 *Religion and the Decline of Magic*. Charles Scribner's Sons, New York.

Tozzer, Alfred
1907 *A Comparative Study of the Mayas and Lacandones*. Macmillan, New York.

Trigger, Bruce
1980 Archaeology and the Image of the American Indian. *American Antiquity* 45(4): 662–676.

Trouillot, Michel-Rolph
1995 *Silencing the Past: Power and the Production of History*. Beacon Press, Boston.

Trueblood, Beatrice (editor)
1968 *The National Museum of Anthropology, Mexico*. Alexis Gregory, New York.

Umberger, Emily
1987 Antiquities, Revivals, and References to the Past in Aztec Art. *Res: Anthropology and Aesthetics* 13:62–105.

Watanabe, John M.
2004 Some Models in a Muddle: Lineage and House in Classic Maya Social Organization. *Ancient Mesoamerica* 15(1):159–166.

Watkins, Joe
2000 *Indigenous Archaeology: American Indian Values and Scientific Practice.* Alta Mira Press, New York.

Workinger, Andrew G.
2002 Coastal/Highland Interaction in Prehispanic Oaxaca: The Perspective from San Francisco de Arriba. Unpublished Ph.D. Dissertation, Department of Anthropology, Vanderbilt University. Nashville, Tennessee.

PART III

Continuity and Abandonment of Houses in the Valley of Oaxaca

LAMBITYECO AND MACUILXÓCHITL

5

Michael D. Lind

The Classic to Postclassic at Lambityeco

Archaeologists specialize in the study of culture change (Plog 1974). Traditional archaeological approaches to the study of culture change involve the use of stratigraphic test pit excavations, block excavations, and surface or settlement pattern surveys. Long continuous archaeological sequences are broken up into discrete blocks of time or phases on the basis of observed changes in artifact types found in stratigraphic contexts. Collections of diagnostic artifact types are used to determine the number of sites in a region and their size, complexity, and geographical spacing for each phase. The changes in these archaeological data from one phase to the next have served as the basis for reconstructing the cultural evolution of ancient civilizations.

This traditional approach might be labeled "stratigraphic segregation" or "sequential segregation" because it involves the use of stratigraphically or sequentially segregated phases or time periods. It has been used effectively by Valley of Oaxaca survey projects, although one glaring error is relevant to the topic of this book. These projects (Blanton 1978; Finsten 1995; Kowalewski et al. 1989) have incorrectly separated the Xoo phase into two phases, which they call Monte Albán IIIB and IV. This error has been dealt with extensively (Chapters 2 and 3; Lind

1991–1992; Markens 2004; Martínez et al. 2000; Winter 1989). However, it will be treated in a limited fashion in this chapter because it relates directly to Lambityeco and the Classic and Postclassic periods.

The problem with a sequential segregation approach is that, although each phase is frequently from 150 to 400 years' duration, archaeologists treat it as if it were a static and unchanging time period within the history of an ancient civilization. The study of culture change, then, has meant interpreting the changes from one sequentially segregated phase to the next. Discussions often center on the transition from one phase to another; but, as Kent Flannery was fond of remarking, every phase is a transition. Every archaeologist knows that a considerable amount of change may take place within a phase of 150 to 400 years and that a study of the continuous developments within a phase is necessary to more fully comprehend the reasons for changes from one phase to another. Nevertheless, few archaeologists have developed research strategies for elucidating the trends and trajectories within phases.

The archaeological approach to culture change in this study might be called "stratigraphic integration" or "sequential integration" because it focuses on the continuous change within a phase. Continuous change is revealed in the stratigraphic patterning of the archaeological remains. Stratigraphic patterning is the sequential interrelationships among features and artifacts. A simple example is house remains. A house may be built, remodeled, added to, and rebuilt. These continuous remodelings, additions, and rebuildings of the house, together with the artifacts and features associated with them, constitute the stratigraphic patterning in the archaeological remains; since the persons who effected the successive changes found in the house remains were functioning members of an ancient culture, these changes reflect the ongoing changes in their cultural system (Lind 1977, 1979, 1987). Later in this chapter a sequential integration approach will be used with regard to the Classic to Postclassic remains at Lambityeco.

LAMBITYECO

From 1961 to 1976, personnel from the Instituto de Estudios Oaxaqueños under the direction of John Paddock conducted archaeological investigations at the site of Lambityeco near Tlacolula in the Valley of Oaxaca, Mexico (Figure 5.1). The investigation included a thorough surface survey of the site and extensive excavations in selected areas.

The surface survey, conducted in the field by David Peterson (1976), revealed that Lambityeco was occupied initially during the Late Formative Rosario phase when it covered little more than two hectares (see Table 5.1)—although a few sherds belonging to the earlier Guadalupe phase were found. The site grew to six and a half hectares in the Danibaan phase (Early Monte Albán I) and to thirteen

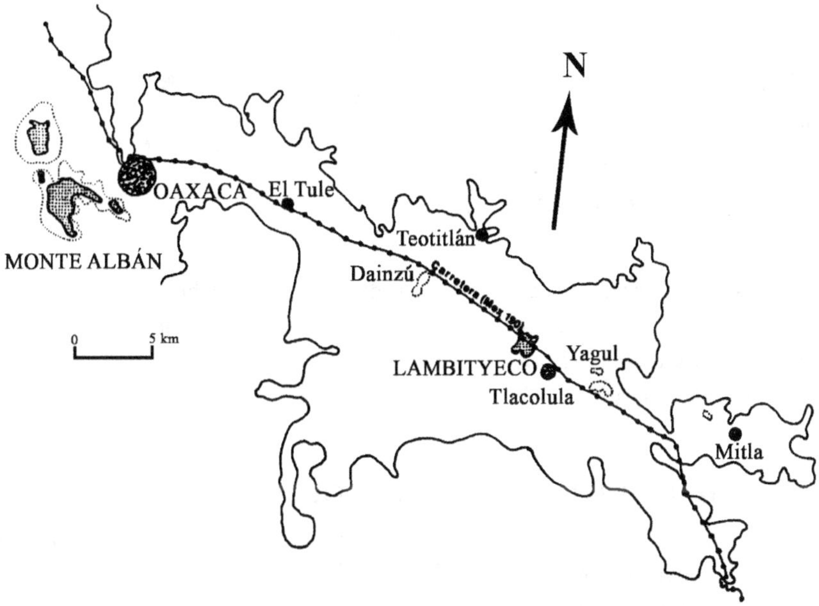

5.1 Location of Lambityeco in the Valley of Oaxaca.

Table 5.1 Lambityeco: Size in hectares through time

Phases	*Dates**	*Hectares†*
Rosario	700–500 BCE	2.25
Danibaan (Early I)	500–300 BCE	6.50
Pe (Late I)	300–100 BCE	13.00
Nisa/Tani (II)	100 BCE–350 CE	8.00
Pitao/Peche (IIIA)	350–600 CE	6.75
Xoo (IIIB/IV)	600–800 CE	63.75
Liobaa (Early V)	800–1200 CE	35.75
Chila (Late V)	1200–1521 CE	18.75

*See dates in Chapter 2.
†After Peterson 1976.

hectares in the Pe phase (Late Monte Albán I; see Figure 2.1 for chronology correlation). During the Niza phase it declined to about eight hectares and then, in the Pitao phase, to little more than six hectares—being virtually abandoned.

Lambityeco was resettled and reached its maximum size during the Late Classic Xoo phase when 147 of its 206 mounds were occupied and the site covered nearly sixty-four hectares. During the Postclassic Liobaa phase the site declined to about thirty-six hectares and in the later Chila phase to nineteen hectares. The Liobaa and Chila occupation at Lambityeco appears to be restricted to salt production

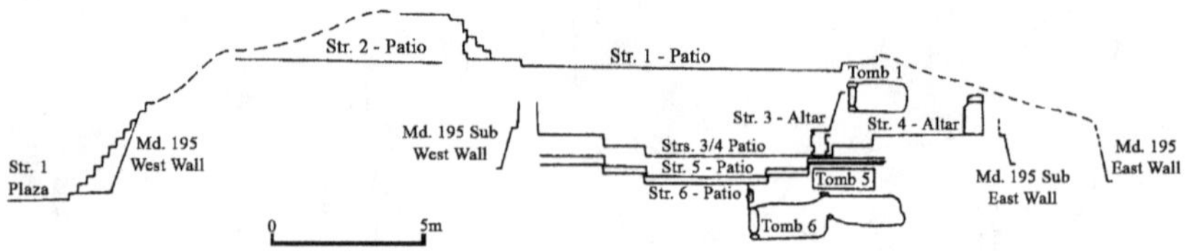

5.2 Sequence of elite houses in Mound 195.

activities—Lambityeco was a major salt-producing site throughout its history. The site was virtually abandoned as a functioning community during the Postclassic, and no Liobaa or Chila houses or temples have been found at Lambityeco (Peterson, personal communication, 1979).

CLASSIC TO POSTCLASSIC CHRONOLOGY AT LAMBITYECO

A thorough excavation of two large Xoo phase mounds—Mound 195 and Mound 190—and a smaller mound (Mound 92) provides insight into the Late Classic to Postclassic transition at Lambityeco. Explorations within Mound 195 revealed that it consists of a series of six superimposed Xoo phase elite houses (Figure 5.2). Absolute dates associated with Mound 195 and nearby Mound 190, which has a sequence of five superimposed elite houses that partially parallels the sequence of houses in Mound 195, indicate that the structures date within the Xoo phase from about 600–800 CE (Table 5.2).

The final structure (Structure 1) built atop Mound 195, and which has an adjoining plaza with platforms around it, was a civic-residential structure that was never completed before being abandoned (Figure 5.3). Two radiocarbon dates of 730 and 755 CE, and one archaeomagnetic date of 725 CE, date this final structure and indicate that it was probably abandoned between 750 and 800 CE.

Following the abandonment of Mound 195 and neighboring Mound 190, evidence for salt production activities occurs in the already abandoned and disintegrating ruins of the last Xoo phase structures. Fires, built over the dirt from disintegrating adobe walls of the last structures, served to boil brine in *ollas* to extract salt. Associated with these areas of salt production were vessels of Silho or X Fine Orange. A Silho Fine Orange hemispherical bowl and olla were found in the plaza adjoining Mound 195 in an area associated with salt production (Figure 5.4).

A Silho Fine Orange tripod *cajete* was found in association with salt-production activities atop Mound 190 (Figure 5.4). Three archaeomagnetic dates of 1035, 1050, and 1065 CE (Wolfman 1973) were obtained in association with the salt production activity, indicating it took place 200 to 300 years after the abandonment of the last Xoo phase structures of Mound 190 and Mound 195.

Table 5.2 Absolute dates associated with Mound 195 and Mound 190*

Mound 195 Superimposed Houses	*Absolute Dates*	*Mound 190 Superimposed Houses*
Post-abandonment	1065 CE*	Post-abandonment
Silho Fine Orange	1050 CE*	Silho Fine Orange
	1035 CE*	
Structure 195-1	755 + 90 CE	Structure 190-1
	730 + 100 CE	
Structure 195-2	720 + 100 CE	Structure 190-2
	700 + 95 CE	
Structure 195-3	690 + 100 CE	Structure 190-3
Structure 195-4	640 + 100 CE	Structure 190-4
Structure 195-5	---	Structure 190-5
Structure 195-6	---	(No structure)

*Indicates archaeomagnetic dates; C-14 dates not calibrated.

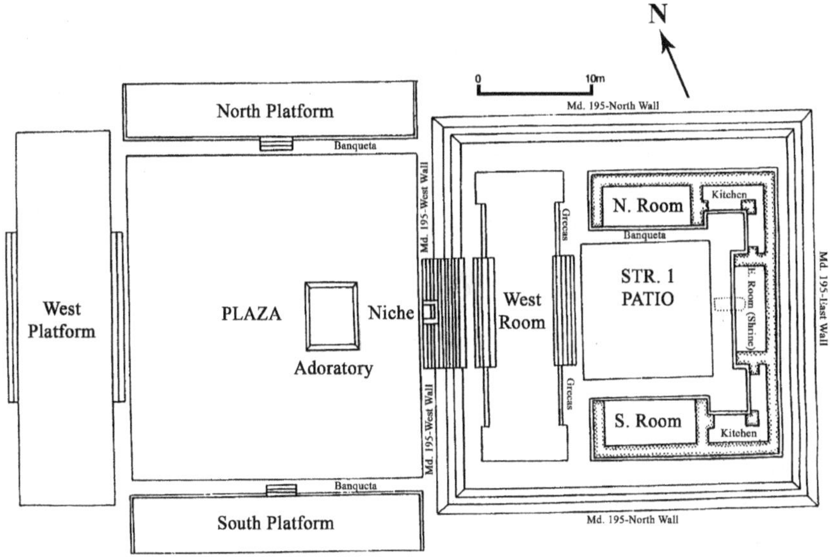

5.3 Reconstruction of Mound 195, Structure 1.

In addition, a burial (68-2) occurred in association with the zone of salt production atop Mound 190 (Figure 5.5). The burial was of a child, six to eight years old, who was placed in a fetal or flexed position with a gray hemispherical bowl on

5.4 Silho or X Fine Orange Vessels from Lambityeco.

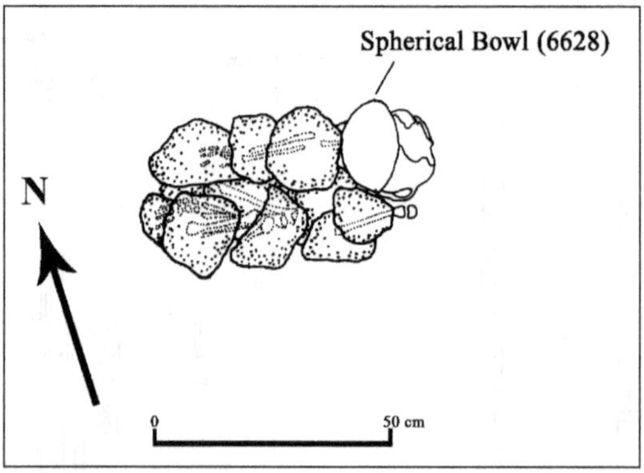

5.5 Burial 68-2, Mound 190, Lambityeco. After Urcid 1983.

his head (Urcid 1983). The bowl, identified by Paddock as Monte Albán V, certainly belongs to the Liobaa phase.

Finally, in a small Xoo phase mound (Mound 92) with an associated tomb (Tomb 8), a Liobaa or Chila phase burial (72-2) was discovered (Figure 5.6). The burial had been placed in a circular hole dug through the ruins of the house and accidentally penetrated the roof of the tomb. It was the flexed burial of an adult male, thirty to forty years old, who had a well-burnished tripod pyriform (pear-shaped) olla placed as an offering (Urcid 1983). Paddock identified the olla as Monte Albán V and it probably dates to either the Liobaa or Chila phase. Both the burial of the child in Mound 190 and the burial of the adult in Mound 92 were flexed, which makes them very distinctive from the extended burials of the Xoo phase.

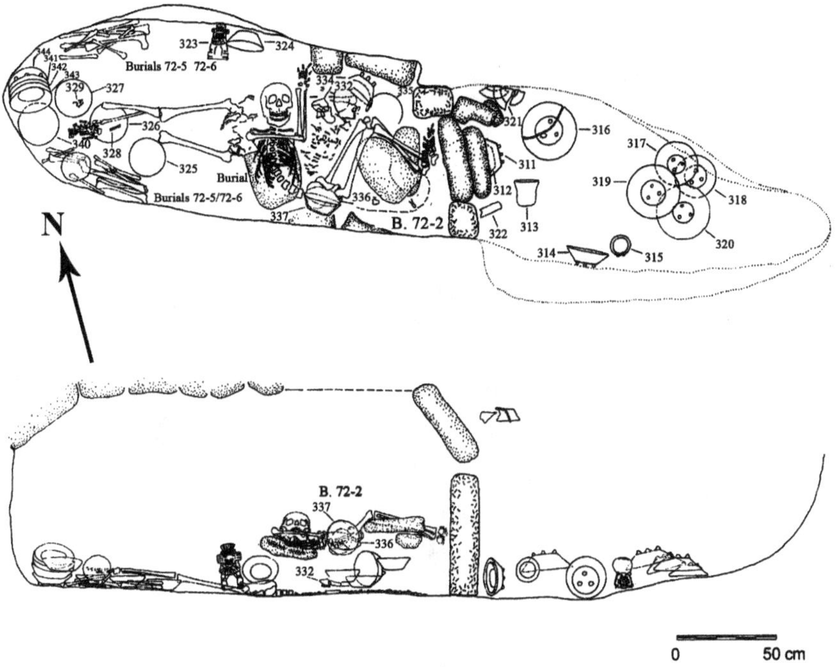

5.6 Intrusive burial (72-2), Tomb 8, Mound 92, Lambityeco.

Kowalewski and his colleagues (1989) have stated that Lambityeco was what they call a "Monte Albán IV" period site, that is, a site that survived the collapse of Monte Albán and grew to its maximum size following the demise of that city. However, in their excavations at Monte Albán, Caso and Bernal (1952:372) reported a stratigraphic sequence that precisely parallels that of Lambityeco outlined above:

> We call . . . IIIB the last period in which temples and palaces were constructed . . . and we call IV the period in which the city had been partially abandoned and offerings in temples and burials were made above the stucco floors in the rubble from the collapsed roofs and walls. Probably this epoch ends with Tula because in tombs and offerings plumbate and Fine Orange pottery have been found which are very characteristic types of the Toltec era; therefore, Period IV should correspond to the period of Tula . . . 900 or 1000 CE. (translated from the original Spanish by the author)

The parallel sequences at Lambityeco and Monte Albán demonstrate that they were contemporaneous during the Xoo phase and largely abandoned during the following Liobaa phase ("IV"). At both sites, Late Classic Xoo phase ceramics are

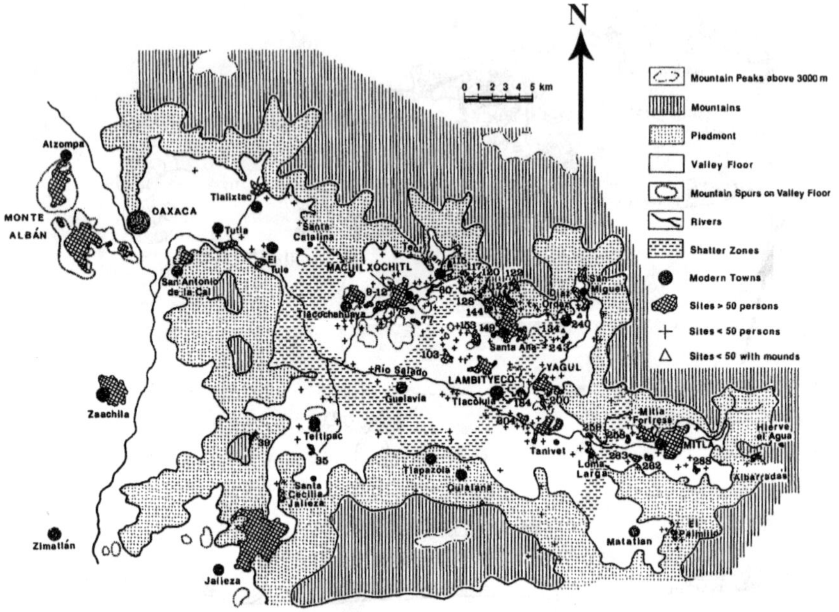

5.7 Xoo phase settlements in the Tlacolula Valley. Base map and locations of modern towns adapted from Welte 1965; site locations approximated from Kowalewski et al. 1989:maps 6–7.

associated with the final periods of construction, and Silho Fine Orange pottery occurs in the collapsed and disintegrating ruins of these Xoo phase buildings. Excavations in Mound 195 and Mound 190 have provided absolute dates for these time periods, which Caso and Bernal did not have from Monte Albán (Bernal 1965:806). More recently, Marcus Winter (1994b) has obtained radiocarbon dates for the Xoo phase from Monte Albán that correspond well with the radiocarbon dates from Lambityeco. The idea that Lambityeco was a "Period IV" site, then, is an error that must be put to rest.

Monte Albán and Lambityeco were contemporaneous during the Xoo phase, a time period during which ancient Zapotec civilization reached its greatest extent and then collapsed (Winter 1990:58–60; 1994a:23–24). Monte Albán was probably the capital of a unified state in the Valley of Oaxaca during the Xoo phase with Lambityeco, Macuilxóchitl, Yagul, and Mitla as district capitals or "secondary administrative centers" in the Tlacolula arm of the valley (Figure 5.7), as I have discussed elsewhere (Lind 1994).

At the end of the Xoo phase, Monte Albán lost political control of the Valley of Oaxaca, and Classic Zapotec civilization—especially the elite component (see

Chapters 1, 6, and 7)—ceased to exist, or was drastically transformed. It is possible, but not yet demonstrated, that Monte Albán continued in the Liobaa phase as the capital of an independent kingdom in the Valley of Oaxaca, but its population would have been reduced considerably and the former capital was abandoned before the arrival of the Spaniards. Some former Xoo phase district capitals (such as Macuilxóchitl, Yagul, and Mitla, which were located in defensible positions in the Tlacolula arm of the valley) remained occupied during the Liobaa and Chila phases and were the capitals of independent kingdoms at the time of the Spanish Conquest (Chapter 6). On the other hand, Lambityeco, which is located on the flat valley floor without natural defenses, was abandoned at the end of the Xoo phase. A number of changes took place at Lambityeco during the Xoo phase that led up to its abandonment. Some of these changes will be highlighted by following a sequential integration approach to the archaeological remains.

XOO PHASE CHANGES IN SALT PRODUCTION AT LAMBITYECO

Lambityeco was a major salt-producing center for the Valley of Oaxaca during the Xoo phase. Peterson (1976:113–115) estimates that Lambityeco produced 90 percent of the salt consumed by the Valley of Oaxaca population during the Xoo phase. A salt marsh occurs along the southern edge of the site and it is bordered by saline soils (Figure 5.8). Salt was produced by obtaining brine from the salt marsh and enriching it by filtering it through saline soils. The enriched brine was boiled over open fires in ollas, which functioned as salt boilers, and once the brine evaporated, the salt was scraped from the ollas.

Peterson's survey of Lambityeco succeeded in locating a number of houses of salt producers scattered throughout the site (Figure 5.8), which led to the conclusion that salt production at Lambityeco was an individual household activity. However, additional surveys and excavations in a 7,500-square-meter area near the salt deposits—where no house mounds occur—yielded apparently contradictory evidence. This area was a Xoo phase salt production workshop in which salt boilers were placed in ovens, instead of over open fires, to evaporate the brine. Peterson hypothesized that the ovens were probably a later innovation in salt production and therefore that the salt workshop was later in the Xoo phase.

The excavation of Mound 91, a series of stratified house remains occupied by salt producers, resolved the apparent contradiction and supported Peterson's hypothesis that the salt workshop occurred later in the Xoo phase. Using a sequential integration approach, Urcid (1983:117–133) has analyzed the features in Mound 91 as part of his study of the Lambityeco tombs and burials. To understand how this analysis was carried out, it is necessary to provide some background information. Each Xoo phase household had a tomb and only the household head

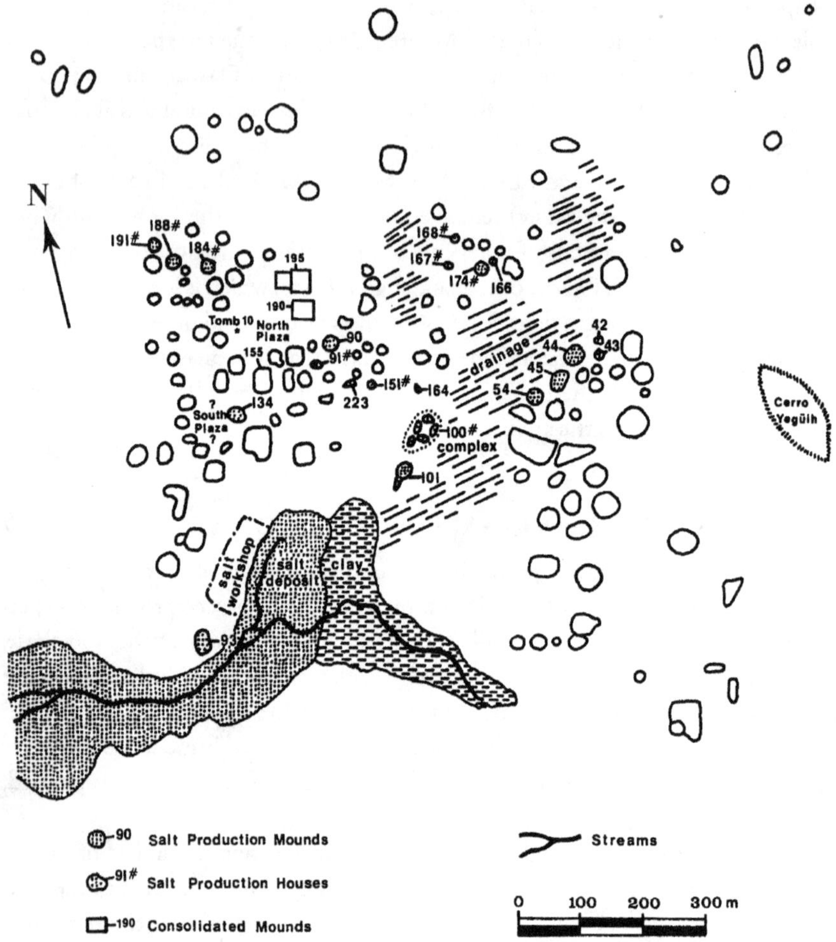

5.8 Xoo phase Lambityeco. Based on data provided by David A. Peterson.

and his principal wife were buried in the household tomb (Lind and Urcid 1983; Winter 1974). Other family members were buried under the patio of the house, room floors, or just beyond the confines of the house. Household tombs were retained in houses, usually under the east room that served as a household shrine to the ancestors, while the houses above them underwent repairs, remodelings, additions, and rebuildings.

The stratified salt producers' house remains in Mound 91 included four superimposed houses with an associated tomb (Tomb 9). The presence of six adults in Tomb 9 accounts for three generations who had occupied the three earlier houses while the fourth generation was occupying the final house in the sequence of four superimposed houses. Therefore, the house remains span a period of four generations or, at twenty-five years per generation, approximately one hundred years during the Xoo phase.

The oldest three houses in the sequence have salt boilers associated with them. This is clear evidence that during the seventy-five years these houses were occupied, probably from around 625 to 700 CE, salt production was an individual household activity. The fourth and final house in the sequence has no salt boilers associated with it, indicating that the final generation of salt producers who occupied the last house in Mound 91, probably between about 700 and 725 CE, no longer carried out salt production as an individual household activity. It seems evident that they were working in salt workshops that were probably established around 700–725 CE.

During the early part of the Xoo phase (ca. 600–700 CE), salt production was an individual household activity carried out by numerous households scattered throughout Lambityeco. Near the end of the Xoo phase (ca. 700–750 CE) salt production was organized into a workshop area bordering on the salt deposits (Figure 5.8). The organization of salt production in a workshop area was most likely carried out by governmental authorities as a way to control salt production at Lambityeco.

XOO PHASE CHANGES IN THE MARKET PLAZA AT LAMBITYECO

As a district center and center for economic specialization, Lambityeco might be expected to have had a market plaza where goods could be exchanged on a daily and/or periodic basis. Evidence for a possible market plaza was first discovered by Lind and Joseph Mogor, who were investigating a looted tomb near Mound 134. Nearby, Lind found a stone with a circular hole in its center that reminded him of similar stones used to anchor awning ropes or to support awning poles in the present-day Tlacolula market. According to Peterson (1976:83, plate 18), Martin Diskin (1967), who has made an intensive ethnographic study of the Tlacolula market, refers to these awning supports as "sun stones" because of their use in erecting awnings to protect vendors and their products from the sun. The area (west of Mound 134) in which the "sun stone" was found covers some 100 meters north to south by 50 meters east to west and is flat with no evidence of mounds. Although no intensive study of this area has been done, it is a probable market plaza area and therefore will be referred to as the South Market Plaza (Figure 5.8).

During his surveys of Lambityeco, Peterson located a large, flat, moundless area south of Mound 195 that he thought might be a market plaza. The area measures roughly 125 meters east to west and 75 meters north to south and is "bounded by large high structures on three sides (north, south, and west)" (Peterson 1976:90).

This area will be referred to as the North Market Plaza and, unlike the South Market Plaza, it has been the subject of intensive systematic survey and limited excavation (Figure 5.8).

From a carefully designed systematic survey, Peterson was able to demonstrate that the surface materials in the North Market Plaza were clearly distinct from surface materials in the salt workshop area and from surface materials in areas of domestic habitation. Peterson noted that the absence of *sahumadores* (ladle censers carried in religious ceremonies) in the North Market Plaza would tend to rule out its use as an area of religious ceremonies. In addition, he located two "sun stones" and noted that the North Market Plaza had the highest density of cajetes (open rim bowls) at Lambityeco. Peterson (1976:91–92) observed that the cajetes are of graded sizes and hypothesized that, in the absence of a system of weights in prehispanic Mesoamerican markets, they were used as a systems of graded measures in the market plaza.

Although unrelated to Peterson's work and not designed to test this area as a possible market plaza, William Fowler excavated thirty 2-by-2-meter stratigraphic test pits in the North Market Plaza as part of his random sample test pit project at Lambityeco. He uncovered numerous small holes filled with sherds and ash scattered throughout the North Market Plaza. Peterson considered these mini middens to have been left by transient vendors who, like their present-day counterparts in traditional Zapotec market plazas, build small fires to cook their meals (or food to sell) while attending the market.

Although the North Market Plaza showed no remains of house mounds, in one of his test pits located near the center of the western part of the North Market Plaza, Fowler encountered the remains of a commoner's house and its associated tomb (Tomb 10). This evidence would seem to contradict the idea that the area was a market plaza. However, a sequential integration analysis of the House of Tomb 10 remains by Urcid (1983:134–139) provides clarification.

Urcid's analysis revealed the presence of three superimposed house remains associated with Tomb 10. This tomb contained four individuals and a fifth individual had been buried in a slab-lined grave directly above the tomb, but most of the bones from this burial were removed when the house was abandoned. The sequence of burials indicates that the successive house remains had been occupied over three generations, or about seventy-five years. No radiocarbon dates were obtained in association with the tomb or house remains. The tomb, however, contained a very unusual double cup. The only other double cup of this type has been found in Tomb 6 in Mound 195, dated from ca. 625 to 700 CE. The House of Tomb 10 was probably occupied between ca. 625 and 700 CE.

The most likely reason that the House of Tomb 10 left no house mound, despite being composed of three stratified houses, is that the house was leveled when the

North Market Plaza was built around 700 CE. This is also the probable reason that the bones were removed from the burial in the slab-lined grave above the tomb when the house was abandoned. Two other houses, the House of Tomb 3 and the House of Tomb 4, like the House of Tomb 10, were leveled and left no house mound. Likewise, the bones from the burial in Tomb 4 were removed when the house was abandoned. In this case, however, the Houses of Tombs 3 and 4 were leveled in ca. 700 CE to build the north platform of Structure 195-1 (Figure 5.3). Therefore, the leveling of commoner houses for public projects appears to have been a common practice at Lambityeco late in the Xoo phase.

Some additional evidence indirectly supports the idea that the North Market Plaza was established around 700 CE. Peterson (1976:90) observed that large structures bound the North Market Plaza to the north, south, and west. The last phase of construction of one of these large structures (Mound 195) is known to have occurred between ca. 700 and 750 CE (Figure 5.3). At that time Mound 195 was converted into a large civic-residential system located along the north side of the market plaza. Furthermore, a temple precinct system represented by Lambityeco's largest mound, twelve-meter-high Mound 155, was located along the south side of the market plaza. One of Fowler's test pits was excavated in the plaza of Mound 155 and showed it to be a single phase of construction like the plaza of Mound 195. It is probable, therefore, that Mound 155 was converted into a temple precinct system, or what Winter (1986) has called a TPA, the same time Mound 195 was converted into a civic-residential system—between ca. 700 and 750 CE. The North Market Plaza, situated between these two monumental systems, was probably established coincidental with their construction ca. 700 CE (Figure 5.8).

Since the area where the North Market Plaza was established late in the Xoo phase was probably filled with houses of commoners in the earlier part of the Xoo phase, the location of any possible earlier market plaza remains to be discovered at Lambityeco. The probable location of this early Xoo phase market was most likely the South Market Plaza. Several large mounds occur on the north, south, and east sides of this probable early Xoo phase South Market Plaza (Figure 5.8).

XOO PHASE CHANGES IN THE RULING LINEAGE AT LAMBITYECO

To understand changes in the ruling lineage at Lambityeco, it is first necessary to explore more fully the nature of ancient Monte Albán's government during the Xoo phase. Different forms of government existed in preindustrial states; ethnographic studies have documented some of these forms. In his study of African preindustrial states, Lloyd (1965) has identified three different forms of government; archaeological correlates for these different forms exist, especially expressed in burial practices.

The ancient Zapotec state of Monte Albán probably had the form of government that Lloyd (1965:102) calls "political association," which includes strongly developed patron-client relations among commoners and the local nobility. The archaeological correlates of such an organization include a well-developed cult of the ancestors (Lind and Urcid 1983, 1990)—such as that found among the Dahomey, Benin, and Lozi, who had this form of government.

In a government by political association, the king has the right to appoint anyone in the society as a noble ruler (Lloyd 1965:102). In practice, however, the king usually appoints the most important and respected person in a community or region. This person has attained his importance through patron-client relations. Among Zapotec communities today, these patron-client relations survive in the form of the *guelaguetza*, the "precious gift" (Williams 1979).

To retain the position of noble ruler within the family or lineage, funerary rituals involving the curation of the ancestors' bones are practiced. Among Xoo phase Zapotecs, elaborate tombs were constructed for deceased nobles and their bones were curated by their descendants (Lind and Urcid 1983, 1990). The statement being made to the king by this cult of the dead is that his ancestors had appointed their ancestors as noble rulers; therefore, they have the right to continue as noble rulers. If the king decides that the local nobles are becoming too powerful, he may replace them with other persons of his choice. If he decides to replace them with members of his own royal lineage, the form of government changes to what Lloyd (1965:104) calls a royal aristocracy.

At Xoo phase Lambityeco, Mound 195 became the seat of its noble rulers during the Xoo phase. A sequential integration approach to the stratified remains of their elite houses provides insight into the political power relationships between these local noble rulers and the kings of Monte Albán during the Xoo phase.

Structure 6 was the first or oldest house built within Mound 195 (Lind 2001). It was a substantial house with a patio paved with white plaster and had white plaster room floors. The house was built to Monte Albán elite standards, that is, four rooms arranged around the sides of a central patio with three smaller corner rooms. The fourth corner of the patio contained an entry vestibule reached from the outside by an L-shaped blind corridor (Caso 1938:69, 83–84). Three of the rooms along the sides of the patio were living quarters and the three corner rooms were kitchens, each one associated with one of the living quarters. The noble household head and his principal wife occupied one of the living quarters and associated kitchen, while the other two living quarters and associated kitchens were occupied either by his married sons and their wives and children or his secondary wives and their children. The east room of Structure 6 was the household shrine beneath which was the household tomb (Tomb 5), a single-chamber tomb with stone walls and a white plaster floor (Figure 5.2).

Structure 6 was built and occupied early in the Xoo phase when Lambityeco was being resettled. The household head who built and occupied Structure 6 between ca. 600 and 625 CE was certainly a wealthy individual. A large area of ash and salt boilers directly south of Mound 195 indicates that he was involved in salt production. It seems likely that either he or his son was appointed ruler (*coqui*) of Lambityeco by the Monte Albán king.

If the Structure 6 household head was not appointed ruler of Lambityeco, his son, the Structure 5 household head, probably was. Structure 5 was built directly over Structure 6 (Figure 5.2) atop a platform with a *talud*, or sloping stone wall, faced with red plaster. A new household tomb (Tomb 6) was built beneath the eastern part of the patio. Tomb 6 is a very elaborate tomb built of stone; it has niches in three of its walls and a large façade topped by double cornices. By Monte Albán standards, Tomb 6 was clearly an elite tomb.

The Structure 5 ruler (coqui) and his principal wife (*xonaxi*) occupied their elite house between ca. 625 and 650 CE. This ruler may have appointed or acquired an appointment for his brother as Lambityeco's high priest of Cociyo, the Zapotec deity of rain and lightning (Lind and Urcid 1983:82–84). His brother built an elite house, Structure 190-5, a few meters directly south of Mound 195—initiating the sequence of five superimposed houses within Mound 190 occupied by priests of Cociyo. The coqui also appointed a commoner to be his *golaba*, or tally man, in charge of collecting taxes or tribute and organizing communal labor for public works projects (Lind and Urcid 1983:85–87). This commoner occupied the House of Tomb 3 about forty-five meters northwest of Mound 195.

The power and wealth of the Lambityeco rulers increased with the son of the Structure 5 ruler, the ruler who built and occupied Structure 4 between ca. 650 and 675 CE. The Structure 4 ruler built his house on top of the Structure 5 house but greatly expanded it (Figure 5.2). First, he raised the platform atop which the house was built and extended it. Second, he added a second patio with rooms around it along the north side of the original house. Third, he expanded Tomb 6 from a single-chamber to a double-chamber tomb (Lind 2004). Finally, he built an altar at the back of the east room, or household shrine to the ancestors, which probably had friezes showing his noble lineage. Unfortunately, they were destroyed or removed by later construction activity. His construction activities made Structure 4 larger than most of the elite houses at Monte Albán.

The power and wealth of the Lambityeco rulers increased even more with the son of the Structure 4 ruler, the ruler who built and occupied Structure 3 between ca. 675 and 700 CE. The Structure 3 ruler raised the rooms around the north patio so that all four had to be reached by stairways from the patio below. The walls on either side of the stairways are framed by single cornices. He also raised the rooms along the south side of the south patio, which had to be reached by a stairway from the patio below. The walls on either side of the stairway have panels decorated with grecas and framed by double cornices.

The Structure 3 ruler also had a large altar complex built above Tomb 6 on the east side of the patio (Figure 5.2). The complex includes a square-top altar flanked by sloping stone walls two meters high (Figure 5.9). The bases and tops of the walls on either side of the altar contain panels with friezes framed by double cornices. The upper friezes had been destroyed but the lower friezes are preserved intact and depict married couples with their calendrical names—the ancestors representing the noble lineage of the Structure 3 ruler. Each of the males in the friezes carries a human femur in his hand, the femur of his ancestor, symbolic of his right to rule (Figure 5.9). The altar complex above Tomb 6 was a clearly visible statement by the Structure 3 ruler of his right to rule Lambityeco.

The Structure 3 ruler did not stop with the altar complex above Tomb 6. He also had two life-size plaster portrait heads either of himself and his principal wife or of his parents attached to the façade of Tomb 6 (Figure 5.9). The portrait heads have their calendrical names incorporated into them (Urcid 2001). His name was Lord 1 Lachi (Ballcourt) and her name was Lady 10 Naa (Cornfield). Nothing as elaborate or ostentatious as these portrait heads has ever been found on any tomb at Monte Albán.

It is evident that the local rulers of Lambityeco were becoming more and more wealthy and powerful from ca. 600 to 700 CE. The Structure 3 ruler died in 690 CE, if the radiocarbon date associated with his offering in Tomb 6 is accurate, and his wife probably died about ten years later, ca. 700 CE. Her body was buried rather unceremoniously by way of a hole dug in the center of the flat top altar and through the roof of the main chamber of Tomb 6. The hole in the altar was never repaired and Structure 3 was partially abandoned following her interment in ca. 700 CE.

At this point in the sequence it appears that the Monte Albán king put an end to the ruling noble lineage at Lambityeco and, perhaps, named a member of his royal lineage to rule Lambityeco. The new ruler occupied the rooms around the north patio of Structure 3 while Mound 195 was being built. Once the western half of Mound 195 was built, he abandoned Structure 3 and occupied a temporary residence, Structure 2, atop Mound 195 (Figure 5.2). Structure 3 was buried under construction fill used to raise the eastern half of Mound 195. Once Mound 195 was built, the Structure 1 residence atop Mound 195 was completed and occupied by the new ruler in ca. 725–730 CE.

Structure 1 is a huge civic-residential system that was built to Monte Albán standards (Figure 5.3). It has the same layout and basal measurements as Mound M and System IV on the Main Plaza at Monte Albán (Lind 1994:108) and was probably designed by Monte Albán architects. Structure 1 includes Mound 195, a two-tiered, seven-meter-high pyramidal platform with sloping stone walls around

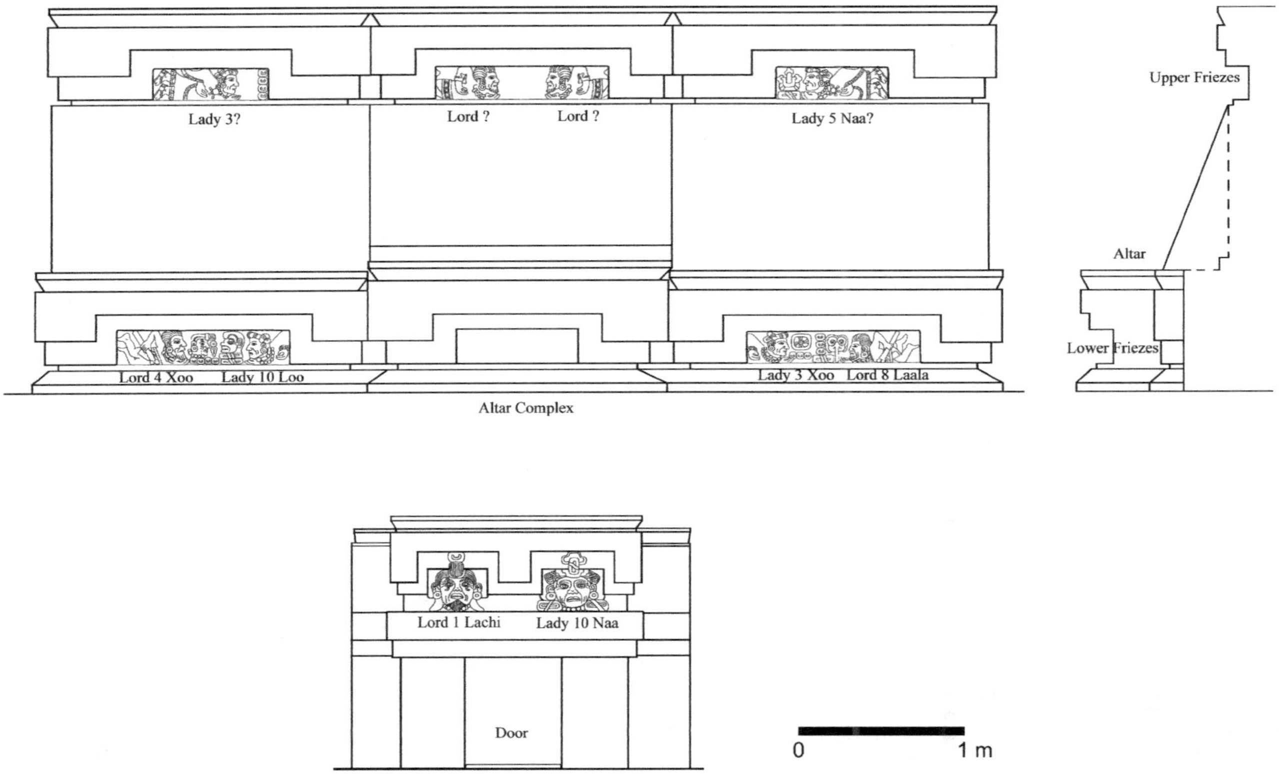

5.9 Reconstruction of altar complex above Tomb 6 in Structure 3. Drawing courtesy of Javier Urcid.

it, atop which the Structure 1 residence was built. The Structure 1 residence has a large patio, nearly twice as large as the Structure 3 patios, with rooms around it that are also nearly twice as large as any of the rooms of Structure 3. A monumental stairway, nine meters wide, descends the west side of Mound 195 into a large plaza surrounded on the other three sides by platforms. The plaza has an adoratory, a small low square platform, within it.

Despite its enormous size, the Structure 1 residence has a very small tomb. Tomb 1 is a single-chamber tomb with stone walls and roof but no real façade; it is a very simple and small tomb when compared to the larger and much more elaborate Tomb 6 associated with the houses of Mound 195-Sub. Furthermore, no evidence of an altar complex showing the ruler's noble lineage was found in Structure 1. There is a niche in the monumental stairway on the west side of Mound 195 that might have been intended to display a carved stone showing the ruler's heritage, but no carved stone was found. The small size of Tomb 1 suggests that, although the Structure 1 civic-residential system was constructed to impress and convey the power of the state, the Structure 1 ruler (coqui) of Lambityeco did not have much personal power within the state.

Interestingly, Structure 1 was a work in progress. It was unfinished when it was abandoned in ca. 750–800 CE. The north and south platforms along the plaza never had walls completed around them. Furthermore, the south and west platforms had piles of construction fill on them, indicating that they were to be raised to higher levels. A large limestone block from which stones were being removed to build walls was left at the southeast corner of Mound 195. A raised and paved walkway or road along the south side of Mound 195 also was never finished.

CONCLUSIONS

A sequential integration approach has been used to elucidate some of the changes evident in the archaeological remains at Lambityeco during the Late Classic Xoo phase (ca. 600–800 CE). Lambityeco was resettled as a salt-producing community at the beginning of the Xoo phase and by ca. 600 CE had become established as a district center for Monte Albán in the Tlacolula arm of the Valley of Oaxaca. A wealthy local noble involved in salt production, and probably heavily invested in patron-client relations, was appointed by the Monte Albán king to be the ruler (coqui) of Lambityeco. Over the next 100 years (ca. 600–700 CE), the successive rulers within this local noble lineage became wealthier and more powerful.

Around 700 CE, a number of dramatic changes took place at Lambityeco. The local ruling lineage was apparently deposed by the ruler of Monte Albán, who probably appointed a member of his own royal lineage to be ruler of Lambityeco. The new ruler established some sweeping economic changes at Lambityeco. Salt production, which had been an individual household activity in the early part of the Xoo phase, was reorganized in a government workshop near the salt deposits. This change made it easier for political authorities to control and tax salt production but probably was not a popular move among salt producers who had enjoyed more independence when salt production was an individual household activity.

Lambityeco's South Market Plaza, located near the salt deposits during the early part of the Xoo phase, was shifted to the North Market Plaza around 700 CE. The establishment of the North Market Plaza resulted in the leveling of a number of commoner houses, probably an unpopular move with the commoners at Lambityeco. The new North Market Plaza was situated between two large government buildings that were newly built and served to control the market plaza.

One of these new government buildings was Mound 195 Structure 1, the civic-residential system occupied by the new ruler of Lambityeco, located along the north side of the new market plaza. It was built over the older houses of the former ruling lineage. Its construction also involved the leveling of some commoner houses. The other new government building was Mound 155, a twelve-meter-high temple that had an adjoining plaza with platforms around it and was located along the south side of the new market plaza. Both of these government buildings were built to Monte Albán standards, or TPAs (temple-patio-adoratory complexes), between ca. 700 and 750 CE.

Structure 1 was never finished before its abandonment around 750–800 CE. It appears that workmen simply stopped working and abandoned construction in progress. The abandonment of Structure 1 coincides with that of Lambityeco at the end of the Xoo phase. Evidently, the commoners at Lambityeco, tied to the former ruling lineage through generations of patron-client relations, rebelled against Monte Albán overlords by leaving the site and fleeing, perhaps to nearby Yagul.

As Arthur Joyce and his colleagues (2001) have pointed out, on the Oaxaca Coast, commoners played an important role in rejecting the political system and its symbols of power. In the Valley of Oaxaca during the Postclassic Liobaa phase, symbols of Classic Zapotec power disappeared. Gone are the funerary urns, state-sponsored images of Cociyo, carved stelae, and large temples, thereby initiating the transformations that led from the Late Classic to Postclassic. The Xoo phase palaces and temples at Lambityeco fell into ruins and were later degraded by commoners who used them as platforms for their salt boilers.

REFERENCES

Bernal, Ignacio

1965 Archaeological Synthesis of Oaxaca. In *Handbook of Middle American Indians,* Vol. 3: *Archaeology of Southern Mesoamerica,* Part 2, edited by R. Wauchope and G. Willey, pp. 788–813. University of Texas Press, Austin.

Blanton, Richard E.

1978 *Monte Albán: Settlement Patterns at the Ancient Zapotec Capital.* Academic Press, New York.

Caso, Alfonso

1938 *Exploraciones en Oaxaca: Quinta y sexta temporadas 1936–1937.* Publicación No. 34. Instituto Panamericano de Geografía e Historia, Mexico City.

Caso, Alfonso, and Ignacio Bernal

1952 *Urnas de Oaxaca.* Memorias del Instituto Nacional de Antropología e Historia, No. 2. INAH, Mexico City.

Diskin, Martin

1967 Economics and Society in Tlacolula, Oaxaca, Mexico. Unpublished Ph.D. Dissertation, Department of Anthropology, University of California, Los Angeles.

Finsten, Laura

1995 *Jalieza, Oaxaca: Activity Specialization at a Hilltop Center.* Vanderbilt University Publications in Anthropology, No. 48. Nashville, Tennessee.

Joyce, Arthur, Laura Arnaud Bustamante, and Marc Levine

2001 Commoner Power: A Case Study from the Classic to the Post-classic Collapse on the Oaxaca Coast. *Journal of Archaeological Method and Theory* 8(4): 343–385.

Kowalewski, Stephen A., Gary M. Feinman, Laura M. Finsten, Richard E. Blanton, and Linda M. Nicholas

1989 *Monte Albán's Hinterland, Part II: Prehispanic Settlement Patterns in Tlacolula, Etla and Ocotlán, the Valley of Oaxaca, Mexico.* Memoirs of the Museum of Anthropology, University of Michigan, No. 23. University of Michigan, Ann Arbor.

Lind, Michael D.

1977 Mixtec Kingdoms in the Nochixtlán Valley: A Preconquest to Postconquest Archaeological Perspective. Unpublished Ph.D. Dissertation, Department of Anthropology, University of Arizona. Tucson.

1979 *Postclassic and Early Colonial Mixtec Houses in the Nochixtlán Valley, Oaxaca.* Vanderbilt University Publications in Anthropology, No. 23. Nashville, Tennessee.

1987 *The Sociocultural Dimensions of Mixtec Ceramics.* Vanderbilt University Publications in Anthropology, No. 33. Nashville, Tennessee.

1991–92 Unos problemas con la cronología de Monte Albán y una nueva serie de nombres para las fases. *Notas Mesoamericanas* 13:177–192.

1994 Monte Albán y el Valle de Oaxaca durante la Fase Xoo. In *Monte Albán: Estudios Recientes,* edited by M. Winter, pp. 99–111. Proyecto Especial Monte Alban 1992–1994, Contribución No. 2. Centro INAH Oaxaca, Oaxaca.

2001 Lambityeco and the Xoo Phase: The Elite Residences of Mound 195. In *Memoria de la Primera Mesa Redonda de Monte Albán: Procesos de cambio y conceptualización del tiempo,* edited by N. Robles, pp. 113–128. CONACULTA-INAH, Mexico City.

2004 Lambityeco, Tomb 6. In *Homenaje a John Paddock*, edited by P. Plunket, pp. 45–66. Universidad de Las Américas, Cholula, Puebla.

Lind, Michael D., and Javier Urcid

1983 The Lords of Lambityeco and Their Nearest Neighbors, *Notas Mesoamericanas* 9:78–111.

1990 La zona arqueológica de Lambityeco. In *Lecturas históricas del Estado de Oaxaca*, Vol.1: *Epoca prehispánica*, edited by M. Winter, pp. 287–307. INAH, Mexico City.

Lloyd, Peter C.

1965 The Political Structure of African Kingdoms. In *Political Systems and the Distribution of Power,* edited by M. Banton, pp. 63–112. Tavistock Publication, London.

Markens, Robert J.

2004 Ceramic Chronology in the Valley of Oaxaca, Mexico, during the Late Classic and Postclassic Periods and the Organization of Ceramic Production. Unpublished Ph.D. Dissertation, Department of Anthropology, Brandeis University. Waltham, Massachusetts.

Martínez, Cira, Robert Markens, Marcus Winter, and Michael Lind

2000 *Cerámica de la Fase Xoo (Monte Albán IIIB–IV) del Valle de Oaxaca.* Proyecto Especial Monte Alban 1992–1994, Contribución No. 8. Centro INAH Oaxaca, Oaxaca.

Peterson, David A.

1976 Ancient Commerce. Unpublished Ph.D. Dissertation, Department of Anthropology, New York State University at Binghamton. Binghamton.

Plog, Fred T.

1974 *The Study of Prehistoric Change.* Academic Press, New York.

Urcid, Javier

1983 The Tombs and Burials from Lambityeco: A Pre-Hispanic Community in the Valley of Oaxaca, Mexico. Unpublished Masters Thesis, Department of Anthropology, Universidad de las Américas. Cholula, Puebla.

2001 *Zapotec Hieroglyphic Writing.* Studies in Pre-Columbian Art and Archaeology, No. 34. Dumbarton Oaks Research Library and Collection, Washington, DC.

Welte, Cecil

1965 Welte's Ready Reference Map of the Valley of Oaxaca. Map on file, Welty Institute, Oaxaca.

Williams, Aubrey

1979 Cohesive Features of the Guelagetza System in Mitla. In *Social, Political, and Economic Life in Contemporary Oaxaca,* edited by A. Williams, pp. 91–101. Vanderbilt University Publications in Anthropology, No. 24. Nashville, Tennessee.

Winter, Marcus

1974 Residential Patterns at Monte Albán, Oaxaca, Mexico. *Science* 186:981–987.

1986 Templo-Patio-Adoratorio: Un conjunto arquitectónico no residencial en el Oaxaca prehispánico. *Cuadernos de Arquitectura Mesoamericana* 7:51–59.

1989 From Classic to Post-Classic in Prehispanic Oaxaca. In *Mesoamerica after the Decline of Teotihuacan, A.D. 700–900,* edited by R. Diehl and J. Berlo, pp. 123–130. Dumbarton Oaks Research Library and Collection, Washington, DC.

1990 Oaxaca Prehispánica: Una Introducción. In *Lecturas históricas del Estado de Oaxaca,* Vol.1: *Epoca prehispánica,* edited by M. Winter, pp. 31–217. INAH, Mexico City.

1994a El Proyecto Especial Monte Albán 1992–1994: Antecedentes, intervenciones y perspectivas. In *Monte Albán: Estudios Recientes,* edited by M. Winter, pp. 1–24. Proyecto Especial Monte Alban 1992–1994, Contribución No. 2. Centro INAH Oaxaca, Oaxaca.

1994b Nuevas determinaciones de radiocarbono de Monte Albán. In *Monte Albán: Estudios Recientes,* edited by M. Winter, pp. 119–120. Proyecto Especial Monte Alban 1992–1994, Contribución No. 2. Centro INAH Oaxaca, Oaxaca.

Wolfman, Daniel

1973 A Re-Evaluation of Mesoamerican Chronology A.D. 1–1200, Unpublished Ph.D. Dissertation, Department of Anthropology, University of Colorado. Colorado Springs.

6

Robert Markens, Marcus Winter, and Cira Martínez López

Ethnohistory, Oral History, and Archaeology at Macuilxóchitl

PERSPECTIVES ON THE POSTCLASSIC PERIOD (800–1521 CE) IN THE VALLEY OF OAXACA

The nature of community organization in the Valley of Oaxaca following the decline of Monte Albán at the end of the Classic period (800 CE) remains obscure, if not invisible, due to longstanding difficulties with the Early Postclassic (800–1200 CE) portion of the regional ceramic chronology (see Chapter 2). A case in point is the issue of how and precisely when the competitive, territorially compact kingdoms or city-states, known to the Spanish in the sixteenth century as cacicazgos, emerged (Chapter 1; Oudijk 2000:10; 2002:73–76). Recently, the regional ceramic chronology for the Classic-Postclassic period transition has been illuminated through excavations at Monte Albán (Herrera Muzgo Torres 2000; Herrera Muzgo Torres et al. 1999; Martínez López et al. 2000) and a ceramic seriation of Oaxaca Valley tomb and grave offerings spanning this interval (Chapter 2; Markens 2004a). These studies divide the Late Classic period into the Peche (500–600 CE) and Xoo phases (600–800 CE). The Liobaa phase (800–1200 CE) corresponds to the Early Postclassic, and the Chila phase (1200–1521 CE) to the Late Postclassic period (Chapter 2, Figure 2.1).

In this chapter we consider the nature of the Early and Late Postclassic period occupation of the Valley of Oaxaca in the light of pertinent ethnohistoric documents,

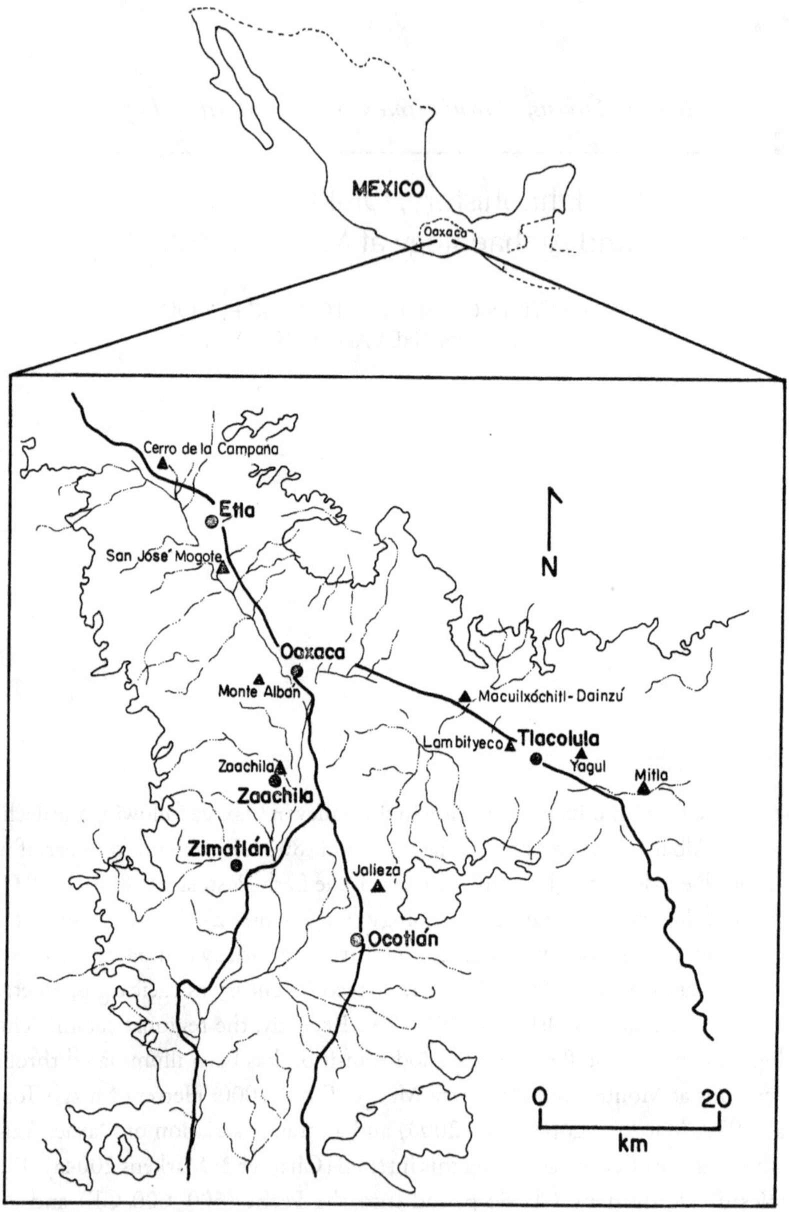

6.1 Map of the Valley of Oaxaca and the principal places mentioned in text.

contemporary oral history from the town of San Mateo Macuilxóchitl, and the findings from a recently completed program of salvage excavations at Macuilxóchitl (Figure 6.1). The excavations took place from April to October 2002 in connection with the widening of the Pan-American Highway (Mexico 190) from Oaxaca to the Isthmus of Tehuantepec.

DOCUMENTS RELATING TO THE VALLEY OF OAXACA FROM THE LATE POSTCLASSIC AND COLONIAL PERIODS

One of the most important sources of insight into Zapotec political organization of the Valley of Oaxaca for the Postclassic are the Colonial period native documents painted on lengths of cotton cloth, known as *lienzos*, which are commonly found in Valley, Sierra and Isthmian communities (Chapter 3). The information provided in them is complemented by a number of the prehispanic codices or screenfold books from the neighboring Mixteca Alta and by the surviving prehispanic codex-style paintings that decorate a number of plastered stone lintels of Mitla's palaces (Pohl 2000). These indigenous sources provide a basis for inferring principles of Postclassic period elite ideology and worldview in Oaxaca, used by individuals of high social standing to legitimize or enhance their power (see Kertzer 1988).

Although conceived and painted with different purposes in mind, the prehispanic codices and Colonial period lienzos overlap to a large extent thematically. They record from a local perspective—that is, from the point of view of the cacicazgo or one of its subject communities—the establishment of the polity's ruling dynasty, the genealogy of the royal family, the deeds of its rulers, and often the territorial extent of its domain and its subject communities. Through these documents there emerges for the Postclassic period the image of an intricate web of political alliances among the cacicazgos of the Valley of Oaxaca and beyond, forged through marriage exchange and episodes of armed conflict, conquest, and political incorporation (Chapters 1 and 3; Oudijk 2002; Pohl and Byland 1994:191; Whitecotton 1990).

One might consider the lienzo known as the *Genealogy of Macuilxóchitl* to be a typical example (Figure 6.2). The document, painted a generation after the Spanish Conquest, records fifteen generations of semi-divine rulers (Whitecotton 1990:15) extending back in time to the threshold of the Late Postclassic period (1200 CE) when the dynasty was founded by Lord 8/11 Rabbit, originating from a mythical place translated as the "Lagoon of Primordial Blood" (Chapter 3; Oudijk 2000:118–119). The document records marriages with the noble families from nearby cacicazgos in the Tlacolula branch of the valley and sometime later with those of Zaachila in the valley's southern arm. Zaachila appears to have been the preeminent political center in the valley throughout much of the Postclassic period (Pohl 2000:35–47). The *Genealogy of Macuilxóchitl* also records that one of the town's rulers, Lord 2 Water, assisted Lord Quixicayo 6 Water of Zaachila with the conquest of the towns of Huitzo and Mazaltepec, in the Etla branch of the valley, by

6.2 A portion of the Genealogy of Macuilxóchitl.

supplying arms and fielding a contingent of warriors in fulfillment of his tributary obligation to Zaachila (Oudijk 2000:119–120).

A complementary document, the 1580 *Relación Geográfica* from Macuilxóchitl (Acuña 1984), which is accompanied by a painted map (Figure 6.3), corroborates the polity's subject status to Zaachila at some point. The document and map specify the extent of Macuilxóchitl's domain by identifying its putative subject communities. The map's Nahuatl gloss records that Macuilxóchitl was at one point governed by a ruler appointed by either Lord Cosijoeza 11 Water of Zaachila or his son, Lord Quixicayo 6 Water (Acuña 1984:330; Oudijk 2000:131–132).

The *Genealogy of Macuilxóchitl* is typical of the lienzos and codices relevant to the Valley of Oaxaca regarding time depth. The genealogies in these documents (e.g., the *Genealogy of Quiaviní*, the *Genealogy of Tabaá*, the *Yale Genealogy*) are, in general, temporally shallow, extending no farther back than the thirteenth century. There is, however, an exception in the instance of the *Genealogy of Quialoo* from Santa Cruz Mixtepec located in the southern branch of the valley. This document records seventeen generations of rulers before the Spanish Conquest, placing the dynasty's founding at the beginning of the twelfth century. Reference is also made to Zaachila, which played an instrumental role in founding Mixtepec's ruling dynasty. This would indicate that Zaachila was already by then a venerable place of authority and a source of legitimacy in the valley.

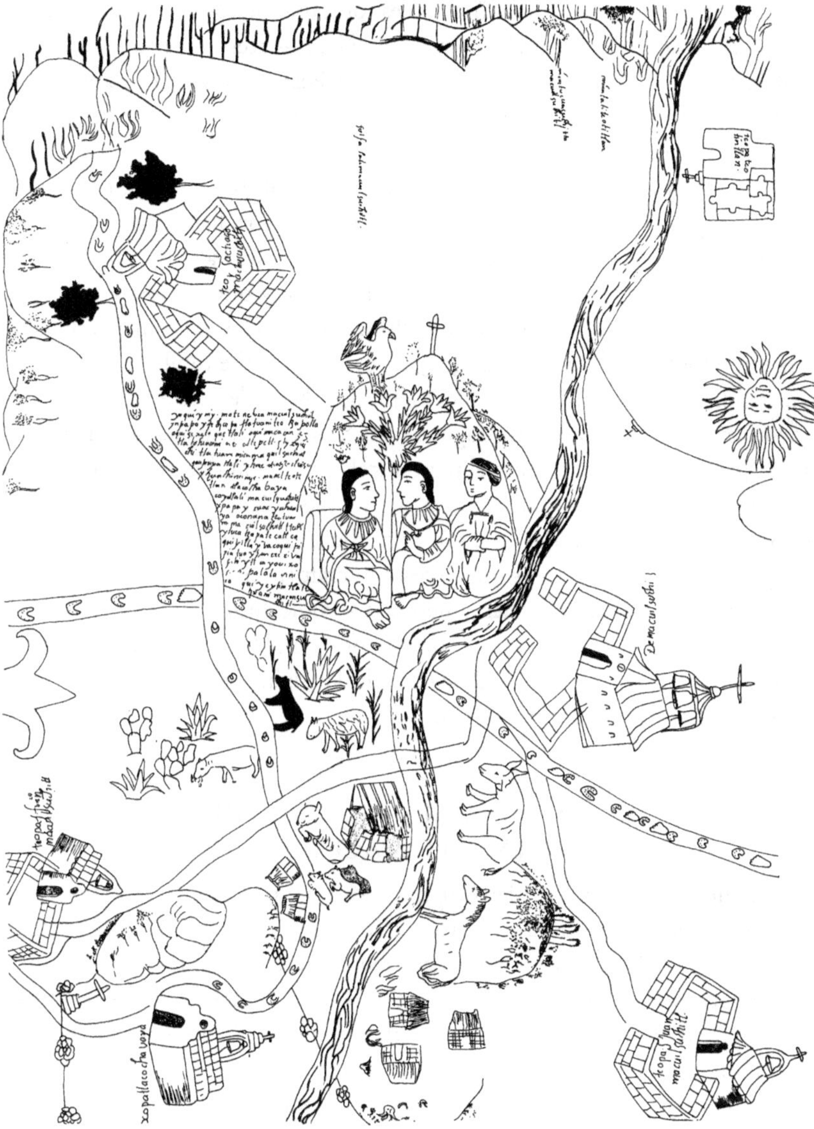

6.3 1580 Map of Macuilxóchitl.

With the exceptions of Mixtepec and Zaachila, the documentary sources indicate that from the thirteenth century on, Zapotec royal houses were established throughout the Valley of Oaxaca, concentrating what may have been a rurally dispersed population during the Early Postclassic period into a number of compact, more densely populated centers. The process of founding royal houses created the political landscape of territorially circumscribed city-states in the valley and coincided in time with the appearance of the Late Postclassic Chila ceramic phase, which is dated by radiocarbon assays to the interval 1200–1521 CE (Chapter 2; Bernal and Gamio 1974:21).

The pottery of the Chila phase is readily identifiable by abundant hemispherical and composite silhouette serving bowls made of a fine, hard gray paste known as G3M; the presence of hollow elongated tripod supports; and the appearance of vividly painted polychrome pottery. Polychrome pottery, often decorated with pan-Mesoamerican religious symbols or embellished with codex-style images (Chapter 1), is often found exclusively or in greatest quantity in the tombs and palaces of high-standing individuals (e.g., Gallegos 1978). The wide extent of this ceramic horizon across the valley and throughout much of Oaxaca would appear to be at least in part the result of intense elite political interaction throughout the region as can be inferred from the Late Postclassic and Colonial period codices and lienzos. Another factor promoting the spread of the Late Postclassic ceramic horizon throughout much of Oaxaca is the increase in craft specialization and commerce, which appears to characterize Mesoamerica as a whole during this time (Smith and Berdan 2003). We now consider the contemporary oral history and archaeological findings from our investigations at Macuilxóchitl in light of the ethnohistoric documents relevant to the Valley of Oaxaca.

CONTEMPORARY ORAL HISTORY FROM SAN MATEO MACUILXÓCHITL

The present-day residents of Macuilxóchitl possess a rich tradition of beliefs and religious practices that appear to be rooted in part in the town's prehispanic past. Although the town's residents are silent about the elite history recorded in its Colonial period documents, recalling only Rey Pacheco, the last in a line of caciques who lived in the nineteenth century, their traditions illuminate aspects of the town's indigenous past related to worldview and ritual practice.

The modern town of Macuilxóchitl lies at the foot of the imposing hill they call Cerro Danush (Figure 6.4), the very one that appears so prominently in the 1580 *Mapa de Macuilxóchitl*. Today a small chapel crowns the ruin of a temple platform that sits atop the hill, and it is here that one of the town's most important annual fiestas takes place: el Día de la Santa Cruz, or Day of the Holy Cross. Celebrated every May 3, just before the onset of the summer rains marking the beginning of the annual planting season, Macuilxóchitl's faithful ascend the summit to leave offerings and to pray for health and prosperity. Among the many things they say about the hill, numerous residents report that it is hollow and contains treasure.

6.4 Photograph of Cerro Danush.

Further, an enormous plumed serpent that dwells within emerges for a few hours each December 31.

Their many observations are part of an elaborate and widespread complex of beliefs recorded by anthropologist Alicia Barabas (2003) in numerous contemporary Zapotec, Chatino, and Mixe communities throughout the state of Oaxaca. The work of Barabas (2003) exemplifies the recent current of research concerned with ritual landscapes. Using as a point of departure the premise that societies define their territory culturally (e.g., Koontz et al. 2001), researchers involved in this enterprise have identified the core organizing principles used to structure the natural and built environment among ancient and contemporary ethnic groups. Archaeologists employing this line of inquiry have identified measurements corresponding to the calendrical cycles common to Mesoamerican groups manifest spatially in the layouts of such centers as Teotihuacan (Sugiyama 2004) and Monte Albán (Peeler and Winter 1995), for example. Others have recognized the long enduring model among Mesoamerican peoples of conceiving hills and temple platforms as sacred mountains embodying the abundance of the natural world (Joyce 2001; Reilly 1999; Schele 1995; Schele and Guernsey Kappelman 2001), and it is here in particular that the work of Bararbas (2003) fits.

According to Barabas, hills like Danush represent sacred mountains embodying the bounty of the natural environment that makes human life possible. Further,

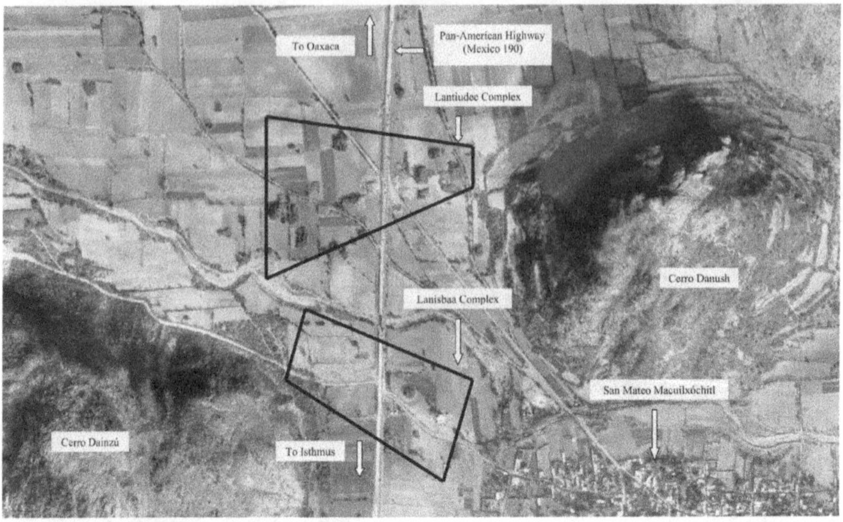

6.5 Aerial photograph of Macuilxóchitl.

they are believed to be hollow and act as portals connecting the heavens with the terrestrial worlds and underworlds. Often, a serpent is thought to be the guardian or owner of the hill and its natural wealth or abundance. The beliefs of the Macuilxóchitl residents have clear antecedents that extend back into the prehispanic era of Mesoamerica in general (McCafferty 2001:279–281; Schele 1995) and Macuilxóchitl in particular, as we explain below.

2002 ARCHAEOLOGICAL EXCAVATIONS AT MACUILXÓCHITL

The Macuilxóchitl archaeological site, in the eastern branch of the Valley of Oaxaca between Oaxaca City and Tlacolula, is one of the largest Late Classic and Postclassic settlements in prehispanic Oaxaca and thus should be ideal for studying Late Classic to Postclassic social transformations (Figure 6.5). In their surface survey carried out in the 1970s, Kowalewski and his colleagues (1989) recorded 148 mounds at Macuilxóchitl. During the Late Classic period, Macuilxóchitl was second after Monte Albán in number of mounds (67) and third after Monte Albán and Jalieza with over 6,000 inhabitants (ibid.:table 9.6); in the Late Postclassic period it was second to Mitla in number of mounds (54) and first in population with an estimated 14,000 inhabitants (ibid.:table 10.2).

Prior to our work, Macuilxóchitl had received relatively little attention from archaeologists except for Ignacio Bernal's excavations in the late 1960s and early 1970s at Dainzú, the center of the Macuilxóchitl site during the Tani (Monte

Albán Late II) and Pitao (Monte Albán IIIA) phases (Bernal and Oliveros 1988). Over fifty-five years ago, Lorenzo Gamio (1947) salvaged a tomb possibly encountered during construction of the Pan-American Highway (Mexico 190). More recently, Enrique Fernández and Susana Gómez (1993) uncovered three Formative residences to the north of the Dainzú sector of the site. In 1996 Robert Markens exposed portions of two Xoo phase residences on the terrace to the west side of Mound 3 (Markens 2004a:fig. 6.2), and in 1999, Victoria Arriola excavated just to the south of the highway in connection with the installation of a fiber optic cable by Teléfonos de México. (For studies concerning the epigraphy and sculpture of Danizú, see Bernal and Seuffert 1979; Oliveros 1997; Orr 1997; Urcid 2001.)

Although we found Rosario, Danibaan (Early Monte Albán I), and Tani (Late Monte Albán II) phase materials, most data recovered in 2002 correspond to the Late Classic Xoo (600–800 CE) and Postclassic Liobaa (800–1200 CE) and Chila (1200–1521 CE) phases. This sequence of phases—Xoo, Liobaa, and Chila—was defined in collaboration with Michael D. Lind using data from the Monte Albán 1992–1994 Special Project excavations (Martínez López et al. 2000) and through Markens's ceramic seriation. The Macuilxóchitl data fit the sequence well and support our conclusions from Monte Albán.

The Macuilxóchitl site centers around an expanse of nearly four square kilometers of alluvial land delimited approximately on the northeast by Cerro Danush, on the east by Cerro Dainzú, on the south by a ridge of low hills, and on the west by low terraces that rise in stepwise fashion toward the Cerro de Tlacochahuaya. The Río Grande, a tributary of the Río Salado, the main river of the Tlacolula Valley, descends from the mountains above Teotitlán del Valle and crosses the Macuilxóchitl alluvial area from northeast to southwest while intermittent streams flow in from the north. At 1,620 meters elevation, Macuilxóchitl is some thirty meters above the Río Salado floodplain and isolated from the salty water and sediments around Lambityeco and further west. Deposits of silt, sand, and gravel found at the bases of several platforms suggest frequent flooding in ancient times (see Kirkby 1973: plates 7a–c). Rocky outcrops and river cobbles provided readily available construction materials, and mountain zone resources were only a few kilometers north of the site.

Our excavations focused on two areas adjacent to the highway: a complex of mainly Xoo phase mounds about 200 meters west of the Río Grande and a Xoo and Chila phase mound about 200 meters east of the river. We also undertook minor explorations on the summit of Cerro Danush in connection with repairs made to the chapel. The first area, the Lantiudee complex (Figure 6.6), includes seven mounds. The three farthest from the highway were not excavated, including Mound 39, the highest structure in the complex, which presumably supported a temple. The remaining mounds, 35, 36, 37, and 55, were extensively explored.

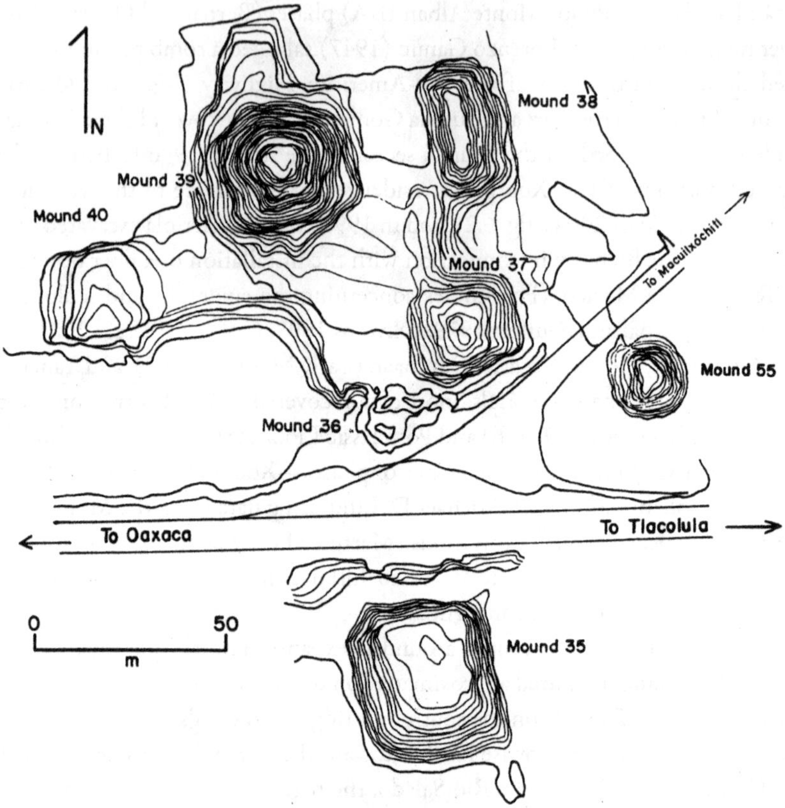

6.6 Plan of the Lantiudee complex, Macuilxóchitl.

Mound 35 is a roughly square platform about forty meters at the base with a wide stairway on the north side. Judging by its form and size, it supported a large residence or palace, although few floors and walls were preserved due to plowing and erosion on the top of the mound. Mound 36, immediately to the north, had been largely destroyed years ago during road construction, although enough of the structure's footprint, platform walls, and stucco floors were preserved to determine that it was a temple with several construction stages oriented with a stairway toward the south. It was linked to Mound 35 by walls thus forming a palace-patio-altar (PPA) complex as defined by Lind (1994) for Lambityeco (Chapter 5).

Mound 37 is a rectangular platform that supported a temple and has a stairway facing east. Mound 55, separated from the complex by about twenty meters, is a nearly square temple platform with a stairway to the west. Part of a large ceramic jaguar head from a hollow figure was found at the base of the stairway, reflecting the ritual activities that took place there (Figure 6.7).

6.7 Photograph of ceramic jaguar head found during excavations of Mound 55, Lantiudee complex, Macuilxóchitl.

A flat plaza-like area in the center of the complex revealed elements of a high-status residence. Structure 37A–Patio in the southwest corner is a small residence with an elegant carved and fitted stone panel and elaborate drain system, but no tombs or burials. Just to the east, removed from its original position, was a large tomb lintel stone (MAC-28) with a crouching jaguar carved on the front and the day or name glyph 5 Rabbit carved on the underside (Figure 6.8). We were unable to completely define this central residential compound and did not find the tomb from which the lintel had been removed.

We interpret the Lantiudee complex as the focus of a high-status family, that is, a residence with associated temples. This kind of *señorío*, or royal house, following the house society model proposed by Lèvi-Strauss and others (see, e.g., Anaya 1996; Carsten and Hugh-Jones 1995), was the basic political unit during the Xoo phase in the Valley of Oaxaca (Chapter 1; Winter 2003).

Our second area of intensive exploration focused on Mound 1 in the Lanisbaa sector (Figure 6.9), about 200 meters east of the Río Grande. Excavations at Mound 1 brought to light a well-preserved residence dating to the Late Postclassic Chila phase, which overlies the remains of an earlier Xoo phase house. The Chila phase residence is striking for its similarity in layout to the palaces of Yagul and the Palace of the Columns at Mitla (see Bernal and Gamio 1974:plan 2; Robles and Moreira

6.8 Photograph of carved lintel MAC-28, Lantiudee complex, Macuilxóchitl.

1990:fig. A9), but, unlike them, it is modest in size, measuring some twenty-five meters in length. The Yagul and Mitla palaces, along with the Mound 1 residence, consist of two patios, each enclosed on three or four sides by rooms and/or walls. Based on details of its architectural layout, the domestic compound was probably divided into private and public areas. The north patio, with more restricted access, appears to have served as the residents' private retreat, whereas the south patio, open on the south side to the community beyond, provided a space for conducting public business as well as serving domestic needs.

The structure located on the north side of the south patio facing the compound's main entrance was most likely the residence of the head of the household. This building contains the household's small tomb, and in this room three other adults were buried beneath the floor, each in a simple grave. The individuals were laid to rest on their backs with legs extended and arms by their sides, or in one case with the hands resting on the pelvis. A fifth adult burial was recovered from beneath the floor of the south patio, adjacent to the structure on the patio's east side; and a sixth interment, that of a child placed in a sitting position with the head resting on the knees, was found just beyond the compound's east wall. The interment of household heads in family tombs and junior members of the family in simple graves beneath house floors is a continuation of Valley of Oaxaca household mortuary practices that began in the Late Formative period.

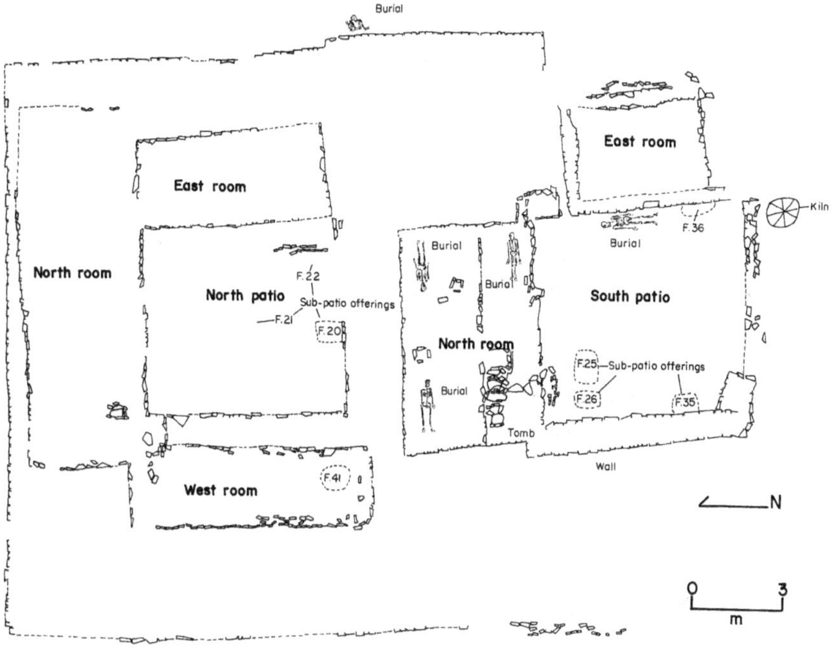

6.9 Plan of Mound 1, Lanisbaa complex, Macuilxóchitl.

Although Zapotec funerary practices are remarkably stable throughout this long duration, evidence from excavations at other Valley of Oaxaca communities shows greater diversity in the treatment of the dead during the Late Postclassic period. In addition to the pattern of burying family heads in tombs and other members of the household in simple pits beneath residence floors as documented for Mound 1, there is also evidence for the secondary burial of large numbers of individuals (approximately fifty) in a single tomb (Bernal and Gamio 1974). In recent excavations at Xaagá in the hinterland of Mitla, a total of fourteen secondary burials were recovered from beneath the floors of two commoner residences (Markens 2004b). Although the meaning of this increase in diversity in funerary practice is unclear, it probably reflects greater flexibility in family organization. One potential factor that may explain this flexibility is the increasing craft specialization and commercialization that is thought to have characterized Mesoamerica during the Late Postclassic period (Smith and Berdan 2003). Families may have adjusted their size in accordance with their economic pursuits.

Each of the adult grave and tomb offerings of Mound 1 consists of three to five pieces of pottery typical of the Chila phase. Common are the fine grayware G3M hemispherical and composite silhouette bowls with or without hollow elongated tripod supports that also abound in the residence's refuse deposits. Small *ollas* with restricted mouths and perforated vertical loop handles attached to the vessel sides made from gray or brown paste are also common in the funerary contexts at Mound 1. Other offerings include beads of greenstone, but these are rare. Although polychrome pottery was absent from all of the funerary contexts, it was present in small quantities in the household debris. Its scarcity at Mound 1 may be one indication that the residents were of non-elite status.

Additional evidence of rituals practiced at the Mound 1 residence consists of over fifty ceramic vessels recovered from beneath the north and south patio floors. The vessels were found in pairs, with an upper vessel inverted to cover the mouth of the one below. These paired vessel offerings occur beneath the patios individually or in groups of up to eight. Each pair appears to have been buried alone, since the vessel pairs are found at slightly varying depths beneath the patio floors. The kinds of vessels most often found in this patio context are brown-paste ollas and boot-shaped jars known as *patojos*; all are heavily blackened by soot. More elegant grayware composite silhouette ollas and medium-size *vasos*, or cups with long supports, are also found. These fancier vessels show signs of heavy use as well, and the tripod supports were almost always broken off. An identical pattern of offerings has been documented for the palaces at Yagul, where similar paired vessels were found buried beneath the floor of Patio B (Bernal and Gamio 1974:37–38, photos 41–49).

Although the meaning of this practice is enigmatic, Elsie Clews Parsons's recounting of a household ritual in Mitla during the 1930s offers a tantalizing analogy (Parsons 1936:76). She documents for Mitla, as well for other Zapotec towns in the valley, the practice of safeguarding the umbilical cord of each newborn using two ceramic vessels with one covering the other. This practice prevents dirt from entering the container, which the villagers believe might damage the child's sight. The vessels are buried beneath the floors of the house.

As Cerro Danush is distant from the path of the Pan-American Highway, intensive exploration there lay beyond the scope of our salvage project. However, we had an opportunity to observe the extensive repairs to the chapel that townspeople undertook. During the construction project, we recorded the features that appeared in the trenches that workers opened on the temple platform and collected pottery samples from the exposed strata.

Cerro Danush lies approximately one kilometer to the north of the Lantiudee complex, and it is on the summit that the Late Classic period religious and political heart of the city is found. Under the modern chapel atop Cerro Danush are the remains of a large temple platform that once formed part of a more extensive Xoo phase temple-patio-altar (TPA) architectural compound, like those found at other contemporary sites, such as Lambityeco Cerro de la Campana and Monte Albán (Chapter 5; Winter 1986). The broad terrace just below and to the south of the

TPA structure is littered with chunks of cut stone and construction debris, probably the remains of what was once a high-status residence or palace. A looted tomb was also documented within the palace compound.

The TPA and palace complex on Danush's crest readily bring to mind the present-day beliefs of which Macuilxóchitl's residents speak, suggesting that notions of Cerro Danush as a sacred mountain of abundance extend back to the Late Classic period, if not earlier (see Joyce 2001:104; Markens 2005; Reilly 1999). If this were the case, it would indicate that Danush was the sacred hub of the ancient community and that the religious and political authority of Macuilxóchitl's rulers was vested in their role as intermediaries between the forces of the natural world and the community. There is perhaps no more vivid and compelling a visual demonstration of this link in the Valley of Oaxaca during the Classic period than the location of the rulers' palace adjacent to the temple that crowns the summit of Danush—Macuilxóchitl's imposing mountain of sustenance. Such an interpretation finds additional support in a recent analysis of the imagery found on two Classic period Valley of Oaxaca Zapotec funerary effigy vessels now stored in Toronto's Royal Ontario Museum. According to Adam Sellen (2002:fig. 1), the individuals portrayed on these vessels are rulers impersonating the storm god Cociyo and involved in rituals related to the agricultural cycle on behalf of the community.

FROM CLASSIC TO POSTCLASSIC AT MACUILXÓCHITL

We now turn to the evidence of change from Xoo to Liobaa and Chila phases that we found in our explorations. The Lantiudee complex was largely abandoned at the end of the Xoo phase. During the subsequent Liobaa phase the major stairway of Mound 35 was blocked and a narrow stairway was built on the southeast corner facing east. A house on top of Mound 35 was represented by a relatively simple tomb containing chipped stone debris and a projectile point, groups of vessels placed beneath the floors as offerings, simple carved stones that resemble Postclassic *penates*, and numerous miniature vessels, especially *sahumadores* (long-handled censers). A seated flexed burial, also with a projectile point and miniature vessels, was found on Mound 36. As we have noted for Monte Albán (Winter et al. 2007), the Liobaa phase is strikingly different from the Xoo phase: population declined, writing disappeared, and no urns or other representations of the Xoo phase gods occur.

At Mound 1 in the Lanisbaa sector, the remains of a well-built middle-status Xoo phase residence came to light beneath the twin-patio Chila phase house. Two long walls forming a corner of the house substructure, well-preserved portions of plastered room floors, and a *tlecuil*, or sunken ceramic hearth, represent the Late Classic period structure. During the Xoo phase the house was remodeled, then at some point it was apparently abandoned and allowed to fall into ruin. Where small patches of floor survived, the stucco was almost entirely eroded away, revealing the underlying foundation of small roughed-out tiles of volcanic rock, set down in mosaic fashion—a common building technique at Macuilxóchitl and Lambityeco during the Classic period. Markens (2004a:317–321) documented the same pattern of abandonment and erosion of house floors in his excavations of a Xoo phase residence on the terrace to the west of Mound 3 some 300 meters east of Mound 1.

During our observation of the repairs made to the chapel on Cerro Danush we documented two superimposed red painted stucco floors, below which we collected abundant pottery dating the structure's construction to the Xoo phase. Although monumental construction on the hill's summit ceased at the end of the Classic period, the temple of Cerro Danush, although probably in a state of ruin, continued through the Postclassic period up to the present day as an object of pilgrimage. Abundant Liobaa and Chila phase sahumadores and braziers were found at the base of the temple platform. The G3M hemispherical serving bowls and other Chila phase domestic ware were present, but in minute quantities.

DISCUSSION

What do these recent excavations tell us about Late Classic to Postclassic sociopolitical transformations at Macuilxóchitl?

1. Late Classic political structure was similar throughout the Valley of Oaxaca and organized around elite families. Local political alliances were forged within and between communities (Chapters 3 and 9). In the Tlacolula Valley, Macuilxóchitl was a major community along with polities centered at Mitla, El Palmillo, San Miguel del Valle, Lambityeco, Yagul, and Tlacochahuaya. How they interrelated remains to be revealed.
2. Around 800 CE Macuilxóchitl, like Monte Albán, was largely abandoned for still-undetermined reasons. Population declined drastically and various cultural elements associated with high-status families dropped out of the archaeological record: large tombs with numerous offerings, carved stone slabs portraying elite individuals in rites of passage, and ceramic effigy vessels or urns depicting elite individuals impersonating deities. This suggests that the leadership collapsed along with its ideological support.
3. During the Late Postclassic Chila phase, Macuilxóchitl regained substantial population (Kowalewski et al. 1989:table 10.2), which appears to coincide with the foundation of a noble ruling house at the community as recounted in the *Genealogy of Macuilxóchitl*. House layouts, burial patterns (individuals in extended position in graves or tombs), and household activities are similar to Xoo phase patterns and suggest continuity in Zapotec culture. Mitla, Yagul, Teotitlán del Valle, Zaachila, and presumably Macuilxóchitl had elite families

> who lived in elegant palaces and buried their dead in tombs with elaborate offerings. In some communities—Yagul, for example—elite compounds were close to temples and ballcourts of earlier Xoo phase construction, and some of these buildings may have been reused. But construction of temples and ballcourts was evidently not the focus of the work and tribute of dependent households, and representations of gods were not revived. Thus, public political and religious ideology had changed while domestic lifeways remained more constant.

One of the great challenges and most intriguing questions facing archaeologists working in Mesoamerica is explaining the demise of a number of civilizations in various regions toward the end of the Classic period. During the last decade or so, a growing number of geophysical studies of lake bed sediments in central Mexico and the Maya area have begun to provide evidence for the onset of a dry interval lasting several hundred years at the end of the Classic period (see Caballero and Ortega Guerrero 1998; Metcalfe et al. 1989; O'Hara and Metcalfe 1997). This information has convinced some archaeologists that changing climatic conditions played a role in the decline of the Classic period civilizations in these regions (Andrews 2003; Smith 2003:56).

At present there are no comparable paleoenvironmental studies for Oaxaca. If Oaxaca also experienced a period of increasing aridity as in other parts of Mesoamerica, this would be consistent with the emerging archaeological and ethnohistoric record for the Early Postclassic period in the Valley of Oaxaca. Increasing aridity may have had the effect of reducing agricultural yields, thereby undermining the system of tribute paid in foodstuffs and labor on which dense nucleated populations and social hierarchy depended. This may constitute one factor explaining the abandonment of Classic period centers, such as Monte Albán, El Palmillo, Lambityeco, and Jalieza, and the possible dispersion of the valley population into smaller communities throughout the valley. Although commoner household social organization, burial ritual, and worldview apparently continued at Macuilxóchitl from the Classic to the Late Postclassic period, there is on the other hand a marked rupture and discontinuity in elite culture for this same interval throughout Oaxaca (see Chapters 1 and 4). Elite culture as it emerged in the Valley of Oaxaca during the Postclassic period is markedly different from that of the Classic period. It is also clear that a possible change in weather conditions did not rule out complex social organization and nucleated settlement altogether, for Epiclassic centers, such as Xochicalco, Cacaxtla, Cholula, and Tula, did flourish during this time. It remains to be demonstrated whether in fact Oaxaca experienced some years of decreased rainfall as in other Mesoamerican regions and if so, what role this climatic change may have played in the abandonment of nucleated centers in the Valley of Oaxaca at the end of the Classic period.

CONCLUSIONS

The end of the Classic period appears to mark the sudden disappearance throughout the Valley of Oaxaca of what one might refer to in Redfield's (1956) terms as the Zapotec "great tradition." Large nucleated communities like Macuilxóchitl, Monte Albán, Lambityeco, and Jalieza appear to have been largely abandoned (Chapter 5). The tradition of using elaborate funerary effigy vessels or urns (Caso and Bernal 1952) to depict individuals impersonating gods (Sellen 2002) comes to an end, as does the use of writing (carved in stone or painted in murals) to record the rites of passage of individuals of exalted status. There is also a marked absence in the archaeological literature for the Early Postclassic period (800–1200 CE) of anything equal to the spacious and opulent tombs known for the Classic (Tombs 103, 104, and 105 from Monte Albán; Tomb 5 from Cerro de la Campana; Tomb 1 from Cuilapan) as well as those for the Late Postclassic (Tombs 1 and 2 from Zaachila, the cruciform tombs from Mitla and Xaagá, Tomb 7 from Monte Albán).

Seen in this light, the Early Postclassic period appears to be a time of political crisis in the Valley of Oaxaca marked by a simplification of the social rank hierarchy and perhaps the dispersion of the valley population into smaller communities. These upheavals may have been precipitated by changes in climate lasting several hundred years that undermined a system of tribute in foodstuffs and labor on which nucleated settlement and social hierarchy depended. This trend, in turn, appears to end by the threshold of the Late Postclassic (1100/1200–1521 CE), for which archaeological and ethnohistoric evidence exist (Oudijk 2000, 2002), documenting the emergence of the territorially compact kingdoms or city-states that the Spaniards described in the sixteenth century (Bernal and Gamio 1974; Gallegos 1978).

ACKNOWLEDGMENTS

The authors thank Javier Urcid and William O. Autry for their helpful comments during the preparation of this chapter. The photographs were taken by Marcus Winter (Figs. 6.7 and 6.8), Robert Markens (Fig. 6.4), and Mark Silverberg (Fig. 6.5). Juan Cruz Pascual skillfully prepared the line drawings.

REFERENCES

Acuña, René

1984 *Relaciones geográficas del siglo XVI: Antequera*. Vols. 1 and 2. Universidad Nacional Autónoma de México, Mexico City.

Anaya, Armando

1996 La noción de *casa* como modelo explicativo del sistema de parentesco del Clásico Maya. In *Cultura y Comunicación: Edmund Leach in memoriam*, edited by J. Jáuregui, M. Olavaria, and V. Franco Pellotier, pp. 129–154. CIESAS and Universidad Autónoma Metropolitana, Mexico City.

Andrews, E. Wyllys
2003 The Fall of Copán and the Collapse of the Lowland Classic Maya. Paper presented at the 102nd Annual Meeting of the American Anthropological Association, Chicago.

Barabas, Alicia M.
2003 Etnoterritorialidad sagrada en Oaxaca. In *Diálogos con el territorio: Simbolizaciones sobre el espacio en las culturas indígenas de México,* Vol. 1, edited by A. Barabas, pp. 37–124. Instituto Nacional de Antropología e Historia, Mexico City.

Bernal, Ignacio, and Lorenzo Gamio
1974 *Yagul: El palacio de los seis patios.* Instituto de Investigaciones Antropológicas, Universidad Nacional Autónoma de México, Mexico City.

Bernal, Ignacio, and Arturo Oliveros
1988 *Exploraciones arqueológicas en Dainzú, Oaxaca.* Colección Científica, No. 167. Instituto Nacional de Antropología e Historia, Mexico City.

Bernal, Ignacio, and Andy Seuffert
1979 *Esculturas asociadas del Valle de Oaxaca.* Corpus Antiquitatum Americanensium, No. 6. Instituto Nacional de Antropología e Historia, Mexico City.

Caballero, Margarita, and Beatriz Ortega Guerrero
1998 Lake Levels since about 40,000 Years Ago at Lake Chalco, near Mexico City. *Quaternary Research* 50:69–79.

Carsten, Janet, and Stephen Hugh-Jones
1995 Introduction: About the House-Lévi-Strauss and Beyond. In *About the House: Lévi- Strauss and Beyond,* edited by J. Carsten and S. Hugh-Jones, pp. 1–46. Cambridge University Press, New York.

Caso, Alfonso, and Ignacio Bernal
1952 *Urnas de Oaxaca.* Memorias del Instituto Nacional de Antropología e Historia, No. 2. INAH, Mexico City.

Fernández Dávila, Enrique, and Susana Gómez Serafín
1993 Un conjunto habitacional del formativo terminal en Dainzú, Valle de Tlacolula, Oaxaca. *Cuadernos del Sur* 5:5–29.

Gallegos Ruiz, Roberto
1978 *El Señor 9 Flor en Zaachila.* Universidad Nacional Autónoma de México, Mexico City.

Gamio, Lorenzo
1947 Informe relacionado con la exploración de una tumba en el pueblo de Teotitlán del Valle, Oaxaca. Archivo de Monumentos Prehispánicos del Instituto Nacional de Antropología e Historia. Tomo 87, vol. 4. Mexico City.

Herrera Muzgo Torres, Alicia

2000 Apéndice G. Algunas categorías de la Fase Liobaa. In *Cerámica de la fase Xoo (Epoca IIIB–IV) del Valle de Oaxaca*, by C. Martínez López, R. Markens, M. Winter, and M. Lind, pp. 299–312. Proyecto Especial Monte Alban 1992–1994, Contribución No. 8. Centro INAH Oaxaca, Oaxaca.

Herrera Muzgo Torres, Alicia, Gustavo Gámez Goytia, Marcus Winter, and Cira Martínez López

1999 Proyecto Especial Monte Albán, 1992–1994, Informe Final: Vol. 8, Exploraciones en la Plataforma Sur. Unpublished report. Centro INAH Oaxaca, Oaxaca.

Joyce, Arthur A.

2001 Poder sacrificial en Oaxaca durante el Formativo Tardío. In *Memoria de la primera mesa redonda de Monte Albán*, edited by N. Robles García, pp. 97–110. CONACULTA-INAH, Mexico City.

Kertzer, David

1988 *Ritual, Politics and Power*. Yale University Press, New Haven, Connecticut.

Kirkby, Anne V.T.

1973 *The Use of Land and Water Resources in the Past and Present Valley of Oaxaca, Mexico*. Memoirs of the Museum of Anthropology, University of Michigan, No. 1. University of Michigan, Ann Arbor.

Koontz, Rex, Kathryn Reese-Taylor, and Annabeth Headrick (editors)

2001 *Landscape and Power in Ancient Mesoamerica*. Westview Press, Boulder.

Kowalewski, Stephen A., Gary M. Feinman, Laura M. Finsten, Richard E. Blanton, and Linda M. Nicholas

1989 *Monte Albán's Hinterland, Part II: Prehispanic Settlement Patterns in Tlacolula, Etla and Ocotlán, the Valley of Oaxaca, Mexico*. Memoirs of the Museum of Anthropology, University of Michigan, No. 23. University of Michigan, Ann Arbor.

Lind, Michael D.

1994 Monte Albán y el Valle de Oaxaca durante la fase Xoo. In *Monte Albán: Estudios recientes*, edited by M. Winter, pp. 99–111. Proyecto Especial Monte Albán 1992–1994, Contribución No. 2. Centro INAH Oaxaca, Oaxaca.

Markens, Robert

2004a Ceramic Chronology in the Valley of Oaxaca, Mexico, during the Late Classic and Postclassic Periods and the Organization of Ceramic Production. Unpublished Ph.D. Dissertation, Department of Anthropology, Brandeis University. Waltham, Massachusetts.

2004b Excavaciones arqueológicas en el Montículo I de Macuilxóchitl: Una residencia del Postclásico Tardío. Paper presented in the symposium Proyecto Salvamento Arqueológico Carretera Oaxaca-Mitla. Parte 1. Sixth Biennial International Symposium for Oaxacan Studies. Oaxaca.

2005 Monte Albán, conceptos de espacio sagrado y urbanismo en el valle de Oaxaca. Paper presented at the 6th Pedro Bosch Gimpera Colloquium. Instituto de Investigaciones Antropológicas de la Universidad Nacional Autónoma de México. Mexico City, June 13–17.

Martínez López, Cira, Robert Markens, Marcus Winter, and Michael Lind
2000 *Cerámica de la Fase Xoo (Monte Albán IIIB–IV) del Valle de Oaxaca*. Proyecto Especial Monte Alban 1992–1994, Contribución No. 8. Centro INAH Oaxaca, Oaxaca.

McCafferty, Geoffrey G.
2001 Mountain of Heaven, Mountain of Earth: The Great Pyramid of Cholula as Sacred Landscape. In *Landscape and Power in Ancient Mesoamerica*, edited by R. Koontz, K. Reese-Taylor, and A. Headrick, pp. 279–316. Westview Press, Boulder.

Metcalfe, S. E., F. A. Street-Perrott, R. B. Brown, P. E. Hales, R. A. Perrott, and F. M. Steininger
1989 Late Holocene Human Impact on Lake Basins in Central Mexico. *Geoarchaeology* 4:119–141.

O'Hara, Sarah L., and Sarah E. Metcalfe
1997 The Climate of Mexico since the Aztec Period. *Quaternary International* 43/44: 25–31.

Oliveros, Arturo
1997 Dainzú-Macuilxóchitl. *Arqueología Mexicana* 5(26):24–29.

Orr, Heather
1997 Power Games in the Late Formative Valley of Oaxaca: The Ballplayer Carvings at Dainzú. Unpublished Ph.D. Dissertation, Department of Art History, University of Texas at Austin.

Oudijk, Michel R.
2000 *Historiography of the Bènizàa: The Postclassic and Early Colonial Periods (1000–1600 A.D.)*. CNWS Publications, Vol. 84. Research School of Asian, African, and Amerindian Studies, University of Leiden, Leiden.
2002 The Zapotec City-state. In *A Comparative Study of Thirty City-state Cultures*, Supplement, edited by M. Hansen, pp. 73–90. The Royal Danish Academy of Sciences and Letters, Copenhagen.

Parsons, Elsie Clews
1936 *Mitla, Town of the Souls and Other Zapoteco-speaking Pueblos of Oaxaca, Mexico*. University of Chicago Press, Chicago.

Peeler, Damon E., and Marcus Winter
1995 Building J at Monte Albán: A Correction and Reassessment of the Astronomical Hypothesis. *Latin American Antiquity* 6(4):362–369.

Pohl, John M.D.
2000 The Lintel Paintings of Mitla and Other Frescoes. Notebook for the Mixtec Pictographic Writing Workshop at Texas. Manuscript on file, Department of Art History, University of Texas, Austin.

Pohl, John M.D., and Bruce E. Byland

1994 The Mixteca-Puebla Style and Early Postclassic Socio-political Interaction. In *Mixteca-Puebla: Discoveries and Research in Mesoamerican Art and Archaeology*, edited by H. Nicholson and E. Quiñones Keber, pp. 189–199. Labyrinthos Press, Culver City, California.

Redfield, Robert

1956 *The Little Community and Peasant Society and Culture*. University of Chicago Press, Chicago.

Reilly, F. Kent, III

1999 Mountains of Creation and Underworld Portals. In *Mesoamerican Architecture as a Cultural Symbol*, edited by J. Kowalski, pp. 15–39. Oxford University Press, New York.

Robles García, Nelly M., and Alfredo J. Moreira Quirós

1990 *Proyecto Mitla: Restauración de la zona arqueológica en su contexto urbano*. Colección Científica, No. 193. Instituto Nacional de Antropología e Historia, Mexico City.

Schele, Linda

1995 The Olmec Mountain and Tree of Creation in Mesoamerican Cosmology. In *The Olmec World: Ritual and Rulership*, edited by J. Guthrie, pp. 105–117. The Art Museum, Princeton University, Princeton, New Jersey.

Schele, Linda, and Julia Guernsey Kappelman

2001 What the Heck's Coatépec? The Formative Roots of an Enduring Mythology. In *Landscape and Power in Ancient Mesoamerica*, edited by R. Koontz, K. Reese-Taylor, and A. Headrick, pp. 29–53. Westview Press, Boulder.

Sellen, Adam T.

2002 Storm-God Impersonators from Ancient Oaxaca. *Ancient Mesoamerica* 13(1): 3–19.

Smith, Michael E.

2003 *The Aztecs*, 2nd edition. Blackwell Publishing, Malden, Massachusetts.

Smith, Michael E., and Frances F. Berdan

2003 Postclassic Mesoamerica. In *The Postclassic Mesoamerican World*, edited by M. Smith and F. Berdan, pp. 3–13. University of Utah Press, Salt Lake City.

Sugiyama, Saburo

2004 Governance and Polity at Classic Teotihuacan. In *Mesoamerican Archaeology: Theory and Practice*, edited by J. Hendon and R. Joyce, pp. 97–123. Blackwell Publishing, Malden, Massachusetts.

Urcid, Javier

2001 *Zapotec Hieroglyphic Writing*. Dumbarton Oaks Research Library and Collection, Washington, DC.

Whitecotton, Joseph W.

1990 *Zapotec Elite Ethnohistory: Pictorial Genealogies from Eastern Oaxaca.* Vanderbilt University Publications in Anthropology, No. 39. Nashville, Tennessee.

Winter, Marcus

1986 Templo-Patio-Adoratorio: Un conjunto arquitectónico no residencial en el Oaxaca prehispánico. *Cuadernos de Arquitectura Mesoamericana* 7:51–59.

1997 Classic to Postclassic in the Valley of Oaxaca: A View from Monte Albán. In *U Mut Maya VI: Reports and Readings Inspired by the Advanced Seminars led by Linda Schele at the University of Texas at Austin 1994–1996,* edited by C. Jones and T. Jones, pp. 21–42. Eureka Printing Company, Bayside, California.

2002 Monte Albán: Su Organización e Impacto Político. Paper presented in the III Mesa Redonda de Monte Albán. Oaxaca.

2003 Monte Albán and Late Classic Site Abandonment in Highland Oaxaca. In *The Archaeology of Settlement Abandonment in Middle America,* edited by T. Inomata and R. Webb, pp. 103–119. University of Utah Press, Salt Lake City.

Winter, Marcus, Robert Markens, Cira Martínez López, and Alicia Herrera Muzgo T.

2007 Shrines, Offerings and Postclassic Continuity in Zapotec Religion. In *Commoner Ritual and Ideology in Ancient Mesoamerica,* edited by N. Gonlin and J. Lohse, pp. 185–212. University Press of Colorado, Boulder.

PART IV

Changing Power Relations and Interaction in the Lower Río Verde Valley

7

Arthur A. Joyce

Domination, Negotiation, and Collapse

A HISTORY OF CENTRALIZED AUTHORITY ON THE OAXACA COAST BEFORE THE LATE POSTCLASSIC

The nature of sociopolitical change during the Classic to Postclassic transition in Mesoamerica has been a source of great research interest and debate. Throughout most of Mesoamerica this period, lasting from about 600 to 1000 CE, was characterized by the fragmentation or collapse of the complex polities that dominated the Classic period (250–800 CE) political landscape. Archaeological, iconographic, and epigraphic research suggests that this period was characterized by dramatic changes in political institutions and ruling ideologies as well as depopulation in some regions (Cowgill 1979; Culbert 1973; Demarest et al. 2004; Diehl and Berlo 1989; Sabloff and Andrews 1986; Webster et al. 2000). Factors that have been implicated in the collapse include warfare, internal revolt, anthropogenic landscape degradation, and climate change. Despite the dramatic sociopolitical changes documented for this period, many questions remain as to their timing, nature, and causes.

Perhaps nowhere in Mesoamerica has the Classic period collapse been as hotly debated as in the southern Mexican state of Oaxaca, where scholars disagree on the nature and timing of demographic and sociopolitical changes (Marcus and Flannery 1990; Winter 1989, 1994). In highland Oaxaca, problems with clearly

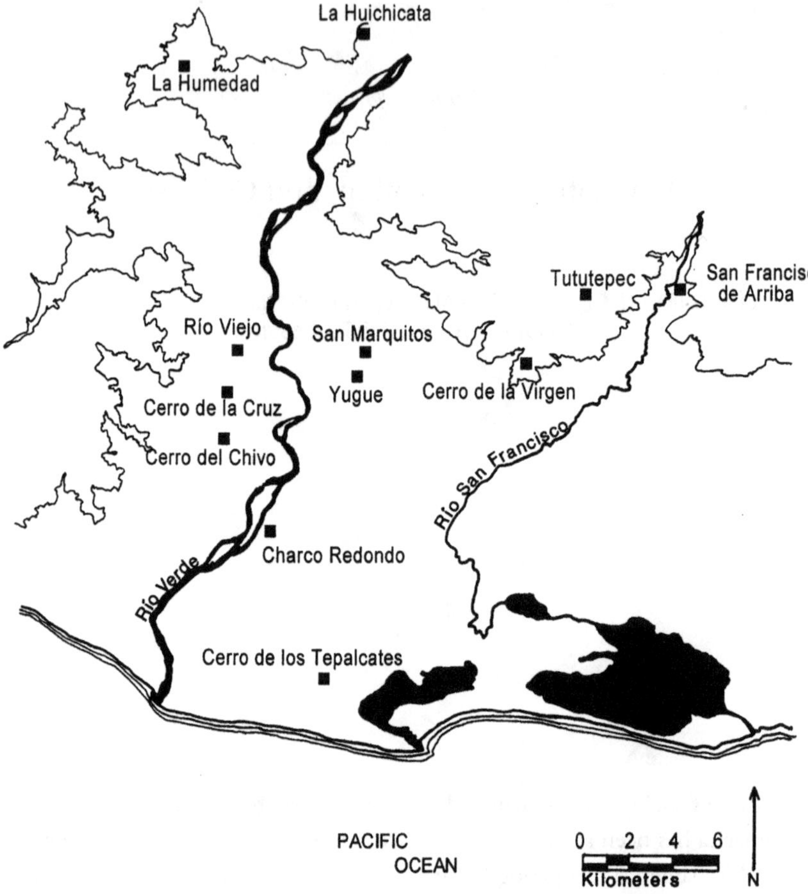

7.1 The lower Río Verde Valley, Oaxaca, showing sites mentioned in the text.

defining a suite of diagnostic ceramic styles for the Early Postclassic, coupled with relatively few radiocarbon dates, have made it difficult for archaeologists to identify sites from this period (Kowalewski et al. 1989:251–254; Lind 1991–1992; Winter 1994), although research by Martínez, Markens, and Winter is beginning to resolve this problem (Chapter 2). Debates over basic questions of chronology have led to widely divergent arguments about the Classic to Postclassic transition, ranging from massive depopulation to political fragmentation with relatively little change in overall population (Chapters 1 and 12).

In this chapter, I address the Classic to Postclassic transition in Oaxaca by examining the Classic period collapse in the lower Río Verde Valley on Oaxaca's western Pacific Coast (Figure 7.1).[1] Recent research in the lower Verde has clarified the nature of demographic and sociopolitical change at this time (Joyce et al.

2001; Joyce et al. 2004; Joyce and King 2001; King 2003). I consider the Classic to Postclassic transition from the perspective of the history of centralized political authority in the lower Río Verde Valley. The history of sociopolitical change in the region has been the focus of interdisciplinary research over the past twenty years (Barber 2005; Grove 1988; Joyce 1991a, 1991b, 1999, 2005; Joyce et al. 1998; Joyce et al. 2001; King 2003; Urcid and Joyce 2001; Workinger 2002). This research has included horizontal and/or block excavations at the sites of Río Viejo, Cerro de la Cruz, San Francisco de Arriba, Yugüe, Cerro de la Virgen, and Tututepec as well as test excavations at thirteen other sites. The entire region has been the focus of a non-systematic surface reconnaissance, and full-coverage surveys have systematically studied an area of 152 square kilometers (Joyce 1999; Joyce et al. 2001; Joyce et al. 2004; Workinger 2002).

The regional data demonstrate an initial period of political centralization toward the end of the Formative period, followed by a political collapse at ca. 250 CE. A second period of centralization occurred during the Late Classic period (500–800 CE) followed by collapse in the Early Postclassic (800–1100 CE). Although not a focus of this chapter, the prehispanic sequence ends with a third period of centralization during the Late Postclassic (1100–1522 CE), which was terminated abruptly by the Spanish Conquest. My historical analysis is based on a poststructural theoretical framework (e.g., Giddens 1979; Janusek 2004; Joyce et al. 2001; Pauketat 2001) and argues that regional political authority in the lower Río Verde Valley was relatively unstable and negotiated and was continuously produced by dynamic, ongoing social relations. Rather than representing the end of a long period of political relations that were overdetermined by a coherent and integrated political structure dominated by the elite (e.g., Fox et al. 1996; Marcus and Flannery 1996:chapter 15; Martin and Grube 2000; Schele and Mathews 1998), the Classic period collapse appears more like a "moment" prefigured, at least in part, by social contradictions and tensions that were inherent in the production of centralized political systems. I argue that archaeologists need to move away from the structuralist societal typologies that have dominated research on political relations in the past. Before discussing the archaeology of the lower Río Verde Valley, I briefly consider the implications of poststructural theory for models of Mesoamerican political organization.

Approaches to the political history of Mesoamerican polities have most often relied on structuralist conceptions of political organization that focus on mechanisms of social organization and integration (Iannone 2002). In these models, ancient Mesoamerican polities are viewed as integrated and cohesive social formations. Recent debate, particularly in the Maya Lowlands, has focused on whether polities were organized in a centralized or decentralized fashion (e.g., Fox et al. 1996; Iannone 2002). Centralized or unitary states are organized and integrated through a centralized bureaucratic state system characterized by a great degree of administrative control over economic, military, and religious matters. Centralized polities are generally seen as larger in territory and population than decentralized ones and are characterized by an endogamous class system. In the decentralized model social integration is achieved largely through kinship and religious practices with rulers as lineage heads. Polities consist of a number of functionally redundant kinship-based units that unite or split apart depending on social conditions, particularly the presence of external threats. In the decentralized model the core political units therefore are kinship groups, usually viewed as lineages, which unite to form larger states that are led by kings who act as ritualists, politicians, and marriage brokers to forge tenuous and often temporary alliances of the social segments. Decentralized states are not characterized by the bureaucracies and large standing armies, often mentioned as features of centralized polities.

Debates over Mesoamerican social organization are increasingly moving toward a middle ground between these two positions that recognizes a continuum in social organization from strongly centralized to decentralized (Iannone 2002; Marcus 1993, 1998). Marcus (1993, 1998) has attempted to integrate both the centralized and decentralized positions through her dynamic model, which argues that complex polities cycle historically between larger-scale and smaller-scale polities. The unification and dissolution of polities are seen as "different stages in the dynamic cycles of the same state" and thus are characteristic of the cultural evolution of complex societies (Marcus 1998:92). The main causes of state cycling are seen as interelite competition and the recognition that "large-scale, asymmetrical, and inegalitarian structures were more fragile and unstable than commonly assumed" (Marcus 1998:94).

Despite the increasing recognition of the dynamism of prehispanic polities, approaches to social organization and political history continue to focus on overarching social and political structures. The decentralized and dynamic models recognize some inherent societal tensions, at least in the larger political formations of the pre-Columbian world, particularly between the institutions of kinship and kingship (see Fox et al. 1996; Iannone 2002). These models, however, continue to focus on the long-term stability, coherence, and integration of large-scale political units, whether the lineage in the decentralized model or the state in the centralized model. The dynamic model further argues that political cycling is part of the inherent structure of complex political systems.

Instead of focusing on the nature of sociopolitical structures, in this chapter I will begin with Marcus's (1998) recognition of the fragility and instability of centralized political systems by exploring social contradictions and tensions that were inherent in the ongoing social relations that constituted the centralized political systems of the lower Río Verde Valley. Rather than representing the end of a long period of stable and uncontested political relations dominated by the nobility—whether viewed as cyclical, centralized, or decentralized—I argue that the Classic period collapse in the lower Río Verde Valley appears more like an outcome of the negotiation of social contradictions and tensions that were inherent in the production of complex political systems.

Poststructural theory argues that political formations including complex societies are instantiations of ongoing social relations simultaneously embedded in and both producing and reproducing historical traditions (e.g., Giddens 1979, 1984; Pauketat 2001). Rather than integrated and coherent, social systems are fragmented and contested to varying degrees such that there is never complete closure in any system of domination. By "social negotiation" I mean that the practices that constitute sociopolitical systems are always negotiations among differently positioned actors characterized by varying identities, interests, emotions, knowledge, outlooks, and dispositions. Political formations therefore are never integrated wholes as represented in most approaches to social organization in Mesoamerican archaeology (see Iannone 2002) but always contain polyvalent and potentially contestable symbols, meanings, actions, and institutions. Political formations therefore are historically constituted through the ongoing interaction of people of different social positions, such as nobles and commoners, women and men, urban and rural dwellers, and people of the core and periphery. Political systems, including ruling ideologies and institutions, are not simple reflections of elite interests imposed on subordinates. The outcome of the negotiation of power may bolster the social position of nobles, but it usually does so in ways that reflect some degree of compromise resulting from the interactions of varied social actors. Subordinates always have some degree of penetration of domination, which can be actualized by engaging with elites in ways that affect systems of domination, by seeking independence from institutions and practices of domination or by opposing domination through resistance (Joyce et al. 2001; Joyce and Weller 2007; Scott 1990). I argue that archaeologists need to move away from the structuralist societal typologies that have dominated research on political relations in the past. Instead, archaeologists need to better problematize ancient political formations by recognizing that all people, including commoners as well as nobles, contributed to the ongoing production and reproduction of political life in ancient Mesoamerican societies.

FORMATIVE-CLASSIC PERIOD POLITICAL CENTRALIZATION AND COLLAPSE

Survey and excavation indicate that the lower Verde began a gradual trend toward political centralization in the Middle Formative (700–400 BCE), which culminated in the Terminal Formative (150 BCE–250 CE) with the emergence of a regional polity with its capital at the urban center of Río Viejo (Barber 2005; Joyce 2003). From 700 BCE until the end of the Formative at ca. 250 CE, population increased greatly as measured by the occupational area in the full-coverage survey. Social complexity also increased as measured by the regional settlement hierarchy, mortuary patterns, residential data, and an increase in the scale of public ceremonies and the construction of monumental buildings (Barber 2005; Barber and Joyce 2007; Joyce 1991a, 1991b, 2003, 2005, 2006; Workinger 2002). The first political center to develop in the region was at Charco Redondo, which grew to sixty-two hectares by the Middle Formative. By the Late Formative period (400–150 BCE), Charco Redondo had grown to seventy hectares, while a second perhaps competing regional center emerged at San Francisco de Arriba, which reached ninety-five hectares. Regional data indicate the development of a three-tiered settlement hierarchy, hereditary social inequality, ritual feasting, communal mortuary ceremonialism, and construction of monumental buildings by the Late Formative. Material expressions of social inequality were restrained, however, and practices such as feasting, public mortuary ceremony in community cemeteries, and the construction of public buildings reproduced and made salient local community identities.

Formative period political centralization culminated during the Terminal Formative with the emergence of an urban center at Río Viejo, which was the capital of a polity that probably incorporated people throughout the entire lower Río Verde region (Barber 2005; Barber and Joyce 2007; Joyce 2003, 2005). Río Viejo increased in size from 25 hectares in the Late Formative to 225 hectares by the early Terminal Formative (150 BCE–100 CE), when it was the primary center of a five-tiered settlement hierarchy. As argued by Barber and Joyce (2007), the development of a regional-scale political formation during the Terminal Formative appears to have been the result of the "scaling up" of communal practices. At the same time, practices that reproduced local community identity persisted. Terminal Formative political relations resemble what Blanton (1998) terms a "corporate pattern," where the exclusionary power of nobles is restricted by a discourse that limits self-aggrandizing impulses of leaders.

During the Terminal Formative, feasting, caching, and mortuary rituals continued to reproduce community identity (Barber 2005; Barber and Joyce 2007). Levine's (2002) analysis of early Terminal Formative ceramics shows a significant increase in the proportion of fancy serving vessels in non-elite ceramic inventories, perhaps indicative of an increase in ritual feasting. At Yugüe, Barber (2005) has found evidence of communal feasting from Terminal Formative midden deposits in public settings. Evidence for the repetitive use of community ceremonial spaces was recovered at both Yugüe and San Francisco de Arriba in the form of ritual caches used to dedicate the construction of public buildings. The most elaborate cache was excavated by Workinger (2002) and included over 500 artifacts of greenstone, rock crystal, iron ore, and pottery. The use of communal cemeteries continued, as shown by Barber's (2005) excavations of a late Terminal Formative cemetery at Yugüe. The excavations recovered the remains of at least forty individuals, both male and female and of varying status levels and ages, buried within a public platform. The repetitive use of the cemetery would have reproduced community identity by referencing community history and reaffirming communal affiliations. The dense placement of burials in the Yugüe cemetery as well as the frequent disturbance and movement of the bones of earlier interments by later ones can be interpreted as an assertion of the collective and a denial of the individual and perhaps of differences among individuals (see Shanks and Tilley 1982). Similar collective mortuary practices were found with a Late Formative cemetery at the site of Cerro de la Cruz (Joyce 1991a).

Social inequality increased during the Terminal Formative as indicated by mortuary patterns, caches, residential evidence, and monumental buildings (Barber 2005; Barber and Joyce 2007; Joyce 2005, 2006). Although most people interred in the Yugüe cemetery were accompanied by few or no offerings, a high-status burial was recovered consisting of a late adolescent male wearing a plaster-backed iron-ore pectoral, probably a mirror, and holding an intricately incised bone flute made from a deer femur. The instrument is the most elaborate flute yet recovered for Terminal Formative Mesoamerica and its incised imagery depicts a skeletal male speaking or inhaling (Barber 2005). Luxury goods like iron ore and greenstone, recovered in caches and as burial offerings, were obtained through networks of interregional exchange among Mesoamerican nobles (Hirth 1984; Joyce 1993). These exchange networks would have linked nobles in the lower Río Verde Valley to elites in other parts of Mesoamerica, contributing to the formation of a distinctive noble identity. In addition to the high-status burial at Yugüe, evidence for increasing social inequality comes from the excavation of a high-status residence at the site of Cerro de la Virgen (Barber 2005). This residence was larger and more elaborate than typical houses of the Oaxacan Formative and was spatially associated with a monumental public plaza.

Beyond the local level, the scale of monumental architecture built during the Terminal Formative indicates the production of supra-community affiliations in some cases probably engaging people within the entire region (Barber 2005; Barber and Joyce 2007; Joyce 2003, 2005). Major communal works projects, including the construction of residential and "mixed-use" platforms as well as public buildings, were carried out at Río Viejo and at second-order and third-order sites in the lower Verde region, such as Charco Redondo, San Francisco de Arriba, and Yugüe (Barber 2005; Levine et al. 2004; Workinger 2002). The scale of monumental construction was considerable even at some lower order sites. For example, at the ten-hectare third-order site of Yugüe, people built a mixed-use platform measuring approximately 300 meters by 200 meters and reaching 10 meters at its highest point. Survey

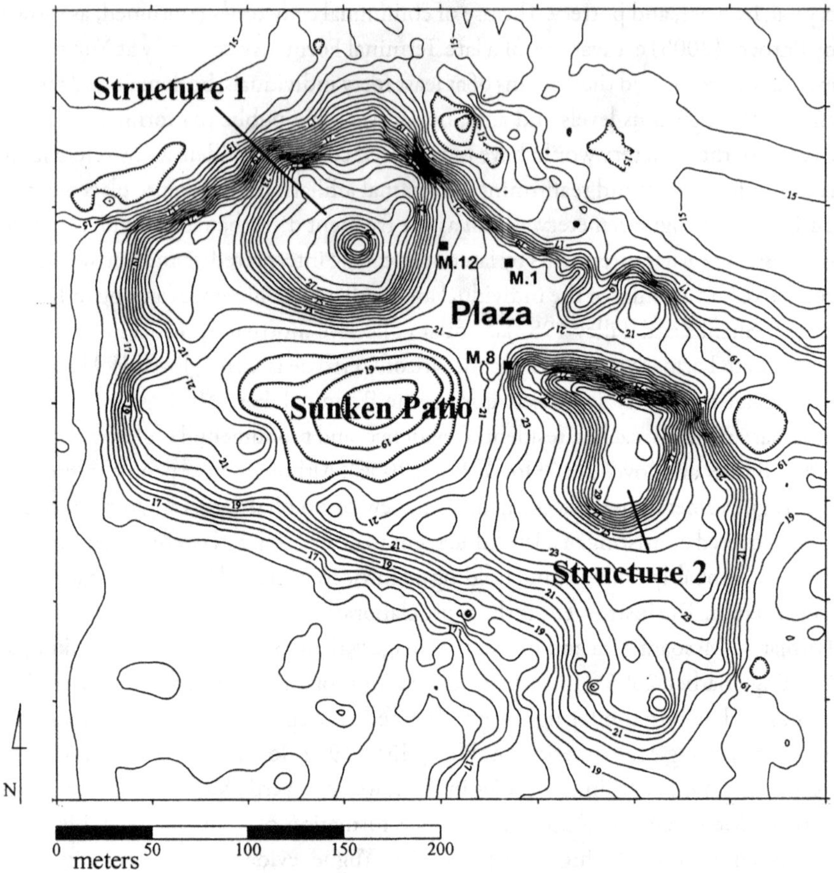

7.2 The Mound 1 acropolis at Río Viejo.

and excavation at Yugüe indicate that except for two ceremonial structures at the summit of the platform, activities and architecture on the mound were residential (Barber 2005; Joyce 1999). The total volume for the platform at Yugüe is estimated at 94,000 to 100,000 cubic meters, demonstrating the scale of labor mobilization required for its construction.

The largest of the monumental buildings was the Mound 1 acropolis at Río Viejo (Figure 7.2), which with an estimated volume of 395,000 cubic meters was one of the largest structures in prehispanic Oaxaca (Joyce 2006; Levine et al. 2004). The platform supports two large substructures. Excavations in Structure 2, the eastern substructure on the acropolis, exposed an area of 242 cubic meters and penetrated in places to a depth of 3.2 meters below the current surface of the mound (Joyce 2003, 2006; Joyce et al. 2001). Although the presence of occasional early

Terminal Formative sherds incidentally incorporated in construction fill leaves open the possibility of an earlier building phase, the excavation data indicate the construction of a single late Terminal Formative (100–250 CE) structure. At that time, Structure 2 consisted of a large stepped platform constructed of adobe blocks and rising approximately fourteen meters above the floodplain. On the summit of the platform, excavations revealed remnants of a poorly preserved adobe building (Joyce 2006). The recovery of pieces of faced stucco that apparently covered portions of the building as well as one piece of painted adobe indicates that it was an architecturally elaborate building. The low density of artifacts and lack of domestic debris indicate that the structure was a public building.

The scale and architectural elaboration of Structure 2 indicate that the acropolis was the civic-ceremonial center of Río Viejo during the late Terminal Formative. The participation of commoners in the construction of the civic-ceremonial center as well as the rituals carried out there, would have contributed to the creation of a new corporate identity centered on the symbols, institutions, and rulers at Río Viejo. Monumental buildings like Río Viejo's acropolis were also visible for great distances so that their power as sacred mountains and political centers would have been present in the everyday lived experiences of people throughout the region. Ritual feasting, perhaps associated with monument construction, was another communal activity that may have engaged large groups of people in ways that contributed to the social production of a larger-scale corporate identity.

Despite the evidence for increasing social inequality and the development of political affiliations and identities at the regional scale, public social practices appear to have continued to materialize social relations as corporate while restraining the expression of noble status (see Barber and Joyce 2007 for an extended discussion). For example, luxury goods obtained through long-distance exchange linked nobles in the lower Río Verde Valley to elites in other parts of Mesoamerica and contributed to the materialization of a noble identity. The use of socially valued goods in community rituals, particularly caches interred in public buildings, however, transformed these objects from prestige items that embodied high status into offerings that materialized corporate identities. Likewise, monumental buildings like Río Viejo's ceremonial center and the mixed-use and residential platforms at several sites were constructed with voluntary labor that would have materialized corporate action and identity as well as political authority. As argued by Barber and Joyce (2007:24): "Monumental architecture embedded regional political authority in place, creating a permanent and highly visible focus for collectivities tied to that authority. In the ritualized context of monument construction, labor became a practice of affiliation that connected regional populations with the physically and morally preeminent forces of regional political authority. Political authority thus was materialized as a scaled-up community." The more egalitarian, corporate, and community-based traditions in the lower Verde therefore constrained the development of more exclusive, regional, and unequal forms of authority during the Terminal Formative. One result was that distinctions between nobles and commoners were not emphasized in public action. When political authority was materialized, such as in the construction of Río Viejo's acropolis or in the interment of the high-status person in the Yugüe cemetery, it was couched in a more traditional corporate and community-based discourse. Unlike later times in the lower Río Verde Valley (see below), Terminal Formative monumental construction was not accompanied by evidence for aggrandizing elites, such as rulers' portraits on carved stone monuments and cemeteries restricted to the nobility.

Although people in the lower Verde participated in practices that produced larger-scale political formations that can probably be described as a state, there undoubtedly were different degrees of compliance and involvement with unifying rulers, institutions, and practices (Barber 2005; Barber and Joyce 2007; Joyce 2003). Terminal Formative social change would not have been driven simply by emerging elites or the new corporate structures of the Río Viejo polity. In addition to cooperative social practices such as the construction of monumental buildings and ritual performances, social change at this time was undoubtedly also an outcome of structural contradictions resulting in struggle, negotiation, and perhaps conflict. One likely point of tension was between the emerging institutions of rulership that were more unequal and regional in scope and the traditional structural principles that were relatively egalitarian and community-based. Both nobles and commoners were increasingly drawn away from traditional sites of social interaction tied to their local communities to participate in practices at the regional center of Río Viejo, including the construction of monumental buildings and large-scale public ritual performances. In addition, nobles were increasingly involved in wider interregional networks of exchange and interaction, which distanced themselves from commoners.

Social tensions surrounding the emerging regional forms of authority and identity are suggested by the mortuary data from the cemeteries at Yugüe and Cerro de la Cruz (Barber 2005; Joyce 1991a). As discussed above, most of the skeletons recovered in the cemeteries were interred in dense concentrations where individual bodies were often rearranged and piled together as a result of successive burial events, thereby losing their individuality and becoming incorporated into the social group at death. Some burials, however, especially high-status ones, were left as intact skeletons, suggesting a more restricted form of authority focused perhaps on individuals or particular kin groups and linked to emerging supra-community political institutions as symbolized, for example, by Río Viejo's acropolis. While the overall pattern of rulership at this time may appear to be corporate, it was not necessarily the result of a structural unity as implied in Blanton's (1998) model but was instead in part an outcome of social negotiations involving traditional communal authority and identity and the newer, more restricted and unequal forms of power.

The tension between traditional and centralized forms of authority could have been a factor contributing to the collapse of the Terminal Formative regional polity (Joyce 2003, 2006). At about 250 CE the elaborate public building on Structure 2 of Río Viejo's acropolis was abandoned. Burned adobes and floor areas suggest that the structure may have been destroyed by fire. The regional settlement data also indicate a dramatic disruption in regional sociopolitical organization. Río Viejo decreased in size from 200 hectares in the late Terminal Formative to 75 hectares in the Early Classic. Several other large Terminal Formative floodplain sites with mounded architecture, including Yugüe, declined significantly in size or were abandoned. The regional settlement hierarchy declined from five to four levels and there is a shift in settlement from the floodplain into the piedmont, perhaps for defense. During the Early Classic (250–500 CE), the region contained as many as eight first-order centers of roughly equivalent size. There is little evidence for monumental building activities. The impression is that the lower Verde region was characterized by multiple and perhaps competing polities. The scale of political control was far reduced from the Terminal Formative when Río Viejo was the single dominant center in the region and from the Late Formative when two first-order centers were present.

Early Classic burials at Río Viejo occur most often as individual interments and there is no evidence of the dense cemeteries of the Formative (Christensen 1999; Joyce 1991a). Two high-status burials have been recovered with offerings of up to twenty-nine ceramic vessels as well as greenstone, shell, and obsidian artifacts (Joyce 1991a:779, 784). The data suggest that Early Classic social organization involved a decrease in the scale of political control, but with more restricted forms of authority. These data suggest that nobles were more successful in consolidating power, developing new forms of rulership within smaller, more traditional community-level scales of control.

At present, the causes of the Early Classic political collapse in the lower Río Verde Valley are only beginning to be investigated. One factor may have been interaction with the powerful Central Mexican state of Teotihuacan (Joyce 2003). Another factor in the collapse, however, could have been social tension over divergent ideologies and forms of authority, leading to the rejection of rulers and ruling institutions by local elites and commoners. One plausible scenario is that the construction of the acropolis was an attempt by Río Viejo's rulers to consolidate regional political authority, which instead became a spark that triggered the rejection of the polity and the resulting political fragmentation of the Early Classic period. It is intriguing that following its abandonment, Structure 2 on the acropolis at Río Viejo lay exposed to the elements for 250 years, resulting in erosion and further disintegration of the building. The ruins of the acropolis would have persisted through the Early Classic as a reminder of the people, institutions, and ideas that sponsored its construction during the Terminal Formative. Based on current data, the acropolis was not reoccupied until the Late Classic during a second period of political centralization.

LATE CLASSIC CENTRALIZATION

The data from the lower Río Verde Valley show that the political fragmentation of the Early Classic was followed in the Late Classic period by population nucleation and political centralization with the regional capital once again situated at Río Viejo (Joyce et al. 2001). The Río Viejo polity shared many features with other centralized polities of Late Classic Mesoamerica, including urbanism, monumental art and architecture, writing, the institution of kingship, craft specialization, and a settlement hierarchy with at least four levels. Río Viejo was one of the largest and most powerful polities in Late Classic Oaxaca.

Late Classic settlement in the full-coverage survey zone consisted of fifty sites, covering 605 hectares. Settlement shifted back toward the floodplain with the occupational area recorded there increasing from 22 percent in the Early Classic to 56 percent by the Late Classic. A seven-tiered settlement hierarchy developed during the Late Classic based on site size, volume of mounded architecture, and the presence/absence of carved stone monuments. Río Viejo was the first-order capital of a regional polity given its large size, monumental architecture, and numerous carved stone monuments. In the current settlement model, second-order sites like Charco Redondo and San Francisco de Arriba range from 52 to 58 hectares and have impressive monumental buildings and carved stones. Third-order sites range in size from 26 to 33 hectares and include Tututepec and Cerro del Chivo within the full-coverage zone and probably La Humedad and La Huichicata outside of the systematic survey. All of the third-order centers have monumental architecture and carved stones. Fourth-order sites range from 10 to 15 hectares, fifth-order sites range from 5 to 9 hectares, sixth-order sites from 2 to 4 hectares, and seventh-tier sites are less than 2 hectares; these sites never have carved stones and rarely include mounded architecture.

By the Late Classic, Río Viejo had grown to its maximum area of 250 hectares and was the capital of a complex polity that dominated the lower Verde (Figure 7.3). Much of the site was artificially raised above the floodplain by a series of large residential and multi-use platforms. All of the platform mounds mapped at Río Viejo have Late Classic occupations, although most of them included redeposited pottery from earlier periods. Mounds 3, 4, 6, 7, 10, 12, 13, and 14 appear to have been large residential platforms based on the presence of building foundations visible on the

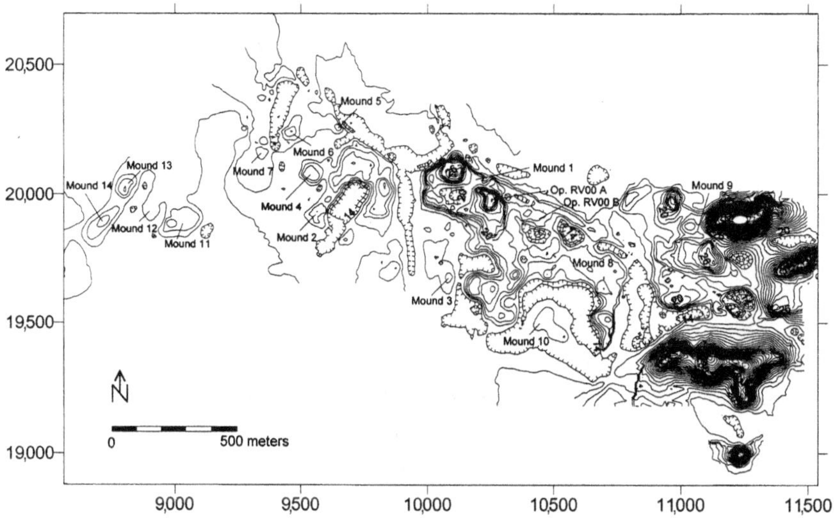

7.3 Plan of Río Viejo showing mounds and excavation areas from the 2000 field season.

surface along with numerous *manos*, *metates*, and utilitarian pottery. Mounds 2, 8, 9, and 11 also supported large structures, probably public buildings, and so should be considered multi-use platforms.

Río Viejo's acropolis was reoccupied during the Late Classic and once again became the site's civic-ceremonial center. Evidence that Mound 1 was a locus of important public ceremonies, and probably the ruler's residence, includes the presence of three Late Classic carved stone monuments depicting rulers (Urcid and Joyce 2001), a plaza spatially situated for large public gatherings, and a sunken patio probably for elite-restricted activities. A test excavation fifty meters south of Mound 1 recovered thick deposits of Late Classic sherds from fancy serving vessels, suggesting elite domestic activities or perhaps feasting (Joyce 1991a:480). Excavations on Structure 2 exposed Late Classic building foundations, although they were very poorly preserved because of the reuse of foundation stones during the Early Postclassic. Excavation and surface collections suggest that the entire acropolis was occupied during the Late Classic.

Although the Late Classic saw the return of centralized rulership in the lower Río Verde Valley, evidence indicates that the nature of political authority varied from the previous period of centralization during the Terminal Formative. The Río Viejo polity no longer was characterized by the corporate political organization and communal building projects that occurred during the Terminal Formative. Excavations at Río Viejo and San Francisco de Arriba indicate that rather than large-scale building projects, construction of monumental public buildings during the Late Classic involved only minor renovations of earlier structures that would not have required large labor forces (Joyce 1999, 2006; Workinger 2002:96–237). For example, Structure 2 on the acropolis was rebuilt by laying down a 0.6-meter-thick deposit of fill over the ruins of the Terminal Formative building and than constructing another building on this surface, this time with a stone foundation and perishable walls.

Iconography from Late Classic carved stone monuments in the lower Río Verde Valley suggests a more exclusionary form of political power legitimated through the aggrandizement of individual rulers, their ancestors, and their place in the line of dynastic succession. A total of thirteen carved stone monuments have been dated stylistically to the Late Classic at Río Viejo (Urcid and Joyce 2001). They are carved in low relief and are made of the local granite. Many of the carved stones depict nobles, probably rulers of Río Viejo, dressed in elaborate costumes and sometimes accompanied by a glyph that represents their name in the 260-day ritual calendar (Figure 7.4). For example, Río Viejo Monument 8 located on the acropolis, depicts a noble wearing an elaborate headdress and the profile head of a jaguar. The personage also wears a jaguar buccal mask with prominent fangs and earspools. To the left of the figure is the individual's hieroglyphic name, 10 Eye. Human sacrifice and bloodletting are referred to on several monuments. In addition to actual depictions of rulers, two carved stones (Monuments 1 and 14) each include only a single glyph, which we hypothesize to be the calendrical name of a ruler. Carved stone monuments at second-order and third-order sites are similar in style to those from Río Viejo and include either depictions of nobles or stones with only the hieroglyphic names of rulers (Jorrín 1974; Urcid and Joyce 2001; Workinger 2002). The nobles referred to on these monuments may be local rulers or members of Río Viejo's ruling dynasty.

The aggrandizement of nobles as well as their physical and symbolic separation from commoners is indicated by data from the hilltop ceremonial site of Cerro de los Tepalcates. Cerro de los Tepalcates is located on a rocky hill overlooking the coastal lagoons. Survey of the site recovered few sherds and no evidence for terraces or building foundations typically visible on hilltop sites in the region. At Cerro de los Tepalcates, hieroglyphic inscriptions are carved into boulders. The inscriptions appear to be calendrical names of nobles. The names often occur in pairs, suggesting that they may represent marital pairs. The site also included a probable looted tomb. Since no tombs have been discovered elsewhere in the region, these data suggest that lower Verde rulers may not have been interred in their communities but rather in cemeteries associated with sacred non-residential sites.

Although few Late Classic burials have been excavated in the lower Verde, the data suggest that like the Early Classic, commoners were buried as individuals or in small family groups near their houses (Christensen 1999) rather than in communal cemeteries as had been done during the Formative. Burials of non-elites have been found in residential settings usually without offerings or accompanied by a small

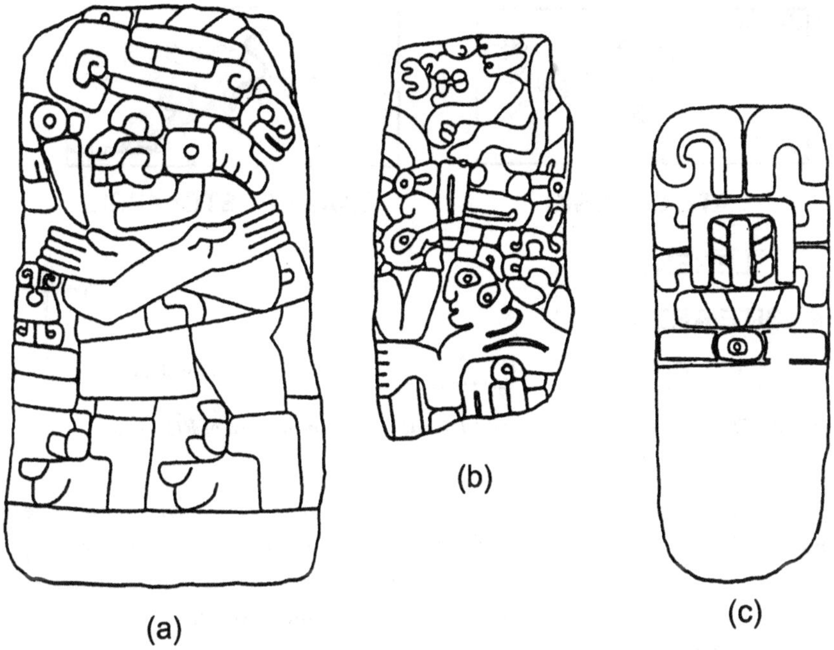

7.4 Late Classic carved stone monuments from Río Viejo: a=Monument 8; b=Monument 11; c=Monument 14. Drawn by Javier Urcid.

number of ceramic vessels, although an adult burial recovered from Mound 7 at Río Viejo was interred with three ceramic vessels, two ground-stone axes, a shell necklace consisting of sixty-nine beads, two bone pendants, two pieces of worked bone, one greenstone bead, and a piece of worked granite (Workinger and Joyce 1999:96–97). Based on the available data, commoners were primarily farmers who lived in modest wattle-and-daub houses, although evidence for specialized production of grayware pottery comes from a test excavation and surface collections on Mound 4 at Río Viejo. Future research in the lower Río Verde Valley needs to explore more fully the dimensions of social difference and identity beyond noble and commoner distinctions and how these differences were implicated in social negotiation and transformation.

The data from the lower Verde indicate a return to centralized political authority during the Late Classic with the reemergence of Río Viejo as the dominant center in the region. In contrast to the Terminal Formative, however, commoners seem to have been less involved in large-scale projects such as the construction of public buildings. Although lower Verde nobles expressed their power in monumental art and architecture, the focus on individual rulers in monumental art and the decrease in public building projects suggest a less communal, more exclusionary ideology

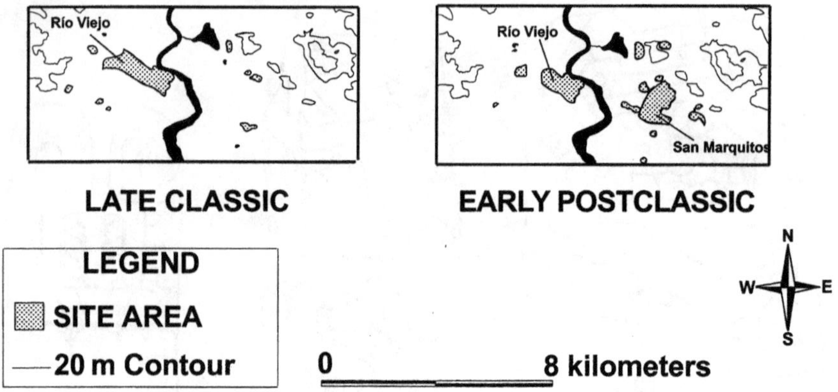

7.5 Late Classic to Early Postclassic settlement change in the area of Río Viejo.

(Joyce 2006; Joyce et al. 2001; Joyce and Weller 2007). Commoners may have been less actively engaged in the kinds of dramatic ritual performances and shared experiences that created a sense of belonging and identity with the polity, including its rulers, ruling institutions, and symbols (Kertzer 1988). At present, we have little evidence for the nature of Late Classic social negotiations or tensions, although data from the Early Postclassic suggest that there may have been a hidden transcript of commoner resistance that only became public once the Río Viejo polity, and its coercive powers, had collapsed (Joyce et al. 2001).

THE CLASSIC PERIOD COLLAPSE

The Late Classic period polity centered at Río Viejo collapsed during the Early Postclassic period (Joyce et al. 2001). The data indicate that a major change in settlement patterns and sociopolitical organization occurred during the Early Postclassic. Regional settlement as measured by the occupational area in the full-coverage survey zone decreased from 605 hectares in the Late Classic to 452 hectares in the Early Postclassic, while the settlement hierarchy decreased from seven to four levels. Río Viejo continued as a first-order center, although settlement at the site declined from 250 to 140 hectares (Figure 7.5).[2] At the same time, another first-order center emerged at San Marquitos, which grew from 7 hectares in the Late Classic to 191 hectares in the Early Postclassic.[3] In the Early Postclassic, second-order sites range from 10 to 21 hectares, third-order sites from 2 to 5 hectares, and fourth-order sites are 1 hectare or less. Regional settlement shifted back toward the piedmont with 62 percent of the occupational area in the full-coverage survey located there, versus only 34 percent during the Late Classic. Excavation and survey have found no evidence for the construction of monumental architecture at Río Viejo and

7.6 Early Postclassic carved stones at Río Viejo: a=Monument 3; b=Jamiltepec Monument 1. Drawn by Javier Urcid.

other sites during the Early Postclassic. The architectural data indicate a cessation of the construction of monumental buildings to house rulers and politico-religious institutions.

The lack of monumental building activities is mirrored in a reduction in monumental art with only three stone monuments recorded at Río Viejo (Figure 7.6) that are tentatively dated stylistically to the Early Postclassic; all of these are sculptures as opposed to flat stelae and orthostats (Urcid and Joyce 2001).[4] The iconography and location of the monuments indicate a shift away from expressions of aggrandizement and dominance in the portrayal of important personages. Early Postclassic sculptures were highly visible and accessible since they were located on a natural hill on the southeastern end of the site as opposed to locations on public buildings or multi-use platforms where Late Classic carved stones were placed. Late Classic monuments depicted individual rulers shown with elaborate elements of royal dress—such as jaguar headdresses and masks, staves of office, and other aspects of personal adornment—and in many cases with their hieroglyphic names and allusions to important rites like sacrifice. The Early Postclassic sculptures depict

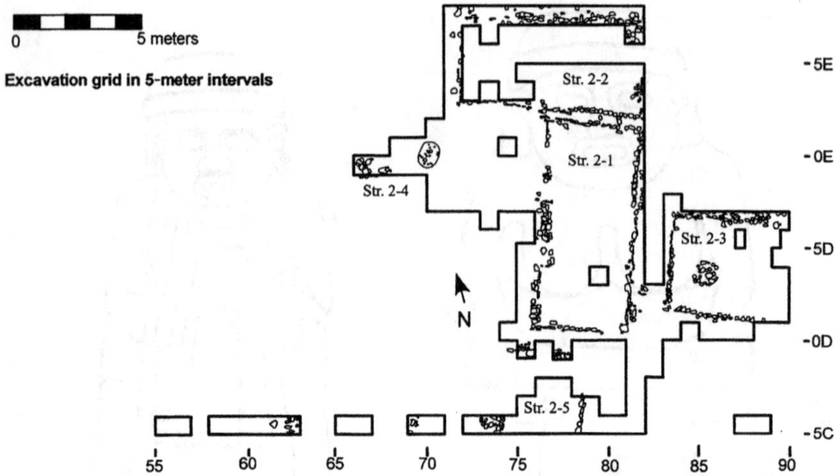

7.7 Plan of Op. RV00 A excavations, Río Viejo, Oaxaca.

personages that lack the glyphs and elaborate ornamentation of the Late Classic carved stones. For example, Monument 3 clearly depicts a topless female wearing a skirt, or *posahuanco*, in the traditional style of the Oaxaca Coast. Urcid and Joyce (2001) suggest that the Early Postclassic stone monuments depict deities, although they cannot rule out living nobles or noble ancestors.

Large-scale horizontal excavations exposed two areas of Río Viejo with the remains of Early Postclassic residences (Operations RV00 A and RV00 B; Joyce 2006; Joyce et al. 2001; Joyce and King 2001; King 2003). Op. RV00 A cleared 242 square meters on Mound 1–Structure 2, the eastern portion of the acropolis (Figure 7.7). Two structures were completely exposed as well as portions of three others. Op. RV00 B exposed portions of seven structures on Mound 8, approximately 180 meters southeast of the acropolis. The Postclassic structures in both operations were low platforms, approximately 0.5 meter high, and supported wattle-and-daub superstructures. The excavations yielded burials along with artifacts, features, and refuse that demonstrate the domestic function of these buildings. The size and form of the buildings in the two areas were virtually identical and the relatively modest architecture and burial offerings indicate commoner status. Dozens of similar structures have been observed on the surface over a broad area of Mound 8 (Joyce and King 2001; King 2003). Survey and test excavations throughout Río Viejo have not recovered material indications of significant wealth distinctions relative to the residences exposed in Ops. RV00 A and RV00 B. The excavations at Río Viejo along with the regional survey data suggest little variation in wealth and power during the Early Postclassic.

The Op. RV00 A excavations show that by the Early Postclassic, the acropolis was no longer the civic-ceremonial center of the site but instead was a locus of commoner residences. The five low platforms excavated on Structure 2 were densely packed, often with less than two meters separating structures. The stones used to construct the platforms were obtained by dismantling the foundations of the Late Classic public building on Structure 2. The deposits that overlay occupational surfaces included concentrations of unfired daub from the decay of wattle-and-daub superstructures. Three primary burials were recovered adjacent to the southwestern corners of two of the structures. Two burials, each containing a single child without offerings, were excavated outside of the southwest corner of Structure 2-1. A flexed burial of an adult male without offerings was excavated beneath the occupational surface immediately outside of the southwestern corner of Structure 2-3.

Midden deposits were excavated from two areas of Op. RV00 A (Joyce et al. 2001). One midden was exposed in the one-meter-wide passage between Structure 2-5 and Structure 2-1 and yielded a radiocarbon date from charcoal of 997 ± 47 bp, or 953 CE (AA37669). Early Postclassic refuse was also used for fill in Structure 2-5, which is stratigraphically earlier than the midden in the passageway, showing that the Early Postclassic domestic occupation of Structure 2 began prior to the mid-tenth century (uncalibrated). Artifacts associated with the Early Postclassic occupation on Mound 1–Structure 2, especially those from the middens, confirm the domestic use of this area. Typical Mesoamerican domestic items included obsidian blades, cores, and debitage; ground-stone axes; hammerstones; mano and metate fragments; chert projectile points and debitage; heat-altered rock; animal bone; shell; charred plant remains; ceramic sherds, figurines, whistles, earflares, stamps, and spindle whorls; bone needles; and carved bone. These data suggest activities such as processing and consumption of food, working of lithics, manufacturing textiles, and performance of household rituals. Imported goods associated with the residences included greenstone beads, a turquoise pendant, obsidian, pumice, possible non-local ceramics, and fragments of at least two alabaster bowls. Since Structure 2 had been the location of public buildings during the Terminal Formative and Late Classic, it is possible that some of these luxury goods were imported into the region prior to the Early Postclassic. A similar set of domestic artifacts and imported goods was recovered from residences excavated in Op. RV00 B on Mound 8, 180 meters southeast of the acropolis (Joyce and King 2001; King 2003; Chapter 8). Overall, the data suggest relatively little variation in social status and roles between the two areas where Early Postclassic residences were excavated. Although the inhabitants of these residences had access to a variety of local and imported prestige goods, the relatively modest architecture and burial offerings indicate commoner status.

Three of the platforms excavated in Op. RV00 A surrounded a patio (Mound 1–Structures 2-1, 2-2, and 2-4). A worked monumental stone measuring 1.42

meter by 1.09 meter by 0.48 was found lying on the surface of the patio; the stone resembles a probable Late Classic altar found on the plaza beneath Structure 2. The upper surface of the stone exhibited fifteen ground or pecked depressions similar to depressions observed on other worked monumental stones and unworked boulders at the site (Urcid and Joyce 2001:205–208). The function of stones like this one is unclear. As discussed by Joyce and his colleagues (2001:358–359), they may have been milling stones or could have had a ceremonial purpose.

A multiple burial was interred beneath the surface of the patio with evidence of an unusual mortuary ritual relative to other Early Postclassic burials (Joyce et al. 2001). The burial included two individuals placed in a pit partially lined with uncut stones; neither was accompanied by offerings. One interment was a secondary burial of an adult male accompanied by red pigment and with several bones exhibiting cut marks, possibly due to a violent death or postmortem preparation of the body (Urcid 2000). The fill in the burial pit also included ash and charcoal indicative of burning. The second individual was a primary interment of an adult female. She was seated and tightly flexed, probably indicative of a bundle burial, and placed directly on top of the first individual. After the burial was covered with sediment, a fire was set over the grave, leaving a layer of burned earth. The mortuary ceremony therefore involved the burial of an adult female probably accompanied by a male ancestor or possibly a sacrificial victim. The data indicate that the mortuary ritual was a restricted household ceremony since it was carried out in a small, enclosed patio space of a residence, although the broader significance of this unusual burial is unclear. The size and form of the Early Postclassic residential structures as well as the associated artifact assemblage and the other burials recovered on Structure 2 do not suggest significant status differences between this domestic unit and the one on Mound 8 east of the acropolis, so it would be difficult to interpret the burial as high status. It is possible that the multiple interment involved a primary female burial accompanied by the reburial of an ancestor removed from another location, since Structure 2 was not a residential area in the Late Classic. The interment could have been part of a termination ceremony desacralizing the acropolis (Kunen et al. 2002; Mock 1998).

The presence of commoner residences on the acropolis shows that Early Postclassic people did not treat the earlier spaces, objects, and buildings associated with rulership with the same reverence they had been afforded in the Late Classic and before (Joyce et al. 2001). During the Late Classic, the acropolis with its public buildings, plaza, sunken patio, and carved stone portraits of rulers was a monument expressing the sacred authority and political power of the nobility. By the Early Postclassic, the occupation of the acropolis by commoners and the dismantling of public buildings for reuse as foundation stones to construct their residences suggest the active denigration of earlier symbols of rulers and ruling institutions.

A more dramatic example of the disjunction between Late Classic and Early Postclassic political discourse is marked by the discovery of a fragment of a Late Classic carved stone monument (Río Viejo Monument 17) reutilized in an Early Postclassic structure wall excavated in Op. RV00 B (Joyce and King 2001; King 2003). The carved stone depicted an elite individual with an elaborate feathered headdress. Prior to its placement in the wall of a commoner residence, this monument had first been broken and then reutilized as a metate. At least four other Classic period carved stones were also reset in walls during terminal, presumably Early Postclassic, construction phases (Urcid and Joyce 2001:201–205). The ground or pecked depressions on the monumental stone recovered in the Early Postclassic residential patio may also represent another example of a utilitarian reuse and symbolic denigration of a Late Classic stone monument, in this case an altar.

Elsewhere in Mesoamerica evidence for the reoccupation of civic-ceremonial centers as well as the reuse and/or destruction of elite art and architecture in the years following the collapse has often been explained as the opportunistic actions of "squatters" (e.g., Culbert 1988:74; Harrison 1999:192–199; Pendergast 1979:183, 199), resulting in a functional change from elite public uses to non-elite residential ones. This view is incomplete in that it assumes that the commoners who reoccupied site centers were unaware of their history or of the ruling ideas and institutions of their immediate ancestors. A view of commoners as people without history or social memory is in sharp contrast to recent arguments concerning practices of Mesoamerican nobles. It is generally accepted by Mesoamerican scholars that acts of destruction and "termination" by nobles should be interpreted as desecrations of defeated regimes, whether deposed political factions or external enemies (Mock 1998). If nobles were aware of the ruling ideas and institutions of their predecessors, common people should also have had a similar awareness of their immediate past. As cogently argued by Hamann (2002, Chapter 4), Mesoamerican peoples, commoners as well as nobles, exhibited historical continuities in meaning and symbolism for hundreds and even thousands of years despite historical ruptures, including the Spanish Conquest (also see R. Joyce 2000; Monaghan 1990). In the case of the dismantling of public buildings and the reuse of a ruler's portrait as a metate, I find it highly unlikely that only a few generations after the collapse of the Río Viejo polity the earlier meanings of these elite places, buildings, and portraits would have been lost and they would simply have been considered as convenient building materials. Even in cases where sites are reoccupied hundreds of years after abandonment, or by outsiders, the reuse or destruction of buildings and monuments would have involved meaningful acts (Chapter 4). To deny common people an understanding of their High Culture or its history is another example of the exclusion of commoners as significant actors in Mesoamerican political history (see also Chapter 4; Graham 2002:413–415; Robin 1999; Sheets 2000).

Another argument that denies historical consciousness to common people involves objections to the use of the category "commoner" to describe Early Postclassic social identity. Since current evidence indicates that inequalities in wealth and power were minimal, King (2003:353) argues that there were no "elites" and therefore use of the term "commoner" is also inappropriate. I argue that the category "commoner" is justified, however, by the historical relations embodied in tradition and social memory, which would have reflected centuries of living under conditions of hierarchical political systems. It is also likely that the immediate descendants of Late Classic noble families continued to embrace an identity as nobles during the Early Postclassic even if these families were no longer distinguished by unusual wealth or political power. In other words, commoner and noble identities were not just a product of the economic relations of the time but were the result of historical relations embodied in people's dispositions. Early Postclassic people in the lower Río Verde Valley also participated in networks of long-distance trade and interaction (Chapter 8), which would have brought them into contact with powerful nobles in other parts of Mesoamerica (see Ringle et al. 1998).

The regional data indicate that the Classic period collapse most dramatically affected rulers, ruling institutions, and the dominant ideologies that legitimated their authority. Río Viejo, the Late Classic capital of the lower Verde polity, was in decline, with a decreasing population, a reduction in the erection of carved stone monuments, and a cessation in the construction of monumental architecture that housed rulers and ruling institutions. The data from the lower Verde not only indicate the collapse of ruling institutions but also the denigration by commoners of objects, symbols, spaces, and buildings associated with Late Classic rulership. At present, there are few data suggesting significant differences in wealth and political power during the Early Postclassic. Although rulers and political institutions were greatly affected by the collapse, the social changes of the Classic to Postclassic transition had a less severe impact on the lives of commoners (Joyce et al. 2001; King 2003). The survey data do not indicate a demographic collapse suggesting large-scale emigration or high mortality rates. Commoners living at Río Viejo in the Early Postclassic participated in a vibrant and diverse domestic economy, suggesting that they were freed from tributary burdens imposed by the nobility. Commoners also had improved access to an array of imported prestige goods, indicating that they had greater involvement in long-distance trade.

CONCLUSIONS

The Classic period collapse in Mesoamerica has been identified as an important research problem for over fifty years. For many years, views of Classic period political history and the collapse, particularly in the Mexican Highlands, were dominated by long-term research on the largest and most powerful political centers, such as Teotihuacan and Monte Albán, which continued as regional powers for hundreds of years, often from as early as the Formative period. Although the fortunes of many Classic period polities waxed and waned, the collapse is usually viewed as the end of a long period of structural stability in ruling institutions and ideologies, despite considerable debate concerning the degree of political centralization, especially in the Maya Lowlands (Fox et al. 1996). Research on the complex polities of Classic period Mesoamerica is increasingly recognizing that in many regions centralized political authority was, in fact, not characterized by long-term stability (Marcus 1998; Sharer 1994). For example, as discussed in this chapter, the Oaxaca coastal polity of Río Viejo went through two periods of centralization and collapse before the Late Postclassic. In highland Oaxaca political centers such as Yucuita, Monte Negro, and Huamelulpan emerge by ca. 300 BCE only to collapse a few hundred years later and many Late Classic Maya polities were relatively short-lived.

The relative instability of political authority has most often been attributed to the unsuccessful outcome of conflict and competition among ruling dynasties. This position reflects the dominant perspective in Mesoamerican archaeology that Classic period political history resulted from the actions of powerful nobles operating within the structural constraints of prehispanic political systems, with little input from commoners and lesser nobles (Joyce et al. 2001; Robin 1999). Fortunately, recent research on Maya polities, particularly models of decentralized states, are beginning to consider structural contradictions and social tensions along with the actions of lesser nobles as important factors in political history (e.g., Fash et al. 2004; Iannone 2002; McAnany 1995). For example, the decentralized models focus attention on conflict between lineage heads and the rulers who periodically attempted to consolidate tenuous affiliations of multiple lineages into states. These models, however, are still focused on structural properties with polities cycling historically between their more centralized and decentralized iterations (e.g., Marcus 1993, 1998). The success or failure of nobles in warfare, trade, the production of wealth items, and the exploitation of commoners moves the polity back and forth along this continuum of relative centralization. Political organization, "dynamism," and the activities of nobles are therefore tightly constrained within the centralized-decentralized continuum. There is relatively little consideration, however, of historical contingency and the ways in which political formations are continuously produced and transformed by ongoing social relations and negotiations.

Another tendency of current models of Mesoamerican political history is to view common people as passive participants in systems of political relations rather than as people who contribute to ongoing social processes and transformations. An impressive body of research has investigated the participation of commoners in domestic and political economies (e.g., Blanton et al. 1996; Fedick 1996; Masson and Freidel 2002), yet, as argued by several researchers, nobles are still seen as having overwhelmingly controlled political economies as well as ruling ideas and institutions (Joyce et al. 2001; Sheets 2000). For example, Graham (2002:413–415) observes that views of elite control of political economy that have dominated archaeological research are problematic:

> I do not believe that the bulk of Maya society passively allowed power to accumulate in the hands of particular elites. I take the view that all of the Maya at all levels—other elites, craftsmen, farmers, traders, fisherfolk—made decisions that bore on economic development. Some of these decisions fostered compliance with elite consolidation of power; others forced it into particular molds; still others consistently and pervasively weakened elite power. (Graham 2002:413)

Although many researchers have considered the ways in which commoners participated in political economy as well as public ceremonies and labor projects, there has been little consideration of the ways in which the actions, interests, dispositions, and traditions of common people affected and altered elite decision making, ruling ideas and institutions, and systems of political economy (for exceptions, see Ashmore et al. 2004; Clark 2004; Joyce et al. 2001; Pyburn 1998; Sheets 2000).

Recent theoretical considerations of complex societies in Mesoamerica and beyond, however, have recognized that systems of domination are always negotiated and that we must consider commoners and non-ruling elites in our models of ancient and modern political systems (Barber 2005; Comaroff 1985; Joyce et al. 2001; Miller et al. 1989; Patterson and Gailey 1987; Scott 1990). Indeed, since the late 1960s research in social history and historical anthropology has emphasized the role of commoners in social transformation and has highlighted the importance of commoner historical consciousness in acts of resistance (Blickle 1981; Guha 1983; Sahlins 1985; Thompson 1963; Wolf 1969). More generally, Giddens (1979:88–94) has argued that all power relations are relations of autonomy and dependence where even the least powerful agents have some ability to act. Ideology, power, and systems of domination need to be problematized not just for times of fragmentation and collapse but for periods marked by long-term continuity in ruling ideologies and institutions. Social and political life is always the outcome of the embodied practices of all members of society, even during periods of apparent stability in social institutions (Giddens 1979; Pauketat 2001; Scott 1990). In ancient Mesoamerica as in all societies, structures of domination were continuously produced in practice and there was always the possibility of negotiating or contesting political relations. Commoners and lesser nobles could contest domination, for example, by claiming that rulers were not meeting their moral responsibilities as politico-religious leaders, by withdrawing support from rulers, by choosing which elite commodities they would acquire from nobles, by voting with their feet and leaving political centers, and by forming competing factions (Ashmore et al. 2004; Joyce 2004; Joyce et al. 2001; Sheets 2000). Political domination was not a given but was part of a dynamic, negotiated history. Of course, a consideration of social negotiation does not negate the potential importance of interelite relations. For example, competition and conflict among nobles of different polities have implications for the negotiation of power among people within polities that should be considered in models of political change.

The research in the lower Río Verde Valley has begun to consider the social negotiation of power and how various forms of domination produced different constraints and opportunities for people differentially situated within these polities. The data from the lower Río Verde Valley show that the Classic period collapse was not the termination of a long and stable tradition of centralized authority. Prior to the Classic period collapse, the region went through an earlier cycle of political centralization and fragmentation. The Formative period in the lower Verde saw a steady increase in population and political centralization, culminating in the development of a complex polity with its capital at the urban center of Río Viejo. Ruling institutions and ideologies were relatively inclusive and corporate with evidence for unifying social practices, such as ritual feasting and the communal construction of monumental buildings. Río Viejo continued as a regional political center through the Terminal Formative, a duration of less than 400 years. At 250 CE, the Terminal Formative Río Viejo polity collapsed, perhaps violently, with the destruction of the site's acropolis. Following a period of political fragmentation during the Early Classic, a centralized polity reemerged at Río Viejo, but it was based on a more exclusionary form of political power legitimated through the aggrandizement of rulers. The Late Classic Río Viejo polity continued for roughly 300 years until its collapse at ca. 800 CE.

The prehispanic history of the lower Río Verde Valley can be described in general terms as a series of cycles of centralization and fragmentation. Unlike Marcus's (1993, 1998) dynamic model, however, I argue that rather than simply cycling between centralized and decentralized "stages" of an overarching political structure, the periods of centralization and fragmentation in the lower Verde were historically contingent and highly variable. In the lower Verde, the periods of centralization during the Terminal Formative and Late Classic, like the periods of fragmentation in the Early Classic and Early Postclassic, differed greatly from one another in terms of political organization, social relations, and ideology.

Although the nature of rulership during the two periods of political centralization appears to have been quite different, the political history of the region suggests that centralization was relatively tenuous and contested (Barber 2005; Barber and Joyce 2007; Joyce 2003; Joyce et al. 2001). Centralized political authority during the Terminal Formative seems to have been built by mobilizing support through the sponsoring of communal rituals and works projects. Ruling institutions did not emphasize the personal or familial power of rulers but rather focused on nobles as part of a larger corporate body. Yet the evidence suggests a contradiction and tension between earlier less hierarchical forms of social organization and the increasing power of Terminal Formative rulers. Rulers seem to have been struggling to negotiate and legitimate rising inequality and political centralization within the context of traditional ideological principles that were more communal, egalitarian, and politically localized. That the acropolis was burned and abandoned shortly after its completion and then left unoccupied for 250 years is intriguing evidence suggesting that the rulers of Río Viejo may have been ultimately unsuccessful in institutionalizing their authority in the long-term and gaining the widespread consent of commoners and local nobles. By the Early Classic, the lower Verde region had fragmented into numerous, probably competing, polities.

Despite the return of centralized political authority and the emergence of a regional polity during the Late Classic, evidence from the Early Postclassic suggests that power continued to be contested. In contrast to political authority in the Terminal Formative, Late Classic rulers set themselves apart from their subjects in monumental art and mortuary practices. The Late Classic acropolis with its plaza, public buildings, and carved monuments of rulers was a sacred space where dominant ideologies were reinforced through symbolism and ritual performance. Relative to the Terminal Formative, however, commoners were less actively engaged in public projects like the construction of monumental buildings. References to sacrifice on carved stone monuments raise the possibility that coercion may have been an important component of Late Classic political authority. Elsewhere in Mesoamerica, a similar trend toward self-aggrandizement of rulers and the exclusion of commoners from state ceremonies and sacred spaces is evident at Monte Albán in the Oaxaca Valley and at several lowland Maya centers (Joyce 2004; Joyce and Weller 2007).

Archaeological research has so far yielded little evidence for the contestation of Late Classic political authority in the lower Río Verde Valley and elsewhere (Joyce et al. 2001; Joyce and Weller 2007), although this may be due to commoners having resisted in subtle ways that did not directly confront authority (see Giddens 1979:145–150; Scott 1990). By the Early Postclassic, however, commoners at Río Viejo were occupying the acropolis, dismantling public buildings, and reusing carved stone monuments for utilitarian purposes, suggesting the active denigration of earlier spaces, objects, and buildings that housed and symbolized rulers and ruling institutions (Joyce et al. 2001). I argue that the destruction, denigration, and reuse of these material symbols of the Late Classic centralized polity were based on social memories of the experiences of subjugation among commoners. By dismantling the public buildings of the Late Classic polity to build their houses, commoners were re-inscribing the acropolis with markers of their identities as freed from the subjugation of the rulers and ruling institutions that were once housed in those buildings. Perhaps the most evocative symbol of this re-inscription was the symbolic act of grinding maize on the head of a Late Classic ruler.

Seen from this perspective, the Classic period collapse appears less like a catastrophic end to stable and deeply embedded institutions of rulership and more like the outcome, at least in part, of social contradictions and tensions that were inherent in the reproduction of more complex regional and centralized political systems. The Classic period collapse in the lower Verde, however, was not an isolated historical transformation but instead was undoubtedly linked to the collapse of political institutions throughout much of Mesoamerica. The fact that numerous polities collapsed from 600 to 900 CE draws us back out to the macroscale and factors that might have affected polities throughout Mesoamerica, such as climate change, widespread warfare, and landscape degradation. In the lower Verde, population decline resulting from environmental factors like landscape degradation or drought are not indicated, although ongoing geomorphological and palynological studies are investigating the possibility of ecological factors in the collapse. The movement of people into defensible piedmont locations and the unusually high frequency of projectile points recovered from Early Postclassic sites suggests the possibility that conflict was a factor in the collapse (Joyce et al. 2001:371–372). It is unclear whether conflict was intraregional, involving members of the fragmented Río Viejo polity, or if it involved incursions by people from outside the region. Another factor was the importance of networks of interregional relations to the negotiation and legitimation of Late Classic political authority (Demarest et al. 2004; Sabloff and Andrews 1986). As polities like Teotihuacan and Monte Albán began to collapse between 600 and 800 CE, networks of trade, alliance, and intermarriage were increasingly disrupted and reoriented (Ringle et al. 1998), which may have begun to undermine Río Viejo's rulers. A similar process may have contributed to the collapse of the Monte Albán polity in the Valley of Oaxaca (Joyce 2004:211–212).

Regardless of the specific set of factors, by ca. 800 CE, Río Viejo's rulers were no longer able to mobilize the support of their followers as people left the political center and ceased participating in political ceremonies at the capital (also see Ashmore et al. 2004). Although the collapse in the lower Verde probably did not involve a commoner rebellion, allegiance to the nobility may have been weak given the exclusive and perhaps coercive character of Late Classic political authority. Commoners may not have supported regional elites in the face of external military incursions, internal factional competition, or economic hardship due to environmental change. The way in which symbols of rulership were treated in the Early Postclassic suggests that commoners increasingly penetrated and perhaps actively resisted the dominant ideology in the years prior to the political collapse. By the Early Postclassic, people were free of the coercive power of Late Classic nobles and were able to publicly oppose and subvert the meanings of traditional symbols of political power.

Although many questions remain concerning the Classic period collapse on the Oaxaca Coast, I have tried in this chapter to drawn attention to the importance of considering political relations in a more dynamic fashion. As in all political systems, the power of Late Classic rulers and ruling institutions was not a given; it was produced and reproduced in practice, negotiated to varying degrees, and sometimes contested or actively resisted. To understand the collapse and prehispanic Mesoamerican political history more generally, archaeologists must adopt a more dynamic view of systems of political domination that recognizes the ways in which all people, commoners as well as nobles, participated in social reproduction and transformation.

ACKNOWLEDGMENTS

I thank the Instituto Nacional de Antropología e Historia; especially the presidents of the Consejo de Arqueología, Joaquín García-Bárcena and Roberto García Moll; and the directors of the Centro INAH Oaxaca, María de la Luz Topete, Ernesto González Licón, and Eduardo López Calzada, who have supported the research in the lower Río Verde Valley, Oaxaca. Funding for the field research in the lower Verde has been provided by grants from the following organizations: National Science Foundation (grants SBR-9729763 and BNS-8716332), Foundation for the Advancement of Mesoamerican Studies (#99012), National Geographic Society (grant 3767-88), Wenner-Gren Foundation (GR. 4988), Vanderbilt University Research Council and Mellon Fund, Fulbright Foundation, H. John Heinz III Charitable Trust, Explorers Club, Sigma Xi, University of Colorado, and Rutgers University. During the writing of this chapter, I was supported by an ACLS/SSRC/NEH International and Area Studies Fellowship and a Faculty Fellowship from the Council on Research and Creative Work, University of Colorado at Boulder. I thank Stacy Barber, Jeff Blomster, Byron Hamann, Scott Hutson, Marilyn Masson, Heather Orr, and Payson Sheets for comments on this chapter. I thank Chris Ward, Gene Wheaton, and Curtis Nepstad-Thornberry for drafting most of the figures. Finally, I thank Jeffrey Blomster for inviting me to contribute to this volume.

NOTES

1. For comparative purposes, researchers in the lower Río Verde Valley (Joyce 1991a, 1991b; Joyce et al. 2001; Levine 2002; Workinger 2002) have followed the convention of archaeologists throughout Oaxaca (see Drennan 1983; Lind 1991–1992; Martínez López

et al. 2000) of basing their ceramic chronologies on uncalibrated radiocarbon dates. The Late Classic in the lower Río Verde Valley is dated to 500–800 CE based on ceramic cross-ties, stratigraphic evidence, and two uncalibrated radiocarbon dates from excavated charcoal deposits at Río Viejo: 1410 ± 180 bp, or 540 CE (Beta-85358), and 1230 ± 70 bp, or 720 CE (Beta-62906). The dating of the Early Postclassic is based on ceramic cross-ties, stratigraphy, and two uncalibrated radiocarbon dates from excavated charcoal deposits at Río Viejo (Joyce et al. 2001): 997 ± 47 bp, or 953 CE (AA37669), and 899 ± 44 bp, or 1051 CE (AA40034). King (Chapter 8) reports an uncalibrated date of 1035 CE from her excavations in Early Postclassic contexts at Río Viejo. Of course, the chronology will be modified as additional radiocarbon determinations are acquired.

2. Early Postclassic Río Viejo includes two components, the main settlement, which covers 140 hectares, and a 20-hectare component along the western end of the site.

3. The San Marquitos site as a whole includes multiple components during both the Late Classic and Early Postclassic. The settlement figures cited here are only for the major Early Postclassic component and its Late Classic precursor.

4. One of these sculptures, Jamiltepec Monument 1, was moved from Río Viejo to Jamiltepec in the late nineteenth or early twentieth century (Urcid and Joyce 2001).

REFERENCES

Ashmore, Wendy, Jason Yaeger, and Cynthia Robin

2004 Commoner Sense: Late and Terminal Classic Social Strategies in the Xunantunich Area. In *The Terminal Classic in the Maya Lowlands: Collapse, Transition, and Transformation*, edited by A. Demarest, P. Rice, and D. Rice, pp. 302–323. University Press of Colorado, Boulder.

Barber, Sarah

2005 Heterogeneity, Identity and Complexity: Negotiating Status and Authority in Terminal Formative Coastal Oaxaca. Unpublished Ph.D. Dissertation, Department of Anthropology, University of Colorado, Boulder.

Barber, Sarah, and Arthur A. Joyce

2007 Polity Produced and Community Consumed: Negotiating Political Centralization in the Lower Río Verde Valley, Oaxaca. In *Mesoamerican Ritual Economy*, edited by E. C. Wells and K. L. Davis-Salazar. University Press of Colorado, Boulder.

Blanton, Richard E.

1998 Beyond Centralization: Steps toward a Theory of Egalitarian Behavior in Archaic States. In *Archaic States*, edited by G. M. Feinman and J. Marcus, pp. 135–172. School of American Research Press, Santa Fe.

Blanton, Richard E., Gary M. Feinman, Stephen A. Kowalewski, and Peter N. Peregrine

1996 A Dual-processual Theory for the Evolution of Mesoamerican Civilization. *Current Anthropology* 37(1):1–14.

Blickle, Peter

1981 *The Revolution of 1525: The German Peasants' War from a New Perspective.* Translated by Thomas A. Brady Jr. and H. C. Erik Midelfort. Johns Hopkins University Press, Baltimore.

Christensen, Alexander

1999 Apéndice 3: Los restos humanos. In El Proyecto Patrones de Asentamiento del Río Verde, edited by A. Joyce, pp. 487–494. Report submitted to the Consejo de Arqueología, Instituto Nacional de Antropología e Historia, Mexico.

Clark, John E.

2004 Mesoamerica Goes Public: Early Ceremonial Centers, Leaders, and Communities. In *Mesoamerican Archaeology*, edited by J. Hendon and R. Joyce, pp. 43–72. Blackwell, Oxford.

Comaroff, Jean

1985 *Body of Power, Spirit of Resistance.* University of Chicago Press, Chicago.

Cowgill, George L.

1979 Teotihuacan, Internal Militaristic Competition, and the Fall of the Classic Maya. In *Maya Archaeology and Ethnohistory,* edited by N. Hammond and G. R. Willey, pp. 51–62. University of Texas Press, Austin.

Culbert, T. Patrick (editor)

1973 *The Classic Maya Collapse.* University of New Mexico Press, Albuquerque.

Culbert, T. Patrick

1988 The Collapse of Classic Maya Civilization. In *The Collapse of Ancient States and Civilizations*, edited by N. Yoffee and G. Cowgill, pp. 69–101. University of Arizona Press, Tucson.

Demarest, Arthur, Prudence M. Rice, and Donald S. Rice (editors)

2004 *The Terminal Classic in the Maya Lowlands: Collapse, Transition, and Transformation.* University Press of Colorado, Boulder.

Diehl, Richard A., and Janet C. Berlo (editors)

1989 *Mesoamerica after the Decline of Teotihuacan, A.D. 700–900.* Dumbarton Oaks Research Library and Collection, Washington, DC.

Drennan, Robert D.

1983 Appendix: Radiocarbon Dates for the Oaxaca Region. In *The Cloud People: Divergent Evolution of the Zapotec and Mixtec Civilizations,* edited by K. Flannery and J. Marcus, pp. 363–370. Academic Press, New York.

Fash, William L., E. Wyllys Andrews, and T. Kam Manahan

2004 Political Decentralization, Dynastic Collapse, and the Early Postclassic in the Urban Center of Copán, Honduras. In *The Terminal Classic in the Maya Lowlands: Collapse, Transition, and Transformation,* edited by A. Demarest, P. M. Rice, and D. S. Rice, pp. 260–287. University Press of Colorado, Boulder.

Fedick, Scott L.

1996 *The Managed Mosaic: Ancient Maya Agriculture and Resource Use*. University of Utah Press, Salt Lake City.

Fox, John W., Garrett W. Cook, Arlen F. Chase, and Diane Z. Chase

1996 Questions of Political and Economic Integration: Segmentary versus Centralized States among the Ancient Maya. *Current Anthropology* 37:795–801.

Giddens, Anthony

1979 *Central Problems in Social Theory*. University of California Press, Berkeley.

1984 *Constitution of Society: Outline of the Theory of Structuration*. University of California Press, Berkeley.

Graham, Elizabeth

2002 Perspectives on Economy and Theory. In *Ancient Maya Political Economies*, edited by M. Masson and D. Freidel, pp. 398–418. Altamira Press, Walnut Creek, California.

Grove, David C.

1988 Archaeological Investigations on the Pacific Coast of Oaxaca, Mexico, 1986. Report submitted to the National Geographic Society, Washington, DC.

Guha, Ranajit

1983 *Elementary Aspects of Peasant Insurgency in Colonial India*. Oxford, Delhi.

Hamann, Byron

2002 The Social Life of Pre-sunrise Things. *Current Anthropology* 43(3):351–382.

Harrison, Peter D.

1999 *The Lords of Tikal: Rulers of an Ancient Maya City*. Thames and Hudson, New York.

Hirth, Kenneth G. (editor)

1984 *Trade and Exchange in Early Mesoamerica*. University of New Mexico Press, Albuquerque.

Iannone, Gyles

2002 Annales History and the Ancient Maya State: Some Observations on the "Dynamic Model." *American Anthropologist* 104(1):68–78.

Janusek, John W.

2004 *Identity and Power in the Ancient Andes: Tiwanaku Cities through Time*. Routledge, New York.

Jorrín, Maria

1974 Stone Monuments. In *The Oaxaca Coast Project Reports: Part I*, edited by D. L. Brockington, M. Jorrín, and J. R. Long, pp. 23–81. Vanderbilt University Publications in Anthropology, No. 8. Nashville, Tennessee.

Joyce, Arthur A.

1991a Formative Period Occupation in the Lower Río Verde Valley, Oaxaca, Mexico: Interregional Interaction and Social Change. Unpublished Ph.D. dissertation, Department of Anthropology, Rutgers University, New Brunswick, New Jersey.

1991b Formative Period Social Change in the Lower Río Verde Valley, Oaxaca, Mexico. *Latin American Antiquity* 2(1):126–150.

1993 Interregional Interaction and Social Development on the Oaxaca Coast. *Ancient Mesoamerica* 4(1):67–84.

1999 El Proyecto Patrones de Asentamiento del Río Verde. Report submitted to the Consejo de Arqueología, Instituto Nacional de Antropología e Historia, Mexico City.

2003 Imperialism in Pre-Aztec Mesoamerica: Monte Albán, Teotihuacan, and the Lower Río Verde Valley. In *Ancient Mesoamerica Warfare*, edited by M. K. Brown and T. M. Stanton, pp. 49–72. AltaMira Press, Walnut Creek, CA.

2004 Sacred Space and Social Relations in the Valley of Oaxaca. In *Mesoamerican Archaeology*, edited by J. Hendon and R. Joyce, pp.192–216. Blackwell, Oxford.

2005 La arqueología del bajo Río Verde. *Acervos* 7(29):16–36.

2006 The Inhabitation of Río Viejo's Acropolis. In *Space and Spatial Analysis in Archaeology*, edited by E. Robertson, J. Siebert, D. Fernandez, and M. Zender, pp. 83–96. University of Calgary Press, Calgary, Alberta, Canada.

Joyce, Arthur A., Laura Arnaud Bustamante, and Marc N. Levine

2001 Commoner Power: A Case Study from the Classic Period Collapse on the Oaxaca Coast. *Journal of Archaeological Method and Theory* 8(4):343–385.

Joyce, Arthur A., and Stacie M. King

2001 Household Archaeology in Coastal Oaxaca, Mexico. Final report submitted to the Foundation for the Advancement of Mesoamerican Studies, Crystal River, Florida.

Joyce, Arthur A., and Errin Weller

2007 Commoner Rituals, Resistance, and the Classic-to-Postclassic Transition. In *Commoner Ritual and Ideology in Ancient Mesoamerica*, edited by N. Gonlin and J. C. Lohse, pp. 143–184. University Press of Colorado, Boulder.

Joyce, Arthur A., Marcus Winter, and Raymond G. Mueller

1998 *Arqueología de la costa de Oaxaca: Asentamientos del periodo Formativo en el valle del Río Verde inferior*. Estudios de Antropología e Historia No. 40. Centro INAH Oaxaca. Oaxaca.

Joyce, Arthur. A., Andrew Workinger, Byron Hamann, Peter Kröfges, Maxine Oland, and Stacie King

2004 Lord 8 Deer "Jaguar Claw" and the Land of the Sky: The Archaeology and History of Tututepec. *Latin American Antiquity* 15(3):273–297.

Joyce, Rosemary

2000 High Culture, Mesoamerican Civilization, and the Classic Maya Tradition. In *Order, Legitimacy, and Wealth in Ancient States*, edited by J. Richards and M. Van Buren, pp. 64–76. Cambridge University Press, Cambridge.

Kertzer, David

1988 *Ritual, Politics, and Power*. Yale University Press, New Haven, Connecticut.

King, Stacie M.

2003 Social Practices and Social Organization in Ancient Coastal Oaxacan Households. Unpublished Ph.D. dissertation, Department of Anthropology, University of California, Berkeley.

Kowalewski, Stephen A., Gary M. Feinman, Linda M. Finsten, Richard E. Blanton, and Linda M. Nicholas

1989 *Monte Albán's Hinterland, Part II: Prehispanic Settlement Patterns in Tlacolula, Etla, and Ocotlán, the Valley of Oaxaca, Mexico*. Memoirs of the Museum of Anthropology, University of Michigan, No. 23. University of Michigan, Ann Arbor.

Kunen, Julie L., Mary Jo Galindo, and Erin Chase

2002 Pits and Bones: Identifying Maya Ritual Behavior in the Archaeological Record. *Ancient Mesoamerica* 13(2):197–211.

Levine, Marc N.

2002 Ceramic Change and Continuity in the Lower Río Verde Region of Oaxaca Mexico: The Late Formative to Early Terminal Formative Transition. Unpublished Masters Thesis, University of Colorado, Boulder.

Levine, Marc N., Arthur A. Joyce, and Paul Goldberg

2004 Earthen Mound Construction at Río Viejo on the Pacific Coast of Oaxaca, Mexico. Poster presented at the 69th Annual Meeting of the Society for American Archaeology, Montreal, Canada.

Lind, Michael D.

1991–92 Unos problemas con la cronología de Monte Albán y una nueva serie de nombres para las fases. *Notas Mesoamericanas* 13:177–192.

Marcus, Joyce

1993 Ancient Maya Political Organization. In *Lowland Maya Civilization in the Eighth Century A.D.*, edited by J. A. Sabloff and J. S. Henderson, pp. 111–183. Dumbarton Oaks Research Library and Collection, Washington, DC.

1998 The Peaks and Valleys of Ancient States: An Extension of the Dynamic Model. In *Archaic States*, edited by G. M. Feinman and J. Marcus, pp. 59–94. School of American Research Press, Santa Fe.

Marcus, Joyce, and Kent Flannery

1990 Science and Science Fiction in Postclassic Oaxaca: Or, "Yes Virginia, there is a Monte Albán IV." In *Debating Oaxaca Archaeology*, edited by J. Marcus, pp. 191–205. Anthropological Papers, No. 84. Museum of Anthropology, University of Michigan, Ann Arbor.

1996 *Zapotec Civilization: How Urban Society Evolved in Mexico's Oaxaca Valley*. Thames and Hudson, New York.

Martin, Simon, and Nikolai Grube

2000 *Chronicle of the Maya Kings and Queens*. Thames and Hudson, New York.

Martínez López, Cira, Robert Markens, Marcus Winter, and Michael D. Lind
2000 *Cerámica de la Fase Xoo (Monte Albán IIIB–IV) del Valle de Oaxaca.* Proyecto Especial Monte Alban 1992–1994, Contribución No. 8. Centro INAH Oaxaca, Oaxaca.

Masson, Marilyn A., and David A. Freidel (editors)
2002 *Ancient Maya Political Economies.* Altamira Press, Walnut Creek, California.

McAnany, Patricia A.
1995 *Living with the Ancestors.* University of Texas Press, Austin.

Miller, Daniel, Michael Rowlands, and Christopher Tilley (editors)
1989 *Domination and Resistance.* Allen and Unwin, London.

Mock, Shirley B. (editor)
1998 *The Sowing and the Dawning: Termination, Dedication, and Transformation in the Archaeological and Ethnohistoric Record of Mesoamerica.* University of New Mexico Press, Albuquerque.

Monaghan, John
1990 Sacrifice, Death, and the Origins of Agriculture in the Codex Vienna. *American Antiquity* 55(3):559–569.

Patterson, Thomas C., and Christine W. Gailey (editors)
1987 *Power Relations and State Formation.* American Anthropological Association, Washington, DC.

Pauketat, Timothy R.
2001 Practice and History in Archaeology: An Emerging Paradigm. *Anthropological Theory* 1:73–98.

Pendergast, David
1979 *Excavations at Altun Ha, Belize, 1964–1970, Vol. 1.* Royal Ontario Museum, Toronto.

Pyburn, K. Anne
1998 Smallholders in the Maya Lowlands: Homage to a Garden Variety Ethnographer. *Human Ecology* 26(2):267–286.

Ringle, William M., Tomás Gallareta Negrón, and George J. Bey III
1998 The Return of Quetzalcoatl: Evidence for the Spread of a World Religion during the Epiclassic Period. *Ancient Mesoamerica* 9(2):183–232.

Robin, Cynthia
1999 Towards an Archaeology of Everyday Life: Maya Farmers of Chan Nóohol and Dos Chombitos Cik'in, Belize. Unpublished Ph.D. Dissertation, Department of Anthropology, University of Pennsylvania, Philadelphia.

Sabloff, Jeremy A., and E. Wyllys Andrews V. (editors)
1986 *Late Lowland Maya Civilization: Classic to Postclassic.* University of New Mexico Press, Albuquerque.

Sahlins, Marshall
1985 *Islands of History*. University of Chicago Press, Chicago.

Schele, Linda, and Peter Mathews
1998 *The Code of Kings*. Scribner, New York.

Scott, John C.
1990 *Domination and the Arts of Resistance*. Yale University Press, New Haven, Connecticut.

Shanks, Michael, and Christopher Tilley
1982 Ideology, Symbolic Power and Ritual Communication: A Reinterpretation of Neolithic Mortuary Practices. In *Symbolic and Structural Archaeology*, edited by I. Hodder, pp. 129–154. Cambridge University Press, Cambridge.

Sharer, Robert J.
1994 *The Ancient Maya*, 5th edition. Stanford University Press, Stanford, California.

Sheets, Payson
2000 Provisioning the Ceren Household: The Vertical Economy, Village Economy, and Household Economy in the Southeastern Maya Periphery. *Ancient Mesoamerica* 11(2):217–230.

Thompson, Edward P.
1963 *The Making of the English Working Class*. Gollancz, London.

Urcid, Javier
2000 Notes on Burial Feature. Manuscript in possession of the author.

Urcid, Javier, and Arthur A. Joyce
2001 Carved Monuments and Calendrical Names: The Rulers of Río Viejo, Oaxaca. *Ancient Mesoamerica* 12(2):199–216.

Webster, David, AnnCorinne Freter, and Nancy Gonlin
2000 *Copán: The Rise and Fall of an Ancient Maya Kingdom*. Harcourt College Publishers, Fort Worth.

Winter, Marcus
1989 From Classic to Post-Classic in Prehispanic Oaxaca. In *Mesoamerica after the Decline of Teotihuacan, A.D. 700–900,* edited by R. Diehl and J. Berlo, pp. 123–130. Dumbarton Oaks Research Library and Collection, Washington, DC.
1994 The Mixteca Prior to the Late Postclassic. In *Mixteca-Puebla: Discoveries and Research in Mesoamerican Art and Archaeology*, edited by H. B. Nicholson and E. Quiñones Keber, pp. 201–221. Labyrinthos, Culver City, California.

Wolf, Eric R.
1969 *Peasant Wars of the Twentieth Century*. Harper & Row, New York.

Workinger, Andrew
2002 Coastal/Highland Interaction in Prehispanic Oaxaca, Mexico: The Perspective from San Francisco de Arriba. Unpublished Ph.D. Dissertation, Department of Anthropology, Vanderbilt University, Nashville, Tennessee.

Workinger, Andrew, and Arthur A. Joyce.
1999 Excavaciones arqueológicas en Río Viejo. In El Proyecto Patrones de Asentamiento del Río Verde, edited by A. Joyce, pp. 51–119. Report submitted to the Consejo de Arqueología, Instituto Nacional de Antropología e Historia, Mexico.

8

Stacie M. King

Interregional Networks of the Oaxacan Early Postclassic

CONNECTING THE COAST AND THE HIGHLANDS

INTRODUCTION

Rulers of successful highland Mesoamerican cities, such as Teotihuacan and Monte Albán, had good reason for establishing and maintaining ties with coastal Oaxacan communities during the prehispanic era. The climatological and ecological regime of coastal Oaxaca made it a highly valuable and politically important region throughout prehispanic and early Colonial Mesoamerica. The raw material for many desirable Mesoamerican luxury goods, such as feathers, marine shell, *pupura* dye, cacao, and cotton were abundantly available in coastal Oaxaca, as were salt and palm products (e.g., oils and fibers) (Byland and Pohl 1994; Feinman and Nicholas 1992; Monaghan 1994; Spores 1993). The lower Río Verde Valley, in particular, has extremely fertile agricultural land owing in part to the alluvial deposition of eroded topsoil from the highlands along the coastal plain (Figure 8.1) (Joyce and Mueller 1992, 1997). The lower Verde site of Río Viejo grew to its largest size and maintained control over a vast coastal area during most of the Classic period (250–800 CE) (Joyce and King 2001; Joyce and Workinger 1996) in part because of the wealth and power generated from managing the export of coastal resources to the highlands.

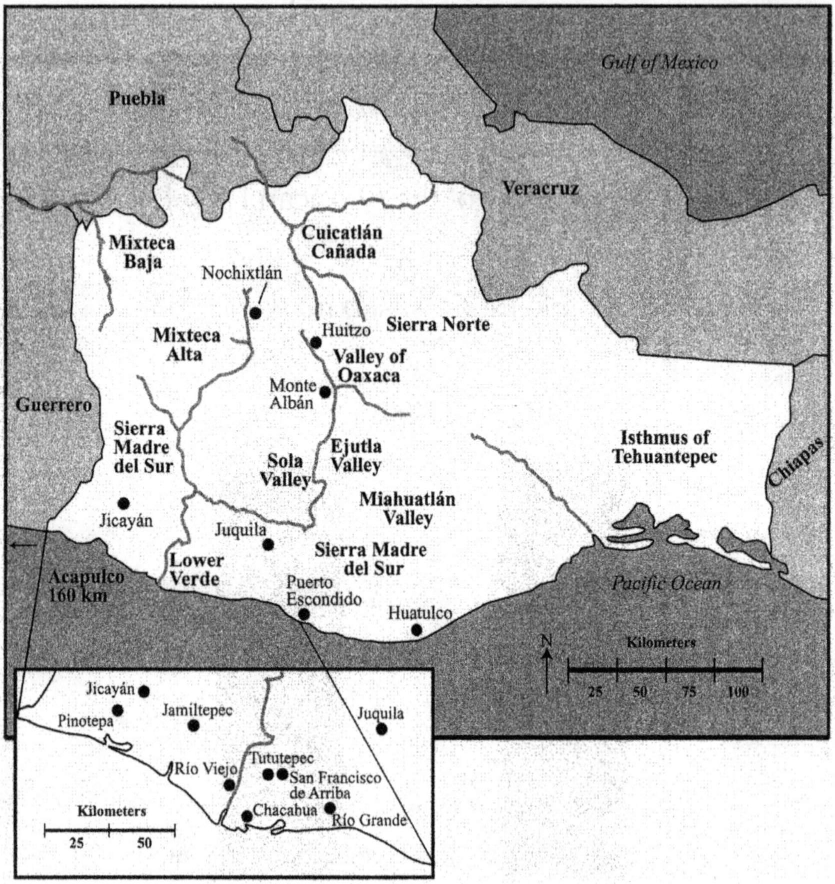

8.1 Map of Oaxaca, showing regions, sites, and towns mentioned in the text.

Based on ethnohistoric documents, we know that exchange networks between the coast and the highlands were important during the Late Postclassic and early Colonial periods. Mixtec Lord 8 Deer Jaguar Claw's choice to establish operations at Tututepec in the twelfth century CE can be viewed as a strategic decision to build his political power and reputation prior to his return to the highlands (Byland and Pohl 1994; Joyce et al. 2004; Smith 1973; Spores 1993). In addition, a coastal ally no doubt ensured highland Mixtec a steady supply of raw materials for elite luxury goods. This chapter addresses the evidence for the continuity and discontinuity in trade relationships between the Classic and Late Postclassic, or following the "collapse" of the Classic period state around 800 CE and prior to Mixtec entry into the coast between 1000 and 1200 CE (see Chapters 1 and 7). I argue for the presence of strong interregional connections between the Oaxaca Coast and the Mixteca Alta during the Early Postclassic and examine the evidence for interregional connections between Early Postclassic coastal Oaxaca and neighboring regions, both within and beyond the borders of contemporary Oaxaca.

Excavations at the coastal site of Río Viejo revealed a vibrant Early Postclassic community that was connected to multiple networks of exchange. Coastal residents were specialists in the production of cotton thread and cloth, which they likely exchanged for obsidian, an important and heavily used highland commodity. I argue that the primary interregional exchange routes used for trade and communication during the Early Postclassic connected the coast to the highlands, and specifically the lower Verde to the Mixteca Alta and beyond to include Cholula and Tula. The coast-highland trade route through the Mixteca Alta was more heavily used than was a transcoastal exchange network or a direct trade relationship with the Valley of Oaxaca.

This discussion is based primarily on an analysis of the domestic artifact assemblage recovered in excavations at Early Postclassic Río Viejo, located along the lower reaches of the Río Verde drainage on the coast of Oaxaca, Mexico. The clustered residences in two neighborhoods of Río Viejo yielded ample evidence of domestic activities, including food preparation, spinning and weaving, ceramic manufacture, and stone tool use and production (Joyce and King 2001; King 2003). The data show that residents of Río Viejo were well connected to multiple networks of interregional exchange through which obsidian was imported, manufacturing and stylistic conventions of ceramic production were shared, and cotton cloth was exported. However, residents lacked access to copper bells produced or distributed by people in other regions of Mesoamerica. Based on this evidence, I suggest that residents of Río Viejo were either distanced from some networks of exchange or were selective about the exchange networks they supported and supplied.

RÍO VIEJO DURING THE EARLY POSTCLASSIC

The cumulative results of work at Río Viejo show that the site was first occupied during the late Middle Formative (500–400 BCE) and grew dramatically during the Terminal Formative (150 BCE–250 CE). During the Late Classic (500–800 CE), Río Viejo reached 250 to 300 hectares, its largest size of any period of occupation, larger than any other site in the region (see Chapter 7 for an extensive discussion of settlement distribution in the lower Verde from the Classic to the Postclassic). Joyce and colleagues (2001) have proposed that Río Viejo was the capital of a state polity during the Late Classic. Seventeen plain and pecked monoliths, carved stone monuments (stelae), and standing three-dimensional stone sculptures have been recorded at Río Viejo, which date to the Classic period (Urcid and Joyce 1999). Four of the carved stones depict elite personages with elaborate headdresses accompanied by glyphs, which presumably represent the calendrical names of these rulers and suggest the presence of a ruling dynasty at Río Viejo during the Late Classic. The ceremonial center of the site was the acropolis, which measured 350 meters by 200 meters, supported several large structures and was elevated up to 15 meters above the floodplain (Joyce and Workinger 1996).

Although it was once presumed that Río Viejo was gradually abandoned following the Late Classic, the results of the 2000 field season show that Río Viejo was reduced to only about half the size, or 140 hectares, during the Early Postclassic (see Chapter 7; Joyce et al. 2001). However, large mound construction and carved stone production ceased by the Early Postclassic, and the once-ruling political regime was no longer in power. Instead, the entire Early Postclassic community of Río Viejo consisted of rather humble residences built on top of Late Classic period platforms and mounds (Joyce and King 2001; King et al. 2000). Joyce and colleagues (2001) have proposed that the Early Postclassic occupants at Río Viejo were commoners who actively resisted Late Classic period elites by restructuring political ideologies and reshaping their community during the Early Postclassic in the heart of the once-sacred ceremonial precinct.

Lower Río Verde Valley sites during the Early Postclassic lacked many of the features commonly associated with political and economic centralization. Ceremonial centers and monumental architecture were absent at all sites, and excavation data showed that socioeconomic status was not sharply differentiated. However, Río Viejo residents were still very much part of the greater Mesoamerican world and had access to ideas and goods from distant regions. Within this period of occupation (most likely between 975 and 1220 CE based on calibrated AMS dates[1]), numerous people and families cycled through the buildings at Río Viejo. Archaeological evidence reveals a rich and varied set of domestic activities, including house construction, food preparation and eating, spinning and weaving cloth, figurine and ceramic production, and performing religious rituals.

The Río Viejo Residence Project was designed in collaboration with Arthur Joyce to investigate the form and nature of Early Postclassic household social organization and included excavations in two separate Early Postclassic residential neighborhoods (Figure 8.2). In all, portions of twelve houses and associated exterior spaces were excavated in both of these Early Postclassic neighborhoods. Large horizontal exposures revealed architectural features, burials, and items used in domestic activities. The artifacts and architecture uncovered in both areas suggested few differences in social roles and status, based on the lack of differentiation in luxury goods and the standardization of domestic assemblages and architecture. Residents of both neighborhoods lived in highly uniform, modest, single-roomed rectangular houses, which were organized into dense barrios with no discernible site center or specialized ceremonial plaza.

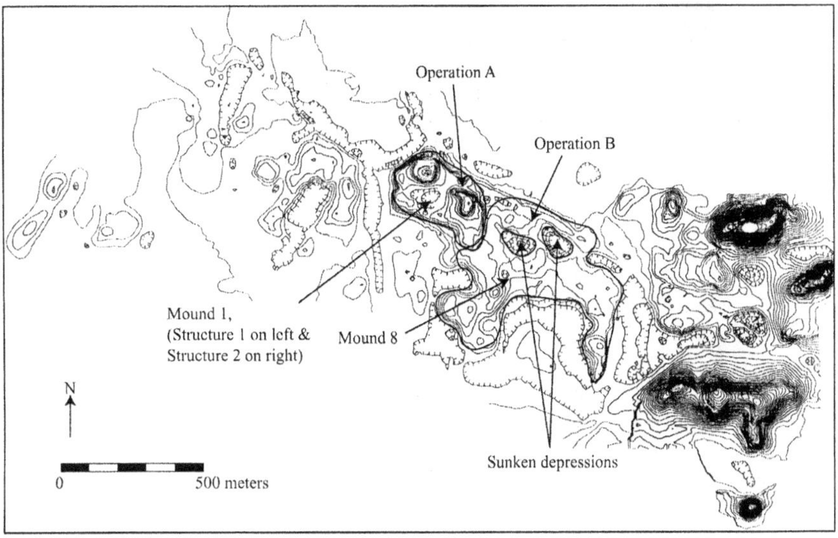

8.2. Map of Río Viejo. Adapted from Joyce et al. 2001.

The Operation B neighborhood of Río Viejo (the subject of this chapter) lies on a low broad platform elevated about five meters above the floodplain. Here, surface visible foundation walls mark the presence of several dozen structures. A total of 284 square meters was excavated in Operation B, including two complete structures, over half of two others, and small portions of another three (Figure 8.3; Joyce and King 2001). This neighborhood encompasses two phases of occupation, three major stages of construction events, and numerous smaller-scale discrete activities (King 2003). Exterior work areas appear to have been relatively limited, especially since even the presumed "patio" space contained remains of yet another structure. The structures all measure roughly five meters by eleven meters and consist of a single room delimited by stone foundation walls. These foundations likely supported perishable superstructures covered in daub, fragments of which were found in the post-abandonment rubble. Four small burn features located in Structures 8-4 and 8-8 show some repetitive use of small fires inside houses. Several buildings were occupied, constructed, and renovated at different times during the Early Postclassic, as is evident from fill deposits in the houses. The data used in this chapter are drawn from the Operation B excavations, which I directed.

OBSIDIAN ASSEMBLAGE OF EARLY POSTCLASSIC RÍO VIEJO

The primary imported material at Early Postclassic Río Viejo was obsidian. Residents likely had easy access to the material and its interregional exchange networks based

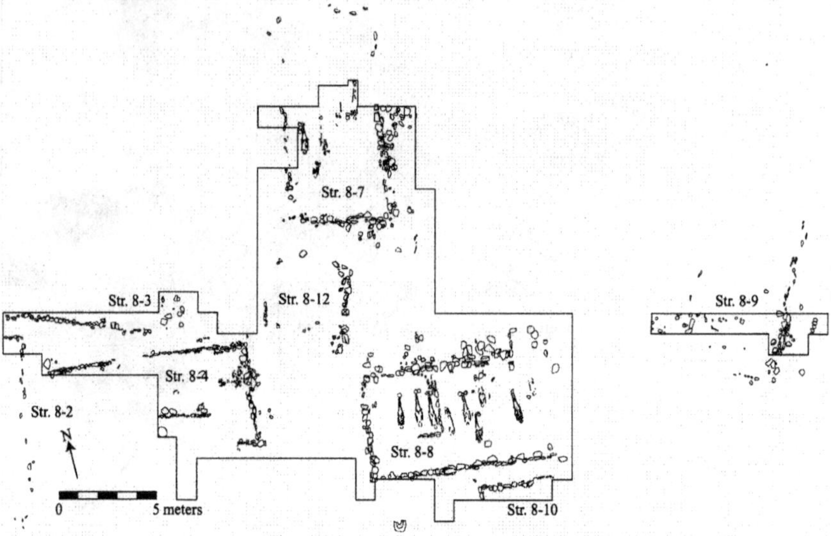

8.3 Operation B plan, Río Viejo.

on the abundance of non-local obsidian in domestic debris. The chipped stone assemblage recovered in Operation B was primarily composed of obsidian blades, small pressure flakes, and chert projectile points. The blades were probably used for a wide variety of cutting purposes since their patterns of discard did not correlate with any defined set of artifacts, and the wear patterns on the blades were not consistent with any specific defined task. The obsidian assemblage is largely composed of finished prismatic blade tools (75.8 percent), which exhibit wear patterns ranging from none to heavy, with a few examples of extensive retouch. Of the total number of obsidian artifacts (n=1058), 77.0 percent were finished tools, 22.9 percent were flakes, and 0.1 percent was a possible core fragment.

Obsidian found in lower Verde sites was either imported in the form of prepared cores and prismatic blades were manufactured locally, or it was directly imported in the form of prismatic blades. Joyce and colleagues (1995) proposed that starting in the Classic period, obsidian was imported to the lower Verde in the form of prefinished prismatic blades since prismatic blades overwhelmingly dominated the Classic period obsidian assemblage from test pits excavated in and around Río Viejo. However, given the presence of a few possible primary series blades and one possible spent core, the obsidian at Early Postclassic Río Viejo could have arrived in the lower Verde in the form of prepared polyhedral cores (Santley et al. 1986). The somewhat larger flakes and chunks in the Operation B assemblage could have resulted from corrections of manufacturing errors during blade tool production, and non-blade obsidian debitage was present, indicating that some amount of manufacture took place on site. Workinger (2002:134) also tentatively concluded that obsidian arrived to the nearby lower Verde site of San Francisco de Arriba in the form of polyhedral cores during the Early Classic.

The density of obsidian found at Early Postclassic Río Viejo averaged 18.2 pieces of obsidian per cubic meter. This exceeds the 9.6 per cubic meter site average calculated by Workinger (2002) for San Francisco de Arriba, located sixteen kilometers away. The difference in the average obsidian densities likely reflects an overall increase in obsidian utilization during the Postclassic (Healan et al. 1983; Rice 1987).

Manufacture, use, and disposal occurred throughout the Operation B residential neighborhood. Early Postclassic lithic debitage was distributed throughout fill deposits, occupation debris, and middens, without apparent concern for treading on sharp objects. Workinger has argued that blades were probably produced from cores in distinct locations at the site of San Francisco de Arriba, since a lithic dumpsite contained high density manufacturing and consumption debris (48.3 per cubic meter) (Workinger 2002:135). None of the excavated contexts at Early Postclassic Río Viejo suggests a specialized obsidian refuse dump, and obsidian debris was mixed with many other kinds of household trash.

Although both chert and obsidian were imported resources, Río Viejo residents relied more heavily on imported obsidian at a ratio of 18:1. This pattern is similar to San Francisco de Arriba, where obsidian comprised 97 percent of the overall lithic assemblage (dating from the Middle Formative to Late Postclassic) (Workinger 2002:295). Obsidian and chert raw materials were used most often to fashion distinct types of tools. The choice of raw material primarily reflects structural differences in mineralogy, hardness, and workability of both materials. However, the use of both obsidian and chert for projectile points shows that some crossover in application existed. Of the fifty-nine chert artifacts found in Early Postclassic contexts, finished tools comprised 33.9 percent of the assemblage, 50.8 percent were utilized and unutilized flakes, and 15.3 percent were cores/chunks. Projectile points were the most common type of chert tool, comprising 25.4 percent of the chert artifacts, with an additional drill, side scraper, and two perforators. In addition, the color of the chert raw material varied and included white, orange, brown, gray, and red varieties, which were often streaked with two or more of these colors. Although specific sources for the chert raw materials are unknown, chert is present throughout the Sierra Madre del Sur range and in the Oaxaca highlands. The Río Viejo chert may have been acquired opportunistically while traveling or trading, or perhaps the swift waters of the Río Verde carried small cobbles of chert downstream, which were then recovered for local use from secondary lag deposits. The presence of large chunks and unutilized flakes with cortex suggest that chert tools were sometimes manufactured on site from start to finish. Nonetheless, the amount of obsidian far exceeded chert in the Early Postclassic chipped stone assemblage.

Joyce and colleagues (1995) suggest that obsidian prismatic blades were luxury items in the lower Verde during the Classic period, since they were possibly manufactured by specialists elsewhere and imported over long distances. The high density of imported obsidian at Early Postclassic Río Viejo, in contrast, suggests that obsidian was relatively inexpensive and readily available, in spite of the long distance it had to travel. The composition of the obsidian assemblage, with large numbers of used and worn blades, shows that Río Viejo residents were major consumers of blades and did not necessarily control the distribution of obsidian to other Early Postclassic communities in the lower Verde. Most blades showed some degree of wear (81.1 percent), although only a few (1.6 percent) exhibited retouch. The relatively low number of retouched blades further supports the interpretation that obsidian was easy to acquire; as blades were worn down through use, they were apparently discarded rather than retouched to extend their use-life.

Studies of Postclassic period obsidian utilization in the Valley of Oaxaca are based largely on surface artifacts recovered during survey projects, which could not reliably separate Postclassic deposits into distinct Early and Late components (e.g., Appel 1982; Blanton 1978; Feinman and Nicholas 2004; Parry 1990). Nonetheless, Valley of Oaxaca studies show increased amounts of obsidian during the Postclassic as a whole (Parry 1990).

Obsidian at Río Viejo was imported from multiple sources. Of the 810 obsidian blade fragments pertaining to Early Postclassic contexts, clear and green obsidian together comprise greater than 50 percent of the assemblage. Transparent gray, opaque black, and opaque gray obsidian are also represented (Table 8.1). Of the 1,058 fragments of all obsidian from Early Postclassic contexts at Río Viejo, 30 percent were clear, 21.7 percent were green, 20 percent were transparent gray, 20 percent were black, and 8.1 percent were opaque gray. Workinger (2002:339) conducted obsidian source analysis using Instrumental Neutron Activation Analysis (INAA) on excavated material from the coastal site of San Francisco de Arriba. Workinger found that visual identification of green and clear/streaked obsidian correctly identified the Pachuca, Hidalgo, and Pico de Orizaba sources, respectively (see also Braswell et al. 2000). The remaining three kinds of obsidian (blacks and grays) could have been derived from a number of sources, which cannot be reliably identified based on visual inspection but could include the Guadalupe Victoria, Otumba, Ucaréo, and Zaragoza sources, identified by INAA in Workinger's study.

If the visual sourcing of green and clear obsidian is accurate, Río Viejo residents were importing obsidian from the Pachuca, Hidalgo, and Pico de Orizaba sources, located on the border between Puebla and Veracruz. Further, if the visual identification of at least five distinct colors of obsidian can be used as a proxy for different

Table 8.1 Early Postclassic obsidian blade fragment color varieties

Obsidian Color	*Blade Fragments (n)*	%
Clear	238	29.4
Green	213	26.3
Transparent gray	147	18.1
Opaque black	143	17.7
Opaque gray	69	8.5
Total	810	100

parent materials, then Early Postclassic residents acquired obsidian from a number of different sources, which might have entailed forging and/or maintaining connections with multiple highland exchange partners.

R. Zeitlin's (1982) study of Early Postclassic obsidian utilization on the southern Isthmus of Tehuantepec, which relies on chemical sourcing, showed that 52 percent of the obsidian was imported from Pico de Orizaba, followed by smaller percentages from a variety of Puebla/Veracruz, Basin of Mexico, and Guatemalan sources. Pico de Orizaba is the nearest obsidian source to the southern Isthmus (385 kilometers) (as it is for the lower Verde at 325 kilometers) and proximity, he argued, may in part explain its heavy utilization. Although no one knows for sure who was mining the Pico de Orizaba obsidian, Mixteca-Puebla ceramics have been found in the Cotaxtla region near the Pico de Orizaba source. Based on the presence of these wares, Daneels (1997) has hypothesized that Postclassic utilization of Pico de Orizaba obsidian might be linked to increasing demand from Cholula. Also, in the nearby Mixtequilla region of Veracruz, 87 percent of the obsidian in contexts dating from 1200 to 1350 CE has been sourced to Pico de Orizaba (Heller and Stark 1998). During the Early Postclassic, increased production at the Pachuca source was possibly linked to demand for obsidian at Tula (Braswell 2003; Healan 1993). The presence of Pico de Orizaba obsidian from both the Puebla/Veracruz region and Pachuca obsidian from Hidalgo in coastal assemblages, therefore, could suggest that coastal residents had connections to the same market networks that supplied the Early Postclassic centers of Cholula and Tula. The variety of obsidian sources used in both the lower Verde and the Isthmus demonstrates that more than one region, center, or trade network likely controlled the Early Postclassic obsidian trade (R. Zeitlin 1982). Lower Verde traders might have been able to negotiate independently with multiple highland Mexican communities or merchants to acquire obsidian from a diverse set of sources. Feinman and Nicholas (2004) report a similar degree of independence in obsidian acquisition in the Tlacolula region of the Valley of Oaxaca during the Classic and Postclassic periods.

In the Operation B obsidian assemblage, most obsidian blade striking platforms exhibited ground surfaces. Large, ground platforms on polyhedral cores were an invention of the Middle Classic that allowed for more efficient production of larger blades (Santley et al. 1986). Tolstoy (1971:274) notes that ground platforms were more common during the Postclassic period than earlier. In this assemblage, among the blades where ground platforms were present (n=93), 59.1 percent were made from clear obsidian and only 1.1 percent were green obsidian. Conversely, among the examples made from cores with flat, mirror-like platforms (n=30), 66.7 percent were manufactured from green obsidian, and only one fragment (3.3 percent) was clear. This suggests that the green and clear obsidian cores were made with different production techniques. Since the majority of blades date to the Early Postclassic, specialists in the source regions were likely employing distinct technologies for processing cores around the same time. The technological differences further support a scenario of multiple exchange partners and trade networks.

By the Late Postclassic, the amount of Pachuca obsidian on the Southern Isthmus accounts for almost half of the overall assemblage, which R. Zeitlin (1982) associates with Aztec expansion and control over the Pachuca source, as well as increased traffic along the Gulf Coast / Veracruz / Soconusco corridor to which the Isthmus was tied (Chapter 12). However, Orizaba obsidian was also still heavily used during the Late Postclassic, accounting for another 45 percent of the sample. Workinger (2002), too, notes the heavy use of both Orizaba and Pachuca obsidian during the Late Postclassic (at 50 percent and 35 percent, respectively) and proposes that Late Postclassic residents of San Francisco de Arriba were probably tapping into the Gulf Coast / Veracruz / Soconusco network of trade via the Isthmus. I argue below that Early Postclassic trade was most likely conducted via the Mixteca Alta, and it is likely that obsidian also traveled along these networks. If true, then Late Postclassic lower Verde communities would have likely been able to access materials using long-standing Mixteca Alta routes.

CERAMICS OF THE COASTAL EARLY POSTCLASSIC

Ceramic ties to Cholula and the Mixteca Alta corroborate a coastal / Mixteca Alta / Cholula connection during the Early Postclassic, even though the ceramic industry itself involved local manufacture and local ceramic tradition (Chapter 1). Serving vessels shift from gray and orange conical bowls with incised designs during the Late Classic to fine-paste bowls with painted decoration during the Early Postclassic (Joyce et al. 2001). However, other features of Early Postclassic vessels (e.g., effigy supports) exhibit stylistic continuities with Late Classic ceramics of the lower Río Verde Valley. Utilitarian wares of coarse brown paste were produced during both the Late Classic and Early Postclassic, supporting the argument of cultural continuity, and are thus poor indicators of a transition between the Classic and Postclassic.

Table 8.2 Analyzed sample of Early Postclassic ceramic assemblage (16.3 percent, or n=115 contexts)

	Bowls	*Tecomates*	*Jars*	*Comales*	*Other/ Undefined*	*Body Sherds*	*Total*
Total Count	1,906	12	79	67	1,628	36,941	40,633
Total Weight (g)	23,035.1	128.6	3,285.1	1,427.7	9,563.4	222,080.7	259,520.6
Percentage by Count	4.7	0.0	0.2	0.2	4.0	90.9	
Percentage by Weight	8.9	0.0	1.3	0.6	3.7	85.6	
Identified forms:							
Percentage by Count	92.3	0.6	3.8	3.2			2,064
Percentage by Weight	82.6	0.5	11.8	5.1			27,876.5

An analysis of twenty-nine complete or nearly complete ceramic vessels found during the course of Operation B excavations suggests some degree of connection between lowland and highland Oaxaca. The majority (n=21) were found in primary depositional contexts as offerings in Early Postclassic burials. Additionally, three large fragments were found within Early Postclassic architectural fill between Burials 34 and 35 beneath the floor of Structure 8-8b and fragments of another five vessels were found in primary context within the Early Postclassic midden located in the narrow path between two Early Postclassic house structures (Structure 8-8b and 8-10; see Figure 8.3).

An analyzed sample of the overall ceramic assemblage from Early Postclassic contexts (n=115, or 16.3 percent, including 40,633 vessel fragments) shows that fine-paste serving vessels, such as those represented in the complete vessel sample, make up the largest portion of the Early Postclassic ceramic assemblage (Table 8.2). Coarse pastes were more often used in the manufacture of utilitarian cooking and storage vessels (jars and *comales*). Utilitarian vessels make up a far smaller part of the overall ceramic assemblage (3.8 and 3.2 percent by count, and 11.8 and 5.1 percent by weight) and are not represented in the complete vessel sample used in this study.

The similarities in vessel shape and design are perhaps the best indicators of near contemporaneity of the sub-floor burial events and provide us with complete examples to compare to the broken pottery found throughout the architectural fill and occupational debris associated with the Early Postclassic occupation of the platform. All of the vessels are thin-walled, averaging 5.2 millimeters thick, and are made with a fine paste that when fired appears gray or orange. Controlling the firing conditions creates the color variation between the interior and exterior sides of the vessels, or between the exterior base, wall, and rim. In the latter case, the rim of

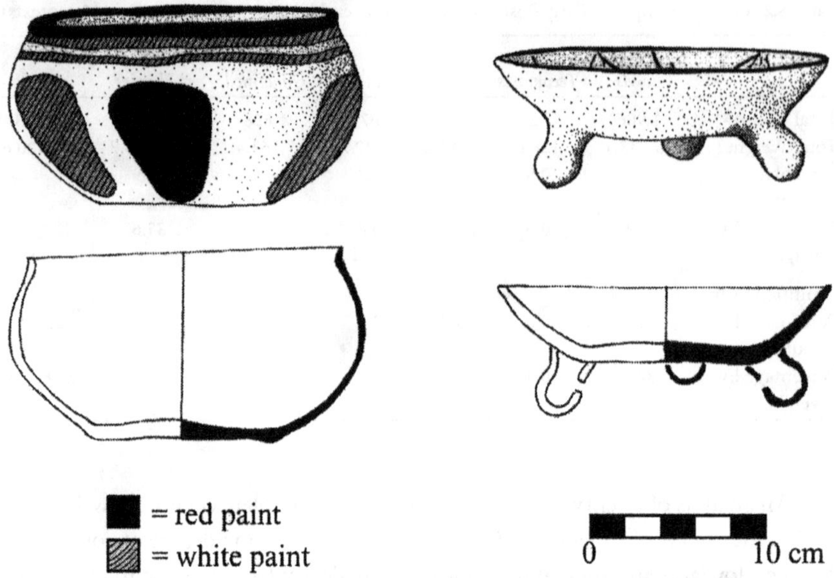

8.4 High-walled and low-walled hemispherical bowls.

the vessel was likely placed upside down into the earth during firing to create thin bands of gray along the rim, and vessels were stacked upside down on top of one another during the firing process, creating thick bands of oxidized orange circling the circumference of the higher walled bowls. This method also left the rim and vessel interior, as well as the exterior base (and sometimes the feet) of the bowls, gray in color.

Differential firing was the means by which these Early Postclassic vessels were made to appear polychrome. Differential firing also occurs on Natividad phase (1000 to 1520 CE) fine creamwares from the Mixteca Alta, as described by Spores (1972:27), where rim-body and interior-exterior "contrast patterns" make up much of the decoration. Although only red and white paints were used to decorate the Río Viejo vessels, the skilled use of differential firing creates the effect of five different colors: white (paint), red (paint on oxidized surface), orange (oxidized area), gray (unoxidized area), and a dark brown/black, which is created by applying the red paint to a surface that is left unoxidized during firing.

High-walled and low-walled varieties of hemispherical bowls are the vessel forms found with Early Postclassic burials (Figure 8.4). Seventeen of twenty-nine examples (58.6 percent) are low-walled tripod hemispherical bowls. The low-walled bowls average 3.9 centimeters in height and are always tripod, making the overall height average 6.6 centimeters. The supports are either bulbous or rounded, or are molded into the form of the head of an unidentifiable animal. The animal-head effigy

8.5 Vessel supports.

supports typically have narrow hollow interiors, whereas the bulbous and rounded supports are wider with clay pellet rattles in the feet (Figure 8.5). Two low-walled bowls were originally tripod, but the supports were broken prior to placement with

8.6 Tripod bowls with broken supports.

the deceased (Figure 8.6). The scars where the supports would have been attached are still visible but highly eroded, suggesting that the breakage occurred well before placement as a burial offering. The different vessel supports are found in roughly equal frequencies, with eight examples of hollow supports with rattles and five examples with solid animal-head supports.

The low-walled bowls were often decorated on the interior with painted geometric or zoomorphic designs using red and white paint (Figure 8.7). The vessels average 17.5 centimeters in diameter with outcurving or slightly outcurving rims and flat or slightly convex bases, providing broad interior surfaces for elaboration. Designs were painted on both the interior walls and interior bases of the low-walled bowls and include birds, stars, scorpions, bar/dot patterns, and unidentifiable animals, possibly monkeys.

Four of the low-walled tripod vessels are *molcajetes*, which were scored with crosshatched or squiggly lines in the interior base of the bowl for grinding. These incised lines, in all cases, show light to moderate wear, indicating that the vessels had been used prior to interment with the deceased. Two additional hemispherical bowls have higher walls (6.5 to 7.5 centimeters) with tripod supports. One molcajete had three small animal-head appliqués applied to the exterior lip of the

8.7 Painted designs on Early Postclassic bowls.

rim (Figure 8.8). This decorative technique is used in some examples of modern pottery from Atzompa, Oaxaca, but is, to my knowledge, unattested archaeologically. The major differences between the two kinds of ceramic serving vessels are, thus, interior versus exterior decoration and tripod supports versus no supports.

The eight non-tripod higher-walled semispherical bowls average 7.2 centimeters tall and reach their maximum diameters halfway up the wall of the bowl before they begin to curve inward. The rims of the bowls are high, narrowed, and finished with some slight outcurving, a form that has been described as "super-hemispherical" (G. McCafferty 2001:24, fig. 3.1) or "convergent incurving walled" (Joyce et al. 2001:376) bowls. The average maximum diameter of these vessels is 18 centimeters and the average rim diameter is 16.7 centimeter. The base of these vessels was generally flattened or raised slightly concave to provide a flat surface to keep the bowls from rolling.

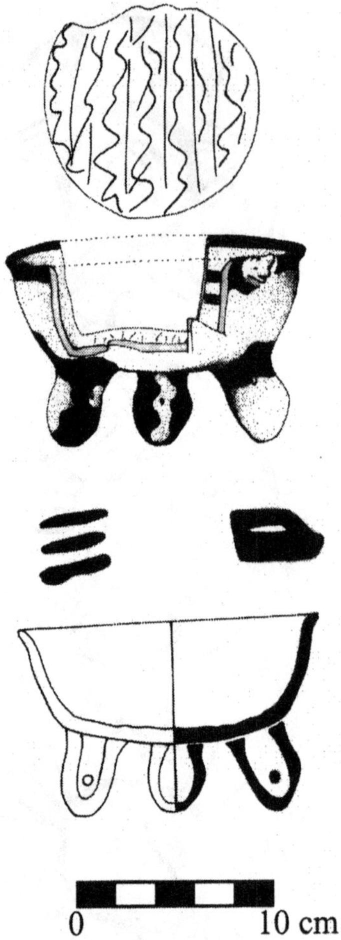

8.8 Molcajete, with animal head appliqué on rim.

The high-walled hemispherical bowls were decorated along the exterior circumference of the vessel and the rim. In these cases, the oxidized band often served as the border for the painted designs, creating images that are skillfully framed by the unoxidized rim and base. The most striking design that occurs in two different vessels is a hand motif (Figure 8.9). The hand is depicted palm-side down with fingernails in white, which in both cases is repeated twice around the perimeter. These higher-walled bowls include our finest examples of Early Postclassic vessel design.

Although no clear pattern exists for explaining how these two kinds of bowls were distributed as burial offerings, it does seem to be the case that high-walled bowls were always accompanied by one or more low-walled bowls and never by themselves. Although no obvious contents were visible in the base of the bowls, sediment samples taken from the interior of the vessels for microanalysis contained (in at least one case) maize phytoliths, as well as somewhat higher pH levels indica-

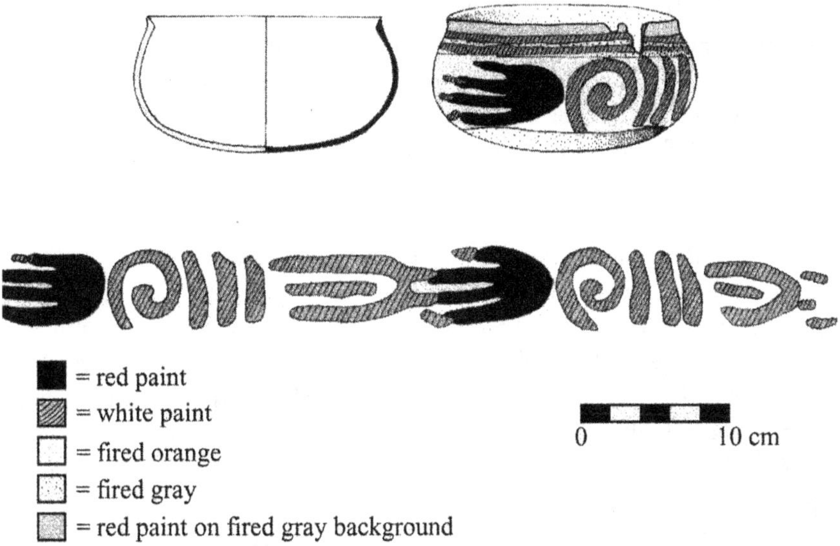

8.9 High-walled hemispherical bowl with hand motif.

tive of ash, showing that burned organics or prepared food was placed in the vessels (King 2003).

Along the coast of Oaxaca, somewhat similar ceramics are found at Río Grande, located twenty kilometers east of Río Viejo (Zárate Morán 1995). Considerably further east, at the site of Carrizal, located about twenty kilometers west of Salina Cruz on the Isthmus (and 270 kilometers east of Río Viejo), Brockington (1974:28, fig. 8) illustrates a vessel that closely resembles the Early Postclassic Río Viejo tripod bowls. He describes this vessel as a rare type in the Isthmus region, a statement that is confirmed through comparisons with published reports of roughly contemporaneous archaeological deposits from Puerto Escondido to the Isthmus of Tehuantepec (Delgado 1965; Fernández Dávila and Gómez Serafín 1988; Long 1974; J. Zeitlin 1978).

Similarly, west of Río Viejo, Early Postclassic ceramics bear little resemblance to wares found in Acapulco and coastal Guerrero (Brush 1969). Ceramic similarities in design motifs and vessel forms with more distant highland regions, however, are clearer. Design motifs were shared between Río Viejo ceramics and highland Mixteca Alta, Valley of Oaxaca, and materials found at the sites of Tula and Cholula. For example, the hand motif, which on the coast is represented realistically, is depicted more abstractly on Huitzo Polished Cream vessels of the Valley of Oaxaca (Paddock 1966:208, fig. 260), on vessels from a tomb in Loma Yutendahue in Suchilquitongo, Valley of Oaxaca (Winter and Guevara Hernández 2000), and vessels from Tula (Cobean 1990:309, plate 153). The hemispherical bowl form is also shared among coastal Oaxaca, Puebla, the Mixteca Alta, northern Guerrero, and the northwestern Valley of Oaxaca, as are many of the decorative motifs employed on their interior and exterior surfaces. Geometric designs, parallel lines, spirals, and volutes are found on Natividad phase fine creamwares of the Nochixtlán Valley and Mixteca Alta (Lind 1987:33–40; Spores 1972:32–33, figs. 4–5), as well as on various Early Postclassic wares from Cholula, including Cocoyotla Black-on-Natural, Ocotlán Red Rim (Lind's [1994] Catalina), and Torre Red and Orange on White (Lind's [1994] Albina) (Lind 1994:82, fig. 3d, 84, fig. 9a; G. McCafferty 1994:65, fig. 15; 1996:309, fig. 10; 2001:55–58). Bird motifs, which are common images represented on the interior of the coastal *cajetes* (bowls), are also commonly represented in the Mixteca Alta Comiyuchi variety of Yanhuitlán Red-on-Creamwares, which are most similar to Huitzo Polished Cream vessels (Lind 1987:35).

Tripod bowls with effigy head supports are found throughout highland Mesoamerica during the Early Postclassic, and some of the closest formal resemblances occur between coastal Oaxaca, the Soconusco region, and highland Guatemala (Voorhies and Gasco 2004:fig. 6.12; Wauchope 1941:fig. 68; Woodbury and Trik 1953:159, 409, fig. 245). Somewhat similar examples have also been found in Morelos at the site of Tetla (Norr 1987b:528, fig. 1.2) and in Michoacan (Chadwick 1971:686, fig. 24). Short, unpainted bat effigy supports are principal diagnostics of the Late Classic period lower Río Verde Valley (Joyce et al. 2001:365, fig. 11), and the Early Postclassic version seems to be a muted, less carefully modeled version of the earlier variety. These effigy supports differ markedly from the elongated painted Late Postclassic serpent head supports common in Late Postclassic Mixteca-Puebla pottery, which are found throughout a wide area of Oaxaca and beyond (Caso et al. 1967:plate 19).

Hollow rounded or elongated supports containing clay pellet rattles are also common during the Early Postclassic across Mesoamerica from Michoacán to Guatemala (e.g., Chadwick 1971:686; Markman 1981:94; Shepard 1948:12; Wauchope 1941:222). We located 142 loose clay balls during the excavations, and complete vessels with intact rattle supports indicate that a primary use of these pellets was in supports for noisemaking. This differs from the common interpretation of clay balls as "blowgun pellets," although the difference in interpretation may be based on the diameter of the clay balls, with larger balls more often interpreted as blowgun pellets. The Operation B sample includes primarily small-diameter pellets with unimodal clustering for both weight and diameter. The mean diameter of the clay pellet rattles is 11.5 millimeters (standard deviation 3.11) and mean weight is 1.41 grams (standard deviation 1.32).

Some of the Río Viejo Early Postclassic vessels have incised interior bases typical of molcajetes. These too are a common marker of the Early Postclassic across wider regions of Mesoamerica. Río Viejo molcajete bases are incised with designs similar to the burnished designs on the bases of conical bowls illustrated by Caso et al. (1967:391, fig. 322) and Martínez López et al. (2000: Lam. 13, fig. 14), which are attributed to the Late Classic period (Xoo phase) of Monte Albán (see Chapter 2). Late Classic period Valley of Oaxaca motifs may have influenced the design of Río Viejo Early Postclassic molcajetes, demonstrating a continuity of ideas across regions and through time.

Stylistic comparisons, then, hint that coastal Río Viejo communicated more closely with highland Oaxacan communities than it did with coastal communities to the east or to the west, although shared ideas spread even farther from and to coastal and highland Guatemala and northern Guerrero and Michoacán. Río Viejo was likely connected to this communication network through the Mixteca Alta, given the shared stylistic traits and the position of the Mixteca Alta with respect to neighboring highland Mexican communities that had an obvious influence on coastal ceramic design. Mixteca Alta Yanhuitlán Red-on-Creamwares, which are stylistically more closely connected to coastal ceramics, were uncommon in the Valley of Oaxaca (Paddock 1983). This indicates that Mixteca Alta communities might have had more direct contact with the Oaxaca Coast than with communities in the Valley of Oaxaca during the Early Postclassic. However, it is important to note that a conceptual difference between polychrome ceramics and differentially fired "polychromes" likely existed.

Absent from the Río Viejo ceramics samples are plumbate wares (see Chapter 1). Plumbate pottery was traded throughout Mesoamerica during the Early Postclassic, beginning around 900 CE and ending rather abruptly around 1250 CE (Neff and Bishop 1988), making it a useful marker of the Early Postclassic across regions. Plumbates are also rare in the Valley of Oaxaca but have been found on the Isthmus of Tehuantepec (Chapter 12; Cortés Vilchis and Winter 2006; Delgado 1965:33), perhaps showing that the Isthmus was in some way involved in a network of exchange extending eastward along the coast. Río Viejo residents did not participate in a coastal network of exchange for plumbate pottery (or for other Isthmus goods, for that matter), suggesting that either this connection was not well established or that plumbate pottery was not a desired commodity of Río Viejo residents.

SPINNING AND WEAVING AT RÍO VIEJO

Whereas obsidian was the primary imported material recovered in coastal Oaxacan archaeological collections, cotton thread and finished cloth were the primary Early Postclassic exports. This industry depended on the productivity of coyuche cotton plants native to the region and is widely attested in ethnohistoric documents (see

Table 8.3 Spindle whorls from the Operation B neighborhood, Río Viejo (n=86)

	Diameter (mm)	*Height (mm)*	*Weight (g)*	*Hole Diameter (mm)*	*Shape Index (diameter/height)*
Type A	25.8	16.7	10.3	4.9	0.65
n=22, 26.5%	(20.2–30.3)	(11.3–21.3)	(5.0–17.0)	(3.8–6.4)	(0.43–0.81)
Hemispherical, trapezoidal, flat					
Type B	24.1	20.9	9.9	4.7	0.86
n=48, 57.8%	(16.3–27.3)	(11.7–26.6)	(3–16)	(3.5–7.0)	(0.72–1.01)
Spherical, circular					
Type C	25.8	23.1	13.0	4.9	0.90
n=13, 15.7%	(22.5–29.3)	(18.3–30.9)	(6.0–18.0)	(4.2–6.4)	(0.72–1.37)
Globular					
Totals	24.9	20.0	10.5	4.8	0.80
n complete	80	78	75	86	75
Std. Dev.	2.37	3.56	3.49	0.68	0.14
Range	(16.3–30.3)	(11.3–30.9)	(3.0–18.3)	(3.5–7.0)	(0.43–1.37)

below). Evidence for spinning and weaving is based on eighty-six spindle whorls and approximately ten bone needle fragments recovered in Early Postclassic deposits in the Operation B neighborhood at Río Viejo.

The Río Viejo whorls were distributed relatively evenly across the excavated area in Early Postclassic architectural fill, occupation debris, and midden contexts (King 2003). Many of these whorls (n=71, 82 percent) were decorated with incised geometric designs that repeat around the circumference of the whorl. The abundance of whorls in the artifact assemblage shows that spinning thread was a common activity at Río Viejo and was important to the economy and social life of this coastal community. Made of coarse orange and fine orange pastes in 77.6 percent (n=60) of the cases, the spindle whorls average 20 millimeters in height and 25 millimeters in diameter, and weigh about 10.5 grams (Table 8.3). The holes of these whorls average 4.8 millimeters in diameter. Three principal shapes are present, which correspond to three "types": (1) hemispherical, trapezoidal, or flat; (2) spherical or circular; and (3) globular (Figure 8.10).

A few similar whorls were found in surface collection contexts at the site of Río Grande, east of the lower Verde (Zárate Morán 1995:29). Coastal whorls, however, are markedly different from highland Oaxacan whorls in both size and shape, where they were often flatter and undecorated, conical, or informally manufactured using broken ceramic sherds (Caso 1969:159; Caso et al. 1967:465; Feinman et al. 2002a; Spores 1972:72). The reported number of whorls in most highland Oaxacan artifact assemblages is lower than Río Viejo (Caso 1969:157–158; Caso et al. 1967:465; Finsten 1995; Spores 1972:70). The sites of Ejutla and El Palmillo,

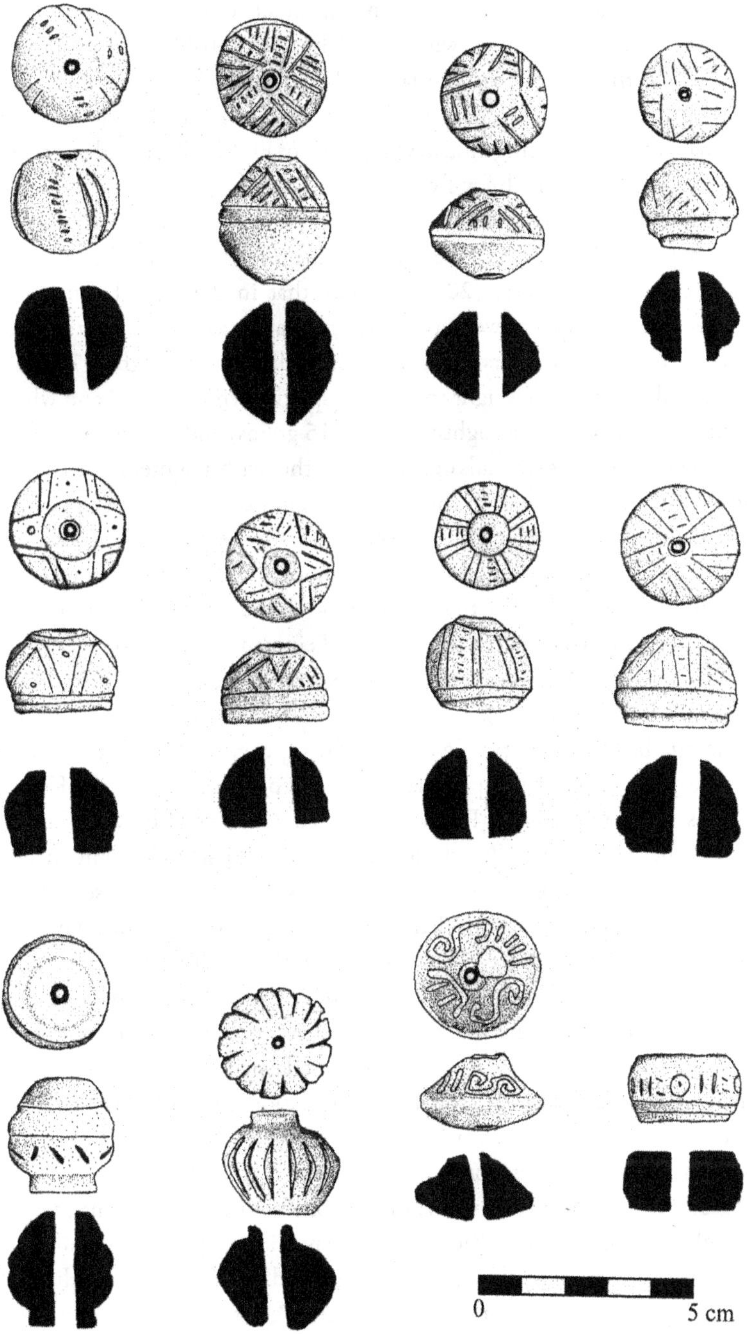

8.10 Spindle whorls.

located in highland Oaxaca, are exceptions. At the site of Ejutla were found around fifty Classic period cotton fiber whorls, which were probably used to spin cotton imported from the eastern coast of Oaxaca (Feinman and Nicholas 2000; Feinman et al. 1994). Feinman and colleagues (2002a, 2002b) further argue for a Classic period maguey fiber spinning industry at the site of El Palmillo, based in part on the presence of approximately thirty-five whorls.

The formal differences observed in spindle whorls are closely related to both the kind of fiber being spun and the quality of the resultant thread (Brumfiel 1996). McCafferty and McCafferty (2000:46) note that in the coastal community of Jamiltepec, Oaxaca, modern weavers use whorls that are as tall or taller than they are wide, averaging 24 millimeters in diameter, 25 millimeters in height, a 7-millimeter hole size, and 12 grams in weight to support-spin brown (coyuche) and white cotton. The same weavers use a slightly heavier (15 grams) and slightly taller (31-millimeter) whorl to ply two threads of cotton together with a tighter twist. The whorls at Río Viejo more closely match these modern Jamiltepec whorls in all dimensions than they do any of the other whorl dimensions presented in published whorl analyses, indicating that the thread produced by modern coastal Oaxacan weavers may be similar in kind and quality to the thread produced by Río Viejo residents during the Early Postclassic (see Brumfiel 1996; Feinman et al. 2002a; S. McCafferty and McCafferty 2000; Nichols et al. 2000; Norr 1987b; Parsons 1972; Smith and Hirth 1988; Stark et al. 1998).

The number and density of whorls in the Operation B artifact assemblage is suggestive of household-level specialization in cotton fiber production (King 2003, 2004). As mentioned above, Río Viejo yielded a high number of whorls compared to other Classic and Postclassic period Oaxacan sites. In comparison with sites where intensive fiber production industries have been proposed, Río Viejo deposits have yielded some of the densest reported deposits, with one whorl per 3.6 square meters.[2] This far exceeds the density whorls at El Palmillo (one whorl per 18.9 square meters) (Feinman et al. 2002a, 2002b), is close to the density recorded at Classic period Ejutla (one whorl per 3.8 square meters) (Feinman et al. 1994), but is still below the whorl density at Early Postclassic Cholula (one whorl per 1.5 square meters) (McCafferty, personal communication, 2004). The thread and cloth production in coastal Oaxaca would have been of sufficient intensity to supply Río Viejo residents with surplus cloth to export to the highlands.

Based on comparisons of whorl dimensions with cotton and maguey whorls from highland Mexican sites, Río Viejo residents likely produced a kind of thread that was different from the thread spun in highland Mexico. The tight clustering in all whorl dimensions suggests that the Río Viejo whorls were manufactured specifically for the production of a particular kind of thread, with relatively minor variation in quality, thickness, and tightness. The coastal cotton thread was thicker than the cotton thread being spun in many communities in the highlands, perhaps two-ply, and was also more tightly woven. Therefore, the unique thread, most likely spun from indigenous coyuche cotton, and the finished woven cloth produced at Río Viejo might have had its own market niche in the highland communities.

CERAMIC BELLS

The ceramic bells present a different scenario of interregional interaction. The twelve bells found in Operation B are unique, since bells have not been found in any other archaeological collection of the lower Verde. Bells from Operation B have hand-modeled looped handles for hanging. The walls of the bell chambers are thin, averaging 2.93 millimeters thick. One complete and still functioning example of a bell was recovered with the molded clay pellet rattle still inside the chamber. The overall dimensions of this example are 28.7 millimeters tall (length) and 20.8 millimeters in diameter (across the chamber) (Figure 8.11). Two examples have molded bird heads forming the handle.

These bells are similar in design to the elongated copper bells that are some of the earliest bell forms found in West Mexico, which have parallels in coastal South America (Chapter 1; Hosler 1994:fig 3.5, Type 11a; Pendergast 1962a:527, fig. 7; 1962b:378, Type ICIa). Copper bells were traded to neighboring regions during the Early Postclassic, moving west to east. During the Late Postclassic, new forms of bells were manufactured across Mesoamerica. Metallurgy was first introduced to West Mexico around 800 CE, and copper objects are found archaeologically throughout the West Mexican region from Sinaloa to northwestern Guerrero prior to 1200 CE (Hosler 1994; Mountjoy 1969; Pendergast 1962a). However, after 1200 CE, copper and metal alloy implements and decorative ornaments are found more widely across highland Mesoamerica, including highland Oaxaca (e.g., Batres 1902:fig. 26; Caso 1965, 1969:339).

On the Pacific Coast, we have archaeological evidence for copper materials from Río Grande (Zárate Morán 1995) as well as from archaeological sites in Acapulco and west along the Costa Grande in Guerrero where the elongated bell was a common form (Lister 1971:628), as well as in the vicinity of Puerto Escondido (personal observation). In recent excavations, copper was recovered at Tututepec (Levine 2006). These collections likely postdate 1200 CE, when metallurgy was present in many regions of Mesoamerica, and thus the absence of copper bells at Río Viejo might be explained based on chronology. But we should also consider that even though copper bells were not widely produced and traded during the Early Postclassic, coastal artisans likely had knowledge of the bells manufactured farther west. Although Hosler (1994:122) suggests that bells made from clay predate the introduction of metallurgy to Mexico, the only dated examples of clay bells are from Terminal Classic and Early Postclassic contexts in coastal Guatemala (Shook 1965:192), highland Morelos (Smith 1996: 90; 2002) and Early Postclas-sic Río Viejo (King 2003), which are contemporaneous with early West Mexican copper bell manufacture.

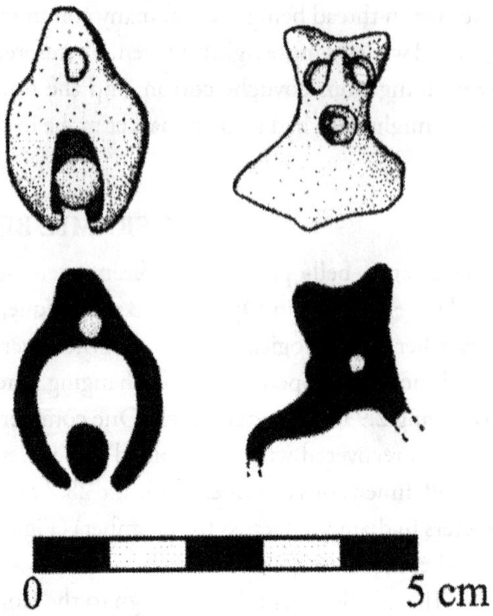

8.11 Clay bells.

The collection of bells from Río Viejo is small but perhaps indicative of the character of interregional connections between the Oaxaca Coast and the highlands. Trade for obsidian was well established and coastal residents likely traded cotton thread or finished textiles northward in exchange for this obsidian. Ideas about ceramic stylistic motifs and manufacture circulated along these networks, although the actual pottery did not. Coastal residents did not or could not access networks of copper trade but probably had knowledge about the bells being produced farther west. Without access to these goods, they fashioned their own versions of copper bells using clay, as did rural artisans elsewhere in Mesoamerica. This break suggests that coastal Río Viejo was to a certain degree distanced from some exchange networks, whether by choice or by circumstance.

CONNECTING HIGHLAND AND LOWLAND OAXACA

Trade routes connecting diverse regions of Mesoamerica were established as early as the Early Formative period (1300–900 BCE). Highland Oaxaca actively participated in these networks from their inception, and interaction among the Valley of Oaxaca, Mixteca Alta, Gulf Coast, and Central Mexico is demonstrated throughout the Formative period. The lower Verde was a participant in long-distance exchange by the Late Formative period, when Monte Albán was first established in the highlands of Oaxaca (Joyce 1993). Trade routes between the coast and highland valleys bridged differing geographical and ecological zones, and coastal resources—such as shells, cotton, cacao, and feathers—were likely exchanged for highland products, including maguey, pulque, and obsidian (Monaghan 1994; Spores 1967:5–7).

From the Late Formative to Classic period, residents of the coast were involved in exchange with both highland Oaxaca and Central Mexico (Brockington 1973; Feinman and Nicholas 1993; Joyce 1993; R. Zeitlin 1993).

Once Teotihuacan was well established, residents of the western coast of Oaxaca may have traded more directly with Teotihuacan for some products (primarily for obsidian) (Joyce 2003). Trade routes connecting the western coast with Central Mexico, which remained in place into the Late Postclassic, could have traveled through the modern state of Guerrero and the Mixteca Alta (Whitecotton 1992). At the same time, the eastern coast (Pochutla/Huatulco to the Isthmus) was probably connected to trade networks that traveled through Monte Albán or traversed the lowland Veracruz Gulf Coast and crossed the Isthmus, thereby bypassing highland Oaxaca altogether (R. Zeitlin 1978). Eastern coastal Oaxacan communities were more tied into trade networks linking the lowland Maya region and Soconusco coast with the rest of western Mesoamerica (Fernández Dávila and Gómez Serafín 1988; Whitecotton 1992).

Ball and Brockington (1978) argued that three exchange systems were in place in Oaxaca at the time of conquest: (1) an Aztec tribute collection network in the highlands and Isthmus, (2) a northwest-southeast coastal network focusing on luxury goods, and (3) a highland-lowland network linking diverse ecological zones that also further connected the two previous networks. The Aztec tribute collection network did not directly affect the west coast but instead involved the Oaxaca highlands, the Sierra, and the Isthmus of Tehuantepec. Along the coastal route, copper and bronze objects and tropical luxury goods were likely exchanged from as far west as the Tarascan Empire to the Chiapanec kingdom, Soconusco coast, and Nicaragua beyond. Miahuatlán may have linked the highland Valley of Oaxaca with the coastal trade networks, as shell from the Pacific Coast is found at some Miahuatlán and Ejutla sites (Brockington 1973; see also Feinman and Nicholas 1992). However, Ball and Brockington (1978) suggest that in the Late Postclassic, Tututepec was vying with Miahuatlán for control of highland-lowland trade. After allying with the Aztecs, occupants of Miahuatlán successfully defended themselves from conquest by Tututepec, and Tututepec also successfully resisted any Aztec incursion until the arrival of the Spanish (Davies 1968; Gerhard 1972).

The ceramic data suggest that, following the decline of Classic period centers, we should look for increasingly stronger connections between the western coast and the Mixteca Alta. Although coastal products are well represented in Classic period assemblages from sites in the Ejutla and Miahuatlán valleys (which are stopovers on the Valley of Oaxaca–Pochutla route) (Brockington 1973; Feinman and Nicholas 1992, 1993), different regions along the coast may have been linked to highland communities via numerous lowland-highland footpaths. That coastal

Early Postclassic ceramics at Río Viejo show some similarity to highland Oaxaca ceramics may indicate some continued travel along the Río Verde drainage.

Early Postclassic material from Sipolite (Pochutla area), Huatulco, and east to the Isthmus is quite different from that of Río Grande and Río Viejo (Brockington 1982; Brockington et al. 1974; Fernández Dávila and Gómez Serafín 1988; Zárate Morán 1995; J. Zeitlin 1978; R. Zeitlin 1979). Instead, the Río Viejo ceramics look more like the ceramics of the Mixteca Alta. By the Late Postclassic the connections between the lower Verde and Mixteca Alta were much deeper, when most of western Oaxaca fell under the authority of Mixtec nobility (see Chapter 1). The Mixteca Alta at this time was a clear center of political and commercial activity. During the Late Postclassic, highland Mixtecs likely controlled trade and tribute collection from subject communities up and down the west coast through Jicayan, Putla, and even Tututepec (Spores 1984, 1993).

Río Viejo's trade connections, thus, may have shifted during the Early Postclassic to include increased interaction with residents of the Mixteca Alta. Notably, however, coastal Oaxacans were *not* connected to some Early Postclassic period trade networks. For example, we found no Tohil Plumbate pottery at Río Viejo, and residents did not venture along a coastal route to access the West Mexico copper network. This could suggest that Río Viejo's residents opted out of particular trade networks. Another scenario is that Río Viejo was not directly connected to the network of elites that shared ideas, symbolism, and luxury objects. In spite of the lack of access, obsidian from Central Mexico was readily available to Río Viejo's occupants. The most appropriate place to look for comparative data on the Early Postclassic may thus be in highland Mixtec and intermediary regions, which is the most obvious route connecting the western coast and Central Mexico.

DISCUSSION AND CONCLUSION

The tierra caliente (hot lands) of the lower Verde were renowned for their richness and fertility, in spite of the difficulties caused by heat and insect life. In the sixteenth century, chroniclers reported that the lands of the lower Verde provided cacao, cane, cotton, fish, salts, and ample space for cattle (Paso y Troncoso 1905b:247, 301). Most of the communities up and down the coast of Oaxaca were required to provide tribute to the Crown in the form of cotton, finished weavings, cacao, and cane, in addition to many pesos worth of gold dust ("*oro en polvo*") (Paso y Troncoso 1905a). Salt is listed as a product of Tututepec in the *suma de visitas* (Paso y Troncoso 1905b:247), and presumably the salt flats present along the lagoons and estuaries of the coastline could have been used during the Early Postclassic. According to the documents, the lower Verde and nearby western Oaxaca Coast regions also supplied cotton and cloth to Nochixtlán, in the Mixteca Alta, and the northwestern Valley of Oaxaca community of Huitzo (Paso y Troncoso 1905a).

Coastal peoples produced and supplied the highlands with a variety of agricultural products, exotic tropical goods, and marine resources, including cotton, salt, marine shell, and feathers. Coastal products were likely exchanged for highland products, such as maguey, pulque, and obsidian. Maguey, pulque, feathers, salt, cotton, and fish are organic products that are obviously difficult to recover in the archaeological record. Spindle whorls, often made of better-preserved fired clay, provide an indirect material means of examining cotton thread production. Salt flats used in the historic period are present in the lower Verde region, but as yet they have not been associated with Early Postclassic activity. Further, the faunal assemblage from Operation B contains only a small proportion of fish remains (King 2003). Even acknowledging the preservation issues related to fish bones as compared to larger animals, the underrepresentation of fish, along with the terrestrial and agricultural focus of Río Viejo throughout its history, suggests that fishing and drying fish were not substantial components of Río Viejo's export economy. Feathers or jaguar pelts, although possibilities as export products, are more difficult to trace and are not attested in these excavations. Macrobotanical remains of cotton were not identified in the paleoethnobotanical analysis conducted for Operation B Río Viejo (King 2003). Nonetheless, the fertile lands, agricultural productivity, access to marine resources, and success of cotton were keys to the lower Verde's long-standing preeminence and success.

Given the evidence from excavations at Early Postclassic Río Viejo, I argue that lower Verde residents were not well connected to coastal exchange networks. Indeed, I have doubts that a strong littoral network of interaction was in place during the Early Postclassic, as Ball and Brockington (1978) propose for the Late Postclassic. The evidence so far from Río Viejo suggests that for all time periods prior to the Late Postclassic, coastal routes were never heavily utilized for long-distance exchange purposes, whether accessed overland or by sea. Río Viejo itself is not a good candidate as a stop in a seafaring model of coastal exchange, given its inland location (Ball and Brockington 1978:108) and what seems to be a continuing orientation toward agriculture and a dependence on terrestrial resources established centuries earlier (Joyce 1991). The overland route is heavily bisected by large and at times impassable rivers flowing to the ocean. Further study along the coast of Oaxaca and Guerrero would help to clarify the existence and magnitude of coastal trade relationships.

Río Viejo residents preferentially forged trade relationships with highland Mexican trade partners or retained preexisting highland relations, primarily through the Mixteca Alta. In exchange for obsidian, Río Viejo residents produced a kind of cloth that was different from that available from other cloth-producing communities, and residents may have chosen to produce surplus amounts of this cloth in response to an active Early Postclassic long-distance market demand for their goods. But these networks only allowed them to acquire certain kinds of materials. Residents manufactured clay bells that elsewhere were manufactured in copper. They may have chosen to make them at home out of local materials because the cost of access was too great or because those trade networks did not yet exist. The skill of Río Viejo artisans in producing intricately designed costume ornaments may have influenced the choice to add small bells to their productive repertoire, and the distance and independence of coastal Río Viejo, in spite of its highland connections, might help to explain why local social practices and social organization in this region were in some ways unique (King 2003). Río Viejo, with its well-dated Early Postclassic occupation from 1000 to 1200 CE, gives us a clear example of the form of socioeconomic organization in Early Postclassic Oaxaca and provides us with the possibility to interpret the relationships between the Early Postclassic communities of Oaxaca in new ways.

ACKNOWLEDGMENTS

The field excavations associated with the Río Viejo Residence Project were generously supported by the Foundation for the Advancement of Mesoamerican Studies, Inc., Grant #99012 (with Arthur Joyce); the Stahl Endowment of the Archaeological Research Facility, University of California, Berkeley; and the Lowie-Olson Fund of the Department of Anthropology, University of California, Berkeley. In addition, National Science Foundation Doctoral Dissertation Improvement Grant #0122226 supported some of the laboratory analysis discussed in this study. This chapter is a topic addressed in my dissertation and, as such, has benefited from the comments and suggestions provided by Rosemary Joyce, Christine Hastorf, and Harvey Doner. I also thank the editor of this volume and outside reviewers for insightful comments on earlier drafts of this chapter, and the session organizers and fellow participants for sharing their ideas.

NOTES

1. This is based on three published dates: 1022 CE (975–1161 CE calibrated, AA37669, reported in Joyce et al. 2001) and 1035 CE (1035–1187 CE calibrated, AA40040, reported in King 2003) from Early Postclassic middens in each of the neighborhoods at Río Viejo, and 1051 CE (1026–1220 CE calibrated, AA40034, reported in Joyce et al. 2001) from a final phase floor surface.

2. Density measures for spindle whorls are rarely calculated based on volume of excavated deposits and rarely are both the number of whorls and the total volume of excavated

deposits reported in publication. In addition, many spindle whorl studies are based in whole or in part on surface collected whorls. Another widely used method, calculating density as a ratio of whorls to overall ceramic assemblage, is pending completed ceramic analysis. Here I have calculated density based on the number of whorls and the total area excavated / surface collected, if reported (see King 2003 for further discussion).

REFERENCES

Appel, Jill

1982 Political and Economic Organization in the Late Postclassic Valley of Oaxaca, Mexico. Unpublished Ph.D. Dissertation, Department of Sociology and Anthropology, Purdue University. West Lafayette, Indiana.

Ball, Hugh G., and Donald L. Brockington

1978 Trade and Travel in Prehispanic Oaxaca. In *Mesoamerican Communication Routes and Cultural Contacts*, edited by T. Lee Jr. and C. Nararrete, pp. 107–114. Papers of the New World Archaeological Foundation, No. 40. Brigham Young University, Provo, Utah.

Batres, Leopoldo

1902 *Exploraciones de Monte Albán*. Casa Editorial Gante, Mexico City.

Blanton, Richard E.

1978 *Monte Albán: Settlement Patterns at the Ancient Zapotec Capital*. Academic Press, New York.

Braswell, Geoffrey E.

2003 Obsidian Exchange Spheres. In *The Postclassic Mesoamerica World*, edited by M. Smith and F. Berdan, pp. 131–158. University of Utah Press, Salt Lake City.

Braswell, Geoffrey E., John E. Clark, Kazuo Aoyama, Heather I. McKillop, and Michael D. Glascock

2000 Determining the Geological Provenance of Obsidian Artifacts from the Maya Region: A Test of the Efficacy of Visual Sourcing. *Latin American Antiquity* 11(3):269–282.

Brockington, Donald L.

1973 *Archaeological Investigations at Miahuatlan, Oaxaca*. Vanderbilt University Publications in Anthropology, No. 7. Nashville, Tennessee.

1974 Reconnaissance from the Río Tonameca to Salina Cruz. In *The Oaxaca Coast Project Reports: Part II*, edited by D. Brockington and J. Long, pp. 3–33. Vanderbilt University Publications in Anthropology, No. 9. Nashville, Tennessee.

1982 Spatial and Temporal Variations of the Mixtec-Style Ceramics in Southern Oaxaca. In *Aspects of the Mixteca-Puebla Style and Mixtec and Central Mexican Culture in Southern Mesoamerica*, edited by D. Stone, pp. 7–14. Middle American Research Institute Occasional Paper, No. 4. Tulane University, New Orleans.

Brockington, Donald L., María Jorrín, and J. Robert Long
1974 *The Oaxaca Coast Project Reports: Part I*. Vanderbilt University Publications in Anthropology, No. 8. Nashville, Tennessee.

Brumfiel, Elizabeth M.
1996 The Quality of Tribute Cloth: The Place of Evidence in Archaeological Argument. *American Antiquity* 61(3):453–462.

Brush, Charles
1969 A Contribution to the Archaeology of Coastal Guerrero, Mexico. Unpublished Ph.D. Dissertation, Department of Anthropology, Columbia University, New York.

Byland, Bruce E., and John M.D. Pohl
1994 *In the Realm of 8 Deer: The Archaeology of the Mixtec Codices*. University of Oklahoma Press, Norman.

Caso, Alfonso
1965 Lapidary Work, Goldwork, and Copperwork from Oaxaca. In *Handbook of Middle American Indians,* Vol. 3: *Archaeology of Southern Mesoamerica,* Part 2, edited by R. Wauchope and G. Willey, pp. 896–930. University of Texas Press, Austin.
1969 *El tesoro de Monte Albán*. Memorias del Instituto Nacional de Antropología e Historia, No. 3. INAH, Mexico City.

Caso, Alfonso, Ignacio Bernal, and Jorge R. Acosta
1967 *La cerámica de Monte Albán*. Memorias del Instituto Nacional de Antropología e Historia, No. 13. INAH, Mexico City.

Chadwick, Robert
1971 Archaeological Synthesis of Michoacan and Adjacent Regions. In *Handbook of Middle American Indians,* Vol. 11: *Archaeology of Northern Mesoamerica,* Part 2, edited by R. Wauchope, G. Ekholm, and I. Bernal, pp. 657–693. University of Texas Press, Austin.

Cobean, Robert H.
1990 *La cerámica de Tula, Hidalgo*. Estudios sobre Tula 2. Instituto Nacional de Antropología e Historia, Mexico City.

Cortés Vilchis, Marisol Yadira, and Marcus Winter
2006 El Posclásico del Valle de Jalapa del Marques, Región del Istmo, Oaxaca. Paper presented at the 71st Annual Meeting of the Society for American Archaeology, San Juan, Puerto Rico.

Daneels, Anick
1997 Settlement History in the Lower Cotaxtla Basin. In *Olmec to Aztec: Settlement Patterns in the Ancient Gulf Lowlands*, edited by B. Stark and P. Arnold III, pp. 206–252. University of Arizona Press, Tucson.

Davies, Nigel

1968 *Los señorios independientes del imperio Azteca*. Serie Historia XIX. Instituto Nacional de Antropología e Historia, Mexico City.

Delgado, Agustin

1965 *Archaeological Reconnaissance in the Region of Tehuantepec, Oaxaca, Mexico*. Papers of the New World Archaeological Foundation, No. 18. Brigham Young University, Provo, Utah.

Feinman, Gary M., and Linda M. Nicholas

1992 Pre-Hispanic Interregional Interaction in Southern Mexico: The Valley of Oaxaca and the Ejutla Valley. In *Resources, Power, and Interregional Interaction*, edited by E. Schortman and P. Urban, pp. 75–116. Plenum Publishers, New York.

1993 Shell-Ornament Production in Ejutla: Implications for Highland-Coastal Interaction in Ancient Oaxaca. *Ancient Mesoamerica* 4(1):103–119.

2000 High-Intensity Household-Scale Production in Ancient Mesoamerica: A Perspective from Ejutla, Oaxaca. In *Cultural Evolution: Contemporary Viewpoints*, edited by G. Feinman and L. Manzanilla, pp. 119–142. Kluwer Academic / Plenum Publishers, New York.

2004 *Hilltop Terrace Sites of Oaxaca, Mexico: Intensive Surface Survey at Guirún, El Palmillo and the Mitla Fortress*. Fieldiana, Anthropology New Series, No. 37. Field Museum of Natural History, Chicago.

Feinman, Gary M., Linda M. Nicholas, and Helen R. Haines

2002a Houses on a Hill: Classic Period Life at El Palmillo, Oaxaca, Mexico. *Latin American Antiquity* 13(3):251–278.

2002b Mexico's Wonder Plant. *Archaeology* 55(5):32–35.

Feinman, Gary M., Linda M. Nicholas, and William D. Middleton

1994 Craft Activities at the Prehispanic Ejutla Site, Oaxaca, Mexico. *Mexicon* 15(2):33–41.

Fernández Dávila, Enrique, and Susana Gómez Serafín

1988 *Arqueología de Huatulco, Oaxaca: Memoria de la primera temporada de campo del proyecto arqueológico Bahías de Huatulco*. Colección Científica, No. 171. Instituto Nacional de Antropología e Historia, Mexico City.

Finsten, Laura

1995 *Jalieza, Oaxaca: Activity Specialization at a Hilltop Center*. Vanderbilt University Publications in Anthropology, No. 48. Nashville, Tennessee.

Gerhard, Peter

1972 *A Guide to the Historical Geography of New Spain*. Cambridge University Press, New York.

Healan, Dan M.

1993 Local Versus Non-local Obsidian Exchange at Tula and Its Implications for Post-Formative Mesoamerica. *World Archaeology* 24:449–466.

Healan, Dan M., Janet M. Kerley, and George J. Bey III

1983 Excavation and Preliminary Analysis of an Obsidian Workshop in Tula, Hidalgo, Mexico. *Journal of Field Archaeology* 10:127–145.

Heller, Lynette, and Barbara L. Stark

1998 Classic and Postclassic Obsidian Tool Production and Consumption: A Regional Perspective from the Mixtequilla, Veracruz. *Mexicon* 20:119–128.

Hosler, Dorothy

1994 *The Sounds and Colors of Power: The Sacred Metallurgical Technology of Ancient West Mexico*. MIT Press, Cambridge, Massachusetts.

Joyce, Arthur A.

1991 Formative Period Social Change in the Lower Río Verde Valley, Oaxaca, Mexico. *Latin American Antiquity* 2(1):126–150.

1993 Interregional Interaction and Social Development on the Oaxaca Coast. *Ancient Mesoamerica* 4(1):67–84.

2003 Imperialism in Pre-Aztec Mesoamerica: Monte Albán, Teotihuacan, and the Lower Río Verde Valley. In *Warfare and Conflict in Ancient Mesoamerica*, edited by M. Brown and T. Stanton, pp. 49–72. Altamira Press, Walnut Creek, California.

Joyce, Arthur A., Laura Arnaud Bustamante, and Marc N. Levine

2001 Commoner Power: A Case Study from the Classic Period Collapse on the Oaxaca Coast. *Journal of Archaeological Method and Theory* 8(4):343–385.

Joyce, Arthur A., J. Michael Elam, Michael D. Glascock, Hector Neff, and Marcus Winter

1995 Exchange Implications of Obsidian Source Analysis from the Lower Río Verde Valley, Oaxaca, Mexico. *Latin American Antiquity* 6(1):3–15.

Joyce, Arthur A., and Stacie M. King

2001 Household Archaeology in Coastal Oaxaca, México. Report on file with the Foundation for the Advancement of Mesoamerican Studies, Crystal River, Florida.

Joyce, Arthur A., and Raymond G. Mueller

1992 The Social Impact of Anthropogenic Landscape Modification in the Río Verde Drainage Basin, Oaxaca, Mexico. *Geoarchaeology* 7(6):503–526.

1997 Prehispanic Human Ecology of the Río Verde Drainage Basin. *World Archaeology* 29(1):74–96.

Joyce, Arthur A., and Andrew G. Workinger

1996 Río Viejo: A Prehispanic Urban Center on the Oaxaca Coast. Paper presented at the 61st Annual Meeting of the Society for American Archaeology, New Orleans.

Joyce, Arthur A., Andrew G. Workinger, Byron E. Hamann, Peter Kröfges, Maxine Oland, and Stacie M. King

2004 Lord 8 Deer "Jaguar Claw" and the Land of the Sky: The Archaeology and History of Tututepec. *Latin American Antiquity* 15(3):273–297.

King, Stacie M.

2003 Social Practices and Social Organization in Ancient Coastal Oaxacan Households. Unpublished Ph.D. Dissertation, Department of Anthropology, University of California, Berkeley.

2004 Spinning and Weaving in Early Postclassic Coastal Oaxaca. Paper presented at the 69th Annual Meeting of the Society for American Archaeology, Montreal.

King, Stacie M., Arthur A. Joyce, and Laura Arnaud Bustamante

2000 Investigaciones recientes en la región del Río Verde inferior: Resultados preliminares de las excavaciones en unidades domésticas del postclásico temprano en Río Viejo. Paper presented at the 4th Biennial Symposium of Oaxacan Studies, Oaxaca.

Levine, Marc N.

2006 Preliminary Findings from Residential Excavations at Tututepec, a Late Postclassic Mixtec Capital on the Coast of Oaxaca. Paper presented at the 71st Annual Meeting of the Society for American Archaeology, San Juan, Puerto Rico.

Lind, Michael D.

1987 *The Sociocultural Dimensions of Mixtecs Ceramics*. Vanderbilt University Publications in Anthropology, No. 33. Nashville, Tennessee.

1994 Cholula and Mixteca Polychromes: Two Mixteca-Puebla Regional Substyles. In *Mixteca-Puebla: Discoveries and Research in Mesoamerican Art and Archaeology*, edited by H. Nicholson and E. Quiñones Keber, pp. 79–99. Labyrinthos, Culver City, California.

Lister, Robert H.

1971 Archaeological Synthesis of Guerrero. In *Handbook of Middle American Indians,* Vol. 11: *Archaeology of Northern Mesoamerica,* Part 2, edited by R. Wauchope, G. Ekholm, and I. Bernal, pp. 619–631. University of Texas Press, Austin.

Long, J. Robert

1974 The Late Classic and Early Postclassic Ceramics from the Eastern Portion of the Coast. In *The Oaxaca Coast Project Reports: Part II*, edited by D. Brockington and J. Long, pp. 39–98. Vanderbilt University Publications in Anthropology, No. 9. Nashville, Tennessee.

Markman, Charles W.

1981 *Prehispanic Settlement Dynamics in Central Oaxaca, Mexico: A View from the Miahuatlan Valley*. Vanderbilt University Publications in Anthropology, No. 26. Nashville, Tennessee.

Martínez López, Cira, Robert Markens, Marcus Winter, and Michael D. Lind

2000 *Cerámica de la Fase Xoo (Monte Albán IIIB–IV) del Valle de Oaxaca.* Proyecto Especial Monte Alban 1992–1994, Contribución No. 8. Centro INAH Oaxaca, Oaxaca.

McCafferty, Geoffrey G.

1994 The Mixteca-Puebla Stylistic Tradition at Early Postclassic Cholula. In *Mixteca-Puebla: Discoveries and Research in Mesoamerican Art and Archaeology*, edited by H. Nicholson and E. Quiñones Keber, pp. 53–77. Labyrinthos, Culver City, California.

2001 *Ceramics of Postclassic Cholula, Mexico: Typology and Seriation of Pottery from the UA-1 Domestic Compound.* Cotsen Institute of Archaeology, Monograph 43. University of California, Los Angeles.

McCafferty, Sharisse D., and Geoffrey G. McCafferty

2000 Textile Production in Postclassic Cholula, Mexico. *Ancient Mesoamerica* 11(1): 39–54.

Monaghan, John

1994 Irrigation and Ecological Complementarity in Mixtec Cacicazgos. In *Caciques and Their People: A Volume in Honor of Ronald Spores,* edited by J. Marcus and J. Zeitlin, pp. 143–161. Anthropological Papers, No. 89. Museum of Anthropology, University of Michigan, Ann Arbor.

Mountjoy, Joseph B.

1969 On the Origin of West Mexican Metallurgy. In *Pre-Columbian Contact within Nuclear America,* edited by J. Kelley and C. Riley, pp. 26–42. Mesoamerican Studies, No. 4. University Museum, Southern Illinois University, Carbondale.

Neff, Hector, and Ronald L. Bishop

1988 Plumbate Origins and Development. *American Antiquity* 53(3):505–522.

Nichols, Deborah L., Mary Jane McLaughlin, and Maura Benton

2000 Production Intensification and Regional Specialization: Maguey Fibers and Textiles in the Aztec City-State of Otumba. *Ancient Mesoamerica* 11(2):267–291.

Norr, Lynette

1987a The Excavation of a Postclassic House at Tetla. In *Ancient Chalcatzingo,* edited by D. Grove, pp. 400–408. University of Texas Press, Austin.

1987b Postclassic Artifacts from Tetla. In *Ancient Chalcatzingo,* edited by D. Grove, pp. 525–546. University of Texas Press, Austin.

Paddock, John

1983 Mixtec Impact on the Postclassic Valley of Oaxaca. In *The Cloud People: Divergent Evolution of the Zapotec and Mixtec Civilizations,* edited by K. Flannery and J. Marcus, pp. 272–277. Academic Press, New York.

Paddock, John (editor)

1966 *Ancient Oaxaca: Discoveries in Mexican Archeology and History.* Stanford University Press, Stanford, California.

Parry, William J.

1990 Postclassic Chipped Stone Tools from the Valley of Oaxaca, Mexico: Indications of Differential Access to Obsidian. In *Nuevos enfoques en el estudio de la lítica,* edited by M. de los Dolores Soto de Arechavaleta, pp. 331–345. Universidad Autónoma de México, Mexico City.

Parsons, Mary Hrones

1972 Spindle Whorls from the Teotihuacan Valley, Mexico. In *Miscellaneous Studies in Mexican Prehistory*, edited by M. Spence, J. Parsons, and M. Parsons, pp. 45–69. Anthropological Papers, No. 45. Museum of Anthropology, University of Michigan, Ann Arbor.

Paso y Troncoso, Francisco del

1905a *Relaciones Geográficas de la Diócesis de Oaxaca*. Papeles de Nueva España, Geografía y Estadística, Vol. 4. Est. Tipográfico Sucesores de Rivadeneyra, Madrid.

1905b *Suma de Visitas de Pueblos por Orden Alfabético*. Papeles de Nueva España, Geografía y Estadística, Vol. 1. Est. Tipográfico Sucesores de Rivadeneyra, Madrid.

Pendergast, David M.

1962a Metal Artifacts from Amapa, Nayarit, Mexico. *American Antiquity* 27(3):370–379.

1962b Metal Artifacts in Prehispanic Mesoamerica. *American Antiquity* 27(4):520–544.

Rice, Prudence M.

1987 Economic Change in the Lowland Maya Late Classic Period. In *Specialization, Exchange, and Complex Societies*, edited by E. Brumfiel and T. Earle, pp. 76–85. Cambridge University Press, New York.

Santley, Robert S., J. Kerley, and Ronald R. Kneebone

1986 Obsidian Working, Long-Distance Exchange, and the Politico-Economic Organization of Early State in Central Mexico. In *Economic Aspects of Prehispanic Highland Mexico*, edited by B. Isaac, pp. 101–132. Research in Economic Anthropology, Supplement 2. JAI Press, Greenwich, Connecticut.

Shepard, Anna O.

1948 *Plumbate, a Mesoamerican Trade Ware*. Publication 573. Carnegie Institution of Washington, Washington, DC.

Shook, Edwin M.

1965 Archaeological Survey of the Pacific Coast of Guatemala. In *Handbook of Middle American Indians,* Vol. 2: *Archaeology of Southern Mesoamerica,* Part 1, edited by R. Wauchope and G. Willey, pp. 180–194. University of Texas Press, Austin.

Smith, Mary Elizabeth

1973 *Picture Writing from Ancient Southern Mexico: Mixtec Place Signs and Maps*. University of Oklahoma Press, Norman.

Smith, Michael E.

1996 *The Aztecs*. Blackwell Publishing, Malden, Massachusetts.

2002 Domestic Ritual at Aztec Provincial Sites in Morelos. In *Domestic Ritual in Ancient Mesoamerica*, edited by P. Plunket, pp. 93–114. Cotsen Institute of Archaeology, Monograph 46. University of California, Los Angeles.

Smith, Michael E., and Kenneth G. Hirth

1988 The Development of Prehispanic Cotton-Spinning Technology in Western Morelos, Mexico. *Journal of Field Archaeology* 15:349–358.

Spores, Ronald

1967 *The Mixtec Kings and Their People.* University of Oklahoma Press, Norman.

1972 *An Archaeological Settlement Survey of the Nochixtlán Valley, Oaxaca.* Vanderbilt University Publications in Anthropology, No. 1. Nashville, Tennessee.

1984 *The Mixtecs in Ancient and Colonial Times.* University of Oklahoma Press, Norman.

1993 Tututepec: A Postclassic Period Mixtec Conquest State. *Ancient Mesoamerica* 4(1):167–174.

Stark, Barbara L., Lynette Heller, and Michael A. Ohnersorgen

1998 People with Cloth: Mesoamerican Economic Change from the Perspective of Cotton in South-Central Veracruz. *Latin American Antiquity* 9(1):7–36.

Tolstoy, Paul

1971 Utilitarian Artifacts of Central Mexico. In *Handbook of Middle American Indians,* Vol. 10: *Archaeology of Northern Mesoamerica,* Part 1, edited by R. Wauchope, G. Ekholm, and I. Bernal, pp. 270–296. University of Texas Press, Austin.

Urcid, Javier, and Arthur A. Joyce

1999 Monumentos grabados y nombres calendáricos: Los antiguos gobernantes de Río Viejo, Oaxaca. *Arqueología* 22:17–39.

Voorhies, Barbara, and Janine Gasco

2004 *Postclassic Soconusco Society: The Late Prehistory of the Coast of Chiapas, Mexico.* Institute for Mesoamerican Studies, Publication 14. State University of New York at Albany, Albany.

Wauchope, Robert

1941 Effigy Head Vessel Supports from Zacualpa, Guatemala. In *Los Mayas Antiguos,* edited by C. Lizardo Ramos, pp. 211–232. El Colegio de México, Mexico City.

Whitecotton, Joseph W.

1992 Culture and Exchange in Postclassic Oaxaca: A World-System Perspective. In *Resource, Power, and Interregional Interaction*, edited by E. Schortman and P. Urban, pp. 51–74. Plenum Publishers, New York.

Winter, Marcus, and Jorge Guevara Hernández

2000 Apéndice E: Una tumba postclasica (Tumba 1986-1) de Loma Yutendahue, Santiago Suchilquitongo, Etla, Oaxaca. In *Ceramica de la Fase Xoo (Epoca Monte Alban IIIB–IV) del Valle de Oaxaca*, by Cira Martínez López, Robert Markens, Marcus Winter and Michael D. Lind, pp. 287–297. Proyecto Especial Monte Alban 1992–1994, Contribución No. 8. Centro INAH Oaxaca, Oaxaca.

Woodbury, Richard B., and Aubrey S. Trik
1953 *The Ruins of Zaculeu, Guatemala, Vol. 1.* United Fruit Company, New York.

Workinger, Andrew G.
2002 Coastal/Highland Interaction in Prehispanic Oaxaca, Mexico: The Perspective from San Francisco de Arriba. Unpublished Ph.D. Dissertation, Department of Anthropology, Vanderbilt University. Nashville, Tennessee.

Zárate Morán, Roberto
1995 El Corozal, un sitio arqueológico en la costa del Pacífico de Oaxaca. *Cuadernos del Sur* 10:10–36.

Zeitlin, Judith F.
1978 Community Distribution and Local Economy on the Southern Isthmus of Tehuantepec: An Archaeological and Ethnohistorical Investigation. Unpublished Ph.D. Dissertation, Department of Anthropology, Yale University. New Haven, Connecticut.

Zeitlin, Robert N.
1978 Long-Distance Exchange and the Growth of a Regional Center on the Southern Isthmus of Tehuantepec, Mexico. In *Prehistoric Coastal Adaptations: The Economy and Ecology of Maritime Middle America*, edited by B. Stark and B. Voorhies, pp. 183–210. Academic Press, New York.
1979 Prehistoric Long-Distance Exchange on the Southern Isthmus of Tehuantepec. Unpublished Ph.D. Dissertation, Department of Anthropology, Yale University. New Haven, Connecticut.
1982 Toward a More Comprehensive Model of Interregional Commodity Distribution: Political Variables and Prehistoric Obsidian Procurement in Mesoamerica. *American Antiquity* 47(2):260–275.
1993 Pacific Coastal Laguna Zope: A Regional Center in the Terminal Formative Hinterlands of Monte Albán. *Ancient Mesoamerica* 4(1):85–101.

PART V

Sacred History and Legitimization in the Mixteca Alta

9

Jeffrey P. Blomster

Legitimization, Negotiation, and Appropriation in Postclassic Oaxaca

MIXTEC STONE CODICES

Postclassic politics of the Mixteca Alta epitomize the sociopolitical transformations that characterize Oaxaca and other parts of Mesoamerica after the decline of large Late Classic states. Although it is ill-advised to associate a specific ethnic group with a geographic area, especially during the Late Classic through Postclassic periods (see Chapter 1), here I focus on Mixtec city-states, or cacicazgos, in the Valley of Nochixtlán. In the wake of the collapse of large states, factional competition prevailed within and between cacicazgos. Mixtecs saw opportunities for new alliances and new ways in which to inscribe changing political power and legitimacy. Invoking external relationships and phenomena formed one strategy to bolster and sacralize internal authority.

Postclassic Oaxaca has been characterized as a series of small competing city-states. After the eclipse of Monte Albán as a major polity, a transformation in sociopolitical organization occurred as small centers arose throughout the Valley of Oaxaca, with no center dominating the entire valley (Chapter 1). Classic centers in the Mixteca Alta, such as Yucuñudahui, were less nucleated than Monte Albán; Ronald Spores (1984) has credited this to the Mixtec "montane production strategy," resulting in a more dispersed population and less centralized elite administrative complex. Although not at the scale of Monte Albán, Yucuñudahui integrated much of the Nochixtlán Valley; this dominance ended by the Late Classic / Postclassic transition, as already ascendant cacicazgos become the primary political organization throughout the Mixteca. Unlike the Basin of Mexico, which experienced an influential conquest/mercantile state in the Early Postclassic (the Toltecs) and a tribute-based empire in the Late Postclassic (the Aztecs), sociopolitical organization in Oaxaca remained a series of competing cacicazgos throughout the Postclassic. Although some cacicazgos, such as that controlled by Lord 8 Deer Jaguar Claw of Tilantongo, incorporated populations in disparate regions of Oaxaca, these ephemeral unions were tied to the fortunes of specific dynasties. In this sense, Oaxaca corresponds with a pattern seen throughout much of Postclassic Mesoamerica, such as in the Quiché region of Guatemala, where occasional and fluid central control over certain competing kingdoms was fleetingly achieved by centers such as Utatlán (Chapter 1; Carmack 1981). Despite the differing scale, city-states throughout Mesoamerica shared basic ideological principles, especially concerning elite leadership rituals and imagery, and both the Toltecs and the Aztecs had significant—if not always direct—impacts throughout parts of Oaxaca (Smith and Berdan 2003).

With some exceptions (Byland and Pohl 1994; Winter 1989), archaeology has generally paid insufficient attention to internal political dynamics within and between the city-states of the Mixteca Alta. It has primarily been through studies of the Mixtec codices that the dynastic struggles and political machinations of the ruling factions of some Mixtec centers have been explored (see Chapter 10 for an example of the rich political narrative that can be gleaned from codices). Despite their many intellectual benefits, codices, however, present a serious problem to understanding the political history of the Mixteca Alta as a region, and the Nochixtlán Valley in particular. Each Mixtec codex presents a selective narrative of elite history, commissioned by royal lineages. Whereas prehispanic Mixtec codices depict the genealogies of dynasties (often intermarried) from different towns, colonial documents generally present the history of only one family in order to be more closely aligned with the realities of the Spanish legal system (Smith 1994). Thus, by their nature, the codices are biased and incomplete in their coverage of competing cacicazgos. These elite chronicles detail the conquests, alliances, and occasionally defeats of select ruling families and noble heroes. In a sense, these are heroic histories (Sahlins 1985), in which the actions of particular heroes and elite families are made representative of Mixtec society in general; at the same time they reinforce the divinely sanctioned status of the ruling class (Joyce et al. 2004; Pohl 2003). Codices promote the achievements of particular towns and dynasties, which paints non-allied competing centers and dynasties, if mentioned, in a negative light. For example, because Lord 8 Deer Jaguar Claw of Tilantongo is prominently featured in several codices (such as the *Codex Nuttall* and *Colombino-Becker I*), he appears to be enormously influential. In other codices, however, he plays only a fleeting role. In the *Codex Selden*, closely tied with the Mixtec center of Jaltepec (in the southern portion of the Nochixtlán Valley), Lord 8 Deer makes only a brief cameo appearance, as the father-in-law of sons from the main lineage in the *Selden* who marry three of his daughters (Caso 1964, 1966; Jansen and Pérez Jiménez 2000; Smith 1983:261). Based solely on the *Codex Selden*, it would be impossible to reconstruct the disparate territories dominated by Lord 8 Deer and his importance in the founding of Tututepec.

Thus, the potential political importance of some Postclassic Mixtec centers, and the powers of their ruling dynasty, has been vastly underestimated for those centers and dynasties whose fortunes are not recorded in the pages of the surviving Mixtec codices. Archaeology must play a crucial role in understanding the impact and roles of such centers. To this point, however, archaeology has not provided substantial material evidence to understand how competing centers and their rulers negotiated these relationships and promoted the power of both their place and lineage.

Archaeology has also provided scant data on the participation of the Mixteca in larger spheres of Postclassic Mesoamerican activity. Although the supposed Postclassic "invasion" by the Mixtecs of other parts of Oaxaca has been linked by some with the fall of Tula and the cessation of Toltec control or influence (see Bernal 1966:365), interpretations on the importance of external alliances and influences throughout the Postclassic—from "Toltec" to Aztec—derive primarily from codical histories and Colonial period documents in both Spanish and indigenous languages. Archaeological data from an important Postclassic center in the Nochixtlán Valley, Etlatongo, can be used to explore questions of internal sociopolitical competition and involvement in larger Mesoamerican realms.

Excavations at the site of Etlatongo were designed to document the emergence of social complexity and interregional interaction during the Early Formative period. Another goal of the research, however, was to determine the occupational history of the site—to establish the changing size of this multi-component place through time (Blomster 1995, 1998). The 1992 project at Etlatongo documented the large size of this site during the Postclassic period, or Natividad phase (900–1521 CE; see Chapter 2, Figure 2.1). In this chapter I explore both the Postclassic occupation of this site and the participation of social actors at Etlatongo in the display and manipulation of symbols associated with both earlier and contemporaneous states throughout Mesoamerica.

ETLATONGO AND THE NOCHIXTLÁN VALLEY DURING THE POSTCLASSIC PERIOD

Etlatongo is located in the Nochixtlán Valley north of the confluence of the Yucuita and Yanhuitlán Rivers (Fig. 9.1). Ronald Spores documented Etlatongo as two sites

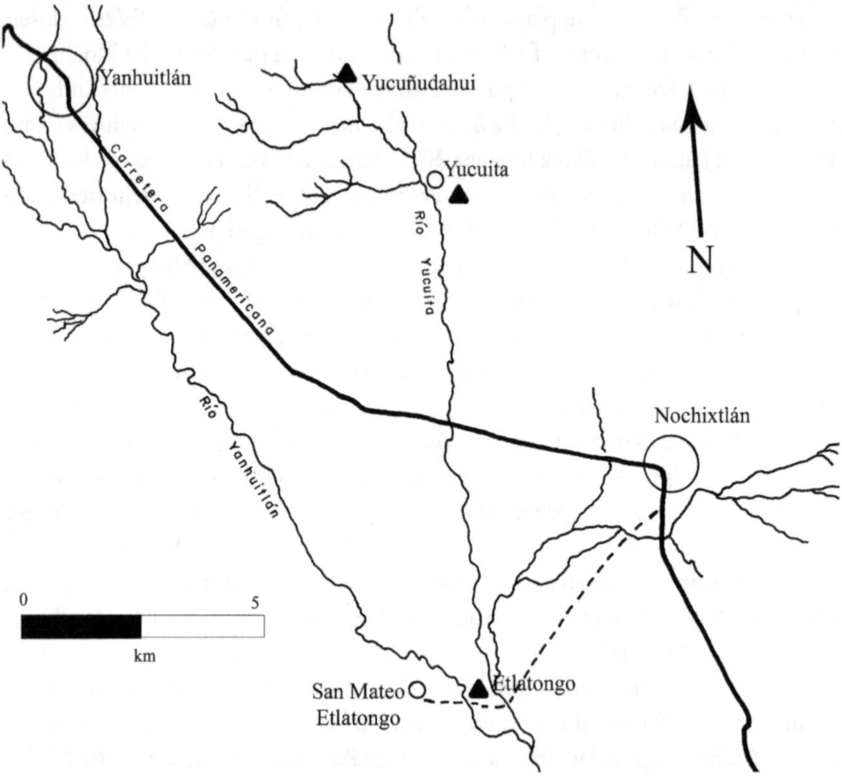

9.1 Map of the central region of the Nochixtlán Valley, showing the rivers and location of Etlatongo relative to other sites. The dashed line represents a road connecting Etlatongo to Nochixtlán. Circles (roughly proportional in size to population) represent modern villages; triangles represent archaeological sites. Adapted from Blomster 2004:fig. 2.3.

separated by a zone of less than half a kilometer of land: one site (N802) atop a hill and a lower site (N810) between the confluence of two rivers to the south (Spores 1972:150–153). Spores interpreted the hilltop site primarily as occupied in the Classic and Postclassic periods, whereas both Spores's survey and a subsequent program of archaeological testing by Roberto Zárate Morán (1987) showed the lower site, N810, to have been occupied primarily during the Early to Late Formative periods.

The 1992 Etlatongo project contributes significant data regarding the size of the Postclassic Etlatongo center. Systematic surface survey, in addition to test units, documents continuous occupation between what had been referred to as two separate sites (Blomster 1998, 2004). The Postclassic occupation of the site was also larger than anticipated, as extensive Natividad phase ceramics were recovered in

N810, in addition to the high frequencies expected on the hill based on Spores's survey. In fact, Etlatongo would have been at its largest extent during the Postclassic, when all of the land surveyed in 1992 would have been occupied (Figure 9.2). The drastic population increase Spores (1972:190) has proposed for the Mixteca Alta is supported at Etlatongo by the presence of Natividad occupations directly over bedrock at the base of test units in previously unoccupied parts of the site.

Postclassic Etlatongo covered at least 208.2 hectares (514.2 acres or 2.08 square kilometers). The projected size of this urban center only includes the area most densely occupied. Small satellite hamlets or ranches—which continue to be a vital part of how residents of the modern town of San Mateo Etlatongo conceptualize their community—as well as much of the surrounding land would also have been part of Postclassic Etlatongo (Blomster 2004). Recent reconnaissance around the modern town of San Mateo Etlatongo—over one kilometer away from the archaeological site—reveals traces of a Postclassic occupation, especially in the area near the town cemetery. This may represent an extension of Postclassic Etlatongo, dramatically increasing the size of this center, or this cluster may represent yet another hamlet or ranch subject to prehispanic Etlatongo.

The Nochixtlán Valley ceramic sequence is not sufficiently sensitive to chronological change to detect additional diachronic divisions within the long Natividad phase, except for a probable division between the early and late portions of this sequence (Lind 1987). Recent refinements of the ceramic sequences of the Valley of Oaxaca (Chapter 2) and lower Río Verde area support such a division. Until the chronology is better understood, it is not clear how much of Etlatongo was simultaneously occupied. Based on a few sensitive ceramic markers, the occupation appears to have been particularly intense during the Late Postclassic—an interpretation that corresponds well with Late Postclassic demographics from throughout Oaxaca (Chapter 1).

Alas, this important Postclassic city is not the subject of any surviving codex. The archaeologically defined site represents the Late Postclassic center of Etlatongo, one of the Nochixtlán Valley kingdoms known primarily from colonial administrative and legal documents (Spores 1967). The number of Late Postclassic Nochixtlán Valley kingdoms varies based on how these documents are interpreted. For example, Spores (1972:191) cites seven Nochixtlán Valley kingdoms: Yanhuitlán, Nochixtlán, Etlatongo, Chachoapan, Soyaltepec, Jaltepec, and Tiltepec. All settlements in the Nochixtlán Valley were subject to one of these centers. In a later publication, Spores (1983:257) pares the list down to five major Nochixtlán Valley kingdoms: Yanhuitlán, Chachoapan, Nochixtlán, Etlatongo, and Jaltepec. Thus, although the precise number of Postclassic Nochixtlán Valley kingdoms documented through colonial sources (not archaeology) varies, Etlatongo is consistently cited as one of them.

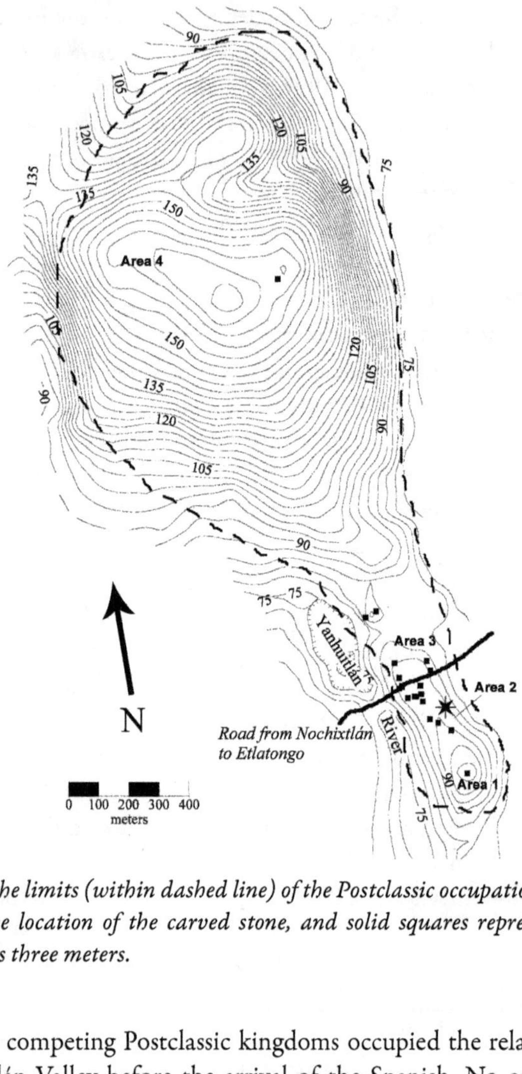

9.2 Map showing the limits (within dashed line) of the Postclassic occupation at Etlatongo; the star marks the location of the carved stone, and solid squares represent test units. Contour interval is three meters.

At least five competing Postclassic kingdoms occupied the relatively circumscribed Nochixtlán Valley before the arrival of the Spanish. No center emerged that controlled all of the Nochixtlán Valley; these five kingdoms competed with each other for power and prestige. As recorded during the Colonial epoch, the Nochixtlán Valley kingdoms had numerous subject towns, and Etlatongo was associated with eight such hamlets in the 1540s (Spores 1967:100). Etlatongo is not listed as one of the centers in the Mixteca Alta with a population of over 10,000 people; only one Nochixtlán Valley site—Yanhuitlán—had a contact era population greater than that. The remaining three Mixtec centers (Coixtlahuaca, Teposcolula, and Tlaxiaco) with the largest contact era populations fall outside of the Nochixtlán Valley (Spores 1967:101). Population at Etlatongo plummeted after the Conquest, with 642 people listed from 1547–1548 (Spores 1984:105) and only 300 people from 1565–1570 (Spores 1967:240).

As evinced by both population figures and other colonial documents, Yanhuitlán appears to have been the largest and most powerful of these Late Postclassic Nochixtlán Valley kingdoms. The early colonial ruler of Yanhuitlán, Don Gabriel de Guzmán, included tracts of land in Etlatongo as part of the holdings to which he claimed title in 1580 as the royal patrimony of his rule (Spores 1967:165). It is not possible to assess if Guzmán's claim to Etlatongo lands is based on a prehispanic precedent. The validity of his claims may also be suspect; perhaps Guzmán attempted to exploit the Spanish legal system for his own ends as he negotiated a stronger role for himself and his community in the colonial world. The amount of legal action directed against Guzmán by neighboring towns such as Etlatongo suggests he may have, in fact, manipulated the system to annex lands previously not under the control of Yanhuitlán. Such legal action reflects a long chain of contested lands and histories by competing Nochixtlán Valley kingdoms. Indeed, the Spanish Conquest and subsequent legal possibilities may have provided avenues for people from a variety of places and socioeconomic backgrounds to negotiate new identities and positions for themselves in ancient and contemporaneous disputes, such as manifested in the Yanhuitlán idolatry trials from 1544 to 1546, in which Etlatongo residents served as hostile witnesses.

In terms of indigenous Mixtec manuscripts, Etlatongo is mentioned briefly in only a few codices, primarily the *Selden*, *Bodley*, and *Muro*. The few references to Etlatongo should not indicate lack of importance; merely no codex produced at Etlatongo or any of its significant allies survives that celebrates the heroic history of its dynasty. The Etlatongo place glyph, thought to mean "hill or place of beans" or "temple of beans" (Smith 1988), is a direct glyphic representation of the site's name, showing several black beans arranged on a temple in profile (Figure 9.3). These codices reveal little of the dynasties and politics of Postclassic Etlatongo.

CONTEXT AND DISCOVERY OF THE ETLATONGO CARVED STONE

Information that contributes to understanding Postclassic politics in the Nochixtlán Valley emerged serendipitously during the 1992 research at Etlatongo. Independent of the 1992 excavations, a farmer from San Mateo Etlatongo uncovered first a wall and then a carved stone immediately to the east of a large raised platform in the lower portion of the site (Figure 9.2), in an area interpreted by previous investigations as primarily Formative (pre-200 BCE) period (Spores 1972). Expanding his fields that lay approximately one meter below this platform, the farmer exposed a large section of an extremely well-constructed masonry wall, as well as thick, stucco

9.3 The glyph in the Mixtec codices for Etlatongo—Hill/Temple of the Beans—as it appears in Codex Selden *(13). Redrawn from Mary Smith 1988:fig. 1.*

floors visible in the adjacent soil profile (Figure 9.4). Mixed with these structural remains were large concentrations of Late Postclassic sherds, especially large fragments of Yanhuitlán Red-on-Cream bowls, diagnostic of the later portion of the Natividad phase in the Nochixtlán Valley (Spores 1972:30–33).

The wall as visible in May 1992 was composed of a series of shaped square or rectangular slabs of worked limestone, each approximately forty centimeters or larger in length. Some slabs resembled what is referred to locally as "*endeque*." Softer than limestone, endeque is a tough caliche-like material, which resembles chalk in consistency and appearance and hardens once exposed to the air (see Kirkby 1972:15). As a material, endeque would be much easier to quarry and shape than limestone. Although such shaped stones, when discovered, are often recycled for new construction projects (Blomster 1998), ten stones remained in situ when I examined this spot. Several thick stucco floors exposed to the north of this wall could be traced for fifteen to twenty meters. One of these floors nearly came into direct contact with the wall stones and was probably directly associated with the wall as an exterior patio or plaza. Based on the thick stucco floors, some of which were painted red, and well-constructed wall, I interpret this largely destroyed structure as a possible Postclassic palace. Remains of Postclassic palaces have been documented in the Valley of Oaxaca and elsewhere in the Nochixtlán Valley (such as Yucuita and Chachoapan) and feature endeque or limestone blocks that face adobe walls, with red or white plaster floors (Lind 1979, 1987)—a common pattern for elite residences throughout Postclassic Oaxaca. The portions of these palaces exposed feature rooms arranged around a series of courtyards. The superimposed palace structures at Chachoapan extend from the Postclassic into the Colonial period, suggesting a strong continuity in the location of a noble lineage (Lind 1987:10).

The Etlatongo carved stone (Figure 9.5) lay outside this wall by just over a meter to the east. Although made of the same kind of endeque or soft limestone as some of the wall stones, it does not appear to have been incorporated into the row of stones defining this probable Postclassic palace. Not only is the carved stone smaller than any of the exposed in situ wall stones, it is less square—that is, it is longer than it is high. In order to properly document the context of this carved stone, a one-by-two-meter test unit was excavated at the location of the carved stone. The first deposit excavated contained a small eroded stone fragment that appeared to

9.4 Stone wall approximately one meter to the west of the location of the Etlatongo carved stone.

match the one found by the farmer. Several pieces of painted stucco and numerous Natividad ceramic fragments came from this deposit. Although highly disturbed, the deposit from which the carved stone came may have served as constructional fill for the stucco floor above it. Not only was the stone not in its original context, it apparently was reused, incorporated into fill. Thus, context alone is not enough to determine that the stone is Late Postclassic; that designation comes primarily from stylistic comparisons.

IMAGERY OF THE ETLATONGO CARVED STONE

Unfortunately, the Etlatongo stone is eroded, obscuring crucial details of the image (Figure 9.5). The drawing (Figure 9.6) is based only on those parts still visible under close scrutiny; reconstructions of damaged portions of the stone were not attempted.

As preserved, the stone has a maximum height of twenty-nine centimeters. Although key pieces of the image are missing, it appears as if the stone's height is roughly intact. The base appears to have been carefully made and is well preserved. The length is more difficult to assess—possibly forty centimeters or more. The stone

9.5 Photograph of the Etlatongo carved stone immediately after discovery in 1992.

itself is thin but demonstrates marked depth in relief; the average depth of the carving is seven centimeters. The stone's thinness also argues against it playing a structural role in architecture. Stylistically, the carved stone resembles other examples of Late Postclassic imagery in the Mixteca-Puebla style (see Chapter 1) executed in stone, ceramics, and codices; although I draw upon these sources in my interpretation, an image may not necessarily be represented in the same way on different media.

The stone probably depicts a male, based solely on costume; the image, as preserved, exhibits neither primary nor secondary sexual characteristics. Biological sexual characteristics are seldom indicated in the codices, where identification of male or female is usually based on costume. Loincloths invariably indicate male gender. He walks in profile, traveling from the viewer's right to left (all directions are from the viewer's perspective). The feet are clearly visible and encased in sandals. A banner/ribbon projects from the leg, just above the ankle, on the figure's well-preserved right leg; a similar configuration is visible on the damaged left leg.

A huge headdress rises above and to the left of the figure—the direction in which he walks. The lower portion of the headdress contains a curling element, with a partially visible circular element behind it; this feature is probably part of what some researchers (Byron Hamann, personal communication, 2003) refer to as a butterfly-proboscis headband, with the circular element an associated eye (see *Codex Nuttall* 1975:14, 21, 30, 54, 75). Feathers adorn the Etlatongo figure's head-

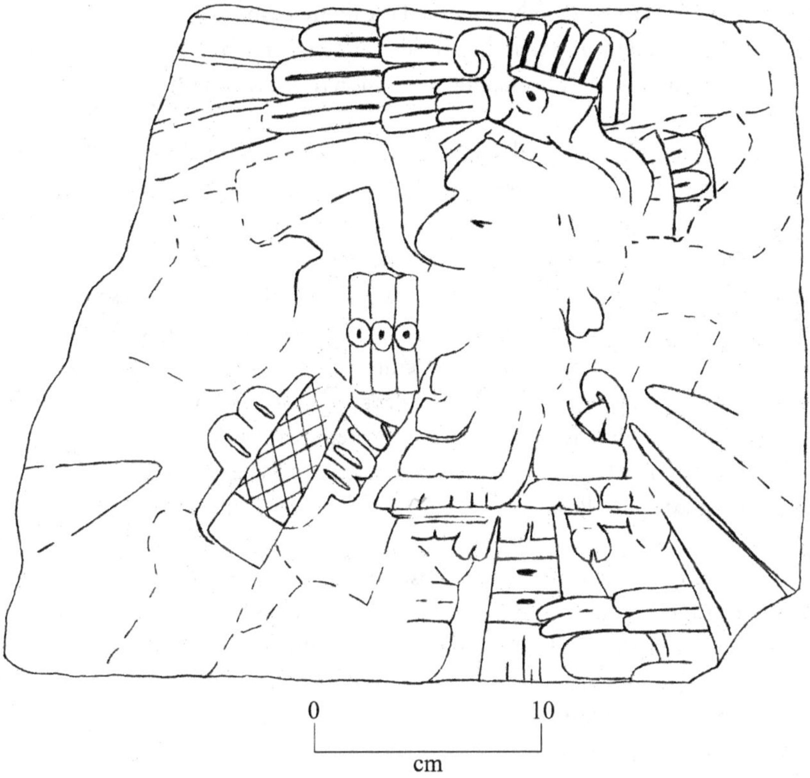

9.6 Drawing of the Etlatongo carved stone; dashed lines indicate only approximate shape visible due to erosion.

dress. Several types of feathers constitute the portion of the headdress that extends to the left of the figure, with the length of the feathers increasing with distance from the figure's head; central shafts are clearly indicated on the larger feathers.

Little remains preserved of the figure's face. Similar to Mixtec codices, a pronounced groove separates the forehead from the nose, which is quite large, leaving little space for the mouth—which has been totally obscured. Hair protrudes from the base of the headdress, with bangs projecting in front of the figure, visible in profile atop his forehead. A possible speech scroll originates in the mouth area; the size of the upper portion of the speech scroll indicates it contained additional embellishments related to the nature of the speech or sounds made by this individual. Highly ornamented speech scrolls often distinguish the nature of Late Postclassic sounds, such as the speech glyphs meaning "war" uttered by the deity impersonators flanking the sun disc on the Aztec Teocalli ("temple" or "throne") of Sacred War (Townsend 1979:55). The raised surface to the left of, and partially in contact with, the speech scroll probably contained the figure's name glyph, a location for his calendric name identical to that on a similar carved stone from Tilantongo (Figure 9.7 and see below). A faint horizontal depression to the right of his nose may represent the remnants of the eye.

The excessive damage to the face and name glyph presents the possibility that this may have been intentional effacement. Although all portions of the stone exhibit the deleterious effects of wear and erosion, the face and name glyph have been completely eliminated, possibly ground off of the stone. Clear evidence of grinding is visible behind the figure as well. There is a tradition throughout Mesoamerica of challenging an individual's status or identity by desecrating images of them, or in the case of the Maya, actually placing architecture in a way that blocked access or changed the orientation of a previous ruler's structures, such as at Palenque and Tikal (Harrison 1999). Such defacement may represent either the machinations of rival factions or, as a Classic period stone depicting a leader from Río Viejo reused as a grinding stone in a Postclassic context (see Chapter 7) illustrates, resistance and critique of the public transcript.

Only portions of the individual's costume are visible. From below the fringe of the main garment, a decorated loincloth drops between his legs. Preservation precluded illustrating the complete design; the two circles indicated on Figure 9.6 also may be related to imperfections in the slab. The back of the loincloth—as well as at least one streamer or additional costume element—projects from behind the figure, attached by an apparent knot to the rear of his costume. Also dangling beneath the fringe, above each leg, is a circular object with a vertical slit—a copper bell, examples of which also appear on the Tilantongo stone (Figure 9.7). Copper bells were important items of elite paraphernalia throughout Mesoamerica (see Chapters 1 and 8). As with the Tilantongo stone, the bells may appear as pairs above each leg, as suggested by the possible second bell on the rear leg. Although the details visible on the torso suggest "T-shaped" elements shown sometimes as pectorals in the codices, the preservation is simply too poor for any definitive identifications.

The paraphernalia held by the figure remain extremely difficult to interpret, due to the fragmentary nature of the preserved image. A basic problem centers on the inability to determine the position of the arms. The only truly analogous stone image is from Tilantongo, which depicts the individual's arms extended on either side of the body and perpendicular to it. The codices show, however, that arms from the same individual can be in various and contrasting positions. Thus, one arm raised in front of the figure may be holding the object described below, while the other may lie adjacent to it or in the opposite direction. An important clue to the position of at least one arm is the three ribbons that envelop something perpendicular to the body. Ribbons, often in groups of three and tied with circles in the middle, occur in the codices on staffs—such as in sacrifice scenes in the *Codex*

9.7 Drawing by Javier Urcid of the Tilantongo carved stone, with a breakdown (bottom) of the different costume elements and paraphernalia held by Lord 5 Death.

Nuttall (1975)—or wrapped around an element worn on the back of headdresses. These ribbons, however, are also commonly depicted on arms, often around the biceps (*Codex Vaticanus* 70, 78).

Thus, if the three ribbons wrap around the figure's arm, it cannot be extended perpendicular and in front of the body; there simply is not enough space before the name glyph. In codical art, images do not overlap. Following a suggestion by Byron Hamann (personal communication, 2003), there is a strong possibility that the arm with the ribbons on it is folded in front of his body, an arm position that is fairly common in the codices (such as Lord 10 Vulture in *Codex Nuttall* 1975:9, lower left; see Figure 9.8a). In the codices, different arm positions on the same figure are unusual, with one exception: bloodletting scenes (ibid.; Figure 9.8a). The knotted ribbons reinforce the association with bloodletting. If the positions of the arms relate to bloodletting, the other arm may be holding and employing the vertical element (visible below the headdress on the figure's right side) that ends in a rounded feature, which may represent the distal end of a long bone (either a femur or humerus), used as an awl to perforate the ear; images of such activity abound in Late Postclassic codical and sculptural art. Unfortunately, the poor preservation of this feature does not exclude other possibilities, such as the possibility that it may represent an elaborate ear ornament.

An object hangs diagonally from one arm, probably gripped by or attached to it. This relatively well-preserved portion of the stone is particularly vexing, and several interpretations appear possible for this crosshatched, long, rectangular object. Nothing directly similar to this object appears in codices and other carved stones, although crosshatched patterns sometimes indicate netlike containers. In plate 19 of the *Codex Borgia* (1993), a figure with Quetzalcoatl imagery bears on his arm a diagonal crosshatched object, which Eduard Seler (1963:plate 36) identified as a mantle or jacket (*tlaquimiloli*) for wrapping the wind bundle, which is composed of other similar pieces. Also, pendants or streamers often appear on figures in the codices who wear the knotted bands, often oriented diagonally from the bands. Lord 4 Jaguar, the "Toltec" (see Chapter 1) who aided Lord 8 Deer in his ambitions, wears the whole ensemble, or elements of it, in several consecutive pages of the *Codex Nuttall* (1975:78–80). The figures noted above from the *Codex Vaticanus* (70 and 78) who wear the triple bicep knots also have diagonal streamers coming from the knots. Netted objects, however, can also be not pliable; one way of depicting a *pulque* container is as a "netted" object with foam on top of the vessel orifice (Anders et al. 1992:240). The diagonal object on the Etlatongo stone is probably too rigid to be cloth and has additional elements associated with it that appear to preclude identifying it as such. Also, it appears to have a solid rectangle at its lower tip, which furthers the impression of rigidity.

An earlier precedent for such an object occurs on a carved stone, dating to the Late Classic/Xoo phase, from the Valley of Oaxaca cacicazgo of Zaachila (Urcid 1995). A supernatural ancestral figure, wearing a bird's beak, descends from the sky, holding a key-shaped netted object that appears to be an important aspect of his paraphernalia. One of the four seated figures that receive the beaked ancestor holds an eroded version of the same object—perhaps representing the transfer of a title or office. Another Xoo phase example of the netted object is held by a figure from a stone reused in the church of Santa Inés Yatzechi (ibid:fig. 14).

Two additional elements attached to its long sides further complicate this feature. They appear on the long sides of the object as thin rectangles with two circular features that resemble finger holes. I would say these could be highly stylized *atlatls* (spear throwers) drawn in profile (although the finger holes appear disproportionately large), but artists never depicted throwing sticks this way in codices or among the vast array of Postclassic atlatl images compiled by Zelia Nuttall (1891). The depiction of an atlatl on the Tilantongo stone corresponds with depictions in the

9.8 Three images of materials comparable to that being held by the figure on the Etlatongo stone. (a) Lord 10 Vulture, from the Codex Nuttall *(1975:9, lower left), offers blood from his ear. Note position of arms, and objects held in crook of arm, including a jaguar paw vessel. (b) Long "pouch-like" object in* Codex Selden *(14, third band from bottom). (c) Detail of a wooden atlatl in the National Museum of the American Indian; note round shield at bottom has two possible finger holes on left side. Redrawn from* Codex Nuttall *1975:9; Jansen and Pérez Jímenez 2000:279; and Saville 1925:plate 8.*

codices (Figure 9.7). On Mixteca-Puebla-style polychrome ceramics, sacrificial bone awls are sometimes shown in a similar way but with only one hole (Lind 1994:94). Although the possibility remains that the artist illustrated elements such as an atlatl or awl but in a way that differs from other preserved representations, such double bumps often appear in the codices to indicate hard things, such as hills, tree bark, and the stone men.

I conclude there are at least two identifications (which are not mutually exclusive) for the diagonal object, and they share related themes. The first interpretation views the diagonal object as a container or pouch. As Hamann (personal communication, 2003) notes, in both the codices and Aztec sculptural art, figures that have a folded arm in front of the body often have a pouch, probably containing bloodletting tools, hanging (sometimes diagonally) from the elbow. Lord 10 Vulture lets blood from his ears in the *Codex Nuttall* (1975:9; see Figure 9.8a), and a pouch and jaguar paw (perhaps representing the small ceramic vessels in the shape of jaguar paws associated with blood offerings in the Xoo phase, and more rarely beyond, at Monte Albán; see Figure 2.8) dangle from his elbow. Additional examples of long pouches occur throughout the codices; of special interest is one from *Codex Selden* (14), where the pouch appears to be made from a woven material and is connected to an adze (Figure 9.8b). If the Etlatongo example is a pouch, the objects attached to it may actually represent items held within the pouch, as the Mixtec often deployed X-ray cutaway conventions. A related identification for this object that also entails an autosacrificial theme is the close resemblance of this hatch-marked rectangle with a defined rectangle on the tip with the way in which maguey spine bloodletters are depicted in the *Codex Vaticanus* (6), where they are shown in pouches/bundles with other bloodletting accoutrements, such as flint knives and human femora. Indeed, although too fragmentary to be conclusively identified, the possible awl held in the figure's other hand certainly supports such an interpretation, with the awl being one of the objects stored in such a pouch. A rectangular netted object—perhaps also a pouch—appears in the headdress of the figure who holds the key-shaped netted object on the Xoo phase Yatzechi stone (see above).

The second interpretation combines the crosshatched object and at least one set of "finger holes." Together these may represent a kind of rectangular shield, shown in profile, which appears in iconography as early as Classic Teotihuacán. In addition to depictions on painted murals, ceramic fragments from Teotihuacán also show hands holding shields with crosshatching, although none of the examples illustrated by Von Winning (1987:fig. 4j) are complete. Additional ceramic fragments from Azcapotzalco illustrated by Von Winning (1987:fig. 1a) apparently show atlatls with handles decorated by crosshatching. Finger holes are not clearly depicted. Von Winning (1987:81) notes that such elaborate weapons are probably ceremonial. Rectangular shields also occur at several Maya sites with supposed "Teotihuacan influence," such as Stela 31 from the Petén site of Tikal. Carved on four surfaces, the sides show a warrior (possibly a Teotihuacano) in profile holding a rectangular shield (with a Tlaloc-like image) in frontal view (Miller 1999:fig. 76). Similar to the atlatl from Azcapotzalco sherds, the small portion visible of the atlatl's handle held by this figure in his right hand is crosshatched.

Turning to shields more contemporaneous with the Etlatongo stone, the closest example comes from the Mural of the Chimales at Postclassic Tehuacán Viejo, Puebla. Painted in the style of the *Codex Borgia*, seven preserved circular shields have pairs of lances crossing diagonally behind them (Sisson and Lilly 1994:figs. 2–8). In each case, a banner hangs from one of the lances, looking very similar to the diagonal object on the Etlatongo stone, providing another possibility as to that object's identification. On a Late Postclassic Aztec bench in the Eagle House, Tenochtitlán, a figure holds what appears to be a rectangular shield (Broda 1987: plate 23). Rectangular shields also occur in the Late Postclassic Santa Rita murals of Belize (Quirarte 1982). Finally, a round crosshatched shield with two finger holes appears on a wooden atlatl (Figure 9.8c) carved in the Mixteca-Puebla style (Saville 1925). Unfortunately, rectangular shields do not appear in the Mixtec codices (Hamann, personal communication, 2003).

Thus, I cannot provide a definitive interpretation for the diagonal object, which is so crucial in understanding the overall image. The stone depicts a male high-ranking lord and/or warrior. The paraphernalia held by the striding figure on the Etlatongo stone pertain to two related themes: blood sacrifice and warfare.

COMPARISONS FROM OAXACA: THE TILANTONGO STONE

The carved stone closest to the Etlatongo example in terms of geography and image originates from Tilantongo, less than twenty kilometers to the southwest of Etlatongo but separated from it by mountainous terrain. First reported by Alfonso Caso (1938), this stone was found by Jorge Acosta during excavations of a building—probably a palace (Byland, personal communication, 2003)—near the Tilantongo church. The stone came from above the first and oldest wall in a series of three superimposed occupations from this mound; it was probably reused as construction material in the fill above this wall made of alternating vertical and horizontal rows of flat stones (Caso 1938:56–57). Further evidence of reutilization of this stone derives from the stucco that covered parts it when found, obscuring much of the carved design. Similar to the Etlatongo example, the Tilantongo stone is made of a soft, highly friable limestone-like material.

The image on the Tilantongo carved stone is much better preserved and bears a series of similarities to that from Etlatongo. Javier Urcid's drawing (Figure 9.7) of the Tilantongo stone shows a warrior striding in profile from left to right. He wears a headdress similar in terms of feather orientation to that illustrated in the Etlatongo example, ending with four large feathers that extend in front of his body. Arms are raised perpendicular to his body, and in one he holds a shield with spears behind it. The deep recessed area in the center of the shield—now empty—probably originally contained an inset object made of a material different from this stone. His other hand clutches an atlatl, and a pouch or bag is slung on the arm. A jade collar dangles in front of his chest, and sandals encase his feet. He wears a central garment quite distinct from that worn by the Etlatongo figure and features a much smaller sash or loincloth. The garment, however, has four copper bells that extend from it (the fourth is assumed to be present behind the pectoral). Caso (1938) identified the glyph next to the figure's forehead as representing the individual's name, Lord 5 Death.

In terms of original context and function, several possibilities can be provisionally excluded based on the shapes of both stones. Both the Etlatongo and Tilantongo stones are thin and probably were not placed at a prominent part of a large structure. The lack of carving that continues onto the limited sides of each stone further excludes them from serving as cornerstones in a public structure, in the way many Classic Zapotec stones appear to have originally been placed. The horizontal, rather than vertical, orientation of both stones also argues against them serving previously as tomb jambs. Examples of tomb jambs from both the Nochixtlán Valley (Yanhuitlán) and the Valley of Oaxaca (Huitzo) demonstrate a recessed border that would have received the sealing slab of the tomb (Urcid, personal communication, 2003). The extreme vertical orientation of the Yanhuitlán stone and its well-defined boundaries suggest that it was not part of a larger composition (Figure 9.9). Each of the two reused tomb jams from Huitzo (one of which was placed upside down) also features a figure carrying a shield and an atlatl (Moser 1969).

The clue to the Tilantongo stone's original context—and probably that of the Etlatongo stone as well—lies in the upper left corner of the stone. What appears to be the back of a headdress is clearly visible. Caso (1938:58) originally interpreted this as part of a figure facing and fighting the preserved figure—perhaps comparable to the bench frieze analyzed by Hermann Beyer (1955) from Tenochtitlán, where the central figures face each other, although not in combat. Based on Toltec and Aztec images discussed below, I instead interpret this top left element on the Tilantongo stone as probably the headdress of a figure striding in procession in front of the individual preserved. I interpret the Tilantongo and Etlatongo stones as portions of larger processional images, probably of a series of striding elites and/or warriors that would have been on the sloping or vertical surface of a bench or banquette. On the Etlatongo stone, the largely destroyed features to the left of the enigmatic diagonal object held by the figure probably pertain to costume elements—streamers or the back of a loincloth—from the back of a figure advancing in the procession.

For both the Early and Late Postclassic periods, correlates of such processional images are known from Central Mexico and Yucatan. The so-called Warrior Benches of the Toltecs of Tula and the Aztecs of Tenochtitlán are most similar, whereas the bench relief from the so-called Mercado at Chichén Itzá appears to show bound figures on the sculpted altar or dais (Ruppert 1943:fig. 22) and may actually predate those of Tula, based on the recent revision of Chichén Itzá as primarily a Terminal Classic center (Andrews et al. 2003). The chronological placement of the "Toltec" elements at Chichén Itzá, however, remains debated, as does the focus on Tula and Chichén Itzá as the primary nexus of such features (see Chapter 1). Peter Schmidt's (2007) recent research at Chichén Itzá, for example, documents the eleventh-century occupation of Chichén Itzá and that Toltec features temporally overlap with those at Tula. I focus, however, below on examples from Central Mexico throughout the Postclassic, due to greater similarity of the imagery with the Mixtec carved stones.

BENCH FRIEZES: FROM TOLTEC TO AZTEC

Many of the artistic and architectural traits associated with the Aztecs actually originated at the Toltec capital of Tula, whose art—and legacy—the Aztecs actively appropriated. At Tula, Toltec iconography and sculpture appear between around 950 CE with the transition to decorated façades. Some scholars (Bey and Ringle 2007:414) focus on the adoption of Toltec elements at Tula as an already complete stylistic package, without much internal evolution and change, furthering their argument for a non-Tula origin for these features. As noted above and in Chapter

9.9 The Yanhuitlán stone. Originally a tomb jamb, the stone has been incorporated into a colonial shrine and wall east of the church and ex-convent of Yanhuitlán.

1, elements considered Toltec were reused and redeployed at Tula not only from distant centers in northwest Mexico, but also from places earlier in time, such as elements of the "Toltec Military Outfit," which recycles and evokes Teotihuacan imagery (Kowalski 2007:296). Benches and altars (either as extensions of benches or freestanding constructs) predate Tula, with a notable example of a polychrome painted altar at Xochicalco, Morelos (Garza Tarazona and González Crespo 1995:123), and possible precursors at Teotihuacán. Benches with carved processional reliefs, however, appear to be a Toltec innovation, although the revised dating of Chichén Itzá (see above) suggests that the format, if not the actual style, may have existed prior to the Toltecs. The processional imagery from Tula and Chichén Itzá differs from earlier processional imagery due to its placement on actual architectural elements used in ritual, whereas at Classic period Teotihuacan, for example, the imagery occurs on *taluds* projecting from lower walls (Kristan-Graham and Kowalski 2007:59).

Benches at Tula

Beginning in 1940, Jorge Acosta (1945, 1961) excavated for over twenty years in the monumental zone of Tula, Hidalgo, the early Postclassic Toltec capital, where he exposed fragments of several benches or banquettes with carved reliefs. The Toltecs deployed large benches with scenes of warrior processions at positions that lay in the sacred sector of Tula. These appear in "palaces" and vestibules adjacent or close to Pyramid B (Diehl 1983; Mastache et al. 2002). Acosta (1945) found the most complete bench in the South Vestibule of Pyramid B. Stretching for over eight meters in length, the well-preserved portion of this bench features figures carved on the *tablero*—or vertical surface—of the bench. The vertical surface rises for fifty centimeters above the floor; the bench provides a horizontal surface that extends just over one meter from the sloping talud behind it, which connects the bench to the main wall (Acosta 1945:fig.21). The bench runs along three interior walls of

9.10 Detail of two figures from the "Friso de los caciques," a processional bench at Tula. Adapted from Acosta 1945:fig. 25.

the vestibule and has an altar-like projection; Acosta (1945:41) estimated that the bench originally covered twenty-three meters.

The well-preserved portion of the carved relief in the northwest corner of the South Vestibule, labeled the Friso de los Caciques (Acosta 1945; Jiménez García 1998; Moedano Köer 1947), illustrates nineteen male figures above which serpents undulate (Figure 9.10). The nineteen human figures walk or march in a procession from left to right, until reaching a staircase. Each figure, approximately thirty-five centimeters high, is similar in size (about seven centimeters higher) to the figure on the Etlatongo stone. The overly large heads depict different physiognomies—perhaps indicating specific individuals (Acosta 1945). Different headdresses and pectorals further distinguish the nineteen figures. Many of the figures wear costume elements that appear elsewhere at Tula, such as butterfly pectorals. All carry a shield with arrows in one hand and a staff in the other; none carry atlatls. Additional differences appear in costume elements and paraphernalia. One figure carries a fan, while the final preserved figure wears a crown or diadem (Moedano Köer 1947).

Interpretations of the cacique frieze have varied. In his study of this frieze, Hugo Moedano Köer (1947:133) associated the fan held by one figure with the long-distance merchants known as the *pochteca* among the Aztecs, but he suggested the processional frieze showed important elites and towns subject to the Toltecs. Richard Diehl (1983:65) suggests that the frieze illustrates events that actually occurred in the rooms they decorate. In terms of the nature of these rituals, a recent interpretation by Cynthia Kristan-Graham (1993) focuses on the lack of purely military paraphernalia (such as atlatls and cotton armor) and posits that the frieze depicts merchants engaged in trade-related ceremonies. In addition to the fan noted by Moedano Köer, she identifies one figure as wearing a backpack—generally a diagnostic trait of merchants and celebrated in a mural at the Terminal Classic trading center of Cacaxtla.

Comparison with other Tula benches may assist in understanding the meaning of this narrative. Additional bench reliefs have been found in Building 4 (the Palace to the East of the Vestibule) and the so-called Palacio Quemado (Burned Palace), west of Pyramid B (de la Fuente et al. 1988). The richly garbed personages in the procession from the Palace to the East of the Vestibule may include a Toltec ruler, with the figures converging on a now-absent central motif. The scene has been interpreted as featuring elites from other regions arriving to greet a new ruler, similar to the investiture ceremonies related to Aztec kings (Mastache et al. 2002).

The fragments from the north and south sides of Sala 2 in the Palacio Quemado apparently show two different processions, one of warriors and another of non-warriors (including musicians). The groups meet at the main entrance to the south, although the dichotomy between these two converging processions (Mastache et al. 2002:122) may be exaggerated. Based on the context, iconography, and surrounding offerings, Alba Guadalupe Mastache, Robert Cobean, and Dan Healan (2002:123) associate this scene with a Tlaloc (the Central Mexican rain god) ceremony similar to an ethnohistoric example described for the Aztecs. Although the specifics of the depiction can be debated, the overall theme of elite investiture ceremonies and rituals link royal dynasties throughout Postclassic Mesoamerica (Ringle 2004; Ringle et al. 1998).

Although the meaning of the Cacique Frieze narrative remains elusive, a close analysis of the associated paraphernalia reveals that some figures do, in fact, wear military elements (such as the butterfly pectorals and so-called fending sticks, or slashing weapons). Shields, of course, are not the exclusive domain of warriors, and all objects may have multivalent meanings, based on context and audience. As with the interpretations of the paraphernalia held by the figure on the Etlatongo stone, the distinction between warrior and one engaged in bloodletting rituals is fluid, as warriors, after all, were the ultimate suppliers of blood-sacrificial offerings. Among the Aztecs, a fictive kin relationship was established between the captor and his captive, who lived with the captor's family until the time for sacrifice, almost as if the victorious warrior would be offering his own blood. Based on other examples both at Tula and Tenochtitlán, I support an interpretation that focuses on the depiction of rituals related to martial and autosacrificial ceremonies.

Benches at Tenochtitlán

The Aztecs used processional friezes on benches as part of their program to draw legitimacy from the revered Toltec past by reviving the art from Tula, a place they both venerated and looted (Sahagún 1950–1982, 10:165). Emily Umberger (1987) argues that few actual objects from Tula have been found at Tenochtitlán; instead, she cites use of Toltec costume details on a chacmool as evidence of conscious archaizing by the Aztecs. Fragments of a procession occur on the bench relief (or banquette frieze), reconstructed from twenty carved stones found in 1913 by Manuel Gamio in construction fill near the southwest corner of the Templo Mayor, the double temple at the heart of Tenochtitlán and the Aztec Empire (Beyer 1955). Additional slabs that may pertain to this frieze had been found in 1901 near the Calle de Guatemala. As reconstructed, the bench has an overhanging upper surface with undulating serpents and sloping base on which the figures stride. Similar in size and style to those from Tula, this represents an additional example of Aztec archaizing. The figures converge on a central object—probably in this case three bloodied perforators (for autosacrifice) embedded in a smoking grass ball, what Beyer (1955) referred to as a *zacatapalloli*.

Hermann Beyer (1955) identified the figures as warriors, although he noted that some figures with "crowns" are nobles. Most hold shields, atlatls, and lances. Speech scrolls emerge from the mouth of most figures. Many figures hold banners, some of which are incorporated into backpack-like objects. The figure to the left of the grass ball is probably the Aztec ruler (*huey tlatoani*)—in this case Itzcoatl, indicating the scene, if not the actual relief itself, probably dates to his reign, from 1427 to 1440 (Beyer 1955). Following Beyer's suggestion that this resembles a feast described in the ethnohistoric sources and similar to her interpretation of the eagle bench, Cecilia Klein (1987:304) has interpreted this scene as showing preparation for autosacrificial rituals in celebration of a military victory.

A similar frieze has been uncovered in its original context—as benches or banquettes around the walls of three rooms surrounding the inner patio of the Temple of the Eagles (or Eagle House), just to the north of the Templo Mayor (Figure 9.11). Each bench features a complete series of walking human figures, with snakes undulating above them, converging on a small altar with a central image, probably a zacatapalloli from which bloodletting instruments project (Matos Moctezuma 1990). The figures all hold shields and staffs, although each image contains slightly different details—indicating specific individuals (Broda 1987:82). Although some figures may represent warriors, clearly individuals of various ranks and social positions are shown, as indicated by differences in costume and paraphernalia. These bench processions have been dated to 1485 CE, from Tizoc's reign (Matos Moctezuma 1988); they also represent Toltec style and were found with archaic, Toltec-style Tlaloc braziers.

The benches appear to represent what actually transpired in these rooms, which included rituals related to autosacrifice, the aftermath of battles, and probably the investiture of the king, or *tlatoani* (Klein 1987:307). The benches served not only as places for sitting—perhaps for close association and bonding of triumphant and penitent warriors—but also as altars where spoils of war, including captives, could be displayed and offered. The processional relief depicts both the king and his advisors/cabinet, which includes his successor; the image specifically shows the celebration of the king's inaugural war victory, part of his coronation rites (Klein 1987:317–318). Successive bloodletting in this ritually encoded space further validated the new king's right to rule and, after his death, could ensure the legitimacy of his successor.

Archaeology provides support for the performance of penitent and autosacrificial rites. Archaeologists found awls and maguey perforators during the excavations, and recent chemical analysis of residues from the Eagle House shows the presence

9.11 Two figures from an Aztec processional bench in the House of the Eagles, at the Templo Mayor, Tenochtitlán.

of blood in this space (Barba et al. 1998). Ash and vegetal residues concentrate in front of the altar in the bench frieze, where the procession meets—the actual rituals may have corresponded closely to those shown in the frieze.

MIXTEC STONE CODICES: APPROPRIATION AND NEGOTIATION

The exploration of Toltec and Aztec carved benches provides insight into how the carved stone from Etlatongo may have been utilized, although direct correlations may not be appropriate between such disparate political entities. The stone falls within the Mixtec-Puebla style; although it was probably reused, the basic information on context and its style suggest a Late Postclassic date. In terms of connections with Central Mexico, no evidence exists that the Etlatongo stone represents an Aztec (and certainly not a Toltec) imposition. Although the Aztecs required tribute from Nochixtlán Valley centers, their impact on internal political dynamics appears limited (Spores 1967:174). The patron(s) who commissioned the stone appropriated ideology in a physical manifestation that dates to the Toltecs as a statement of legitimization. By constructing this piece, Mixtec elites at Etlatongo participated in part of a larger practice throughout contemporaneous Oaxaca—and Mesoamerica—of deploying "Toltec" imagery as part of negotiating and expressing an enhanced social identity for their ruling lineage within a context of contested internal dynastic claims and external competitive ruling houses.

Toltec Imagery in Postclassic Oaxaca and Mesoamerica

As noted above and in Chapter 1, concepts and terms such as "Tollan" and "Toltec" used in codices and ethnohistoric sources do not automatically signify the archaeological site of Tula in Hildago state. Tollan conceptualizes a sacred place associated with legitimacy and civilization; thus, various Tollans existed at the same time in the Early Postclassic and beyond (and probably earlier as well; see Ringle 2004). Although there were multiple—and earlier—Tollans, or places of the reeds, scholars continue to recognize Tula as an important place associated with origins (Kristan-Graham and Kowalski 2007:26); spatially closer and more contemporaneous Tollans, however, may have provided more salient reference points for Mixtecs in the Nochixtlán Valley. For elites in Oaxaca, Cholula may have been the most significant Tollan (see Chapters 1 and 3), although Bruce Byland (Chapter 10) associates Lord 4 Jaguar with the Mixtec center of Coixtlahuaca, which may have been considered a local Tollan. References to Toltec lords occur in the codices in association with alliances and the founding of new dynastic lineages, such as the arrival of Atonal, the founder of the ruling house at Coixtlahuaca, along with the Toltec warrior Lord 4 Jaguar, sometime after 1086 CE. The association with Cholula appears especially important in both this narrative as well as those involving the marriages and alliances arranged by Lord 8 Deer, who was also closely associated with Lord 4 Jaguar (Chapter 3).

Thus, based on codical images, it appears that Oaxacan elites shared the Postclassic obsession with the Toltecs as a legitimating and civilizing force. Unlike the Aztecs, however, who created abundant archaizing art inspired by the Toltecs (in which the ruins of Tula formed an important material referent for Tollan), such imagery is scant in Oaxaca outside of the codices. The surviving fragments of the Mitla murals, closely related to the codices, apparently show the important Toltec founding deity/lord Camaxtli-Mixcoatl (the Cloud Serpent). Pohl (1999:184) identifies this figure, and others, as Toltec by the black "lone ranger mask," which probably originates from smearing the female deity Itzpapalotl's ashes on the face. Indeed, an actual freestanding monolithic sculpture from coastal Tututepec may represent this fierce goddess. The columnar Tututepec Monument 6 differs from Postclassic Mixtec or Zapotec sculpture and resembles the colossal atlantid warriors that would have supported the roof of Tula's Pyramid B—offering material corroboration for the Toltec connections of Lord 8 Deer, who was the city's founder (Joyce et al. 2004; Pohl 1999). A subsequent ruler, however, proclaimed these connections through Monument 6; the florescence of Tututepec was the Late Postclassic, long after the collapse of Tula and its Toltecs (see Chapter 7). Monument 6 reportedly was positioned in front of the palace of Tututepec's cacique at the time of the Spanish Invasion (Joyce et al. 2004:289). Monument 6 represents an archaizing of the Toltec past in Oaxaca comparable to that performed by the Aztecs.

Invocation and representation of Toltec themes connected Oaxacan elites with a web of ruling dynasties throughout Mesoamerica who both channeled legitimacy from venerated allies, past and present, often expressed in the Mixteca-Puebla style. Much of this imagery appears later in the Postclassic, after the fall of Tula. Northwest of Oaxaca, in Tlaxcala state, more symbolic representations in the Mixteca-Puebla style were painted on altars and benches at Ocotelolco and Tizatlán, showing skulls, hands, hearts, and shields, and deity figures are also included on the Tizatlán altar (Pohl 1998). Far to the east, in the highlands of Guatemala, the Quiché utilized decorative elements related to the Mixteca-Puebla style and also included human figures in this style in murals at Iximché and Utatlán (Carmack 1969, 1981). The striding figure in the mural from the Cawek palace at Utatlán, for example, holds a shield in one hand, a rattle in the other, and is probably part of a procession. Robert Carmack (1981:299) interprets this figure as a warrior, perhaps engaged in a ritual dance. As with Oaxaca, it appears that it was the elites who were steeped in their interpretation of Toltec culture; they invoked Toltec sacredness and acquired Toltec icons as one strategy in competition between lineages (ibid.:374). These invocations combined general notions of a sacred past and ancestors with locally constructed notions of foreignness as the elites both forged and adopted an ideology of past Toltecs. Although the rituals and images varied, places marked by Mixteca-Puebla images connected elites across Mesoamerica while also celebrating external variation and internal factionalism. Indeed, Pohl (1998) sees the painted altars at Ocotelolco and Tizatlán as loci for Aztec feasts that celebrated factionalism and social violence, whereas the Mitla murals illustrate contrasting Mixtec, Zapotec, and Toltec cosmogonies (Pohl 1999:192).

Procession, Invocation, and Investiture at Etlatongo

I suggest that the Etlatongo carved stone was part of a processional relief, most likely from a bench or banquette, based on size and context compared with examples from Central Mexico. Comparable to elites throughout Mesoamerica, ruling dynasties from at least two Mixtec centers, Etlatongo and Tilantongo, appropriated an architectural form that probably had a Central Mexican origin in the Terminal Classic and executed a processional relief following Mixteca-Puebla stylistic conventions. These benches constituted important power symbols and represented the triumphs and heroic histories of ruling lineages. The procession bench at Etlatongo, of which we only have one stone, may have shown allies (both past and present) and ancestors of the patron of this bench, and may have represented the individual's investiture rituals. As part of a decreasing emphasis on large public monuments in the Postclassic period (Spores 1984), relief-covered banquettes presented many of the same themes as in codices but materialized them in a more permanent and visible medium. The small size of the imagery portrayed on the benches may have precluded them from being represented—at least in a realistic manner—as architectural elements in painted codices. Instead, the codices depicted the actual procession. Scenes of standing figures in processions appear in several codices, such as on the reverse of the *Codex Bodley* and in numerous processions in the *Codex Nuttall* (6, 19, 36, 76), which often portray figures arrayed for marriages or presenting objects as offerings. The Etlatongo stone is probably from a bench that commemorated a similar event—a stone codex.

Indeed, although the bench format may have been novel, arrangements of stones to form a larger narrative occur both contemporaneously and earlier in the Valley of Oaxaca. In addition to the Classic period stelae from the corners of the South Platform of Monte Albán, which Javier Urcid (2005) reconstructs as originally forming a larger narrative scene of a costumed ruler and prisoners, Urcid (2005:fig. 1.12) suggests nine Late Postclassic monolith fragments from Teotitlán del Valle also formed a monumental narrative, probably of a procession. The stones from Teotitlán are much larger than the one from Etlatongo and perhaps were incorporated directly into the façade of a palace or public structure.

Although not found in primary context, the archaeological settings of the Etlatongo and Tilantongo stones suggest these stone codices occurred close to palaces. This reflects a fundamental sociopolitical difference between the large Aztec Empire and the city-states of the Mixteca Alta; a Mixtec *cabecera* (capital city) did not have a massive public-ceremonial complex such as the Aztec Templo Mayor. Whereas the processional reliefs at Tenochtitlán lay in a sacred and restricted context, the Mixtec examples may have been located adjacent to a palace structure, as visible manifestations of the power and legitimacy of the ruling dynasty and a strong message to competing factions. Depicting allies and perhaps rivals, the ruling lineage at Etlatongo could construct such scenes in a way most conducive to enhancing their legitimacy—which may have involved a variety of strategies, from invoking ancient Toltec allies to conquests (real or imagined) of the current ruler. Indeed, perhaps such benches inscribed powerful foreign alliances that had been crucial in the origin of the royal dynasty and the investiture of the Etlatongo ruler, comparable to the importance of "Toltec" connections for both Lord 8 Deer and the royal lineage at Coixtlahuaca (Doesburg and van Buren 1997). As with the bench from the Eagle House in Tenochtitlán that witnessed and inscribed the promotion of the Aztec tlatoani from lord to emperor, benches could serve as a permanent referent to such ceremonies.

Such visible statements may have been especially important in the factious Nochixtlán Valley political context, where by 1200 CE emerging great houses engaged in competitive reciprocity systems to strengthen their position in alliance networks (Pohl 2003). As a demonstration of the power and conquests of a ruling family, such benches may have been installed as expressions of political aggrandizement and served as places for the ruler to gather with supporters as well as factions to display his legitimacy, as the scene may actually have depicted the ruler's investiture. Supporting the idea of internal factions that may have contested the legitimacy of the bench's patrons is the extensive damage to this individual's face and name glyph, which have been practically eliminated from the stone, possibly by rivals. As elites constantly strove to "marry up" by linking their lineage with a more prestigious one, such public statements advertised—and possibly exaggerated—the accomplishments of the lineage head depicted on the bench, while showing powerful allies and ancestors. Additional ideological benefits may have accrued from selecting a format for this imagery tied to larger expansionist states in Central Mexico.

Similar to the Aztecs, Mixtecs manipulated historical and external phenomena as important symbols of legitimization. In addition to Etlatongo, another example comes from the Tilantongo bench fragment; the exotic alliances of Lord 8 Deer, the ruler of Tilantongo, are supported by codical narratives. In the *Codex Nuttall* (Anders et al. 1992) and other codices, Lord 8 Deer meets with Lord 4 Jaguar, whose connections to Central Mexican authority are indicated by costume elements, face paint, hairstyle, and paraphernalia (see above and Byland and Pohl 1994:142). Lord 4 Jaguar may be an actual priest from "Tollan" (probably Cholula), or he may be a Mixtec representing a locally reconfigured version of a Toltec cult, in which case the place of legitimization may lie within the Mixteca, such as Coixtlahuaca (Byland and Pohl 1994:144). By referencing an external alliance and affiliation with a larger Mesoamerican entity, Lord 8 Deer attempted to legitimize his claim to the vacant throne of Tilantongo and elevate his dynasty's standing outside the typical rituals of the Mixtec dynastic system. A similar process is evident at Etlatongo, where the bench infused a palace context with some of the foreign sanctity surrounding the place(s) where nose-piercing ceremonies occurred.

Indeed, there were probably a variety of props and paraphernalia used in investiture rituals that linked elites across Postclassic Mesoamerica. What William Ringle (2004) refers to as the "Cult of Quetzalcoatl" is a suite of shared imagery, beliefs, and practices associated with the ideology of leadership and the investiture of rulers. The different Tollans throughout Mesoamerica played an important role in the investiture of client elites, with major Tollans such as Chichén Itzá, Cholula, and Tula acting as centers of legitimization for large areas. Although this practice is a pronounced pattern in the Postclassic, with local variants of the Mixteca-Puebla style expressing these connections, Ringle (2004:214) sees the basic format extending back to Teotihuacan, with the Temple of Quetzalcoatl/Ciudadela complex as a setting for investiture and the "arrival of strangers," referred to in Classic period Maya texts, signifying the arrival of Quetzalcoatl cult imagery as a means of legitimizing local leadership.

At Etlatongo, the bench represented by the carved stone materialized the ruling lineage's connection with this broader network of relationships. An additional line of material evidence excavated at Etlatongo is suggestive of connections with "Tollan." A ceramic vessel fragment in the Mixteca-Puebla codex style depicts an individual holding a staff or spear (Figure 9.12). The "lone ranger mask" (see above) worn by the figure, as well as his gray and black-striped body paint, suggests the image represents a mostly human "Toltec" dressed as Camaxtli-Mixcoatl, a costume worn by important personages, as discussed above for the Mitla murals (Pohl 1999). Although images of supernatural Cloud Serpent figures in the Mixtec screenfolds always wear white and red striped body paint, gray and black striped body paint is worn only by Lord 4 Jaguar, Lord 8 Deer's Toltec ally (*Codex Nuttall* 1975:52, 70, 79, 80; Hamann, personal communication, 2003). Polychrome codex-style pots were highly valued objects used to promote alliances and also served as props in ancestor rituals (Pohl 1999:192). Together, the archaizing bench fragment from Etlatongo and the codex-style sherd represent the first archaeological manifestations of the Postclassic Mixtec obsession with the Toltecs, previously documented only through codices.

CONCLUSION

Without a regional center holding sway, Postclassic Nochixtlán Valley politics transformed as city-states competed and attempted to enhance their prestige relative to each other. Different strategies may have been deployed to promote the heroic history and legitimacy of the ruling dynasty over both internal factions and external competitors. At Etlatongo, the ruling dynasty materialized the power and authority of temporally and spatially distant alliances, real or invented, by erecting a banquette carved with a processional relief, of which one stone has been recovered. The procession scene itself probably included the ruler, ancestors, and members of his lineage, as well as both internal and external allies, representing a heroic history of his dynasty and place. The individuals may have been depicted holding martial implements or engaged in bloodletting rituals—or some combination of the two.

The Late Classic to Postclassic represented a time of rupture, disjunction, and political transformation that heavily impacted elites throughout Oaxaca. Elites devised new strategies to negotiate their position in Postclassic society. In some cases, such as invoking the ruins of Classic sites that surrounded them, an ideology that elevated their status may have been developed in cooperation with commoners. Depending on the social identity of the viewer, the ruins may have represented the

9.12 Polychrome codex-style vessel fragment from Etlatongo.

failings of past elites while focusing on the importance of the elites in negotiating an end to the tenth-century War that Came From Heaven (contemporaneous with the rise of the Toltecs), which emphasized elites' roles—in the past as well as present—in facilitating agriculture and thus the civilization in which both elites and commoners lived (Chapter 4).

Elites also manipulated imagery that tied them in with larger Mesoamerican phenomena and elevated their claims to legitimacy. The bench at Etlatongo may have represented the investiture of a ruler and illustrated leadership rituals that linked this ruler with a larger network of Postclassic Mesoamerican elites, broadcasting an important legitimating message to internal factions and external rivals.

Carmack (1981:374) details how the Quiché Maya used Toltec connections both to claim legitimacy for the development of their state (with Quichés noting in retrospect that such societal changes required foreign symbols) and, once political control of the Quiché basin had been achieved, in political competition within and between Quiché lineages. In Oaxaca, various methods existed to reference contact with this legitimating force. Although sculpture diminishes in frequency in Postclassic Oaxaca, legitimating themes from the codices found a more public expression in objects such as the hypothesized bench or banquette from which this stone comes. The extensive damage to the face and name glyph of the Etlatongo stone's figure may represent factional challenges to the transcript presented on the banquette.

Because studies of codical histories can only reveal the narratives of those places whose dynasties happen to appear in the seven surviving Mixtec codices, archaeologists must explore other, more permanent imagery that inscribes related themes. Processional images, in this case on a bench, related to elite leadership rituals throughout Postclassic Mesoamerica represent one strategy used in Late Postclassic negotiations of status and power. Although the format—a bench—may have been novel, the image is executed in the Mixteca-Puebla style, with both specific elements (such as the netted object) and overall narrative (a procession) having referents in both earlier and contemporaneous Oaxacan art.

ACKNOWLEDGMENTS

I acknowledge the assistance of the Rodriguez family for bringing this stone to my attention and ensuring its recording and preservation. The fieldwork would not have been completed without the assistance of numerous residents of San Mateo Etlatongo. For permission and support throughout the fieldwork and subsequent analysis, I thank the Centro INAH Oaxaca (and its directors Ernesto González Licón and Eduardo López Calzada) and the Consejo de Arqueología of INAH, especially its presidents Lorena Mirambell and Joaquín García-Bárcena. The fieldwork was supported by a Fulbright (IIE) Fellowship. Numerous colleagues have generously looked at the photos and drawings of the Etlatongo stone, two of whom merit special citation. Javier Urcid compared the Etlatongo image with those from his corpus of Mixtec stones and provided a drawing of the Tilantongo stone. The fecund mind of Byron Hamann also provided a source of inspiration, as he diligently noted comparable images in a variety of Mixtec codices and provided possible identifications for the paraphernalia depicted on the carved stone. I continue to benefit from the SURFER wizardry of Andrew Workinger. Hamann, Arthur Joyce, Mickey Lind, Marilyn Masson, and Marcus Winter all commented on drafts of this chapter. I remain solely responsible for any errors.

REFERENCES

Acosta, Jorge R.

1945 La cuarta y quinta temporadas de exploraciones arqueológicas en Tula, Hgo. *Revista Mexicana de Estudios Antropológicos* 7:23–64.

1961 La indumentaria de los cariátides de Tula. In *Homenaje a Pablo Martínez del Rio*, pp. 221–228. Instituto Nacional de Antropología e Historia, Mexico City.

Anders, Ferdinand, Maarten Jansen, and Gabina Aurora Pérez Jiménez

1992 *Crónica Mixteca: El rey 8 Venado, Garra de Jaguar, y la dinastía de Teozacualco-Zaachila: Libro explicativo del llamado Códice Zouche-Nuttall.* ADEVA/Fondo de Cultura Económica, Mexico City.

Andrews, Anthony P., E. Wyllys Andrews, and Fernando Robles Castellanos

2003 The Northern Maya Collapse and Its Aftermath. *Ancient Mesoamerica* 14(1): 151–156.

Barba, Luis, Luz Lazos, Karl F. Link, Agustín Ortiz, and Leonardo López Luján

1998 Arqueometría en la Casa de las Águilas. *Arqueología Mexicana* 6(31):20–27.

Bernal, Ignacio

1966 The Mixtecs in the Archaeology of the Valley of Oaxaca. In *Ancient Oaxaca: Discoveries in Mexican Archaeology and History*, edited by J. Paddock, pp. 345–366. Stanford University Press, Stanford, California.

Bey, George J., III, and William M. Ringle

2007 From the Bottom Up: The Timing and Nature of the Tula–Chichén Itzá Exchange. In *Twin Tollans: Chichén Itzá, Tula, and the Epiclassic to Early Postclassic Mesoamerican World,* edited by J. Kowalski and C. Kristan-Graham, pp. 377–427. Dumbarton Oaks Research Library and Collection, Washington, DC.

Beyer, Hermann

1955 La procesión de los señores. *El México Antiguo* 8:8–42.

Blomster, Jeffrey P.

1995 Micro-settlement Patterning and Demographic Change at Etlatongo, Oaxaca, Mexico. Paper presented at the 60th Annual Meeting of the Society for American Archaeology, Minneapolis.

1998 At the Bean Hill in the Land of the Mixtec: Early Formative Social Complexity and Interregional Interaction at Etlatongo, Oaxaca, Mexico. Unpublished Ph.D. Dissertation, Department of Anthropology, Yale University. New Haven, Connecticut.

2004 *Etlatongo: Social Complexity, Interaction, and Village Life in the Mixteca Alta, Oaxaca, Mexico*. Wadsworth, Belmont, California.

Broda, Johanna

1987 Templo Mayor as Ritual Space. In *The Great Temple of Tenochtitlán: Center and Periphery in the Aztec World*, by J. Broda, D. Carrasco, and E. Matos Moctezuma, pp. 61–123. University of California Press, Berkeley.

Byland, Bruce E., and John M.D. Pohl

1994 *In the Realm of 8 Deer: The Archaeology of the Mixtec Codices*. University of Oklahoma Press, Norman.

Carmack, Robert M.

1969 Quichean Art: A Mixteca-Puebla Variant. *Katunob* 7(3):12–35.

1981 *The Quiché Mayas of Utatlán*. University of Oklahoma Press, Norman.

Caso, Alfonso

1938 *Exploraciones en Oaxaca: Quinta y sexta temporadas 1936–1937*. Publicación No. 34. Instituto Panamericano de Geografía e Historia, Mexico City.

1964 *Interpretación del Códice Selden 3135 (A.2)*. Sociedad Mexicana de Antropología, Mexico City.

1966 The Lords of Yanhuitlán. In *Ancient Oaxaca: Discoveries in Mexican Archaeology and History*, edited by J. Paddock, pp. 313–335. Stanford University Press, Stanford, California.

Codex Borgia

1993 *The Codex Borgia: A Full-Color Restoration of the Ancient Mexican Manuscript*, reconstructed by Gisele Díaz and Alan Rodgers; introduction and commentary by Bruce E. Byland. Dover Publications, New York.

Codex Nuttall

1975 *The Codex Nuttall: A Picture Manuscript from Ancient Mexico*, edited by Zelia Nuttall, notes by Arthur Miller. Dover Publications, New York.

de la Fuente, Beatriz, Silvia Trejo, and Nelly Gutiérrez Solana

1988 *Escultura en Piedra de Tula: Catálogo*. Instituto de Investigaciones Estéticas, Universidad Nacional Autónoma de México, Mexico City.

Diehl, Richard A.

1983 *Tula: The Toltec Capital of Ancient Mexico*. Thames and Hudson, New York.

Doesburg, Sebastian van, and Olivier van Buren

1997 The Prehispanic History of the Valley of Coixtlahuaca, Oaxaca. In *Códices, Caciques y Comunidades*, edited by M. Jansen and L. Reyes García, pp. 103–160. Cuadernos de Historia Latinoamericana, No. 5. AHILA, Ridderkerk.

Garza Tarazona, Silvia, and Norberto González Crespo

1995 Xochicalco: Una cima cultural. In *La Acrópolis de Xochicalco*, edited by J. Wimer, pp. 89–144. Instituto de Cultura Morelos, Mexico City.

Harrison, Peter D.

1999 *The Lords of Tikal: Rulers of an Ancient Maya City*. Thames and Hudson, New York.

Jansen, Maarten, and Gabina Aurora Pérez Jiménez

2000 *La Dinastía de Añute: Historia, literatura e ideología de un reino mixteco*. CNWS Publications, Vol. 87. Research School of Asian, African, and Amerindian Studies, University of Leiden, Leiden.

Jiménez García, Elizabeth
1998 *Iconografía de Tula: El caso de la escultura.* Colección Científica, No. 364. Instituto Nacional de Antropología e Historia, Mexico City.

Joyce, Arthur A., Andrew G. Workinger, Byron Hamann, Peter Kröfges, Maxine Oland, and Stacie M. King
2004 Lord 8 Deer "Jaguar Claw" and the Land of the Sky: The Archaeology and History of Tututepec. *Latin American Antiquity* 15(3):273–297.

Kirkby, Michael
1972 *The Physical Environment of the Nochixtlán Valley, Oaxaca.* Vanderbilt University Publications in Anthropology, No. 2. Nashville, Tennessee.

Klein, Cecilia F.
1987 The Ideology of Autosacrifice at the Templo Mayor. In *The Aztec Templo Mayor,* edited by E. Boone, pp. 293–370. Dumbarton Oaks Research Library and Collection, Washington, DC.

Kowalski, Jeff Karl
2007 What's "Toltec" at Uxmal and Chichén Itzá? Merging Maya and Mesoamerican Worldviews and World Systems in Terminal Classic to Early Postclassic Yucatan. In *Twin Tollans: Chichén Itzá, Tula, and the Epiclassic to Early Postclassic Mesoamerican World,* edited by J. Kowalski and C. Kristan-Graham, pp. 251–313. Dumbarton Oaks Research Library and Collection, Washington, DC.

Kristan-Graham, Cynthia
1993 The Business of Narrative at Tula: An Analysis of the Vestibule Frieze, Trade, and Ritual. *Latin American Antiquity* 4(1):3–21.

Kristan-Graham, Cynthia, and Jeff Karl Kowalski
2007 Chichén Itzá, Tula, and Tollan: Changing Perspectives on a Recurring Problem in Mesoamerican Archaeology and Art History. In *Twin Tollans: Chichén Itzá, Tula, and the Epiclassic to Early Postclassic Mesoamerican World,* edited by J. Kowalski and C. Kristan-Graham, pp. 13–83. Dumbarton Oaks Research Library and Collection, Washington, DC.

Lind, Michael
1979 *Postclassic and Early Colonial Mixtec Houses in the Nochixtlán Valley, Oaxaca.* Vanderbilt University Publications in Anthropology, No. 23. Nashville, Tennessee.
1987 *The Sociocultural Dimensions of Mixtec Ceramics.* Vanderbilt University Publications in Anthropology, No. 33. Nashville, Tennessee.
1994 Cholula and Mixteca Polychromes: Two Mixteca-Puebla Regional Sub-styles. In *Mixteca-Puebla: Discoveries and Research in Mesoamerican Art and Archaeology,* edited by H. Nicholson and E. Quiñones Keber, pp. 79–99. Labyrinthos, Culver City, California.

Mastache, Alba Guadalupe, Robert Cobean, and Dan Healan
2002 *Ancient Tollan: Tula and the Toltec Heartland*. University Press of Colorado, Boulder.

Matos Moctezuma, Eduardo
1988 *The Great Temple of the Aztecs: Treasures of Tenochtitlán*. Thames and Hudson, New York.
1990 *Treasures of the Great Temple*. Alti Publishing, La Jolla, California.

Miller, Mary E.
1999 *Maya Art and Architecture*. Thames and Hudson, New York.

Moedano Köer, Hugo
1947 El friso de los caciques. *Anales del INAH* 2:113–136.

Moser, Christopher L.
1969 La Tumba 1 del Barrio del Rosario, Huitzo, Oaxaca. *Boletín del INAH* 36:41–47.

Nuttall, Zelia
1891 *The Atlatl or Spear-Thrower of the Ancient Mexicans*. Archaeological and Ethnological Papers of the Peabody Museum Vol. 1, No. 3. Peabody Museum of American Archaeology and Ethnology, Cambridge, Massachusetts.

Pohl, John M.D.
1998 Themes of Drunkenness, Violence, and Factionalism in Tlaxcalan Altar Paintings. *Res: Anthropology and Aesthetics* 33:184–207.
1999 The Lintel Paintings of Mitla and the Function of the Mitla Palaces. In *Mesoamerican Architecture as a Cultural Symbol*, edited by J. Kowalski, pp. 176–197. Oxford University Press, New York.
2003 Creation Stories, Hero Cults, and Alliance Building: Confederacies of Central and Southern Mexico. In *The Postclassic Mesoamerican World*, edited by M. Smith and F. Berdan, pp. 61–66. University of Utah Press, Salt Lake City.

Quirarte, Jacinto
1982 The Santa Rita Murals: A Review. In *Aspects of the Mixteca-Puebla Style and Mixtec and Central Mexican Culture in Southern Mesoamerica*, edited by J. Brown and E. Andrews V, pp. 43–59. Middle American Research Institute, Occasional Paper 4. Tulane University, New Orleans.

Ringle, William M.
2004 On the Political Organization of Chichen Itza. *Ancient Mesoamerica* 15(2): 167–218.

Ringle, William M., Tomás Gallareta Negrón, and George J. Bey III
1998 The Return of Quetzalcoatl: Evidence for the Spread of a World Religion during the Epiclassic Period. *Ancient Mesoamerica* 9(2):193–232.

Ruppert, Karl
1943 *The Mercado, Chichén Itza, Yucatán*. Publication 546. Carnegie Institution of Washington, Washington, DC.

Sahagún, Bernardino de

1950–82 *Florentine Codex: General History of the Things of New Spain,* vols. 1–13 [1547–1579]. Edited and translated by A. Anderson and C. Dibble. University of Utah Press, Salt Lake City.

Sahlins, Marshall

1985 Other Times, Other Customs: The Anthropology of History. In *Islands of History,* pp. 32–72. University of Chicago Press, Chicago.

Saville, Marshall

1925 *The Woodcarver's Art in Ancient Mexico*. Contributions from the Museum of the American Indian, Vol. 9. Heye Foundation, New York.

Schmidt, Peter J.

2007 Birds, Ceramics, and Cacao: New Excavations at Chichén Itzá, Yucatan. In *Twin Tollans: Chichén Itzá, Tula, and the Epiclassic to Early Postclassic Mesoamerican World,* edited by J. Kowalski and C. Kristan-Graham, pp. 151–203. Dumbarton Oaks Research Library and Collection, Washington, DC.

Seler, Eduard

1963 *Comentarios al Códice Borgia*. Mariana Frenk, translator. 3 volumes. Fondo de Cultura Económica, Mexico City.

Sisson, Edward B., and T. Gerald Lilly

1994 The Mural of the Chimales and the Codex Borgia. In *Mixteca-Puebla: Discoveries and Research in Mesoamerican Art and Archaeology,* edited by H. Nicholson and E. Quiñones Keber, pp. 25–44. Labyrinthos, Culver City, California.

Smith, Mary Elizabeth

1983 Regional Points of View in the Mixtec Codices. In *The Cloud People: Divergent Evolution of the Zapotec and Mixtec Civilizations,* edited by K. Flannery and J. Marcus, pp. 260–266. Academic Press, New York.

1988 It Doesn't Amount to a Hill of Beans: The Frijol Motif in Mixtec Place Signs. In *Smoke and Mist: Mesoamerican Studies in Memory of Thelma D. Sullivan,* edited by J. Josserand and K. Dakin, pp. 696–710. British Archaeological Reports International Series 402. Oxford.

1994 Why the Second Codex Selden Was Painted. In *Caciques and Their People: A Volume in Honor of Ronald Spores,* edited by J. Marcus and J. Zeitlin, pp. 111–141. Anthropological Papers, No. 89. Museum of Anthropology, University of Michigan, Ann Arbor.

Smith, Michael E., and Francis F. Berdan

2003 Postclassic Mesoamerica. In *The Postclassic Mesoamerican World,* edited by M. Smith and F. Berdan, pp. 3–13. University of Utah Press, Salt Lake City.

Spores, Ronald

1967 *The Mixtec Kings and Their People*. University of Oklahoma Press, Norman.

1972 *An Archaeological Settlement Survey of the Nochixtlán Valley, Oaxaca*. Vanderbilt University Publications in Anthropology, No. 1. Nashville, Tennessee.

1983 Postclassic Mixtec Kingdoms: Ethnohistoric and Archaeological Evidence. In *The Cloud People: Divergent Evolution of the Zapotec and Mixtec Civilizations*, edited by K. Flannery and J. Marcus, pp. 255–260. Academic Press, New York.

1984 *The Mixtecs in Ancient and Colonial Times*. University of Oklahoma Press, Norman.

Townsend, Richard F.

1979 *State and Cosmos in the Art of Tenochtitlan*. Studies in Pre-Columbian Art and Archaeology, No. 20. Dumbarton Oaks, Washington, DC.

Umberger, Emily

1987 Antiquities, Revivals, and References to the Past in Aztec Art. *Res: Anthropology and Aesthetics* 13:62–105.

Urcid, Javier

1995 Comentarios a una lápida zapoteca en el Museo Nacional de Historia Natural del Instituto Smithsonian. *Cuadernos del Sur* 3(8–9):9–27.

2005 Zapotec Writing: Knowledge, Power, and Memory in Ancient Oaxaca. Monograph submitted to the Foundation for the Advancement of Mesoamerican Studies.

Von Winning, Hasso

1987 *La Iconografía de Teotihuacan: Los Dioses y Los Signos*. Vol. 1. Instituto de Investigaciones Estéticas, UNAM, Mexico City.

Winter, Marcus

1989 *Oaxaca: The Archaeological Record*. Minutiae Mexicana, Mexico.

Zárate Morán, Roberto

1987 *Excavaciones de un sitio preclásico en San Mateo Etlatongo, Nochixtlán, Oaxaca, México*. British Archaeological Reports International Series 322. Oxford.

10

Bruce E. Byland

Tree Birth, the Solar Oracle, and Achiutla

MIXTEC SACRED HISTORY AND THE CLASSIC TO POSTCLASSIC TRANSITION

The culture of the Mixtec people of Oaxaca, Mexico, during and after the transition between Classic and Postclassic periods in Mesoamerican history has engendered significant interest among archaeologists working in southern Mexico (see Spores 2001 for discussion). This work has been greatly aided by the complementary research of their allies in the ethnohistoric and epigraphic fields (Jansen 1982, 1996, 1998; Monaghan 1995; Pohl 1994a, 1994b; Rincón Mautner 1997, 1999, 2000; Smith 1983a; Spores 1993; Terraciano 2001). The Classic-Postclassic transition has traditionally been seen as a period of sudden transformation of governments from the large centers of the Classic period to the smaller, more dispersed centers of the early Postclassic (see Chapter 1). The timing of the Classic to Postclassic transition has traditionally been placed variously at about 750 CE in the Basin of Mexico when Teotihuacan suffered its greatest decline (Sanders et al. 1979), or about 800 CE in the Valley of Oaxaca when the South Platform at Monte Albán was abandoned (Marcus Winter, personal communication, 2003) and at about 900 CE in the Maya region when the major centers stopped erecting new dated stelae commemorating the life-crisis events of their rulers (Coe 1999). This broad span of time clearly suggests that the political processes that were operative in the transition took place at different times in different areas, and also that the transition from one form of political organization to another through the breadth of Mesoamerica involved a lengthy, complex process of transformation rather than any sort of short-term or simple shift in structure.

In the effort to understand these processes, some archaeologists have focused on the evidence for internal and external conflict as this transition occurred and the consequent movement of people away from Classic centers and into other areas. Others have emphasized the social and cultural reorganization that occurred as the transition happened (see Chapters 1, 5, and 7). Still others have emphasized ecological and environmental changes that affected subsistence systems near the great centers (see Chapter 12; Gill 2000; Hamblin and Pitcher 1980; Redman 1999; Rice and Rice 1990; Sanders et al. 1979; Thompson 1954; Webster 2002). These views have almost universally been based on archaeological evidence in conjunction with ecological information. I believe that another important aspect of understanding this process can be accomplished by considering cultural information derived from ethnohistoric sources, including the native texts of the Mixtec historical codices (compare with Chapters 3 and 4).

Emphasis has long been placed on the demise of long-established settlement systems that had been dominated by macro-regionally important political centers and the subsequent creation of new systems of regional integration centered on emergent communities that assumed newly important roles in the political scene. There has been little study of the transition at smaller centers located at greater distances from these major centers. I believe that new light can be shed on the cultural processes operating in this most important of historical transitions by looking at smaller communities that are peripheral to the largest centers. Many smaller centers were independent actors that made their own decisions in the context of the broader political scales of Mesoamerican interaction at the time (see Chapters 9, 11, and 12). The combination of archaeological, ethnohistorical, and epigraphic sources of information available for some of them can further illuminate the transition. These smaller centers can serve as models of cultural behavior related to the processes of change.

One such locale might be the Mixtec region of Oaxaca, Mexico, and its environs (Figure 10.1). The Mixteca Alta has been the focus of a series of extensive archaeological surveys conducted during the last several decades (Balkansky et al. 2000; Byland 1980; Byland and Pohl 1994; Finsten et al. 1996; Plunkett 1983, 1990; Spores 1972, 2001; Stiver 2001). Although surveys have grown, only a few excavations of Classic or Postclassic contexts have occurred (see Chapter 9; Bernal 1949; Gaxiola 1984; Lind 1979; Pérez Rodríguez 2003; Spores 1974a). From this work I can now identify and begin to understand a variety of Classic period communities that existed in various valleys of the Mixteca Alta and nearby parts of the Mixteca Baja and Mixteca de la Costa.

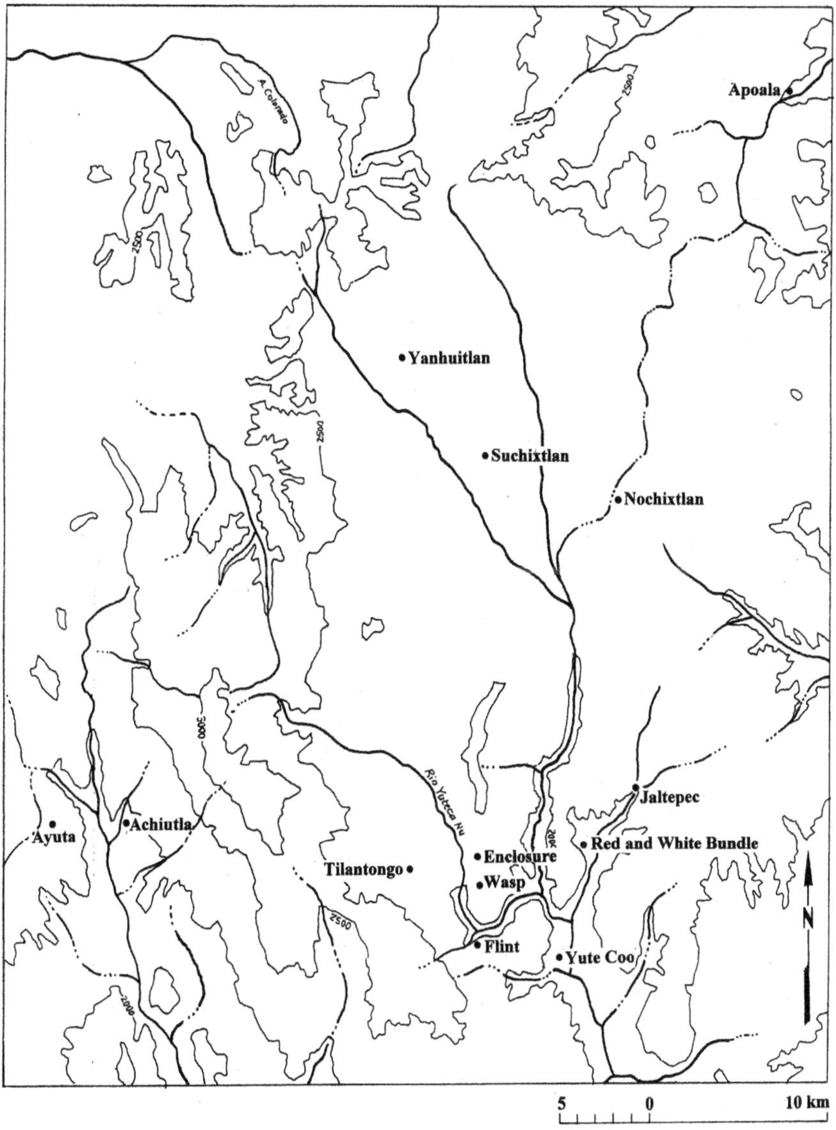

10.1 Map of the eastern Mixteca Alta showing the locations of sites mentioned in text.

HISTORICAL CODICES

The uniqueness of the Mixteca Alta in Mesoamerican archaeology is that in this area archaeological research can be augmented by a study of the remarkable documentary history of the region (see Chapter 9 for a discussion of relevant issues).

That documentary history includes Colonial period manuscripts written in Spanish as well as in Mixtec (Hamann 2002; Spores 2001; Terraciano 2001). It also includes a remarkable collection of native tradition pictorial documents from the early Colonial period as well entirely indigenous documents from before the first Spanish contact (Chapter 1).

Among these native tradition documents is the largest corpus of surviving indigenous pre- and peri-conquest historical documents known from Mesoamerica. I refer, of course, to the Mixtec historical codices, a group of five principal and three additional painted screenfold documents including the *Codices Bodley* (Caso 1960), *Colombino-Becker I* (León-Portilla 1996), *Nuttall* (Anders et al. 1992a; Troike 1987), *Vienna* (Anders et al. 1992b), and *Selden* (Caso 1964) in the principal group and *Codices Becker II* (Nowotny 1964), *Egerton* (Burland 1965), and *Muro* (Smith 1973) in the extended group. The first four of these are clearly pre-conquest in age and the others were painted after the conquest but retain, to varying degrees, the indigenous style. Together, these documents, and a variety of other postconquest *lienzos* and maps provide an account of Mixtec history that begins before 940 CE and extends through a period well after the Spanish Conquest. Each codex presents a version of history relevant to its place of origin and to the noble families of that place (Smith 1983a, 1983b). Even knowing this, I cannot assume that we fully understand the reasons for the inclusion or omission of particular events or perspectives in each of the various documents. The historical nature of these documents, nevertheless, makes it possible to track local events involved in the Classic to Postclassic transition and their consequences over a fairly long period. The codices, then, provide a nuanced view of the dynamics of the transition process that is not available in most other areas of Mesoamerica where archaeological resources alone are the principal line of evidence.

The codices are complex documents that undoubtedly had multiple purposes and uses for their authors. Among the roles of the codices were the recounting of family trees of current people that would link them to heroic figures from the ancient times of Mixtec history and the recounting of earlier political conflicts and alliances between polities to establish the context of their current relationships, a kind of political spin on the past to serve the political purposes of the present. Some parts of these documents were undoubtedly meant to be written versions of oral or dramatic performances of the texts. Others, perhaps, are records of relationships between communities and their noble families that served particular diplomatic purposes. To the extent that the codices are historical in nature, and to the extent that I can read and understand them, they can provide a foundation for the reconstruction of an indigenous account of the events of the Classic to Postclassic transition in Mesoamerica.

SACRED HISTORY

Among the apparent functions of the historical codices was the presentation of sacred history, or history interpreted within a politico-religious structure. Some of the events that are depicted are clearly not the sort of events that have historical reality as we now understand the material world. Certainly, some passages in the documents recount entirely or partly supernatural events that are all depicted in the historical codices on an equal footing with the more mundane events of daily life. I cannot say that to the Mixtec authors of these works these events were categorically different from more readily recognizable historical occurrences. Indeed, I must conclude that they were seen as having a clear historical relevance. Today these sorts of events are described as being part of a "sacred history." I choose that term rather than "mythological history" because the word "myth" tends to connote a separation from reality, a fictional quality that calls upon us, as enlightened citizens of a modern world, to not believe. "Myth" implies a falseness rather than a transcendent reality that is supernatural in nature. "Sacred history" honors the sincere belief of its authors whether or not one chooses to accept its "historical" nature. It affirms the historical value of human perceptions of the supernatural, whatever the physical validity of these perceptions.

There are many sacred histories of origin in the literature of the Mixtec people. The living traditions of the people, the Spanish language documents of the last five centuries, and the Mixtec language documents of their earlier history (from both before and after the arrival of the Spaniards) all contain histories of the origin of the Ñuu Dzavui, the people of "The Land of the God of Rain." I will use the sacred histories of the time of origins, as recorded in the Mixtec historical codices, to better understand the dynamic changes that were occurring in the political world of the Classic to Postclassic periods.

Among the sacred histories of origin of people in Mixtec literature are two that are well-known in the Nochixtlán Valley and throughout the Mixteca Alta. One is the tree birth story of the origin of Mixtec people connected most commonly to Apoala (Jansen 1979; Reyes 1976) although sometimes also to Achiutla (Figure 10.1) and other places (Byland and Pohl 1994:111, 115). The other is the stone or earth birth story related to the creation of the Mixtec people and the stone men. This history has been tentatively connected to Jaltepec, Mitlatongo, and communities located in the southern end of the Nochixtlán Valley (Byland and Pohl 1994:116).

The codices place the sacred histories of origin at the beginning of a long historical sequence of events. Before genealogical accounts of the families of historical figures can be given, the sacred history of the origin of those families and their kingdoms is typically established. Identifying the localities involved in the sacred histories with real historical places can serve to identify specific functions of the sacred history for the actors in later political history.

The surviving Mixtec historical codices were not intended to be dispassionate histories relating the events of the past to simply preserve them. Rather, they were instruments of current political action. So, why did the Mixtec leaders of the fifteenth and sixteenth centuries have them made? I contend that the purpose of writing what were then modern political documents that appealed both to sacred history and to current political relationships was substantially about their current political effect. The codices were made, and their content was chosen, in order to effectuate the purposes of leaders in power at the time that they were written. Those leaders were purposefully making reference to the political transformations that took place during the Classic to Postclassic transition (see Chapter 4). They were defining those events as sacred history.

THE WAR OF HEAVEN: BRIDGING SACRED AND POLITICAL HISTORIES IN THE CODICES

One important bridging event between the origin stories and the documentary history is the War of Heaven, an event that is described twice in the *Codex Nuttall* and once in the *Codex Bodley* (see Caso 1960; Rabin 1979). Careful examination of the story of the War of Heaven will help us to understand the meaning of the sacred histories to the flesh-and-blood actors in the intercommunity politics of later times (Chapter 4).

The War of Heaven is a political and military conflict between tree-born people, earth- or stone-born people, sky-born people, supernatural figures, and others. The historical reality of the various participants in the war, their home places, and the events of the war have long been subject to question.

To what extent is the War of Heaven meant to portray real events in real history? These events can be placed in time with some confidence. Emily Rabin, in her masterly study of Mixtec codex chronology, puts the War of Heaven between 963 and 991 CE (see Rabin 1979; 2004:103). I believe that the locations in which the events of the war occur are also well established (Byland and Pohl 1994, but see Jansen et al. 1998 for an alternate view). Some of the characters are clearly historical figures who have descendants. Nevertheless, the absolute historicity of the War of Heaven is still insecure because some parts of the conflict and the characters involved in it appear to be supernatural rather than real. Some of the warriors are apparently supernaturals, including Lord 9 Wind Flint Helmet and Lady 9 Grass. In addition, some of the participants claim supernatural origins, as the stone men who are shown as being literally composed of earth and stone and the red-and-white-striped men who enter the battle directly from the skyband (*Nuttall* 3, 4, 20, 21).

It is necessary to examine the sacred history of birth of Mixtec people from trees and consider the implications of that origin in order to understand the later history of political conflict. I will then look at the newly recognized role of Achiutla and the character seated as ruler of that place, Lord 1 Death. He has been variously interpreted as either a solar deity or an oracular priest representing the deity. I generally favor the more human role of "oracular priest" because of the evident political consequences of his interactions with other real, historical characters. The implications of his role for political history are quite substantial. I will consider the new meanings of sacred history in the context of political history as informed by archaeological, ethnohistoric, and documentary sources. I hope that this very parochial view of the historical events surrounding the transition from the Classic to the Postclassic in a small part of the Mixteca Alta will serve to illuminate the larger questions of political dynamics during this important episode in Mesoamerican history.

THE SACRED HISTORIES OF TREE BIRTH

The birth of people from trees (*Codex Vienna* Obverse 37-b) is placed in sacred context as a culminating event in the creation of the world (Figure 10.2) (Furst 1977, 1978a, 1978b:62, 132–142). The creation story is introduced with the events of the first page of the *Codex Vienna*, *Vienna* 52, in which ritual prayer and offering bring forth the fundamental characteristics and qualities of the world (Boone 2000; Furst 1978b:55–56; Jansen 1982). Immediately after this basic creation appears a primordial couple, Lord 1 Deer and Lady 1 Deer, in the presence of four unnamed supernaturals on *Vienna* 52-b–51-a. The offerings of powdered tobacco and incense made by the primordial couple bring forth a host of other more elaborated characteristics and inhabitants of both the natural and supernatural worlds. The end of this segment of the creation story comes with the birth of Lord 9 Wind Flint Helmet from a personified flint knife (Furst 1978b:95–109). This Mixtec supernatural is iconographically similar to the Aztec deity Quetzalcoatl/Ehecatl (Nicholson 1978). He is a generative deity who reveals and establishes the physical world. In another important aspect, he is the wind deity. His birth is from a sacrificial instrument that is an element of the earth, a stone knife that is decorated with the multicolored stripes that indicate earth and with the twin bumps that are shown typically on hills or other large masses of land.

Lord 9 Wind embarks on a sacred mission to create the physical world of the Mixtec. He visits the skyband and receives the trappings of power from two unnamed supernaturals who appear to be the same as two of the four present at the creation of the primordial couple on *Vienna* 52-b. Using these power objects, he reveals or attends the creation and naming of hundreds of places in the Mixtec landscape. He is recognized across Mesoamerica as being involved in the making and naming of places (Rincón Mautner 1997:130). After the creation of the physical

10.2 Codex Vienna *Obverse 37b. Two priests are shown opening a sacred birth tree. Primordial male and female figures are being born from the center of the tree in a generative act that is beginning the population of the world. All codex drawings by Bruce E. Byland.*

world, Lord 9 Wind causes the sacred tree, at a place long presumed to be Apoala, to be cut open (Figure 10.2). Viewers are witness to the birth first of two elemental figures, one male and the other female. Then a host of other people arrives, including several who are identified elsewhere as lineage ancestors. Included in this birth sequence are figures that seem to be human but who have characteristics that are clearly not human. These are often seen as representing the qualities and characteristics of people and of supernatural characters (Boone 2000:92–94; Furst 1977, 1978b; Jansen 1979, 1982; Nowotny 1948; Rabin 2004:104–106). The tree birth appears to be a critical part of the establishment of the real world. It is fundamental to the establishment of the Mixtec people, the real Mixtec people of the historical period as well as their sacred ancestors. It is not simply a "myth" that can be separated from physical history but "sacred history" that is integral to the Mixtec understanding of physical history.

Most accounts of the sacred history of creation would then separate the sacred history from the historical accounts that follow. I find it illuminating to look for the connection between this time of sacred creation and the actual political conflicts and machinations of the period of historical time.

Two other examples of the sacred birth of people from trees that are found on *Codex Selden* 2-I and *Codex Bodley* 1-V can help in that effort (Figure 10.3). In each of these two instances, the birth of an ancestral figure is shown as happening at a place of tree birth marked by a flame. On *Selden* 2-I (Figure 10.3a) the tree from which Lord 2 Grass Skull Headdress is born is shown growing from a multicolored frieze marked by a red oval with three fingers of flame rising from it. Lord 2 Grass is a progenitor of the Jaltepec royal lineage. On *Bodley* 1-V (Figure 10.3b), the birth of Lady 1 Death Solar Shield, Feather Fan, is shown from a tree upon which rests a red oval with three fingers of flame rising from it. She is the progenitor of the first dynasty of Tilantongo. The Flame Place is identified as San Miguel Achiutla, and I believe, consequently, that each of these tree births is intended to be placed at the town of Achiutla. It is Achiutla, rather than Apoala, that is the source of the tree-born lineages that rule at Tilantongo and Jaltepec.

A fourth example of a tree birth is found on *Codex Nuttall* 9-II in the aftermath of a conflict that occurred at Jaltepec a short while before (Figure 10.4). In this scene an unnamed person is emerging from a tree identified with a sun disc. The solar disc is also a marker for Achiutla, and so this tree is at Achiutla as well, the place of birth of Lady 1 Death Solar Shield, Feather Fan, and the site of the Solar Oracle, Lord 1 Death. It is an important Mixtec place (Pérez Rodríguez 2001). The figure born from the tree is wearing red body paint, similar to that worn by the lords of Zaachila (Byland and Pohl 1994:167; Jansen 1998). Immediately below, a child named Lord 3 Reed, wearing gray body paint, is presented to an adult figure wearing the same red paint as the figure born from the Achiutla tree. He is seated in a temple that I believe to be at Zaachila in the Valley of Oaxaca, an important Zapotec center. The temple is identified as on a bent hill that bears a green crested bird and is beside a rain deity jewel. Those identifiers are remarkably similar to the well-known place sign of Zaachila on *Nuttall* 33, which is composed of a temple with a Xipe priest wearing red body paint and a rain deity mask. That temple is placed on a bent hill and a river containing a green crested bird. It is interesting to speculate that the figure seated at the new Postclassic center of Zaachila may have been the product of a sacred birth that occurred at Achiutla in the Mixteca Alta, a community

a

b

10.3 (a) Codex Selden *2-I and (b)* Codex Bodley *1-V. Two more examples of tree birth. In the more elaborate* Codex Selden *scene, Lord 2 Grass is being born from the center of a sacred tree that is growing from the flame frieze place of Achiutla. Note that Achiutla and its sacred tree are shown in a river. The simpler image from* Codex Bodley *shows Lady 1 Death Solar Shield, Feathered Fan being born from a sacred tree with the same flame marking. These two sacred births start two great lineages that rule at Mixtec kingdoms for generations afterward.*

10.4 Nuttall *9-II. This scene shows the birth of a figure in red body paint from the center of a sacred tree that is identified not by a flame but by a solar disc, another signifier of Achiutla. This tree grows in a river. Below the tree birth scene, a child named 3 Reed is presented to a priest wearing red body paint who sits in a temple on a hill that is identified as the Zapotec center of Zaachila, a kingdom in the Valley of Oaxaca. The name of a Mixtec lord, Lord 5 Deer Warband Arrow, surrounds the scene.*

with Classic roots that endured into the Postclassic period (Chapter 1).

Zaachila was clearly a site of great secular and sacred authority in Postclassic Valley of Oaxaca society (Appel 1982:62–65; Burgoa 1934; Jansen 1998). It is also noteworthy that an unusual ancestral statement is made with the presentation of young Lord 3 Reed at the temple of Zaachila. The name of one of the lords who makes offerings to the family of Lord 8 Wind, the powerful ruler of Suchixtlán, is placed on either side of the Zaachila temple. Lord 5 Deer Warband Arrow is positioned either as a follower making an offering to or as a child of the mighty Lord 8 Wind (see *Nuttall* 6-III). The presence of his name in this context emphasizes the Mixtec identity of the boy, Lord 3 Reed, at the Zapotec temple. It seems then that two places that were important ethnically distinct centers in the years of the transition from the Classic to the Postclassic are referred to in this brief passage. One, Achiutla, is Mixtec and the other, Zaachila, is Zapotec.

Two scenes in the *Nuttall* illustrate a meeting in which a Solar Deity settles a dispute between two conflicting lords (*Nuttall* 10-I and 78-II, III; Figure 10.5). This unspecified dispute, and its resolution through the intervention of the Solar Deity, is placed in the context of the Mixtec tree birth at Achiutla, the Zapotec temple at Zaachila and the heritage of Lord 3 Reed in relation to the very influential ruler of Suchixtlán. This foreshadows events to come.

a

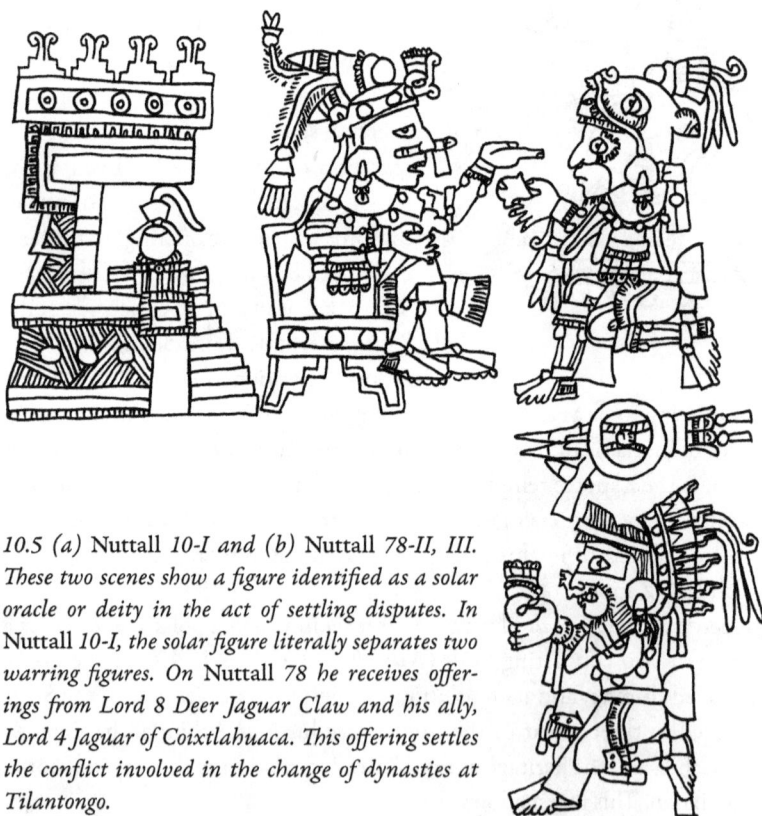

b

10.5 (a) Nuttall *10-I and (b)* Nuttall *78-II, III. These two scenes show a figure identified as a solar oracle or deity in the act of settling disputes. In* Nuttall *10-I, the solar figure literally separates two warring figures. On* Nuttall *78 he receives offerings from Lord 8 Deer Jaguar Claw and his ally, Lord 4 Jaguar of Coixtlahuaca. This offering settles the conflict involved in the change of dynasties at Tilantongo.*

ALLIANCES WITH ACHIUTLA

Achiutla had two important roles in the supernatural world of the Mixteca. Each of these two roles has profound political effects in the very real political reorganization that occurred in the Mixteca Alta at the time of the Classic to Postclassic transition.

First, it was the seat of an oracular shrine presided by a powerful priest, Lord 1 Death, who was an impersonator of the Solar Deity, also named Lord 1 Death (Caso 1979, 2:143). Achiutla functioned as a preeminent sacred and political center of the Mixteca (Dahlgren 1979:263–264, 266–268). This priest had both sacred authority and secular power. His authority was such that it seems to have been equal to or, at times, greater than that of ordinary rulers. Indeed, his imprimatur was sought by Mixtec royalty at times of dynastic change even at the time of the Spanish Conquest (Burgoa 1934, 1:276) and, according to the codices, during the transition between the Classic and Postclassic when he settled disputes between other authorities (Figure 10.5).

Second, Achiutla was also the home of the sacred ancestor, Lady 1 Death, who was born from a sacred tree. Lady 1 Death was one of the key ancestors of the first dynasty that ruled at Tilantongo. Although she exhibits supernatural qualities (her parent was, after all, a tree), she acts like a normal human. She marries and has at least one daughter, Lady 1 Vulture, and a granddaughter, Lady 5 Reed, who, with Lord 9 Wind Stone Skull, founded the first dynasty of Tilantongo in 990 CE. She served as a sacred ancestor of the Tilantongo line, linking that line directly to the supernatural. Achiutla, like Apoala, is a place of sacred birth.

The marriages of Lady 1 Death's descendants reveal the growing political influence of Achiutla on other communities (Figure 10.6). She marries Lord 4 Crocodile Eagle Drinking Blood, who is from a place identified by a rain deity and a walled enclosure (*Bodley* 1-IV, III; *Vienna* Reverse 1-I; see Caso 1979, 2:145–146). Such royal marriages are usually interpreted as alliance-building efforts (Spores 1974b). I believe the Rain Deity / Enclosure place to be the site known as Yucu Yuhua, or Hill of the Enclosure, a site located on the same ridgeline as Hill of the Wasp, also known as Mountain that Opens / Bee (Byland and Pohl 1994:98–100; Caso 1960:28, 1979, 2:145). On *Nuttall* 19 this site is shown as a walled enclosure associated with a temple that bears a distinctive Rain Deity tripod vessel. It is suggestive that a Lady 1 Death is shown at Hill of the Enclosure on *Nuttall* 19, although she is not given a personal name here and therefore cannot be positively associated with the Lady 1 Death Solar Shield from Achiutla. It is possible that the reference here is not to the specific individual but rather to a position that carries that title. The reciprocal references to both members of the couple and a place with two identifying images make a strong case for its identity. Her presence also emphasizes the role of Achiutla in the alliance between the adjacent sites of Wasp and Enclosure and

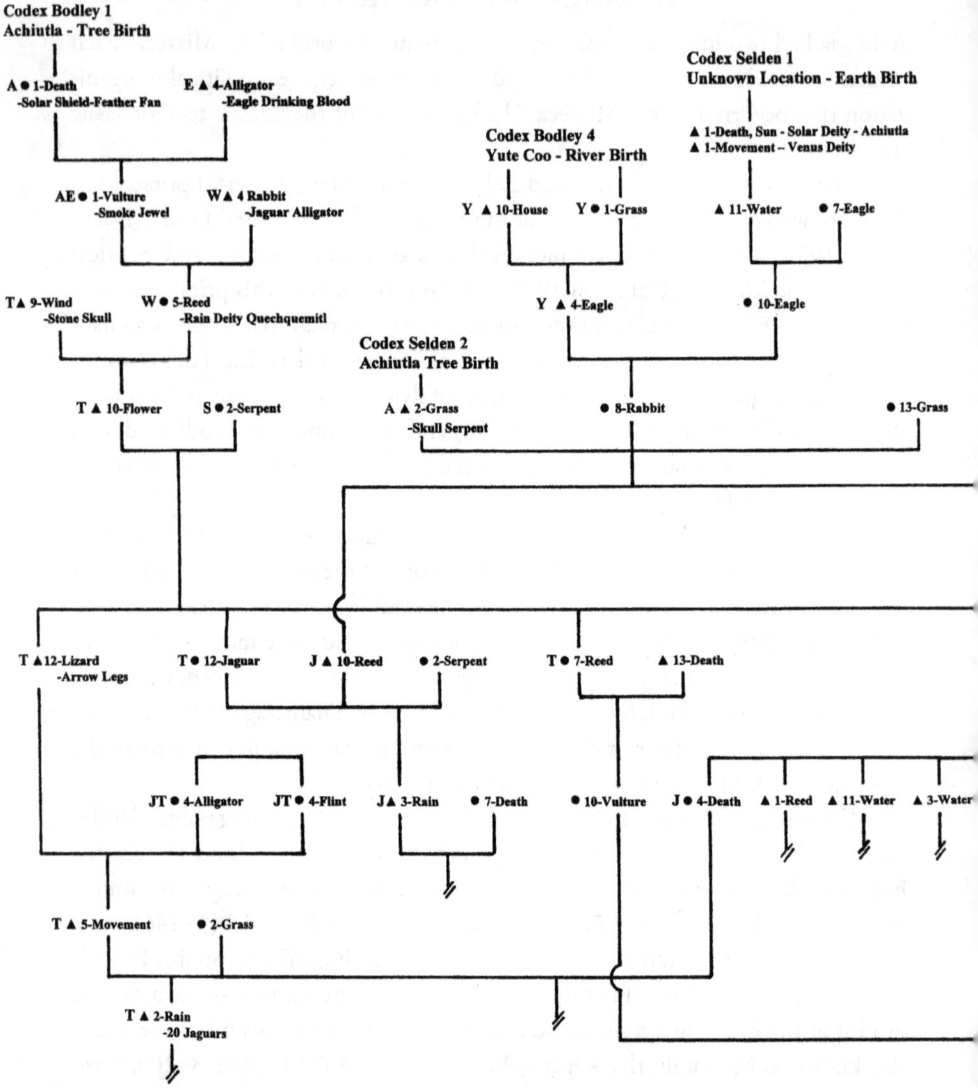

10.6 Genealogy of families descended from two Sacred Tree births at Achiutla and the family of Lord 8 Deer. The communities associated with each individual on the diagram are indicated with bold-faced letters before their names. The calendric and personal names of the people are given next. Only essential individuals are included.

the site of Achiutla. The royal marriages recorded in the codices allow us to make inferences about the processes of political integration of communities in this portion of the Mixteca Alta.

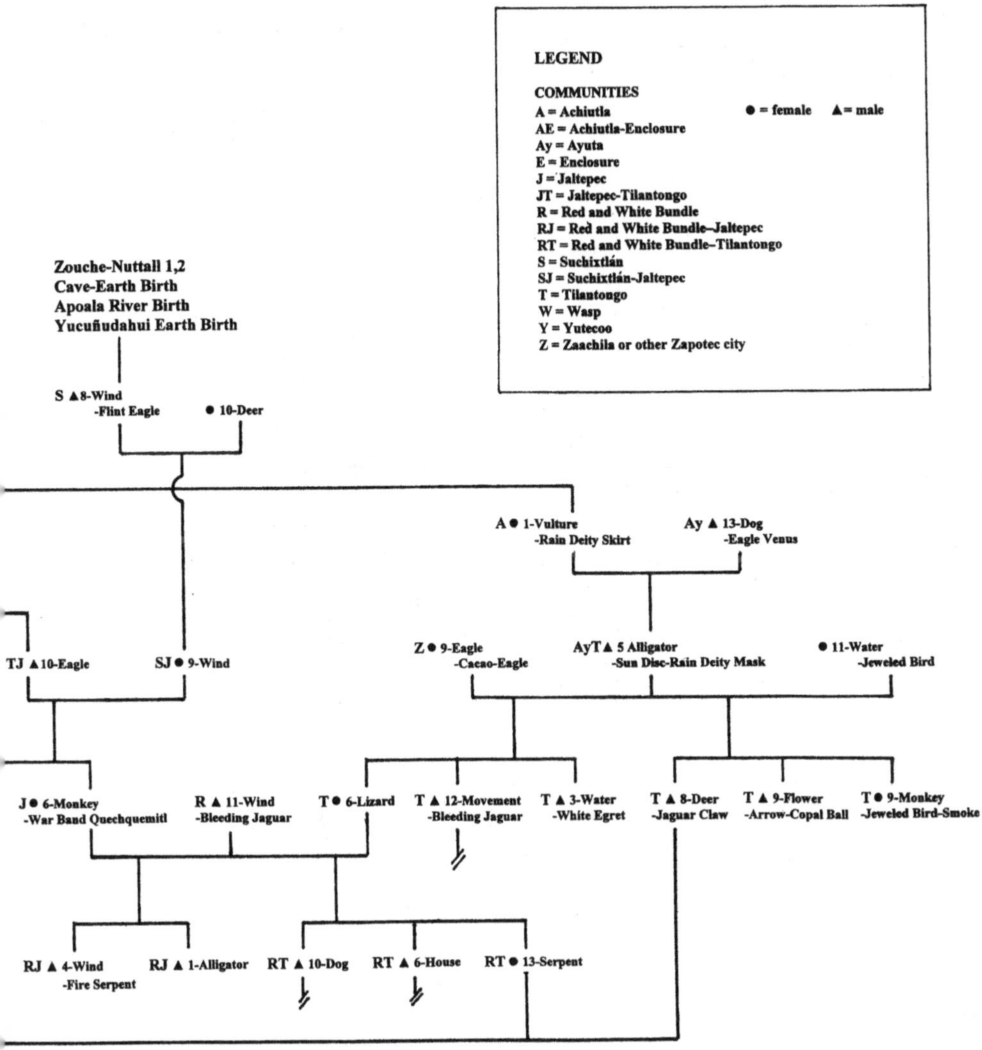

The first child born to the union of Achiutla's Lady 1 Death and Lord 4 Crocodile is Lady 1 Vulture. She marries Lord 4 Rabbit, who is from Hill of the Wasp (*Bodley* 3-I; Byland and Pohl 1994:94–98; Caso 1979, 2). This marriage completes two generations of alliance building between Achiutla and the communities surrounding Hill of the Wasp, but the interweaving of their histories does not stop there. The intermarriage between Achiutla and other sites can be viewed as establishing or cementing political alliances in which members of less important lineages become associated with a place regarded as having supernatural sanction or imprimatur. Such an association could bolster the claims to the throne by lineages from other communities (see Chapter 9 for other tactics).

There were four daughters born to the marriage of Lady 1 Vulture of Achiutla to Lord 4 Rabbit of Hill of the Wasp. Their names are Lady 5 Reed, Lady 10 Crocodile, Lady 4 Jaguar, and Lady 5 Jaguar. Lady 10 Crocodile marries a Lord 9 Deer who comes from the site of Red and White Bundle, a town that, through this marriage, reaches into the alliance structure developing between the Wasp ridge system and the oracular site of Achiutla (*Bodley* 4-I). This site has been identified as the site of Huachino, located in the valley of Jaltepec just east of Hill of the Wasp (Byland and Pohl 1994:66–73). The archaeological Huachino is notable for its extensive Classic period ceramic and architectural connections with the Zapotec communities of the Valley of Oaxaca (Byland and Pohl 1994:56–60). Lady 5 Jaguar also marries a lord from Red and White Bundle (*Bodley* 4-I, II). These marriages are placed in the narrative before the beginning of the War of Heaven.

The next marriage pair shown in *Codex Bodley* is between Lord 12 Lizard and Lady 12 Vulture (*Bodley* 3, 4-II). He is shown as coming from Valley that Is Opened / Hill of the Wasp and she is from Achiutla, Hill of the Sun. Their parents are not clearly indicated although they clearly represent the continuation of the alliance system between these two important sites. That they should be contemporaries of Lady 1 Vulture and Lord 4 Rabbit is evident because they have sons who die in the War of Heaven. Lady 12 Vulture could even be a sister of Lady 1 Vulture. I note that she is shown holding the personal name symbol of Lady 1 Death, the solar shield and fan in what may be an unusual parentage statement. In any case, their marriage reinforces the notion of a strong alliance between the centers on the Wasp ridge and Achiutla.

THE WAR OF HEAVEN

The War of Heaven represents the acts, real and metaphorical, that signaled the beginning of the transition between Classic modes and Postclassic modes of political and social organization (Byland and Pohl 1994:109–114). The Classic period, or Las Flores phase in the Mixteca Alta, saw the preeminence of a variety of important centers in the Nochixtlán Valley, including Jaltepec, Cerro Jasmín, Yucuñudahui, Huachino, and others. Other centers existed in various parts of the Mixteca Alta: Huamelulpan, Achiutla, Teposcolula, and Tlaxiaco among them (see Balkansky et al. 2000). The Postclassic Natividad phase saw the decline of many of these communities; the expansion of a few of them, including Jaltepec and Teposcolula; and the rise of some new centers, including Tilantongo and Yanhuitlán (Byland and Pohl 1994:56–64; Spores 1972). I recognize the absence of well-dated stratigraphic material from this period of transition in the Mixteca Alta and the limitations that are thus imposed on interpretation of the archaeological record. The Las Flores phase in the Mixteca is often considered to run from about 200 until 1000 or 1100 CE. Those termination dates put the end of the Classic period in the Mixteca Alta somewhat after the pan-Mesoamerican perception of the end of the Classic, a transition positioned variously between 750 and 900 CE.

The events related to the resolution of the War of Heaven, a conflict of epic proportions that took place from 963 to 979 CE, are related in the codices in three passages, twice in the *Codex Nuttall* (*Nuttall* 3–5, 21–22) and once in *Codex Bodley* (*Bodley* 3–4). The second presentation of the war in *Nuttall* is focused on events and participants connected to the southern part of the Nochixtlán Valley and to the town of Tilantongo. The last battle shown in this version of the war takes place at the White Hill of Flints (*Nuttall* 21-I) (Byland and Pohl 1994:92, plate 2).

The resolution of the conflict occupies the next page and a half. The process of resolution begins with the protagonist, Lord 12 Wind Smoking Eye, visiting a temple located on top of a hill identified by an elaborate solar disc (*Nuttall* 21-II; Figure 10.7). Standing on the hill are Lord 4 Crocodile Eagle Drinking Blood and Lady 1 Death Solar Shield, Feather Fan, the founding male and female ancestors of Achiutla. In a courtyard in front of the temple, Lord 4 Crocodile Eagle Drinking Blood again stands before a sacred bundle and fire-making apparatus in the temple. Because of these associations, it is clear that this Hill of the Sun with its temple is indeed the community of Achiutla. Lord 12 Wind is carrying the burden of the community to the temple, an action that signifies the establishment of a new community authority (see Pohl 1984 for discussion) and the resolution of the War of Heaven through the founding of the town of Tilantongo.

A key aspect of this scene is the fact that the name of Lord 9 Wind is placed in the roof of this temple that is so clearly located at Achiutla (Figure 10.7). Lord 9 Wind Flint Helmet is the ancestral deity of Tilantongo and is also the Mixtec wind deity who is conceptually related to the Nahuatl deity Quetzalcoatl/Ehecatl. Why is a Tilantongo figure located at Achiutla? Why is the wind deity located at a temple dedicated to the Solar Deity, Lord 1 Death? I suggest that this supernatural association has to do with the importance of the political and genealogical alliance between these two important centers, with the resolution of the genealogical conflict embodied by the War of Heaven. Consequently, this scene depicts a pivotal point in the transition from the Classic political regime to the new, repositioned Postclassic regime.

The connection between Achiutla and Tilantongo is solidified on the next page, where Lord 12 Wind Smoking Eye and two companions carry sacred symbols of power from Achiutla on page 21 to the famous full-page hill sign that depicts several places in the Tilantongo Valley on page 22 (Pohl and Byland 1990).

10.7 Nuttall *21-II. This scene shows the beginning of the end of the War of Heaven at Achiutla. The Hill of Achiutla is indicated by the large solar shield at its summit and the presence of its two founding ancestors, Lady 1 Death and Lord 4 Crocodile Eagle Drinking Blood. Atop the hill is a temple with Lord 9 Wind's name in its roof. It is attended by Lord 4 Crocodile Eagle Drinking Blood and is being approached by Lord 12 Wind Smoke Eye who is carrying the burden of community on his way to Tilantongo.*

I contend that the resolution of the War of Heaven involved a transfer of the authority that had formerly resided at Mountain that Is Opened / Hill of the Wasp to the community of Tilantongo. The War of Heaven ended with the deaths of the last two important figures from Mountain that Is Opened /Hill of the Wasp, Lord 12 Lizard and Lady 12 Vulture, and their children. This important relocation of symbols of authority, and indeed of the authority itself, could only be accomplished with the aid of the ancestral site, the solar oracle from the place of the miraculous birth of the lineages, the site of Achiutla. Indeed, in the aftermath of the War of Heaven, eleven years after the last battle, the firstborn daughter from Mountain that is Opened / Hill of the Wasp, Lady 5 Reed, was married to the founding ancestor of the royal lineage at Tilantongo, Lord 9 Wind Stone Skull (*Bodley* 4-V). This cementing of the alliance through royal marriage is the culmination of the transfer of power and authority formerly associated with Hill of the Wasp / Mountain that Is Opened, and Hill of the Enclosure to the new lineage seated at Tilantongo and is also a key element in the transition from a Classic period organizational structure to a Postclassic one.

In terms of the Classic to Postclassic transition, these events mark the beginning of the change in the Mixteca Alta. Access to indigenous documentary records allows us to understand this transformation and to see into these processes with far greater clarity than has ever been the case before. Classic centers, both large and small, that rose in earlier parts of the Las Flores phase remained stable and locally powerful throughout that long period. The mutual dependence and involvement between Achiutla and Mountain that Is Opened / Hill of the Wasp in this politically and religiously charged environment is apparent in the documentary record and their physical stability is clear in the archaeological record. The alliance is long-term and is intricately established. It is affirmed and reaffirmed through multiple marriages between figures from each of the communities. The War of Heaven, between 963 and 979 CE, marks the end of stability and the beginning of a period of unrest and change that would last until the time of Lord 8 Deer's (born in 1063 CE) assault on Red and White Bundle, the site of Huachino, in 1101 CE. The dramatic events of the War of Heaven, and the important efforts to resolve the conflict and animosity that attended these events, seem now to involve the relationship between two small sacred and political authorities in the Mixteca Alta, the communities of Achiutla and Mountain that Is Opened / Hill of the Wasp.

Achiutla had a long established alliance with the early center of Mountain that Is Opened / Hill of the Wasp, cemented by multiple generations of intermarriages and redundant, contemporaneous marital connections at key moments in history. Lord 8 Deer's family came from a town located near Achiutla and apparently dependent on, or allied to, Tilantongo. Hill of the Wasp had set the War of Heaven into motion by beginning a program of marital alliances with a community that had not been part of the earlier alliance scheme, the site of Red and White Bundle (Huachino), the community that Caso had called "Xipe Bundle" (Caso 1960). This was a political miscalculation of extraordinary proportions. To the extent that Red and White Bundle was allied to the nascent power of the emerging Zapotec state at Zaachilla, it was dependent on a distant and not overly strong ally. They were up against the rising power of Tilantongo and its powerful ally, the oracular site of sacred origins, the site of Achiutla. The end of the War of Heaven saw the dismantling of the ruling lineage of Mountain that Is Opened / Hill of the Wasp and the movement of both alliance and authority to the new lineage of Tilantongo, its first recorded dynasty. It is important to note here that though Hill of the Wasp / Mountain that Is Opened, and Place of the Enclosure were defeated and destroyed in this conflict, the site of Red and White Bundle was not. It continued to thrive and had a legitimate connection to the royal bloodline of Hill of the Wasp / Mountain that Is Opened, and Place of the Enclosure, and, through them, to Achiutla.

LORD 8 DEER'S FAMILY

The first dynasty of Tilantongo endured for barely a century. It was established as a result of conflict within a Classic period political alliance system, conflict that exposed weakness in the system and led the way to the emergence of a new Postclassic organization (see Chapters 5 and 7 for perspectives from other parts of Oaxaca). Achiutla stepped in when an outside force, the site of Red and White Bundle with its relationship to external Zapotec influences, intervened in the established network of alliances between Mixtec kingdoms. Tilantongo was founded to reestablish the Mixtec alliance system and to reestablish the orderly system that had prevailed.

The first dynasty ended with the death of Lord 2 Rain Twenty Jaguars, the last male heir of the founder, Lord 9 Wind Stone Skull, in 1096 CE. The rise of the second dynasty—with the seating of Lord 8 Deer, in 1097 CE, and his defeat of Red and White Bundle in 1101 CE—marked the end of the great transitional period in this part of the Mixteca Alta. This may correspond with the transition from the Early Postclassic to the Late Postclassic.

The genealogies of the ruling families of these Mixtec communities and of Lord 8 Deer's family, all the way back to the sacred births from trees, are key to understanding the historical dynamics that were taking place (see Figure 10.6). The ability to understand the transition that occurred rests on the genealogical relationships of the various actors. If we can recognize why some individuals had key roles and others did not, we may be able to better understand the deeper political significance of the events depicted in the codices. Why, for example, did 8 Deer's older half brother, Lord 12 Movement Bleeding Jaguar, not assume the position of new leader at Tilantongo when the first dynasty ended? Why was Lord 8 Deer the one who stepped up instead? Finally, these genealogies will help us to establish the historical foundation for the role of Achiutla as the oracle chosen to legitimize the local changes that marked a great reorganization of power and authority in this part of Mesoamerica.

Lord 13 Dog, the grandfather of Lord 8 Deer Jaguar Claw, was seated at Ayuta (the modern community of Atoyaquillo), a small community across the river from Achiutla, and dependent on it, but connected also to Tilantongo (Pohl 1984:202–

10.8 Bodley *6-I. Lord 13 Dog and Lady 1 Vulture, the grandparents of Lord 8 Deer Jaguar Claw, are seated at Ayuta (Atoyaquillo), suggesting that they are rulers of that place. The birth of their son, Lord 5 Crocodile, at that place directly connects his son, Lord 8 Deer, to the realm of Achiutla and thus establishes a tie to its lineage of tree-born people. This scene establishes Lord 8 Deer's genealogical connection to the Achiutla realm.*

203; see Figure 10.8). There he married a Lady 1 Vulture and she gave birth to Lord 5 Crocodile Sun Disc, Rain Deity Mask (*Bodley* 6-I). This sun disc, interpreted widely as being part of his personal name and by us also as an heirloom insignia, is an apparent reference to his Achiutla origin. The date of his birth is not given, and the date following his birth is damaged in the codex, although it probably corresponds to the Year 13 House Day 10 Flower, or 1025 CE. On that date begins an elaborate ceremony in which Lord 5 Crocodile receives instruction from his parents and from a variety of other individuals. This ceremony prepares him to leave his home and take up a new office in the town of Tilantongo.

Lord 5 Crocodile visits the River of the Serpent, Yute Coo, the place of origin for the first lord of the initial dynasty of Tilantongo, the famous Lord 9 Wind Stone Skull (*Bodley* 4-V). It is also the place at which Lord 2 Rain Twenty Jaguars will rise up to the heavens after his apparent demise, ending the first dynasty of Tilantongo in 1096 CE, some seventy-one years later (*Bodley* 5, 6-I). The visit by Lord 5 Crocodile to Yute Coo is therefore fraught with significance as a reference to the past and a portent of the future. Immediately after that visit he offers tobacco before two figures, one holding a flaming torch and the other blowing a conch-shell trumpet, a traditional Mixtec call to the community. The ceremonial cycle ends with his burning incense at what I believe to be the Temple of Heaven at Tilantongo (*Bodley* 8-II). This identification would put his obeisance at the River of the Serpent into context as an act honoring the ancestors of the community that he is now being dedicated to serve.

Next, in a series of events that occur in the years 6 Reed (1031 CE), 10 Reed (1035 CE), 12 House (1037 CE), and 1 Reed (1039 CE), he participates in four ceremonies (*Bodley* 7-II, III; *Nuttall* 25-III), each involving two sacrificial knives, a red *xicolli* (shirt), and other items. I believe that these mark his ascension through the council of four priests responsible for the mummy bundles of the rulers of

Tilantongo and, ultimately, his accession as leader of the council (Byland and Pohl 1994:132–134; Pohl 1984; Rabin 2004:114). He had received that title no later than the year 1 Reed, or 1039 CE (*Nuttall* 25-III). In a final bloodletting ceremony in the year 5 Reed (1043 CE), Lord 5 Crocodile becomes free to marry and start a family (*Nuttall* 25-III, 26-I). This ceremony may have marked his retirement from the priestly role; after this date his genealogical position is mentioned and his priestly role is not. He promptly married Lady 9 Eagle (*Nuttall* 26-I, 42-I; *Bodley* 7-III), and she gave birth to his first son, Lord 12 Movement Bleeding Jaguar, in the year 7 House, 1045 CE.

Lord 5 Crocodile had been associated by birth with Ayuta (Atoyaquillo), a central dependency of Achiutla. He was later connected to Tilantongo through a ceremonial cycle that began in the year 1025 CE. He ascended through the priestly ranks while serving there, married twice, and had a variety of offspring. He died a peaceful death in 1082 CE (*Vienna* Reverse 7-I). I do not know who was the leader of the council of four bundle priests at Tilantongo after Lord 5 Crocodile started his family in 1043 CE, nor is the identity of the chief bundle priest between 1082 and 1096 CE clear, when the first Tilantongo dynasty ended.

THE RISE OF 8 DEER

When Lord 2 Rain died in the year 6 Flint (1096 CE), at the age of twenty-one, his connection to the original sacred tree birth at Achiutla was distant indeed. Lord 2 Rain's great grandfather's mother was the granddaughter of Lady 1 Death, who had been miraculously born from the tree at Achiutla. That is a span of seven generations back to the miraculous origin of the lineage. When Lord 2 Rain died and the dynasty came to an end, Lord 8 Deer claimed the right to rule at Tilantongo and began a struggle to secure his position that would take five years to complete. To take control Lord 8 Deer had to return from his mission to Tututepec and insert himself into the conflict in the Mixteca Alta.

To understand why Lord 8 Deer was the one who became head of his lineage and his older half brother, Lord 12 Movement, was passed over for this position, we must look at their respective family trees. Lord 8 Deer and Lord 12 Movement had the same father, but they had different mothers. Their suitability for particular roles was affected by both sides of their ancestry. Lady 9 Eagle, the mother of Lord 12 Movement, seems to be of Zapotec ancestry or affiliation. She is shown in *Nuttall* 42-II with face paint related to Xipe Totec, a Zapotec deity. She shares that face paint with the rulers of Zaachila elsewhere in *Codex Nuttall* (33-III, 34-II, 35-II, III, IV). Lord 12 Movement and his sister, Lady 6 Lizard, were therefore related by descent to the foreign allies of Red and White Bundle. That meant that they had an ancestral allegiance to the losing side in the War of Heaven. They were on the losing side of the historic conflict between Achiutla, Suchixtlán, and Tilantongo on the one hand and the ruling lines of Hill of the Wasp and Red and White Bundle on the other. From the perspective of the codices, the legitimate authority of the dynasty at Hill of the Wasp had been transferred to Tilantongo with the marriage of Lady 5 Reed to Lord 9 Wind Stone Skull at the beginning of the first dynasty. Despite competing claims to that legitimacy on the part of Red and White Bundle through its marriages to Lady 5 Reed's sisters, the Tilantongo point of view would have been that they alone were legitimate heirs to the alliance. Lord 12 Movement's ancestry, and the fact that his sister, Lady 6 Lizard, was married to the ruler of Red and White Bundle, Lord 11 Wind, would have been problematic at best and could have made his allegiance to the ancient alliance suspect.

Lord 8 Deer's claim to power in Tilantongo was stronger, but it too was certainly questionable. Despite Caso's belief that Lord 8 Deer was related to the first royal lineage at Tilantongo, he was not a member of that line (Rabin 2004:112). Rather he was a son of the former leader of the council of four bundle priests of Tilantongo and Lady 11 Water, a Mixtec noblewoman, and was descended from a noble, or principal, line connected to Achiutla. We do know that he sought outside help to establish his claim by making an alliance with Lord 4 Jaguar, a great warrior and lineage head from the Coixtlahuaca Basin (Byland and Pohl 1994:138–150; Rincón Mautner 1997, 1999, 2000). Together, they participated in a number of military conquests. At the end of these joint campaigns he was conferred a nose ornament by Lord 4 Jaguar in a traditional, yet distinct, Tolteca-Chichimeca ceremony that was performed to raise warriors to the rank of lords, or *tecuhtli*. This happened in the year 7 House, or 1097 CE, at a Place of Reeds (see Chapters 1, 3, and 9 for discussions of "Tollan").

It has been possible to corroborate that the Lord 4 Jaguar who appears on a series of Coixtlahuaca-area maps lived at the same time as Lord 8 Deer. Lord 4 Jaguar, like Lord 8 Deer, was actively pursuing the establishment of his lineage and the political integration of settlements in the neighboring Coixtlahuaca Basin (Rincón Mautner 1997:139–142; 1999:332–334; 2000:39–41). The specific identity of the Place of Reeds is uncertain (Chapters 1 and 9). I believe it to have been in the Coixtlahuaca realm, but others have argued that it was at the more distant site of the Toltec capital at Cholula (Chapter 3; Jansen 1996).

Lord 8 Deer subsequently conquered a few places and ultimately, seated with his half brother, Lord 12 Movement Bleeding Jaguar, received 112 lords (*Nuttall* 54–68). In a strictly political world this would seem to have established his legitimate right to rule. In the next year or two Lord 8 Deer asserted his political power by visiting and conquering a series of places. Somehow, however, all this was not enough to completely legitimize his position. Consequently, in 1099 CE he began a sacred journey to Achiutla to visit the Solar Oracle/Deity, Lord 1 Death (*Nuttall*

75–80). This journey is rich with supernatural elements as well as seemingly mundane events. It was concluded with a successful visit to Lord 1 Death in the year 10 Flint (1100 CE), four long and contentious years after the failure of the first dynasty of Tilantongo.

Why did Lord 8 Deer seek the approval of the Solar Oracle/Deity from Achiutla at this point? It would seem that his right to rule was already well-established by conquest, yet he embarked on a perilous journey to meet Lord 1 Death. It now seems that Lord 8 Deer and his external ally, Lord 4 Jaguar of Coixtlahuaca, were appealing to an ancestral Mixtec authority to validate their alliance and Lord 8 Deer's new position. With secular power in their hands, why was this additional sanction necessary? Not until the sacred journey was accomplished could they assert an undeniable claim. The sacred history of tree birth that originated at Achiutla was linked to the establishment of the royal lineage at Tilantongo. It was also tied, through the place sign of Lord 8 Deer's grandfather and father, to the lineage of Lord 8 Deer. Furthermore, the sacred and secular authority at Achiutla had a long-standing connection with the secular and religious center of Zaachila. Much like the role ascribed to the high priest at Mitla over the Zapotec kings of the Valley of Oaxaca (Pohl 1994a:75), the authorities at Achiutla and Zaachila appear to have served as mediators of disputes between Mixtec communities and Zapotec ones, respectively, and to have mediated interaction between these two linguistic and ethnic groups. When Tilantongo's first dynastic line failed, it experienced a crisis of leadership and of legitimacy. The alliance with Achiutla could not prevent the death of the heir to the throne.

The traditional anthropological view of politics (Fried 1967) suggests that the capacity to take power and the fact of having seized it should be sufficient to define an absolute shift in power. An essentially political change can be accomplished simply through the application of power in political relations. What I have found in this archaeological and ethnohistoric study of the reorganization of power during the transition from the Classic to the Postclassic in the Mixteca Alta is that the actors in this political drama are not simply the wielders of secular power. They are also part of a cultural tradition that is bound up in a sacred history that requires supernatural support for political action. No matter how much political power 8 Deer had, and was able to wield in the years following his usurpation of the throne in Tilantongo, he could not finish the job, establish his legitimacy, and impose a final settlement to this episode of unrest in the region without binding himself to the sacred history of creation and the foundation of lineage in the Mixteca Alta.

Lord 8 Deer was able to take up the reins and assert control of Tilantongo for at least three reasons. First, he had the experience necessary for the task and the personal qualities of character required to carry the mission through to success. I find that he had these qualities because the codices relate that he had acquired military experience as a young man while he was living in Tututepec. When he traveled to Tututepec as a twenty year old in 1083 CE, he was apparently a member of a group of four exchange and sacrifice priests from Tilantongo (Byland and Pohl 1994:85–90; Jansen and Winter 1980; Pohl 1994a:43–47; Smith 1973:60–64). These priests were known as Yaha-Yahui, or Eagle-Fire Serpent, priests. Lord 8 Deer was wearing part of the costume of this priestly order at the famous meeting with Lady 9 Grass at Chalcatongo (*Nuttall* 44-I–III). He went to Tututepec on the Oaxaca Coast as a Yaha-Yahui priest and, while there, engaged in extensive military conquest. *Codex Nuttall* (44–50) lists some twenty-five places that he conquered while stationed at Tututepec, as well as five that he conquered before he left Tilantongo in 1083 CE. When he returned to Tilantongo in 1097 CE he was dressed as a senior Yaha-Yahui priest, was a seasoned warrior, and was apparently dedicated to the establishment of a new dynasty in Tilantongo.

Second, he appears to have formed a new alliance with a strong outside force, Lord 4 Jaguar of Coixtlahuaca (see Byland and Pohl 1994:138–151). Lord 8 Deer returned from Tututepec to Tilantongo in 1097 CE, the year after the death of Lord 2 Rain Twenty Jaguars, the presumed heir to the throne (see Rabin 2004:112 for an interesting alternative possibility). Upon his return, he immediately sought to establish a foundation of legitimacy to allow him to assume the role of ruler. Part of that effort was a prompt attempt to create an alliance with the powerful lord of Coixtlahuaca, Lord 4 Jaguar. Once that alliance was cemented by the nose ornament ceremony that elevated Lord 8 Deer to the rank of tecuhtli, Lord 8 Deer and his brother were able to receive the 112 lords.

Third, he was descended from a principal line originally seated at Achiutla's dependency of Ayuta. Because his father had been sent to Tilantongo from a community that belonged to Achiutla, Lord 8 Deer was closely allied to that complex source of sacred authority. Indeed, his connection to the place of sacred tree birth and the home of the solar oracle was much more immediate than that of Lord 2 Rain. He was only one generation removed from Achiutla and, thus, he could claim legitimate standing to seek the support of the sacred and secular leadership at Achiutla, the sacred place of origins and the home of the politically potent solar oracle, for his new position as ruler of Tilantongo.

DEATH OF LORD 12 MOVEMENT

It was in the year 10 Flint (1100 CE), following Lord 8 Deer's journey to see Lord 1 Death at Achiutla and his final establishment of control in Tilantongo, that his half brother, Lord 12 Movement, was assassinated in a steam bath near the place of Red and White Bundle (*Nuttall* 81; Byland and Pohl 1994:70). His death has been puzzling because the identity of his murderer is not given and the motive for his killing is not clear. Alternative explanations have been proposed (Anders et al. 1992a:241; Rabin 2004:115–116; Troike 1974). One possibility is that he was killed by someone from Red and White Bundle. That would explain why Lord 8 Deer attacked Red and White Bundle the following year and then proceeded to sacrifice its ruler, his second wife, and his own two half nephews. Another possibility is that Lord 8 Deer was behind his own half brother's death. Lord 8 Deer may have mistrusted his half brother because of his affiliations with the community of Red and White Bundle. This position could be explained by the alliance situation discussed here. Lord 8 Deer could not have been comfortable as ruler with an ally of his enemy sitting at his side. If Lord 12 Movement supported his sister and her husband, he could not have offered undivided support to his half brother. In that case Lord 8 Deer might have ruthlessly caused his half brother's death to simplify the political stance of his own house. Other theories of the crime are certainly possible. I cannot determine who killed Lord 12 Movement or why. I know only that Lord 8 Deer's effort to end the heritage of alliance between Tilantongo and Red and White Bundle was successful. He was able, through his military prowess, strategic alliances, and supernatural support, to end the alliance, assume the power, and reorganize government in the Mixteca Alta, thus marking the completion of the transition between the Classic and the Postclassic in this region.

DEATH OF LORD 8 DEER

A scant thirteen years after the destruction of Red and White Bundle and the bulk of its ruling lineage, Lord 8 Deer met his own violent demise at the hands of Lord 4 Wind in an act of apparent revenge that took place in the year 12 Reed, 1115 CE (*Colombino* 16-II; *Bodley* 14-V–IV; see Byland and Pohl 1994:167–171 and Troike 1974 for discussion). This Lord 4 Wind was one of the young boys from Jaltepec that 8 Deer had spared in the great bloodletting at Red and White Bundle; he was a son of the executed rulers of that community. Three years after Lord 8 Deer's assassination, the same Lord 4 Jaguar of Coixtlahuaca, who had been allied with him, got involved in the dispute over his killing. In *Codex Bodley* 34, 33-III, Lord 4 Jaguar pursued Lord 4 Wind into a steambath place. He captured Lord 4 Wind and bound his arms behind him. Thus bound, Lord 4 Wind was taken to a place marked by flames, certainly the site of Achiutla. There he enters the flames in a sacred journey and reappears on *Bodley* 33-II in one hand of Lord 1 Death, the Solar Oracle/Deity, and with Lord 4 Jaguar in the other hand (Figure 10.9). The Solar Oracle/Deity seems again to be settling a dispute over legitimacy.

Codex scholars have long recognized that the meeting described here is parallel to an earlier meeting between Lord 8 Deer, Lord 4 Jaguar, and Lord 1 Death of Achiutla (*Codex Nuttall* 78-II, III). Both meetings functioned as appeals for legiti-

10.9 Bodley *33-II. Here the Solar Oracle-Deity, Lord 1 Death, is again involved in settling a dispute, this time between Lord 4 Wind and Lord 4 Jaguar. He separates them in a pose reminiscent of the scene from* Nuttall *10-I in Figure 10.5. Lord 4 Wind had been involved in the assassination of Lord 8 Deer and was brought to see the Solar Oracle / Deity of Achiutla by Lord 8 Deer's erstwhile ally, Lord 4 Jaguar. Following this scene, Lord 4 Jaguar gives a* tecuhtli *nose ornament to Lord 4 Wind, raising him up to lineage-head status, just as he had earlier done for Lord 8 Deer.*

macy and reconciliation by combatants involved in the complex historical struggle for power and authority in the southern Mixteca Alta. A monumental change had been building in the southern Nochixtlán Valley in the Mixteca Alta since the beginning of the War of Heaven in 963 CE. Although the Classic may have ended earlier in the major centers of Teotihuacan and Monte Albán, in the Mixteca the political structures that had characterized the Classic had persisted at sites like Achiutla, Red and White Bundle, Suchixtlán, and Jaltepec. The War of Heaven was precipitated by the violation of an alliance scheme that was predicated on the old forms of power relations in the region. When Mountain that Is Opened / Hill of the Wasp chose to abandon its alliance with the old centers of Achiutla and Suchixtlán and create a new tie to the site of Red and White Bundle, it was breaking with the past. The growth of Tilantongo as a new center of power was begun when it led the successful fight against Mountain that Is Opened / Hill of the Wasp. The great transition from Classic forms of political structure to new Postclassic ones had begun.

These changes continued to develop as Lord 8 Deer and his allies destroyed the town of Red and White Bundle and established the new dynasty at Tilantongo. That new political structure could not be accepted as legitimate without the sanction and approval of the Solar Deity/Oracle, Lord 1 Death from Achiutla. This fact, above all, suggests that the transition from the Classic to the Postclassic was not an abrupt break in the chain of history. Legitimacy was still based on the heritage of the ancestors. The transition to the Postclassic in the southern Mixteca Alta was a process that took at least 140 years. Some centers of political power, like Mountain that Is Opened / Hill of the Wasp, were quickly destroyed and abandoned (see

Chapter 1). Others persisted for a time but ultimately met the same fate, like Red and White Bundle. A few were born during this time of transition and grew to prominence, like Tilantongo. Still others maintained their population and influence across the boundary of the Classic to Postclassic transition, like Achiutla and, to a lesser degree, Jaltepec.

Interestingly, this period of transition is consistent with the very scant archaeological information about the end of the Classic in the Nochixtlán Valley mentioned by Spores (1983:207) when he estimates the end of the period at between 900 and 1100 CE.

The persistence of Achiutla in this context seems not to have been based on its great secular or military power but rather on its appeal to the supernatural power rooted in its very special place in the sacred history of the region. Achiutla was the place where the local actors believed that their primordial ancestor, Lady 1 Death, had been miraculously born from the sacred tree. It was also the home of the great Solar Oracle/Deity Lord 1 Death, the arbiter of peace between disputing royal families.

CONCLUSION

Ultimately, I can now say that the sacred history of the Mixtec people of Achiutla was important in the secular historical decisions made by political figures for generations after the beginning times of the Mixtec codices. The town of Achiutla had two important roles in the sacred history of the Mixteca Alta. One is that it was the place where the original ancestors of royal lineages were supernaturally born from trees. Achiutla was the birthplace of Lady 1 Death. The second role was that Achiutla was the home of the Solar Oracle/Deity known as Lord 1 Death. In the first role, that of the place of sacred birth from trees, Achiutla gave birth to the ruling lineages of both Tilantongo and Jaltepec. In the second, as the home of the Solar Deity and his oracle, Achiutla played a mediating role in the process of settling disputes between kingdoms including, certainly, Tilantongo and Jaltepec but also other towns with whom those places had dealings including Red and White Bundle (Huachino) and Mountain that Is Opened / Hill of the Wasp (Yucu Yoco).

The transition from the Classic to the Postclassic in the Mixteca Alta occurred in the context of local political action. Alliances were built and dashed. Conflict was raging between old powers and new ones. The forces of cultural continuity that were embodied in Achiutla were critical in the transition from the Classic to the Postclassic in the Mixteca Alta. The long-term roles of Achiutla and its oracular priest/king in the changes that were brokered by Lord 8 Deer have been unappreciated. Indeed, the role of sacred history and deeply held belief systems in the transformation of profoundly historical and political systems has been under appreciated. I propose that the recognition of these roles helps to inform a much more satisfying interpretation of several significant events described in codical history. Indeed, I think that an understanding of the process of the transition in Mesoamerica generally can be informed by a consideration of the internal view of the transition, to the extent that it can be recognized, provided by the Mixtec historical codices (Chapter 4). These events do not directly inform the causes for the decline of the major centers of Teotihuacan, Monte Albán, and Tikal, but they do help to create a cultural context for those processes. If the transition from the Classic to the Postclassic in the Mixteca Alta was a product of sacred historical validation of long-term political and economic transformations, then those processes may be relevant to the transitions in the larger centers as well.

REFERENCES

Anders, Ferdinand, Maarten Jansen, and Gabina Aurora Pérez Jiménez

1992a *Crónica Mixteca: El rey 8 Venado, Garra de Jaguar, y la dinastía de Teozacualco-Zaachila: Libro explicativo del llamado Códice Zouche-Nuttall.* ADEVA/Fondo de Cultura Económica, Mexico City.

1992b *Origen e historia de los reyes Mixtecos: Libro explicativo del llamado Códice Vindobonensis Mexicanus I.* ADEVA/Fondo de Cultura Económica, Mexico City.

Appel, Jill

1982 Political and Economic Organization in the Late Postclassic Valley of Oaxaca, Mexico. Unpublished Ph.D. Dissertation, Department of Sociology and Anthropology, Purdue University. West Lafayette, Indiana.

Balkansky, Andrew, Stephen A. Kowalewski, Verónica Pérez Rodríguez, Thomas J. Plechaha, Charlotte A. Smith, Laura R. Stiver, Dmitri Beliaev, John F. Chamblee, Verenice Y. Heredia E., and Roberto Santos P.

2000 Archaeological Survey in the Mixteca Alta of Oaxaca, Mexico. *Journal of Field Archaeology* 27(4):365–389.

Bernal, Ignacio

1949 Exploraciones en Coixtlahuaca, Oaxaca. *Revista Mexicana de Estudios Antropológicos* 10:5–76.

Boone, Elizabeth

2000 *Stories in Red and Black.* University of Texas Press, Austin.

Burgoa, Fray Francisco de

1934 *Geográfica descripción* [1674]. 2 vols. Publicaciones, vols. 25–26. Archivo General de la Nación, Mexico City.

Burland, Cottie A.

1965 *Codex Egerton 2895 (Codex Waecker Götter).* Facsimile with commentary. Akademische Druck-u. Verlagsanstalt, Graz.

Byland, Bruce
1980 Political and Economic Evolution in the Tamazulapan Valley, Mixteca Alta, Oaxaca, Mexico: A Regional Approach. Unpublished Ph. D. Dissertation, Department of Anthropology, Pennsylvania State University. State College.

Byland, Bruce, and John M.D. Pohl
1994 *In the Realm of Eight Deer: The Archaeology of the Mixtec Codices.* University of Oklahoma Press, Norman.

Caso, Alfonso
1960 *Interpretation of the Codex Bodley 2858.* Translated by Ruth Morales and revised by John Paddock. Sociedad Mexicana de Antropología, Mexico City.
1964 *Interpretación del Códice Selden 3135 (A.2).* Sociedad Mexicana de Antropología, Mexico City.
1979 *Reyes y reinos de la Mixteca,* Vol. 2: *Diccionario biográfico de los señores mixtecos.* Fondo de Cultura Económica, Mexico City.

Coe, Michael
1999 *The Maya,* 6th edition. Thames and Hudson, New York.

Dahlgren de Jordan, Barbro
1979 *La Mixteca: Su cultura e historia prehispánicas.* Gobierno del Estado de Oaxaca, Oaxaca.

Finsten, Laura, Stephen A. Kowalewski, Charlotte A. Smith, Mark D. Borland, and Richard D. Garvin
1996 Circular Architecture and Symbolic Boundaries in the Mixteca Sierra, Oaxaca. *Ancient Mesoamerica* 7(1):19–35.

Fried, Morton H.
1967 *The Evolution of Political Society: An Essay in Political Anthropology.* Random House, New York.

Furst, Jill
1977 The Tree Birth Tradition in the Mixteca, Mexico. *Journal of Latin American Lore* 3(2):183–226
1978a The Year 1 Reed, Day 1 Alligator: A Mixtec Metaphor. *Journal of Latin American Lore* 4(1):93–128.
1978b *Codex Vindobonensis Mexicanus I: A Commentary.* Institute for Mesoamerican Studies, Publication 4. State University of New York at Albany, Albany.

Gaxiola González, Margarita
1984 *Huamelulpan: Un centro urbano de la Mixteca Alta.* Colección Científica, No. 114. Instituto Nacional de Antropología e Historia, Mexico City.

Gill, Richardson
2000 *The Great Maya Drought.* University of New Mexico Press, Albuquerque.

Hamann, Byron
2002 The Social Life of Pre-sunrise Things. *Current Anthropology* 43(3):351–382.

Hamblin, Robert L., and Brian L. Pitcher
1980 The Classic Maya Collapse: Testing Class Conflict Hypotheses. *American Antiquity* 45:246–267.

Jansen, Maarten
1979 Apoala y su importancia para la interpretacion de los codices Vindobonensis y Nuttall. *42nd International Congress of Americanists, Paris 1976,* 7:161–171.
1982 *Huisi Tacu: Estudio Interpretivo de un libro mixteco antiguo: Codice Vindobonensis Mexicanus 1.* Incidentale Publicaties 24, vols. 1 and 2. Centro de Estudios y Documentación Latinoamericanos, Amsterdam.
1996 Lord 8 Deer and Nacxitl Topiltzin. *Mexicon* 18:2.
1998 Monte Albán y Zaachila en los Códices Mixtecos. In *The Shadow of Monte Alban: Politics and Historiography in Postclassic Oaxaca, Mexico,* edited by M. Jansen, P. Kröfges, and M. Oudijk, pp. 67–122. CNWS Publications, Vol. 64. Research School of Asian, African, and Amerindian Studies, University of Leiden, Leiden.

Jansen, Maarten, Peter Kröfges, and Michel R. Oudijk (editors)
1998 *The Shadow of Monte Albán: Politics and Historiography in Postclassic Oaxaca, Mexico.* CNWS Publications, Vol. 64. Research School of Asian, African, and Amerindian Studies, University of Leiden, Leiden.

Jansen, Maarten, and Marcus Winter
1980 Un relieve de Tilantongo, Oaxaca, del año 13 Búho. *Antropología e Historia* Epoca III 30:3–19.

León-Portilla, Miguel
1996 *Códice Alfonso Caso: La vida de 8-Venado, Garra de Tigre* (Colombino-Becker I). Patronato Indígena, Mexico City.

Lind, Michael
1979 *Postclassic and Early Colonial Mixtec Houses in the Nochixtlán Valley, Oaxaca.* Vanderbilt University Publications in Anthropology, No. 23. Nashville, Tennessee.

Monaghan, John
1995 *The Covenants with Earth and Rain: Exchange, Sacrifice, and Revelation in Mixtec Sociality.* University of Oklahoma Press, Norman.

Nicholson, Henry B.
1978 The Deity 9 Wind "Ehecatl-Quetzalcoatl' in the Mixteca Pictorials. *Journal of Latin American Lore* 4(1):61–92.

Nowotny, Karl Anton
1948 Erlauterungen zum Codex Vindobonensis (Vorderseite). *Archiv fur Volkerkunde* 3:156–200.
1964 *Codices Becker I/II: Comentario, descripción y corección.* Translated by Baron W. v. Humbolt. Instituto Nacional de Antropología e Historia, Mexico City.

Pérez Rodríguez, Verónica

2001 Achiutla and Yanhuitlán: History and Configuration of Two Cacicazgos. Paper presented at the 66th Annual Meeting of the Society for American Archaeology, New Orleans.

2003 Household Intensification in the Mixtec Cacicazgo: Excavation of a House and Terraced Fields. Final report submitted to the Foundation for the Advancement of Mesoamerican Studies, Crystal River, Florida.

Plunket, Patricia

1983 An Intensive Survey in the Yucuita Sector of the Nochixtlán Valley, Oaxaca, Mexico. Unpublished Ph.D. Dissertation, Department of Anthropology, Tulane University. New Orleans.

1990 Patrones de asentamiento en el Valle de Nochixtlán y su aportación a la evolución cultural en la Mixteca Alta. In *Lecturas históricas del Estado de Oaxaca*, Vol. 1: *Epoca prehispánica*, edited by M. Winter, pp. 349–378. Instituto Nacional de Antropología e Historia, Mexico City.

Pohl, John M.D.

1984 The Earth Lords: Politics and Symbolism of the Mixtec Codices. Unpublished Ph.D. Dissertation, Department of Anthropology, University of California, Los Angeles.

1994a *The Politics of Symbolism in the Mixtec Codices*. Vanderbilt University Publications in Anthropology, No. 46. Nashville, Tennessee.

1994b Mexican Codices, Maps, and Lienzos as Social Contracts. In *Writing Without Words: Alternative Literacies in Mesoamerica and the Andes*, edited by W. Mignolo and E. Boone, pp. 137–160. Duke University Press, Durham, North Carolina.

Pohl, John M.D., and Bruce Byland

1990 Mixtec Landscape Perception and Archaeological Settlement Patterns. *Ancient Mesoamerica* 1(1):113–131.

Rabin, Emily

1979 The War of Heaven in Codices Zouche-Nuttall and Bodley: A Preliminary Study. In *42nd International Congress of Americanists, Paris 1976,* 7:171–182.

2004 Toward a Unified Chronology of the Historical Codices and Pictorial Manuscripts of the Mixteca Alta, Costa, and Baja: An Overview. In *Homenaje a John Paddock*, edited by P. Plunket, pp. 101–136. Universidad de las Américas, Cholula, Puebla.

Redman, Charles

1999 *Human Impact on Ancient Environments*. University of Arizona Press, Tucson.

Reyes, Fray Antonio de los

1976 *Arte en lengua mixteca por Antonio de los Reyes 1593* [1593]. Vanderbilt University Publications in Anthropology, No. 14. Nashville, Tennessee.

Rice, Don S., and Prudence M. Rice

1990 Population Size and Population Change in the Central Lakes Region, Guatemala. In *Precolumbian Population History in the Maya Lowlands,* edited by T. Culbert and D. Rice, pp. 123–148. University of New Mexico Press, Albuquerque.

Rincón Mautner, Carlos

1997 Reading the History of Place-Becoming in the Codices from the Coixtlahuaca Basin. In *Messages and Meanings,* edited by M. Preuss, pp. 129–148. Labyrinthos, Culver City, California.

1999 Man and the Environment in the Coixtlahuaca Basin of Northwestern Oaxaca, Mexico: Two Thousand Years of Historical Ecology. Unpublished Ph.D. Dissertation, Department of Geography, University of Texas at Austin.

2000 La reconstrucción cronológica del linaje principal de Coixtlahuaca. In *Códices y Documentos Sobre México, Tercer Simposio,* edited by C. Vega, pp. 25–43. Serie Historia. Instituto Nacional de Antropología e Historia, Mexico City.

Sanders, William T., Jeffrey Parsons, and Robert Santley

1979 *The Basin of Mexico: Ecological Processes in the Evolution of a Civilization.* Academic Press, New York.

Smith, Mary Elizabeth

1973 The Relationship between Mixtec Manuscript Painting and the Mixtec Language: A Study of Some Personal Names in Codices Muro and Sánchez Solís. In *Mesoamerican Writing Systems,* edited by E. Benson, pp. 47–98. Dumbarton Oaks Research Library and Collection, Washington, DC.

1983a Regional Points of View in the Mixtec Codices. In *The Cloud People: Divergent Evolution of the Zapotec and Mixtec Civilizations,* edited by K. Flannery and J. Marcus, pp. 260–266. Academic Press, New York.

1983b Codex Selden: A Manuscript from the Valley of Nochixtlán? In *The Cloud People: Divergent Evolution of the Zapotec and Mixtec Civilizations,* edited by K. Flannery and J. Marcus, pp. 248–255. Academic Press, New York.

Spores, Ronald

1972 *An Archaeological Settlement Survey of the Nochixtlán Valley, Oaxaca.* Vanderbilt University Publications in Anthropology, No. 1. Nashville, Tennessee.

1974a *Stratigraphic Excavations in the Nochixtlán Valley, Oaxaca.* Vanderbilt University Publications in Anthropology, No. 11. Nashville, Tennessee.

1974b Marital Alliance in the Political Integration of Mixtec Kingdoms. *American Anthropologist* 76:297–311.

1983 The Mixteca Alta at the End of Las Flores. In *The Cloud People: Divergent Evolution of the Zapotec and Mixtec Civilizations,* edited by K. Flannery and J. Marcus, p. 207. Academic Press, New York.

1993 Tututepec: A Postclassic Period Mixtec Conquest State. *Ancient Mesoamerica* 4(1):167–174.

2001 Estudios mixtecos, ayer, hoy y mañana: Dónde estábamos, dónde estamos, hacia dónde vamos? In *Memoria de la Primera Mesa Redonda de Monte Albán:*

Procesos de cambio y conceptualización del Tiempo, edited by N. Robles, pp. 167–181. CONACULTA-INAH, Mexico City.

Stiver, Laura R.
2001 Prehispanic Mixtec Settlement and State in the Teposcolula Valley of Oaxaca, Mexico. Unpublished Ph.D. Dissertation, Department of Anthropology, Vanderbilt University. Nashville, Tennessee.

Terraciano, Kevin
2001 *The Mixtecs of Colonial Oaxaca: Ñudzahui History, Sixteenth through Eighteenth Centuries*. Stanford University Press, Stanford, California.

Thompson, J.E.S.
1954 *The Rise and Fall of Maya Civilization*. University of Oklahoma Press, Norman.

Troike, Nancy
1974 The Codex Colombino-Becker. Unpublished Ph.D. Dissertation, University of London.
1987 *Codex Zouche-Nuttall (British Museum ADD.MSS 39671)*. Akademische Druck-u. Verlagsanstalt, Graz, Austria.

Webster, David
2002 *The Fall of the Ancient Maya: Solving the Mystery of the Maya Collapse*. Thames and Hudson, New York.

PART VI

New Research Frontiers in Oaxaca and Eastern Guerrero

11

Gerardo Gutiérrez

Classic and Postclassic Archaeological Features of the Mixteca-Tlapaneca-Nahua Region of Guerrero

WHY DIDN'T ANYONE TELL ME THE CLASSIC PERIOD WAS OVER?

This chapter focuses on archaeological data from eastern Guerrero, an area along the western border of Oaxaca in the so-called La Montaña region and municipalities of the Costa Chica (Figure 11.1). Presented here are preliminary findings as related to settlement patterns, ceramic distributions, and sculpture. I argue that eastern Guerrero demonstrates a strong continuity of archaeological features from the Classic to Postclassic periods, especially in settlement patterns and the calendrical system. Eastern Guerrero archaeology provides a case study to compare and contrast some proposed hypotheses and ideas on the cultural development of neighboring Oaxaca cultures (Kowalewski et al. 1989), especially with the Mixteca Alta and Baja (Moser 1977) regions (see Chapter 1). Archaeological study in eastern Guerrero is essential for understanding the spatial and social reach of Zapotec expansion during the Classic period, as well as the development and expansion of the Mixtecs in the Postclassic.

BACKGROUND

Early scholarship subsumed the Mexican state of Guerrero into the West Mexico cultural region as part of the regionalization of Mesoamerica into discrete, self-

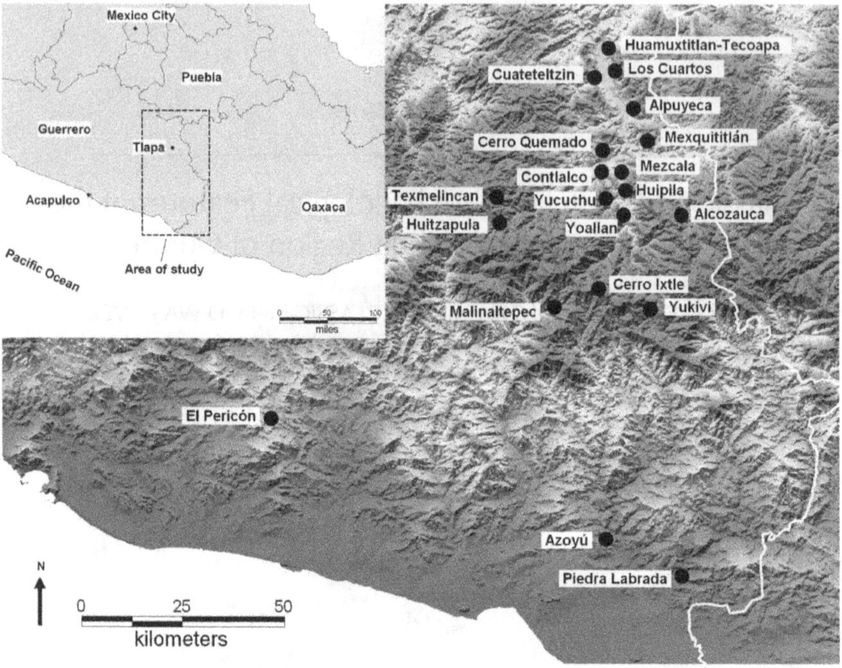

11.1 Area of study in eastern Guerrero and distribution of Classic period sites.

containing cultural areas (Sociedad de Antropología 1948). Unfortunately, this notion remains in the literature, museum displays, and Web pages. Although academics, particularly specialists who work in Colima, Jalisco, Michoacan, and Nayarit, have begun leaving Guerrero out of this regional construct, other venues, like the West Mexico Archaeological Cultures Room (Sala de Occidente) of the National Museum of Anthropology in Mexico City, promote it. The Sala de Occidente displays an important collection of archaeological objects from across Guerrero, together with shaft-tombs from Colima and Jalisco and cave paintings from Baja California. This heuristic construct would not be too problematic if not for the fact that objects from Guerrero show stronger relationships with Central Mexico and Oaxaca styles and traditions, which clearly demonstrates that Guerrero should be integrated into the Mesoamerican cultural area.

Given an odd combination of factors, among them difficult topography, lack of highways, social unrest, and, until recently, the paucity of attention Guerrero has received by archaeologists, most research has centered on individual sites in the central region and incidental salvage projects related to dam construction, irrigation districts, or urban development. To date, there have been few systematic surveys and those so far attempted have embraced specific river valleys or principal roads. This coverage has produced a fragmentary knowledge of Guerrero's prehistory insufficient for providing an archaeological framework.

Additionally, this record has resulted in the proposal of some interesting and occasionally farfetched hypotheses about Guerrero's cultural development. As is often the case with unknown areas, Guerrero's archaeological cultures have been characterized as peripheral, marginal, non-urban, pre-state, and so forth. I recognize that researchers specializing in this area, myself included, have helped to magnify these erroneous visions. Published work on Guerrero tends toward the high-profile archaeological discoveries, particularly those related to Formative period mural paintings, sculpture, and portable objects (Gay 1967; Grove 1970; Martínez Donjuan 1982, 1994; Reyna Robles 1996; Villela 1989). Perhaps we are afraid that our colleagues in other regions will not read our articles unless we write about "Olmec" jades and mural paintings.

For the Postclassic and Colonial periods, rich ethnohistorical evidence from Guerrero creates another research bias—we focus on colorful codices and lienzos rather than on related documentation (e.g., land litigations). Also, there have been few attempts to utilize this ethnohistoric data together with archaeology, for example, locating sites mentioned as place names in codices. Instead, it has become a weekend hobby for some to wander into indigenous communities asking for local colonial codices and/or caves with "Olmec" murals. In my opinion, Guerrero deserves more than that.

Based on my interest in the Tlapanec codices of Azoyú[1] and the Spanish colonial officer Diego Pardo's account of the Yope rebellion of 1531, I began working in two regions of Guerrero in 1997: the Mixteca-Tlapaneca-Nahua and the Costa Chica, which together embrace some 9,000 square kilometers from mountains to the Pacific Coast. The objective of this first-stage research was to understand political and territorial competition during the Postclassic period through systematic reconnaissance in both the La Montaña and Costa Chica. Although my research was initially focused on Postclassic and Colonial developments, archaeological sites from all time periods were located and mapped. To date, more than 200 sites have been recorded.

ECOLOGICAL FRAMEWORK

Eastern Guerrero can be conceptualized as two symbiotic regions: La Montaña and the Costa Chica. Altitude, together with the hydrological system of the Pacific Ocean, creates rainfall shadow on the leeward side of the Sierra Madre del Sur. This phenomenon produces five distinct ecological tiers, which ascend parallel to the Pacific coastal plain up the leeward face of the mountain range: tierra caliente windward, tierra templada windward, tierra fría, tierra templada leeward, and tierra caliente leeward. Air temperature and precipitation indices vary greatly depending on which face of the mountain any given tier is located. The windward slope of the Sierra Madre receives heavy rainfall, whereas the leeward slopes tend to be arid, especially the tierra caliente leeward. Each tier also displays distinct soil and vegetation types.

Rainfall in eastern Guerrero is seasonal, with a six-month cycle of alternating heavy precipitation and practically no rainfall. During the dry season, which corresponds to the cooler months of December through April, the coast and the leeward sector of the mountain range receive scarcely 25 to 50 millimeters of rain. Since cultivated plants cannot thrive with less than 400 millimeters during a growth cycle, agriculture becomes impracticable during winter, except in irrigated fields. Precipitation is so scarce that only the main tributaries of the Tlapaneco, Omitlán, Marquelia, Santa Catarina, and Quetzala Rivers continue carrying water; the remainder dry up. This phenomenon has heavily influenced agricultural practices and archaeological settlement patterns, which tend to concentrate along these rivers and near permanent water sources.

I have identified two zones of high agricultural production (up to two metric tons of maize per hectare) in eastern Guerrero: the first is located along the irrigated riverbanks of the upper and middle Tlapaneco River Basin, and the other is the Amuzgo-Mixteca area in the floodplains of the Santa Catarina and Quetzala Rivers (Gutiérrez 2002:75–79). Apart from these two zones, the average maize production per hectare is less than the annual average consumption for a six-member family.[2] In order to balance maize production deficits, settlements in the tierra fría and tierra templada leeward tiers must trade with those communities located along the valleys of the Tlapaneco River and the Ometepec-Azoyú area.

Another critical feature of eastern Guerrero's environment is the preponderance of Precambrian metamorphic rocks (gneiss) in contact with Paleozoic intrusive igneous rocks (granite). This dynamic provides the conditions for the formation of pegmatite deposits abundant in gemstones and other valuable minerals used by prehispanic societies.

These ecological characteristics have influenced the milieu in which local prehispanic rulers operated. Since at least the Formative period, trade corridors were established through the ecological tiers of eastern Guerrero (Gutiérrez 2002; Niederberger 2002; Pye and Gutiérrez 2007). There were two primary trade networks in the area: one following a horizontal or east-west direction, linking several points within the same ecological tier; and a second oriented in a vertical or north-south direction, connecting various ecological tiers between the Costa Chica and La Montaña. Political units competed to control these corridors. Competition was marked for those polities located within the same tiers as they sought trade partners from other ecological tiers and struggled to reroute trade flows through corridors under their control. Some examples of competing sites occupying the same tier would have been Chilapa and Tlapa in eastern Guerrero, Juxtlahuaca and Tlaxiaco in western Oaxaca, and Ometepec and Azoyú in the Costa Chica of Guerrero.

LINGUISTICS

During the Postclassic period, a myriad of languages are reported to have been spoken in eastern Guerrero (Mason 1977). Many purportedly disappeared during colonial times. Allowing for the possible disappearance of a few, I argue that most of these supposedly extinct tongues were actually local variants of one of the four major languages present today in the area: Mixtec, Tlapanec, Amuzgo, and Nahuatl. Notably, linguistic groups did not necessarily correlate to political units, and typically political units were multilingual and multi-ethnic. A local dynasty controlled villages and other corporate groups based on political allegiances irrespective of language. There were no Tlapanec, Mixtec, or Amuzgo nations.

PREVIOUS ARCHAEOLOGICAL RESEARCH IN EASTERN GUERRERO

Despite the many pictorial documents from eastern Guerrero, the entire area has remained largely unexplored archaeologically. The little that is known of its prehistory has come from a few reports by INAH (Instituto Nacional de Antropología e Historia) inspectors in the wake of large-scale looting. Nevertheless, the materials rescued by these inspectors provided primary clues about the cultures that inhabited the region. Although never fully corroborated, two Teotihuacan-style masks were believed found in a burial near the town of Malinaltepec in 1920 (Aguirre 1922; Ethnos 1922). One of the masks was richly decorated with jadeite, shell, quartz crystals, and turquoise. Such elite objects indicate some kind of interaction with Classic period Teotihuacan and the Basin of Mexico.

In 1932 a tomb was looted at the site of Texmelincan. Some of the objects (jadeite figurines, gold discs, *chalchihuite* beads, alabaster vessels, obsidian blades, copper rings, shell collars, carved bones, and amber) found their way into the National Museum of Anthropology, where archaeologists related them stylistically to objects found in Tomb 7 at Monte Albán (Noguera 1933), perhaps indicating direct contact with Oaxacan cultures. Texmelincan turned out to be a large archaeological site with twenty mounds arranged in three sectors, each with a ballcourt. Four stelae with Classic-Epiclassic calendrical dates were also recorded (Figure 11.2).

In the Costa Chica, Román Piña Chán (1960) reported several Classic period stelae at the site of Piedra Labrada, municipality of Ometepec, and these stelae also display an important connection with the sculptural tradition of the Pacific Coast

11.2 Slab number 1 from Texmelincan, depicting a character named 5 or 7 Vulture. After García Payón 1941:356.

of Oaxaca. Other scholars (Manzanilla 1995; Urcid and Joyce 2001) revisited the site to better record these monuments, but none has tried to place the site of Piedra Labrada within a regional context or explain its role in the settlement network of the Santa Catarina–Quetzala Basin. Jane Rosenthal (1963) undertook explorations and excavations throughout the Costa Chica in the early 1960s; unfortunately, she died prior to publishing her results; hence, we have only a brief report indicating the importance of this region and her research.

During 2000 and 2001, I undertook seven months of systematic archaeological reconnaissance in eastern Guerrero, exploring both the La Montaña and Costa Chica areas. The information presented here is based on this field research.

CLASSIC PERIOD TRAITS OF EASTERN GUERRERO

Given that eastern Guerrero's archaeology is unknown to the vast majority of scholars and general public, I review its general characteristics through presentation of a few key sites.

Ometepec–Piedra Labrada

Region: Costa Chica (Amuzgo area)
Ecological tier: tierra caliente windward

Piedra Labrada is a large site covering at least forty-nine hectares. It lies 150 meters above the valley of the Santa Catarina River, atop a ridge projecting from an escarpment of the Sierra Madre del Sur. First reported by Piña Chán in 1960, it has been visited sporadically by archaeologists interested in the epigraphy found on sculptures there.

The modern community of Piedra Labrada has settled on top of the site, destroying and covering over its architectural layout. What can be observed are three large mounds and a ballcourt. The main mound, with a thirty-meter-diameter base, was built on the highest point and reaches a height of six meters. To the west of this primary mound are two smaller structures. One was cut in half, revealing its core and the yellow clays used in a single construction episode. Many one-meter-high platforms are seen across the site, which the current inhabitants have used to build their houses. There is a well-preserved I-shaped ballcourt, which measures fifty-three meters long and nine meters wide.

A dozen perfectly carved stelae and sculptures are scattered throughout the site. Some are of sedimentary rock, but others were carved from granite. Piedra Labrada sculptures depict diverse themes with an abundance of zoomorphic and anthropomorphic representations. Large serpent heads, turtles, and felines are the most common elements. Anthropomorphic sculptures depict hunchbacks, porters bearing calendar glyphs, men wearing jaguar masks, and ballcourt markers, some showing a man bent backward with his hands tied behind him. There are also slabs depicting Mesoamerican deities, Tlaloc being the most conspicuous. At least five stelae have calendrical symbols, primarily year bearers. The year bearer *ollin* (Movement)

11.3 Piedra Labrada, Monument 13; sculpture of a tiger depicting the probable calendrical date 10 Movement.

is the most frequently represented, appearing on three different monuments, and two others display the same date, 10 Movement, with two bars representing five units each. Based on their formal attributes (Figure 11.3), Piña Chán (1960) dated these sculptures to the Classic period, contemporaneous with Teotihuacan. I propose a time window ranging from 400 to 800 CE (see Chapter 2 for a review of the chronology). Ceramics recovered from the surface are similar to Monte Albán IIIA (Pitao phase) and IIIB (Peche and Xoo phases) types (G.23, G.35, and C.17 types; see Caso et al. 1967), although Piedra Labrada also had earlier occupations.

Azoyú-Tenconahualle

Region: Costa Chica (Tlapanec area)
Ecological tier: tierra caliente windward

Tenconahualle covers forty-three hectares and is found in the low, hilly Pacific coastal plain, near a tributary of the Quetzala River. The ancient inhabitants leveled some hills to build low mounds, platforms, and plazas.

Tenconahualle is centered on a main plaza (which measures sixty-six by forty-two meters). On its east and west side, there are natural hills (twenty meters high), whose summits were leveled to build platforms 1.5 meters high with bases measuring fourteen by eight meters. North and south of this plaza are other modified hills with platforms of similar dimensions. An important architectural trait is the paving of platforms and plazas with stone slabs. The paved area is estimated to cover some 10,000 square meters. A similar pattern was reported by Rosenthal (1963) at the site of Capulín Chocolate, near San Luis Acatlán.

Ceramics and sculptures from various periods have been recovered from the site. I have seen dozens of miniature pots with lids in one particular private collection. There are vases with modeled human faces, typically depicting human emotions: some cry, others smile, show regret, or anger (Figure 11.4). Abundant quantities of Formative and Classic period clay figurines have also been found at Tenconahualle and in the Azoyú area.

There is a large serpent-head sculpture that had formerly been located in the ballcourt, the typical pattern of eastern Guerrero. Serpent-head sculptures have also been found in the ballcourts at Cochoapa-Yu kivi, Huitzapula, Texmelincan, and Piedra Labrada. The ballcourt at Tenconahualle measures fifty by eight meters and it is oriented at a twenty-three-degree deviation from true north, the common orientation for ballcourts on the Costa Chica.

Based on a bead necklace from a tomb at Teconahualle, it is presumed that the prehispanic inhabitants used local gemstones (aquamarines, garnets, quartz crystals, amethysts, and opals). In addition, common artifacts in eastern Guerrero are deep-welled grinding stones (mortars), typically fifty by forty centimeters. A hard material, not maize, was crushed and ground in them with such frequency and force that many have perforated bottoms. These grinding mortars are also seen at Piedra Labrada and Texmelincan.

11.4 Ceramic form from Azoyú-Tenconahualle.

El Pericón–Yopes

Region: La Montaña (Yopetzinco area)
Ecological tier: tierra templada windward

El Pericón–Yopes covers at least sixty-four hectares and is located halfway between Tierra Colorada and Ayutla de los Libres, in the heart of what used to be the Postclassic Yope region.

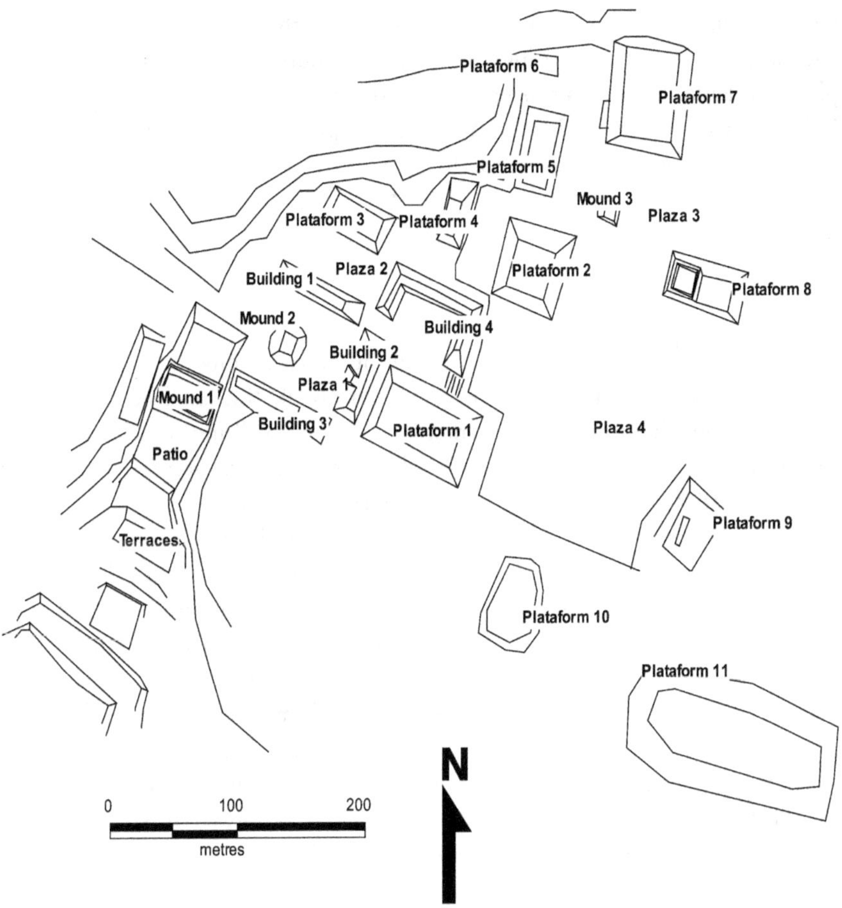

11.5 Regal-ritual core of Pericón-Yopes.

Its ceremonial core consists of several platforms, mounds, and terraces organized in four plaza groups (Figure 11.5). The architectural layout is one of the best planned in eastern Guerrero, with mounds and platforms distributed evenly, forming large open spaces. All structures are generally oriented at a twenty- to twenty-three-degree deviation from true north. Again, the same orientation is seen at other sites in the Costa Chica, including ballcourts at Piedra Labrada and Azoyú-Tenconahualle (Gutiérrez 2003). The dominant ceramics are similar to the Monte Albán C.17 type reported at Piedra Labrada and other sites of the Classic period of La Montaña, like Cerro de Ixtle and Yu kivi.

Another trait here common to other sites is the architectural set of mound-patio-platform, specifically a patio of modest dimensions (forty by forth meters on average) closed on its north side (or sometimes the east) by a mound three or more meters high, and the southern edge (or sometimes the west) is closed by a rectangular platform two meters high. Usually a ballcourt is embedded in one of the platform flanks. Sites with this pattern are Yu Cuchu (Cerro Machete), Cerro de Ixtle, Yu kivi, Huitzapula, Igualita-Yoallan, Mexquititlán-Organal, Huamuxtitlan-Tecoapa, and Coyahualco-Cuateteltzin.

Cochoapa–Yu kivi

Region: La Montaña (Mixtec area)
Ecological tier: tierra fría

Cochoapa–Yu kivi is located at the bottom of a ravine along the upper basin of the Igualita River (a tributary of the Tlapaneco River). This small site covers 1.75 hectares, although this is only its ceremonial core. This small area is enclosed on two sides by torrential rivers with the only possible access through a very steep mountain ridge, dramatically reducing land available for residential areas.

The structures are organized around a sunken central patio (measuring twenty-seven by twenty-five meters). To the north of this sunken patio is an I-shaped ballcourt (forty-three by nine meters), with the lateral structures measuring 18.6 meters long and 6.5 meters wide. Amazingly, this ballcourt still has two marker rings in situ, which are sculpted in the round and display anthropomorphic figures similar to the Piedra Labrada ballcourt—men who are bent backward with hands tied behind them to the rings of the ballcourt (Figure 11.6). In the same ballcourt, there was also a serpent-head sculpture carved similarly to those at Huitzapula, Texmelincan, and Piedra Labrada. These sculptures of Yu kivi date the site to the Classic period. The ceramics here are similar to the Monte Albán C.17 type.

To the north of the ballcourt are two small terraces (thirteen by thirteen meters). Forming the southern side of the sunken patio is an enormous terrace (sixty by eighteen meters), which probably was a high-status residential unit. Crossing one of the rivers north of the site, there is a small rock shelter with ceramic remains; the presence of nearby caves is yet another distinct cultural pattern in this area, as at other sites (Ocoapan, Chiepetepec and Texmelincan).

Texmelincan-Tezquilcatemic

Region: La Montaña (Tlapanec-Nahuatl area)
Ecological tier: tierra fría

Texmelincan was described by García Payón (1941) after his 1937 exploration; I present here the current conditions at the site.

Texmelincan covers approximately fifty-seven hectares, occupying the whole southeastern side of the Tezquilcatemic Mountain. Nonetheless, this is not a continuous area, and the site is segmented by deep ravines creating sectors with various

11.6 Ballcourt marker ring of Cochoapa-Yu kivi.

Nahuatl names: Ixcuintomahuacan, Texmelincan, Tiuhuapanco and Tlachihualtepec, and Tequixca. Three of these names are related to rocks and mining.

Although Texmelincan is extensive, its architectural layout is of average dimensions compared with other sites in the region; for example, its mounds are small, some ten to fifteen meters in diameter and one-half to two meters high. These are not comparable in size to those observed at Contlalco, Cerro Quemado–La Coquera, Huamuxtitlan-Tecoapa, Los Cuartos, Alpuyeca, or Alcozauca (Gutiérrez 2003). The interesting feature at Texmelincan is the presence of at least five I-shaped ballcourts, the most at any site recorded to date in eastern Guerrero.

The most important sector of Texmelincan is called Ixcuintomahuacan and consists of a mound group, four levels of terraces, and one ballcourt. The latter measures forty by nine meters and is limited to the southeast by a lateral mound measuring thirty by ten meters and three meters high. Its northwest edge is defined by the retention wall of a terrace (fifty by thirty-five meters). In the center of the main terrace, south of the ballcourt, is a two-meter-high platform with a base of thirty by twenty meters. García Payón located within it the remains of four bas-relief-carved slabs (Stones 1 through 4), which depict warriors and calendrical glyphs. García Payón also found in situ a fragment of the *tlachtemalacatl*, or ring marker, of the ballcourt.

Texmelincan was an important site in the regional settlement of eastern Guerrero. Nonetheless, it is unclear when the primary occupation occurred and what its relationship was with other sites in the area, especially with those located along the Tlapaneco River. From the sculpture, one may deduce that Stone 1 (Figure 11.2) is in late Classic period style (600–800 CE), whereas the other slabs were carved during the Epiclassic / Early Postclassic (900–1100 CE). In general, these carved monuments have a style associated with Xochicalco, indicating a strong relationship with the Valley of Morelos. During my survey, I noted the presence of local red-paste ceramics with sand temper, also seen at Yu kivi and Cerro de Ixtle.

During the Postclassic, the region where Texmelincan is located was under the political control of the Tlahuiscalera rulers, a powerful dynasty that formerly controlled the towns of Zapotitlan Tablas, Huitzapula, Teocuitlapan, and Acatepec and the area of Copanatoyac (Gutiérrez 2002).

Alcozauca

Region: La Montaña (Mixtec area)
Ecological tier: tierra templada leeward

Alcozauca's ceremonial center consists of a plaza of 110 by 78 meters; its northern and southern sides defined by deep ravines. The western edge of the plaza has two platforms measuring 1.7 meter high and 110 by 50 meters.

Just off center of the plaza was a low mound largely destroyed by agricultural machinery. The eastern side of the plaza is demarcated by an enormous mound composed of three terraces. The first, at the base of the mound, is 102 by 30 meters. From this terrace a talus wall emerges, 89 meters long and 8 meters high, which rises to a second L-shaped terrace, 66 by 22 meters for the longer arm and 57 by 11 meters for the shorter. From this terrace emerges a third, consisting of a platform that is 1.40 meters high and 70 by 23 meters. This mound covers one hectare, making it the second largest structure found to date in eastern Guerrero after the *tecpan* (palace) of Contlalco (1.1 hectares).

Crossing the southern ravine there are several terraces that have leveled the hillside. The extent of Alcozauca is 21.5 hectares, although this is probably a low estimate given that the modern community of Alcozauca has covered large portions of the site. Graywares (Monte Albán types G.3, G.4, and G.35) have been documented here, indicating a Classic period occupation. No ballcourt was apparent.

Contlalco

Region: La Montaña (Tlapaneco River Valley)
Ecological tier: tierra caliente leeward

Contlalco covers some eighty-five hectares. Its ceremonial core is built on the northern slope of an eighty-meter-high hill. The northern face of the hillside has been totally modified by a staggering pattern of terraces that ascend upward, simulating a stepped pyramid. A narrow creek divides the talus of the hill in half, as well as dividing the site itself into eastern and western sectors.

The western sector has a large plaza, 185 by 81 meters, covering 1.5 hectares. The main mounds of the site are found on this plaza (Figure 11.7). The western edge of the plaza has an I-shaped ballcourt (seventy-four by sixteen meters); the ballcourt is formed by two lateral structures measuring sixty by twenty-two meters, with a height of four meters. There are four other mounds in the plaza. These rectangular platforms have varied heights, ranging from less than one meter to two meters.

The northern side of the plaza is closed off by a mound of great volume and dimensions, with a base measuring 112 by 103 meters and a height of up to 15 meters. On top are four patios constructed at different levels, with a total surface of 4,578 square meters. Patio 1, the largest, is constructed at the highest point of the mound. The forty-degree slopes of this mound are supported with stone and lime plastering, providing structural stability.

Contlalco is a site with a long occupational sequence from Formative to Postclassic periods, and at this point, it is difficult to estimate the occupation and construction by period. Based on the presence of talud-tablero architectural features and Teotihuacan-style censers, it was an important site during the Classic period, and to date it is the largest site reported for eastern Guerrero and western Oaxaca.

Huamuxtitlan-Tecoapa

Region: La Montaña (Cañada de Huamuxtitlan, Nahua area)
Ecological tier: tierra caliente leeward

This site is located south of the town of Huamuxtitlan, on the eastern bank of the Tlapaneco River. It embraces a total surface of thirty hectares.

The architectural core of the site was built along a ridge and the main buildings surround a sunken patio of sixty-two by fifty-six meters. The northern, southern,

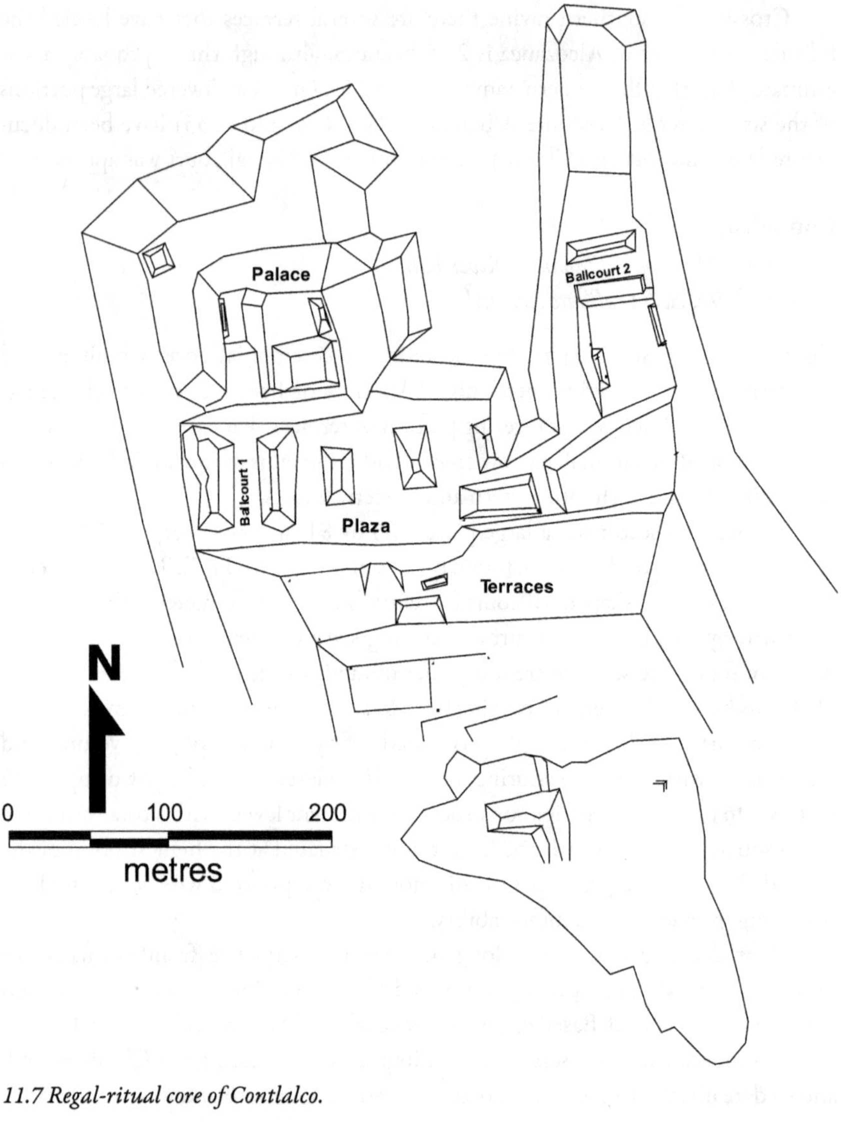

11.7 Regal-ritual core of Contlalco.

and western sides of the sunken patio are enclosed by walls (1.5 meters high and 10 meters wide); the top of these walls were also used as walkways around the sunken patio and controlled the access to other sectors of the site (Figure 11.8). North of the sunken patio there is a descending slope that arrives at a large plaza (ninety by ninety meters). The eastern side of the sunken patio is edged by a mound with a forty-three-meter-diameter base and seven meters high; the core is stone and lime plaster, and unfortunately the upper level has been totally destroyed by looters. The

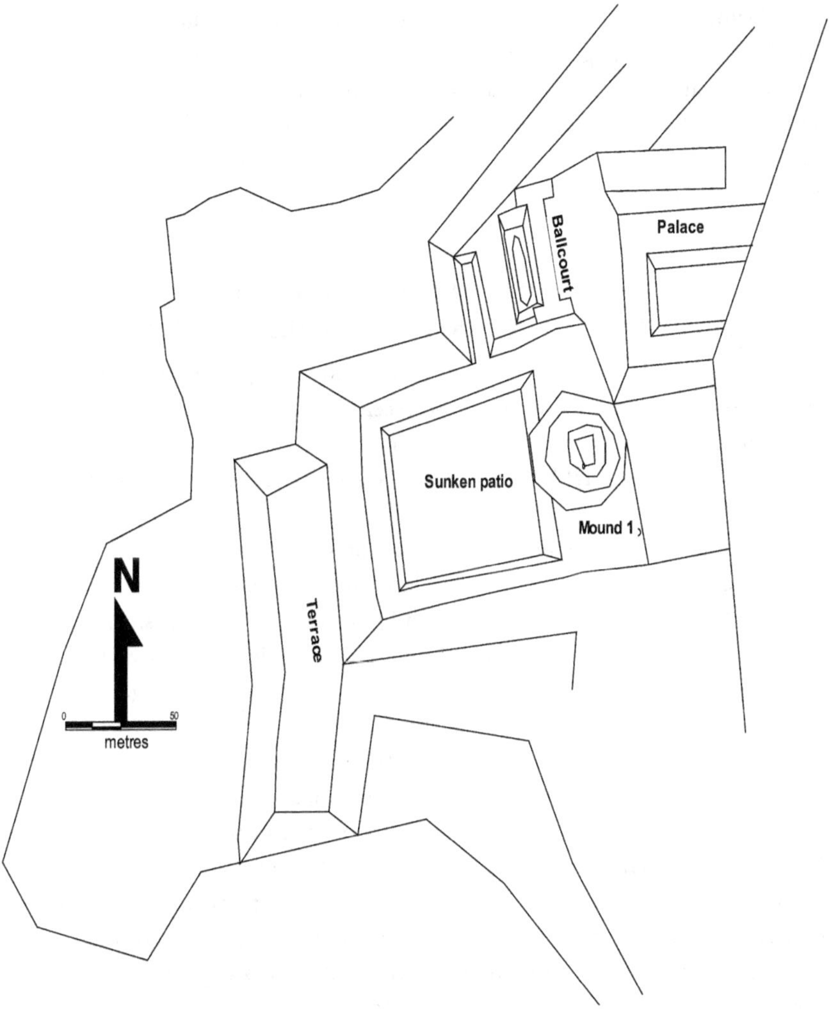

11.8. Regal-ritual core of Huamuxtitlan-Tecoapa.

architectural layout of "sunken patio-mound" is similar to the archaeological site of Coyahualco-Cuateteltzin (5.2 kilometers to the southwest).

Fifty meters north of the main mound, there is an I-shaped ballcourt, which measures forty-nine by eight meters. The court is accompanied by a lateral structure that shapes its western flank, measuring thirty by eight meters. These buildings are aligned at a 350-degree deviation from true north, which appears to be the local pattern for the Huamuxtitlan Valley—all sites with ballcourts have that orientation (Cuateteltzin, Los Cuartos, and Alpuyeca).

Huamuxtitlan-Tecopa is the largest site reported for the Huamuxtitlan Valley, and although not as large as Contlalco, it is still an impressive site. It was occupied from the Formative period (perhaps Monte Albán II, G.12 ceramic type) continuously into the Classic (Monte Albán G.4 and G.35 ceramic types). Sculptures recovered from the site depict Tlaloc wearing a decorated headdress with the Mixtec year glyph. Postclassic sculptures of kneeling women are also present.

GENERAL PATTERNS FOR THE CLASSIC PERIOD IN EASTERN GUERRERO (200–800 CE)

Eastern Guerrero is located equidistantly from Teotihuacan and Monte Albán (200 lineal kilometers), thus close enough to receive influences from both centers but far enough to display strong local developments. Graywares with traits similar to those of Monte Albán IIIA / Pitao phase (G.4, G.23, and G.35 ceramic types), as well as Teotihuacan-style censers and Teotihuacan III (Tlamimilolpan-Xolalpan) and Teotihuacan IV (Metepec) figurines, are present throughout the La Montaña and Costa Chica regions. Fragments of large Teotihuacan-style censers have been reported from La Soledad and Contlalco (Jiménez 2000). In the small village of Mezcala in the municipality of Tlapa, I was given a complete censer, which had been recovered from a burial during the construction of the town's kindergarten (Figure 11.9). Thermoluminescence dating of the Teotihuacan censer from Mezcala, near Tlapa, dated to 450–650 CE (Gutiérrez 2007). The many artifacts uncovered to date suggest a strong interaction with Teotihuacan, and although trade was probably a primary component, the precise nature of the interaction between Central Mexico and Guerrero will require excavation to elucidate. Whatever the case, it is likely that local polities copied and replicated some Monte Albán and Teotihuacan traits, and the area seems to have synthesized both traditions into its own.

It seems that most Formative sites continued to be occupied into the Classic period (see Figure 11.1). This is understandable given the environmental limits dictated by the aridness of the region during the dry season. Thus, the presence of springs and permanent sources of running water were important components that dictated settlement patterns. There is a quantitative increase in the number of Classic period sites that could be correlated to an increase in population size. Judging from site sizes, I believe that the ceremonial centers of Contlalco, Texmelincan, Cerro Quemado, Alcozauca, Huamuxtitlan-Tecoapa, Coyahualco-Cuateteltzin, Alpuyeca, El Pericón–Yopes, Cerro Ixtle, and Yu kivi played dominant political roles in the region. As for architectural patterns, these site centers all had an I-shaped ballcourt and a small patio delimited by a mound at one end and a large low platform on the other. The ballcourt rings, where present, were sculptures depicting what looked to be a human captive—a man bent backward with

11.9 Teotihuacan-style censer from Mezcala, municipality of Tlapa.

his hands tied behind him. Carved serpent heads are also found in association with ballcourts. In the Costa Chica, the Classic sites are paved with rock slabs and the ballcourts are oriented twenty to twenty-three degrees deviation from true north. In the Huamuxtitlan Valley, the orientation of the ballcourt is 350 degrees deviation from true north, and the sunken patio is a typical feature.

THE POSTCLASSIC PERIOD

Thanks to ethnohistorical research by Constanza Vega Sosa (1991), we have more insight into the societies of eastern Guerrero during this period. The emergence of Tlapa-Tlachinollan as the most powerful polity in eastern Guerrero is the key sociocultural development of this period. Within a 160-year span, it came to dominate most of its neighbors south of the Tlapaneco River Valley. At its greatest extent, it controlled some 100,000 people over more than 6,000 square kilometers, extending as far as Alpuyeca to the north, Alcozauca to the east, the Costa Chica to the south, and Atlixtac-Hueycatenango to the west (Gutiérrez 2002).

The presence of Yestla-Naranjo and Aztec III ceramics and metallurgy are used to date Postclassic occupation. Other local Postclassic ceramic types include a thick, grayish brown ceramic with large fragments of schist and calcite for temper and a porous redware with abundant mica-like flakes that shine in sunlight (Gutiérrez 2003).

Ethnohistorical references also provide clues for dating archaeological sites in the region. More than forty distinct place names are recorded in various documents corresponding to actual Postclassic settlements in the region. I found imported Aztec III and IV ceramics, as well as local imitations, at the sites of Ahucatitlan (Mexquititlan-Organera), Tecoyo–La vuelta de las Pilas, Cerro Machete, Yoso None, Alpuyeca–Las Minas, Huamuxtitlan-Tecoapa, Huamuxtitlan–Los Cuartos, Alcozauca, Atlamajac, Axoxuca, Xocotla, Aserradero, and Cerro Quemado (Coquera). Nevertheless, in most collections Aztec ceramics are scarce. From 127 Postclassic sites, only 19 sites (15 percent) contain Aztec sherds and the frequency was low, from three to four sherds collected per site. Of the 5,457 sherds recovered from throughout the region, only 71 (1.3 percent) are Aztec ceramics, 60 percent of which are probably local imitations.

Another Postclassic ceramic type is Yestla-Naranjo, which is rarer than Aztec wares; only four sherds have been found at two sites: Loma UPN and Conhuaxo 7. Notably, 116 sites have local Postclassic wares (T1BGB, T2BL, T3BLM, and T14 MO), representing a huge settlement increase after the Classic period.

As mentioned previously, mineral extraction was an important activity in the region, which was further confirmed by the *Codices Azoyú II* and *Mendoza*. Gold and green gemstones are mentioned as tribute items for the provinces of Tlapa and Quiauhteopan-Olinala. Sahagún (1975:608) was informed of these activities by the Aztecs: "These (Tlapanecs) are rich . . . and they were living in sterile and poor lands, with great needs, rugged and rough lands, but they know the rich stones and their virtues."

CLASSIC TO POSTCLASSIC TRANSITION

Settlement Patterns

The collapse of the Classic period polities of Teotihuacan and Monte Albán was felt throughout central and southern Mexico. What were the consequences of this sociopolitical breakdown in eastern Guerrero? Based on the archaeological record, I think not very dramatic. Sites were not abandoned but instead continued to be inhabited into colonial times and, were it not for the indigenous resettlements ordered by the Spanish Crown, perhaps they would still be occupied today. It is generally believed that militarism increased during the Postclassic period, with fortified sites built on ridge tops. Notably, Classic period iconography in eastern Guerrero is full of representations of violence and warriors, in exactly the same way that local codices depict war events during the Postclassic period. I argue that there was no significant increase in militarism from Classic to Postclassic eras. Additionally, Piedra Labrada, Huamuxtitlan-Tecoapa, Azoyú-Tenconahualle, Alcozauca, Contlalco, and many other Classic sites of eastern Guerrero are built in strategic defensive positions in river bottoms and on ridge tops. It seems that in eastern Guerrero "balkanization" did not occur after the collapse of the "Teotihuacan-Monte Albán world" but was instead an endemic part of the Classic period, the era of the "super-powers" (see Chapter 1).

The demise of Teotihuacan, more than the demise of Monte Albán, affected, at least temporarily, the flow of trade goods between Central Mexico and eastern Guerrero: less demand for coastal materials (such as cacao, gemstones, and maritime products) from Teotihuacan would have translated into a smaller input of Central Mexican goods (green obsidian and other prestige items) into eastern Guerrero's economic system. Local production of luxury goods, however, probably flourished and replaced Teotihuacan's imports. Perhaps an increase in production of items like finely decorated gourds and wooden chests occurred during this period and, subsequently, these items became popular in Postclassic times. The abundance of late local imitations of Teotihuacan censers in the region could be the archaeological indicator of this changing long-distance and prestige exchange network. Coastal materials were again in demand by the political successors of Teotihuacan—Xochicalco, Tula, and, later, the Aztecs, so trade was never completely interrupted. Interestingly, after the breakdown of Classic period societies, metallurgy was introduced in Mesoamerica and the mining tradition of eastern Guerrero found a new economic niche with gold extraction.

Thus, a combination of factors such as extreme aridity during the dry season, fertile irrigated agricultural lands in the Tlapaneco and Santa Catarina–Quetzala River Basins, intense inter-polity competition, monopoly of segments of a critical trade route, and the adaptation of the production and export of prestige items to a more locally oriented market (by increasing the variety and the volume of local production) kept eastern Guerrero from suffering a major sociopolitical collapse.[3]

Regional powers produced cyclical processes of political expansions and retreats. The last expansionist process undertaken by a local polity was that of Tlapa-Tlachinollan, whose capital was located close to the archaeological site of Classic period Contlalco but embraced a larger area that includes portions of the modern city of Tlapa.

The Calendar

Settlement patterns were not the only cultural feature that remained practically unaltered from Classic to Postclassic periods. Perhaps the best documented is the calendar system.

Specifically, the year bearer ollin (Movement) depicted on two sculptures from Piedra Labrada (as the date 10 Movement), and on the Tlaloc sculpture from Chilpancingo (with the date 4 Movement), has also been used in the calendar system of the Colonial *Codices Azoyú I* and *II,* which were found in the Tlapanec town of Azoyú, located twenty-five kilometers west of Piedra Labrada. These codices used the year bearers *ehecatl* (wind), *mazatl* (deer), *malinalli* (grass), and ollin (movement) in combination with numerals 2 through 14, instead of the Postclassic period Aztec and Mixtec year bearers *calli* (house), *tochtli* (rabbit), *acatl* (reed), and *tecpatl* (flint), with numerals from 1 to 13. The eastern Guerrero Classic period calendrical system seemingly survived well into the Colonial period (1565 CE). If such is the case, what does this longevity mean?[4] If calendrical iconography endured for 1,000 years, it may indicate permanency and stability for the ideological institutions of eastern Guerrero's societies.

If there was in fact calendrical continuity from Classic to Postclassic period, then we should be able to use the synchronology proposed for the codices of Azoyú (Toscano 1943) to date Classic period monuments in eastern Guerrero, at least as an estimate. Based on folio 32 (front) of *Codex Azoyú I,* which depicts the arrival of the Spaniards to Tlapa,[5] Toscano determined that the Tlapanec year, 3 Wind, corresponded to the Julian calendar year of 1521 CE. Unfortunately, the same year bearer and numeral repeats every fifty-two years and does not have a true zero. Nevertheless, if the synchronicity of the Azoyú codices applies to the carved slabs of Piedra Labrada, the year 10 Movement in the Classic period would correspond to one of the following possibilities: 228, 280, 332, 384, 436, 488, 540, 592, 644, 696, 748, or 800 CE. As one may appreciate, this dating method is not exact, but in conjunction with radiocarbon dates and a better ceramic chronology from these sites, the year bearers may help to further refine the chronology of eastern Guerrero.

CONCLUSIONS

Archaeological research indicates that Guerrero is a region with a strong local development but also demonstrates an impressive blending of cultural traditions from neighboring areas, including the Basin of Mexico, Mixteca Baja and Costa, Tlaxcala-Puebla, Morelos and Toluca Valleys, as well as West Mexico. Perhaps more than any other area, Guerrero will prove to be the "melting pot" or "salad bowl" of Mesoamerican archaeological traditions and therefore will need to be considered itself a primary regional core of Middle America.

Evidence for prehistoric occupants in eastern Guerrero may date to the early preceramic period, given the presence of unique carvings found in the Totomixtlahuaca area (Gutiérrez 2002), and the area has likely participated in the Mesoamerican exchange system since then. Its settlement patterns have been heavily influenced by the arid conditions of the leeward Montaña, concentrating the majority of sites along the permanent tributaries of the Tlapaneco River.

The region was in contact with other Formative societies, as demonstrated by Olmec style and influence in murals and other features (Gay 1967; Grove 1970; Gutiérrez 2007). Archaeological data also attest to strong links with the Classic period cultures of Teotihuacan and Monte Albán (especially ceramics), as well as with Postclassic period Aztec society. Notwithstanding, we must not force archaeological evidence from eastern Guerrero into pan-Mesoamerican sequences to obtain questionable chronology for our sites. Instead, we must first understand the local evolutionary sequence, so that it can then be used to test its relationship to other Mesoamerican cultural and processual developments. Until the area is fully surveyed and excavations undertaken, it remains problematic to adopt wholesale sequences from other parts of Mesoamerica, especially the Mixteca Baja and Mixteca Alta, or lump the area with the distinctive traditions of West Mexico. The paucity of archaeological research in eastern Guerrero provides, ironically, the rare opportunity to test many of John Paddock's original proposals for the cultural development of the Tetlamixteca region (Paddock 1966), as well as other hypotheses from previous projects in the Mixteca and the valleys of Oaxaca.

NOTES

1. The Azoyú codices are a group of three pictorial documents (*Codex Azoyú I, Codex Azoyú II,* and the Genealogical Lienzo of Tlapa-Azoyú) painted during the first decades of Spanish colonial rule, 1521–1565 CE, which depict the political history of the ancient polity of Tlapa-Tlachinollan in eastern Guerrero.

2. This figure was developed by Matías (1997:83) as 1,920 kilograms of maize and includes an average consumption rate of six family members and domestic animals.

3. Nonetheless, some sites that were not able to adapt to the market changes were abandoned, resulting in the demise of some gateway communities, specifically Yu kivi, Cerro de Ixtle, and even Piedra Labrada. This may explain why these sites have Classic period monuments still in place, and why the sites were not covered by tons of later Postclassic period occupation.

4. These are not the only documents that use the year bearers ehecatl, mazatl, malinalli and ollin; the Cuicatec codices, the *Porfirio Díaz* and *Fernández Leal,* have the same year bearers, but their numerical systems range from 1 to 13.

5. Perhaps this was the exploratory trip made by Bernadino Vásquez de Tapia under Cortes's orders.

REFERENCES

Aguirre, Porfirio

1922 Informe del ayudante: Sobre una máscara de turquesa y jade encontrada en Malinaltepec, Guerrero. *Boletín del Museo Nacional de Antropología, Historia e Etnología* Época 4, 1(3):34–35.

Caso, Alfonso, Ignacio Bernal, and Jorge Acosta

1967 *La cerámica de Monte Albán*. Memorias del Instituto Nacional de Antropología e Historia, No. 13. INAH, Mexico City.

Ethnos

1922 A Counterfeit Mosaic Mask. *Ethnos* 1(8–12):263–264.

García Payón, José

1941 Estudio preliminar de la zona arqueológica de Texmelincan, Estado de Guerrero. *El México Antiguo*. 5:361–364.

Gay, Carlo

1967 Oldest Paintings in the New World. *Natural History* 75(8):28–35.

Grove, David

1970 The Olmec Paintings of Oxtotitlán Cave, Guerrero. *Studies in Pre-Columbian Art and Archaeology*, No. 6. Dumbarton Oaks Research Library and Collection, Washington, DC.

Gutiérrez, Gerardo

2002 The Expanding Polity: Patterns of the Territorial Expansion of the Post-Classic Señorío of Tlapa-Tlachinollan in the Mixteca-Nahua-Tlapaneca Region of Guerrero. Unpublished Ph.D Dissertation, Department of Anthropology, Pennsylvania State University, State College.

2003 Informe técnico presentado al Consejo de Arqueología del INAH acerca de las actividades del proyecto: Arqueología y Etnohistoria en la Montaña de Guerrero: Patrones de Expansión Política-Territorial de un Señorío Post-Clásico en La Mixteca-Náhuatl-Tlapaneca; temporada 2000. Manuscript on file. Archivo Técnico del Instituto Nacional de Antropología e Historia, Mexico City.

2007 *Catálogo de sitios arqueológicos de las regiones Mixteca-Tlapaneca-Nahua y Costa Chica de Guerrero*. CIESAS, Mexico. Available as a CD-ROM and online at the FAMSI Web site: http://www.famsi.org/spanish/research/gutierrez/index.html.

Jiménez, García Elizabeth

2000 La Arqueología de Tlapa. In *Tlapa: Origen y memoria histórica*, edited by M. Martínez Rescalvo, pp. 15–42. Universidad Autónoma de Guerrero and H. Ayuntamiento de Tlapa de Comonfort, Chilpancingo, Guerrero.

Kowalewski, Stephen A., Gary M. Feinman, Laura M. Finsten, Richard E. Blanton, and Linda M. Nicholas

1989 *Monte Albán's Hinterland, Part II: Prehispanic Settlement Patterns in Tlacolula, Etla and Ocotlán, the Valley of Oaxaca, Mexico*. Memoirs of the Museum of

Anthropology, University of Michigan, No. 23. University of Michigan, Ann Arbor.

Manzanilla López, Rubén

1995 Nuevas apreciaciones sobre el sitio de Piedra Labrada, Municipio de Ometepec, Costa Chica de Guerrero. In *Presencias y encuentros: Investigaciones arqueológicas de salvamento*, pp. 309–318. Instituto Nacional de Antropología e Historia, Mexico City.

Martínez Donjuan, Guadalupe

1982 Teopantecuanitlan, Guerrero: Un sitio olmeca. *Revista Mexicana de Estudios Antropológicos* 28:123–132.

1994 Los olmecas en el estado de Guerrero. *Los olmecas en Mesoamérica*, edited by J. Clark, pp. 143–163. El Equilibrista, Mexico City.

Mason, Alden J.

1977 The Native Languages of Middle America [1940]. In *The Maya and Their Neighbors, Essays on Middle American Anthropology and Archaeology*, edited by C. Hay, R. Linton, S. Lothrop, H. Shapiro, and G. Vaillant, pp. 52–87. Dover Publications, New York.

Matias Alonso, Marcos

1997 *La agricultura indígena en La Montaña de Guerrero*. Asociación Alemana para la Educación de Adultos, Programa de Apoyo a las Culturas Municipales y Comunitarias, and Altepetl Nahuas de la Montaña de Guerrero, Mexico.

Moser, Christopher L.

1977 *Ñuiñe Writing and Iconography of the Mixteca Baja*. Vanderbilt University Publications in Anthropology, No. 19. Nashville, Tennessee.

Niederberger, Christine

2002 Nácar, "jade" y cinabrio: Guerrero y las redes de intercambio. In *El Pasado Arqueológico de Guerrero*, edited by C. Niederberger and R. M. Reyna Robles, pp. 175–223. CEMCA, Gobierno del Estado de Guerrero, and Instituto Nacional de Antropología e Historia, Mexico City.

Noguera, Eduardo

1933 Importancia arqueológica del descubrimiento de objetos en Temexlican, Guerrero. *Boletín del Museo Nacional*, época II, 2:42–44.

Paddock, John

1966 *Ancient Oaxaca: Discoveries in Mexican Archaeology and History*. Stanford University Press, Stanford, California.

Piña Chán, Román

1960 Algunos sitios arqueológicos de Oaxaca y Guerrero. *Revista Mexicana de Estudios Antropológicos* 16:65–76.

Pye, Mary E., and Gerardo Gutiérrez

2007 The Pacific Coast Trade Route of Mesoamerica: Iconographic Connections between Guatemala and Guerrero. In *Archaeology, Art, and Ethnogenesis in*

Mesoamerican Prehistory: Papers in Honor of Gareth W. Lowe, edited by L. Lowe and M. Pye, pp. 229–275. Papers of the New World Archaeological Foundation, No. 68. Brigham Young University, Provo, Utah.

Reyna Robles, Rosa María
1996 *Cerámica de época olmeca en Teopantecuanitlán, Guerrero*. Instituto Nacional de Antropología e Historia, Mexico City.

Rosenthal, Jane Powell
1963 Exploring Ancient Guerrero. *Brooklyn Museum of Art Annual Report*, pp. 6–17. Brooklyn, New York.

Sahagún, Fray Bernardino de
1975 *Historia general de las cosas de la Nueva España*. Editorial Porrúa, Mexico City.

Sociedad Mexicana de Antropología
1948 *El Occidente de México*. Cuarta reunión de mesa redonda sobre problemas antropológicos de México y Centro América. Sociedad Mexicana de Antropología, Mexico City.

Toscano, Salvador
1943 Los códices Tlapanecas de Azoyú. *Cuadernos Americanos* 10:127–136.

Urcid, Javier, and Arthur Joyce
2001 Carved Monuments from Coastal Oaxaca. *Ancient Mesoamerica* 12(1):1–18.

Vega Sosa, Constanza
1991 *Códice Azoyú 1: El reino de Tlachinollan*. Fondo de la Calle Económica, Mexico City.

Villela, Flores Samuel
1989 Nuevo testimonio rupestre olmeca en el oriente de Guerrero. *Arqueología* (2da época) 2:149–172.

12

Marcus Winter

Classic to Postclassic in Four Oaxaca Regions

THE MAZATECA, THE CHINANTLA, THE MIXE REGION, AND THE SOUTHERN ISTHMUS

In the early sixteenth century, at the time of the Spanish Conquest, an estimated 1.5 to 3 million people representing at least sixteen distinct ethnic and linguistic groups lived in what is now the state of Oaxaca in southern Mexico (see Figure 1.2). Tracing the culture history of these groups has been a challenge to archaeologists. In theory, all sixteen groups and perhaps others, such as the now extinct Papabuco, are represented by prehispanic remains. In fact, several groups are practically undocumented archaeologically since many regions of Oaxaca have yet to be explored.

Zapotecs and Mixtecs are Oaxaca's two most numerous indigenous populations today and are also the best known from archaeological evidence (Marcus and Flannery 1996; Paddock 1966; Winter 1989a) and ethnohistorical sources (Oudijk 2000; Romero Frizzi 1996; Spores 1984). Zapotecs are commonly linked with Monte Albán, Mitla, Yagul, Zaachila, and other sites in the Valley of Oaxaca and with Guiengola in the Isthmus of Tehuantepec. Mixtecs are usually associated with the Mixtec codices and with places like Apoala, Tilantongo, and Tututepec, mainly in the Mixteca Alta and along the Pacific Coast (see Chapter 1). Both groups are mentioned in relation to Tomb 7 at Monte Albán, since the tomb was originally built and used by Zapotecs during the Classic and then reused by Mixtecs, or by a family of mixed ethnic and linguistic descent, during the Postclassic (see Chapter 2 for an overview of chronology).

Although Oaxaca archaeology is often represented only by Zapotecs and Mixtecs (Flannery and Marcus 1983; Smith and Berdan 2003a), survey and minor excavations show that archaeological sites are common throughout the state as early as the Classic period (300 CE), and that by the Late Postclassic period (1250 CE) even the most remote Oaxaca regions were inhabited. Thus Zapotec and Mixtec archaeological remains represent only a portion of prehispanic Oaxaca. The correlation of archaeological remains with ethnic groups and geographic locations is an undertheorized and problematic area of archaeological research. In Oaxaca, historical information, including glottochronology, can be used to trace present-day groups back into Colonial and Postclassic times, although connections become increasingly vague and hypothetical as one goes farther into the past.

In this chapter I first describe some Classic and Postclassic archaeological finds from four lesser known Oaxaca regions (Figure 12.1). The initial goal is simply to document this material and thus begin to fill in the culture history of these regions. I then briefly compare the data from these regions with what we know about the Late Classic to Postclassic transition elsewhere in Oaxaca, specifically in portions of the Zapotec and Mixtec regions where it has been studied. The idea is to determine whether pan-regional patterns exist, and if so, whether they can be ascribed to the same cause. Finally, a third goal is to consider to what extent the modified world systems model of the Late Postclassic recently proposed by Michael E. Smith and Frances F. Berdan (2003b) helps account for the archaeological evidence from these Oaxaca regions.

THE MAZATEC REGION

The Mazateca in northern Oaxaca, occupied today by the Mazatec ethnic and linguistic group, includes to the south an area of high karst mountains and some of the world's deepest caves, and to the north a lower area of piedmont and river valleys opening to the Gulf Coast lowlands. Like several Oaxacan culture areas, the Mazatec region encompasses a wide range of climates, from tierra caliente to tierra fria, which means that people of this ethnic and linguistic group have had access to resources in various zones, either directly or through exchange. Group territories in Oaxaca frequently include many ecological zones, and this pattern may have originated in early times by a founding community that established settlements in areas of strategic resources outside their immediate local setting. This kind of "verticality" has been recognized in Chiapas (Culbert 1965) and in Peru (Murra 1985) but not in Oaxaca, and consequently some archaeological surveys have proceeded horizontally, omitting high mountain zones and thus missing sites.

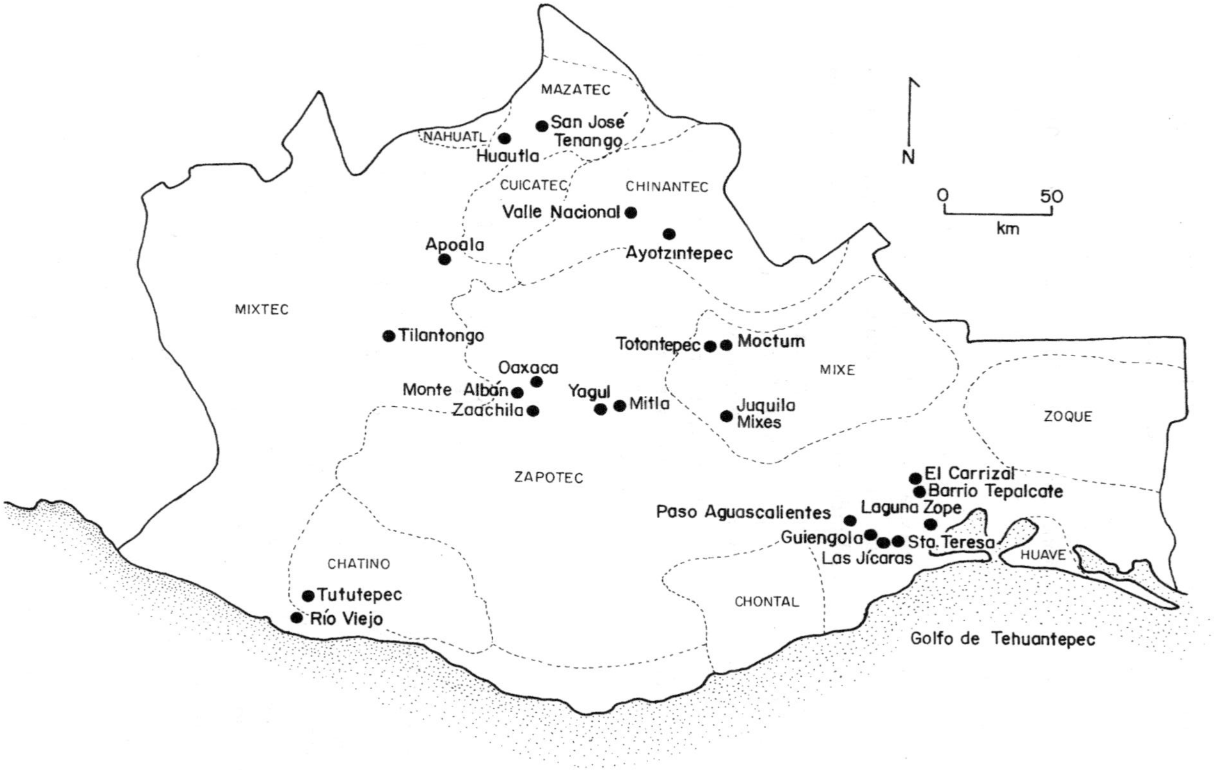

12.1 Map of Oaxaca with regions discussed in the text. Redrawn from Barabas and Bartolomé 1999.

The Mazatec region has not received systematic archaeological study. I hypothesize that early permanent occupations in the region will eventually be found in the lowland riverine environment north of the Sierra Mazateca. Similar settings characterized by rich, cultivable alluvium have revealed Early Formative village occupations elsewhere in Mesoamerica, including in the Olmec region about 250 kilometers to the east. To date, however, the oldest archaeological remains documented from the Mazatec region are a Late Classic carved human mandible and some associated pottery from Eloxochitlán (Winter and Urcid 1990). A tomb at Loma Maguey near Huauhtla may also be Late Classic, based on photographs of the offerings (Munn n.d.).

Clearly dated Early Postclassic materials have not been identified in the Mazateca. I would argue for a Classic collapse and population decline followed by in situ Late Postclassic population growth and cultural flourishing, based on favorable agricultural conditions and independent political development. Late Postclassic data are abundant, documented from burial caves in the region near Huauhtla (Steele 1987), San José Tenango, and San Martín Caballero (Hapka and Rouvinez 1995). Human burials accompanied by ceramic vessels, which probably contained offerings of food and drink, occur in pits and tombs inside horizontal caves and in the mouths of deep vertical caves and sinkholes. Offerings and stone structures of undetermined function indicate practice of rituals and other non-mortuary activities in some caves.

Cueva de Tenango

The most significant archaeological discovery in the Mazateca is the Cueva de Tenango in the municipio of San José Tenango in the heart of the region. The Tenango town center is in a narrow valley at about 600 meters above sea level. My brief unsystematic survey around Tenango suggests that the prehispanic occupation was concentrated in the area immediately north of the town center where the valley expands to several hundred meters in width and forms relatively flat cultivable terraces. Smaller terraces on the surrounding slopes probably functioned as residential spaces. A looted Classic or Postclassic tomb constructed of stone blocks is exposed on one terrace.

The Cueva de Tenango, discovered in 1983 by Lucio Martínez Terán, a young man from the town, is a horizontal cave in the steep limestone outcrops on the west side of the valley high above the town center. A small entrance gives access to the cave, and after a four-meter drop the cave opens out and one can stand up and walk inside. The cave measures about six meters in width and four meters in height near the entrance and then becomes larger and extends about 40 meters to the west, sloping down at an angle of about thirty degrees. Stalactites hang from the roof of the humid interior and narrow lateral niches lead off the main chamber. Fresh air in

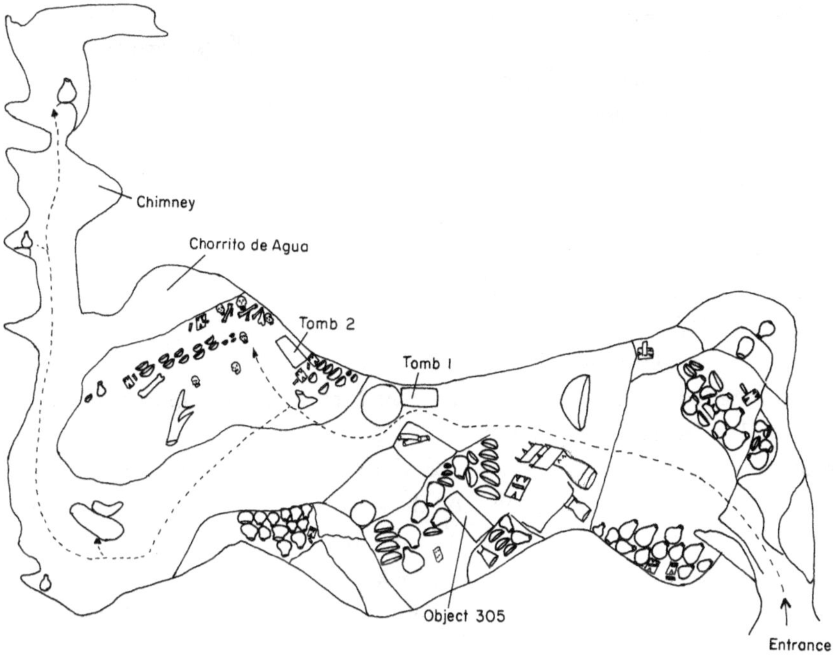

12.2 The Cueva de Tenango with location of finds; based on a drawing by Lucio Martínez Terán.

the cave indicates the presence of a chimney and cracks connecting to the surface, although the interior is totally dark and no other entrances have been found.

The cave contained osteological remains of portions of a minimum of twenty-two individuals, both male and female, ranging in age from four to twenty-seven years. Only nine skulls were recovered. Artifacts included more than 300 ceramic vessels; hundreds of shell, stone, and metal ornaments; a wooden shield with turquoise inlay; obsidian blades; carved animal bones; a carved stone slab; and remains of a hollowed-out tree trunk stained with powdered red hematite that may have served as a funeral bier for transporting a body to the cave, and may represent a symbolic means of transport to the afterworld, as suggested by Henry Munn (personal communication, 2004). A Late Postclassic date for the Cueva de Tenango material is based on design motifs on ceramics, triangular notched arrow points, the inlaid shield, metal ornaments, and three artifacts with codex-style designs.

Verbal descriptions and a sketch made by the discoverer helped determine the original locations of some objects in the cave (Figure 12.2). Groups of ceramic vessels had been placed in irregularities in the rock formation along the sides of the passageway, and three artifact concentrations, designated Tomb 1, Tomb 2, and the

Chorrito de Agua, toward the back of the main chamber, were focal points of prehispanic activity. The two tombs had been almost totally destroyed prior to our intervention by townspeople who visited the cave after the municipal authorities learned of the discovery.

Tomb 1. Located about fifteen meters from the entrance to the cave, Tomb 1 was a masonry construction in the form of a cell incorporated into the natural cave wall. A white stain on the north wall indicated the approximate shape and size, 2.7 meters wide and 1.5 meters high. The irregular cave floor had been modified by placing a bed of rounded stones to make a flat surface about ten square meters. Slabs of slate brought into the cave and covered with white stucco plaster formed the floor of the tomb. The walls were of roughly rectangular stone blocks joined with mortar. The dirt remaining in the area of the tomb contained human bone fragments, some jadeite and gold beads, and turquoise, jadeite, and greenstone mosaic fragments that had apparently fallen off the wooden shield. According to the cave's discoverer, the carved stone slab was found in this area in vertical position. Traces of stucco plaster on the base of the stone suggest it was standing in the area of the stuccoed floor. Tomb 1 was evidently built to bury a high-status individual, probably the principal individual interred in the cave.

Tomb 2. Located ten meters further into the passageway, Tomb 2 was constructed on the side of a rise of carbonate stone deposited by water flowing out of a crack in the north wall of the cave. The tomb walls had been destroyed during the sacking of the cave but foundation stones remained stuck to the rise by carbonates, indicating that the tomb was rectangular and measured approximately 3 meters in length by 1.5 meters in width. In this area the cave roof is only one meter above the rock floor, so the maximum height of the tomb was less than that. Slate slabs scattered in the area apparently formed a tomb roof and probably also a floor covered with white stucco plaster. Mud around the tomb foundation contained shell beads, obsidian blades, copper bells (*cascabeles*), copper rings, and other artifacts. Similar objects were recovered in the Chorrito de Agua immediately northwest of this tomb.

The Chorrito de Agua. A small constant flow of water from a crack in the roof of the cave had formed a pool several meters in diameter, and from there the water trickled out toward the back of the cave. Hundreds of shell beads had been deposited in the pool and human skeletal remains had been placed around the edge. The bones were not found in anatomical position and their taphonomy is unclear. The individuals may have been sacrificed in the cave or brought in as corpses and left as primary (later disturbed) or secondary burials. Some bones may have been moved

Table 12.1 Classification of 280 complete vessels from the Cueva de Tenango.

Group	*Examples (n)*	*Forms*	*Functions*	*Comments*
Sandy paste	76	olla, jar, patojo, comal	storage	
Fine gray	80	bowl, plate, cántaro	service	
Fine yellow	19	bowl, plate	service	some with black paint
Yellow-orange, decorated	41	bowl, olla	service	bichrome, polychrome
Cream-slip; red or black decoration	32	bowl	service	

Note. The majority of the 280 complete ceramic vessels from the cave correspond to five groups:
1. Sandy paste. Mostly utilitarian vessels: undecorated ollas, jars, patojos, comales.
2. Gray paste. Predominantly bowls and plates (some with incised decoration and red paint); some cántaros.
3. Yellow paste. Mostly bowls and plates; some with black painted decoration.
4. Yellow-orange group. Mostly bowls, some ollas. Almost all are decorated, bichrome (black and red) or polychrome (black, red, and white).
5. Cream-slip group. Bowls with cream slip and red or black decoration.

Terminology: olla=jar; comal=tortilla griddle; patojo=shoe-shaped vessel; cántaro=water jar.

from their original positions by recent visitors; others were stuck to the rock by carbonates. Beyond the Chorrito de Agua the cave floor slopes down toward the back of the cave, where we found more human bones, remains of a turtle carapace drum and deer antler drumstick, and bases of ceramic bowls that had been stuck to the rock by carbonates but then removed by looters.

The majority of the 280 complete ceramic vessels from the cave correspond to five groups (Table 12.1). I consider these to be local Mazatec ceramics because they are relatively abundant in the collection and are not recognized as imports from other regions. They may have been made in Tenango or in a community with which the ancient Tenanguenses had frequent contact. Twenty-nine additional vessels probably originated outside the Mazatec region since similar ceramics are documented from other regions; three vessels are of unknown origin (Table 12.2).

Three artifacts from the cave exhibit codex-style designs (Figures 12.3–12.5):

1. A slate slab carved on both sides in low relief (Object 305; height 94 centimeters, width 35 centimeters, thickness 3.2 centimeters). Side A depicts a standing warrior with one foot slightly raised; he wears a quetzal feather headdress and holds a cone with feathers in his right hand and a shield and darts in the other hand. The figure is framed by a celestial band with stars above and horizontal lines, perhaps indicating the earth, below. Side B shows a feathered serpent framed by a band with jade beads and flints above and irregular horizontal groundlines below. Today in Tenango people make offerings using a paper cone containing gold dust and ideally a quetzal feather, although often a macaw or parrot feather is substituted. The slab may represent a Mazatec man making an offering related to human sacrifice.

Table 12.2 Classification of non-local vessels from the Cueva de Tenango.

Group	*Examples (n)*	*Forms*	*Possible Area of Origin*
Chinantla polychrome	10	tripod olla; pedestal base olla	common in the Chinantla
Other polychrome	2	tripod olla; spouted olla	possibly from Puebla
Dark red slip	4	hemispherical bowl	Altiplano Central
Clear light red slip	2	hemispherical bowl	Altiplano Central
Sandy paste	5	hemispherical bowl; cylindrical bowl	common in Teotitlán de Flores Magón (MacNeish et al. 1970)
Teotitlán incised	2	bridge-spout jar; hemispherical bowl	known from Teotitlán de Flores Magón (MacNeish et al. 1970)
Red-on-Cream	1	hemispherical bowl	Nochixtlán Valley, Mixteca Alta (see Lind 1987)
Braziers with 2 supports and a handle	3		Mixteca Alta (Lind 1987)
Unknown	3		

2. An incised deer-femur handle (Object 366; length 17.4 centimeters). The shaft was cut on one end and the process discarded. Four perforations just above the cut served to attach feathers or some other perishable material in the socket, so the bone served as a handle. Finely incised motifs on the shaft show a divided panel with three persons and two heads above, possibly representing a scene of sacrifice, and a geometric design below. Two similar incised bone handles are known, one purportedly from El Puente, Tequixtepec, in the Chocho area of the Mixteca Alta (Parmenter 1991, cited by Rincón Mautner 1995), and one on display in the Postclassic Mixtec section of the Oaxaca room in the National Museum of Anthropology, Mexico City.
3. A trapezoidal pendant made of an unidentified hard organic material covered with white stucco and painted with linear designs on both surfaces (Object 367; approximately 8.5 centimeters wide, 5.5 centimeters high, and 1 centimeter thick). Both sides represent a human head in profile framed within a structure, perhaps a temple. The object exhibits remains of red, yellow, and green or turquoise paint.

Since Tenango is in the heart of the Mazatec region, I believe that the cave and associated objects were used by Mazatecs. The tombs and associated gold beads, carved stone, and mosaic-inlaid shield suggest that the Cueva de Tenango was used for burial of high-status individuals. The bones found near the pool may represent lower-status people, Mazatecs, or non-local individuals, possibly sacrificed in rituals related to water and the underworld.

Relatively simple Late Postclassic burials have been found in caves elsewhere in the Mazatec region near Huauhtla, so use of caves for burials seems to be a com-

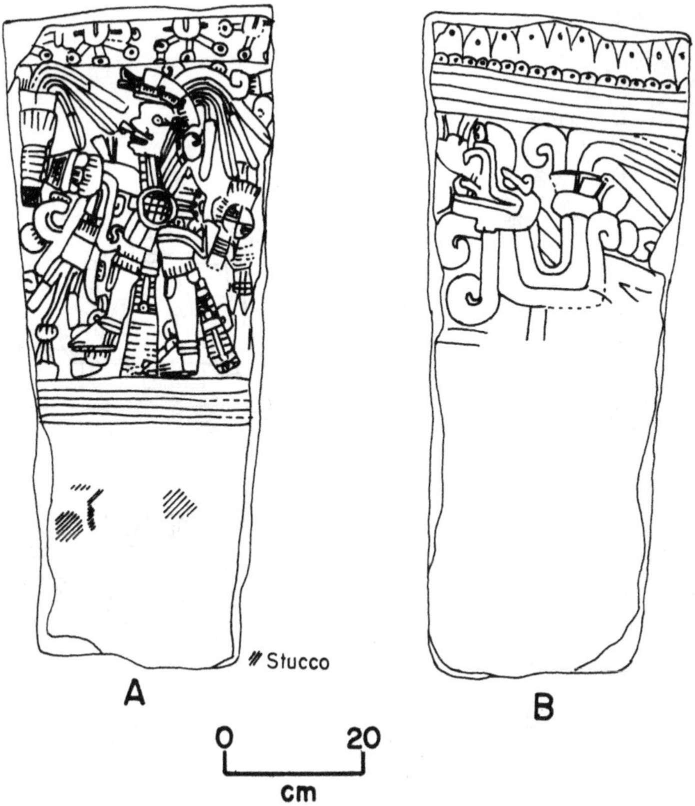

12.3 Carved stone slab from the Cueva de Tenango.

mon Mazatec pattern. At the same time, the carved stone and the offerings in the pool of water suggest additional ritual use of the Cueva de Tenango, perhaps related to the water in the cave. The three objects with codex-style symbols indicate participation of the Mazatec elite in the wider Mesoamerican world. Two artifacts are portable and may have been imported to the area, but the carved slab was made locally, judging by the stone, which in turn indicates local firsthand knowledge of wider patterns.

Houses, burials, and implements related to food preparation are among the archaeological remains most likely to mark ethnic distinctions. Prehispanic houses and cooking implements have not been documented in the Mazateca; for now, some vessel types from the Cueva de Tenango along with the common use of caves for burials are the best indicators of ethnicity for the region.

In sum, although evidence for Classic occupation in the Mazateca is still sparse, the large Late Postclassic populations had distinctive mortuary practices and

12.4 Carved bone from the Cueva de Tenango.

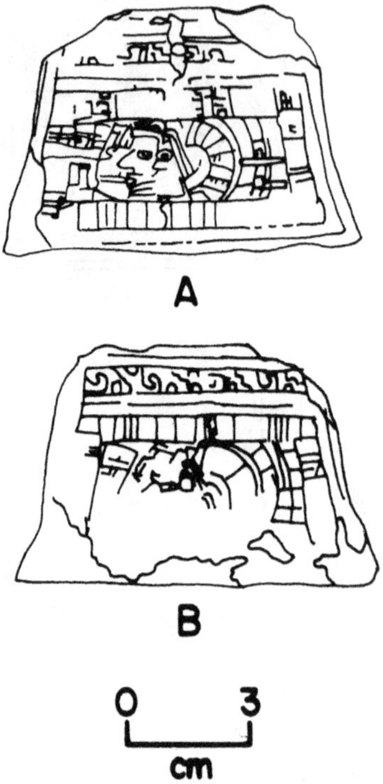

12.5 Trapezoidal pendent from the Cueva de Tenango.

participated in pan-Mesoamerican networks of trade in obsidian and shell and use of Mixteca-Puebla-style symbols.

THE CHINANTLA

Some twenty-five kilometers east of Tenango is the western limit of the Chinantla region, which parallels the Mazateca geographically. To the south is the mountainous Chinantla Alta and to the north is the Chinantla Baja, bordering the Gulf Coastal Plain (Figure 12.1). Some archaeological work has been carried out in the Chinantla Baja. Agustín Delgado (1966) reported sites near Ojitlán and Valle Nacional and Late Postclassic tombs at Cerro Bobo farther east. Raúl Matadamas

Díaz (1995) salvaged a Late Postclassic tomb at Cerro Marín near Valle Nacional and later helped establish a community museum incorporating archaeological pieces from the tomb. Late Postclassic archaeological remains are also known from caves near Usila, and recently a high-status tomb was found near the town.

Ayotzintepec

More extensive evidence comes from the town of Ayotzintepec located two valleys east of Valle Nacional. In late 1973 or early 1974, the town, located next to the lower Río Cajonos, was destroyed by a deluge. Government agencies intervened and the village was relocated to higher ground on a nearby plateau. A formal grid of house lots was laid out, and as machines removed topsoil to delineate the streets, archaeological materials began to appear: the new settlement had been placed on top of a major prehispanic site. Town authorities contacted officials of the Instituto Nacional de Antropología e Historia (INAH), and between January 1974 and February 1977 personnel of the Centro INAH Oaxaca made eight visits to Ayotzintepec to salvage and protect the archaeological remains.

The Ayotzintepec Valley opens up just north of the town, forming a wide alluvial plain that was undoubtedly the principal agricultural area for the ancient population, as it is for today's villagers. This riverine location may have been ideal for an Early or Middle Formative village settlement, although the earliest ceramics found in the 1970s are Late Formative white-rimmed blackware similar to material from Veracruz, the southern Isthmus, and Chiapas. A few Classic period grayware bowl sherds with incised exterior designs indicate at least a small occupation during that period. No Early Postclassic ceramics were recognized, but Late Postclassic material is abundant and suggests the Ayotzintepec population increased markedly in the Late Postclassic, as it did throughout Oaxaca.

The Ayotzintepec site (Figure 12.6) includes at least one large conical mound (probably a temple platform) about twenty meters high, lower mounds and mound groups that may be palace complexes, and a ballcourt. The site covers a minimum of eighty-five hectares, but it has not been carefully surveyed or mapped.

The INAH interventions registered eleven Late Postclassic features, designated "tombs," and a few miscellaneous collections taken from cut banks and recent construction exposures. The "tombs" actually include three types of burial facilities (Figures 12.7 and 12.8). Tomb 1974-1 is a stone masonry rectangular tomb, like the tombs from several other Oaxaca regions and the Late Postclassic Cerro Marín tomb. Nine examples are boot-shaped subterranean pits dug into the underlying hard sediments. In form they resemble some relatively shallow West Mexican shaft tombs (it is unlikely that the regions had direct connections) and are also similar to Postclassic *sótano* burials from the Mixteca Alta, although sótanos are usually symmetrical, like Formative bell-shaped pits, lacking the toe of the boot. These

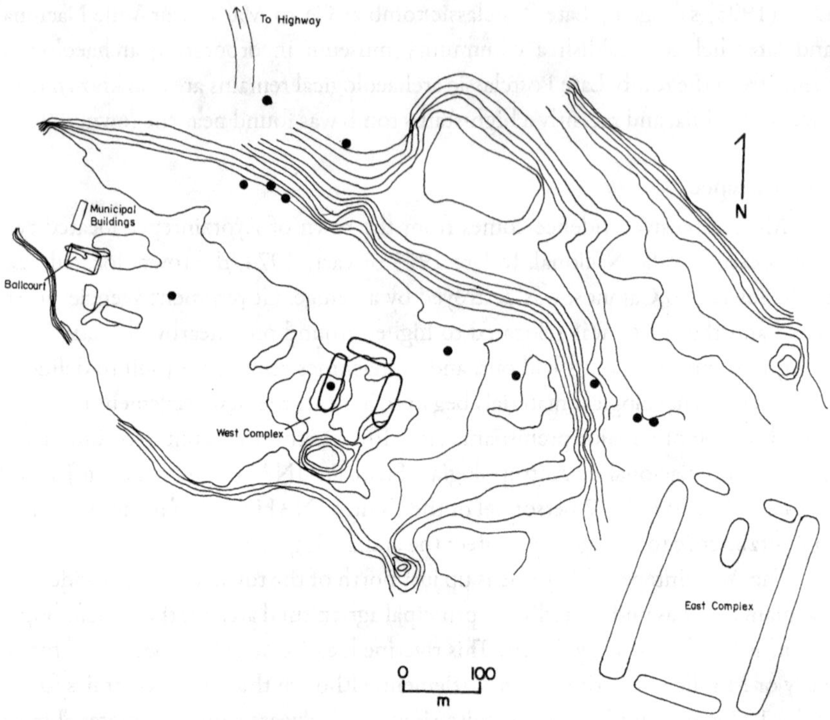

12.6 Sketch map of the Ayotzintepec site showing locations of tombs and burials (solid circles).

features are more like burials than tombs, and each one was probably used in a single event. Tomb 1975-8 is a boot-shaped cavity with a rectangular tomb-like grave dug into the center of the floor. The burials were presumably associated with wooden, thatched-roof houses, but we found no direct evidence of house construction. Table 12.3 summarizes the data on the tombs and their contents. The Ayotzintepec sample documents both simple and high-status burials, distinguished by the variation in burial facilities and in quantity and type of grave goods. Cave burials have also been reported from the Chinantla, although how these compare to the boot-shaped burials remains to be determined.

As in the Mazateca, distinctive local ceramics are present in the Chinantla, including brown-on-yellow fine-paste bowls and thin-walled, orange-paste polychrome pottery with painted decoration in red, black, white, and orange. The Ayotzintepec polychrome vessels exhibit some Mixteca-Puebla motifs (see Chapter 1), such as the step-fret motif and feathers; no codex-style personages appear on the recovered objects or on others reported from the region. This may be due to small

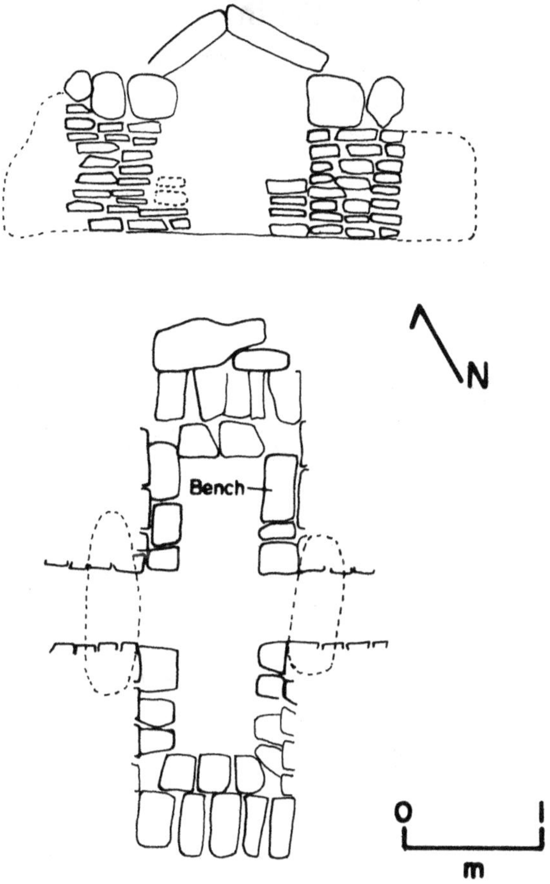

12.7 Ayotzintepec Tomb 1975-1; plan and profile showing wall construction in east and west chambers.

sample size; however, Chinantla polychrome vessels in museum collections similarly lack the codex-style elements. The Tomb 1 offering included three mano and metate sets, each with a rectangular tripod basalt metate and an elongated basalt mano. Similar sets have been found in the Cuicatlán Cañada. Their careful manufacture and standardized forms indicate that these artifacts derive from the same specialized workshop, yet to be located.

The large number of Late Postclassic burials at Ayotzintepec contrasts with the relative paucity of Late Classic material, which in turn suggests there was not a gradual Classic to Postclassic transition. There may have been a population decline and site collapse following the Classic, paralleling some other Oaxaca regions.

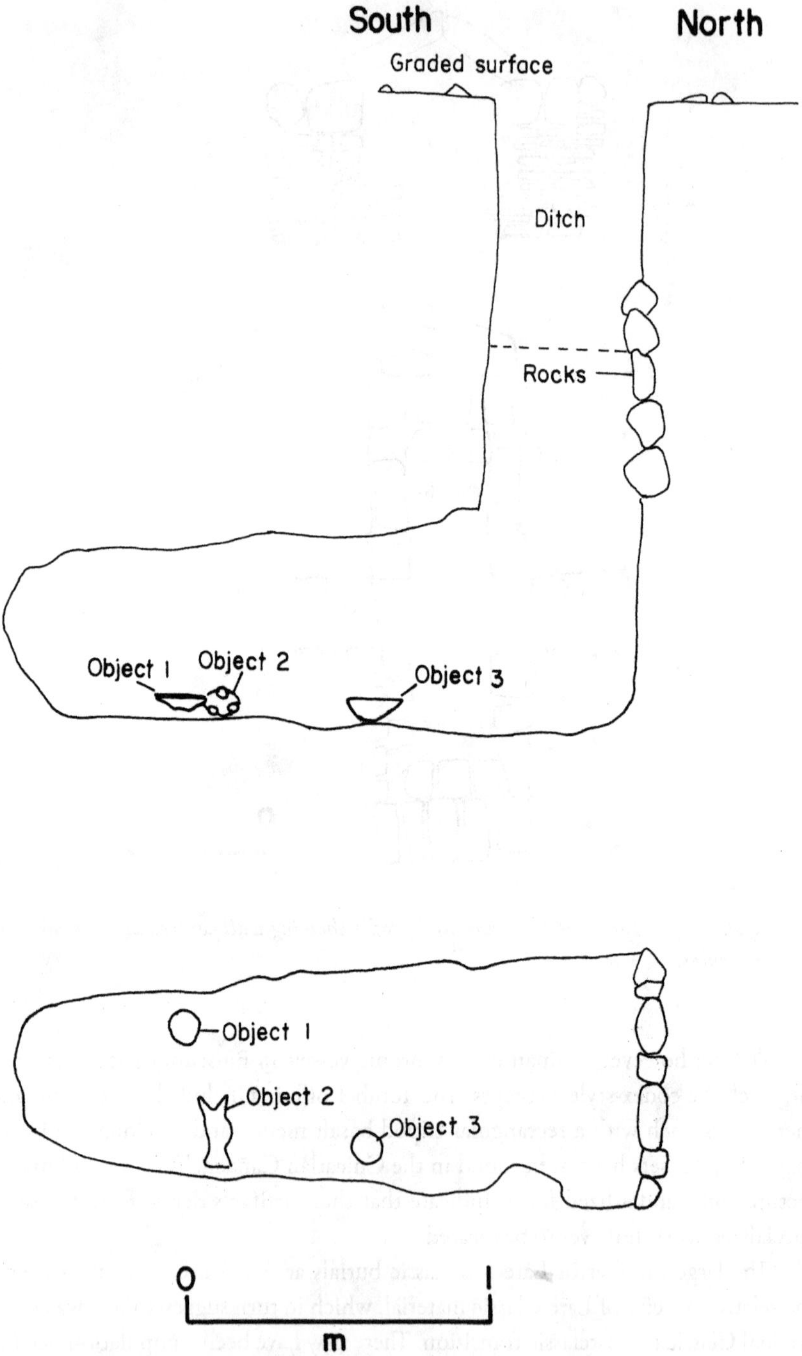

12.8 Ayotzintepec boot-shaped burial (Tomb 1975-9); profile and plan.

Table 12.3 Summary of data from Ayotzintepec tombs and burials

Designation	*Type of Burial Facility*	*Contents*	*Comments*
Tomb 1974-1	rectangular masonry tomb	3 manos, 3 metates, 69 ceramic vessels	recovered after looting
Tomb 1975-2	boot-shaped pit	5 ceramic vessels	
Tomb 1975-3	boot-shaped pit	looted	
Tomb 1975-4	boot-shaped pit	6 ceramic vessels	
Tomb 1975-5	boot-shaped pit	2 ceramics vessels	additional vessels looted
Tomb 1975-6	boot-shaped pit	7 ceramic vessels	
Tomb 1975-7	boot-shaped pit	?	
Tomb 1975-8	boot-shaped pit, with a rectangular tomb in the bottom	30 ceramic vessels, 27 metal objects (copper rings, one gold ring), 10 ceramic beads, 3 fragments of obsidian (perhaps not offerings)	
Tomb 1975-9	boot-shaped pit	?	
Tomb 1977-10	boot-shaped pit	2 ceramic vessels	
Tomb 1977-11	boot-shaped pit	6 ceramic vessels	

THE MIXE REGION

The Mixe region, like the Mazateca and the Chinantla, is generally mountainous and includes a high zone to the west and a lower zone dropping down toward the Isthmus of Tehuantepec to the east (Figure 12.1). Like the other regions it ranges from pine forest to cloud forest to humid tropical lowlands.

The prehispanic past in the Mixe region is known from some collections and brief site inspections. In the 1950s, Walter Miller of the Summer Institute of Linguistics made a large collection of artifacts later donated to the Centro INAH Oaxaca. Some materials are from excavations made around his house in Juquila Mixes; the remainder include objects from other Mixe towns and from undocumented provenance. The Juquila Mixes ceramics date to the Late Formative and include red-on-white decorated bowls analogous to material from the southern Isthmus Kuak phase (200 BCE–1 CE) and the Valley of Oaxaca Nisa phase (100 BCE–200 CE). Brown-paste figurines and ocarinas (Winter and Martínez López 1994) closely resemble Isthmus forms. Ceramics in the collection from other sites include mostly Classic and Postclassic material. Polychrome pottery and artifacts with codex-style designs are absent, and I know of no other artifacts from the region with codex-style designs, although this may be due to sample size. Ethnographic studies document ritual use of caves in the Mixe region (Lipp 1991), and in August 2004, local Oaxaca newspapers reported that conflicts over water rights between the towns of Ayutla and Tamazulapan led to the discovery of human skeletons and ceramic offerings in the cave where the contested spring originates. Judging by the photographs, the ceramics are Postclassic so this cave seems to parallel the cave burials in the Mazatec region.

San Marcos Móctum

A major Classic period site occurs at San Marcos Móctum, an *agencia municipal* of Totontepec in the highlands (Gómez Bravo 2004). The site center, approximately five kilometers south of Totontepec at about 1560 meters elevation in a wet temperate zone, is constructed on a peninsula-like shelf that protrudes out toward the south from the mountain side, forming a relatively flat space. The panoramic 180-degree view includes Totontepec to the west where an extensive area of partly natural terraces slopes down from west to east. This east-facing slope, watered by springs and with plenty of sunlight, provides optimum growing conditions for the area. Today a variety of corn nearly five meters high grows here. House foundations and ceramics appear on the terraces; this must have been the agricultural sustaining area for the Móctum center.

Possible antecedents to Móctum are known from Rancho Santa Cruz below Totontepec and from La Candelaria, an agencia municipal of Zacatepec, the Mixe district capital. Metates, a *molcajete*, obsidian flakes, and ceramics from these sites indicate Late Formative occupations.

Three principal groups form the Móctum site center: the Planicie Oeste, the Plaza, and the Patio Hundido (Figure 12.9). The Planicie Oeste is a natural terrace extending west from the main center. An old church, the agencia office, a basketball court, and a health center now cover much of the surface, but a long, low platform is visible on the southwest edge. A carved tenon with effigy serpent head, typical of some other Late Classic highland Oaxaca sites, was found here during construction.

The plaza is square, about seventy meters on a side and surrounded by mounds and platforms. At 45° to 225° magnetic, the complex appears to be oriented with the natural slope and view, like Ñuiñe centers of the Mixteca Baja, rather than with astronomical phenomena as is the case at Monte Albán and Teotihuacan. The north mound is the highest structure and probably incorporates part of the natural mountainside. The northwest and southeast limits of the plaza are formed by long low mounds approximately one to three meters high. Spaces in the east and west corners provide access to the plaza. Above the plaza and just northeast of the highest mound is the Sunken Patio complex: a square patio delimited by structures, perhaps a palace, with a ballcourt on the southwest side. This entire complex resembles Late Classic Valley of Oaxaca elite residential complexes that include a palace, a ballcourt, a temple, and an open market space (see Chapters 5 and 6) and may be the seat of a royal family. Residential terraces surround the Móctum site center on different levels; to the west are two especially large and wide terraces about three to five meters below the plaza level.

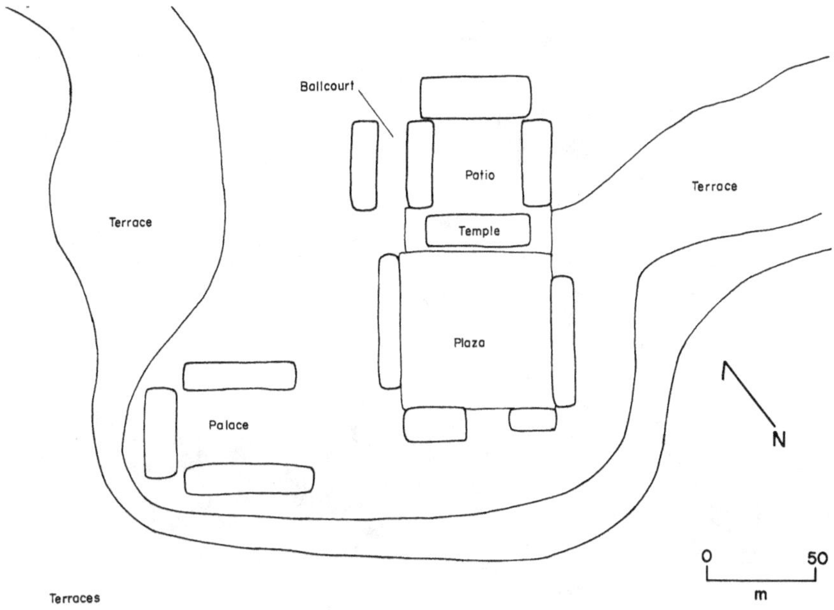

12.9 Schematic map of Móctum site.

At Móctum, ceramics that might help date the structures are scarce; clean fill may have been used for construction, although it is unusual that ceramics are absent on the surface. However, architectural similarities with other Oaxaca sites indicate a Classic period date. Walls of cut-stone blocks are exposed on top of Mound 1, and a small stone statue representing a ballplayer was found inside the mound. Carved stones formerly embedded in the church wall show anthropomorphic and geometric motifs but no glyphs or dates.

No evidence of a Classic to Postclassic transition was found at Móctum, and the site appears to have been largely abandoned after the Classic. Postclassic occupation at Móctum is documented on the terrace just northwest of the site center where two rectangular cists made of stone slabs and containing ceramic offerings were uncovered about a meter below the ground surface (Table 12.4; Figure 12.10). The cists were probably used for burials although no bones were found; high humidity may have caused their disintegration. The vessels from both cists are Postclassic forms. Cist A contained a shoe-shaped vessel (*patojo*) of micaceous brownware and a composite silhouette bowl of fine-paste grayware. Cist B contained a hemispherical bowl of fine yellow paste with brown-orange burnished slip and a greenish gray stone celt (*hacha*).

Additional Postclassic material from Totontepec includes fine white-paste hemispherical bowls and gray-paste composite silhouette bowls. Small stone sculptures

12.10 Postclassic cists and offerings in the patio of Sr. Antonio Reyes Cortés, Móctum.

Table 12.4 Rectangular burial cists at Móctum.

Designation	*Length (cm)*	*Width (cm)*	*Height (cm)*	*Orientation*	*Contents*
Cist A	70	45	65	east-west	2 ceramic vessels
Cist B	65	45	60	55°–235° magnetic	1 ceramic vessel; 1 celt

are fairly common in the Mixe region. Some tall thin ones represent human figures and are Classic period in date. Others are shorter, thicker, and squarish; also have anthropomorphic representations; and may be of Postclassic date (Figure 12.11). Examples are known from Móctum, Totontepec, Tlahuitoltepec, and unspecified locales near Zempoatepetl (Winter 1989a). Thus the Postclassic of the Mixe region is characterized by cist burials, white to yellowish fine-paste ceramics, distinctive stone sculptures, and burials in caves.

THE SOUTHERN ISTHMUS

East of the Mixe region is the 210-kilometer-wide Isthmus of Tehuantepec separating the Atlantic and Pacific Oceans (Figure 12.1). Geographically it includes the

12.11 Stone sculptures from Móctum. Left: ballplayer holding staff; height 8.2 centimeters; courtesy Sr. Melitón González. Right: seated figure; height 22.0 centimeters; courtesy Sr. Estéban González.

Gulf Coastal Plain to the north, an area of low mountains in the center (flanked by higher mountains to the west in Oaxaca and to the east in Chiapas), and the flat, dry Pacific coastal plain and lagoons to the south. In the last area, the southern Isthmus, the crescent-shaped Pacific coastal plain reaches some thirty kilometers in width (north-south) and is cut by the Tehuantepec and Los Perros Rivers, which rise in the rugged metamorphic and limestone mountains to the west and north and flow to the Pacific.

Today the southern Isthmus is one of Oaxaca's most complex regions, ethnically and linguistically. Huaves live along the Pacific Coast, Chontals in the mountains to the west (originally their territory may have extended to the coast), Mixes to the north and west, and Zoques to the east and northeast, whereas Zapotecs dominate in many coastal plain communities, such as Tehuantepec, Juchitán, and Ixtepec, and in some adjacent mountainous areas, such as Petapa and Guevea de Humboldt. Historical documents and linguistic uniformity suggest the Zapotecs were late arrivals. How the distribution of groups changed over time is still unclear.

Archaeologically, the southern Isthmus is better documented than the regions discussed above (for a review, see Zeitlin and Zeitlin 1990). Paleoindian and

Archaic occupations have yet to be discovered in the region. If the New World was colonized by land from north to south, as many archaeologists believe, then nomadic hunter-gatherers must have passed through the Isthmus and presumably left some traces.

The earliest known occupations in the southern Isthmus, dating from around 1400–1250 BCE, are village settlements at Laguna Zope and Barrio Tepalcate along the Los Perros River (Winter 2004). Ceramics are closer in style to those from the Pacific Coast of Chiapas about 200 kilometers southeast and the Gulf Coast of Veracruz some 150 kilometers to the north than to those from the highland Valley of Oaxaca 200 kilometers west, so the southern Isthmus may have been colonized from one or both of the former regions. Village occupations continued during the Early Olmec Horizon (1150–900 BCE) and Late Olmec Horizon (900–500 BCE). During the Late Formative (Goma [400–200 BCE] and Kuak [200 BCE–1 CE] phases), a widespread regional cultural manifestation, probably associated with Mixe-Zoque speakers, is present at the sites of Laguna Zope, El Carrizal, and San Pablo along the Los Perros River and at Las Jícaras and Santa Teresa on the Tehuantepec River. Excavations at El Carrizal uncovered elements of this distinctive southern Isthmus culture: for example, groups of rectangular wattle-and-daub houses, infant burials in large composite silhouette ceramic vessels, adult burials in flexed position, open-air cooking ovens, ceramic ladles for serving liquids, and absence of *comales*. Ceramic affinities continue to be stronger with Chiapas and Veracruz than with the Valley of Oaxaca.

This Late Formative complex ends with abandonment of some communities, a possible hiatus, and then establishment of some new sites along the Los Perros River. New ceramic styles include locally made red-on-fine-white-paste vessels and appearance of elegant resist-decorated pottery and Maya-style figurines similar to those from Jaina. Infant burials are found in jars, and comals, for preparing tortillas, are still absent. Residential patterns have yet to be defined. A somewhat different ceramic complex appears along the Tehuantepec River. At San José del Palmar near Tehuantepec, for example, an Early Classic tomb had a Zapotec-style urn and some grayware conical bowls with exterior incising. Similar pottery, especially grayware bowls with exterior incising, similar to G.23 bowls from the Valley of Oaxaca but with incised rather than excised exteriors and panels with red paint, also occurs at Santa Teresa and at sites in the Jalapa del Marqués Valley.

The region appears to have been depopulated if not abandoned at the end of the Classic. The Early Postclassic (Aguadas phase, 900–1300 CE) is not well represented at coastal plain sites. However, recent explorations in the Jalapa del Marqués Valley, formed by the juncture of the Tequisistlán and Tehuantepec Rivers and also considered to be part of the southern Isthmus region, located substantial Early Postclassic occupation at the site of Paso Aguascalientes. The twenty-five-hectare site center has at least ten mounds and two ballcourts. Test excavations in three mounds exposed probable residential complexes of long, narrow rooms with white stucco floors and adjoining square rooms. A fourth structure is a two-room temple on a platform adjacent to a possible residential structure. Human burials found in extended position in front of the temple stairway were accompanied by offerings that included imported Tohil Plumbate vessels (both plain and effigy), locally made vessels, and jadeite beads and carved plaques similar to those found at Monte Albán (Paddock 1966), Tula (Acosta 1955), Xochicalco (Hirth 2000), and many other sites (Solar Valverde 2002). Whether these remains represent Zapotecs, Mixe-Zoques, or a colony of Chiapaneco, Maya, or Huave merchants who moved along the Pacific coastal lagoon system then travelled up the Tehuantepec River remains to be determined.

During the Late Postclassic, Zapotecs moved into the southern Isthmus, and other groups, at least Huaves, were also present. This period includes the Ulam phase (1300–1521 CE) and the contemporaneous but distinct Lagarto ceramic complex present along the coast and possibly associated with Huaves (Zeitlin and Zeitlin 1990). The Late Postclassic mountaintop-fortified urban center of Guiengola (Peterson 1990) overlooking the Tehuantepec River, with its main plaza flanked by two temple platforms, a ballcourt, and a palace complex, is reminiscent of Classic Zapotec architecture in the Valley of Oaxaca. The recently discovered site of Cerro Negro above the Los Perros River near Laollaga may be an analogous naturally fortified Zapotec center. Cerro Padre López in Tehuantepec was the seat of a Postclassic Zapotec *señorío*, and some structures had stone slabs carved with step-fret greca motifs similar to examples found at Guiengola. An elite tomb, salvaged in 1966 in Tehuantepec, contained at least forty-seven ceramic vessels including Valley of Oaxaca–style polychromes now in the Museo de las Culturas in Oaxaca City. The Cerro Remolino site near Laollaga has revealed polychrome pottery similar to that from the Valley of Oaxaca and the Chinantla.

Downriver from Laollaga at Barrio Tepalcate just outside Ixtepec, we recently salvaged a Late Postclassic Ulam phase tomb, Tomb 2003-1, rectangular in shape, two meters long and seventy centimeters wide, with block-and-slab wall construction similar to some Valley of Oaxaca structures and a red-painted stucco floor (Figure 12.12). The tomb contained bones of at least one adult individual and several ceramic vessels including a polychrome tripod-necked *olla* of fine white paste with orange, red, and black painted decoration; step-fret motifs on the basal exterior of the rim; a feather motif on the neck; and pinched-end supports (Figure 12.13). The form and decoration are typically Late Postclassic, the thin walls resemble Chinantla polychrome tripod ollas, and the fine white paste is characteristic of Mixe and Zoque ceramics, so this may be a distinctive type of polychrome produced by one of those groups. Grayware vessels from the tomb include two forms reminiscent of valley

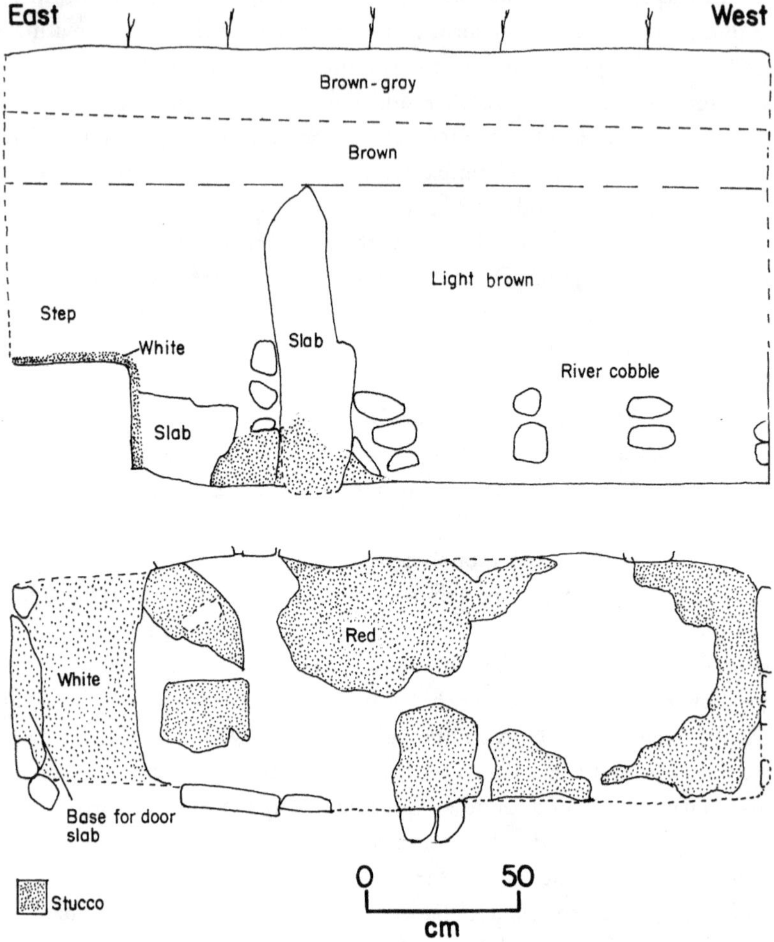

12.12 Tomb 2003-1 at Barrio Tepalcate, Ixtepec.

Zapotec ceramics: small bottles (*cántaros*) like Xoo phase bottles but with round rather than ovoid bases and two hemispherical bowls that closely resemble in form and finish specimens found in burials 1994-69 and 1994-70 at Monte Albán (Martínez López et al. 1995). Three other forms, a fine gray tripod olla, a small orange-paste bottle (*ollita*) with perforated nubbin handles, and two small bottles (cántaros), also suggest Zapotec affiliations. Thus, although the tomb architecture and majority of vessels suggest Zapotec affiliation, the polychrome olla indicates contact with neighboring ethnic groups.

Pictographs in red paint appear in the southern Isthmus from at least Guiengola to Tolostoque on rocky outcrops along the juncture between the coastal plain and

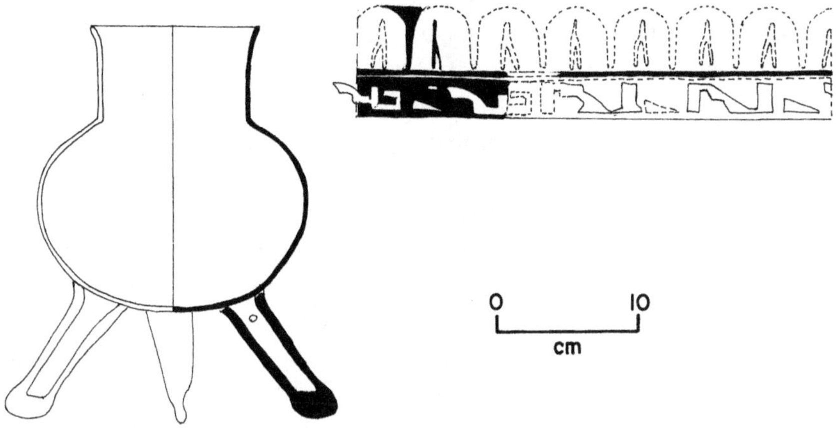

12.13 Polychrome vessel from Tomb 2003-1, Barrio Tepalcate, Ixtepec.

the mountains. Some include codex-style human figures with calendrical dates and glyphs (Zárate Morán 2003). Whether these correspond to Zapotec, Huave, or other groups has not been determined.

The multi-ethnic cultural panorama makes the southern Isthmus one of Oaxaca's most interesting regions. A disjunction occurs between the Classic and Postclassic with the abandonment of major Classic sites. Neither Paso Aguascalientes nor Guiengola are underlain by Classic components. The region may have been partially abandoned at the end of the Classic, but Paso Aguascalientes may indicate movement of groups into the region in the Early Postclassic whereas Guiengola reflects Zapotec incursions in the Late Postclassic. Mixteca-Puebla-style design motifs appear in the Late Postclassic and are not necessarily limited to any one group.

THE CLASSIC TO POSTCLASSIC TRANSITION

The Classic to Postclassic transition is well documented in only two Oaxaca regions, the Valley of Oaxaca and the lower Río Verde Valley. Both regional sequences show an overall pattern of abandonment with variation in process and timing. In the Valley of Oaxaca, Monte Albán and other urban centers such as Cerro de la Campana, Lambityeco, and Macuilxóchitl collapsed at the end of the Classic Xoo phase around 800 CE and population declined drastically (see Chapter 5). Early Postclassic Liobaa phase (800–1200 CE) occupations are sparse and had reduced cultural inventories compared to the immediately previous Xoo phase occupations. Urns, carved stones, writing, elaborate tombs, and temples drop out of the archaeological record. Liobaa phase ceramics are relatively simple and rustic and pottery figurines are rare or absent (Chapter 2). This reduced cultural inventory suggests little economic specialization as well as absence of an elite group (see Chapter 6). During the Late Postclassic Chila phase (1200–1521 CE) population increased again; señoríos such as Mitla, Yagul, and Zaachila flourished, and both nucleated and dispersed settlements occurred widely in the valley. A parallel pattern seems to occur in the Mixteca region but the Early Postclassic is not well defined.

In the lower Río Verde Valley, population also declined after the Late Classic but, in contrast to the Valley of Oaxaca, occupation continued at some sites, most notably the large urban center of Río Viejo, until approximately 900–1100 CE (Chapters 7 and 8; Joyce et al. 2001; Joyce et al. 2004; King 2003). Here the Early Postclassic occupation has a remarkably rich material culture inventory with elegant bichrome ceramics, pottery figurines, flutes, earspools, and abundant spindle whorls reflecting textile production (Chapter 8). Both the Classic and Late Classic occupants at Río Viejo correspond to the Chatino ethnic and linguistic group. They finally left or died out around 1100 CE, and Mixtecs moved into the region a century or two later.

Two contrasting models, one of climate change and the other of sociopolitical change, could explain the variation in these two regional trajectories. The climate change model postulates that a drought adversely affected agricultural potential and productivity, leading to population decline and cultural collapse. Direct evidence from Oaxaca for a drought is lacking, and little paleoclimatological work has been done in the state. However, evidence of climate change for this time period has been accumulating in the Maya region (Gunn et al. 2002; Robichaux 2002; Shaw 2003) and in Central Mexico (Smith 2003:56) and may help explain pan-Mesoamerican collapse of Classic centers. Widespread climate change would have affected Oaxaca as well and could help explain the collapse of Monte Albán and other centers in the Valley of Oaxaca and the Mixteca (see Chapters 1 and 6). The climate model predicts simultaneous collapse in various regions. The lower Río Verde may have been one of the few exceptional regions where the extensive highland drainage basin and the lagoon system near the coast may have provided water and offered agricultural potential while other areas were too dry to sustain more than dispersed families or small communities.

The political model holds that Classic period Zapotec and Mixtec cultures collapsed for sociopolitical reasons: the elite lost political control and the power to exact tribute payments from their dependents; the hierarchical structure broke down; and elite-controlled writing, arts, craft specialization, and elaborate religious ceremonies were no longer practiced (Chapter 6; Joyce 2004). Populations did not necessarily decline, so there could be large sites and many residences, although elite-related artifacts such as urns and carved stones disappeared from the archaeological record. The possible cause of an initial collapse is less clear. For the Valley of Oaxaca, Joyce and Winter (1996) suggest that polities weakened as elite energy was directed to competition, and commoners became increasingly disengaged from religious and political life in the urban centers. The destruction of central Teotihuacan around 550 CE, or events at Cholula sometime later, may have triggered widespread reactions or a domino effect (Chapter 1). The political model predicts some local variation in rates and timing of collapse and allows for cases where no collapse occurred. One could argue, for example, that the lower Río Verde was geographically and politically isolated and thus immune to outside stress, at least for two or three centuries prior to the Late Postclassic.

Data on the Classic to Postclassic transition from the regions discussed in this chapter are uneven. Little is known about the Classic in the Chinantla and the Mazateca whereas in the Mixe region the Móctum site provides more data for the Classic in that region than are available for the Postclassic. Glottochronological evidence suggests considerable time depth of at least 2,000 years for all three groups, Mazatecs, Chinantecs, and Mixe (Hopkins 1984), so unless people emigrated from elsewhere we would expect Classic sites to be present in each area. Since the Late Postclassic occupations do not appear to develop directly out of Classic or Early Postclassic antecedents, for these regions I argue for a population decline and cultural collapse similar to the Zapotec and Mixtec regions, presumably caused by a drought.

The Isthmus data present a different scenario but similar patterns. The Late Classic Tixum phase (600–900 CE) is known from several medium to large sites such as Saltillo in Juchitán and La Huana in Ixtepec. These sites declined or were abandoned at the end of the Classic, so one could argue for the same kind of depopulation as elsewhere. However, as noted above, there is a clear Early Postclassic occupation at Paso Aguascalientes in the Jalapa del Marqués Valley. The structures are built over sterile soil (a Late Formative component appears in some areas), possibly indicating a local settlement shift or colonization by an outside group, which would be the first documented case from Oaxaca of the kind of population movement often considered characteristic of Mesoamerica's Epiclassic. Early Postclassic structures at Paso Aguascalientes were used for a few generations at most and then reused in the Late Postclassic, possibly by Zapotecs.

How this case corresponds to the hypothesized drought elsewhere in Oaxaca is unclear. It is possible that the narrow canyon at the end of the Jalapa del Marqués Valley (now closed off by the Benito Juárez Dam) served to retain water from the Tequisistlán and Tehuantepec Rivers, creating a viable agricultural area in the valley during the Early Postclassic even though sites on the coastal plain were abandoned.

To summarize, the Classic to Postclassic transition is a complex period in Oaxaca as elsewhere and involves population dynamics that are still incompletely understood. There is little evidence for the kind of regional variation immediately after the Classic predicted by the political change model; a widespread drought seems to offer a better explanation for pan-regional population decline. This could be further tested through excavation and precise dating of Late Classic deposits in various regions: if the climate change model holds, we would expect Late Classic sites to end at nearly the same time.

LATE POSTCLASSIC DIVERSITY IN OAXACA

The data in this chapter document the presence of diverse ethnic and linguistic groups during the Late Postclassic in Oaxaca. To conclude, I now turn to the question of what kind of model might account for this diversity.

In some areas of Mesoamerica, for example in the Sayula Basin of Jalisco, since historical data on ethnic groups are absent, archaeologists hesitate to assign their finds to specific peoples (Susana Ramírez, personal communication, 2004). In Oaxaca, however, temporal continuity links today's ethnic groups with their Colonial period and prehispanic ancestors, making Oaxaca an ideal setting for studying the emergence of these groups. Several general features characterize Oaxaca's prehispanic ethnic groups. Each one usually occupies a relatively extensive territory encompassing several communities, so the ethnic group is a level of integration more inclusive than the polity. Historically each group must have had a center of origin, probably going back to pre-Olmec population concentrations in environmental settings favorable for corn agriculture. Shared language is usually taken as the clearest indicator of common ethnicity and in simple terms implies relatively more contact, at least at some time in the past, among speakers of a common language than with those of other languages. An important feature in the process of formation of ethnicities is the emergence of status differentiation between communities. Large centers such as San José Mogote and Etlatongo in the Early Formative and Monte Albán and Móctum in the Classic were political centers and foci of innovation that served to generate distinctive cultural patterns on a local if not regional level.

In their recent attempt to account for the complexity of Postclassic Mesoamerica, Smith and Berdan (2003b) propose adopting a modified world-systems perspective that emphasizes three features: (1) core-periphery model of site distribution in which certain population concentrations are dominant and more powerful than others; (2) emphasis on commerce that cut across all regions and groups; and (3) widespread presence of an international symbol set of design elements with religious significance.

For three of the regions treated in this chapter—the Mazateca, the Chinantla, and the southern Isthmus—both commerce and the international symbol set (elements in the Mixteca-Puebla style) were clearly important but variable from region to region (Figure 12.14). The fourth region discussed here—the Mixe region—lacks these features. Obsidian, a non-local material, was found in the Cueva de Tenango (Mazateca), at Ayotzintepec (Chinantla), and in the Isthmus sites and is common in most Oaxaca regions, although none was found at Móctum and it appears to be scarce in general in the Mixe region. Metal objects show a similar pattern: present in the Cueva de Tenango, frequent in Postclassic contexts in the Chinantla, and known from the Isthmus, although again scarce or absent in the Mixe region.

Commerce was present but complex and variable from group to group or community to community (Chapters 1 and 8). Obsidian, metal, and many other products were obtained through trade but the mechanisms and networks varied. Obsidian blades were available in most Oaxaca regions to all Late Postclassic households and may have been brought in by itinerant merchants (Winter 1989b). Metal objects were associated with the elite and metal ornaments probably moved through elite exchanges. Shell for purpura dye and salt, both present at locales along the Pacific Coast, may have been exploited seasonally by families of different ethnic groups who migrated temporarily to the resource areas and then brought the materials back to their communities without elite intervention. Some products, such as woven textiles, were made by women, at least in the highlands (Hamann 1997; McCafferty and McCafferty 1994), for domestic purposes as well as for tribute payment.

Presence of the international symbol set (the Mixteca-Puebla style) was also manifested differently in the four regions described here. The Cueva de Tenango (Mazateca) showed the most varied and sophisticated iconographic elements (carved slab, mosaic shield, carved bone, trapezoidal pendant, ceramics), whereas other regions had simpler manifestations, such as motifs on ceramics (Isthmus, Chinantla) or none at all (Mixe). Although this variation may be due in part to sampling error, there is no reason to expect each region to reflect the same patterns. The possibility of obtaining finely crafted luxury goods probably depended on elite leaders' abilities to control local wealth and craft specialists and to negotiate with their peers. Appearance of symbols in public context is rare in the four regions discussed here, except for the carved slabs with grecas at Guiengola and Cerro Padre López in the southern Isthmus.

Although commerce and common symbols are widespread in the Late Postclassic, their differential distribution requires explanation. In their recent synthesis, Berdan, Kepecs, and Smith (2003) claim that Late Postclassic Mesoamerica had four core areas: Tlaxcala/Cholula, the Basin of Mexico, Lake Pátzcuaro, and the Mixteca / Valley of Oaxaca. The Late Postclassic Zapotec and Mixtec populations, as noted at the beginning of this chapter, were large and widespread, but there were hundreds of Zapotec and Mixtec communities and it is not even clear that they were unified as two ethnic groups. During the Early Postclassic, the Mixtec ruler 8 Deer Jaguar Claw apparently unified many Mixteca communities into a tribute-

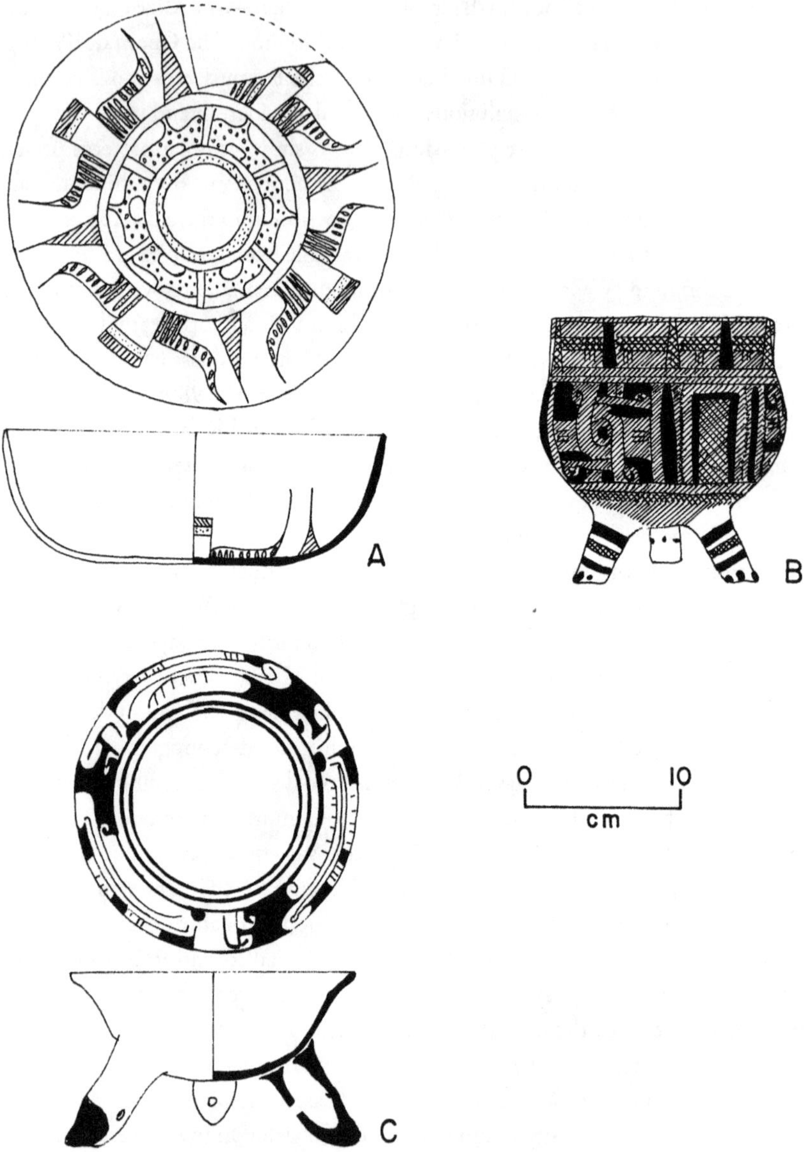

12.14 Polychrome vessels from (a) the Mazatec region, (b) the Chinantla, and (c) the Isthmus (Tehuantepec), drawn to the same scale.

paying political entity for some years, and later the Zapotecs and Mixtecs forged an alliance to fight off the Aztec invaders at Guiengola in the Isthmus, but evidence of wide-ranging or long-lasting integration is lacking. During the Late Postclassic the

Aztecs established a garrison at Tuxtepec; the Chinantecs at Ayotzintepec, only fifty kilometers to the south, may have fallen under Aztec domination and been incorporated into their trade and tribute networks. The Mixe, protected by their rugged terrain, had a reputation for ferocity and resisted outside control even into Colonial times (Maldonado Alvarado and Cortés Márquez 1999). Thus, there is no evidence that Zapotecs and Mixtecs dominated all of Oaxaca. To claim that all of Oaxaca was under one of four core groups relegates the distinct Oaxacan ethnic groups to lesser importance or invisibility.

Elsewhere in the same book on Postclassic Mesoamerica, Smith and Berdan (2003c:26) characterize the Mixteca Alta and the Valley of Oaxaca as "affluent production zones," that is, "areas of high populations and intensive economic activity . . . that lacked the powerful polities and large urban centers found in core zones." Whether as core zones or simply as affluent production zones, there is no evidence that the Mixteca Alta and Valley of Oaxaca dominated the inhabitants of the four regions discussed in this chapter. The latter must have known about and probably traded with Zapotecs and Mixtecs, but they also had links to groups to the west (Guererro and Puebla), to the north (Veracruz), and to the east (Chiapas). Portions of these regions if better known might even qualify as affluent production zones themselves, or at least "resource-extraction zones" (Smith and Berdan 2003c).

Lack of knowledge of these regions precludes a full understanding of Late Classic and Postclassic dynamics within Oaxaca. An additional little-known region is the present-day Huave area along the barrier beaches of the southern Isthmus, said to have numerous archaeological sites with abundant obsidian and polychrome pottery. The Late Postclassic Huave were perhaps not only traders but producers of salt, shell, dried fish, and other basic commodities exchanged among Oaxacan groups.

The focus on ethnic groups has both a particularistic, historical dimension as well as a comparative character, since it involves comparison of material cultural complexes from different communities (archaeological sites) and ethnic identity is partly defined through contrast with other groups (see Chapter 1). The Postclassic data from Oaxaca reflect a complex panorama of multiple ethnic groups. Future research could try to clarify the strategies used by community leaders and other individuals to further the survival of their families and towns within the Mesoamerican context of commerce and symbols. The Late Postclassic clearly is not composed just of multiple polities, some dominant and some not, but of multiple ethnic groups on a level above the polity. All regions had connections outside their local polities and outside the ethnic group and thus could obtain imported obsidian, metal, pan-Mesoamerican symbols, and others elements.

An adequate explanation requires a multi-ethnic approach and historical framework in which all groups have at least some if not equal weight, or are at least considered, although they may have had different roles. The ancestors of the lesser known groups are relevant to their present-day descendants. If absorbed through the archaeologists' theories or pens into an Aztec or Zapotec-Mixtec core, their identity is lost. Instead, however, each can be studied on its own terms. Only if the trajectory of each ethnic group is known will reliable results be obtained as general social theory is tested in the archaeological record.

ACKNOWLEDGMENTS

I thank my colleagues in the Centro INAH Oaxaca, Teresa Morales and Raúl Matadamas for providing information on Cerro Marín, and Juan Cruz Pascual for preparing the final line drawings. I thank Jeffrey Blomster and especially Robert Markens for reading and providing perceptive comments, which improved the content of this chapter.

REFERENCES

Acosta, Jorge R.
1955 Resumen de los informes de las Exploraciones Arqueológicas en Tula, Hgo, durante las IX y X Temporadas, 1953–1954. *Anales del Instituto Nacional de Antropología e Historia* 9(38):37–115.

Barabas, Alicia Mabel, and Miguel Alberto Bartolomé
1999 Las protagonistas de las alternativas autonómicas. In *Configuraciones étnicas en Oaxaca*, edited by A. Barabas and M. Bartolomé, 1:15–57. Instituto Nacional de Antropología e Historia, Mexico City.

Berdan, Frances F., Susan Kepecs, and Michael E. Smith
2003 A Perspective on Late Postclassic Mesoamerica. In *The Postclassic Mesoamerican World*, edited by M. Smith and F. Berdan, pp. 313–317. University of Utah Press, Salt Lake City.

Culbert, T. Patrick
1965 *The Ceramic History of the Central Highlands of Chiapas, Mexico*. Papers of the New World Archaeological Foundation, No. 19. Brigham Young University, Provo, Utah.

Delgado, Agustín
1966 Arqueología de la Chinantla, Noreste de Oaxaca, Mexico: Su secuencia actual. In *Suma antropológica en homenaje a Roberto J. Weitlaner*, pp. 81–90. Instituto Nacional de Antropología e Historia, Mexico City.

Flannery, Kent V., and Joyce Marcus (editors)
1983 *The Cloud People: Divergent Evolution of the Zapotec and Mixtec Civilizations*. Academic Press, New York.

Gómez Bravo, Noemí
2004 *Móctum: Antigua grandeza del un pueblo mixe*. Fonca, Oaxaca.

Gunn, Joel T., Ray T. Matheny, and William J. Folan
2002 Climate-change studies in the Maya area. *Ancient Mesoamerica* 13(1):79–84.

Hamann, Byron
1997 Weaving and the Iconography of Prestige: The Royal Gender Symbolism of Lord 5 Flower's/Lady 4 Rabbit's Family. In *Women in Prehistory: North America and Mesoamerica*, edited by C. Claassen and R. Joyce, pp. 153–172. University of Pennsylvania Press, Philadelphia.

Hapka, Roman, and Fabienne Rouvinez
1995 Prospection archéologique des grottes du Cerro Rabón, Oaxaca, Mexico. In *Proyecto Cerro Rabón 1990–1994*, edited by T. Bitterli, pp. 57–69. Speleo Projects, Basil.

Hirth, Kenneth
2000 *Ancient Urbanism at Xochicalco*. University of Utah Press, Salt Lake City.

Hopkins, Nicholas A.
1984 Otomanguean Linguistic Prehistory. In *Essays in Otomanguean Culture History*, edited by J. Josserand, M. Winter, and N. Hopkins, pp. 25–64. Vanderbilt University Publications in Anthropology, No. 31. Nashville, Tennessee.

Joyce, Arthur A.
2004 Sacred Space and Social Relations in the Valley of Oaxaca. In *Mesoamerican Archaeology: Theory and Practice*, edited by J. Hendon and R. Joyce, pp. 192–216. Blackwell Publishing, Malden, Massachusetts.

Joyce, Arthur A., Laura Arnaud Bustamante, and Marc N. Levine
2001 Commoner Power: A Case Study from the Classic Period Collapse on the Oaxaca Coast. *Journal of Archaeological Method and Theory* 8(4):343–385.

Joyce, Arthur A., Andrew G. Workinger, Byron Hamann, Peter Kröfges, Maxine Oland, and Stacie M. King
2004 Lord 8 Deer "Jaguar Claw" and the Land of the Sky: The Archaeology and History of Tututepec. *Latin American Antiquity* 15(3):273–297.

Joyce, Arthur A., and Marcus Winter
1996 Ideology, Power, and Urban Society in Prehispanic Oaxaca. *Current Anthropology* 37(1):33–86.

King, Stacie M.
2003 Social Practices and Household Organization in Ancient Coastal Oaxacan Households. Unpublished Ph.D. Dissertation, Department of Anthropology, University of California, Berkeley.

Lind, Michael
1987 *The Sociocultural Dimensions of Mixtec Ceramics*. Vanderbilt University Publications in Anthropology, No. 33. Nashville, Tennessee.

Lipp, Frank J.
1991 *The Mixe of Oaxaca: Religion, Ritual, and Healing.* University of Texas Press, Austin.

MacNeish, Richard S., Frederick A. Peterson, and Kent V. Flannery
1970 *The Prehistory of the Tehuacan Valley,* Vol. 3: *Ceramics.* University of Texas Press, Austin.

Maldonado Alvarado, Benjamín, and Margarita M. Cortés Márquez
1999 La gente de la palabra sagrada: El grupo etnolingüístico *ayuuk ja'ay* (mixe). In *Configuraciones étnicas en Oaxaca,* Vol. 2, edited by A. Barabas and M. Bartolomé, pp. 97–145. Instituto Nacional de Antropología e Historia, Mexico City.

Marcus, Joyce, and Kent V. Flannery
1996 *Zapotec Civilization: How Urban Society Evolved in Mexico's Oaxaca Valley.* Thames and Hudson, New York.

Martínez López, Cira, Marcus Winter, and Pedro Antonio Juárez
1995 Entierros Humanos del Proyecto Especial Monte Alban 1992–1994. In *Entierros humanos de Monte Alban: Dos estudios,* edited by M. Winter, pp. 79–247. Proyecto Especial Monte Alban 1992–1994, Contribución No. 7. Centro INAH Oaxaca, Oaxaca.

Matadamas Díaz, Raúl
1995 Rescate arqueológico de una tumba en Cerro Marín, Valle Nacional, Oaxaca. Unpublished report on file at the Centro INAH Oaxaca.

McCafferty, Sharisse D., and Geoffrey G. McCafferty
1994 Engendering Tomb 7 at Monte Albán: Respinning an Old Yarn. *Current Anthropology* 35(2):143–166.

Munn, Henry
n.d. Vislumbres de la Sierra Mazateca en Tiempos Prehispánicos. In *Investigaciones Arqueológicas Recientes en Oaxaca,* edited by M. Winter. Manuscript in preparation.

Murra, John
1985 The Limits and Limitations of the "Vertical Archipelago" in the Andes. In *Andean Ecology and Civilization,* edited by S. Masuda, I. Shimada, and C. Morris, pp. 15–20. University of Tokyo Press, Tokyo.

Oudijk, Michel R.
2000 *Historiography of the Bènizàa: The Postclassic and Early Colonial Periods (1000–1600 A.D.).* CNWS Publications, Vol. 84. Research School of Asian, African, and Amerindian Studies, University of Leiden, Leiden.

Paddock, John
1966 Oaxaca in Ancient Mesoamerica. In *Ancient Oaxaca: Discoveries in Mexican Archeology and History,* edited by J. Paddock, pp. 83–242. Stanford University Press, Stanford, California.

Parmenter, Ross

1991 Un hueso esgrafiado al estilo códice mixteca. Unpublished manuscript in possession of the author.

Peterson, David A.

1990 Guiengola: Fortaleza Zapoteca en el Istmo de Tehuantepec. In *Lecturas históricas del Estado de Oaxaca*, Vol. 1: *Epoca prehispánica*, edited by M. Winter, pp. 455–488. Instituto Nacional de Antropología e Historia, Mexico City.

Rincón Mautner, Carlos

1995 The Ñuiñe Codex from the Colossal Natural Bridge on the Ndaxagua: An Early Pictographic Text from the Coixtlahuaca Basin. *Institute of Maya Studies Journal* 1(2):41–66.

Robichaux, Hubert R.

2002 On the Compatibility of Epigraphic, Geologic and Archaeological Data, with a Drought-Based Explanation for the Classic Maya Collapse. *Ancient Mesoamerica* 13(2):341–345.

Romero Frizzi, María de los Angeles

1996 *El sol y la cruz: Los pueblos indios de Oaxaca colonial.* CIESAS/INI, Mexico City.

Shaw, Justine M.

2003 Climate Change and Deforestation: Implications for the Maya Collapse. *Ancient Mesoamerica* 14(1):157–167.

Smith, Michael E.

2003 *The Aztecs*, 2nd edition. Blackwell Publishing, Malden, Massachusetts.

Smith, Michael E., and Frances F. Berdan (editors)

2003a *The Postclassic Mesoamerican World.* University of Utah Press, Salt Lake City.

Smith, Michael E., and Frances F. Berdan

2003b Postclassic Mesoamerica. In *The Postclassic Mesoamerican World*, edited by M. Smith and F. Berdan, pp. 3–13. University of Utah Press, Salt Lake City.

2003c Spatial Structure of the Mesoamerican World System. In *The Postclassic Mesoamerican World*, edited by M. Smith and F. Berdan, pp. 21–31. University of Utah Press, Salt Lake City.

Solar Valverde, Laura

2002 Interacción interregional en Mesoamérica: Una aproximación a la dinámica del Epíclásico. Unpublished Licenciatura thesis, Escuela Nacional de Antropología e Historia. Instituto Nacional de Antropología e Historia, Mexico City.

Spores, Ronald

1984 *The Mixtecs in Ancient and Colonial Times.* University of Oklahoma Press, Norman.

Steele, Janet F.

1987 Blade Cave: An Archaeological Preservation Study in the Mazatec Region, Oaxaca, Mexico. Unpublished Master's Thesis, Department of Anthropology, University of Texas at San Antonio.

Winter, Marcus
1989a *Oaxaca: The Archaeological Record.* Minutiae Mexicana, Mexico City.
1989b La obsidiana en Oaxaca prehispánica. In *La obsidiana en Mesoamérica*, edited by M. Gaxiola G. and J. Clark, pp. 345–361. Colección Científica, No. 176. Instituto Nacional de Antropología e Historia, Mexico City.
2004 Excavaciones Arqueológicas en El Carrizal, Ixtepec, Oaxaca. In *Palabras de luz, palabras floridas*, edited by V. Marcial Cerqueda, pp. 17–48. Universidad del Istmo, Tehuantepec.

Winter, Marcus, and Cira Martínez López
1994 Figurillas y silbatos prehispánicos de Juquila Mixes, Oaxaca. *Oaxaca Ayer y Hoy* 1(1):9–13.

Winter, Marcus, and Javier Urcid
1990 Una Mandíbula Humana Grabada de la Sierra Mazateca, Oaxaca. *Notas Mesoamericanas* 12:39–49. Universidad de las Américas–Puebla, Cholula.

Zárate Morán, Roberto
2003 Una forma de escritura: Las pinturas rupestres del Istmo de Tehuantepec. In *Escritura zapoteca*, edited by M. Romero Frizzi, pp. 143–169. CONACULTA-INAH, Mexico City.

Zeitlin, Judith F., and Robert N. Zeitlin
1990 Arqueología y Epoca Prehispánica en el Sur del Istmo de Tehuantepec. In *Lecturas históricas del Estado de Oaxaca*, Vol. 1: *Epoca prehispánica*, edited by M. Winter, pp. 393–454. INAH, Mexico City.

Contributors

Jeffrey P. Blomster, Department of Anthropology, George Washington University, Washington, DC, blomster@gwu.edu.

Bruce E. Byland, Department of Anthropology, City University of New York, Hunter College, Bronx, New York, BByland@aol.com.

Gerardo Gutiérrez, Centro de Investigaciones y Estudios Superiores en Antropología Social, Mexico City, gxg153@hotmail.com.

Byron Ellsworth Hamann, Department of Anthropology and History, University of Chicago, Illinois, behamann@uchicago.edu.

Arthur A. Joyce, Department of Anthropology, University of Colorado at Boulder, Arthur.Joyce@colorado.edu.

Stacie M. King, Department of Anthropology, Indiana University, Bloomington, Indiana, kingsm@indiana.edu.

Michael D. Lind, Santa Ana Unified School District (Retired), Santa Ana, California, mikemyrn@sbcglobal.net.

Robert Markens, Centro INAH Oaxaca, Pino Suárez 715, Oaxaca, Mexico, rmarkens@hotmail.com.

Cira Martínez López, Centro INAH Oaxaca, Pino Suárez 715, Oaxaca, Mexico, rmarkens@hotmail.com.

Michel R. Oudijk, Instituto de Investigaciones Filológicas, Universidad Nacional Autónoma de México, Mexico City, mroudyk@hotmail.com.

Marcus Winter, Centro INAH Oaxaca, Pino Suárez 715, Oaxaca, Mexico, winteroax@prodigy.net.mx.

Index

www.ingramcontent.com/pod-product-compliance
Lightning Source LLC
Chambersburg PA
CBHW060018030426
42334CB00019B/2089